SEEING THE LORD'S GLORY

SEEING THE LORD'S GLORY

KYRIOCENTRIC VISIONS AND THE DILEMMA OF EARLY CHRISTOLOGY

CHRISTOPHER BARINA KAISER

Fortress Press
Minneapolis

SEEING THE LORD'S GLORY

Kyriocentric Visions and the Dilemma of Early Christology

Cover image: *The Saviour's Transfiguration*, courtesy of Wikimedia Commons

Cover design: Tory Herman

Library of Congress Cataloging-in-Publication Data is available

Print ISBN: 978-1-4514-7034-5

eBook ISBN: 978-1-4514-8429-8

The paper used in this publication meets the minimum requirements of American National Standard for Information Sciences — Permanence of Paper for Printed Library Materials, ANSI Z329.48-1984.

Manufactured in the U.S.A.

This book was produced using PressBooks.com, and PDF rendering was done by PrinceXML.

CONTENTS

Abbreviations

PERIODICALS, SERIES, AND DICTIONARIES

AB Anchor Bible

ABD Anchor Bible Dictionary. Edited by D. N. Freedman. 6 vols. New York, 1992.

ABRL Anchor Bible Reference Library

ACW Ancient Christian Writers

AJS Review Association for Jewish Studies Review

ANF Ante-Nicene Fathers

ATR Anglican Theological Review

AYB Anchor Yale Bible Commentary Series

AGAJU Arbeiten zur Geschichte des antiken Judentums und des Urchristentums

BHT Beiträge zur historischen Theologie

BJRL Bulletin of the John Rylands University Library of Manchester

BJS Brown Judaic Studies

BTB Biblical Theology Bulletin

BZ Biblische Zeitschrift

BZAW Beihefte zur Zeitschrift für die alttestamentliche Wissenschaft

BZNW Beihefte zur Zeitschrift für die neutestamentliche Wissenschaft

CBQ Catholic Biblical Quarterly

CH Church History

CRINT Compendia rerum iudaicarum ad Novum Testamentum

DSD Dead Sea Discoveries

ExpTim Expository Times

HR History of Religions

HTR Harvard Theological Review

HUCA Hebrew Union College Annual

JBL Journal of Biblical Literature

JEH Journal of Ecclesiastical History

JPST Jewish Publication Society Tanakh

JQR Jewish Quarterly Review

JR Journal of Religion

JSHJ Journal for the Study of the Historical Jesus

JSJ Journal for the Study of Judaism in the Persian, Hellenistic, and Roman Periods

JSJ Supplement Supplements to the Journal for the Study of Judaism

JSNT Journal for the Study of the New Testament

JSNTSup Journal for the Study of the New Testament Supplement Series

JSOTSup Journal for the Study of the Old Testament Supplement Series

JSP Journal for the Study of the Pseudepigrapha

JSRI Journal for the Study of Religions and Ideologies

JSQ Jewish Studies Quarterly

JTS Journal of Theological Studies

LCC Library of Christian Classics

MPPB *My People's Prayer Book*

NETS New English Translation of the Septuagint

NICNT New International Commentary on the New Testament

NIGTC New International Greek Testament Commentary

NovT Sup Supplements to Novum Testamentum

NPNF[1, 2] *Nicene and Post-Nicene Fathers*, First and Second Series

NTOA Novum Testamentum et Orbis Antiquus

NTS New Testament Studies

OTP Old Testament Pseudepigrapha. Edited by J. H. Charlesworth. 2 vols. New York, 1983, 1985.

RRJ Review of Rabbinic Judaism

SBLMS Society of Biblical Literature Monograph Series

SBLSP Society of Biblical Literature Seminar Papers

SBLSS Society of Biblical Literature Symposium Series

SJ Studia Judaica

SJLA Studies in Judaism in Late Antiquity

SJSJ Supplements to the Journal for the Study of Judaism

SJOT Scandinavian Journal of the Old Testament

SJT Scottish Journal of Theology

SVTP Studia in Veteris Testamenti pseudepigraphica

TBN Themes in Biblical Narrative

TDNT Theological Dictionary of the New Testament. Edited by G. Kittel and G. Friedrich. Translated by G.W. Bromiley. 10 vols. Grand Rapids, 1964–1976.

TS Theological Studies

TSAJ Texte und Studien zum antiken Judentum (Texts and Studies in Ancient Judaism)

VC Vigiliae christianae

VCSup Vigiliae christianae Supplement Series

VT Vetus Testamentum

WUNT Wissenschaftliche Untersuchungen zum Neuen Testament

ZAW Zeitschrift für alttestamentliche Wissenschaft

Old Testament Pseudepigrapha

1 En. 1 Enoch (Ethiopic Apocalypse)

2 En. 2 Enoch

2 Bar. 2 Baruch

Apoc. Ab. Apocalypse of Abraham

Apoc. Elijah Apocalypse of Elijah

Apoc. Zeph. Apocalypse of Zephaniah

Ascen. Isa. Ascension of Isaiah

Jos. Asen Joseph and Aseneth

Jub. Jubilees

L.A.B. Liber antiquitatum biblicarum (Pseudo-Philo)

Let. Aris. Letter of Aristeas

Odes Sol. Odes of Solomon

Pss. Sol. Psalms of Solomon

Sirach MS B Hebrew manuscript B of the Wisdom of Jesus, son of Sirach (ben Sira)

T. Dan. Testament of Dan

T. Job Testament of Job

T. Mos. Testament of Moses

New Testament Apocrypha and Apostolic Fathers

Diog. Epistle to Diognetus

GH Gospel of the Hebrews

Gos. Pet. Gospel of Peter

GT Gospel of Thomas

Herm. Shepherd of Hermas

Mishnah, Talmud, and Related Literature

b. (Babylonian Talmud) y. (Jerusalem Talmud) t. (Tosefta) m. (Mishnah)

b. B. Bat Bava Batra

b. B. Qam. Bava Qamma

b. Ber. Berakhot

b. Eruv. Eruvin

b. Git. Gittin

b. Hag. Hagigah

b. Pesah. Pesahim

b. Sanh. Sanhedrin

b. Sukkah Sukkah

b. Tem. Temurah

Cant. R. Canticle Rabbah

Exod. R. Exodus Rabbah

Gen. R. Genesis Rabbah

Lev. R. Leviticus Rabbah

m. Avot Avot

m. Ber Berakhot

m. Ed. Eduyyot

m. Pesah. Pesahim

m. Sanh. Sanhedrin

m. Shab. Shabbat

m. Sot. Sotah

m. Sukkah Sukkah

m. Ta'an. Ta'anit

m. Tamid Tamid

m. Yoma Yoma

Midr. Tanh. Midrash Tanhuma

MRI Mekilta of Rabbi Ishmael

MRS Mekilta of Rabbi Shimon bar Yohai

Pesiq. Rab. Pesiqta Rabbati

t. Ber. Berakhot

t. Hag. Hagigah

t. Hullin Hullin

t. Maksh. Makhshirin

t. Pesah. Pesahim

t. Sanh.   *Sanhedrin*
t. Shab.   *Shabbat*
t. Sotah   *Sotah*
t. Sukkah   *Sukkah*
t. Ta'an.   *Ta'anit*
y. Ber.   *Berakhot*

Targumic Texts

Tg. Isa.   *Targum Isaiah*
Tg. Neof.   *Targum Neofiti*
Tg. Tos.   *Targumic Tosefta*

Early Jewish, Christian, and Pagan Writers

Augustine, *Conf.* *Confessions*
Augustine, *Ep.* *Epistle*
Cassian, *Inst.* *Institutes of the Coenobia*
Clement of Alexandria, *Strom.* *Stromateis*
Gregory of Nazianzus, *Ep.* *Epistulae*
Gregory of Nazianzus, *Or.* *Oratio in laudem Basilii*
Josephus, *Ant.* *Jewish Antiquities*
Josephus, *J.W.* *Jewish War*
Justin, *Dial.* *Dialogue*
Justin, *1 Apol.* *First Apology*
Ignatius, *Eph.* *To the Ephesians*
Ignatius, *Magn.* *To the Magnesians*
Ignatius, *Phld.* *To the Philadelphians*
Ignatius, *Rom.* *To the Romans*
Ignatius, *Smyr.* *To the Smyrnaeans*
Ignatius, *Trall.* *To the Trallians*
Irenaeus, *Haer.* *Against Heresies*
Mart. Pol. *Martyrdom of Polycarp*
Paulinus of Nola, *Ep.* *Epistle*
Philo, *Agriculture* *On Agriculture*
Philo, *Confusion of Tongues* *On the Confusion of Tongues*
Philo, *Contempl.* *Life On the Contemplative Life*

Philo, *Dreams On Dreams*
Philo, *Flaccus Against Flaccus*
Philo, *Flight On Flight and Finding*
Philo, *Names On the Change of Names*
Philo, *Moses On the Life of Moses*
Philo, *On the Creation On the Creation of the World*
Philo, *QG Questions and Answers on Genesis 1, 2, 3, 4*
Philo, *Rewards and Punishments On Rewards and Punishments*
Philo, *Spec. Laws On the Special Laws 1, 2, 3, 4*
Pliny the Younger, *Ep. Epistulae*

MANUSCRIPTS AND PAPYRI

P[46] Papyrus 46 of the Letters of Paul
PGM Greek Magical Papyri
BG Papyrus Berolinensis

Deity Christology in a Jewish Context

There is a dilemma at the heart of New Testament Christology: How could deity Christology arise among pious Jews whose tradition consistently opposed the exaltation of any living human being to equality with God?

Following the execution of Jesus,[1] according to New Testament accounts, the disciples "saw the Lord" (1 Cor. 9:1; Acts 9:17, 27; 26:16; John 20:18, 20) and "beheld his glory" (2 Cor. 3:18; cf. Luke 9:32; John 1:14; 12:41). When taken in the context of early Judaism, these phrases are unambiguous descriptions of *YHWH/Adonai*,[2] revelatory visions and auditions[3] like those described in Exodus 33:18-19, 22 (LXX[4]); Numbers 12:8 (LXX); 14:22;[5] Isaiah 6:1, 3, 5, 8;[6] and Amos 9:1. When read in the flow of New Testament narratives, however, they all refer to Jesus as clearly stated in most of the texts just cited. In other words, early disciples of Jesus[7] talked about him in the exact same way that Jews of their time talked about YHWH. They affirmed that:

- Jesus is "Lord of all" (a confessional formula in Rom. 10:12; Acts 10:36; cf. Eph. 4:6).
- Jesus is to be invoked as the Lord who saves (1 Cor. 1:2; Rom. 10:9-13; Matt. 8:25; 14:30; 15:25; Acts 2:21; 4:12; 7:59; 9:14, 21; 22:16).
- Jesus is the Lord to whom unbelievers must turn as a sign of repentance (2 Cor. 3:16; Acts 9:35; 11:21b).
- Jesus is called upon and visualized as the Lord who comes to save and to judge (1 Cor. 16:22 [Aramaic *mar*];[8] Rev. 22:20; *Did.* 10:6, all with probable eucharistic settings).

The identification with YHWH, the Lord God of Israel, is unmistakable in these texts. In fact, the primary Christian confession was *Kyrios Iēsous*, "The Lord is Jesus" (1 Cor. 8:6; 12:3) long before the Council of Nicea (325 CE).[9] As Jewish biblical scholar Moshe Weinfeld has astutely concluded: "The eschatological aspirations of Judaism were adopted by the early Christians, but the object of the aspirations changed from 'Lord God' to 'Lord Jesus.'"[10]

This early development of deity Christology is now agreed upon among most scholars of the New Testament.[11] The problem is explaining how this could have happened within the context of early Judaism.[12] Doing the work of rethinking Christian origins will require a strong sense of the urgency of this problem. Unless it is addressed, we will be forced either to abandon the Jewishness of the early disciples or to deny the historicity of their belief in a truly divine Lord.

Even given the limitations of our knowledge, limited for the most part to surviving texts, we know that early Judaism was a complex historical phenomenon.[13] There was such a diversity of sects, especially prior to the rise of "normative Judaism" under the leadership of the Rabbis,[14] that many scholars today speak of a diversity of systems or dialects within a "complex common Judaism."[15] At the risk of barbarism, some scholars have even referred to a plurality of "Judaisms."[16] On the other hand, there were common features like adherence to the Law of Moses as a gracious gift from *HaShem* ("The Name," a respectful substitute for the Tetragrammaton) and belief that the God who had appeared to the patriarchs and matriarchs of Israel was Israel's only Lord and savior. New forms of Judaism (of which early Christianity was just one) were free to innovate in new directions, but the initial impulse for such a movement, the downbeat as it were, must have been consistent with what we know of the early dialects of "common Judaism."

Good historical explanations for the origin of deity Christology are hard to come by. Most Christians would not regard them as being particularly relevant to Christian faith and life. Yet the issue should not be written off as a matter of pure speculation. In the process of investigation, I reframe the way we think about early Jewish and Christian practices like liturgical performances and prayer (especially in chs. 1, 3, 6, 9).

Our main objective, however, will be to reexamine the origin and meaning of the most fundamental Christian affirmation, the Lordship of Jesus. Most readers of a book like this will have been exposed to earlier accounts of the origin of beliefs about Jesus' divine identity. Before proceeding with my own suggestion, I shall review three of these scenarios: one that is based on the resurrection of Jesus, another that invokes outside influence from gentile polytheism, and a third that derives the divine identity of Jesus from binitarian features already present in biblical Judaism. Assessing the strengths and weaknesses of each of these treatments will point the way to my own suggestion.

A Resurrection Scenario (from below): N. T. Wright

The most familiar way to account for the deity Christology of the New Testament is to trace it back to those disciples who first experienced Jesus as risen from the dead. A leading current proponent of this view is N. T. Wright, according to whom the disciples encountered Jesus in an "empirical" way. It was not just a vision (with its psychological, spiritualist associations),[17] but a physical body perceived by the five senses—hence, what New Testament scholars often refer to as a Christology developed "from below."

Jesus' coming back to life after his death demonstrated to the disciples that he truly was the Messiah that he (supposedly) claimed to be. In fact, he was a special kind of Messiah who had been glorified and who now exercised universal dominion at the "right hand of God" (Ps. 110:1).[18] Such elevation and lordship placed him on the same level as God the Father in heaven and soon led to affirmations of Jesus own identity as "Lord" (YHWH). In short, the early disciples leveraged the resurrection appearances and arrived at a deity Christology using a bootstrap hermeneutic—each inferential step placing them just within reach of the next. As Wright puts it: "The creator God has raised Jesus from the dead, and he was therefore Israel's Messiah, the world's true Lord, and [therefore] the strange second self of Israel's God himself."[19]

Wright's proposal is perhaps the most comprehensive scenario yet developed, encompassing everything from the historical life of Jesus to the early creedal formulas of the New Testament, all the time avoiding the kind of subjectivism that non-empirical, visionary scenarios usually imply.[20] In this respect, Wright has set a standard for other scholars to emulate. Moreover, each step in his reconstruction seems plausible enough, at least, provided one tacitly assumes the inevitability of the outcome. Early Christians did in fact conclude that Jesus was the "strange second self of Israel's God."

However, most of the inferential steps that Wright attributes to the first disciples would not have been so obvious at the time of the early disciples. Wright's scenario entangles us in a thicket of difficult questions regarding historical plausibility:

- Would any purely empirical experience have led the disciples to infer the unaided resurrection of an individual human being (an act of God)—something for which there was no clear, pre-Christian expectation and no good parallel in the history of Judaism?[21]
- In contrast to theophanies, for which there were biblical precedents and expectations, would reliance on the empirical nature of an

> individual "resurrection body" not immediately remove early Christian faith from its context in early Judaism?
> - Beyond that, what would the occurrence of a unique, individual resurrection event have to do with pre-Christian beliefs about a coming Messiah (cf. Mark 6:14, 16 on the resurrection of John the Baptist)?[22]
> - What precedent did the disciples have for inferring universal lordship from a physical resurrection,[23] or even from Jewish messiahship (cf. Ps. 89:25)?[24]
> - Would any first-century Jew who was familiar with scriptural traditions have attributed deity to their teacher and identified him with YHWH as a "strange second self," even if they believed that he was a Messiah,[25] seated at the "right hand of God"?[26]

I have no reason to deny that any of these inferential steps actually occurred at some point. Evidently they all did, at least, as seen in retrospect (we shall return to these points in ch. 7). However, I question whether they constitute a coherent *historical* explanation of the origin of deity Christology. Such things can be stated as brute facts based on the available texts, but historians prefer to work with plausible, contextual scenarios, in which prominent features of the text are seen to follow from sufficient (if not necessary) causes. Our second reconstruction does just that: it provides a more plausible scenario by appealing to influences on the disciples coming from outside of Judaism.

An Externalist Historical Scenario (from Outside Traditional Judaism): Maurice Casey

The implausibility of a deity Christology emerging within the context of Judaism so soon after the execution of Jesus has led scholars like Maurice Casey to posit a longer-range development that makes room for polytheistic gentile influence (in the train of earlier historians of religion like Wilhelm Bousset).[27] The decisive impetus needed for deity Christology was not "from below" (and certainly not "from above") but from outside the bounds of traditional Judaism.

The plausibility of this scenario is often enhanced by assuming that deity Christology did not emerge until the writing of the Gospel of John in the late first century ce.[28] In contrast to earlier New Testament documents, John clearly portrays Jesus as the divine Logos (Word) and a "Son of God" who enjoys some degree of parity with God the Father (John 1:1; 17:5, passim). In one passage of the Gospel, Jesus is actually acclaimed as "my Lord and my God" (the confession of Thomas in John 20:28).[29] These features are not found in the earlier "synoptic" Gospels (Matthew, Mark, and Luke) and may well have emerged decades after the life and death of the historic Jesus.

The popularity of such a gradualist scenario is also enhanced by a priori preference for progressive, evolutionary ways of thinking. In biological evolution, innovative traits often emerge through a long series of steps that have relatively simple beginnings. This reconstruction does not suffer, therefore, from the implausibility of the inferential steps that N. T. Wright's resurrection scenario does (as outlined above). In fact, the great strength of Casey's scenario is its attention to historical, as well as exegetical, considerations.

Nonetheless, there are a number of major problems with Casey's externalist scenario. One problem, as pointed out by Richard Bauckham and Larry Hurtado, is that deity Christology developed much earlier than the Gospel of John. Even our earlier New Testament documents describe Jesus with "Yahweh texts"—texts that describe the coming of YHWH, the God of Israel, in the Hebrew Bible (or the lxx)[30]–and Aramaic formulas like *Marana tha* ("Our Lord, come!" 1 Cor. 16:22) date back to the Jerusalem church.[31] Moreover, binitarian formulas that exhibit just as much parity as that in the Gospel of John are present in the earliest New Testament documents (Paul, Mark, and Q[32]). Phenomena like these push deity Christology back into the 30s and 40s ce,[33] prior to the time that gentile influence would have been a significant factor, and do not allow time for a gradual process lasting many decades.[34]

This early date for the origin of deity Christology accentuates the dilemma of early Christology, however. We not only need to explain how deity Christology could have arisen in the context of early Judaism (without significant gentile influence), but we must explain how it could have happened in a matter of years. We need to posit a historical process that could produce such a result on a short timescale and that relies only on known features of early Judaism. Until a plausible scenario can be worked out, however, a significant number of cautious scholars will continue to favor a gradualist approach like Casey's and will even be skeptical that any appeal to evidence for early deity Christology is confessionally motivated.[35] As Kevin Sullivan has aptly stated: "It seems unnecessarily implausible to suggest that Jesus was immediately incorporated into the divine identity as part of an unprecedented move in Jewish theology."[36]

A more fundamental problem with scenarios like Casey's is that they rely too much on a dynamic of "influences" to explain major developments in history. Such appeals do not explain *why* people willingly respond to some influences rather than to others (or to none). Religious people are normally subject to influences from many directions, but they do not respond positively in every case. Even if they seek to communicate their ideas in language that others will understand, they do not select terminology that they deem incompatible with their basic values.

The question that still needs to be addressed is why the early disciples favored (and cultivated) one influence or term over against another. What were the issues *within the community* that generated the quest for helpful ideas—regardless of where those ideas came from? What are the criteria by which a community decides to borrow some ideas and reject others?[37] In other words, an adequate historical explanation must consider the demand-side (or the "demand system") as well as the supply of beliefs and practices from which selection was made. Simply put, the reasons why communities select and develop traditions are never stated in the traditions themselves (the supply)—they derive from the challenges facing the community (the demand).[38] In the scenario to be developed in this book, major features of early Christology will be explained as attempts to resolve to problems generated by a revelatory event that echoed the visions and auditions of earlier Judaism.

Before we move on, one other possibility should be considered. Perhaps the solution to our dilemma was readymade in the binitarian pattern of prior Jewish beliefs about their Deity. If early Judaism was not strictly monotheistic and entertained various ideas about a second god alongside *HaShem*, early Christians may simply have developed a new variant of Jewish binitarianism.

A Continuing Binitarianism Scenario (from above): Margaret Barker

All of these difficulties we have encountered can be avoided by an alternative offered by Margaret Barker. Barker argues that most all of the New Testament beliefs about Jesus as a divine figure go back to an ancient, originally Canaanite depiction of YHWH as a special "son of God," also known as the "Great Angel," who (along with other sons and angels) was subordinate to *El*, God Most High.[39] For Barker, there is no need to appeal to a postmortem resurrection or to gentile influence on the early Christians—external influences were part of Israelite religion from the outset.

Barker's scenario has two great advantages over the more familiar explanations described above—advantages that I hope to maintain in our subsequent investigation.

First, there is no major discontinuity between biblical Judaism (at least, as Barker envisions it) and early Christian beliefs about Jesus—there is no need to postulate various inferences or stages of development or influences from outside the Jewish tradition. Nor is there any need to bring in a miraculous event like the resurrection of Jesus to move things along. What happened, according to Barker, was simply that "the Lord continued to appear to his people," now in the form of Jesus.[40]

Second, Barker gives a breathtaking explanation for the binitarian formulas in the New Testament: binitarian liturgical formulas (Rom. 1:7 and elsewhere), binitarian adaptations of a confessional formula known as the *Shema* (1 Cor. 8:6 and elsewhere),[41] and binitarian visions (Acts 7:55-56 and elsewhere). These formulas actually belong to traditional Judaism—they carried on the binitarian beliefs of the Old Testament[42] (as Barker reads it), for which YHWH was a second God alongside the Most High.[43] In short, Jesus was recognized as YHWH (he actually saw himself as YHWH[44]), the Lord God of Israel, and cultic devotion to Jesus and the application of "Yahweh texts" followed accordingly, as evidenced in the New Testament and demonstrated by other New Testament scholars. As Barker states it, "the first Christians recognized that Jesus was Yahweh, not that he was in some way equivalent, but not identical [to Yahweh]."[45] This scenario clearly derives New Testament Christology "from above" (i.e., from the traditional theology of Israel).[46]

Now for the problems: one major issue with Barker's explanation lies in its exegetical basis in the Old Testament. As Richard Bauckham has shown in some detail, Barker's interpretation is based on untenable readings of the *Shema* (especially Deut. 6:4) and of Moses' song about the distribution of nations on earth (Deut. 32:8-9).[47] Any viable reconstruction of the origin of deity Christology surely must avoid such novel readings, if for no other reason than just to avoid the suggestion that the data are being molded to fit the theory.

Another problem is that there are only a few suggestive, potentially binitarian passages in the Hebrew/Aramaic Bible (e.g., Prov. 8 and Dan. 7), and there is no indication of any binitarian liturgical formulas or confessions like those in the New Testament. Nor is there any precedent for the identification of YHWH with a particular, historical human being. Barker's scenario only gains credibility if one is already convinced that the Hebrew religion was originally binitarian (rather than strictly monotheistic), that the canonical Scriptures were edited in such a way as to cover up more pluralistic statements about the Deity, and that older, pluralistic views survived among the common people until the dawn of the Common Era. There may be merit to some of these historical speculations, but it is inadvisable at this stage to use them as a foundation for reconstructing Christian origins. The dilemma of early Christology—the veneration of a deceased man in terms of eschatological and doxological phrases that were otherwise directed to YHWH—is still not quite resolved.

I believe that the benefits of Barker's reconstruction can profitably be preserved, however. Continuity with Judaism still can be maintained, even if the Lord who was identified with Jesus in the New Testament was not a "second power in heaven," as Barker claims, but the one true God, the Most High God, as the *Shema* requires (beginning with Deut. 6:4).

In the following chapters, I contend that a Kyriocentric vision (or a series of visions) following the death of Jesus resulted in the one true God (YHWH) being identified with the name and the face of Jesus,[48] and that this Lord-Jesus identification was itself the origin of early deity Christology.[49] Devotion to Jesus, healing and prophesying in his name, and the use of "Yahweh texts" followed as a continuation of regular Jewish devotion to YHWH, the one true God.[50] As a result, the binitarian formulas and visions of the New Testament must have been secondary in the historical sense,[51] though no less necessary for a credible expression of the faith,[52] even if they did have some precedent in earlier Judaism (on the supply side). Such formulas were necessitated (on the demand side) by the synthesis of Kyriocentric visions with traditions about Jesus' prayers to his *Abba* ("Father") and his teachings about his Father in heaven.[53] We shall treat this matter in detail in chapter 7.

Toward a Resolution of the Dilemma— A Conjecture concerning Kyriocentric Visions

My purpose in this study is not to argue all the points raised by these three scenarios (each of which will actually play a positive role in this study), but to offer an alternative reconstruction that maintains the historical continuity assayed in Barker's version, thereby avoiding the complications of deriving a deity Christology either from an anachronistic emphasis on gentile influence or from improbable inferences based on post-crucifixion encounters with Jesus.

Evidently, something did happen following the execution of Jesus that altered the disciples' understanding of who he was and revised the way that they remembered the teachings of the Old Testament. But these disciples were working-class men and women, not trained sages or professional scribes who might experiment with novel exegeses of their Scriptures. Any major shift in their thinking as Jews could only have stemmed from one source, what they believed to be a revelation of (or from) YHWH, their one and only true God—a revelation and commissioning comparable to the appearance of YHWH to Moses at the burning bush or to Samuel in the tabernacle or to Isaiah in the temple (Exod. 3:2-10; 1 Sam. 3:10-14; Isa. 6:1-13).[54] Subsequent narration of such a revelation would require the disciples to mine their traditions (their prayers, binitarian templates, and known passages from the Hebrew Scriptures) and reformulate their own proclamations and prayers so as to address challenges and criticisms that would inevitably arise among their Jewish associates.[55]

To restate a point made earlier, I have no interest in denying that there were seemingly physical encounters with Jesus or that he was raised bodily from the dead. In order to explain the sudden origin of deity Christology, however, we must begin with a manifestation (vision, audition) of the Deity—a revelation experienced as coming from above—in the context of Jewish devotional practices, before relating it to more "empirical" traditions concerning the life and death of Jesus (from below).

Given some sort of revelation (or revelations) as the starting point, a resolution can readily be formulated as a conjecture, which is a working hypothesis.[56] The simplest explanation for the fact that Jesus was confessed as YHWH in the New Testament would be that *the first disciples experienced a manifestation of YHWH in a glorious anthropic (humanlike) form and that (at some point) they recognized the face and voice as those of their teacher.*[57] Early Christian affirmations of deity Christology can be viewed as relics of such a founding revelation (based on subsequent reenactments).

According to the proposed conjecture, the disciples did not see Jesus as YHWH (as most often stated). Instead, they saw YHWH (the Lord in embodied form) as Jesus. I shall argue (in ch. 4) that the latter proposition (in contrast to the former) fits fairly comfortably within the parameters of early Judaism. The Lord-Jesus identification was therefore based on traditions concerning theophanies (or kyriophanies) that came "from above." In narrative terms, it was based on the continued appearance of the God of Israel "from behind," that is, as an extension of the history of his covenant relations with Israel (in line with Barker's continuity thesis).[58]

If this is so, we may take at face value the confessional formula *Kyrios Iēsous* (1 Cor. 8:6; 12:3; Rom. 10:9; Phil. 2:11; passim).[59] The Christian confession was not primarily that "Jesus is Lord"—a formula that by itself, as translated into English, suggests some sort of elevation from below. The confession and proclamation of the early disciples was primarily that 'The Lord is Jesus.'"[60] It is only when we turn the problem around and start from the traditions concerning the life of Jesus (as the Gospel narratives do) that we get the obverse meaning, "Jesus is Lord."

How to Test the Conjecture

The subject at hand is a conjecture. It cannot be proved inductively by accumulating any amount of evidence. It can only be tested for across-the-board plausibility (or implausibility) against what we know about early Judaism, the New Testament, and the development of early Christianity.[61] At first blush, this admission might sound like a serious weakness. As indicated above, however, the standard approaches are also based on conjectures. Their only advantage, a priori, stems from their having been repeated in the literature to the point of serving as working assumptions by virtue of their familiarity.

It is relatively easy to support our conjecture with a heuristic argument. If the first followers of Jesus were pious Jews, then the initial impulse, the downbeat for early Christology, must have been something that was well attested in Jewish tradition and that was anticipated to recur in the near future. A postmortem encounter with a recently executed man would not fulfill this requirement, but a Kyriocentric vision would. If, therefore, the New Testament does reflect visions of YHWH like those of the prophets, we have *the advantage of the shortest line of reasoning* from biblical Judaism to the deity Christology as evidenced in the New Testament—no appeals to inferential steps, progressive stages, external influences, or revisions of Jewish monotheism, at least, not as far as the origin of deity Christology is concerned.[62]

In principle, it might be enough to offer an alternative scenario like this that avoids most of the difficulties of the existing reconstructions. Heuristics aside, however, it is necessary to think through the implications of the conjecture with regard to the evidence, particularly with regard to Jewish visionary practices, the continuation of these practices in the New Testament era, and the subsequent development of various Christologies in early Christianity. The value of a conjecture should lie in its fruitfulness: whether it generates meaningful exploration of the texts and shows them in a different light than standard approaches have done heretofore.

The implications of the Kyriocentric conjecture can be developed by raising questions about the context in which early Christology developed and assessing the plausibility of the conjecture thereby. These questions will be addressed in the following chapters.

The first three chapters (Part 1) establish a framework in early Judaism by placing visionary practice in the empirical context of oral performances.

In chapter 1, we examine the nature of the evidence we seek for visionary practices in early Jewish and Christian literature: were these visions experiential or were they merely literary motifs? I shall argue that they were both—mental scripts for visionary performances that were subsequently incorporated into narratives and other literary forms.

Chapter 2 summarizes the evidence for performance of Kyriocentric visions before, during, and after the New Testament period. I shall analyze seven apocalyptic texts, six early (Tannaitic) rabbinic texts, and two Heikalot hymns, thereby embedding the New Testament era in a matrix of earlier and later material.

In chapter 3, we describe the practical contexts that were associated with the performance of Kyriocentric visions in the resulting narratives: could such practices have provided the context for Kyriocentric visions among the early followers of Jesus? I conclude that the most frequent literary context was prayer, whether laudatory or petitionary, normally performed in a corporate, liturgical setting.

The next three chapters (Part 2) deal with the central issue: is it conceivable that the anthropic form of YHWH could reveal itself as a deceased human being and what evidence is there for this kind of Kyriocentric visions in the New Testament?

Chapter 4 explores the conditions under which such a Kyriocentric vision could have been identified with a deceased human being. I shall argue that the reenactment of visionary performances could lead to such identification following the violent death of a revered teacher, concluding with a discussion of "fortuitous uniqueness" and the development of a detailed scenario based on the Kyriocentric conjecture.

In chapter 5, we shall look for traces of these Kyriocentric visions in the New Testament itself. If the traces are there in an altered form, what were the exegetical and theological pressures exerted in the process of narrativization and textualization? I shall review several texts discussed by other New Testament scholars and add a few others (six in all).

Chapter 6 turns to prayers and devotional motifs associated with Kyriocentric visions that carry over to the Lord Jesus in New Testament communities: which motifs carry over, which do not, and why not? I find that devotional motifs that were most closely associated with the primary revelation were dedicated to the Lord Jesus. Those that were reserved for God the Father appear to have been constrained by Jesus traditions, particularly those concerning institution of the Eucharist.

The last three chapters (Part 3) build on this scenario to show how both some features of New Testament Christology that were later deemed orthodox and some alternative tradition histories can be understood as consequences of the Kyriocentric visions and the Lord-Jesus identification.

In chapter 7, we ask whether the Kyriocentric scenario can account for other the prominence of features of New Testament Christology, particularly those that the standard explanations rely on: belief in the resurrection of Jesus and binitarian formulas. We also approach beliefs concerning the timing of the union of the Lord with the man Jesus and about the role of the crucifixion in God's plan. Granted that these beliefs were all based on Jewish traditions, I argue that these traditions were selected and adapted in such a way as to address acute problems raised by the Kyriocentric visions. Each of these beliefs resolved a serious problem, and each of them in turn raised new problems that led to further clarifications. This generative approach to early Christology is one of the major strengths of the Kyriocentric conjecture.

Chapter 8 shifts away from such familiar, proto-orthodox beliefs to other early christological traditions that were later judged to be unorthodox. I shall argue that the complex texture of early Kyriocentric Christology allowed for a variety of emphases and that such diverse emphases could be tolerated in the Church (during the late second, third, and fourth centuries) as long as they were not systematized to the point of negating other traditions.

In chapter 9, we conclude the investigation by asking when and why Church leaders became uneasy with the idea of the Lord God having an anthropic form. I shall summarize three early developments that moved the church from an anthropic Deity to an aniconic (apophatic) one. These movements took place over a period of three centuries and were motivated by challenges from formative Judaism, Gnosticism, and Arianism, respectively.

Evaluation of the Kyriocentric conjecture requires addressing these nine questions in some detail. So as not to raise unrealistic expectations, I will say at the outset that I am not entirely satisfied with all of the answers I have been able to develop (some anomalies are listed in the Conclusion). I believe, however, that a new approach to the problem is needed and hope that others will take up the challenge either to improve on the answers presented here or to devise further scenarios that may help to resolve the dilemma of early deity Christology. Doing justice to this question will require a creative spirit like that of the first disciples and their Jewish associates.

Notes

1. Prior to the discussion in ch. 7, I shall use the term "execution" rather than "crucifixion." The latter is historically correct, but is also fraught with an accumulation of theological (soteriological) connotations that developed over time.

2. I shall use YHWH (the unpronounced Tetragrammaton) and *Kyrios* as transliterations of the divine names in the Hebrew Bible and the Greek New Testament, respectively, and use "the

Lord" for English translations of these texts. For propriety, the Tetragrammaton should be read as *Adonai* in Scripture (and in prayers). According to the *Avot [Fathers] of Rabbi Nathan*, the Rabbis taught that "those who pronounce God's name according to its proper consonants have no share in the world to come" (*Avot of Rabbi Nathan*, version A, 36). In discussing Rabbinic and Heikalot texts, however, I shall use *HaShem*, meaning "The [Divine] Name," which stands for the Tetragrammaton.

3. Post-Enlightenment scholars are often caught in the disparity between the richness of contextually appropriate ("emic") terms like "revelation" or "theophany" and the strictures of scholarly ("etic") language. For the most part, I shall restrict myself to neutral, phenomenological terms like "vision," keeping in mind that "visions" were normally accompanied (or preceded) by auditions (e.g., Job 4:12-16; 2 Cor. 12:1, 9), and "performance," the reenactment of classic visions. "Theophanies" and "revelations" would be more "emic" terms to use because visionaries believed what they reported seeing and hearing was real, but these terms have the disadvantage of assuming an ontology that is foreign to post-Enlightenment scholarship. "Encounter" is another possible term, as argued by Philip S. Alexander, "Jewish Believers in Early Rabbinic Literature (2d to 5th Centuries)," in *Jewish Believers in Jesus: The Early Centuries*, ed. Oskar Skarsaune and Reidar Hvalvik (Peabody, MA: Hendrickson, 2007), 659–709 (684). To my ears, however, it still seems to carry too much ontological (and existential) weight.

4. LXX (the Roman numeral for seventy) stands for the LXX, which is the Greek translation of the Old Testament that was widely used in the first century. The Hebrew texts on which it was based were different in places from the Masoretic Hebrew texts that are translated in English Bibles. Manuscripts of the LXX also include several "apocryphal" or "deuterocanonical" texts that are not included in the Masoretic canon. For an English translation, see Albert Pietersma and Benjamin G. Wright, eds., *A New English Translation of the Septuagint and the Other Greek Translations Traditionally Included Under That Title* (New York: Oxford University Press, 2007). Abbreviated NETS.

5. The Isaiah and Amos visions were both staged in the Temple. Some Rabbinic *midrashim* (exegetical "inquiries") insisted that *HaShem*'s self-revelations always occurred in the Temple (once it was constructed); *Sifrei* Num. 6:23; Reuven Hammer, trans., *The Classic Midrash: Tannaitic Commentaries on the Bible*, Classics of Western Spirituality (New York: Paulist, 1995), 223. Non-Rabbinic Jewish traditions, like that in *1 Enoch* 14, located such revelations in a temple in heaven, which was accessible to righteous people like Enoch.

6. On 1 Cor. 9:1 in relation to Isa. 6:1, 8, see Seyoon Kim, *The Origin of Paul's Gospel* (Tübingen: Mohr Siebeck, 1981), 94; Kim, *Paul and the New Perspective: Second Thoughts on the Origin of Paul's Gospel* (Grand Rapids: Eerdmans, 2002), 241. On John 12:41(*eiden tēn doxan autou*) in relation to Isa. 6:1, 3, see Nils Alstrup Dahl, "The Johannine Church and History," in *Current Issues in New Testament Interpretation: Essays in Honor of Otto A. Piper*, ed. William Klassen and Graydon F. Snyder (New York: Harper, 1962), 124–42 (131–32); Anthony T. Hanson, *Jesus Christ in the Old Testament* (London: SPCK, 1965), 104–8; Martin McNamara, *Targum and Testament: Aramaic Paraphrases of the Hebrew Bible: A Light on the New Testament* (Shannon: Irish University Press, 1972), 49, 99; Riemer Roukema, "Jesus and the Divine Name in the Gospel of John," in *The Revelation of the Name YHWH to Moses: Perspectives from Judaism, the Pagan Graeco-Roman World, and Early Christianity*, ed. George H. Kooten, TBN 9 (Leiden: Brill, 2006), 207–33 (210–11). See also the parallels charted in Gary T. Manning, *Echoes of a Prophet: The Use of Ezekiel in the Gospel of John and in the Literature of the Second Temple Period* (London: T&T Clark, 2004), 150–57. Adriana Destro and Mauro Pesce argue for dependence of John 12:41on *Ascen. Isa.* 6–11 (which is in itself based on a performance of Isa. 6); Destro and Pesce, "The Heavenly Journey in Paul: Tradition in a Jewish Apocalyptic Literary Genre of Cultural Practice in a Hellenistic-Roman Context?" in *Paul's Jewish Matrix*, Studies in Judaism and Christianity, ed. Thomas G. Casey and Justin Taylor (Rome: Gregorian & Biblical Press, 2012), 167–200 (194 n. 46 and sources cited there).

7. The earliest disciples of Jesus were not yet called "Christians" (cf. Acts 11:26) or even "Jewish Christians" or "Nazarenes." A useful term is "Jewish believers in Jesus," the earliest precedent for which comes from the Gospel of John (8:31); Oskar Skarsaune, "Jewish Believers in Jesus in Antiquity: Problems of Definition, Method, and Sources," in Jewish Believers in Jesus: The Early Centuries, 3–21 (5). However, disciples were more than "believers," and their focus was just as much on prayer and practice. Among others, Philip R. Davies has pointed out the danger in defining Jewish sects only in terms of their theological beliefs; Davies, "Sects from Texts: On the Problem of Doing a Sociology of the Qumran Literature," in New Directions in Qumran Studies, Library of Second Temple Studies 52, ed. Jonathan G. Campbell, William John Lyons, and Lloyd K. Pietersen (London: T&T Clark, 2005), 69–82 (72). Moshe Idel criticizes Jewish scholars for a similar (Christian influenced!) emphasis on theology; Idel, Enchanted Chains: Techniques and Rituals in Jewish Mysticism (Los Angeles: Cherub, 2005), 19–25.

8. I cannot agree with Charles Talbert's lumping 1 Cor. 16:22 together with texts like Acts 17:31 that portray Jesus as a man taken up into heaven who will function in the end time but is not a present benefactor; Talbert, The Development of Christology during the First Hundred Years and Other Essays on Early Christian Christology, NovT Sup 140 (Leiden: Brill, 2011), 16. I do agree with Talbert on the diversity of models (or rather, performances and narratives) in the NT, but his inductive procedure (constructing categories of models and using them, together with their soteriological implications, to explain the origin of Christology) is radically different from the hypothetico-deductive method and demand-side hermeneutic that will be developed here.

9. Andrew Chester nicely sums up the point (with respect to 1 Cor. 8:6) in a recent review of early Christology scholarship: "Christ is given the supreme, distinctive divine name YHWH (denoted as kýrios). . . . the fact that he [Paul] uses the Shema shows that beyond any doubt. Thus he makes Christ fully one with God, in the strongest possible Jewish terms, sharing in the divine name as well as the divine act of creation"; Chester, "High Christology—Whence, When and Why?" Early Christianity 2 (2011): 22–50 (36–37).

10. Moshe Weinfeld, "The Day of the Lord: Aspirations for the Kingdom of God in the Bible and Jewish Literature," in Studies in Bible, Scripta Hierosolymitana 31, ed. Sara Japhet (Jerusalem: Magnes, 1986), 345–72 (371). The results of the present investigation imply that the "change" Weinfeld refers to was the accretion of a new name (Jesus), not a transfer of attributes from HaShem to Jesus as a surrogate god; cf. David Frankfurter, "Beyond 'Jewish Christianity': Continuing Religious Sub-Cultures of the Second and Third Centuries and Their Documents," in The Ways that Never Parted: Jews and Christians in Late Antiquity and the Early Middle Ages, TSAJ 95, ed. Adam H. Becker and Annette Yoshiko Reed (Tübingen: Mohr Siebeck, 2003), 131–43 (139).

11. The magisterial work on this topic is Larry W. Hurtado, Lord Jesus Christ: Devotion to Jesus in Earliest Christianity (Grand Rapids: Eerdmans, 2003). Hurtado dates the "big bang" of deity Christology to the 30s ce; ibid., 135, 136.

12. A few representative theories will be discussed below. Even if early Judaism did allow some multiplicity within the Godhead and occasionally assigned divine attributes to ideal figures like the apocalyptic Son of Man, deity was never attributed to a human being of recent historical memory and doxological formulas like "Save, Lord!" were exclusively directed to the Lord God of Israel (discussed further in ch. 6).

13. George Nickelsburg and Robert Kraft define the provenance of "early" or "postbiblical" Judaism as the period from Alexander the Great (c. 330 bce) to Hadrian (c. 138 ce); Nickelsburg and Kraft, introduction to Early Judaism and its Modern Interpreters, ed. Robert A. Kraft and George W. E. Nickelsburg, Bible and its Modern Interpreters 2 (Atlanta: Scholars, 1986), 1–30 (2). Other scholars would extend the period one more century in order to include the Tannaitic era and the redaction of the Mishnah (early third century).

14. The term rabbi could be used merely as an honorary title; see Lee I. Levine, The Rabbinic Class of Roman Palestine in Late Antiquity (New York: Jewish Theological Seminary of America, 1989), 49 n. 32. I shall use the capitalized form Rabbis to designate the scholarly class whose ideas

are discussed in Mishnah, Tosefta, Talmud, and midrash. The term *Sages* (*Hakhamim*) is normally used for exponents of the majority opinion among the Rabbis (e.g., *t. Maksh.* 3:4) and so may not do justice to the diversity of interests in this early period.

15. E.g., Seth Schwartz, *Imperialism and Jewish Society: 200 B.C.E. to 640 C.E.* (Princeton, NJ: Princeton University Press, 2001), 77, 86 (ideologies within a single complex); Daniel Boyarin, "Semantic Differences," in *The Ways that Never Parted*, 65–85 (76, 79, dialects); Stuart S. Miller, *Sages and Commoners in Late Antique 'Erez Israel: A Philological Inquiry into Local Traditions in Talmud Yerushalmi*, TSAJ 111 (Tübingen: Mohr Siebeck, 2006), 21–28 (complex common Judaism); Arkady Kovelman, *Between Alexandria and Jerusalem: The Dynamic of Jewish and Hellenistic Culture*, Brill Reference Library of Judaism 21 (Leiden: Brill, 2005), xii (stylistic systems).

16. See, for example, Daniel Boyarin, *Dying for God: Martyrdom and the Making of Christianity and Judaism* (Stanford, CA: Stanford University Press, 1999), 8–11. In more recent writing, Boyarin prefers the phrase *polyform Judaism*, judging that the term *Judaisms* suggests separate social groups; Boyarin, "Beyond Judaisms: Metatron and the Divine Polymorphy of Ancient Judaism," *JSJ* 41 (2010): 323–65 (325, 328, 360).

17. Wright allows that Paul may have *interpreted* his initiatory vision as the expected appearance of the divine Glory (Isa. 40:1), but he denies that this recognition was the "initial primary meaning of the event"; rather it was an inference based on Paul's prior conviction that Jesus had been vindicated as Messiah and "the world's true Lord" (based on Dan. 7:13; Ps. 110:1); Wright, *The Resurrection of the Son of God*, Christian Origins and the Question of God 3 (Minneapolis: Fortress Press, 2003), 394–95, 397. Andrew Chester appropriately points out that Wright's construction of the Pauline vision in terms of messiahship is "question-begging"; Chester, "The Christ of Paul," in *Redemption and Resistance: The Messianic Hopes of Jews and Christians in Antiquity*, ed. William Horbury, Markus Bockmuehl, and James Carleton Paget (London: T&T Clark, 2007), 109–21 (114).

18. See also Richard Bauckham on the exaltation of Jesus and the use of Psalm 110; Bauckham, *Jesus and the God of Israel: God Crucified and Other Studies on the New Testament's Christology of Divine Identity* (Grand Rapids: Eerdmans, 2008), 128, 138, 234–36. Similar chains of events have been posited by the late Jewish scholar Alan Segal in *Paul the Convert: The Apostolate and Apostasy of Saul the Pharisee* (New Haven, CT: Yale University Press, 1990), 56–57; James D. G. Dunn, *Did the First Christians Worship Jesus? The New Testament Evidence* (Louisville: Westminster John Knox, 2010), 101–3; and Larry W. Hurtado, *God in New Testament Theology*, Library of Biblical Theology (Nashville: Abingdon, 2010), 62, 64.

19. N. T. Wright, "Resurrecting Old Arguments: Responding to Four Essays," *JSHJ* 3 (2005): 209–31 (230); cf. Wright, *The Resurrection of the Son of God*, 25, 394–98, 554, 563, 571, 577.

20. The burden of chapters 1 and 2 will be that visionary texts were actually rooted in the community-based performance of ancient vision traditions. In terms of performance theory, there is no dichotomy between empirical and spiritual as Wright appears to assume.

21. Healing prophets like Elijah and Elisha (and Jesus himself) were believed to have raised the dead, but these raisings were signs of the status of the prophets, not of the dead. Dan. 12:13 promises the resurrection of Daniel at the "end of days," but only as a member of the class of *maskilim* (cf. 12:3-4, 10). Some of the followers of the Lubavitcher Rebbe, Menachem Mendel Schneerson, affirmed that he had risen from the dead following his death in 1994. Messianic expectations and Christian influence may have played a role in this case, so, unlike Joel Marcus, I still do not see it as a useful parallel to New Testament affirmations about the resurrection of Jesus; Marcus, "The Once and Future Messiah in Early Christianity and Chabad," *NTS* 47 (2001): 381–401 (396–97).

22. Wright himself states that "There are no traditions about a Messiah being [martyred and] raised to life"; Wright, *The Resurrection of the Son of God*, 205. New Testament scholars should pay more attention to counterexamples like the putative resurrection of John the Baptist

(Mark 6:14). As Eduard Schweizer pointed out in his commentary, "One could be fully convinced of the possibility of John's resurrection and yet not honor him as the Messiah"; Schweizer, *The Good News According to Mark*, trans. Donald H. Madvig (Atlanta: John Knox, 1970), 133. One might add that John was probably thought to be the Messiah by at least some of his followers (cf. John 1:8, 20). Another counterexample would be the expected bodily resurrection of the two witnesses in Rev. 11—there are no messianic implications here either; cf. Dale C. Allison, Jr., *Constructing Jesus: Memory, Imagination, and History* (Grand Rapids: Baker Academic, 2010), 242–43. Nor did the raising of R. Kahana by R. Yohanan (*b. B. Qam.* 117b) lead to any thought about (either of them) being the Messiah. Jesus being raised from the dead might be viewed as confirming his claims (or his disciples' hopes) about himself—whatever they were; so, for example, Allison, *Constructing Jesus*, 243–44. But Jesus' claims to messiahship were implicit at best, even as presented in the Gospels, so there is little for the historian to work with here; see, e.g., Petr Pokorny, *The Genesis of Christology* (Edinburgh: T&T Clark, 1987), 84, 88 (here discussing Q); Allison, *Constructing Jesus*, 286–88 (on Jesus traditions in general). The latter point will be discussed further in ch. 7. Wright's case might be strengthened if Israel Knohl were correct in reading the "Gabriel Revelation" (*Hazon Gabriel*, an inscribed tablet from the late first century bce), lines 80-81, as saying, "In three days you [prince of princes] shall live"; Knohl, "'By Three Days Live': Messiahs, Resurrection, and Ascent to Heaven in *Hazon Gabriel*," *JR* 88 (2008): 147–58 (155–57). However, see the critique of Knohl's reading in John Collins, "Gabriel and David: Some Reflections on an Enigmatic Text," in *Hazon Gabriel: New Readings*, Early Judaism and its Literature 29, ed. Matthias Henze and John J. Collins (Atlanta: SBL, 2011), 99–112 (107–8).

23. As Larry Hurtado states, "Jesus' resurrection is not really presented as an expression of Jesus' inherent power of divinity so much as the exercise of 'God's' power on Jesus' behalf"; Hurtado, *God in New Testament Theology*, 57.

24. The Similitudes of Enoch portray the kings of the earth as paying homage—thereby attributing suzerainty—to the Son of Man (*1 En.* 62:9). As Dale Allison points out, however, the expectation of a Messiah is rather marginal in the Similitudes as a whole (appearing only in *1 En.* 48:10; 52:4); Allison, *Constructing Jesus*, 288. Relying on the Similitudes would also require addressing the problems of dating this late addition to the Enoch corpus.

25. In a footnote that concludes a lengthy chapter on the origin of Christology, Dale Allison suggests that a "very high Christology," including deity "in a qualified sense," was implicated in the Apostles' recognition of his being Messiah; Allison, *Constructing Jesus*, 304 n. 349. William Horbury cites *1 En.* 52:6 and *4 Ezra* (part of *2 Esdras*) 13:3-4 as evidence that divine attributes could be transferred to the Messiah or Son of Man; Horbury, *Jewish Messianism and the Cult of Christ* (London: SCM, 1998), 103–4; on *4 Ezra* 13, cf. Daniel Boyarin, *The Jewish Gospels: The Story of the Jewish Christ* (New York: New Press, 2012), 96–99. Clearly there are important associations here, but we need to pay more attention to counterexamples in the history of Judaism. For example, Hayyim Vital dreamt that he was elevated to the presence of *HaShem* and even invited to sit at his right hand, a place that was specially prepared for him (thereby supplanting Joseph Karo); Vital, *Sefer ha-Hezyonot* ("Book of Visions") 2.5, ET in Morris M. Faierstein, trans., *Jewish Mystical Autobiographies: Book of Visions and Book of Secrets*, Classics of Western Spirituality (New York: Paulist, 1999), 81; cf. R. J. Zwi Werblowsky, *Joseph Karo: Lawyer and Mystic*, 2nd ed. (Philadelphia: Jewish Publication Society of America, 1977), 144. The messianic overtones are clear, but there is not even a hint of identification with *HaShem* as in the case of Jesus. As Ada Rapoport-Albert has pointed out with regard to Hasidic masters: "The Zaddik was never deified; he never became the object of worship in his own right"; Rapoport-Albert, "God and the Zaddik as the Two Focal Points of Hasidic Worship," *History of Religions* 18 (1979): 296–325 (322).

26. According to Epiphanius, *Panarion* ("Medicine Chest") 30.3.4, some Ebionites held that Christ was the "lord of all," and yet was created by God. Arians and Eunomians also held this view.

27. Maurice Casey, *From Jewish Prophet to Gentile God: The Origins and Development of New Testament Christology* (Cambridge: James Clarke, 1991), 163–65. Wilhelm Bousset's classic work

Kyrios Christos was first published in German just over a century ago (1913). His argument for a Hellenistic cult origin of the title *Kyrios* is found in ch. 3; Bousset, *Kyrios Christos*, trans. John E. Steely (Nashville: Abingdon, 1970), 119–52.

28. For example, James Crossley states in his review of Hurtado, *Lord Jesus Christ* that "There is nothing like the Johannine material in the earlier documents, thereby suggesting they did not have such a 'high' Christology"; *JEH* 56 (2006): 118–20 (119).

29. Casey, *From Jewish Prophet to Gentile God*, 156–59.

30. The compound term *Yahweh text* goes back to David B. Capes, *Old Testament Yahweh Texts in Paul's Christology*, WUNT 47 (Tübingen: Mohr, 1992). While credit goes to Capes for popularizing the phrase, the basic idea had been developed decades earlier by scholars like Lucien Cerfaux, "*Kyrios* dans les citations pauliniennes de l'Ancien Testament," *Ephemerides Theologicae Lovanienses* 20 (1943): 5–17; and J. C. O'Neill, "The Use of *Kyrios* in the Book of Acts," *SJT* 8 (1955): 155–74. James D. G. Dunn has used the less succinct but more descriptive phrase "scriptural *kýrios* = Yahweh references"; Dunn, *The Theology of Paul the Apostle* (Grand Rapids: Eerdmans, 1998), 249. I shall place *Yahweh text* in quotation marks in recognition of its use as a stock phrase in New Testament literature and the divine name being used adjectivally.

31. Matthew Black, "The Maranatha Invocation and Jude 14, 15 (I Enoch 1:9)," in *Christ and Spirit in the New Testament*, ed. Barnabas Lindars and Stephen S. Smalley (Cambridge: Cambridge University Press, 1973), 189–96.

32. "Q" stands for *Quelle*, the German word for the hypothetical "source" of non-Markan material that is common to the Gospels of Matthew and Luke. Q is usually dated to the 50s CE but may have strata of various dates. Following standard introductions to the New Testament, I shall list texts in their chronological order (as far as known), rather than in their canonical order.

33. Martin Hengel opined that the entire process took less than five years; Hengel, *Between Jesus and Paul: Studies in the History of Earliest Christianity*, trans. John Bowden (Minneapolis: Fortress Press, 1983), 39–47.

34. Hurtado, *Lord Jesus Christ*, 136.

35. When Casey reviewed Larry Hurtado's *Lord Jesus Christ*, he charged Hurtado with using "evangelical" categories and took the author to task for appealing to "revelatory religious experience," rather than providing an explanatory historical account in terms of Jewish traditions; Casey, "Lord Jesus Christ: A Response to Professor Hurtado," *JSNT* 27 (2004): 83–96 (86, 89).

36. Kevin P. Sullivan, *Wrestling with Angels: A Study of the Relationship between Angels and Humans in Ancient Jewish Literature and the New Testament*, Arbeiten zur Geschichte des antiken Judentums und des Urchristentums 55 (Leiden: Brill, 2004), 235. Here Sullivan is responding to Richard Bauckham's advocacy of early deity Christology, but his statement is based on a misreading of Bauckham's idea of "incorporation" as "addition"; cf. Bauckham, *Jesus and the God of Israel*, 101, 185, and most clearly on 213: "Paul is not adding to the one God of the *Shema* . . . . He is identifying Jesus as the 'Lord' (*YHWH*) whom the *Shema* affirms to be one."

37. Werner H. Schmidt calls for a similar explication of criteria in the case of ancient Israel's borrowing of ideas from Canaanite cults; Schmidt, *The Faith of the Old Testament: A History*, trans. John Sturdy (Oxford: Blackwell, 1983), 180–81. Richard Bauckham has pointed out that Schmidt's suggestion could be useful in explaining the development of New Testament Christology; Bauckham, *Jesus and the God of Israel*, 75–78.

38. I am arguing for a simplified version of *Rezeptionsgeschichte*, as distinct from traditional *Wirkungsgeschichte*; cf. Beate Pongratz-Leisten, "When the Gods are Speaking: Toward Defining the Interface between Polytheism and Monotheism," in *Propheten in Mari, Assyrien und Israel*, ed. Von Matthias Köckert and Martii Nissinen (Göttingen: Vandenhoeck & Ruprecht, 2003), 132–68 (140–41, 160–61). The matter is stated clearly by John Ashton: "authors borrow for a reason and the reason is never to be found in the text that is borrowed"; Ashton, "The Johannine Son of Man: A New Proposal," *NTS* 57 (2011): 508–29 (525). For a brilliant application of this "generative problematic" in the formation of the Mishnah, see Jacob Neusner, *Oral Tradition in Judaism: The*

Case of the Mishnah (Garland Reference Library of the Humanities 764, New York: Garland, 1987), 136 (cf. 139–40): "the critical problematic at the center always exercises influence over the peripheral facts, dictating how they are chosen arranged, utilized."

39. Margaret Barker, *The Great Angel: A Study of Israel's Second God* (Louisville: Westminster John Knox, 1992).

40. Barker, *Temple Themes in Christian Worship* (London: T&T Clark, 2007), 137.

41. The standard view is that the "one Lord" in 1 Cor. 8:6 is taken from a Greek version of Deut. 6:4, which is the first verse of the *Shema*. James F. McGrath's spirited critique falters on the dubious suggestion that Paul held Jesus as Lord only on earth; McGrath, *The Only True God: Early Christian Monotheism in its Jewish Context* (Urbana: University of Illinois Press, 2009), 41. To the contrary, Paul clearly affirmed Jesus to be "Lord over all," Rom. 9:5; cf. 1 Cor. 15:27 ("all things in subjection"); Phil. 2:10-11 ("every knee in heaven and on earth"); Col. 1:15-20 ("all creation . . . all things in heaven and on earth . . . all things whether on earth or in heaven"). The standard view of 1 Cor. 8:6 holds up quite well in this respect.

42. In spite of the potentially anti-Judaic associations with the term *Old Testament*, it is the only phrase in common currency that includes the Hebrew Tanakh, the Aramaic Targumim, and the Greek Septuagint with its deuterocanonical additions.

43. Similar views have been argued by scholars like Crispin H. T. Fletcher-Lewis, "The Real Presence of the Son before Christ: Revisiting an Old Approach to Old Testament Christology," *Concordia Theological Quarterly* 68 (2004): 105–26; Steven Richard Scott, "The Binitarian Nature of the *Book of Similitudes*," *JSP* 18 (2008): 55–78 (based on the figure of the Son of Man in the Similitudes of Enoch); Daniel Boyarin, *The Jewish Gospels* (based on the Son of Man in Daniel 7 and the Similitudes of Enoch).

44. Barker locates Jesus' recognition of his identity as the Great Angel at his baptism, during which he knew himself to be taken up into the vision and deified; Barker, *The Risen Lord: The Jesus of History as the Christ of Faith* (London: T&T Clark, 1996), 107–8, 110; Barker, *The Hidden Tradition of the Kingdom of God* (London: SPCK, 2007), 92–94, 96. As a parallel, she cites the "Self-Glorification Hymn" from Qumran (4Q427; personal e-mail dated 16 Feb 2009).

45. Barker, *The Great Angel*, 221.

46. There are many variations of this binitarian scenario in current scholarship, some of which have been argued particularly in response to Larry Hurtado. Hurtado had argued for the novelty of binitarian visions in the New Testament like that of the Son of Man at the right hand of God (Acts 7:56; cf. Mark 14:62) or the Lamb before the throne (Rev. 4:6-7); Hurtado, *Lord Jesus Christ*, 176; Hurtado, *How On Earth Did Jesus Become a God?* (Grand Rapids: Eerdmans, 2005), 199–201. William Horbury justly critiques Hurtado for treating the early Christian visions "with emphasis on their innovatory potential rather than their reflection of existing [Jewish] loyalties"; Horbury documents such loyalties by positing Jewish belief in a divine Messiah; Horbury's review of Hurtado, *Lord Jesus Christ*, in *JTS* 56 (2005): 531–39 (538). Steven Richard Scott also makes the point that mystical visions have normally fit the parameters of their host religion; he finds precedent for binitarian visions in the Similitudes of Enoch; Scott, "The Binitarian Nature of the Book of Similitudes," 58, 60. On the "divinity" of the expected Messiah, see the more balanced treatment of Adela Yarbro Collins and John J. Collins, *King and Messiah as Son of God: Divine, Human and Angelic Messianic Figures in Biblical and Related Literature* (Grand Rapids: Eerdmans, 2008), 20–22, 57–58, 100, 172, 204. In contrast, my own approach will be to start with the most common accounts of Jewish visions, those centered on YHWH in anthropic form, and generate the distinctive Christian beliefs from the superposition of this with the remembered portrait of Jesus as Jewish *hasid* at a secondary level (ch. 7).

47. Richard Bauckham, *Jesus and the God of Israel*, 95, 112–13. One can appreciate Bauckham's basic point without insisting on all of his strictures on YHWH's participation in the divine council and the veneration of angelic (divine) beings.

48. I adopt the term "Kyriocentric" as a way of stressing the primary interest of most texts (apocalypses and Psalms) in the presence of YHWH (*Kyrios*) while allowing for accompaniment

by any number of angels, or even an angelic Son of Man. As Charles Gieschen has stated, "Although Jewish and early Christian apocalyptic literature includes a visionary experience of a wide variety of subjects . . . nevertheless the visible image of YHWH especially on his throne, is often the central visionary experience in apocalyptic documents"; see Gieschen's contribution, "'Early Jewish and Christian Mysticism': A Collage of Working Definitions," *Society of Biblical Literature Seminar Papers* 40, ed. April DeConick (2001): 278–304 (287). The use of Kyriocentric language has been critiqued by feminist theologians like Elisabeth Schüssler Fiorenza, who points out that it actively, performatively constructs an androcentric world, defined in terms of male imagery; Fiorenza, *Transforming Vision: Explorations in Feminist Theology* (Minneapolis: Fortress Press, 2011), 222. Even though this archaic language does not meet modern standards of inclusiveness, it still conforms to those of biblical writers, who shared a more hierarchical understanding of the world than we do (Fiorenza, *Transforming Vision*, 17). I discuss this important matter further in the Conclusion.

49. The Lord-Jesus identification *Kyrios Iēsous* was a primary confessional formula that encapsulated the new bodily manifestation of YHWH with the face and voice of Jesus.

50. Early identifications of the anthropic form as Jesus constituted a primary "revelation" for the sectarian movement that they engendered. As discussed in chapters 1 and 2, such revelations were originally rehearsals of earlier theophanies. The "primary revelations" are therefore part of an ongoing series of performances and revelations.

51. My primary-secondary distinction is similar to James M. Robinson's between primary and secondary stages in accounts of Christ's appearances (luminous visualizations and depictions of a physically resurrected human, respectively); Robinson, "Jesus from Easter to Valentinus (or the Apostles' Creed)," *JBL* 101 (1982): 5–37 (12–13, 16). The main difference is that I identify the primary (luminous) appearances as kyriophanies (or Kyriocentric visions) rather than appearances of a transformed Jesus. As Andrew Chester states, " . . . the early Christians struggling to make full sense of the extraordinary nature of Christ, as this had been revealed to them, may well, within their Jewish context, have found knowledge of such [intermediary figure] traditions helpful in enabling them to articulate the significance of Christ . . ."; Chester, "High Christology," 41–42.

52. One of the best parallels in the history of Judaism is R. Eleazah ben Yehudah ben Kalomymus of Worms (c. 1165–1230), who distinguished the Glory that appeared to Isaiah, Ezekiel, and Daniel from the Creator of the world who has "no limit or boundary" (*Ein Sof*), while maintaining the ontological continuity of the two; see Elliot R. Wolfson, *Through a Speculum that Shines: Vision and Imagination in Medieval Jewish Mysticism* (Princeton, NJ: Princeton University Press, 1994), 231. Philo of Alexandria had similarly distinguished the "Lord" who was seen by Abraham in Gen. 17:1 from the invisible Cause of all (e.g., *Change of Names* 15), but Philo was not so clear about the ontological continuity between the two (cf. *Abraham* 124). This confusion will be discussed in ch. 8 (the subordinationist, proto-Arian option).

53. Compare Arthur W. Wainwright's discussion of the New Testament distinction between the titles "God" and "Lord" (1 Cor. 8:6; Phil. 2:11) or the titles "Father" and "Son"; Wainwright, *The Trinity in the New Testament* (London: SCM, 1962), 92, 171–72. In saying that binitarian formulas were necessitated by Jesus traditions, I bypass for the time being the "modalist" option, according to which the difference between Jesus and the Father was only apparent. This particular tradition history will also be discussed in ch. 8, "The Proto-modalist Option."

54. As explained in an earlier note, "revelation" was an appropriate term in the context of the biblical worldview. Once the main idea is established, I shall use terms like "performance" and "vision."

55. Gershom Scholem's classic description of the dynamics of "mystical experience" is helpful in spite of recent criticisms. According to Scholem, revelatory experiences must be communicated in terms of traditional symbols, but they can also transform the content of that tradition and give new meaning to old forms; Scholem, *On the Kabbalah and its Symbolism*, trans. Ralph Manheim (New York: Schocken Books, 1965), 7–9. Scholem cites Paul's Damascus Road revelation as an example of such transformation; ibid., 14–15. Rachel Elior puts it this way

(assuming a culture of written manuscripts): "The visionary reads and internalizes visions for the sacred literary text, inserts new imagery into the original visions, and thus transforms them into a living reality within himself"; Elior, *Jewish Mysticism: The Infinity Expression of Freedom*, trans. Yudith Nave and Arthur B. Millman (Oxford: Littman Library of Jewish Civilization, 1997), 89. Moshe Idel has developed a similar analysis of mystical phenomena. He stresses the role of ritual and praxis, which, he states, is more inclusive and open to "unexpected experiences" than theological symbols are; Idel, *Enchanted Chains*, 35–37. As any athlete or thespian knows, performances often take on their own momentum with unpredictable results.

56. Similarly, Lawrence Hoffman explores the meaning of statutory Jewish prayers in terms of a liturgical "field of meaning," in which the devout can "intuit a worshipful relationship with the divine." From the perspective of the modern scholar, this liturgical field is a "hypothetical construct" or set of "nonempirically derived propositions"; Hoffman, *Beyond the Text: A Holistic Approach to Liturgy* (Bloomington: Indiana University Press, 1987), 148–50. An analogy from modern cosmology would be reconstructing the state of the universe prior to its earliest observable feature, the cosmic microwave background. Cosmologists hypothesize cosmic inflation in order to build models that reproduce what we do observe at a later stage of development.

57. Alan Segal once stated that the manifestation was not YHWH in person, but rather the divine *Kavod* ("Glory") in human form; Segal, *Paul the Convert*, 57, 61, 154, 157. However, these two modes of appearance are not readily differentiated within the context of pre-Christian Judaism (e.g., Exod. 16:10-11; 24:16-17; Num. 16:42-4; Isa. 40:5, 10; 60:1-2; Ezek. 1:26-8; 3:12; 11:22-3; 43:2-7; 2 Macc. 2:8; Palestinian Targumim to Exod. 24:10; 33:23; 34:5-7; Tg. 1 Kgs. 22:19; Tg. Isa. 6:1, 5); see Gerhard von Rad, "Doxa," *TDNT* 2:232-55 (244). Elliot Wolfson has come closer to the mark in stating that "The possibility of encountering the visible form of the invisible God was appropriated by some of the earlier followers of Jesus and the Jewish mystical doctrines are [were] applied to him"; See Wolfson's contribution, "'Early Jewish and Christian Mysticism': A Collage of Working Definitions," *SBLSP* 40, 299.

58. Dutch theologian Hendrikus Berkhof argued for a Christology "from behind," that is, from the narrative of the people of Israel and the Holy One of Israel; Berkhof, *Christian Faith: An Introduction to the Study of the Faith*, trans. Sierd Woudstra (Grand Rapids: Eerdmans, 1979), 28. See the helpful interpretation of Berkhof's idea in Klaas Runia, *The Present-Day Christological Debate* (Leicester: Inter-Varsity Press, 1984), 72.

59. The normal Pauline word order places the title Kyrios first; Gordon Fee, *Pauline Christology: An Exegetical-Theological Study* (Peabody, MA: Hendrickson, 2007), 123–34, 399–400. The alternate word order in 2 Cor. 4:5 and Phil. 3:8 shows that the identification was reversible, but Paul's normal usage began with his adherence to the Lord as confessed in the *Shema*; cf. 1 Cor. 8:6; Rom. 10:9.

60. The *Kyrios Iēsous* (or *Kyrios Christos*) form is found at least twenty-four times in the New Testament, the earliest being 1 Cor. 8:6; 12:3, 5. The reverse order is found only four or five times (2 Cor. 4:5; Phil. 3:8; Col. 2:6; 1 Pet. 2:3, and possibly Luke 2:11).

61. Karl Popper's classic method of conjecture and refutation has long since replaced the earlier positivist ideal of "verification"; Popper, *Conjectures and Refutations: The Growth of Scientific Knowledge* (London: Routledge & Kegan Paul, 1963). In all but the simplest, most formalized cases, however, strict refutation is no more possible than strict verification, and it is better to work with the category of plausibility. Even though predictions that are not verified or even contradicted by the evidence can be accommodated by modifications of the original conjecture, such "epicycles" make the conjecture far less plausible than desired (unless they can be independently observed and verified).

62. This part of the argument has been forcefully argued by earlier scholars, one of whom is Bert Jan Lietaert Peerbolte, who once stated that "In Phil 2:11 . . . Jesus is identified as the Lord God of the Jewish bible, as YHWH"; Peerbolte, "The Name above All Names (Philippians 2:9)," in *The Revelation of the Name YHWH to Moses*, 187–206 (203). It appears that Prof. Peerbolte reversed himself in a later (otherwise most helpful) article: "But given the fact that Paul apparently

saw Christ, and not *YHWH*, as the main character of his vision, the content of what he communicates . . . differs strongly from comparable descriptions in other Jewish sources" (173); Peerbolte, "Paul's Rapture: 2 Corinthians 12:2-4 and the Language of Mystics," in *Experientia, Volume I: Inquiry into Religious Experience in Early Judaism and Christianity*, ed. Frances Flannery, Colleen Shantz, and Rodney A. Werline (Atlanta: SBL, 2008), 159–76. The point of the present essay will be to vindicate the former (2006) statement against the latter (2008).

PART I

Kyriocentric Visions in the Context of Crisis and Performative Prayer

1

Kyriocentric Visions in Early Judaism: Experiential, Literary, or Performative?

The Kyriocentric conjecture proposed here is based on the assumption that turn-of-the-era Jews experienced visions of YHWH coming to reassure and to save. Is this a realistic assumption? Several eminent scholars of Jewish literature doubt that such an assumption can be supported from the texts at hand (reasons for which are discussed below). So, is it possible that we are only left with literary allusions to visionary motifs that have no historical verisimilitude?

First, let us clarify some of the options to be considered. First-century Jews certainly believed that holy men and women *could have* visions of their God appearing to them—and speaking to them—in human form. They believed that Kyriocentric visions (also known as theophanies) had been granted to their forebears: the patriarchs and matriarchs, the exodus generation, and the prophets.[1] According to the Septuagint (LXX) rendering of theophany texts in Exodus and Numbers, the Lord (*Kyrios*) was seen in the Tabernacle—and, by inference, in the Temple—particularly in association with the high-priestly blessing.[2] A public Kyriocentric vision had also been granted to the citizens of Jerusalem who had suffered under one of the Ptolemies (3 Macc. 5:51; 6:17-18).[3] According to later, Amoraic Rabbis (third–fifth century), *HaShem* was clearly visible in the Temple: visible to the high priest and also to pilgrims who were allowed into the sanctified priestly area.[4] What are we to make of these beliefs? Did they correspond to anything in the practices of their communities?

In much of Christian literature, Old Testament representations of the Deity in bodily form have been treated as figures of speech or anthropomorphisms. Since the pioneering work of people like James Barr, Johannes Lindblom, Arthur Marmorstein, Ulrich Mauser, Anthony Hanson, Tryggve Mettinger, and Terence Fretheim,[5] however, scholars have begun to take the concrete nature of divine epiphanies more seriously.[6] There were early Jews and Christians who spiritualized the anthropic (humanlike) features of the Deity, but they were clearly in the minority until the late fourth century of the Common Era (a story to be taken up in ch. 9).[7]

Not only did first-century Jews believe that Kyriocentric visions were possible. Eschatologically minded Jews, at least, expected that the Kyriocentric visions of their patriarchs and prophets would be renewed in the near future. As they looked forward to the liberation of Israel, they centered their expectations of a public appearance of YHWH (or the glory of YHWH) in anthropic form.[8]

Present-day discussions, particularly those among Christian and Jewish scholars, generally focus their attention on expectations on the coming of a Messiah.[9] For the Old Testament and Second Temple literature,[10] on the other hand, the predominant eschatological focus was not the Messiah, but rather the coming of the YHWH, Lord God of Israel (Pss. 50:2-3; 80:1-3; 102:16; passim[11]).[12] In view of this widespread expectation,[13] the distribution of this eschatological motif among various strata of the Gospels can be cited as evidence for this expectation among the Jesus' disciples (Mark 13:35-37; Q [Luke] 12:43-46; Matt. 21:40; 25:6; Luke 12:36-38[14]).

In view of the diversity of Jewish beliefs and practices in this era (as described in the Introduction), we need to avoid any suggestion that all the "dialects" were visionary (some like the Sadducees were evidently not). It will be sufficient for our purposes to show that visionary practices may well have occurred among some early Jewish groups, not that they are a universal feature. From an a priori standpoint, such limited occurrence is certainly plausible, but is there any evidence that this was indeed the case? This part of the question is more difficult to answer.[15]

METHODOLOGICAL REASONS FOR POSTPONING DISCUSSION OF NEW TESTAMENT TEXTS

The simplest way to answer our question would be to cite the New Testament itself, which contains a variety of visionary accounts. In one of the earliest of these, 2 Corinthians 12:1, for example, Paul clearly states that he had "visions and revelations of the Lord," and such experiences may well have been shared by the Corinthian Christians whom he mimics. If, as argued here, apocalyptic (revelatory) visions were normally Kyriocentric, Paul likely meant just that—a vision in which YHWH was the central figure. Taken on its own, however, this text is filled with grammatical and semantic ambiguities: "visions of the Lord" might simply mean revelations granted by the Lord.[16]

There are a number of other texts in the New Testament that can be viewed as traces of Kyriocentric visions, but most of them could also be interpreted in terms of (empirical) resurrection appearances or two-power traditions.[17] It is methodologically inadvisable, therefore, to make such accounts our starting point.

Once we have secured the basic idea of visionary performances (and their relevance to early Christology), we will be in a better position to examine some of these texts. Such an examination will come in chapter 5—our conjecture must, after all, be consistent with the texts.[18] Given the lack of clarity about the practical milieu of these texts, however, it makes more sense to use the proffered conjecture as grounds for performative readings of the texts (hypothetico-deductively), rather than to argue (inductively) from texts themselves.

An inductive approach will not suffice by itself if the texts are byproducts, rather than literal descriptions, of the life of a community. They are more like chips from a large block (or many different "building blocks") taken from a quarry of faith and practice,[19] and they have as much to do with the common practices of Jewish communities as they do with the special issues that arose in Christian churches.[20] I shall try to show how inductive methods can be supplemented with hypothetico-deductive ones[21] and bolster this top-down methodology with recent research concerning traditions of oral-performance that lie behind the texts.[22]

If we cannot begin with the New Testament itself, where shall we begin? Outside the New Testament and early Christian literature, there are at least four comparable corpora (bodies) of literature in which Kyriocentric visions are clearly described: canonical Hebrew Bible texts, Second Temple apocalypses, [23] early Rabbinic literature, and early texts that celebrate the Heikalot ("Celestial Palaces" or "Sanctuaries").[24] We shall look at particular texts from each of these corpora of literature in the following chapter, but first we need to assess their relevance for the question at hand.

At first glance, it might not seem that an argument for first-century visions could be based on any of these texts: most Old Testament texts originated centuries earlier, the earliest Rabbinic and Heikalot literature is several centuries later (third century at the earliest), and apocalyptic texts are seemingly literary creations.

Such minimalism is based on a dubious assumption, however. It envisions these four corpora as sitting on different shelves of a library and quite separate from each other. In the context of modern academic specialization, requiring expertise in distinct dialects of Hebrew and Aramaic, such demarcations are necessary, but in terms of the history of religious communities they must be questioned. First-century Jews may have thought of themselves as living somewhere between the time of prophetic visions and that of eschatological renewal, but this in-between space and time was not experienced as a gap so much as an overlap between living memories and anticipated renewal.[25] I shall illustrate this overlap for the biblical-apocalyptic case first, and then for Rabbinic and Heikalot literature.

APOCALYPTIC TEXTS AND THE PERFORMANCE OF HEBREW BIBLE VISIONS

To illustrate this overlap between prophetic visions and eschatological renewal, consider first apocalyptic literature, major texts of which clearly do overlap the New Testament era.[26] For several decades now, prominent scholars have argued that these apocalypses originated in communities that did, in fact, celebrate ancient models of prophetic activity. Michael E. Stone argued already in 1971 that the apocalyptic accounts of the late Second Temple period reflected a "tradition of active, living ecstatic experience."[27] A decade later, Christopher Rowland suggested that apocalyptic accounts originated among prophetic circles that rehearsed visions as a way of understanding God's will (note the communal dimension here).[28] In 1990, Alan Segal argued that scholars must assume such visionary practices in order to make sense of the statements of the Apostle Paul (like those reviewed above).[29] More recently, visionary practices have been examined from a cross-cultural perspective. Howard Jackson (2000) has built a strong case for the prevalence of visions of the "form of the divine stature" (shi'ur qomah) in the first century CE in continuity with earlier Egyptian traditions of dream-incubation.[30] Frances Flannery-Dailey has demonstrated the presence of Greco-Roman dream cults in Syria-Palestine and suggested that the authors of the pseudepigrapha (texts written in the name of heroes of the past) were familiar with such conventions concerning the incubation and interpretation of Kyriocentric visions.[31] If one were to listen only to these scholars, our conjecture would seem to be obvious. However, it is not quite that simple.

The main thing that gives scholars pause in this visionary program is the necessity of relying exclusively on literary texts of apocalypses, most of which were pseudepigraphical. Apocalyptic texts were not written as spiritual autobiographies or even as eyewitness accounts of journeys through the heavens. There is no way, therefore, to induce the practices of the communities from the texts alone. [32] I think we must accept these demurrals at face value.

Even if we do accept them at face value, however, we are not at a loss. Apocalyptic texts were certainly literary creations, but like all such creations they were reworkings of earlier sources, whether oral or written (or both), sources that were themselves developed for narrative and ritual performance. The most familiar example of this trajectory between performance, literary text, and continued performance is the *Shema*. Christian Bible readers know it primarily as a single verse, "Hear, O Israel, the Lord is our God, the Lord alone" (Deut. 6:4), but the *Shema* actually involves the oral recitation of verses taken from Deuteronomy and Numbers (Deut. 6:4-9; 11:13-21; Num. 15:37-41), and it has continued to be performed, along with a series of accompanying blessings, to the present time.[33] Therefore, observations about the literary nature of our written texts are in no way a stopper as far as the performative nature of the contexts in which they originated is concerned. I shall try to bolster this argument in the remainder of this chapter and look at some specific examples in the next.

If, as most scholars would agree, the communities that were responsible for the composition of apocalypses cherished the visions of their patriarchs and prophets, it is plausible to suppose (even if it cannot be proven from the texts) that those visions were actually dramatized and rehearsed in communal settings (so Rowland on prophetic circles).[34] In other words, the "compositional building blocks" for the apocalypses included oral "scripts" for such performances. In the process of composition, these scripts were integrated into narratives (and other forms) and were eventually written up in our texts.[35] The critical point is that even though the texts of ancient apocalypses were new literary creations, they were not entirely fictional—that is, they were not unrepresentative of the practices of their communities.

Our sharp distinction between performative and literary activities of the communities may seem to make the actual life of ancient communities rather remote. This cognitive cost is counterbalanced, however, by the fact that we can wed the idea of visionary experience to that of ritual performance. In post-Enlightenment society, we normally think of visions happening to isolated individuals and coming out of the blue—jokes about "this is God speaking" can sometimes even be funny. Religious rituals, on the other hand, are motions that people go through without expecting anything to happen at all—particularly when they are governed by the clock. This separation of visionary experience and ritual performance is one of the most serious gaps in our worldview that must be overcome if we are to understand non-Enlightenment cultures in which performance is a primary mode of communal activity. The visions with which we are concerned here were scripted far more than we would expect (even in accounts of ecstatic visions), and the rituals involved were performative in ways we are not used to. There was no gap between the two.

What we may hope to find in extant apocalyptic texts, therefore, is not accounts of "historical" visionary experiences, but traces of these "mental scripts" for performances, now embedded in larger narratives.[36] We must expect at the outset that the performative material underwent considerable modification in the processes of narrativization, compilation, and redaction. Unfortunately for us, the writers did not share our anthropological approach to folk traditions. They had more urgent matters to deal with. The people who composed apocalyptic texts had no idea that later generations might consult their works in order to learn about their daily practices. They were invested in issues concerning the wellbeing of their communities, which were largely matters of cohesion, self-propagation, and defection.[37] And what traces they left of their practices were not carefully labeled as such. In short, we cannot expect much by way of inductive proof with regard to the practices that underlie the texts and must rely on what we know from performance theory and studies of extrabiblical literature, particularly that from early Judaism.

If this generalized description sounds unduly contorted and foreign to life as we know it today, perhaps an analogy will help. The challenge we face in retrieving practices from later documents is something like that of finding the features of horse-drawn wagons in later automobiles (or typewriters with QWERTY keyboards in laptops). The features are there, and you easily can find them if you have some idea what you are looking for. It would not be such a simple matter, however, if older wagons had left no material traces like the ones we enjoy looking at on "old home days" in the countryside.

In the case of biblical texts, the situation is rather similar. In Old Testament narratives, we frequently read of people "blessing the Lord" for having delivered or guided either themselves or others on whose behalf they pray. For example, we hear the priest Melchizedek blessing God Most High for giving Abraham victory over his foes (Gen. 14:20). Abraham's servant blessed the Lord, the God of his master, for guiding him on his mission to Haran (Gen. 24:27, 48). Even if we take these narratives to be literary constructs rather than historical fact, we are safe in assuming that the Israelites were religious about everyday affairs and often did utter blessings like these.[38] Even though collecting any number of narrative texts like these would not suffice to prove the fact, we understand that the narratives would have been incomprehensible to their listeners if they made no contact with their own practices.

In short, it is not implausible to suppose that we can use the results of current research to know what we are looking for and thereby to trace at least some apocalyptic texts back to the oral performances they reflect and thereby to lend plausibility (a priori) to the conjecture we have offered.

A great deal of our problem in thinking about the performance of traditions today is that we have learned (particularly since Renaissance humanism) to view texts as distant voices that need to be exegeted.[39] Clearly, apocalyptic circles did not relate to their scriptures in this way. They did not think of themselves as working with (exegeting) texts at all. Rather, as Michael Stone and Christopher Rowland already conjectured, they were rehearsing narratives concerning legendary heroes in whom their hopes and ideals were personified.[40] For the most part, these rehearsals were done from memory, and communities sought to re-experience the visions of some of their heroes, particularly those of prophets like Moses, Miriam, Isaiah, Ezekiel, and Daniel.[41] Their God was "not a God of the dead, but of the living" (Mark 12:27).

In other words, apocalyptic circles carried on the practice, already witnessed in canonical texts like Second and Third Isaiah, of adopting a spiritual giant of the past as their model for performance.[42] The Kyriocentric visions they attributed to earlier prophets functioned as models of the visionary ecstasy to which they aspired and which they sometimes authentically experienced.[43] Even if their descriptions were not written as descriptions of actual prophetic visions, they therefore have historical verisimilitude in the sense that they evidence the occurrence of such visions in the apocalyptic community and count toward the plausibility (or at least, the non-implausibility) that we seek to establish. In fact, the best evidence for vital interest in such visions in the New Testament era is the proliferation and preservation of apocalyptic texts (many of them in Christian Jewish circles), at great expenditure in terms of money and resources.[44]

So what can I say to literary-minded readers who might think that most of this discussion is based on mere supposition? For starters, I would point out that supposition is necessary for any research project, particularly in its early stages—it only sticks out like this when the research challenges longstanding methods of reading and interpreting texts. Beyond that, I would argue that the oral performance of prophetic and apocalyptic visions is a good supposition: it coheres with what we know of semi-literate societies; it maintains contact with Jewish scholarship of the development of Rabbinic texts (from whom we shall hear more); it holds out the promise of explaining the form of apocalyptic visionary texts (to be examined in chs. 2, 3); and, most importantly for our purposes, it can provide a realistic scenario for the emergence of deity Christology among the early disciples of Jesus (chs. 4, 5). The main values that will guide our investigation are plausibility and fruitfulness.

Rabbis, Heikalot Adepts, and the Performance of Hebrew Bible Visions

What about appealing to classic, "Tannaitic" Rabbinic sources like the Mishnah, Tosefta,[45] *Sifra*, *Sifrei*, and *Mekilta* (composed in the third to fourth century)?[46] As often stated, these texts often reflect conditions that arose following the destruction of the Herodian Temple and the failure of the Bar Kokhba restoration (130s CE). True enough, but they were not independent constructions, emerging in isolation from the practices of previous generations (or from other sectors of contemporary Judaism).

Early Rabbinic groups continued to recite the *Shema* and the Psalms (e.g., the *Hallel*), and they based their formal invocations and benedictions on Old Testament forms that had been passed on in oral (not yet formalized) modes of prayer.[47] As in the case of apocalyptic communities, there was more overlap than a gap with their biblical traditions. While we cannot reason backwards from the Rabbis to the New Testament, we can hope to corroborate our conjecture about the visionary practices of earlier communities. The complete absence of such material, at any rate, would make our conjecture less plausible than desired.

Throughout the Rabbinic era, Scripture was known primarily from oral recitation.[48] It would therefore be a serious mistake to sequester biblical texts to the life and times of ancient, "historical" Israel. The prophets continued to be recited, re-imagined, and rehearsed in the Common Era. The Psalms continued to be prayed or sung—sometimes in Hebrew, but also in Aramaic, Greek, and other languages. The wording in which they were recited might sometimes match canonical forms only in places, mostly in stock phrases used to address and describe the Deity. Jesus' recitations of Psalm verses in the Gospel narratives are familiar examples (Mark 15:34; Luke 23:46). The virtual explosion of biblical phrases and motifs in the *Aleinu* prayer is a good example from the siddur.[49] These prayer forms were more like scripture bytes than what we know as formal scripture readings. We shall run into them again when we consider the prayer forms of the New Testament in chapter 6.

If we take the reception of biblical texts by the Rabbis into consideration, therefore, we may think of them not simply as the product of the times in which they were composed, but as the spiritual language of succeeding generations—the language of prayer, the stuff of imagination, and the models for fresh visions of *HaShem*.

The same considerations hold true for the communities responsible for the Heikalot ("Celestial Palaces") texts. For the most part, these texts are far too late to help in our project, but some of the hymnic material they contain is likely to be much earlier (as discussed in the following chapter). Heikalot communities developed biblical and apocalyptic traditions in ways that diverged from the Rabbis who produced "normative Judaism." As pious Jews, however, they overlapped with their normative colleagues in Torah observance and liturgical practice.[50] Again, we look for corroboration, not for proof.

Notes

1. Examples are Gen. 3:8; 15:16; 16:13 (Hagar); 18:1-3; 26:2; 28:13; 32:24-30; Exod. 3:4-6; 17:6; 24:9-18; 33:9—34:7; 1 Kgs. 22:19; Pss. 16:8; 27:8; 42:2; 63:3; Isa. 6:1-3; Ezek. 1:26-8; 3:23-4; 8:2-4; 43:2-5; Dan. 7:9-10, 22; Amos 9:1; *1 En.* 89:16; 89:22; 89:30-31 (Dream/Animal Visions of appearances to Moses and the Israelites). Ithamar Gruenwald lists six characteristic features of these visions, the first two of which are (1) that YHWH sits on a throne, and (2) that he has the appearance of a man; Gruenwald, *Apocalyptic and Merkavah Mysticism*, AGAJU 14 (Leiden: Brill, 1980), 31. Andrew Dearman aptly states the possibility of tracing early Christology to this theophanic tradition: "the anthropomorphism of the Old Testament can be understood as divine preparation, pointing forward to a Christophany/theophany in which the difficulty of 'seeing' God has given way to the Lord who appears in the fullness of time"; Dearman, "Theophany, Anthropomorphism, and the *Imago Dei*: Some Observations about the Incarnation in the Light of the Old Testament," in *The Incarnation: An Interdisciplinary Symposium on the Incarnation of the Son of God*, ed. Stephen T. Davis, Daniel Kendall, and Gerald O'Collins (Oxford: Oxford University Press, 2002), 31–46 (44). Whereas Dearman concludes that the connection he describes was simply the disciples' way of understanding the person of Jesus in the context of Old Testament theophanies, I shall argue that it was rather due to the rehearsal of theophanies in the context (or sequel) of the life and death of Jesus.

2. See particularly LXX Exod. 25:8; Num. 6:25; cf. C. T. R. Hayward, "Understanding of the Temple Service in the LXX Pentateuch," in *Temple and Worship in Biblical Israel: Proceedings of the Oxford Old Testament Seminar*, ed. John Day, Library of Hebrew Bible/Old Testament Studies 422 (London: T&T Clark, 2005), 385–400 (386–88, 391–92, 397, conclusion #1). Hayward makes an important point of associating these epiphanies with invocational prayer; ibid., 388–95, 397, conclusions #2–3. We take up the topic of prayer in ch. 2.

3. I am unable to account for the claim that late Second Temple literature avoided portraying the coming or appearance of YHWH and consistently substituted an intermediary angel; e.g., John E. Alsup, *The Post-Resurrection Appearance Stories of the Gospel Tradition*, Calwer Theologische Monographien A 5 (Stuttgart: Calwer, 1975), 264. Alsup assumes that the Gospel traditions had to "reach back" to the ancient tradition complex in order to utilize visionary language (ibid.); cf. Dearman, "Theophany, Anthropomorphism, and the *Imago Dei*," 45–46. Alsup and Dearman overlook the continued performance of Kyriocentric visions.

4. *Mekilta of Rabbi Shimon bar Yohai* 79:5 to Exod. 23:17 (pilgrims); *Sifrei Devarim* 143 (pilgrims); *Sifra* 16:12-13 (the high priest); cf. Max Kadushin, *The Rabbinic Mind*, 3rd ed. (New York: Bloch, 1972), 240–41, 245–48. On traditions concerning the admission of pilgrims to the sanctified area of the temple, Israel Knohl's article is helpful even though he overstated the historicity of these traditions with respect to the Second Temple era; Knohl, "Post-Biblical Sectarianism and Priestly Schools of the Pentateuch: The Issue of Popular Participation in the Temple Cult on Festivals," in *The Madrid Qumran Congress: Proceedings of the International Congress on the Dead Sea Scrolls, Madrid, 18–21 March, 1991*, ed. Julio Trebolle Barrera and Luis Vegas Montaner, 2 vols. (Leiden: Brill, 1992), 2:601–9 (602–3). For critique on the latter point, see

Steven D. Fraade, "The Temple as a Marker of Jewish Identity Before and After 70 C.E.: The Role of the Holy Vessels in Rabbinic Memory and Imagination," in *Jewish Identities in Antiquity: Studies in Memory of Menahem Stern*, Texts and Studies in Ancient Judaism 130, ed. Lee I. Levine and Daniel R. Schwartz (Tübingen: Mohr Siebeck, 2009), 235–63 (244, 247).

5. James Barr, "Theophany and Anthropomorphism in the Old Testament," *Congress Volume: Oxford 1959*, VTSup 7 (1960): 31–38; Johannes Lindblom, "Theophanies in Holy Places in Hebrew Religion," *HUCA* 21 (1961): 91–106; Arthur Marmorstein, *The Old Rabbinic Doctrine of God*, Vol. 2: Essays in Anthropomorphism (New York: Ktav, 1968), 49, 51–52; Ulrich Mauser, "Image of God and Incarnation," *Interpretation* 24 (1970): 336–56; Anthony T. Hanson, *The Image of the Invisible God* (London: SCM, 1982), 121–43; Tryggve N. D. Mettinger, *The Dethronement of Sabaoth: Studies in the Shem and Kabod Theologies*, Coniectanea Biblica, Old Testament Series 18 (Lund: CWK Gleerup, 1982), 15, 23–4; Terence Fretheim, *The Suffering God: An Old Testament Perspective* (Minneapolis: Fortress Press, 1984), 79–106.

6. It is well known that the concreteness of the divine presence is more muted (ambiguous, abstract) in Deuteronomy and the Deuteronomistic history than in other parts of the Hebrew Bible, apparently due to a concern for limitations that could be inferred from the destruction of the temple; cf. Michael Hundley, "To Be or Not to Be: A Reexamination of Name Language in Deuteronomy and the Deuteronomistic history," *VT* 59 (2009): 533–55 (552–55). Anthropic concreteness is there nonetheless (e.g., Deut. 12:7, 11-12, 18; 23:14; 1 Sam. 3:10; 2 Sam. 7:6; 1 Kgs. 3:5; 8:13; 9:2).

7. The anthropic imagination of Talmudic-era Jews is strikingly confirmed by depictions of the "Binding of Isaac" like those in the entablature above the Torah shrine of third-century Dura Europos on the Euphrates and the mosaic floor of the sixth-century Beth Alpha (Kirbet Beit Ilfa) synagogue in Galilee. Both depictions clearly show the hand of *HaShem* reaching out from heaven to prevent Abraham from striking his son; see the plates and descriptions in Erwin Ramsdell Goodenough, *Jewish Symbols in the Greco-Roman Period*, 13 vols. (Princeton, NJ: Princeton University Press, 1953–68), 1:231, 246–8; vol. 3, figures 602, 638; Avigdor Shinan, "Synagogues in the Land of Israel: The Literature of the Ancient Synagogue and Synagogue Archaeology," in *Sacred Realm: The Emergence of the Synagogue in the Ancient World*, ed. Steven Fine (New York: Oxford University Press, 1996), 130–52 (131, 134, 146). The fact that the divine form is largely hidden (indicated only by the hand reaching through the firmament) clearly evokes the looming presence of the gigantic anthropic form of YHWH in keeping with the promise in Gen. 22:14 ("The Lord will provide . . . on the mountain of the Lord"; cf. the LXX, "On the mountain the Lord appeared") and the traditional blessing cited in *m. Ta'an.* 2:4, 5 ("May he that answered Abraham our father at Mount Moriah answer you and hearken to the voice of your crying this day!"). Note that this anthropic motif is not among those assigned to Christian influence by Zeev Weiss, "Between Rome and Byzantium: Pagan Motifs in Synagogue Art and Their Place in the Judeo-Christian Controversy," in *Jewish Identities in Antiquity: Studies in Memory of Menahem Stern*, TSAJ 130, ed. Lee I. Levine and Daniel R. Schwartz (Tübingen: Mohr Siebeck, 2009), 366–90 (377–81).

8. As Jewish scholars like Moshe Weinfeld and Alan F. Segal have argued, the *Shekinah* Glory was commonly visualized in a human form; Weinfeld, *Deuteronomy and the Deuteronomic School* (Oxford: Clarendon, 1972), 200–201; Segal, *Paul the Convert: The Apostolate and Apostasy of Saul the Pharisee* (New Haven, CT: Yale University Press, 1990), 61; Segal, "The Resurrection: Faith or History," in *The Resurrection of Jesus: John Dominic Crossan and N.T. Wright in Dialogue*, ed. Robert B. Stewart (Minneapolis: Fortress Press, 2006), 121–38, 210–12 (126). Texts like Exod. 24:16-17; Isa. 40:10; 60:2 (from the Jerusalemite temple theology) parallel the appearance of Glory with that of the visible form of YHWH; cf. see Tryggve Mettinger, *The Dethronement of Sabaoth*, 15, 32–36, 110, 112, 133. Mettinger's program was to recover the role of iconic visualization in Old Testament theology; cf. Mettinger, *No Graven Image? Israelite Aniconism in its Ancient Near Eastern Context* (Stockholm: Almqvist & Wiksell, 1995), 20; Mettinger, "Israelite Aniconism: Developments and Origins," in *The Image and the Book: Iconic Cults, Aniconism, and the Rise of Book*

Religion in Israel and the Ancient Near East, ed. Karel van der Toorn (Leuven: Peeters, 1997), 173–204 (187).

9. See, for example, Jacob Neusner, William Scott Green, and Ernest S. Frerichs, *Judaisms and Their Messiahs at the Turn of the Christian Era* (Cambridge: Cambridge University Press, 1987).

10. Late Second Temple literature is Jewish literature dating (approximately) from the third century BCE to the first century CE. It includes portions of canonical books like Daniel and deuterocanonical ones like *1 Enoch*.

11. See also Isa. 35:4 LXX; 40:5, 10; 52:8; 60:1-3; 66:15; Jer. 4:13; Hos. 6:3; Mic. 1:3; Joel 2:28, 32; Hab. 2:3 Greek LXX; Zech. 14:5; *1 En.* 1:3-4, 9; 25:3 (Book of Watchers); 90:15 (Visions of Enoch); *Jub.* 1:26, 28; *T. Moses* 10:3, 7. For methodological simplicity, I am limiting citations of noncanonical ("intertestamental") material to texts regarded "beyond reasonable doubt" as (non-Christian) Jewish rather than Christian (Jewish); James R. Davila, *The Provenance of the Pseudepigrapha: Jewish, Christian, or Other?*, SJSJ 105 (Leiden: Brill, 2005). Davila's rigorous research yields a short list (in addition to the standard Old Testament Apocrypha) including *1 Enoch* (including the Similitudes), *4 Ezra, 2 Bar., T. Moses, Jub.,* Pseudo-Philo (*L.A.B.*), 3–4 Macc., and the *Psalms of Solomon;* summarized in Davila, "The Old Testament Pseudepigrapha as Background to the New Testament," *Expository Times* 117 (2005): 53–57 (56b). As far as we are concerned, it is best not to add to the risks of this study by basing the case on texts whose provenance is debatable.

12. A possible counterexample from the early Middle Ages could be helpful here. *Pesiqta Rabbati* describes an eschatologically minded group of "Mourners for Zion," who acted out the words of Isa. 61 as a way of invoking the appearance of the Messiah ben Ephraim (*Pesiq. Rab.* 34:2, following the numbering of William G. Braude, trans., *Pesikta Rabbati: Discourses for Feasts, Fasts and Special Sabbaths,* Yale Judaica Series 18, 2 vols. [New Haven, CT: Yale University Press, 1968]). As Rivka Ulmer has shown, the messianic contours of the text were developed in the twelfth and thirteenth centuries to counter the challenges of European Christianity; Ulmer, "The Contours of the Messiah in *Pesiqta Rabbati*," HTR 106 (2013): 115–44 (128–29; cf. 121, 124, 134). This powerful text is not an exception to our Kyriocentric rule, however, because its hoped for eschaton is still centered in the revelation of the glory and kingship of *HaShem* (*Pesiq. Rab.* 1:2 [citing Ps. 42:2]; 35:2 [Zech. 2:9]; 35:3 [Mic. 2:13]; 36:2 [Isa. 60:1]), and nothing is said about the Mourners having a vision of their Messiah. In our terms, the main difference is that there was more of an eschatological "gap" in this period than there was in first-century Palestine.

13. As Frances Flannery-Dailey states, Jewish dreams and visions of the Hellenistic and Roman eras typically culminated in the pseudepigraphic hero being granted a vision of YHWH; Flannery-Dailey, *Dreamers, Scribes, and Priests: Jewish Dreams in the Hellenistic and Roman Eras,* SJSJ 90 (Leiden: Brill, 2004), 122, 203, 262. In addition to *1 Enoch* and rewritten Scripture texts, Flannery-Dailey cites examples from *2 Enoch, T. Levi,* and the *Ladder of Jacob* even though they are not independent of Christian influence in their present forms.

14. The New Testament also looks forward to the coming of the Son of Man, usually identified with Jesus (e.g., Mark 13:26). I shall argue in chs. 6 and 7 that these eschatological Son of Man texts were originally modeled on visions of the coming Lord.

15. Of course, if we were to accept the contrarian view that visions and prophecies had ceased in Israel (according to *t. Sotah* 13:3, this happened right after the prophet Malachi), it would be necessary to settle for an unprecedented renewal of these spiritual gifts among the early disciples. In that case, Christian Judaism would be qualitatively different from other contemporary Judaisms from the outset. It is well known, however, that the gift of prophecy was attributed to the Essenes (Josephus, *J. W.* 2.159), and several of the Dead Sea Scrolls claimed gifts of the Spirit and visionary phenomena for the Dead Sea Covenanters (particularly in 1QS, CD, and 1QH).

16. Concerning the problematic grammar, see Victor Furnish, for example, who interprets the genitive as a "subjective" one of origin (a vision granted by the Lord) and confidently states that "the experience . . . seems to have involved no appearing of Christ to Paul"; Furnish, *II Corinthians,* Anchor Bible 32A (Garden City, NY: Doubleday, 1984), 524. One might reduce the

grammatical ambiguity in favor of an objective genitive by appealing to the similar grammatical difficulty in Gal. 1:12 (*apokalypsis Iēsou Christou*) in parallel with Gal. 1:16 (*apokalypsai ton huion en emoi*), or simply appealing to the criterion for Paul's apostleship in 1 Cor. 9:1 (*Iēsoun ton kyrion hēmōn eoraka*); so Bert Jan Lietaert Peerbolte, "Paul's Rapture: 2 Corinthians 12:2-4 and the Language of Mystics," in *Experientia, Volume I: Inquiry into Religious Experience in Early Judaism and Christianity*, SBLSS 40, ed. Frances Flannery, Colleen Shantz, and Rodney A. Werline (Atlanta: SBL, 2008), 159–76 (168–69). But that would only heighten the semantic difficulty. Working a parallel with Paul's temple vision in Acts 22:17, as Christopher Morray-Jones does, leads to the same result; Christopher R. A. Morray-Jones, "Paradise Revisited (2 Cor. 12:1-12): The Jewish Mystical Background of Paul's Apostolate," *HTR* 86 (1993): 177–217, 265–92 (285–6). A better way to resolve the ambiguity on both fronts would be to work from the clear verbal parallels in Ezek. 1:1; 8:2-4. Although the Hebrew, *mar'ot elohim*, probably originally meant visions granted by God (a subjective genitive; cf. Ezek. 8:3; 40:2), the reader anticipates that the narrative will eventuate in a vision of the divine glory; so Peter Schäfer, *The Origins of Jewish Mysticism* (Tübingen: Mohr Siebeck, 2009), 37.

17. The oft-noted difference between the Gospel narratives of encounters with Jesus and first-person visionary descriptions in Paul and the Revelation of John could largely be a matter of genre. Gospel appearance texts like Mark 13:26; Matt. 28:8-10, 16-20; John 1:14; 20:18-21 can be read as references to Kyriocentric visions that were later reinterpreted in terms of the Danielic Son of Man, the Logos, or the resurrected Jesus in order to differentiate the Lord Jesus from God the Father and to emphasize the flesh-and-blood character of Jesus' resurrection body. This "spin-down" of early deity Christology will be treated in ch. 7.

18. There are also visions in the New Testament that are not Kyriocentric. The Deity is sometimes assumed to be in the background, evidenced only by the divine voice (e.g., Mark 1:11; Acts 10:13-14), but these visions are not centered on YHWH.

19. According to one early chronology, *Seder Olam Rabbah* 21 (46a), every city in the land of Israel had its prophets, but only those whose prophecies were intended for future generations were actually written down; Abraham Heschel, *Prophetic Inspiration after the Prophets: Maimonides and Others Medieval Authorities* (Hoboken, NJ: Ktav, 1996), 7 n. 10. The *Seder* nicely captures the historical reality that lies behind the seemingly authoritative nature of the few written texts that have survived. John Miles Foley similarly described written versions of ancient poems as "textual shards of a once-living work of verbal art"; Foley, *How to Read an Oral Poem* (Urbana: University of Illinois Press, 2002), 47. Foley's work makes the case for imagining "voices from the past" as a "realistic representation of what we know" from surviving texts while remaining agnostic about their original composition and subsequent literary history; ibid., 47–49.

20. An inductive method like form criticism searches a variety of documents to discern a group or family (*Gattung*) based on common patterns and attempts to trace those patterns back to an original *Sitz im Leben* in the early Christian community. For example, John E. Alsup finds an "appearance story *Gattung*" that includes the group appearances (Matt. 28:16-20; Luke 24:36-49; John 20:19-29), the Emmaus story (Luke 24:13-35), the Galilean appearance story in John (John 21:1-14), and the story of Mary Magdalene (John 20:14-18); Alsup, *Post-Resurrection Appearance*, 146, 190, 211–13). From a historian's viewpoint, the adequacy of this method depends on the likelihood that the New Testament documents exhibit the great majority of patterns known to the community in practice. It is often necessary to postulate the existence of other patterns and practices where needed to explain features of the New Testament that cannot otherwise be accounted for (anomalies like the dilemma of early high Christology). As Martin Jaffee states for the parallel case of Rabbinic texts: "We may at best offer a fictionalized representation or reconstruction of the multi-tonal quality of the living tradition. That is, on the basis of written survivals of oral-traditional material in performance, we seek to reconstruct the echoes lost from the tradition as it was transformed into manuscript"; Jaffee, "What Difference Does the 'Orality' of Rabbinic Writing Make for the Interpretation of Rabbinic Writings?" in *How Should Rabbinic*

Literature Be Read in the Modern World? ed. Matthew Kraus (Piscataway, NJ: Gorgias, 2006), 11–33 (18).

21. As I see it, coordinating inductive and hypothetico-deductive methods is like digging a tunnel from both sides of a body of water. The objective is to meet somewhere in the middle (depending on obstacles in the way). I work out a case of this sort in ch. 6, dealing with the controversial question of prayers to Jesus.

22. It is fairly standard today to view biblical texts as scripts for performances. Such performances involved what Scott C. Mackie has termed "mystical visuality," or recollection of past (historical) encounters in order to provoke a new theophany (as in the reading of the Epistle to the Hebrews); Mackie, "Heavenly Sanctuary Mysticism in the Epistle to the Hebrews," *JTS* 62 (2011): 77–117 (79, 97, 99, 117). In contrast to Mackie, I suppose that communities did not shift into performance mode only after they wrote their texts. The oral-ritual life out of which the texts emerged was already performative; see, for instance, Werner H. Kelber, "Modalities of Communication, Cognition, and Physiology of Perception: Orality, Rhetoric, Scribality," *Semeia* 65 (1994): 193–216 (esp. 210–11 on Homeric orality and classical rhetoric); Christopher R. A. Morray-Jones, *A Transparent Illusion: The Dangerous Vision of Water in Hekhalot Mysticism*, SJSJ 59 (Leiden: Brill, 2002), 217, 224 ("guided imagination," "performative exegesis"). As David Nelson phrases it (in speaking of Rabbinic oral traditions), written texts represent "fleeting glimpses of traditions that were otherwise fluid, dynamic, and ever changing"; W. David Nelson, "Oral Orthography: Oral and Written Transmission of Parallel Midrashic Tradition in the *Mekilta of Rabbi Shimon bar Yohai* and the *Mekilta of Rabbi Ishmael*," *AJS Review* 29 (2005): 1–32 (30). In the absence of firsthand reports about such performances (with a very few possible exceptions like Philo's report of the Therapeutae), the best way imaginatively to reconstruct the details of such practices is to study Jewish writings from later periods when firsthand accounts were more common. See, for example, descriptions of individual and community performances among Isaac Luria and his disciples in the sixteenth-century Safed, many of which were based on received (oral) texts; Lawrence Fine, *Physician of the Soul, Healer of the Cosmos: Isaac Luria and his Kabbalistic Fellowship* (Stanford, CA: Stanford University Press, 2003), 113 (performing incidents from the *Zohar*), 233 (reciting Ps. 67), 242–4 (reciting Ps. 25 in the context of prayer), 249 (reciting Pss. 29, 92, 93). On the reticence of Jewish mystics to describe their own experiences prior to the sixteenth century, see Louis Jacobs, *Jewish Mystical Testimonies* (New York: Schocken Books, 1996), 4–7 (citing Gershom Scholem); and Morris M. Faierstein, trans., *Jewish Mystical Autobiographies: Book of Visions and Book of Secrets*, Classics of Western Spirituality (New York: Paulist, 1999), xi, 3–4.

23. Limiting our purview to Second Temple apocalypses should not be taken to imply that such literary endeavor was later abandoned by Judaism. For an introduction and texts of Jewish apocalypses of the seventh to the thirteenth century, see John C. Reeves, *Trajectories in Near Eastern Apocalyptic: A Postrabbinic Jewish Apocalyptic Reader*, Resources for Biblical Study (Atlanta: SBL, 2005).

24. There are no descriptions of Kyriocentric visions in Qumran literature (aside from copies of *1 Enoch* and possibly missing sections of Pseudo- (Second) Ezekiel [4Q385] and the *Testament of Levi*). Nor are there any in Josephus (largely historical) or in Philo (largely exegetical), although noetic apperceptions of God are described in general, idealized terms in *Drunkenness* 152 (*thean tou agenētou*); *Contempl. Life* 11 (*tēs tou ontos theas*), and perhaps, more vaguely in *Names* 81–2; *Dreams* 1.165; *Spec. Laws* 1.165. Philo was undoubtedly aware of visionary performances (like those of the Therapeutae), but was uncomfortable with the concreteness of biblical anthropomorphisms, at least, when he was addressing a sophisticated, philosophically trained audience. So he attributed visual, biblical theophanies to the Logos and/or the two Powers (creative and executive), and he directed the mind of the reader to the Archetype that is beyond all forms (*ta paradeigmata kai tas ideas, ta eidē*); *Creation* 71; *Questions on Genesis* 4.1, 4. Scott C. Mackie aptly refers to Philo's practice as "noetic visuality"; Mackie, "Seeing God in Philo of Alexandria: Means, Methods and Mysticism," *JSJ* 43 (2012): 147–79 (159–60).

25. As Brevard Childs explained half a century ago, Israelite memory bridged the gap with the patriarchs and matriarchs and actualized the past; Childs, *Memory and Tradition in Israel*, Studies in Biblical Theology 37 (London: SCM, 1962), 74.

26. The most widely accepted definition of the genre of apocalypse is that of the Apocalypse Group of the SBL Genres Project; see John J. Collins, "Introduction: Towards the Morphology of a Genre," in J. J. Collins, ed. *Apocalypse: The Morphology of a Genre*, Semeia 14 (Missoula, MT: Scholars, 1979), 1–20 (9–10). The important part of the definition for our purposes is the dramatic disclosure of a transcendent, supernatural reality that promises and mediates eschatological salvation.

27. Michael E. Stone's 1974 lecture, "Apocalyptic—Vision or Hallucination?" reprinted in his *Selected Studies in Pseudepigrapha and Apocrypha with Special Reference to the Armenian Tradition*, SVTP 9 (Leiden: Brill, 1991), 419–28 (421, 428). Stone's view is updated in his *Ancient Judaism: New Visions and Views* (Grand Rapids: Eerdmans, 2011), esp. 104, 116. I differ from Stone by seeing in the texts echoes of oral scripts for the performance of visionary experiences, rather than the experiences themselves.

28. Christopher Rowland, *The Open Heaven: A Study of Apocalyptic in Judaism and Early Christianity* (New York: Crossroad, 1982), 226, 246; Rowland, "Visions of God in Apocalyptic Literature," *JSJ* 10 (1979): 137–54 (153). Rowland viewed such practices belonging to mainstream Judaism (ibid., 246). Unfortunately, the apparent opposition in mainstream texts like Jesus ben Sira (Sir. 3:21-24; 24:5, 23) prevents us from settling this issue.

29. As Alan Segal stated in a recent article, "Paul's visions make most sense as a new Christian development within an established Jewish apocalyptic and mystical tradition. . . . Only the identification of the Christ as the figure on the throne was novel by most Jewish standards, yet that [identification] would have been normative in the Christian community"; Segal, "The Afterlife as Mirror of the Self," in *Experientia, Volume I: Inquiry into Religious Experience in Early Judaism and Christianity*, SBLSS 40, ed. Frances Flannery, Colleen Shantz, and Rodney A. Werline (Atlanta: SBL, 2008), 19–40 (24 n. 10); cf. Segal, *Paul the Convert*, 58. The hypothesis of this essay simply extends Segal's important insight about Paul and the "Christian community" to the events during the few weeks after the execution of Jesus.

30. Howard M. Jackson, "The Origins and Development of *Shi'ur Qomah* Revelation in Jewish Mysticism," *JSJ* 31 (2000): 373–415 (389–91, 394–95, 398–99, 407). Significantly, Jackson argues that social contexts of acute uncertainty (particularly military uncertainty) tended to foster visions with greater visual, bodily (even numerical) specificity as assurances that the Deity was still accessible to his people; ibid., 401–4, 407–8.

31. Flannery-Dailey, *Dreamers, Scribes, and Priests*, 261–62. Flannery-Dailey points out the prominence of temple and priestly themes in Kyriocentric dream-visions and concludes that many of the authors were of priestly lineage, even if they lived and operated outside the Jerusalem temple; ibid., 258–59, 262–63, 269. A similar conclusion is entertained by Benjamin G. Wright III, particularly with respect to Enoch's ready access to the inner sanctum of the heavenly temple (and his subsequent Kyriocentric vision) in *1 Enoch* 14; Wright, "*Sirach* and *1 Enoch*: Some Further Considerations," in *The Origins of Enochic Judaism, Proceedings of the First Enoch Seminar, University of Michigan, Sesto Fiorentino, Italy, June 19–23, 2001*, Henoch 24, ed. Gabriele Boccaccini (Torino: Silvio Zamorani Editore, 2002), 179–87 (180–2). Scribal features like Enoch's writing down a memorial prayer, thus operating outside the Jerusalem temple, in *1 Enoch* 13 have been noted by David W. Suter, "Revisiting 'Fallen Angel, Fallen Priest,'" in *The Origins of Enochic Judaism*, 137–42 (141). Unfortunately, we have very little information on how lay groups outside of Jerusalem could have accessed these priestly traditions prior to the destruction of the Second Temple. According to Luke 1:5-23, John the Baptist was a holy man of priestly lineage, whose father was remembered to have witnessed a vision of the archangel Gabriel in the temple, and who made disciples in the Judean wilderness. Qumran influence is another possibility to consider, particularly in view of the emphasis on prayer as parallel to temple sacrifice in its liturgies; see, for instance, Shemaryahu Talmon, "The Emergence of Institutionalized Prayer in Israel in Light of

Qumran Literature," in *The World of Qumran from Within* (Jerusalem: Magnes, 1989), 200–43 (209, 239). The problem with positing a Qumran connection, however, is the relative lack of theophanic visions in the sectarian scrolls (as noted in note 24 and in ch. 2). Mishnah traditions may also be relevant even if they are not strictly historical. According to *m. Tam.* 5:1, the priests recited the *Shema* and its blessings (a model of visionary prayer for "pietists," as discussed in ch. 2) along with the people (cf. Philo, *Spec. Laws* 1.97). A similar mixing of Levites and "men of piety" is described in *m. Sukkah* 5:4, where they chant the words "our eyes are turned to the Lord."

32. Martha Himmelfarb, for example, has argued that the visions in apocalyptic texts are fictional narratives and do not give any information about actual experience; Himmelfarb, *Ascent to Heaven in Jewish and Christian Apocalypses* (New York: Oxford University Press, 1993), 105–6. Himmelfarb specifically rules out the possibility that apocalyptic narratives could be oral performances; ibid., 102–4, 110–14. Her critique is supported by Schäfer, *The Origins of Jewish Mysticism*, 63–65, 84, which is discussed in more detail below.

33. The *Shema* will be found in any siddur (prayer book). Its component parts are nicely laid out and explained in *My People's Prayer Book* (hereafter MPPB), ed. Lawrence A. Hoffman, 10 vols. (Woodstock, VT: Jewish Lights, 1997–2013), vol. 1.

34. As Christopher Rowland comments, "The way in which other biblical imagery merges into the production of the various visions may all point to a seeing in which a free meditation took place on the chariot-chapter [Ezek. 1], so that as in Rev[elation], the visionary's own experience could make an important contribution to the 'seeing again' of Ezekiel's vision"; Rowland, "Visions of God in Apocalyptic Literature," *JSJ* 10 (1979): 137–54 (153). Rowland further comments, "The visions would have arisen within a situation where an individual started with the scriptural description of God's glory of Ezekiel 1 and, on the basis of this passage, believed that he saw again the vision which had once appeared to the prophet"; Rowland, *Open Heaven*, 226). See also the insightful (though oppositional) comments of Schäfer, *Origins of Jewish Mysticism*, 338–9. This performative mode of vision carried over into other bodies of literature that we shall cite. Daniel Boyarin sees in the Psalms (Pss. 48:14 [15]; 105:1-2) and in midrashim like *Mekilta of Rabbi Ishmael* the desire to relive the vision of the Presence of God that Israel enjoyed at the Red Sea and at Sinai; "The [seemingly] absent moment of theophany is thus transformed into an evocation of a present moment of vision of God . . ."; Boyarin, "The Eye in the Torah: Ocular Desire in Midrashic Hermeneutic," *Critical Inquiry* 16 (1990): 532–50 (546). Elliot Wolfson reviews both Rowland's and Boyarin's analyses and applies them to merkavah visionaries and medieval kabbalists who sought to re-experience Ezekiel's vision of the chariot in what he calls the "pneumatic interpretation" of Scripture; Wolfson, *Through a Speculum that Shines: Vision and Imagination in Medieval Jewish Mysticism* (Princeton, NJ: Princeton University Press, 1994), 119–22, 326–9. According to Wolfson, "Study [of Ezek. 1] was viewed as a mode of 'visual meditation' . . . in which there is an imaginative recreation of the prophetic vision within the mystic's own consciousness"; ibid., 331. Joel Hecker develops Wolfson's terminology and describes mystical practices of the kabbalists in the *Zohar* in terms of "pneumatic" or "experiential hermeneutics," which he define as "the imaginative capacity to place oneself in the very scene of the text being read"; Hecker, "Eating Gestures and the Ritualized Body in Medieval Jewish Mysticism," *HR* 40 (2000): 125–52 (128, 143); Hecker, "Mystical Eating and Food Practices in the *Zohar*," in *Judaism in Practice from the Middle Ages through the Early Modern Period*, ed. Lawrence Fine (Princeton, NJ: Princeton University Press, 2001), 353–63 (354); Hecker, *Mystical Bodies, Mystical Meals: Eating and Embodiment in Medieval Kabbalah* (Detroit: Wayne State University Press, 2005), 5–6. It should be noted, however, that even in medieval times practitioners cited biblical and Rabbinic texts from memory, rather than by consulting written texts; cf. Gershom G. Scholem, *Major Trends in Jewish Mysticism* (New York: Schocken Books, 1941), 172–3; Elliot R. Wolfson, *The Book of the Pomegranate: Moses De Leon's Sefer Ha-Rimmon*, BJS (Atlanta: Scholars, 1988), 34.

35. The idea of the "compositional building blocks" of oral tradition was developed by Albert Lord and has been applied to the role of oral traditions in the Mishnah by Elizabeth Shanks

Alexander, *Transmitting Mishnah: The Shaping Influence of Oral Tradition* (Cambridge: Cambridge University Press, 2006), 13, 38–40, 74. Shanks Alexander agrees with Steven Fraade and Martin Jaffee that oral and literary modes of distribution overlapped and influenced each other in Rabbinic texts; ibid., 15–17, 22–4. Even after it is stabilized, therefore, the text is still "performative" in that it invites readers to reenact the exercises (in this case, legal analysis) that its wording presents; ibid., 169, 221–2. On the quest for pre-literary "building blocks" in the Talmud, originating in the context of a master and his circle of disciples, see Baruch M. Bokser, *Post-Mishnaic Judaism in Transition: Samuel on Berakhot and the Beginnings of Gemara*, BJS (Chico, CA: Scholars, 1980), 471–84.

36. I adapt the phrase *mental script* (or *mental text*) from studies of oral performance, such as Minna Skafte Jensen, "Performance," in *A Companion to Ancient Epic*, ed. John Miles Foley (Malden, MA: Blackwell, 2005), 45–54 (49). A mental script differs from a written script in that it is stored in (collective) memory and performed in ways that may vary from one rehearsal to the next. However, the adjective *mental*, by itself, may not do justice to the active, participatory nature of these "scripts." Empirically speaking, the scripts only exist in performances (aided in some cases by written notes).

37. Paul Heger points out that *1 Enoch* was compiled as a means of preaching with the aim of instilling hope in the righteous and persuading sinners to repent; Heger, "*1 Enoch*—Complementary of Alternative to Mosaic Torah?" *JSJ* 41 (2010): 29–62 (57–58).

38. In this particular case, of course, it helps that we find similar blessings in liturgical documents like the Psalms (Pss. 18:46; 28:6; 31:21; 41:13; passim).

39. Again, I have to play with words. Since the European Renaissance, we view texts as artifacts of bygone times and we try to exegete them. Exegesis is not the only mode of interpretation, however. For example, an actor interprets a role by embodying it, not just by studying it. Interpretation is therefore a broader category than exegesis.

40. Compare Rebecca Lesses's point about prayers and adjurations in the Heikalot literature—they were meant to be performed, not read as literature (and were recorded only as talismans); Lesses, *Ritual Practices to Gain Power: Angels, Incantations, and Revelation in Early Jewish Mysticism*, Harvard Theological Studies 44 (Harrisburg, PA: Trinity Press International, 1998), 161–62 (citing Sam Gill's work on Navajo prayers). The idea that ancient biblical texts are collections of oral *traditions* is as old as form criticism itself, going back to Hermann Gunkel, *The Legends of Genesis: The Biblical Saga and History*, trans. W. H. Carruth (Chicago: University of Chicago Press, 1901), 124–5. The more recent focus on oral *performance* takes us beyond Gunkel's idea of orality as folk tradition, impersonally handed down in a fixed genre (*Gattung*) for a given social context (*Sitz im Leben*); cf. Richard S. Sarason, "On the Use of Method in the Modern Study of Jewish Liturgy," in *Approaches to Ancient Judaism: Theory and Practice*, Brown Judaic Studies, ed. William Scott Green, 6 vols. (Missoula, MT: Scholars, 1978–85 [1978]), 1:97–172 (131–7). Instead, we view orality more as live performances, creatively acted out in concrete devotional events. In contrast to Gunkel, current scholars also allow more freedom of reformulation to the redactors (based on redaction criticism) making reconstruction of oral traditions (based on stereotyped patterns) a more tentative procedure than Gunkel's scientific classification. Oral performance does not completely negate the results of form criticism (especially the identification of genre) or redaction criticism, but it does add another dimension—construal of texts in terms of liturgical practice.

41. We have a fairly clear example of such leadership in Luke 4:16-22, where Luke's Jesus performs the synagogue Haftarah reading from the prophet Isaiah (Isa. 61:1-2). Since this account is missing from earlier strata of the Gospels, the historical basis is more likely to be a prayer leader of Luke's personal acquaintance (perhaps Paul; cf. Acts 13:14-16) than an authentic Jesus tradition.

42. For example, the servant of Second Isaiah (Isa. 40–55) was probably a representative of the righteous remnant, perhaps the "tremblers" (*haredim*) described in Isa. 66:2, 5; George W. E. Nickelsburg, *Ancient Judaism and Christian Origins: Diversity, Continuity, and Transformation* (Minneapolis: Fortress Press, 2003), 24; Joseph Blenkinsopp, *Isaiah 56–66: A New Translation*, AB

19B (New York: Doubleday, 2003), 51–53; Blenkinsopp, "The Qumran Sect in the Context of Second Temple Sectarianism," in *New Directions in Qumran Studies*, Library of Second Temple Studies 52, ed. Jonathan G. Campbell et al. (London: T&T Clark, 2005), 10–25 (14–15). Similarly, the seer Daniel represented those gifted with wisdom (*hakhamim*) in Dan. 1:4; 2:20-23; cf. 12:3 (*maskilim*). The model for such praxis could also be a celestial figure, for example, the heavenly "one like a son of man," who was depicted as a heavenly counterpart to the community of holy/ righteous ones on earth in Dan. 7:10c-14, 22; *1 Enoch* (Similitudes) 38:6; cf. Sigmund Mowinckel, *He that Cometh*, trans. G. W. Anderson (Nashville: Abingdon, 1954), 384–85. The angels (seraphim and cherubim) were the model for Israel's antiphonal praise of YHWH at Qumran (e.g., 1QH 11:22-23) and in the third blessing of the *Amidah* benedictions (which cites Isa. 6:3; Ezek. 3:12). From this perspective, I must agree with Seth L. Sanders's treatment of the illumination of Moses (Exod. 34) and the glorification of the Servant (Isa. 52–53) as models for corporate ritual practice in the Hellenistic era, although I doubt his assumption that such practice was a Hellenistic-era novelty; Sanders, "Performative Exegesis," in *Paradise Now: Essays on Early Jewish and Christian Mysticism*, SBLSS 11, ed. April D. DeConick (Atlanta: SBL, 2006), 57–79 (67–70). It is just as reasonable to view the biblical Moses as the historicization of a liturgical role, as the reverse (Sanders follows the historicization tack in treating Exod. 15 as a "liturgical piece" embedded in a narrative; ibid., 73).

43. According to Moshe Idel, Enoch was a "paradigm for attaining experiences similar to his in the present"; Idel, "Adam and Enoch According to St. Ephrem the Syrian," *Kabbalah* 6 (2001): 183–205 (193). Note the correspondence between Enoch, the "righteous and blessed one," and the blessed righteous ones in the superscription, *1 En.* 1:1-2. Pierluigi Piovanelli's socio-rhetorical analysis of the Book of Watchers similarly concludes that "the text [in this case, *1 En.* 13:7-8] shows the path to be followed to the practitioners that would imitate Enoch's approach, namely, triggering oneiric, visionary, ecstatic, and other altered state of consciousness experiences . . ."; Piovanelli, "'Sitting by the Waters of Dan,' or the 'Tricky Business' of Tracing the Social Profile of the Communities that Produced the Earliest Enochic Texts," in *The Early Enoch Literature*, JSJSup 121, ed. Gabrielle Boccaccini and John J. Collins (Leiden: Brill, 2007), 257–81 (277–8). It should be noted, however, that treating Enoch as a model visionary does not require viewing him to be the model in all parts of the Enoch narratives. For example, the narrative of Enoch's acquisition of esoteric knowledge could be for the edification of the community (e.g., *1 En.* 36:4), rather than for their emulation; cf. Flannery-Dailey, *Dreamers, Scribes, and Priests*, 274–75; Annette Yoshiko Reed, "Heavenly Ascent, Angelic Descent, and the Transmission of Knowledge in 1 Enoch 6-16," in *Heavenly Realms and Earthly Realities in Late Antique Religions*, ed. Ra'anan S. Boustan and Annette Yoshiko Reed (Cambridge: Cambridge University Press, 2004), 47–66 (65–66).

44. Methodologically our approach to history is what Jacob Neusner termed a "post-structuralist reversion to questions of a fundamentally historical character," the purpose of which is "not to tell a one-time event, but to create a paradigm" within a particular, historical social context; Neusner, *Judaism: The Evidence of the Mishnah* (Chicago: University of Chicago Press, 1981), 310, 316, 323.

45. The Mishnah and Tosefta are said to be "Tannaitic" in the sense that most of their material is attributed to the Tannaim ("Repeaters" or "Rehearsers") of the first two centuries of the Common Era. Talmudic lemmas taken from the Mishnah do show a moderate degree of fluidity, but the current recension of the Mishnah can safely be dated to the third century; Martin S. Jaffee, "Writing and Rabbinic Oral Tradition: On Mishnaic Narrative, Lists and Mnemonics," *Journal of Jewish Thought and Philosophy* 1 (1991): 123–46 (123 n. 1).

46. Midrashim of the early Palestinian Amoraic era (c. 220–400) are similarly Tannaitic in the sense that much of their material is continuous with the historical Tannaim. Although they are classified as "halakic" (*midrashei halachah*) because they focus on the interpretation of scriptural law, they also contain homilies and haggadic commentaries much like the later amoraic "haggadic midrashim" (*midrashei 'aggadah*). Reuven Hammer suggests that the least confusing title for these

early (Tannaitic) texts is simply "classic midrash"; Hammer, trans., *The Classic Midrash: Tannaitic Commentaries on the Bible*, Classics of Western Spirituality (New York: Paulist, 1995), 16.

47. On the recitation of the *Shema* and Psalms in private prayer as well as in public services associated with the temple, see Stefan Reif, *Judaism and Hebrew Prayer: New Perspectives on Jewish Liturgical History* (Cambridge: Cambridge University Press, 1993), 57–58, 76. 83. Other synagogue prayers that were probably inherited from Second Temple times include the Kedushah and the Kaddish. Marc Brettler and Lawrence Hoffmann suggest that the Kaddish was composed as early as the first century; MPPB 6:152–3 (cf. 160).

48. In formal synagogue settings, the Torah, prophets (*Haftarah*), and Esther (*Megillah*) were read aloud from Hebrew scrolls; *m. Shabb.* 16:1; *m. Meg.* 1:1; 4:3, 4; *t. Shabb.* 13:1; cf. Luke 4:16-17; Acts 13:15. The Talmud actually forbade the audible recitation of Torah portions by heart (*b. Git.* 60b; *b. Tem.* 14b). The Aramaic translation (*Targum*) and the homily would have been recited, however, as were the congregational recitations of the *Shema*. Evidence from medieval Europe indicates that biblical verses included in prayer services (the *Shema, pesukei de-zimrah* [including the *Hallel* and the Song of the Sea], the sacrificial portions, etc.) were often recited by memory by the congregation; Ephraim Kanarfogel, "Prayer, Literacy, and Literary Memory in the Jewish communities of Medieval Europe," in *Jewish Studies at the Crossroads of Anthropology and History: Authority, Diaspora, Tradition*, Jewish Culture and Contexts, ed. Ra'anan S. Boustan, Oren Kosansky, and Marina Rustow (Philadelphia: University of Pennsylvania Press, 2011), 250–70, 397–404 (254–6, 265).

49. MPPB 6:133.

50. Peter Schäfer, "The Aim and Purpose of Early Jewish Mysticism," in his *Hekhalot-Studien*, TSAJ 19 (Tübingen: Mohr Siebeck, 1988), 277–95 (294); Schäfer, "Jewish Liturgy and Magic," in *Geschichte, Tradition, Reflexion: Festschrift für Martin Hengel zum 70. Geburtstag*, ed. Hubert Cancik, Hermann Lichtenberger, and Peter Schäfer, 3 vols. (Tübingen: Mohr Siebeck, 1996), 1:541–56 (esp. 552–3).

2

Motifs Associated with Kyriocentric Visions in Apocalyptic and Early Rabbinic Literature

Our starting point is a dilemma at the heart of New Testament Christology: deity Christology arose among pious Jews whose tradition consistently opposed the exaltation of any living human being to equality with God. Having stressed the urgency of this problem and reviewed the major options (based on the resurrection of Jesus, gentile influence, and Jewish binitarianism), I have proposed that the primary impetus needed for early deity Christology was the disciples' visions of the God of Israel in bodily form and the recognition therein of the voice and face of Jesus. From that point on, they believed "The Lord is Jesus."

In order to evaluate this conjecture, we began by discussing the nature of Kyriocentric visions in early Judaism and argued that they occurred in the context of the scripted rehearsal of visions and auditions that were attributed to the patriarchs and prophets—visions that are known to us from the Hebrew Bible and other Old Testament texts (ch. 1). This chapter will examine several examples of such rehearsals as they appear in apocalyptic texts and early Rabbinic and Heikalot literature. Here we hope to identify some of the motifs that should reappear in the New Testament if our Kyriocentric vision conjecture is realistic. In the following chapter, we shall do the same for devotional practices associated with these visions.

VISIONARY MOTIFS AND PRACTICES IN JEWISH APOCALYPSES

Ancient apocalypses were visions and revelations (Greek, *apokalypseis*) of hidden dimensions of the world (e.g., 2 Cor. 12:1). Those dimensions included the plan

43

of future events, but were focused primarily on the operations of the heavens and visions of the divine world.

There are at least three apocalypses that date from the Second Temple era and include material recalling and rehearsing visions of the Lord: the Book of the Watchers (*1 En.* 1–36, third century BCE or earlier);[1] the book of Daniel 7–11 (second century BCE); and the Similitudes of Enoch (*1 En.* 37–71, first century CE).[2]

Notably absent for this short list of apocalypses are the Dead Sea Scrolls, associated with the archaeological site of Qumran.[3] There are no clearly Kyriocentric visions described in the Qumran corpus, at least, not in the texts that are assigned to the Yahad (the Community of the Renewed Covenant) on the basis of its distinctive vocabulary.[4] The reason for the absence of concrete theophanies in these texts is something of a puzzle.[5] It might have something to do with the relationship of priestly leaders of the Yahad to the Temple in Jerusalem, which for priestly classes like the "sons of Zadok" was still the "house of God" in spite of its many corruptions.[6] Otherwise, the theophanic presence may have been diffused through a hierarchy of angels, as suggested by Elliot Wolfson.[7] Another possibility would be to allow that Kyriocentric visions were rehearsed in the Yahad, but the language needed to describe them was restricted to the angels in heaven (cf. 2 Cor. 12:4).[8] Whatever the reason for this absence, I must bypass Qumran texts in this part of the study. (They will be more helpful when we examine prayers and devotional practices in ch. 6.)

Before discussing individual apocalyptic texts, I summarize the results in a table in order to give an overview of the material and to relegate some technical matters to footnotes. Table 1 arranges these texts in roughly chronological order in the left-hand column[9] and lists the Kyriocentric visions that constitute the tradition pool from which these texts drew in the right-hand column. Texts with superscript EI and DO are allusions that have already been noted in the margins of E. Isaac's (*OTP*)[10] and Daniel Olson's translations of *1 Enoch*, respectively.[11] Readers who are already familiar with the texts and their background models cited may readily draw their own conclusions from the table by itself.

Table 1. Kyriocentric visions in apocalyptic texts and their background models

Apocalyptic Text and Brief Description[12]	Kyriocentric Vision Models Superscript EI indicates *OTP* citations Superscript DO indicates Olson citations
1 En. 14:18—15:2 (Book of the Watchers)[13] Enoch (first person) sees YHWH (Great Glory[14]) enthroned and surrounded by cherubim and flaming fire; he prostrates himself, but is lifted up (by an angel) and commissioned by YHWH.	Isa. 6:1a[EI DO];[15] 1 Kgs. 22:19b[EI] (lofty throne) Ezek. 1:22, 26[DO] (throne like crystal) Ezek. 1:15-16 (gleaming wheels) Ezek. 1:5, 15; cf. 10:15 (cherubim)[16] Ezek. 1:26[EI] (human form enthroned) Ezek. 1:27a (something like fire all around) Ezek. 1:28—2:3 (the seer falls on his face, but is summoned and lifted up and commissioned by YHWH)[17] Isa. 6:8-9; Ezek. 2:2b-3 (the seer hears the voice of YHWH commissioning him to prophecy)
Dan. 7:9-10 Daniel (first person) sees YHWH (Ancient of Days) enthroned and wearing a snow-white robe, with fiery wheels and a stream of fire, and surrounded by myriads of angels, all leading up to a judgment scene (and	Ezek. 1:26a, *1 En.* 14:20 (human form/ glory enthroned) *1 En.* 14:20 (gown whiter than snow)[18] Ezek. 1:15b, *1 En.* 14:18 (throne's wheels like the sun) *1 En.* 14:19 (streams of fire from the throne) *1 En.* 14:22 (myriads of angels)[19]

subsequently a scene featuring "one like a son of man".	*1 En.* 15:2—16:3 (judgment passed on the Watchers)
1 En. 39:9—40:2 (Similitudes)[20] Enoch (first person) gazes at the place beneath the wings of YHWH (Lord of spirits), the latter being surrounded by angels; he witnesses the angelic Sanctus and Benedictus and is transformed in order to see more clearly (preceded by a scene featuring the "elect one of righteousness" in 39:6-8).	Isa. 6:3[DO] (Sanctus) ?Ezek. 3:12 (Benedictus)[21] *1 En.* 14:19-22[22]
1 En. 46:1-3 (Similitudes)[23] Enoch (first person) sees YHWH (One who has a head of days, Lord of Spirits) traveling somewhere with the Son of Man beside him;[24] attention shifts to the secondary figure.	Dan. 7:9[DO] (Ancient of Days enthroned with hair like pure wool)[25] Dan. 7:13[DO] (a second figure like a son of man)
1 En. 47:3 (Similitudes)[26] Enoch (first person) sees YHWH (Head of Days) enthroned and surrounded by the hosts of heaven (no Son of Man here until 48:2).	Dan. 7:9[DO] (Ancient of Days enthroned)[27] Isa. 6:1a; Ezek. 1:26; *1 En.* 14:20 (YHWH seated on a "throne of glory") Dan. 7:10c (books opened in the presence of myriads of angels)[28]

1 En. 60:2-4 (Book of Noah?)[29] Enoch/Noah[30] (first person) sees YHWH (Head of Days), enthroned and surrounded by myriads of angels and righteous ones (no Son of Man here); he falls on his face and is lifted up (by an angel).	Dan. 7:9 (Ancient of Days enthroned)[31] Isa. 6:1a; Ezek. 1:26; *1 En.* 14:20 (YHWH seated on a "throne of glory") Dan. 7:10b; 1 Kgs. 22:19c; *1 En.* 14:22 (surrounded by myriads of angels)[32] Ezek. 1:28—2:3; *1 En.* 14:24—15:1 (the seer falls on his face, but is summoned by *YHWH* and lifted up by a spirit)
1 En. 71:9-14a (appendix to Similitudes?)[33] Enoch (first person) sees YHWH (Head of Days) coming with four archangels and countless angels, whereupon he falls on his face and blesses YHWH who in turn greets and commissions him, addressing him as the "Son of Man."[34]	Dan. 7:9[DO] (Ancient of Days with hair like wool)[35] *1 En.* 14:20; cf. Dan. 7:9b (gown brighter than the sun, whiter than snow)[36] Ezek. 1:28—2:3; *1 En.* 14:24—15:1 (the seer falls on his face and is summoned and commissioned by YHWH)[37]

The point of my presenting these texts en masse like this is to show that Kyriocentric visions were not simply commemorated as wonders of the heroic past (as we might think of them today). At least in apocalyptic circles, these visions were models for continued (or renewed) contact with the God of Israel. In each of the cases cited, the vision is narrated in the first person singular, a dramatic feature no doubt intended to help the leader identify with the visionary protagonist (Enoch or Daniel) and also to aid the communities' efforts to relive and share in his visionary experiences.[38] In some cases (Dan. 7 and the Similitudes), this renewed contact was portrayed as a foretaste of an eschatological theophany. Kyriocentric visions thereby connected the community with the glorious age to come as well as with the heavenly world.

Let us look at the texts individually to identify some of the visionary motifs and practices.

First Enoch 14–15 (the *Book of the Watchers*) describes Enoch's initial ascent into heaven, where he passes through the fiery gate of a "great house," only to see a second house, even greater—the structure clearly suggests a celestial Holy of Holies.[39] Within this second house, Enoch sees a crystalline throne with wheels—clear echoes of the visions of Isaiah and Ezekiel[40]—streams of fire issue forth from the throne; Enoch hears the voice of the cherubim, and he describes the appearance of the Great Glory (**YHWH**) robed in a bright white gown:[41]

> And the Great Glory was sitting upon it [the throne]—as for his gown, which was shining more brightly than the sun, it was whiter than any snow.[42]

The Great Glory is thus at the pinnacle of the vision (a Kyriocentric arrangement). The Lord calls Enoch, lifts him up, and commissions him to prophecy to the Watchers.

For our purposes, the order of progression in *1 Enoch* is just as revealing as the details. Roughly speaking, it follows the order of events in Ezekiel 1–2 (shown in the right-hand column of Table 1), but the references are not exact enough to indicate direct intertextual borrowing. Neither should the text be taken as a straightforward account of a visionary event—in actual experience, one does not see a chair and observe details of its composition and appearance before noticing that someone important is sitting upon it or that it is pouring out flames of fire. So this part of the text reads more like directions for an imaginal stage setting: first, envision a house with particular characteristics; then a second house; then a throne, and finally a humanlike form seated on the throne—watch out for that stream of fire! The community that recited these passages were likely using them as guides to their collective imagination rather than analyzing it in terms of intertextual references the way literary scholars do today.[43]

First Enoch 14 is filled with motifs, performances of which were earlier evidenced in Isaiah 6 and Ezekiel 1–2. How can we understand such a combination when the texts of the prophets in our possession are quite separate from each other? Evidently, performances managed to follow one script while drawing lines from others.

In order to find a helpful analogy, we may turn to performances as we know them today: ancient texts are something like playbooks for a team sport. Studying these playbooks would reveal several common formations and shifts even if the compiler of one playbook had never looked at the other ones. The diachronic relationship here is between performances of the team under successive coaches, each of whom brings his or her own contributions. There is no engagement between the playbooks themselves, even though it may appear that way to an outside reader.[44]

What appears to us to be an intertextual reference may therefore have been inter-performative[45] or inter-rehearsal.[46] The resulting difference is that scriptural allusions in inter-rehearsals are entangled into a single new performance: they cannot readily be isolated and labeled the way a sequence of intertextual citations often can. (We shall see some good examples of such entangled citations in New Testament texts like Mark 6 in ch. 5.)

The second example of a Kyriocentric vision listed above, Daniel 7:9-10, is thought to have been composed at least a century later than the *Book of the Watchers* and to have built on some of its themes along with those of Ezekiel 1—arguably another case on inter-performance. As Daniel watches in this familiar text, thrones are put in place, and the "Ancient of Days" (Aramaic, *atik yomin*) takes his seat. His clothing is bright white like that of the Great Glory and a stream of fire issues from his presence as in *1 Enoch*. Like the Great Glory in *1 Enoch*, he is surrounded by many angels (again the Kyriocentric arrangement), and he exercises judgment. Instead of Daniel being called and commissioned, however, the next scene describes the investment of "one like a son of man" (if true to form, this celestial figure must be a counterpart of Daniel and vice versa). As in *1 Enoch*, the seer leads a dramatic performance—a performance that involves his imagination ("a dream and a vision of his head," Dan. 7:1-2) and presumably the imaginations of his audience as well. Whoever the seer may have been in "real life," in this imaginal world he was Daniel.

The five listed selections from the Similitudes of Enoch are probably contemporary with the New Testament documents and may be treated more briefly. They rely on motifs from earlier Kyriocentric visions and develop the idea of a second power, the Elect One or Son of Man, alongside the God of Israel. Much scholarly attention has focused on this mysterious second figure, largely because a similar motif occurs in the New Testament. It should be noted, however, that all five of these visions remain centered in the one God, here called the "Head of Days" (clearly a reference to the Ancient of Days, known to us from Daniel 7:9). In fact, four of these five scenes describe the entourage of the Ancient of Days in terms of angels and righteous ones. Only one of them describes the Son of Man in the context of the Kyriocentric vision itself. We shall return to the mysterious figure of the Son of Man in chapter 7, but for the time being our interest is in the central figure, the Lord.

Looking again at Table 1, one might quibble about the inclusion or omission of this or that text and this or that background model, but the basic picture is fairly clear and probably would not change even if more texts were included. Scanning the right hand column of the table shows that the visionary narratives were based on classic models of Isaiah and Ezekiel, and, for later texts like the Similitudes, those of Enoch and Daniel. These models almost always occur in a blend, which in the context of oral-performance must be thought of as inter-performative.[47]

Also pointing to oral-performance is the fact that none of the citations are exact quotations as we might have expected if the writers were working from fixed (either written or memorized) texts. The *Kedushah* ("Sanctus") in *1 Enoch* 39:12, for example, refers to YHWH as the "Lord of the spirits," rather than the "Lord of hosts" as in our texts of Isaiah 6:3; and the *Berachah* ("Benedictus") in *1 Enoch* 39:14 refers to "the name of the Lord of spirits" (cf. 61:11), rather than the "glory of the Lord" as in Ezekiel 3:12. The pairing of these two formulas clearly suggests a performative, liturgical (rather than strictly exegetical) context for *1 Enoch*.[48]

There are significant analogies here also to another performative aspect of Judaism, the practice of prayer. The repeated use of classic models in our apocalyptic texts indicates that there was a "scripturalization" of visions in late Second Temple times, parallel to the contemporary "scripturalization of prayer" that has been described by Judith Newman.[49] Another similarity is the fact that the selection of models was anthological rather than sequential, parallel to the collective and selective principles of "anthology" that Joseph Tabory had shown are the primary force in the creation of traditional Jewish prayers.[50]

Note also that individual motifs do not regularly appear in our texts in the same order that they did in the background texts to which they are most closely related (note, for example, the shifting order of allusions to Ezek. 1 in *1 En.* 14:18-25). It seems that apocalyptic imagery was based more on internalized ideas and mental scripts from traditions about the prophets[51]—what David Frankfurter has called the language of "Biblicalese"[52]—rather than on immediate access to written texts.[53] I shall argue in the following chapter that these models were known primarily from corporate prayers and liturgies of the circles in which they were rehearsed. If so, the scripturalization of visions—the couching of Kyriocentric visions in scriptural language—was itself a result of the scripturalization of performative prayer.[54]

To sum up: the apocalyptic texts cited point to the re-enactment of prophetic visions in the late Second Temple period, at least, in eschatologically minded circles. Dates of these texts cited range from the third century BCE to the first century CE. In other words, it is extremely likely that Kyriocentric visions were rehearsed and re-lived by pious Jews of the New Testament era. Our modern, post-Enlightenment perspective may not allow us to conclude that these were actual appearances of the Deity (theophanies), but we can still entertain the possibility that they were scripts for real visionary performances.[55] For the purposes of our Kyriocentric conjecture, that much should be sufficient, but it would be helpful to corroborate these results from Jewish literature—primarily Rabbinic—that immediately followed the New Testament era. In the following section, I shall argue that anthropic motifs continued to be celebrated in what Alexander Golitzin has described as a "continuous witness to a mysticism of the divine form" through the apocalyptic and Rabbinic eras.[56]

VISIONARY MOTIFS AND PRACTICES IN RABBINIC LITERATURE

Four major groups of Jewish works derive from the first millennium: the Rabbinic corpus, foundational statutory prayers, the Aramaic Targumim, and Heikalot texts.

In a strictly inductive approach to our problem, it might be deemed hazardous to appeal to any of these texts—the earliest of which date from the third century CE —in order to substantiate events of the first century, particularly with the destruction of the Temple, the failure of the Bar Kokhba revolt, and the dispersion of the populace intervening. From a hypothetico-deductive perspective, however, it is advisable, at least, to consult such works: it would be problematic if there were no evidence at all for Kyriocentric visions in this literature. That eventuality would require an explanation of its own and might thereby weaken the hypothesis offered here.[57] So which of these groups of texts might be helpful in filling out the picture we are constructing?

The foundational prayers (*Shema* and blessings, *Amidah* benedictions, Qaddish, *Hallel*) most likely originated in the late Second Temple period even if their final forms were not standardized until late in the first millennium.[58] In any case, our interest at this point is not so much in the prayers themselves (which will be more helpful to us in ch. 6), but in the way practitioners thought they should be performed and understood, and for that we must turn to early Rabbinic texts.

One might not expect to find much about visionary practices in Rabbinic writings. As many have observed, there is a certain reticence to propound mystical views in this corpus (particularly when compared with the Heikalot texts). In fact, there are midrashim (exegetical "inquiries") like *Mekilta of Rabbi Ishmael* that appear to critique fellow Jews who celebrated the visions of the prophets Isaiah and Ezekiel: even the most unlearned of those who participated in the Sea Deliverance, *Mekilta* insists, saw more than the prophets Isaiah and Ezekiel could.[59] This very opposition, however, can be read as an indication that the Sages did know of visionary practices, even among their own ranks.[60] Well-known cautions against visionary practices in other Rabbinic texts support this conclusion.[61] Jewish scholars like Abraham Heschel, Elliot Wolfson, and Daniel Boyarin have pointed out the ways in which the visionary practices of the "pietists" (*hasidim*) and Sages (*hakamim*) were celebrated in Rabbinic literature—celebrated in ways more subtle than those of the apocalypses,[62] but along clearly participatory lines, nonetheless.[63] We shall explore some of the earliest of these texts below and take leading scholars of early Judaism as our guides.

Because Rabbinic texts were compiled a hundred years or more after the New Testament, I propose to limit the base to Tannaitic sources (dating before 400 ce, hence actually Tannaitic and early amoraic[64]): the Mishnah-Tosefta complex (third century) and "classic" (Tannaitic) midrashim on the Pentateuch: *Mekilta*, *Sifra*, and *Sifrei* (all late third to fourth century[65]). In spite of the destruction of the Temple in 70 ce and the failure of a major restoration effort in 135 ce, these early Rabbinic texts appear to have been continuous with Second Temple materials in most areas.[66]

The earliest of these texts, the Mishnah (c. 200), tended to avoid eschatological topics like cosmic divine intervention and the coming of the Messiah,[67] but the general tenor of Tannaitic literature was eclectic and preservative.[68] So, for example, we find clear parallels to the New Testament use of the "Save, O Lord," formula in *Mishnah Berachot* 4:4 and *Mishnah Sukkah* 4:5 (cf. Matt. 8:25; 14:30).[69] We know this was not an innovation on the part of the Rabbis because it was prominent in the Old Testament, particularly in the Psalms, which continued to be memorized and recited (e.g., Pss. 116, 118, both part of the *Hallel* liturgy; Pss. 120, 130 among the Pilgrimage Psalms; cf. *t. Ber.* 2:4).[70] Other examples will be cited below. The point here is that Jewish prayer traditions tended to be quite conservative, at least, at the level of particular phrases (scripture bytes) and exclamations.[71]

While aware of conversations with disciples of Jesus, early Rabbinic texts are still quite innocent of contemporary christological debates.[72] In order to avoid significant discontinuities with the first century, however, I shall avoid citing texts here that dealt with adjustments to the destruction of the Temple:[73]

for example, the Rabbis' recontextualization of Temple rituals;[74] the special interest of the Rabbis in the study of Torah, written and oral;[75] the lineage of the Palestinian Patriarchate; and the Rabbis exclusion of various sectarians.[76]

The Aramaic Targumim were redacted somewhat later (fourth–eighth century).[77] These Targumim do amplify traditions about scriptural theophanies of Israel's glorious past in order to supplement the reading of weekly portions of the Torah and the haftarot in synagogues. They also describe eschatological theophanies (notably the beautiful "Song of the Four Nights" in the Palestinian Targumim, which we shall revisit in ch. 5). As paraphrases of the Tanakh, some of these amplifications may reflect contemporary performances, but they do not tell us much about visionary practices as such.

The Heikalot ("Celestial Palaces") macroforms (anthologies) are also relatively late and are of Babylonian provenance.[78] They tend to portray *HaShem* in more transcendent and "apathetic" terms[79] than apocalyptic and Rabbinic texts do.[80] However, the hymnic portions, particularly those in *Heikalot Rabbati*, are thought to antedate the macroforms and may well go back to the amoraic period (third to fifth century).[81] Though less relevant to Tannaitic Palestine than other Rabbinic texts, they do provide useful corroboration.

For these reasons, I shall focus our search on Tannaitic texts, and cite only a few later ones from the Talmud to amplify points already suggested in the early ones. I shall also include a few Heikalot hymns in order to broaden the textual basis of discussion beyond strictly Rabbinic material.[82]

Table 2 summarizes a few of these texts (in roughly chronological order) and lists some of the biblical material in the tradition pool from which they drew (in approximate order of citation). In the redacted texts as we have them, most of these allusions are direct quotations.

Table 2: Kyriocentric Visions in Early Rabbinic and Heikalot Texts and their Scriptural Models

Judaic Text with a Brief Description	Kyriocentric Vision Models
m. Ber. 2:1[83] Directing the heart during the recitation of the *Shema Yisrael* ("Hear, O Israel")	Isa. 26:21; Ezek. 3:12; Hos. 5:15; Mic. 1:3 (from/to his place)
m. Ber. 5:1[84] Directing the heart during the recitation of the *Amidah* benedictions just as the "ancient pious ones" did Cf. *t. Ber.* 3:4, 20 Cf. *b. Sanh.* 22a	Isa. 26:21; Ezek. 3:12; Hos. 5:15; Mic. 1:3 (from/to his place) *t. Ber. 3:4* adds Ps. 10:17 (you strengthen their heart) *b. Sanh. 22a* adds Ps. 16:8 (the Lord before me, at my right hand)
Mekilta of Rabbi Shimon to Exod. 17:6[85] *HaShem*'s words to Moses meant that he was present wherever his footprints appeared.	Ezek. 1:26 (the semblance of a throne . . . the semblance of a human form) Exod. 24:10 ("under his feet . . . sapphire")
Sifrei Zuta (*Beha'alotekha* 12:8) to Num. 12:8[86] Moses was not overcome by fear in his encounters with *HaShem*.	Num. 12:8 (with Moses I speak mouth to mouth) Exod. 33:11 (YHWH spoke to Moses face to face)
Sifrei Bamidbar 115:1-2 to Num. 15:37-41[87]	Num. 15:39 (you will see him/it)

Gazing at the fringes (*tzitzit*) is equivalent to receiving the face of *HaShem* just as the ancestors received him at the first Passover in Egypt.[88]	Ezek. 1:26 (the semblance of a throne like sapphire in appearance)
Sifrei Devarim 355 to Deut. 33:26[89] Israelites ask Moses what the glory of the Lord is like on high.	Deut. 33:26 (his majesty on the high vaults) Ezek. 1:28 (the likeness of the glory of the Lord; when I saw it, I fell on my face)
Heikalot Rabbati 8:2 (*Synopse* §159[90]) [91] A hymn describing YHWH enthroned and the danger of gazing at his beauty	1 En. 47:3; 60:2 (Ancient of Days enthroned on the throne of his glory) Dan. 7:9 (Ancient of Days enthroned . . . fiery flames) Isa. 33:17 (see the King in his beauty)
Heikalot Rabbati 25:1 (*Synopse* §253)[92] A hymn describing the King of kings surrounded by radiant angels, and the manifestations of his majesty, beauty, and stature in the heights and depths of creation	Isa. 33:17 (see the King in his beauty) Deut. 33:26 (his majesty on the high vaults)

There are several differences between Rabbinic texts and the apocalyptic texts discussed earlier. None of the texts cited here were written in the first-person singular as the apocalyptic texts were. Rabbinic texts consolidated material suitable for halakic discussion and for the exegesis of Hebrew Bible texts rather than their prophetic reenactment. Prayer was just one of many aspects of Jewish life that received attention.

Given the fact that the Rabbinic corpus was largely devoted to exegesis and halakah, one can hardly expect to find anything as explicit as the visions described in the apocalyptic texts. Rabbinic circles focused on Torah study and legal rulings, with their own devotional practices and those of the synagogue in the background. If I may press my earlier analogy to team sports, Rabbinic texts are something like the scripts of professional commentators: scripts of commentators are less directly related to practice than playbooks are, but they are based on the same game and think in terms of the same rules.[93] A close reading of these texts reveals a keen awareness of the concrete presence of *HaShem* when he was called on in prayer.[94] Rabbinic texts reflected the same visionary practices as apocalyptic (and later Heikalot) texts did.[95] They differ from apocalypses in formulation more than in spirituality.

I shall focus attention on the two *Mishnah Berakhot* passages (the earliest of those cited) and use the Tosefta, *Mekilta*, *Sifrei*, and Heikalot passages as supplements.[96] *Berakhot* is the Hebrew word for "Benedictions": it is the one tractate of the Rabbinic corpus that is devoted to liturgy and formal prayer. Both of the Mishnah passages cited describe the concentration of a worshiper, presumably a trained rabbi or hasid ("godly one," "holy man"), who prays the *Shema* and the *Amidah* (the "Standing" Prayer or "Eighteen Benedictions").

Mishnah Berakhot 2:1[97] describes the recitation of the *Shema* with brief pauses between blessings and Scripture citations.[98] These pauses provided alternating opportunities for directing one's heart (or face)—now toward *HaShem* and then returning the greeting of a neighbor. The important point here is that *HaShem* and the neighbor are placed on exactly the same footing.[99]

The idea of "directing one's heart" is based on Hebrew verb-stem *KWN*,[100] from which we also get the noun *kavanah*, meaning "spiritual concentration." The force of this *kavanah* is to locate *HaShem* in a particular direction in an imaginal space.[101] Various rules are proffered for greeting the neighbor, but they all hinge on the assumed exclusivity of addressing *HaShem* in benediction and addressing the neighbor in greeting: the one is assumed to be as concrete and immediate (for the worshipper) as the other. As Talmudic scholar Tzvee Zahavy has put it, the concentration that the Rabbis mandated for the *Shema* requires the worshiper to evoke "many major components of the symbolic system of Rabbinic Judaism and its images, and reactivates its myths with key words and phrases, allusions and references."[102] Foremost among these images was that of the anthropic form of *HaShem*.[103]

Admittedly, this is a strong reading of *Berakhot* 2:1, but it can be supported by the description of the recitation of the *Amidah* benedictions in our second mishnah, which comes just a few chapters later. In *Berakhot* 5:1, a worshiper is to emulate the ancient hasidim ("pietists")[104] and not to interrupt the prayer, even under the most extreme imaginable circumstances:

> The pious men of old [*hasidim rishonim*] used to wait an hour before they said the *Tefillah* [the *Amidah*], that they might direct their heart toward God [*Maqom*]. Even if the king salutes a man, he may not return the greeting; and even if a snake was twisted around his heel he may not interrupt his prayer.[105]

This is a typical Rabbinic test case (really a pair of tests), designed to impress an important point upon those who aspire to genuine piety.[106] We need to read it in terms of its intended impact rather than as a realistic occurrence. As in the previous mishnah, the worshiper is to "direct the heart" (again *KWN*), thereby locating *HaShem* in a particular direction (in imaginal space).

This dramatic test of concentration is preceded by the assertion that the "ancient pious ones" (*hasidim rishonim*) spent an entire hour preparing their hearts before beginning the *Amidah* in order to achieve the necessary degree of concentration. Although this discipline is ascribed to the earlier generations, the mandate in *Berakhot* 5:1 suggests the existence of concurrent pietistic circles of rabbis who regarded the "ancient pious ones" as models of *kavanah*, much as the apocalyptic circles did with Enoch, in order to intensify their own devotional practices.[107] According to the corresponding Tosefta passage (*t. Ber.* 3:4, also dating from the third century), the Rabbis found scriptural support for this practice in Psalm 10:17, "you will strengthen their heart."[108] The *Bavli* (Babylonian Talmud) repeats this citation (*b. Ber.* 31a)[109] and explains the strengthening of the heart by cross-reference to Psalm 16:8, "I keep the Lord always before me [he is at my right hand; I shall not be moved]" (*b. Sanh.* 22a, here attributed to one Simeon the Pious).[110] In a magisterial survey of the practice of "iconic visualization" among the Rabbis, Elliot Wolfson analyzes these same texts and comments:

> The essential thought underlying the teaching of Simeon the Pious is that prayer is predicated on the imaginary presencing [sic!] of God . . . in iconic form. . . .the worshiper must symbolically represent the divine presence by imagining God anthropomorphically . . . .
> It is plausible that reflected in the statement of Simeon the Pious is an actual praxis performed by a fraternity of pietists to which he belonged.[111]

Wolfson infers from this *Bavli* text that "iconic visualization" was practiced by "apocalyptic and/or mystical fraternities" that had been in existence since the early centuries of the Common Era.[112] His reading is consistent with what we know of the general trend toward formalization of statutory prayers, which did not occur until the formal redaction the *Bavli* (the Stammaim and Savoraim of the sixth and seventh centuries).[113] It is also consistent with the fact that the idea of locating the *Shekinah* in a particular geographic direction (cf. *m. Sukkah* 5:3) aroused considerable opposition in other parts of the Talmud.[114] The implication is that voices like that attributed here to Simeon the Pious were remnants of earlier traditions. Although the *Bavli* itself is too late (c. 600 CE) to allow specific inferences regarding the use of Psalm 16 for the New Testament era, it is worth noting that the same citation occurs in Acts 2:25 (in preparation for baptism), suggesting the possibility that Psalm 16:8 was one of the psalm verses associated with visionary practice already in the first century.[115] We shall return to this idea in chapter 9.

One other feature of *Berakhot* 5:1 that supports Wolfson's reading is its use of the Hebrew term *Maqom* for God.[116] The literal meaning of *maqom* is "place," particularly the Holy Place (cf. 1 Kgs 8:29-30, 35; *m. Ber.* 3:16).[117] Its usage in the Mishnah assumes familiarity with theophany traditions that portray a location in the heavens from which *HaShem* appears on earth and to which he returns (Isa. 26:21; Ezek. 3:12; Hos. 5:15; Mic. 1:3; cf. *t. Ber.* 3:4).[118] The Mishnah's use of *maqom* in combination with *kavanah* (intention, concentration), locates *HaShem* in a particular place toward which the worshipper directs his (or her) face.[119]

These Mishnahs are not as explicit as the apocalyptic visions described above (nor did we expect them to be): they mandate concrete ("iconic") visualization on the part of the worshiper, but they give no indication of any action or voice on the part of the Deity (being closer to Heikalot texts in this respect).[120] However, they do describe the ideal frame of mind of the worshipper, something apocalyptic texts tell us very little about. Commenting on the latter Mishnah (*Ber.* 5:1), Rabbinic scholar Max Kadushin states:

> Evoking [God's presence], accompanying Rabbinic prayers . . . was a sense, more than physical, of God's nearness. . . . Practices like these are practices of men . . . who trustfully expect to have experience of him, and to have it as a concomitant of "ordinary" prayer, prescribed [statutory] prayer.[121]

As in the case of apocalyptic texts, portrayals like this in the Mishnah are idealized and need not be taken as literal descriptions of events. But idealizations were as real in Rabbinic groups as they were in the apocalyptic circles—real in the sense that they provided models for performance. We have evidence here too of the rehearsal of the practices of the prophets and "ancient pious ones" in at least some Rabbinic circles.[122]

A variety of texts from Tannaitic midrashim confirm the general picture sketched from the Mishnah. They include Kyriocentric models based on the Psalms as well as the Prophets. A few brief comments are in order to fill out the picture so as not to rely solely on the Mishnah and Talmudic literature.

Mekilta of Rabbi Shimon to Exod. 17:6 comments on *HaShem*'s promise to appear to Moses and the elders of Israel on the rock of Horeb and to give them water therefrom. Going beyond the biblical lemma, this imaginative midrash broadens the promised theophany to include any location in which human footprints mysteriously appear on the ground:

> He said to him [Moses], "Anywhere you see human footprints—in accordance with what is said in Scripture, '. . . there was the semblance of a human form' [Ezek. 1:26]—there I am standing before you [cf. Exod. 17:6]."

The location of *HaShem*'s feet was also closely associated with the Temple in Jerusalem, "the place of the soles of my feet" (Ezek. 43:7), for which the rock of Horeb was clearly a prototype (cf. Pss. 36:8; 46:4; Ezek. 47:1). Reference to human footprints also suggests peripheral awareness of Exodus 24:10 ("under his feet . . . sapphire") as a supplementary motif—an anthropic form is clearly in view. *Mekilta of Rabbi Shimon* explicitly cites Ezekiel 1:26 ("the semblance of a throne in appearance like sapphire, and on top . . . the semblance of a human form") as a proof text. Presumably these two references to the gemstone sapphire (*sappir*) provided the connection.

Gershom Scholem concluded that the reference to footprints indicated the "image of the heavenly man" like that described in merkavah ("chariot") visions.[123] Scholem's conclusion can be supported by a text from the Tosefta (*t. Meg.* 3:28), according to which those who expound Ezekiel 1 are supposed to form a visual image of the chariot-throne and its rider in their hearts (cf. Rev. 4:2).[124] If this motif reflects knowledge of synagogue sermons (not just academic discussions of the Rabbis), it is likely that a popular tradition concerning the "footprints of *HaShem*" is being invoked here.[125] If so, we have an important indication of the imaginal world of pious laypeople as reflected in Rabbinic discourse.

Another Tannaitic midrash, *Sifrei Zuta* to Numbers 12:8, exegetes *HaShem*'s declaration that he would speak face to face with Moses so that he could see the uncreated form rather than a mere angel. Exodus 33:11 (I speak to Moses as to a friend) is cited here as an intersecting text,[126] and the midrash adds a further citation from Numbers 12:8:

> ". . . and he beholds the form of the Lord" [Num. 12:8b]. Said R. Simeon [bar Yohai], "For he saw the [uncreated] form forthwith [and not through creaturely mediation]."[127]

On the face of it, this daring exegesis is a simple play with words typical of the midrash genre. However, Abraham Heschel understands the description of Moses' intimacy with *HaShem* to reflect the Rabbis' own prayer life. According to Heschel, the indirect nature of the text simply reflects Rabbinic modesty:

> Modesty befits piety. The modest cover their faces [like Moses in Exod. 3:6] and avoid explicit language [about *HaShem*]. They sublimate their experience of their own divine encounter through homilies on the prophetic heroes of the past. In the traditions about Moses and the generations of the wilderness, who saw the Shehhinah, we find a treasure trove in which the Rabbis concealed their own private fantasies and longings.[128]

In other words, the biblical Moses served as a model or representative figure for the Rabbis just as Enoch did for some apocalyptic circles. [129] This practice is consistent with the Rabbinic maxim that leaders of each generation merited the give of the Holy Spirit even if their generations did not (*t. Sotah* 13:3-4 on Hillel and Samuel the Small).

Further evidence of visionary practice comes from *Sifrei Bamidbar* to Numbers 15:37-41, which interprets Moses' command to wear fringes (*tzitzit*) as a model for visionary contemplation (*Sifrei* 115).[130] The rich blue cord at each corner of the garment stands out from the white ones and was intended to remind wearers to keep the Lord's commandments (Num. 15:39)—an obligation that was considered confessional rather than strictly legal (cf. Deut. 6:6-7; 7:9-11; 11:13; 30:6-14). Our midrash interprets the blue cord as representing the sapphire throne of *HaShem* as described in the anthropic vision of Ezekiel 1:26 (the same visionary motif we encountered in *Mekilta of Rabbi Shimon*):

> It does not say: "And you shall look upon *it* [the feminine pronoun]," but "And you shall look upon *him* [the masculine pronoun]" [Num. 15:39a]. . . . those who fulfill the commandment of the tassels [a.k.a. show-fringes], it is as if [*kivyakol*] they welcome [the face of] the divine presence, for the blue of the fringes is like . . . the blue of the throne of glory, as it is said, "And above the firmament over their heads there was the likeness of a throne in appearance like sapphire [Ezek. 1:26]." (*Sifrei* 115)[131]

So gazing on the four blue cords is "as if" (*kivyakol*)[132] one were standing alongside Ezekiel and viewing the human image of the *Shekinah* Glory.[133] The context indicates that this was the same anthropic form that "showed" itself to the Israelites at the Passover (alluding to Exod. 12:13, 23, and citing Cant. 2:8-9)—hence the folk etymology for the name "show-fringes."[134] Here we enter rather deeply the imaginal world of Rabbinic symbolism of which Tzvee Zahavy and Elliot Wolfson spoke.[135]

We conclude our brief discussion of Tannaitic midrashim with *Sifrei Devarim* to Deuteronomy 33:26 ("O Jeshurun, There is none like God. . . . Through the skies is his majesty," JPST). This midrash begins with a terse, fairly standard exegesis, stressing the distance of God when Israel is disobedient,[136] but then it abruptly shifts to an imaginary conversation between Moses and Israel (*Sifrei* 355). The people ask about the "measure of glory" (*middat kavod*)[137] that Moses saw "on high" (on Mount Sinai)—a reasonable question coming from aspiring visionaries. Moses begins his answer by offering a simple comparison: *HaShem*'s glory is even greater than the splendor of the heavens (reading "Above the skies is his majesty"). Then he cites a parable, which can be summarized as follows.

Someone once traveled to the capital city in order to behold the glory of the king (cf. Isa. 33:17a, "Your eyes will see the king in his beauty"). Even before he could enter the city, however, the traveler was transfixed by the splendor of a gem-studded curtain that hung at the entrance. As a result, he collapsed in a swoon, and the city residents laughed at his presumption. The parable does not answer the question (as the prior exegesis did). Instead it issues a warning: those who are not worthy of beholding the beauty of *HaShem* will not only fail. They will also risk their own safety and jeopardize their reputation among the guardian angels.

Although *Sifrei Devarim* is an exegetical treatise, it would be difficult to explain the origin of this parable on exegetical grounds alone.[138] It appears to be an independent lesson, based on idealized discussions (i.e. scripts) among visionary rabbis and their disciples. The part about collapsing at the curtain is another imaginal performance of the vision of Ezekiel, who also swooned when he beheld the likeness of the anthropic Glory (Ezek. 1:26-28). Michael Fishbane's comment is helpful here, beginning with a rhetorical question:

> Can it therefore be that the (esoteric) knowledge which the people [of Israel] in *Sifre* 355 desire is in fact the *middah* of God's *kabod* ["measure of God's glory"] in heaven, viz., the supernal stature (or form) of the divine figure on high? The fact that the "seer" of the parable faints before the radiant *viylon* [curtain], much like the prophet Ezekiel who collapsed after his vision of the divine Glory (*kabod*) "in the likeness (*demut*) of a man" (Ezek. 1:26-28) enhances this possibility.[139]

The least that can be said is that such a reading would make sense in circles where Ezekiel's vision was a model for iconic visualization.

The source of our final two texts is *Heikalot Rabbati* ("The Greater [Anthology of] Heikalot"), a late macroform (that purports to be an instruction manual for aspiring visionaries (*Synopse* §§159, 253). The two hymns cited are very similar to the parable of Moses from *Sifrei Devarim* and may date from the same general era. Like the parable, these hymns tell of the beauty of the stature (or the measure) of the enthroned Deity.

The Heikalot hymns also warn about the danger of gazing at *HaShem*: "Those who gaze at him are instantly torn; those who glimpse his beauty are instantly poured out like a jug" (*Synopse* §159).[140] Our first impression of these warnings might be that they deny the very possibility of "beholding the King in his beauty" (again Isa. 33:17). As Elliot Wolfson and others have pointed out, however, the underlying assumption is that *HaShem* appears to the visionary in a magnificent anthropic form that can be seen by those who are well qualified.[141] In later narrative strata of *Heikalot Rabbati*, *HaShem* actually invites law-observant Israelites to ascend to his palace in peace and to gaze upon his beauty (cf. Exod. 24:9-11).[142] So the warnings are something like those of an athletic coach: if you want to make the team, you really have to work at it. The same point undoubtedly applies to Moses' warning in *Sifrei Devarim*. Moses was an ideal model for such preparation (Exod. 33:18-20; 34:28; Num. 12:8).

One more thing should be noted from the eight texts just examined. In contrast to Kyriocentric visions in apocalyptic (and New Testament) literature, the Rabbis' visionary experiences do not appear to have involved any new content (like inclusion of the Son of Man in the Daniel and the Similitudes of Enoch). As far as their Kyriocentric models are concerned, they were re-presentations in the strict sense, not new revelations. At least, this was the case in the written versions of the texts reviewed.[143]

Our results suggest that deity Christology in the New Testament could have derived from the rehearsal of Kyriocentric visions that were well within the parameters of contemporary, complex common Judaism. In fact, the early disciples of Jesus might turn out to have had as much in common with early Rabbinic circles (eschatology aside) as they did with apocalypticists.

CONCLUSION FROM OUR REVIEW OF APOCALYPTIC AND EARLY RABBINIC LITERATURE

This chapter has been our first step in testing the Kyriocentric vision conjecture. There can be little doubt that Jews of the first century believed that Kyriocentric visions had occurred in the time of the prophets and that they would be renewed in the impending eschaton. Moreover, there is ample evidence in contemporary literature for the rehearsal of model Kyriocentric visions in the centuries before, during, and after the New Testament era. First-century Jews saw themselves in an overlap between living memories and anticipated renewal.

None of the texts cited here can prove that first-century Jews practiced Kyriocentric visions. Other interpretations are possible for every one of them. But the plausibility of visionary practices is supported by the diversity of sources we have cited from the apocalyptic and Rabbinic traditions. They exhibit a variety of emphases, making it unlikely that they reflect a single formal topos or a literary conceit. Our reading is further supported by the range of Jewish scholars (Scholem, Kadushin, Heschel, Wolfson, Zahavy, and Fishbane) who read them in precisely this way. At the very least we can say that the evidence reviewed thus far shows that our Kyriocentric vision conjecture is not an implausible one in the context of early Judaism. Or, to put it the other way around, hypotheses that rely exclusively on the claims about a revered teacher and binitarian models are not the only ones to consider.

It would still be illegitimate to make inferences about early Christian communities without examining the New Testament material in its own terms. In later chapters, we will examine several aspects of New Testament Christology. Indications of oral performance and reference to Old Testament models will help us to identify some of the more likely remnants of Kyriocentric visions in the New Testament (ch. 5). The occurrence of devotional formulas from the Old Testament and early Judaism will yield further evidence of such visions in prayers and hymns of the New Testament as well as in general Christian discourse (ch. 6). Before proceeding to that stage of the argument, however, we need first to review apocalyptic and Rabbinic literature in order to identify the conditions associated with the performance of Kyriocentric visions, particularly the context of petitionary prayer.

Notes

1. Annette Yoshiko Reed has argued that the strictures on transmitting knowledge between heaven and earth make Enoch's experience unique and unrepeatable; Yoshiko Reed, "Heavenly Ascent, Angelic Descent, and the Transmission of Knowledge in 1 Enoch 6–16," in *Heavenly Realms and Earthly Realities in Late Antique Religions*, ed. Ra'anan S. Boustan and Annette Yoshiko Reed (Cambridge: Cambridge University Press, 2004), 47–66 (66). Contrariwise, Pierluigi Piovanelli points out that the detailed information given in the Book of the Watchers would make no sense if it was not supposed to be used by practitioners; Piovanelli, "'Sitting by the Waters of Dan,' or the 'Tricky Business' of Tracing the Social Profile of the Communities that Produced the Earliest Enochic Texts," in *The Early Enoch Literature*, JSJSup 121, ed. Gabriele Boccaccini and John J. Collins (Leiden: Brill, 2007), 257–81 (279–80). Like Piovanelli, we are primarily interested here in the community practices that lie behind the text.

2. Further evidence for the rehearsal of Kyriocentric visions could also be drawn from apocalyptic texts like *2 Enoch*, the *Apocalypse of Abraham* (polemically), the *Testament of Abraham*, the *Testament of Levi*, and the *Ascension of Isaiah*, the original versions of which all date from the early centuries of the Common Era. The problem here is that early Christians preserved and copied these texts. In fact, most of this material survives only in Christian redactions that are centuries later than the period of interest to us here. Much can be learned by studying all of these texts, particularly on topics like kyriophanies where they fill out details of visions already evidenced in earlier material. For simplicity of methodology, however, we shall concentrate on the latter. In any case, indubitably Jewish works like *1 Enoch* will be sufficient to make a preliminary case. Instead of using Christian Jewish sources, we shall supplement the Second Temple texts with early Rabbinic ones, which are arguably as early as the Christian Jewish ones just mentioned, and are definitively Jewish.

3. Whether these scrolls were deposited by the group who inhabited the buildings excavated at Qumran or not is immaterial for this project. The consensus view is that there was a strong connection even though some of the scrolls are based on the work of forerunners of the *Yahad* and associated groups.

4. Unfortunately the climactic theophany in Ezek. 1 is missing in both 4Q74 (4QEzek^b) and 4Q385 (4QpsEz^a frag. 4), but presumably the continuation of the text was similar to the canonical version. The climactic theophany in the Book of the Watchers, *1 En.* 14:18—15:2 (discussed below), is also missing in 4Q204 (4QEn^{c}ar, columns 7–8), but presumably the text was similar to the Ethiopic and Greek versions. In any case, neither of these texts is thought to have originated with the *Yahad* itself; Devorah Dimant, "Apocalyptic Texts at Qumran," in *The Community of the Renewed Covenant: The Notre Dame Symposium on the Dead Sea Scrolls*, Christianity and Judaism in Antiquity Series 10, ed. Eugene Ulrich and James VanderKam (Notre Dame, IN: University of Notre Dame Press, 1994), 177–91 (179, 189). Among texts for further study is the War Scroll, where the singer senses the presence of the King of glory among the congregation, addresses him

in the second person, and invokes his action as divine Warrior using the language of Ps. 24:8 (1QM 12:7-12; 14:16). In the Thanksgiving Hymns, YHWH is said to reveal himself as "perfect light" (1QH 12:6). In the Festival Prayers (nonsectarian?), the Lord is said to have renewed the covenant in the "vision of your glory" (parallels "words of your holy spirit," 1Q34 frag. 3 2:6; 4Q509 frags. 97-98 1:7-8). In the Blessings scroll (4QBer[a]), reference is made to the footstool and chariots of the glory (or glorious footstool and chariots), partly based on the merkavah vision of Ezek. 1 (4Q286 frag. 1 2:1-2). In the noncanonical Psalms, the name of YHWH is invoked and his glory is seen hovering over Jerusalem, apparently reflecting a performance of Isa. 60:2b (4Q380 frag. 1 1:5-6, nonsectarian). In the nonsectarian Songs of the Sabbath Sacrifice, the angels bless the image of the "throne chariot" (merkavah, 4Q405 frags 20-22 1:8). In the Apocryphon of Moses (4QapocrMoses C), the biblical motif of YHWH speaking face to face with Moses (Exod. 33:11) is repeated and extended to all of Israel (4Q377 frag. 1 2:6-12); Florentino García Martínez and Eibert J. C. Tigchelaar, eds., The Dead Sea Scrolls, Study Edition, 2 vols. (Leiden: Brill, 1997), 2:745. In the Songs of the Sage, the maskil invokes the radiance of YHWH to dispel all kinds of demons (4Q510 frag. 1 4; 4Q511 frag. 10 1). In contrast to the canonical Psalms reviewed in the following section of this chapter, however, none of these texts uses clearly theophanic language, only various manifestations like light, glory, chariots (plural), radiance, and throne.

5. Philip S. Alexander argues that Qumran texts like 4QShirShabb (nonsectarian?) stressed the utter transcendence of God and disallowed human ascent beyond preliminary angelification; Alexander, Mystical Texts: Songs of the Sabbath Sacrifice and Related Manuscripts, Companion to the Qumran Scrolls 7 (London: T&T Clark, 2006), 105-8; Alexander, "Qumran and the Genealogy of Western Mysticism," in New Perspectives on Old Texts, STDJ 88, ed. Esther G. Chazon and Betsy Halpern-Amaru (Leiden: Brill, 2010), 215-35 (222-24). On the other side, Angela Kim Harkins argues that the berakhot in 1QH 18-19 imply actual face-to-face reciprocity between the two parties (as in Gen. 47:7, 10); Harkins, Reading with an "I" to the Heavens: Looking at the Qumran Hodayot through the Lens of Visionary Traditions, Ekstasis 3 (Berlin: de Gruyter, 2012), 254-8. While Harkins puts great emphasis on the importance of the "imaginal body" in the Hodayot, however, it is always the persona/body of the hymnist (or reader) that is imagined, never that of HaShem; Harkins, Reading with an "I", 77-78, 87-88, 111, 201-2, 256, 263-64.

6. Among texts found at Qumran that recognize the temple and its liturgy as divine ordinances are 4QFlor. frags. 1-2 1:3-6; 11Q5 (11QPsa) 27:5-8 (nonsectarian); 11Q19 (11QTemplea) 29:8-9 (nonsectarian). The eschatological character of the Temple scroll need not have prevented Qumran readers from imagining themselves in that future reality, rather than in a celestial temple (as in 4QShirShab). Daniel K. Falk has argued in detail against the notion that liturgical (corporate) prayer developed as a substitute for the rituals of the Temple; Falk, "Qumran Prayer Texts and the Temple," in Sapiential, Liturgical, and Poetical Texts from Qumran: Proceedings of the Third Meeting of the International Organization for Qumran Studies, STDJ 35, ed. Daniel K. Falk, Florentino García Martínez, and Eileen M. Schuller (Leiden: Brill, 2000), 106-26 (113-14, 124-26).

7. According to Elliot R. Wolfson, YHWH was viewed as a pleroma of seven angelic powers (4Q403 frag. 1 1:2-3), so that the radiance of the divine face is deflected through the faces of those seven powers; Wolfson, "Seven Mysteries of Knowledge: Qumran E/Soterism Recovered," in The Idea of Biblical Interpretation: Essays in Honor of James Kugel, SJSJ 83, ed. Hindy Najman and Judith H. Newman (Leiden: Brill, 2004), 177-213 (205, 213).

8. On this stricture, see Esther G. Chazon, "Liturgical Communion with the Angels at Qumran," in Sapiential, Liturgical, and Poetical Texts from Qumran: Proceedings of the Third Meeting of the International Organization for Qumran Studies, STDJ 35, ed. Daniel K. Falk, Florentino García Martínez, and Eileen M. Schuller (Leiden: Brill, 2000), 95-105 (99-100, 104). In support of this possibility, note that all but one of the more promising theophany texts listed in note 4 reflect liturgical settings.

9. The chronological order should not be taken to imply dependence of later texts cited on the earlier ones. It only shows the order in which various traditions are evidenced in extant texts. As a result, unprecedented features of later texts are not necessarily later than shared features.

10. E. Isaac, "1 Enoch," in *Old Testament Pseudepigrapha*, ed. James Charlesworth, 2 vols. (Garden City, NY: Doubleday, 1983), 1:13–89.

11. Daniel Olson, *Enoch: A New Translation* (North Richland Hills, TX: BIBAL Press, 2004).

12. I reluctantly omit the vision described in *1 En.* 1:2-9, particularly since parts of it are found in 4QEnoch[a] 1 and 4QEnoch[c] 1, due to problems of text and translation. Compare, the translation by E. Isaac in *OTP* 1:13 with that by George W. E. Nickelsburg and James C. VanderKam, *1 Enoch: A Commentary on the Book of 1 Enoch*, Hermeneia, ed. Klaus Baltzer, 2 vols. (Minneapolis: Fortress Press, 2001, 2012), 1:137, which follows the Greek text (partly modeled on the vision of Balaam in Num. 24:15-17 and Deut. 33:1-3). In any case, the writer of Jude 14-16 (and possibly the apocalypticist of Rev. 1:7) understood it as a Kyriocentric vision that was accessible to believers. I also omit the Kyriocentric visions in the Dream/Animal Visions of Enoch (*1 En.* 89:16; 89:22), which are retellings of the visions of Moses and the Israelites (listed above).

13. For a general exposition of the vision in *1 En.* 14, see, e.g., Ithamar Gruenwald, *Apocalyptic and Merkavah Mysticism*, AGAJU 14 (Leiden: Brill, 1980), 32–7. For greater detail, see Nickelsburg and VanderKam, *1 Enoch*, 1:264; Peter Schäfer, *The Origins of Jewish Mysticism* (Princeton, NJ: Princeton University Press, 2011), 57–62. Schäfer is correct to point out that *1 En.* 14 is not an "account" of the ecstatic experience of Enoch, or even of the author as an individual mystic (ibid., 64–65, 84), but there are unmistakable experiential aspects (fear, trembling, falling) embedded in the narrative as he himself points out (ibid., 63, 64; the fact that these experiences are "standard biblical reactions" is what one would expect from oral performance). In Enoch literature, the focus is on what is experienced (seen and heard) in heaven, not on the experience itself, and it is described in stylistic terms. Schäfer, like Himmelfarb (whose work he invokes), assumes a forced choice between literary (communal) endeavor and mystic (individual) experience and concludes that there is "no exegetical path" leading from one to the other (ibid., 64–65). He thereby provides a good example of the limits of strictly inductive methodologies. This is precisely the issue in debate between Schäfer, *Origins of Jewish Mysticism*, 351–52, and Elliot Wolfson, *Through a Speculum that Shines: Vision and Imagination in Medieval Jewish Mysticism* (Princeton, NJ: Princeton University Press, 1994), 121–24.

14. In *Mekilta of Rabbi Shimon bar Yohai* (hereafter *MRS*), "Great Glory" (Heb. *kavod gadol*) is the divine name for the greatest of the canonical theophanies, that to the people of Israel on Mt. Sinai (Exod. 20:15); Wolfson, *Through a Speculum that Shines*, 38. W. David Nelson translates the name as the "glory of God" (grammatically equivalent); Nelson, trans., *Mekhilta of Rabbi Shimon Bar Yohai* (Philadelphia: Jewish Publication Society of America, 2002), 253.

15. Nickelsburg and VanderKam (*1 Enoch*, 1:255–6, 264) give a detailed treatment of parallels between the theophany in *1 En.* 14 and those in Isa. 6; Ezek. 1; Dan. 7.

16. Schäfer, *Origins of Jewish Mysticism*, 57.

17. Nickelsburg and VanderKam, *1 Enoch*, 1:270.

18. For possible literary dependence of Dan. 7 on *1 Enoch* 14 (or an earlier source), see Matthew Black, *The Book of Enoch or 1 Enoch: A New English Edition with Commentary and Textual Notes*, SVTP 7 (Leiden: Brill, 1985), 149–52; Schäfer, *Origins of Jewish Mysticism*, 60–62; John J. Collins, *Daniel: A Commentary*, Hermeneia (Minneapolis: Fortress Press, 1993), 300. While these observations are helpful, I would see the two texts as independent products of ongoing oral performance traditions.

19. Schäfer, *Origins of Jewish Mysticism*, 61.

20. See Nickelsburg and VanderKam, *1 Enoch*, 2:125, 130. The authors suggest that the vision of the Lord of spirits begins in 40:1, after the prophet's face has been transformed in 39:14 (ibid., 2:129b, 131a). Schäfer, *Origins of Jewish Mysticism*, 72–73, downplays the theophanic aspect of the text, but he does not take into account the repeated emphasis on the place under the wings

of the Lord of spirits (*1 En.* 40:7-8, 13, which indicates Enoch's lowering his eyes to avoid a direct gaze; see below on visual imagination in *1 En.* 14:23, 25) or the angelic Sanctus and Benedictus (40:12, 14).

21. Gruenwald notes the reminiscence to the Benedictus of Ezek. 3:12; Gruenwald, *Apocalyptic and Merkavah Mysticism*, 39; cf. Nickelsburg and VanderKam, *1 Enoch*, 2:128.

22. Nickelsburg and VanderKam view *1 En.* 14:18-22 as the prototype here and suggest that *1 En.* 39–40 shifts the focus of the vision from YHWH to the attendant angels; Nickelsburg and VanderKam, *1 Enoch*, 2:125a, 129b, 131.

23. See ibid., 2:153.

24. Nickelsburg and VanderKam (*1 Enoch*, 2:154a) speak of the Son of Man as "the main character" in the narrative, but in the vision itself, the Son of Man travels with (or beside) the Head of Days (46:2).

25. Nickelsburg and VanderKam, *1 Enoch*, 2:155; Schäfer, *Origins of Jewish Mysticism*, 73. Schäfer tries hard to play down the centrality of the Ancient of Days in *1 En.* 46.

26. See Gruenwald, *Apocalyptic and Merkavah Mysticism*, 42; Nickelsburg and VanderKam, *1 Enoch*, 2:162. For some reason, Schäfer completely ignores this visionary account; Schäfer, *Origins of Jewish Mysticism*, 72–73.

27. Nickelsburg and VanderKam, *1 Enoch*, 2:155a, 164a.

28. Ibid., 2:155a, 164.

29. Ibid., 2:233; Schäfer, *Origins of Jewish Mysticism*, 73–74.

30. Nickelsburg and VanderKam (*1 Enoch*, 2:233, 235b) emend the text from "life of Enoch" to "life of Noah" on the supposition that this was originally Noachic tradition. Apparently Noah once served as an ideal figure in the Enochic communities as he did in 1Q20 (1QapGen.) 6:11-14; cf. Geza Vermes, *The Complete Dead Sea Scrolls in English* (New York: Allen Lane, 1997), 450.

31. Nickelsburg and VanderKam (*1 Enoch*, 2:235–6) list parallels between the theophany in *1 En.* 60 and those in *1 En.* 14–15; Dan. 7.

32. Ibid., 2:235

33. See Gruenwald, *Apocalyptic and Merkavah Mysticism*, 42–45; Nickelsburg and VanderKam, *1 Enoch*, 2:320–21; Schäfer, *Origins of Jewish Mysticism*, 74–76. Even if *1 En.* 70:3—71:17 is a later addition to the Similitudes, it may still date from the later New Testament era; Darrell D. Hannah, "The Elect Son of Man of the *Parables of Enoch*," in *"Who is This Son of Man?" The Latest Scholarship on a Puzzling Expression of the Historical Jesus*, Library of New Testament Studies 390, ed. Larry W. Hurtado and Paul Owen (London: T&T Clark, 2011), 130–58 (158). In any case, omitting the text would not alter the results here.

34. Interpretations of *1 En.* 71:14 are notoriously difficult. Alan Segal, *Paul the Convert: The Apostolate and Apostasy of Saul the Pharisee* (New Haven, CT: Yale University Press, 1990), 46–47, argues that Enoch is engrafted into the body of the Son of Man as a model for adepts of the Enoch circles (cf. Enoch's desire to dwell in the place of the Elect One in 39:8). Nickelsburg and VanderKam (*1 Enoch*, 2:325, 327–28) more modestly refer to 71:14 as a commissioning scene like that in Ps. 2:7. As Segal himself states (ibid., 61), however, we cannot rule out the possibility that *1 En.* 70–71 was a Christian addition to the corpus.

35. Nickelsburg and VanderKam, *1 Enoch*, 2:327a.

36. Ibid.

37. Ibid., 2:324a, 327b.

38. According to Angela Kim Harkins, use of the first-person in such narratives can be seen as a rhetorical means of inducing a like experience in the performative reader; Harkins, *Reading with an "I"*, 3, 80, 87–88, 110–11 (citing Carol Newsom), 112, passim. In her conclusion, Harkins refers to the protagonist not as a reader, but as a "viewer" who works with a store of oral traditions; ibid., 268, 272. In the case of Rabbinic texts, Martin Jaffee describes the latter as the "primary performance setting," as distinct from the "secondary performance setting of the manuscript"; Jaffee, "What Difference Does the 'Orality' of Rabbinic Writing Make for the Interpretation of

Rabbinic Writings?" in *How Should Rabbinic Literature Be Read in the Modern World?* ed. Matthew Kraus (Piscataway, NJ: Gorgias, 2006), 11–31 (17). In the case of *Avodah piyutim* (late antique liturgical poems), Michael Swartz has shown in detail how the *payyetan* (liturgical poet) identified himself with the high priest and performatively led the synagogue congregation through the entrance into the holy of holies to "bask in the divine presence," culminating in their prostration at hearing him pronounce the Tetragrammaton; Swartz, "Judaism and the Idea of Ancient Ritual Theory," in *Jewish Studies at the Crossroads of Anthropology and History: Authority, Diaspora, Tradition,* Jewish Culture and Contexts, ed. Ra'anan S. Boustan, Oren Kosansky, and Marina Rustow (Philadelphia: University of Pennsylvania Press, 2011), 294–317, 404–10 (313–16); cf. Swartz, "Sage, Priest, and Poet: Typologies of Leadership in the Ancient Synagogue," in *Jews, Christians, and Polytheists in the Ancient Synagogue: Cultural Interaction During The Greco-Roman Period,* Baltimore Studies in the History of Judaism, ed. Steven Fine (London: Routledge, 1999), 101–17 (112, "the power to invoke the encounter between the divine and the human . . . in the synagogue, the realm of song and imagination").

39. As Martha Himmelfarb insists, the function of Enoch's vision in the written composition is primarily to legitimate the condemnation of the Watchers; Himmelfarb, *Ascent to Heaven in Jewish and Christian Apocalypses* (New York: Oxford University Press, 1993), 103–4. Our interest here is rather in the visionary practices that the authors could assume were meaningful to their community.

40. These vision performances are evidenced in the visions of Isaiah and Ezekiel but are probably not based on exegesis of the written texts as we have them. It could well be a case of oral performance "all the way down."

41. After Enoch's observing the inside of the second house in *1 En.* 14:18, visual language continues to be used even though Enoch's face is turned down to the ground (14:23, 25). Apparently these visions combine visual imagination with eyesight.

42. *OTP* 1:21.

43. As Christopher Rowland states, "Intertextual connections one can find in a text like Revelation are less deliberate allusions [to the Old Testament] than the manifestation of a visionary culture in which key scriptural texts, like Ezekiel and Daniel, provide the necessary components for the apprehension and comprehension of divine truth"; Rowland and Christopher R.A. Morray-Jones, *The Mystery of God: Early Jewish Mysticism and the New Testament,* CRINT 3, 12 (Leiden: Brill, 2009), 64; cf. David Rhoads, "Performance Criticism: An Emerging Methodology in Second Testament Studies—Part II," *BTB* 36 (2006): 164–84 (167b) on intertextual allusions as "aural echoes of Israel's stories."

44. The phenomenon of multiple performances is widely recognized in the formation of the Old Testament itself. For example, the prophetic promises in Jer. 33:14–26 (not included in the Greek Septuagint) are a reworked version of material in earlier chapters of Jeremiah (Jer. 23:5–6; 31:35–37). Inclusion of the covenant promises to David and the Levites (not just the survival of Israel) indicates that earlier performances had taken on a new focus in the postexilic setting. Cf. Karel van der Toorn, *Scribal Culture and the Making of the Hebrew Bible* (Cambridge, MA: Harvard University Press, 2007), 132, who makes use of Mesopotamian cuneiform tablets as his model.

45. "Inter-performative" events occur when one oral performance—say one of Enoch's visions in the Similitudes, which rehearses elements now found in the Book of the Watchers—incorporates elements from other performances—say that embedded in Exod. 33:21-22 (in *1 En.* 39:7-8), or that in Dan. 7:9-10 (in *1 En.* 71:6-10). Intertextuality, on the other hand, occurs when a narrator or writer expresses an idea by citing a specific written text (examples of which we shall encounter in ch. 7, "How Could the Lord Have Suffered and Been Crucified?"). My main concern here is to get away from a scholar's imagined world in which written texts emerge directly from reading, recital, and commentary on other written texts. Intertextuality remains a primary tool for determining the face value meaning of written texts, but it cannot stand in for a historical scenario. Martin Jaffee still tries to maintain the primacy of the idea of intertextuality by reinterpreting it along "oralist," performative lines; Jaffee, "What Difference

Does the 'Orality' of Rabbinic Writing Make," 20 and n. 12. Fair enough, but for our purposes, such a blend of etic and emic categories would only confuse the issue.

46. In a comprehensive overview of oral performances in the NT, David Rhoads speaks of repeated performances as communal "compositions" in order to stress the variation in gesture and tone of voice; Rhoads, "Performance Criticism: An Emerging Methodology in Second Testament Studies—Part I," *BTB* 36 (2006): 118–33 (127a). From an etic (observer's) perspective this is accurate, but I prefer to speak of rehearsals to stress the community's consciousness of reenacting and re-experiencing the original performance.

47. Oral, liturgical uses of Scripture characteristically blend motifs from various sources in a way that defies precise analysis. Compare the pre-classical *piyutim* in the *Seder Beriyot*, part of the Yom Kippur liturgy, in which visionary motifs from Isa. 6, Ezek. 1, and Dan. 7 are similarly blended; Michael Rand, "More on *Seder Beriyot*," *JSQ* 16 (2009): 183–209 (192–4, 206–9).

48. The pairing of Sanctus and Benedictus also occurs in the "Blessing of the Creator" (*Yotzer*) in the *Shema* prayer service and in the public repetition of the "Sanctification of the Name of *HaShem*" in the *Amidah*. Joseph Tabory views this pairing as an early example of the anthological nature of Jewish prayers; Tabory, "The Prayer Book (Siddur) as an Anthology of Judaism," *Prooftexts* 17 (1997): 115–32 (122–3).

49. Judith Newman, *Praying by the Book: The Scripturalization of Prayer in Second Temple Judaism*, Early Judaism and its Literature 14 (Atlanta: Scholars, 1999). Newman also defines a narrower category, the recombination of biblical phrases to suit a new context as "biblicizing" prayer; ibid., 103–6. She points out how appropriation of Scripture phrases made the creative uses of language possible during the Second Temple era: "old bits of Scripture and interpretation are used as compost to fertilize the new soil and encourage new growth"; Newman, "The Scripturalization of Prayer in Exilic and Second Temple Judaism," in *Prayers that Cite Scripture*, ed. James L. Kugel (Cambridge, MA: Harvard University Press, 2006), 7–24 (24). Newman assumes that these phrases originated in Scripture, but it is also possible that their occurrence in written Scripture was due to the fact that the authors knew them from preexisting prayers.

50. Tabory, "The Prayer Book (Siddur) as an Anthology of Judaism," 116, 126. In contrast to Judith Newman, Tabory is describing the formation of the prayers and study passages of the Siddur (the Jewish prayer book).

51. Judith Newman points out that such "recontextualization" relied on the author's internalization of the words of the prophet and did not require conscious citation of a particular text; Newman, *Praying by the Book*, 13–14, 105 (here termed "biblicizing"), 115 ("internalization").

52. David Frankfurter, "The Legacy of Jewish Apocalypses in Early Christianity," in *The Jewish Apocalyptic Heritage in Early Christianity*, CRINT 3, 4, ed. James C. VanderKam and William Adler (Assen: Van Gorcum, 1996), 129–200 (167). Richard Horsley describes how facility in biblical wording and style could arise in an oral culture of recitation, resulting in a biblical "register of language" that could later be drawn upon without consulting texts; Horsley, *Scribes, Visionaries, and the Politics of Second Temple Judea* (Louisville: Westminster John Knox, 2007), 116–17, 142–3, 158.

53. As Nickelsburg and VanderKam (*1 Enoch* 1:144a) state, the theophanic material in *1 Enoch* similarly reflects "unconscious combination rather than explicit selective citation." In the composition of Rabbinic texts, prior oral performance is characterized by the "transposition" or "mixing and matching" of diverse traditional elements; Jaffee, "What Difference Does the 'Orality' of Rabbinic Writing Make," 30–1.

54. Among the factors that promoted the scripturalization of prayer, James Kugel includes the desire to evoke biblical instances of divine intervention so as to spur new interventions in the present; Kugel, "The Scripturalization of Prayer," in *Prayers that Cite Scripture*, ed. James L. Kugel (Cambridge, MA: Harvard University Press, 2006), 1–5 (3). A perfect example of this expectation for individuals (and families) is found in the fast day instructions in *m. Ta'an* 2:2-4, where a man who is too poor to feed his children is chosen to recite the *zikronot* ("remembrances") and petitionary psalms (Pss. 120; 121; 130; 102, in that order), each one of which is sealed with the

words, "May he who answered Abraham our father in Mount Moriah answer you and hearken to the voice of your crying this day"; Herbert Danby, trans., *The Mishnah Translated from the Hebrew with Introduction and Explanatory Notes* (Oxford: Oxford University Press, 1933), 196.

55. Similarly, Troels Engberg-Pedersen argues for the possibility (and the need) of recovering of Paul's past experiences from his letters, even though these were written largely for rhetorical rather than autobiographical purposes; Engberg-Pedersen, "The Construction of Religious Experience in Paul," in *Experientia, Volume I: Inquiry into Religious Experience in Early Judaism and Christianity*, SBLSS 40, ed. Frances Flannery, Colleen Shantz, and Rodney A. Werline (Atlanta: SBL, 2008), 147–76 (150).

56. Alexander Golitzin, "The Vision of God and the Form of Glory: More Reflections on the Anthropomorphite Controversy of AD 399," in *Abba: The Tradition of Orthodoxy in the West: Festschrift for Bishop Kallistos (Ware) of Diokleia*, ed. John Behr, Andrew Louth, and Dimitri Conomos (Crestwood, NY: St. Vladimir's Seminary Press, 2003), 273–97 (292). The term *mysticism*, of course, is an etic category, not necessarily the way the apocalypticists or rabbis (or the monks) viewed themselves. Daniel Boyarin speaks simply of the "cultural continuity" in visionary practice (particularly in the context of possible martyrdom) from biblical times through the Rabbis and up until the early medieval period; Boyarin, "The Eye in the Torah: Oracular Desire in Midrashic Hermeneutic," *Critical Inquiry* 16 (1990): 532–50 (544 n. 25).

57. The older scholarly notion that the Rabbis were intractably opposed to mystical experience and visionary practice is to be discarded in favor of more nuanced readings that discern a wide diversity of views, ranging from practical formalists to mystical pietists; see, for example, Stefan Reif, *Judaism and Hebrew Prayer: New Perspectives on Jewish Liturgical History* (Cambridge: Cambridge University Press, 1993), 104–7. Scholars can find evidence for mystical practices or exclusive emphasis on formal study depending on their selection of texts.

58. On the prior existence of the phraseology of the statutory prayers, see Joseph Heinemann, *Prayer in the Talmud: Forms and Patterns*, SJ 9 (Berlin: de Gruyter, 1977), 22–26, 219 (citing Sir. 36 and the additions to Sir. 51:12), 286–87. Heinemann argues convincingly that the Rabbis formulated most of the Eighteen Benedictions by selecting from among numerous earlier formulations (with the exception of the *Bonah Yerushalayim* ["Rebuilder of Jerusalem"] benediction); ibid., 37–39, 48–49, 222; cf. Richard S. Sarason, "On the Use of Method in the Modern Study of Jewish Liturgy," in *Approaches to Ancient Judaism: Theory and Practice*, BJS, ed. William Scott Green, 6 vols. (Missoula, MT: Scholars, 1978–85 [1978]), 1:97–172 (145–7); Ruth Langer, "Revisiting Early Rabbinic Liturgy: The Recent Contributions of Ezra Fleischer," *Prooftexts* 19 (1999): 179–94 (180, 186, 190). The more expansive *piyutim* (liturgical poems) also used traditional material, but were composed centuries after the close of the Tannaitic period; Heinemann, *Prayer in the Talmud*, 240, 286.

59. *Mekilta of Rabbi Ishmael* (hereafter *MRI*) Shirata 3:28–30, ET in Jacob Z. Lauterbach, trans., *Mekilta of Rabbi Ishmael*, 3 vols. (Philadelphia: Jewish Publication Society of America, 1933), 2:24. The participants in the Sea Deliverance evidently include living celebrants as well as those who lived at the time of the exodus.

60. Gruenwald cites two other passages from *MRI* (Vayassa' 7 and Bahodesh 9:56–58) as examples of "non-Merkavah mysticism" in Rabbinic literature; Gruenwald, *Apocalyptic and Merkavah Mysticism*, 73 n. 1. Gruenwald concludes that the Tannaim discovered the ecstatic potential of merkavah visions long before the Heikalot texts were composed; ibid., 85–6, 88

61. See, e.g., *m. Hag.* 2:1; *Sifra* to Lev. 1:1; *Sifrei Bamidbar* §§99, 97 to Num.12:1; *Sifrei Devarim* §357 to Deut. 34:10.

62. Lawrence Kaplan points out that the kind of transformational mysticism that is found in Enoch traditions is entirely absent in classical Rabbinic literature and may even be polemicized against; Kaplan, "Adam, Enoch, and Metatron Revisited: A Critical Analysis of Moshe Idel's Method of Reconstruction," *Kabbalah* 6 (2001): 73–119 (76–9). Since Kyriocentric visions are often accompanied by the apotheosis of the visionary, one might expect a similar absence of Kyriocentric visions in early Rabbinic texts. As we shall see below, this is not the case. Even

though the Rabbis muted their knowledge of Kyriocentric visions, absorbing it into halakic and midrashic formats, they did not repress them, perhaps due to their role in prayers like the *Amidah* benedictions.

63. In relation to the New Testament, my use of Rabbinic texts here is strictly phenomenological, intended only to document the possibility of Kyriocentric visions in the early centuries of the Common Era. The argument could be tightened by citing the Rabbis' sense of continuity between prayer practices of their own time and those of the Temple era; see esp. *m. Yoma* 7:1 = *m. Sota* 7:7; amplified in *t. Yoma* 3:18; *t. Sukkah* 4:5; *MRI* Bahodesh 1:42–9. It is unlikely that the Rabbinic ways of relating to the Divine were entirely new constructs; cf. Steven Fine, *This Holy Place: On the Sanctity of the Synagogue during the Greco-Roman Period*, Christianity and Judaism in Antiquity 11 (Notre Dame, IN: University of Notre Dame Press, 1997), 36–37, 41–43, 49–51.

64. On the terms Tannaitic and *Amoraic*, see ch. 1, "Rabbis, Heikalot Adepts, and the Performance of Hebrew Bible Visions."

65. Hermann L. Strack and Günter Stemberger place the final redaction of *MRI* in the last half of the third century; Strack and Stemberger, *Introduction to the Talmud and Midrash*, trans. Markus Bockmuehl (Edinburgh: T&T Clark, 1991), 278–79.

66. It is over twenty years since Lawrence H. Schiffman used Qumran material like 4QMMT to demonstrate halakic continuity between Hasmonean era Pharisees and the early Rabbis; Schiffman, "New Light on the Pharisees," in *Understanding the Dead Sea Scrolls: A Reader from the Biblical Archaeology Review*, ed. Hershel Shanks (New York: Random House, 1992), 217–24 (224). For a recent critique of the notion that Rabbinic Judaism reacted to emerging Christianity in such a way as to become discontinuous with Second Temple Judaism, see Adiel Schremer, *Brothers Estranged: Heresy, Christianity, and Jewish Identity in Late Antiquity* (Oxford: Oxford University Press, 2010), esp. 5–11. Schremer cautions against the trend to read anti-Christian polemic into Tannaitic texts and wisely emphasizes the role of social and communal issues in defining religious boundaries; ibid., 10, 16, 19–21, 106–7, 117–19, 144–45.

67. So Jacob Neusner: "The one thing the Mishnah does not want to tell us is about change"; Neusner, *Judaism: The Evidence of the Mishnah* (Chicago: University of Chicago, 1981), 235; cf. Neusner, *Transformations in Ancient Judaism: Textual Evidence for Creative Responses to Crisis* (Peabody, MA: Hendrickson, 2004), 58, 61.

68. On the eclecticism of the Tannaim, see Albert I. Baumgarten, "The Akiban Opposition," *HUCA* 50 (1979): 179–97 (192–3, 197, synthesizing interests of Akivan party and the Hillelite Patriarchate); Neusner, *Judaism: The Evidence of the Mishnah*, 232–56 (synthesizing the gifts of priests, scribes, and householders); Shaye J. D. Cohen, "The Significance of Yavneh: Pharisees, Rabbis, and the End of Jewish Sectarianism," *HUCA* 55 (1984): 27–53 (31, 47–51, synthesizing the interests of Hillelites and Shammaites); Avigdor Shinan, "Synagogues in the Land of Israel: The Literature of the Ancient Synagogue and Synagogue Archaeology," in *Sacred Realm: The Emergence of the Synagogue in the Ancient World*, ed. Steven Fine (New York: Oxford University Press, 1996), 130–52 (136 on the diversity of prayer forms).

69. Even though the text of the Mishnah may not have been fixed until after the redaction of the *Bavli*, the traditions recorded therein reflect the cultural world of the Tannaim; Elizabeth Shanks Alexander, *Transmitting Mishnah: The Shaping Influence of Oral Tradition* (Cambridge: Cambridge University Press, 2006), 19, 32.

70. As Lawrence Schiffman has argued, the Psalms must have been used liturgically within the *Yahad*; Schiffman, "The Dead Sea Scrolls and the Early History of Jewish Liturgy," in *The Synagogue in Late Antiquity*, ed. Lee I. Levine (Philadelphia: American Schools of Oriental Research, 1987), 33–48 (36). If the chanting of the psalms was corporate (not just done by a cantor), they must have been recited from memory, so the possibility that written texts of the Psalms were only used for private study does not conflict with their liturgical use as sometime supposed.

71. Eileen Schuller explains the commonalities among Jewish prayer texts from Qumran to the Rabbis by pointing out: "The very essence of prayer/hymnic discourse, whether sectarian or non-sectarian, is its dependence on a common stock of stereotypical and formulaic, biblically-based phraseology"; Schuller, "Prayer, Hymnic, and Liturgical Texts from Qumran," in *The Community of the Renewed Covenant: The Notre Dame Symposium on the Dead Sea Scrolls*, Christianity and Judaism in Antiquity 10, ed. Eugene Ulrich and James VanderKam (Notre Dame, IN: University of Notre Dame Press, 1994), 151–71 (170).

72. So Peter Schäfer, *The Jewish Jesus: How Judaism and Christianity Shaped Each Other* (Princeton, NJ: Princeton University Press, 2012), 13, 67, 81. Schäfer argues that some late third or early fourth century Amoraim were in dialogue with christological ideas (ibid., 42–54, 215, 231–34, passim), but the earliest texts he cites (*Genesis Rabbah* and the Jerusalem Talmud) are from the fifth century.

73. Late Mishnah texts like *m. Tamid* 7:3 and *m. Avot* 5:23 (5:20 in Danby, trans., *The Mishnah*) conclude with the entreaty that the Temple be built up again "speedily, in our days." Günter Stemberger suggests that the Mishnah's descriptions of the Second Temple are really idealizations for a restored Temple in the future; Stemberger, "Dating Rabbinic Traditions," in *The New Testament and Rabbinic Literature*, SJSJ 136, ed. Reimund Bieringer (Leiden: Brill, 2010), 79–96 (86).

74. On the ways in which loss of the Temple steered Rabbinic Judaism in new directions of Torah piety, see the insightful study of William Scott Green, "Romancing the Tome: Rabbinic Hermeneutics and the Theory of Literature," *Semeia* 40 (1987): 148–68 (154–8). For a caution against differentiating the Rabbinic understanding of the temple and Torah study from that of Second Temple Jews, see Jonathan Klawans, *Purity, Sacrifice, and The Temple: Symbolism and Supersessionism in the Study of Ancient Judaism* (Oxford: Oxford University Press, 2006), 198–209.

75. Daniel Boyarin, "The Diadoche of the Rabbis; or, Judah the Patriarch at Yavneh," in *Jewish Culture and Society under the Christian Roman* Empire, Interdisciplinary Studies in Ancient Culture and Religion 3, ed. Richard Kalmin and Seth Schwartz (Leuven: Peeters, 2003), 285–318 (294–7). On the novelty of the Rabbinic doctrine of a dual Torah, see Steven D. Fraade, "Literary Composition and Oral Performance in Early Midrashim," *Oral Tradition* 14 (1999): 33–51 (39–42).

76. On sectarian ideas, see, for example, *m. Sanh.* 10:1; *t. Ber.* 3:25; *MRI* Bahodesh 5:19–26; Shirata 4:22; cf. Boyarin, "Justin Martyr Invents Judaism," *Church History* 70 (2001): 427–61 (439–48), 456 n. 97; Boyarin, "Two Powers in Heaven; or, The Making of a Heresy," in *The Idea of Biblical Interpretation: Essays in Honor of James Kugel*, SJSJ 83, ed. Hindy Najman and Judith H. Newman (Leiden: Brill, 2004), 331–70 (343–44, 347).

77. Avigdor Shinan, "The Aramaic Targum as a Mirror of Galilean Jewry," in *The Galilee in Late Antiquity*, ed. Lee I. Levine (New York: Jewish Theological Seminary of America, 1992), 241–51 (245).

78. The dating of the Heikalot texts depends on their relation to Babylonian incantation bowls of the third to the seventh century. James Davila makes them roughly contemporary and so dates the Heikalot texts to the fifth to seventh century; Davila, *Descenders to the Chariot: The People behind the Hekhalot Literature* SJSJ 70 (Leiden: Brill, 2001), 253, 308. Ra'anan S. Boustan dates the texts slightly later than the Babylonian incantation bowls and comes up with a date of 650–950 ce; Boustan, "The Emergence of Pseudonymous Attribution in Heikalot Literature: Empirical Evidence from the Jewish 'Magical' Corpora," *JSQ* 12 (2007): 18–38. Using an entirely different method, Michael D. Swartz dates early Heikalot texts similar to the macroforms we possess to early classical period of *piyutim* (liturgical hymns), from the fifth to the early seventh century; Swartz, "Piyut and Heikalot: Recent Research and its Implications for the History of Ancient Jewish Liturgy and Mysticism," in *The Experience of Jewish Liturgy: Studies Dedicated to Menahem Schmelzer*, Brill Reference Library of Judaism 31, ed. Debra Reed Blank, trans. Dena Ordan (Leiden: Brill, 2011), 263–81 (278).

79. As Michael Swartz points out, "God rarely speaks directly to humans in Hekhalot ascent texts, even if they visit in his throne room. He is usually portrayed anthropomorphically, but not anthropopathically, distinguishing this genre from apocalyptic literature, in which God . . . delivers a message . . . ."; Swartz, "Jewish Visionary Tradition in Rabbinic Literature," in *The Cambridge Companion to the Talmud and Rabbinic Literature*, ed. Charlotte Elisheva Fonrobert and Martin S. Jaffee (Cambridge: Cambridge University Press, 2007), 198–221 (211); cf. Moshe Idel, *Ascensions on High in Jewish Mysticism: Pillars, Lines, Ladders*, CEU Studies in the Humanities 2 (Budapest: Central European University, 2005), 31. I should point out that there are some notable exceptions like *Heikalot Rabbati* §169, *Merkavah Rabbah* §686, "Ozhaya fragment" (TS[Lxx] K1.21.95.C), and *3 Enoch (Sefer Heikalot)* 9:1. I forgo any discussion of *Heikalot Rabbati* §151 because of the idiosyncratic nature of the one manuscript in which it is found (MS New York 8128); see Ra'anan S. Boustan, "Rabbinization and the Making of Early Jewish Mysticism," *JQR* 101 (2011): 482–501 (489–91). Note that the enthroned Deity of the Similitudes of Enoch was already rather more passive than that of the Book of the Watchers (14:24-25; 15:1): even though YHWH sits down on his throne to initiate judgment (47:3) and comes with the angels to welcome Enoch (71:13), subsequent locution is done by one of the angels (71:14-16). However, other arguably first-century texts like 3 Maccabees and the *Apocalypse of Abraham* assigned a more clearly active role to the coming Lord (3 Maccabees 6:18; *Apoc. Ab.* 16:2; 19:1, arguably Christian). It is difficult to make clear-cut differentiations here.

80. The restrained anthropopathism of Heikalot texts may partly be due to Ashkenazi editing in the Middle Ages. Haym Soloveitchik describes the (temporary) shift in the Ashkenazi view of God in *Sefer Hasidim*; Soloveitchik, "The Midrash, *Sefer Hasidim* and the Changing Face of God," in *Creation and Re-Creation in Jewish Thought: Festschrift in Honor of Joseph Dan on the Occasion of His Seventieth Birthday*, ed. Rachel Elior and Peter Schäfer (Tübingen: Mohr Siebeck, 2005), 165–77 (170–5).

81. Ra'anan S. Boustan, *From Martyr to Mystic: Rabbinic Martyrology and the Making of Merkavah Mysticism*, TSAJ 112 (Tübingen: Mohr Siebeck, 2005), 292; Michael D. Swartz, "Mystical Texts," in *The Literature of the Sages, Second Part: Midrash and Targum Liturgy, Poetry, Mysticism Contracts, Inscriptions, Ancient Science, and the Languages of Rabbinic Literature*, ed. Shmuel Safra, CRINT 2, 3b (Minneapolis: Fortress Press, 2006), 393–420 (403, 410–11, 419); Swartz, "Piyut and Heikalot," 266–8.

82. Moshe Idel has argued that mystic ascent was a part of the Rabbinic experience, though a carefully restrained one, with the result that debatable issues in classical Rabbinic texts can often be clarified by material that is preserved in Heikalot literature; Idel, *Kabbalah: New Perspectives* (New Haven, CT: Yale University Press, 1988), 85–87; Idel, *Ben: Sonship and Jewish Mysticism* (London: Continuum, 2007), 120, 243–45. In overcoming the scholarly antithesis of Rabbinic halakah and Heikalot mysticism, Idel was anticipated by earlier scholars like Jacob Neusner, "Jewish Use of Pagan Symbols After 70 C.E.," *JR* 43 (1963): 285–94 (289–91); cf. Michael Swartz, "Jewish Visionary Tradition in Rabbinic Literature," 216–17.

83. *Mishnah Berakhot* 2:1, Hebrew text and paraphrased English in Philip Blackman, ed., *Mishnayoth*, 7 vols. (London: Mishna Press, 1951–56), 1:39; ET in Danby, trans., *The Mishnah*, 3.

84. ET in Danby, trans., *The Mishnah*, 5. Hebrew text and paraphrased English in Blackman, *Mishnayoth*, 1:52.

85. ET in Nelson, trans., *Mekhilta of Rabbi Shimon Bar Yohai*, 183 (citing the Epstein/Melamed edn. [1955, 1979], 118). MRS has been reconstructed from medieval manuscripts of the text and midrashic anthologies like *Midrash ha-Gadol*. Its original redaction has been dated to the fourth century; Strack and Stemberger, *Introduction to the Talmud and Midrash*, 259.

86. ET in Jacob Neusner, trans. *Sifré Zutta to Numbers*, Studies in Judaism (Lanham, MD: University Press of America, 2009), 127 (citing the H. S. Horovitz edition [Leipzig, 1917], p. 276). *Sifrei Zuta* has also been reconstructed from medieval anthologies, particularly *Midrash ha-Gadol*

and *Yalqut Shimoni*. Its original redaction has been dated to the third century (Saul Lieberman); Strack and Stemberger, *Introduction to the Talmud and Midrash*, 369–70.

87. ET in Jacob Neusner, trans. *Sifré to Numbers* (not to be confused with *Sifré Zutta to Numbers*), 2 vols. (Atlanta: Scholars, 1986), 2:176, 178–79. For comparison, see Christopher Rowland, "Visionary Experience in Ancient Judaism and Christianity," in *Paradise Now: Essays on Early Jewish and Christian Mysticism*, SBLSS 11, ed. April D. DeConick (Atlanta: SBL, 2006), 41–56 (49).

88. The Jerusalem Talmud has an almost identical passage in *y. Ber.* 1:2 (citing Ezek. 10:1 rather than 1:26); ET in Jacob Neusner et al., trans., *The Talmud of the Land of Israel*, Chicago Studies in the History of Judaism, 35 vols. (Chicago: University of Chicago Press, 1982–87), 1:31. The *Bavli*, however, transforms the exegetical rationale into a halakic discussion (adding Exod. 24:10 as a proof text) and omits all reference to Passover and receiving the face of *HaShem*. This truncation could be related to the *Bavli*'s polemic against apocalypses and merkavah experiences, as described by Peter Schäfer, *Origins of Jewish Mysticism*, 224, 239–42.

89. ET in Reuven Hammer, trans., *Sifre: A Tannaitic Commentary on the Book of Deuteronomy* Yale Judaica 309 (New Haven, CT: Yale University Press, 1986), 375–76; cf. Jacob Neusner, trans., *Sifre to Deuteronomy*, BJS 124, 2 vols. (Atlanta: Scholars, 1987), 2:448–9. Hammer's translation of *middat kavod* as "what the divine glory is really like" makes better sense than Neusner's translation in view of the biblical lemma ("none like God . . . majestic") and the following parable (curtain/veil with precious stones and pearls).

90. Peter Schäfer, Margarete Schlüter, and Hans Georg von Mutius, eds., *Synopse zur Hekhalot-Literatur*, TSAJ 2 (Tübingen: Mohr Siebeck, 1981), hereafter titled *Synopse* and cited by paragraph (microform) number.

91. ET in Vita Daphna Arbel, *Beholders of Divine Secrets: Mysticism and Myth in the Hekhalot and Merkavah Literature* (Albany: State University of New York Press, 2003), 72–73; cf. Ira Chernus, "Visions of God in Merkabah Mysticism," *JSJ* 13 (1982): 123–46 (128); Schäfer, *Origins of Jewish Mysticism*, 259.

92. ET in David R. Blumenthal, *Understanding Jewish Mysticism: A Source Reader*, Library of Jewish Learning 2 and 4, 2 vols. (New York: Ktav, 1978, 1982), 1:80–81.

93. Compare Martin Jaffee's analogy of the mishnah to a dramatic script or a musical score; Jaffee, "Writing and Rabbinic Oral Tradition: On Mishnaic Narrative, Lists and Mnemonics," *Journal of Jewish Thought and Philosophy* 1 (1991): 123–46 (127). Apocalyptic (and New Testament) texts nicely fit Jaffee's treatment of the narrative-poetic material in *m. Tamid*, with blocks of apparently performative (poetic) material inserted in a prosaic narrative; ibid., 133–35.

94. On the sense of the real presence of the Shekinah in the *Amidah* benedictions, see the exhaustive study by Uri Ehrlich, *The Nonverbal Language of Prayer: A New Approach to Jewish Liturgy*, TSAJ 105, trans. Dena Ordan (Tübingen: Mohr Siebeck, 2004), 237–46.

95. So William Scott Green criticizes the reduction of Rabbinic discourse to hermeneutical practice (the "book-religion model") and the reduction of Rabbinic piety ("engagement with God") to epiphenomena; Green, "Romancing the Tome," 151, 154.

96. The story of the four who entered the *pardes* ("orchard") in *t. Hag.* 2:3 combines visionary themes (glimpsing, danger) with the idea of being an adept (R. Aqiva) and entering into the King's chamber (Song of Songs 1:4). Later traditions in the *Bavli* (*b. Hag.* 14b) and *Heikalot Zutarti* (*Synopse* §408) focus attention more on the marble plates of the celestial palaces than on *HaShem* himself.

97. *Mishnah Berakhot* 2:1, "If . . . the time came to recite the *Shema*, if he directed his heart [toward *HaShem*; cf. 5:1], he has fulfilled his obligation . . . . Between the sections, he may salute a man out of respect and return a greeting . . ." (Danby, trans., *The Mishnah*, 3).

98. The tradition in *m. Ber.* 2:1 is attributed to R. Me'ir, who was a fourth-generation *Tanna* (mid-second century). Although the attribution cannot be demonstrated, the historical location of the Mishnah is probably correct; Stemberger, *Introduction to the Talmud and Midrash*, 57–58;

Stemberger, "Dating Rabbinic Traditions," 87–88. In other words, this Mishnah is contiguous with the New Testament era.

99. *HaShem* is similarly placed on the same footing as the person sitting next to you at table in *Lev. R.* 20:10 (fifth century), which comments on the vision of *HaShem* in Exod. 24:9-11. *Mishnah Berakhot* 4:5 mandates that, whenever possible, one turn the face as well as the heart; so both heart and face are turned in corporate prayer services; cf. Ephraim E. Urbach, *The Sages: Their Concepts and Beliefs* (Cambridge, MA: Harvard University Press, 1987), 58–59; Ehrlich, *The Nonverbal Language of Prayer*, 66–68, 82, 89. Ehrlich points out that this halakah reflects a time when temple imagery still possessed considerable vitality (loc. cit., 84), whereas the Shekinah was less strongly associated with the temple by the time of the redaction of *t. Ber.* 3:16 (late third century, ibid., 86–87). On the whole question of the tension that arose between the centered discourse of the temple cult and the greater mobility of the sacred in the post-Temple era (not just a supersession of the spiritual or textual over the material and spatial), see Ra'anan S. Boustan, "The Dislocation of the Temple Vessels: Mobile Sanctity and Rabbinic Rhetorics of Space," in *Jewish Studies at the Crossroads of Anthropology and History*, 135–46, 365–70 (137–39, 146).

100. Francis Brown, S. R. Driver, and Charles A. Briggs, *Hebrew and English Lexicon of the Old Testament* (Oxford: Clarendon, 1953), 466 (Hiphil 3).

101. I borrow the terms *imaginal space* and *imaginal world* from the work of Elliot Wolfson, "Judaism and Incarnation: The Imaginal Body of God," in *Christianity in Jewish Terms*, ed. Tikva Simone Frymer-Kensky (Boulder, CO: Westview, 2000), 239–54 (240–1, 251). As Wolfson sees it (ibid., 253), imaginal space overlaps with physical space in liturgical settings—in other words, the imaginal is actually "empirical" for those who participate wholeheartedly in the liturgy. David Rhoads has similarly described oral performance in terms of "imaginative seeing"; Rhoads, "Performance Criticism, Part I," 127a. For a history of the idea of the "imaginal world" (*mundus imaginalis*) and a spirited defense of its ontological value, see Corin Braga, "'Imagination', 'Imaginaire', 'Imaginal': Three Concepts for Defining Creative Fantasy," *JSRI* 16 (2007): 59–68 (64–5).

102. Tzvee Zahavy, *Studies in Jewish Prayer*, Studies in Judaism (Lanham, MD: University Press of America, 1990), 113–15. I see no need to limit this emphasis on *kavanah*, as Zahavy does, to the Ushan sages; ibid., 28–9.

103. For the anthropic form, see, for example, *m. Sanh.* 6:5; *m. Avot* 3:6; cf. Elliot Wolfson's comment: "Study is . . . an imaginative process through which the imaginal body of God is conjured"; Wolfson, "Judaism and Incarnation," 248; cf. 243. Confirmation of the fact that leading Jewish teachers of the second century viewed their God in anthropic terms comes from Justin's *Dialogue with Trypho* 114.3 (c. 160 ce), which we discuss in ch. 9. The Rabbinic emphasis on *kavanah* may have compensated for their sense that prophecy had ceased; *m. Sot.* 9:12; *t. Sot.* 13:2.

104. The term *hasidim* was used for groups of pietists already in Ps. 149:1; 1 Macc. 2:42, passim; *Pss. Sol.* 17:16; 11QPsa 18:12; 22:3. David Flusser suggested that these "pietists" were the same as those represented by Simeon and Anna in the Gospel of Luke (2:25, 36-38); Flusser, "Psalms, Hymns and Prayers," in *Jewish Writings of the Second Temple Period: Apocrypha, Pseudepigrapha, Qumran, Sectarian Writings, Philo, Josephus*, CRINT 2, 2, ed. Michael E. Stone (Assen: Van Gorcum, 1984), 551–77 (558, 560, 573).

105. Danby, trans., *The Mishnah*, 35.

106. The need for concentration is dramatically portrayed by a story in the corresponding Tosefta (*t. Ber.* 3:20): the story goes that Hanina was actually bitten by a snake while praying. The snake was the worse off for the encounter, and it did not interrupt Hanina's prayer in the slightest. As in Gen. 3, the snake served as a concrete mental image for personal discipline.

107. Based on Rabbinic texts, we may surmise that these pietistic circles were more closely related to the Pharisees than they were to the Sadducees and Boethusians; see Gary Anderson, "Towards a Theology of the Tabernacle and Its Furniture," in *Text, Thought, and Practice in Qumran and Early Christianity*, STDJ 84, ed. Ruth A. Clements and Daniel R. Schwartz (Leiden:

Brill, 2009), 161–94 (173 [quoting Shlomoh Naeh], 178–80 [citing the Temple Scroll and P. Oxyrhynchus 840]).

108. *Tosefta Rosh HaShanah* 2:18 attributes a time of preparation like that of the "ancient pious ones" (albeit briefer) to the synagogue prayer leader (*sheliah tzibur*).

109. As Elliot Wolfson comments on *b. Ber.* 31a: "Mental iconography (realized in imaginal space) replaces physical geography"; Wolfson, "Iconic Visualization and the Imaginal Body of God: The Role of Intention in the Rabbinic Conception of Prayer," *Modern Theology* 12 (1996): 137–61 (147). On "mental iconography," as opposed to visual, material iconography, in the Hebrew Bible, see Tryggve Mettinger, *No Graven Image? Israelite Aniconism in its Ancient Near Eastern Context*, Coniectanea Biblica, Old Testament Series 42 (Stockholm: Almqvist & Wiksell, 1995), 20.

110. Support from the *Bavli* can also be seen in the famous comment by R. Hanina concerning the overall structure of the *Amidah* benedictions (*b. Ber.* 34a): in the first three benedictions, the worshipper is like a servant addressing a eulogy to his master; in the final three he is a servant who takes his leave of his master. In practice, this final stage includes taking three steps backward and bowing (lit. "bestowing peace," *b. Yoma* 53b), which is the same procedure as taking leave of one's study master. Hence, the real presence of *HaShem* is assumed in the *Amidah* service as a whole; Uri Ehrlich, *The Nonverbal Language of Prayer*, 120–34; Ehrlich, "'In the Last Benedictions He Resembles a Servant Who Has Received a Largess from His Master and Takes His Leave," in *The Experience of Jewish Liturgy*, 41–61 (42–45, 52, 57). Elliot Wolfson similarly relates *kavanah* to gestures of turning and direction; Wolfson, "Iconic Visualization," 140.

111. Wolfson, "Iconic Visualization," 141, 142. Wolfson supports his reading with the instruction to "direct the heart to the Holy of Holies" in *m. Ber.* 4:5; cf. *t Ber.* 3:15-16 = *y. Ber.* 4:5, 8b-c.

112. Wolfson, "Iconic Visualization," 146. Here Wolfson uses the phrase "iconic visualization of God." Writing at about the same time, he also spoke of the "figural corporealization of God" and the "figuration of God as body" within Judaism; Wolfson, "Images of God's Feet: Some Observations on the Divine Body in Judaism," in *People of the Body: Jews and Judaism from an Embodied Perspective*, ed. Howard Eilberg-Schwartz (Albany: State University of New York Press, 1992), 143–81 (143, 147). Wolfson's idea of a "mystical fraternity" is hypothetical for the Talmudic era, but it can be readily documented in sixteenth-century texts like Mosheh Cordovero's *Sefer ha-Gerushin* and El'azar Azikri's *Sefer Haredim*. In the latter text, the "ancient pious ones" of *m. Ber.* 5:1 are cited as a model for the mystic's visualization of the Shekinah resting upon his head and surrounding him with supernatural light; R. J. Zwi Werblowsky, *Joseph Karo: Lawyer and Mystic*, 2nd ed. (Philadelphia: Jewish Publication Society of America, 1977), 51–52, 63–64. The phenomenon of the Lord (or the Shekinah) resting on the head of a worshipper is attested in earlier written sources like *Odes of Solomon* 1:1; passim, and *Otzar Gaonim*, the latter of which cites Ps. 16:8 (Wolfson, "Iconic Visualization," 151) as well as in Ashkenazi interpretations of the use of phylacteries; see Wolfson, *Along the Path: Studies in Kabbalistic Myth, Symbolism, and Hermeneutics* (Albany: State University of New York Press, 1995), 158–59, 166, 221.

113. See Reif, *Judaism and Hebrew Prayer*, 111. In other words, there was still no monolithic approach to prayer, even in the Talmud, and the "pietistic" passages in *Bavli* represented traditional practices over against the "growing tendency to recite fixed formulae"; ibid., 110, 119–20.

114. In *b. B. Bat.* 25a, a biblical text and a Persian loanword are cited to support the idea that the Shekinah is located in the direction of the west. Three other texts (and an individual prayer practice) are cited to show that the Shekinah is in all places at once.

115. Another possible early witness to the visionary use of Psalm 16:8 is *2 Enoch* 24:1, where Enoch is instructed to sit on God's left side, in order to match the words of Ps. 16:8b. The purpose in *2 Enoch* 24 is clearly instructional and devotional ("I did obeisance to the Lord").

116. Danby takes *maqom* to be a euphemism for the divine name and translates it as "God'; Danby, trans., *The Mishnah*, 5. Other manuscripts of the Mishnah substitute "their Father in

heaven" for *maqom*, presumably to protect the transcendence of *HaShem*; cf. Blackman, ed., *Mishnayoth*, 1:52 n. 5.

117. In his classic work, *The Sages: Their Concepts and Beliefs*, Ephraim E. Urbach translated *maqom* as "Omnipresent"; loc. cit., 66–67. Urbach's *Tendenz* to demythologize and spiritualize the Hebrew Deity has been questioned by scholars like Wolfson, "Images of God's Feet," 147. The idea of omnipresence ("the place of the world") does occur, however, in later midrashim like *Gen. R.* 68:9.

118. The anthropic nature of *Maqom* as a divine name is confirmed by the Valentinian use of the equivalent Greek *topos* to refer to the demiurge (modeled on Dan. 7:9-10; *1 En.* 1:19-21; Ps. 110:1); Clement of Alexandria, *Excerpta ex Theodoto* 38:1-3. The Valentinian demiurge was, of course, none other than YHWH/Adonai, the God of Israel; cf. Gershom G. Scholem, *Jewish Gnosticism, Merkabah Mysticism and Talmudic Tradition* (New York: Jewish Theological Seminary of America, 1960), 34–35; Daniel Stökl Ben Ezra, *The Impact of Yom Kippur on Early Christianity: The Day of Atonement from Second Temple Judaism to the Fifth Century*, WUNT 163 (Tübingen: Mohr Siebeck, 2003), 231 n. 16.

119. Ithamar Gruenwald pointed to the Rabbinic use of *maqom* as evidence of mysticism similar to that found in merkavah circles; Gruenwald, *Apocalyptic and Merkavah Mysticism*, 73 n. 2.

120. One major exception to the passivity of *HaShem* in Rabbinic literature is *b. Ber.* 67a, where *HaShem* actually speaks to R. Ishmael, asking the rabbi to bless him. The context imagined here is the offering of incense (prayer) in the innermost part of the Sanctuary. Abraham Heschel suggests that this exception is due to the Rabbis' effort to make contemplation accessible to all of their students, not just to specially gifted ones; Heschel, *Heavenly Torah as Refracted through the Generations*, trans. Gordon Tucker and Leonard Levin (New York: Continuum, 2005), 344–45, and n. 8. Baruch Bokser points out that the Rabbis played down the petitionary aspect of statutory prayer; Bokser, "The Wall Separating God and Israel," *JQR* 73 (1983): 349–74 (359–61, 369–70, 373). Another factor to consider is the less urgent sense of an imminent eschaton in Rabbinic literature compared with apocalyptic texts and the New Testament. Contrast the repeated invocations of *HaShem's* intervention in standard prayer forms like the conclusion of the *Birkat ha-Torah* ("make us walk upright to our land . . . God who performs triumphs"), the *Ge'ullah* blessing after the morning *Shema* ("arise to help Israel"), the fourteenth benediction of the *Amidah* ("rebuild it soon in our days"), and the third benediction following the reading of the Haftarah ("may he come soon"); cf. Heinemann, *Prayer in the Talmud*, 34–6, 238–9.

121. Max Kadushin, *The Rabbinic Mind*, 207–8. Kadushin calls the ordinary experience of God's nearness "normal mysticism" in order to differentiate it from the sensory experiences attributed to Old Testament and Second Temple figures; ibid., 202–3, 228, 252, 257, 265. He states that "Individuals so inclined by temperament could . . . expect or hope for an actual experience of *Gilluy Shekinah* [the appearance of the Shekinah]"; ibid., 238–9.

122. The practice of *kavanah* and visualization of the place of *HaShem* continued well into the modern era. Clear descriptions (again idealized) occur in *Shivhei ha-Besht* ("In Praise of the Baal Shem Tov," first published in 1814), where Ps. 16:8 was still used as rehearsal text (§228). Amazingly, one of these stories (§243) describes a rabbi who concentrated on the *Shema* and suddenly saw Jesus standing before him—something for which the Besht called him to task; see D. Ben-Amos and J. R. Mintz, trans., *In Praise of the Baal Shem Tov* (Bloomington: University of Indiana Press, 1970), 235, 251. No explanation is given for the unfortunate rabbi having such a vision. The story was intended to warn listeners (and readers) against making such associations.

123. Scholem, *Jewish Gnosticism*, 129. Gruenwald argues that this image was already present in *MRI* Bahodesh 9, which deals with the same verse (*MRI* 2:266); Gruenwald, *Apocalyptic and Merkavah Mysticism*, 73 n. 1.

124. Tosefta Megillah 3:28 is elucidated (with some help from *b. Meg.* 24b) by Moshe Halbertal, *Concealment and Revelation: Esotericism in Jewish Thought and Its Philosophical Implications*, trans. Jackie Feldman (Princeton, NJ: Princeton University Press, 2007), 13–14.

125. On the appeal to popular traditions in midrash in general, see Irving Jacobs, *The Midrashic Process: Tradition and Interpretation in Rabbinic Judaism* (Leiden: Brill, 1995), 80–82, 144. Jacobs's assumption of a sermonic origin of midrashic proems (ibid., 17, 169) does not invalidate his basic point about Rabbinic contact with popular traditions. On the manner in which statements addressed to a popular audience could become incorporated into scholastic Rabbinic discourse, see Richard Kalmin, *The Sage in Jewish Society of Late Antiquity* (New York: Routledge, 1999), 33. For a more general argument along these lines, see Galit Hasan-Rokem, *Web of Life: Folklore and Midrash in Rabbinic Literature*, trans. Batya Stein (Stanford, CA: Stanford University Press, 2000), 88, passim.

126. Compare the contemporary *Mekilta* (*MRI* Shirata 4) on Exod. 15:3-4, where R. Judah holds that Moses saw the divine Glory in a mediated form, through a mirror, and not face to face; Heschel, *Heavenly Torah*, 308. These varying interpretations indicate a lively interest in the nature of theophanic visions among the Rabbis.

127. Neusner, trans. *Sifré Zutta to Numbers*, 127, with bracketed material added to make the differentiation more explicit.

128. Heschel, *Heavenly Torah*, 302.

129. The idea of Moses as a model to for re-enactment is clearly stated in *Sifrei Devarim* 335, where Moses' words to Israel are repeated word for word by Rabbi Judah to his own sons; Hammer, trans., *Sifre*, 344–45.

130. ET in Jacob Neusner, trans., *Sifré to Numbers*, 2:176, 179.

131. The second part of this translation is taken from ibid., 2:179. For the first part, however, I follow Christopher Rowland's translation, which brings out the interpersonal, devotional aspect; Rowland, "Visionary Experience in Ancient Judaism and Christianity," 49, with italics and quotation marks added for clarity. Neusner's translation of the first part reads: "What is said is not, 'You shall see them,' but 'You shall see *it*.' . . . whoever carries out the religious duty of wearing show-fringes is credited as if he had received the face of the Presence of god" (loc. cit.). Compare Neusner's translation of the parallel text in *y. Ber.* 1:2, "To look upon it' [using the feminine pronoun] is not what is written here. Rather, 'To look upon it' [using the masculine pronoun]. This suggests to us that it is as if anyone who fulfills the commandment of [wearing] fringes stands in the divine presence"; Neusner et al., trans. *The Talmud of the Land of Israel*, 1:31.

132. Using many examples, Michael Fishbane shows that the use of *kivyakol* (lit. 'as in/by a possibility') implies that the suggestion is so bold in its anthropomorphism that it must be muted, yet it is considered to be real; Fishbane, *Biblical Myth and Rabbinic Mythmaking* (New York: Oxford University Press, 2003), 329, 398–99.

133. This literal reading of Num. 15:39 is confirmed by Justin, *Dial.* 46.5, where he states the purpose of the fringes was not just to remember the commandments (as in the text of Num. 5:39-40), but to "keep God constantly before your eyes" (*hina . . . pro opthalmōn aei exēte ton theon*) and thereby be restrained from injustice and impiety. Justin frequently referred to Jewish traditions about Old Testament theophanies in his apologies.

134. On the reading of *re'item 'oto* as "look upon him," see Rowland, "Visionary Experience in Ancient Judaism and Christianity," 49. On the Passover event as one of four historic nighttime revelations—the fourth of which was yet future—see the "Song of the Four Nights" in Fragment Targum to Exod. 15:18 (MS Paris Hebr. 110; MS Vatican Ebr 440); *Tg. Neofiti* to Exod. 12:42. The number four appears to be arbitrary in the Targumim, but it may have corresponded to the four blue tassels, each of which represented a theophany.

135. The strong interpretation of Num. 15:39 persisted into the early modern era as indicated by the (reported) dying words of Eliyyahu ben Shlomo Zalman, the Gaon of Vilna (1720–97): "How hard is it to depart from this world, where for a few kopeks a man can purchase *tzitzit* and thereby reach such an elevated stage as to meet with the Shekhinah"; Louis Jacobs, *Holy Living: Saints and Saintliness in Judaism* (Northvale, NJ: Aronson, 1990), 115.

136. The feature of Deut. 33:26 that attracts attention is the difference between two parallel expressions, which may be literally translated as "Riding on heavens as your help" and "His majesty on clouds." Why is the help of *HaShem* cited in the first line, but not repeated in the second? The obvious answer is that the first line applies when Israel is worthy of the divine presence and help, and the second points to his transcendence when it is not.

137. Cf. the parallel expression, the "measure of justice" (*middat ha-din*) in *Sifrei* 307; ET in Hammer, trans., *Sifre*, 312.

138. I use "exegetical" here in the post-Enlightenment sense of the discursive analysis of texts. There is ample evidence that early Rabbinic exegesis was a deeply spiritual, and sometimes even a mystical practice; e.g., *m. Avot* 3:6. See Wolfson, "Judaism and Incarnation," 248, in contrast to David Stern, *Midrash and Theory: Ancient Jewish Exegesis and Contemporary Literary Studies* (Evanston, IL: Northwestern University Press, 1996), 30, 33, who maintains that Rabbinic midrash is "almost completely severed from any connection with prophecy or analogous types of revelatory experience" (30). The difference appears to be that Stern bases his view not on the Rabbis actual (performed) exegesis, but rather on what the Rabbis said about themselves, particularly in post-Tannaitic "haggadic" midrashim (e.g., *b. B. Metzi'a* 59a-b). As a result, Stern views the anthropomorphic depiction of *HaShem* in Rabbinic midrashim, as confined to the era of the Temple ("aggadic time and space") and so quite different from the time and space in which the Rabbis lived; ibid., 93. While helpful in making sense of aggadic midrashim, Stern's view overstates the discontinuity between the Temple and Rabbinic eras (cf. ibid., 51, on literary continuity).

139. Michael Fishbane, "The 'Measures' of God's Glory in the Ancient Midrash," in *Messiah and Christos: Studies in the Jewish Origins of Christianity, Presented to David Flusser*, TSAJ 32, ed. Ithamar Gruenwald, Shaul Shaked, and Guy G. Strousma (Tübingen: Mohr, 1992), 53–73 (61–2); reprint in Fishbane, *The Exegetical Imagination: On Jewish Thought and Theology* (Cambridge, MA: Harvard University Press, 1998), 56–72 (63).

140. ET in Arbel, *Beholders of Divine*, 72–73 (modified).

141. "It appears that in the *Heikalot* material the expression 'beauty' (*yofi*) has a more specific theophanic connotation: the luminous presence of the enthroned form. Insofar as this term is applied to the enthroned form of the glory, it connotes at once corporeality and luminosity. . . . To behold the splendid beauty of the glory is to gaze upon the luminous shape of the glorious body"; Wolfson, *Through a Speculum that Shines*, 85–6; cf. Chernus, "Visions of God in Merkabah Mysticism," 127–9, on the need for proper discipline in order to avoid the dangers.

142. See, for instance, *Heikalot Rabbati* 18:3 (*Synopse* §216); ET in Blumenthal, *Understanding Jewish Mysticism*, 1:65.

143. On the performative (transformational) aspects of Tannaitic midrashim (also in the commentaries of Philo), see Steven D. Fraade, *From Tradition to Commentary: Torah and its Interpretation in the Midrash Sifre to Deuteronomy*, SUNY Series in Judaica (Albany: State University of New York Press, 1991), 11–14. At one level, these transformative performances reenacted the interpretive process of the redactors; at another level, they also involved the re-presentation of *HaShem*'s revelation of Torah on Mount Sinai as depicted in Deut. 33:2-4; ibid., 19–20, 25, 63, 124. For an even stronger statement of the visionary nature of Rabbinic midrash, see Daniel Boyarin, "The Eye in the Torah," 546.

3

Kyriocentric Prayers and Devotions as the Context for Visions among Early Disciples of Jesus

Our modus operandi in this study is neither free speculation nor exact demonstration, but the in-between realm of hypotheses and plausibility (or non-implausibility) arguments. Of course, accepting the plausibility of Kyriocentric visions as the origin of New Testament Christology does not prove that this was the actual case, but it can allow us to think more carefully about historical realities like the context of ritual praxis in which post-execution revelations concerning Jesus were experienced and remembered. That context, in turn, can shed light on many of the attributes and invocations in which early Christology is embedded in New Testament documents. Identifying circumstances under which such visions could have occurred among the Jewish followers of Jesus is one way of doing this (the method here being inductive).

Most studies of Jewish "mystical experience" have focused on the nature of the heavenly world and the Deity experienced therein. I shall follow the lead of Moshe Idel in balancing such theological interests with prior attention to the ritual, physiological, and linguistic aspects of visionary experience.[1] Here I shall focus on those ritual and linguistic aspects that are specific to the Kyriocentric nature of the visions we seek to understand.

Identifying such circumstances is easier said than done. The prototypical theophany in Isaiah 6 was set in the context of liturgical performance (Isa. 6:1-4, including the *Kedushah* or Sanctus), but the liturgy was assumed more than described. Some of the early Rabbinic texts reviewed in chapter 2 were concerned with the practice of prayer, either explicitly (*m. Ber.* 2:1; 5:1) or implicitly (*MRS* 43; *Sifrei Bamidbar* 115). Beyond that, we shall find that a handful of Second Temple texts say more about the conditions under which worshippers sought visions. These Second Temple vision texts can be complemented by passages from the Psalms—assuming that the language of the Psalms typified the performative prayers and devotional practices of Jewish visionaries[2]—and further supplemented by some visionary texts from early Christian literature.

Kyriocentric Vision Texts Associated with Ritual Prayer

Conditions associated with the performance of Kyriocentric visions can be seen in some of the very texts that we discussed in chapter 2, all which date from the centuries immediately before and during the New Testament era (third century BCE to the first century CE). First, we shall return to those texts. In the following section we shall add a few others from the Apocrypha and Pseudepigrapha.

Just prior to the inaugural vision of Enoch in the Book of the Watchers (*1 En.* 14, discussed in ch. 2), the prophet describes himself as interceding for a group of condemned angels called the "Watchers." In a most interesting scene, Enoch writes down a petitionary prayer, begging the "Lord of heaven" for forgiveness on behalf of these Watchers. Although Enoch is not a member of the Watcher community, he clearly serves as their representative in this context of crisis and intercession. Accordingly, he recites the prayer, not just once, but over and over again (hypnotically?), until he "falls asleep," whereupon he receives his first vision (*1 Enoch* 13:4-8). As stated earlier, I understand the (written) text to be based on (mental) scripts for liturgical performances of the Enoch community (led by "Enoch").[3]

Although the exact wording of Enoch's prayer is not given, a correlation is clearly intended between the address ("Lord of heaven") and the identity and location of the glorious figure (the "Great Glory") who appears to Enoch and who responds to his request in the following scene (*1 En.* 14:20—15:1; cf. Ps. 11:4-7; 1 Kgs. 8:30; passim). In other words, the prayer ritual establishes both the person (YHWH) and the place (heaven) to which Enoch directs his attention and which he fixes in his imagination—an early example of *kavanah* ("directing the heart"). While the ensuing vision is not a simple projection of Enoch's intention (his request is actually refused), it derives much of its meaning from the initiatory ritual.[4]

Turning to the book of Daniel, we do not find anything about the seers' practices or preparations in the chapter about the vision of the Ancient of Days (Dan. 7). In chapter 9, however, the prophet draws hope for restoration (the end of the Babylonian Exile) from the book of Jeremiah (Jer. 25:11-12) and prays at length for confirmation of that prophecy in the forgiveness of Israel (Dan.

9:2-19, possibly based on an independent composition[5]). Unlike *1 Enoch*, the prayer practice here is not followed by an ascent to heaven and is not correlated with a Kyriocentric vision (which had already occurred in Dan. 7). In fact, Daniel's prayer in chapter 9 is followed by the appearance of the angel Gabriel, who flies down from heaven to speak with the prophet and answer his questions (9:21-23).

What makes Daniel 9 worth our attention is that it is one of the few instances in which the exact working of a petitionary prayer is given. Even though answers eventually come from Gabriel, the prayer itself, from beginning to end, is addressed directly to YHWH (and not to Gabriel; Dan. 9:3, 4, 15, 16, 18, 19). It is also accompanied by fasting and the donning of sackcloth as a sign of mourning (Dan. 9:3; 10:2).[6] Clearly the script includes an emotional component to go along with behavioral and imaginal aspects.

In the first of the Kyriocentric visions in the Similitudes of Enoch that we discussed (*1 En.* 39:9—40:2), Enoch describes himself as praising the name of the Lord of spirits with blessings and praise (*1 En.* 39:9). Significantly, the prophet's prayer and praise occur together with his vision of the place under the protective wings of YHWH—a place where he hears all the righteous ancestors perpetually praising and blessing the Lord (39:7).[7] Enoch believes that he also has a place under those wings, and he longs to dwell there (39:8). This emphasis on intentionality suggests that these features were scripted for the seer and imagined in the process of ritual prayer. The image of YHWH as a protector like a giant mother bird answers the dangers experienced by the author's community (cf. 46:8—47:2 on the persecution of the righteous as the motive for their prayers).[8] As in the Book of Watchers, Enoch prays as an individual, but on behalf of the community he represents. In this case, he also joins the angels in heaven in their offering of the Sanctus and Benedictus (39:12-14).

We do not find any special preparations in the second Similitude vision (*1 En.* 46:1-3)—coincidentally, this is the one in which attention immediately shifts to the Son of Man. Our third Similitude vision, however, is set in the context of urgent prayer in response to intense persecution. Following an alleged murder of one or more of their leaders ("the blood of the righteous one"[9]), the community of the righteous pray for justice (47:1). Their prayers rise to heaven and are reinforced by the prayers and blessings of the holy ones in heaven—all "with one voice" (47:2). In response to these prayers ("in those days"), the "Head of days" appears (as seen by the prophet), seated on a throne of glory, and judgment ensues (47:3).[10] Again the context is intercessory prayer in a situation of violent stress. As we shall see in the following section, the nexus of persecution, urgent prayer, and theophany is a virtual topos in texts of the first century CE.

In short, four of the seven Kyriocentric vision texts we reviewed in chapter 2 are closely associated with the practice of intercessory prayers and blessings. The prayers are either corporate or offered by a leader on behalf of the community he or she represents. One of the texts reviewed (Dan. 9:3) also mentions fasting along with other signs of mourning.

Visions of YHWH Associated with Prayer in Other Second Temple Texts

Three other Second Temple vision texts help to fill out the picture even though they are narrated in the third person (not the first person singular) and do not so directly reflect the performance of Kyriocentric visions.[11]

The Dream Visions of Enoch, another early part of the Enoch corpus (*1 En.* 83—90, mid-second century BCE), give a rapid review of the history of Israel all the way from Adam to the coming of the Messiah. The pivotal moment occurs when YHWH first calls out to Moses and instructs him to warn the Egyptians against persecuting the Israelites (Exod. 3:4-10). For the most part, the dream vision follows the narrative in Exodus here, but there is one significant shift in emphasis. Whereas Exodus only mentions the groaning and prayers of the Israelites once (2:23), the dream vision duly mentions it and then repeats the point, in fact, repeats it twice, and makes the appearance of YHWH to Moses a direct consequence of these prayers. Enoch narrates the scene as follows:

> But I saw the sheep continuing to lament and cry aloud; and they kept praying to their Lord with all their strength [Deut. 6:4] until the Lord of the sheep descended at their entreatment, from a lofty palace, arriving to visit them. (*1 En.* 89:16)[12]

Although this is a clear case of "rewritten Scripture," rather than a new rehearsal of Moses' vision at the burning bush, it is significant that the same nexus of prayer for salvation and theophany is assumed here as in other parts of *1 Enoch*. In all likelihood, the narrative here is informed by the prayer and vision performances of the Enoch community. The message of the vision is clear: if the Lord does not visit you at first, you must continue to lament and cry out and do this "with all your strength" (Deut. 6:4) until he does visit you.

As mentioned in the previous section, the nexus of persecution, urgent prayer, and theophany was a virtual topos in texts of the first century CE. Another exemplary narrative is found in *3 Maccabees* (early first century CE), which describes a scene in which the people of Israel are again persecuted by their enemies (this time the Ptolemaic Egyptians of the late third century BCE). The Israelites prostrate themselves and cry out to YHWH ("Ruler over every power") to manifest himself and to deliver them (3 Macc. 5:7-9, 17). One of their priests, Eleazar, adds his own supplication, calling upon God for mercy and deliverance (6:1, 10, 12). A lengthy prayer is cited, and, from beginning to end, as in Daniel 9, it is addressed directly to YHWH (6:2, 3, 8, 10, 12, 13, 15[2]). In response to all these prayers, the Lord "reveals his holy face" and sends two angels to defend his beloved people (6:18). As in the Dream Visions of Enoch (describing the exodus from Egypt), the prayers offered were specifically for deliverance and were accompanied by lamentations.

The Syriac Apocalypse of Baruch (also known as *2 Baruch*) was composed near the end of the New Testament era (early second century CE[13]). It is pseudepigraphically attributed to the disciple of Jeremiah, who supposedly witnessed the destruction of the Jerusalem temple, but it clearly reflects the conditions of shock and grief after the destruction of the Second Temple in 70 CE. In this narrative, YHWH promises that he will show himself to Baruch provided that he fast for seven days (*2 Bar.* 20:4-6). Baruch fasts as instructed and then offers a long supplicatory prayer (*2 Bar.* 20:4—21:26). From beginning to end, this prayer is addressed to YHWH, here called on as "the Living One" (21:9, 10), and its focus is on the promised appearance of YHWH's glory (21:22, 25).

As soon as Baruch finishes this lengthy prayer, he collapses in exhaustion, whereupon the heavens are opened, he sees it in a vision,[14] and he is strengthened thereby (21:25—22:1). Next he hears the voice of YHWH coming from heaven with the classic double vocative, "Baruch, Baruch, why are you disturbed?" (22:1-2).[15] If the visual content of Baruch's vision had not been left out (or deleted?), we might have included this text among the Kyriocentric visions discussed in chapter 2 (it is similarly narrated in the first-person singular). As it is, YHWH remains in heaven (as far as the text goes), and we only have an audition ("a voice was heard from on high, and it said to me . . ." *2 Bar.* 22:1). Aside from this significant difference, we have the now familiar nexus of persecution, fervent prayer—here accompanied by fasting—and a manifestation of the Lord's glory.

These seven texts cover a span from the third century BCE to the second century CE and show that Kyriocentric visions were associated with times of persecution and were accompanied by fasting and prayers for divine mercy and salvation. This pattern will serve us well when we get around to discussing the New Testament (chs. 5, 6).

Visions of YHWH Associated with Prayer in the Psalms

So far we have looked at texts describing visions and noted their association with ritual prayer. Another way to approach the problem is to turn it around and begin with the prayers of the Jewish people and ascertain whether visionary elements were rehearsed, or at least anticipated, in their context.

Although we do not know much about the exact form of early Jewish prayers, we do know that they were steeped in the language of the canonical psalms (the "scripturalization of prayer" discussed in ch. 2). The singing of psalms among early Jewish followers of Jesus is witnessed in several strata of the New Testament epistles (1 Cor. 14:26; Eph. 5:19; Col. 3:16; James 5:13). Most scholars understand these New Testament "psalms" to have included the canonical Psalms of the Old Testament.[16] Indeed, the disciples of Jesus were not the only group that made the Psalms the basis of their own prayer life: later Jewish prayer books contain large portions of the canonical Psalms among their prayers; this practice is attested as early as the Mishnah (e.g., *m. Pesah.* 5:7; 9:3). In a parallel way, the practice continued among Christian monks, holy men and holy women.[17] The evidence, though fragmentary, suggests a continuous practice of recitation from biblical times through the New Testament period and beyond.

Kyriocentric visions are a well-known feature of many of the canonical Psalms.[18] What concerns us here is the language of prayer used in connection with such visions as a supplement to our findings from the Second Temple texts reviewed above. One of the great scholars of apocalyptic and Heikalot literature, Ithamar Gruenwald, has called attention to three passages that set Kyriocentric visions in the context of crisis (described in fairly general terms) and petitionary prayer.[19] Reviewing these three will suffice for our purposes.

Psalm 18 is a desperate call for help in life-threatening circumstances, followed by heartfelt thanksgiving for deliverance. In the first section (18:1-6), the psalmist calls on the Lord to be saved from his (or her) enemies, here compared to "torrents of perdition," and we are told that the Lord heard his voice (18:3-6). Immediately, there follows a thirteen-verse description of a dramatic theophany (18:7-19), which unfolds as follows. First, YHWH descends riding a cherub from heaven (here described as "his temple"), shines like lightning, and speaks with a voice like thunder (18:6-13; cf. 144:5-6). As commentator Arthur Weiser has pointed out, this dramatic language is really a cultic (liturgical) re-enactment of the theophany of Sinai (cf. Exod. 19:16, 18; 20:18).[20] Then YHWH reaches down to deliver the psalmist from his enemies, again portrayed as watery deeps (18:16-19; cf. 144:7). The Psalm concludes with the psalmist's blessing and praising YHWH for having delivered him from violence (18:46-50).

It is not coincidental that these latter blessings are similar to the benedictions that make up later Jewish prayers like the *Amidah* (cf. *m. Ber.* 5:1 discussed in ch. 2). The inscription at the head of Psalm 18 attributes it to David, and a duplicate version has been inserted into the life of David in 2 Samuel 22, but its language is clearly meant to be typical of the vicissitudes and prayers of all pious Jews. Gruenwald aptly states that "we may see in this call for help an incantation with the function of an invocation [that] aims at experiencing a redeeming theophany."[21] Ongoing use of this Psalm shows how cultic, priestly language (temple, thick darkness, cherubim) could easily become part of a broader, ongoing practice of prayer and visionary imagination.

Psalm 42 is less specific than our previous example. In some of the most famous words of the Bible, the psalmist describes longing to "behold the face of God" as a deer longs for a drink of water (42:2).[22] The context clearly describes the psalmist's grief, which is occasioned by the sense of having been deserted by God (42:3, 9; cf. 43:2). He complains of oppression, compared again to billows of stormy water (42:7, 9; cf. 43:2). There is no explicit description of a theophany here, but the continuation in Psalm 43 enunciates petitions for vindication (43:1) and some sort of intervention involving light that will show the psalmist the way into God's presence (in the temple, 43:3-4). Throughout, the psalmist promises to praise God for deliverance (42:5, 11; 43:5). As Gruenwald states, we should read psalms like this one in the assumed context of prophetic experiences and theophanies.[23]

Finally, **Psalm 68** begins with a petition for God to "rise up" and scatter his enemies (68:1; cf. Num. 10:35 concerning the ark of the covenant). As in Psalm 18, the psalmist uses thunderstorm imagery to portray the Deity as one who "rides upon the clouds" (68:4, 33). Subsequently, two distinct theophanies are described, both based on the Sinai tradition. The first (68:7-14) begins in the past tense with God marching through the wilderness, accompanied by earthquake and rain (68:7-10). Then, suddenly, it shifts to the present tense to describe YHWH scattering the kings of the nations—presumably in response to the initial petition.[24] In a second, much briefer theophany passage (68:16-18), YHWH is described as ascending Mount Zion with thousands of chariots and a long line of captives (cf. 132:13-14).

In contrast to other examples we have discussed, the focus here in Psalm 68 is on the congregation's songs of praise; there is more exultation and less sorrow (68:4, 26, 32-5). It is not clear whether this exultation is a response to the theophany or provides the means for inducing it.[25] YHWH is all over the place:

riding the clouds of heaven, resting on Mount Sinai, sending his voice from the heavens, and residing in his sanctuary (68:4, 8, 18, 33-5, with no particular order).[26] In a time of gentile oppression, it would be hard to imagine a rousing performance of this Psalm that did not occasion the experience of YHWH's arrival and deliverance.

It should be noted that even though the imagery of these theophanies is related to Mount Sinai, there is no mention of the giving of the Law. The mythic mountain was rather a concrete symbol of YHWH's presence and of YHWH's ability to deliver his people. It was a military beachhead on earth from which to launch campaigns from heaven (cf. the Song of Deborah in Judg. 5:4-5). I suggest that this imaginal "Sinai" provided performers of the Psalm with a sense of directionality for *kavanah*, for "directing one's heart," as in the Mishnah's instructions for the recitation of the *Shema* and the *Amidah* (ch. 2). Sinai functioned in the piety of the Psalm much the way the image of the throne of YHWH did in other visionary texts (1 Kgs. 22:19; Isa. 6:1; Ezek. 1:26; *1 En.* 14:18; Dan. 7:9; etc.).

The results of this survey can be summed up in a few words. Not all visionary texts in Second Temple literature indicate the practical context in which Kyriocentric visions were expected to occur, but those that do (including the ongoing recitation of Psalms) all include intercessory prayers. Most often these prayers are occasioned by acute distress and appeal to YHWH to intervene and save, but many of them also include thanksgiving and praise for such intervention. These features can help us hypothetically to reconstruct the context of Kyriocentric visions as oral performances among the Jewish followers of Jesus as explained in the following section.[27]

VISIONS ASSOCIATED WITH PRAYER IN EARLY CHRISTIAN LITERATURE

Exploration of a few texts from the early centuries of the Common Era can help to fill out the picture already established from the biblical and Second Temple texts cited above. It can tell us whether there are grounds for assuming the continuity of practice upon which our conjecture depends. As we have seen in chapter 2, the practice of prayer in Rabbinic circles had an imaginal, visionary dimension (e.g., "directing the heart" during the recitation of the *Amidah*), thereby establishing a degree of continuity on that count. It would be helpful to see whether such practices were also known in early Christian circles.

Early Christian texts were obviously not written to address our questions about praxis any more than the Second Temple texts were. Unless a particularly pressing problem arose, preachers and writers could assume that common practices were well known to their audiences. Nonetheless, we should be able to find some points of contact or else be forced to speculate about reasons for the suppression of such material (which did eventually occur, as discussed in chapter 9). I find indications of a continuous practice of Kyriocentric visions in the context of prayer in the Letters of Paul (tentatively) and the Acts of the Apostles, and I shall supplement these findings with the *Acts of Paul and Thecla*, the Book of Revelation, the *Ascension of Isaiah*, the *Odes of Solomon*, and the Life of Pachomius.

Paul's letters exhibit both of the features that we look for, but not in immediate association with each other. Prayers for intervention and salvation are evidenced in the early Aramaic *Marana tha* ("Lord, come!") in 1 Corinthians 16:22,[28] and also in the practice of calling on the name of the Lord (Jesus) in Romans 10:12-13 (citing Joel 2:32; cf. 1 Cor. 1:2; 2 Tim. 2:19). Both motifs are familiar from the Second Temple and Psalm texts we have just reviewed (esp. *3 Macc.* 6:1; Pss. 18:3, 6; 68:1, 28) and undoubtedly represent some of the earliest prayers of the New Testament era.[29] Prayers of blessing and thanksgiving are also plentiful as they are in the Second Temple texts reviewed (for example, Rom. 1:25; 7:25; 9:5; passim; cf. *1 En.* 39:9; 47:1-2; Ps. 18:46-50; 42:5, 11; 43:5; 68:4, 26, 32-5, all discussed above). Traces of the performance of visions of the Lord (Jesus) are also evidenced in several places, for example, in 2 Corinthians (3:18; 4:6; 12:1). We shall discuss one of these further in chapter 5.

If, as we suppose, there was any overlap between these prayers and vision performances in Pauline churches, it was taken for granted rather than made explicit.[30] The case could be somewhat tightened by supplementing them with later "Pauline" texts like the *Acts of Paul and Thecla*, where Paul and his associates are described as fasting together and praying in an open tomb near Antioch.[31] Bert Jan Lietaert Peerbolte has suggested that this mid-second century text reflected memories of Paul's own asceticism in preparation for visions.[32] The nexus is plausible, but rather tenuous based on these texts alone.

Fortunately, the Acts of the Apostles has a narrative structure and makes some of these connections more explicit. Even though its composition (late first century CE) was decades after the events described and reflects particular theological concerns, the practices described must have seemed realistic for the author and his intended audience in the emerging church. The first two chapters of Acts portray the earliest assembly of Jesus' disciples in Jerusalem in terms very much like those used in early Jewish literature to describe contemporary Rabbinic groups: they meet in the "upper room" of a private house and devote themselves to prayer and the interpretation of Scripture (Acts 1:13-20; 2:1, 16-21).[33] Nothing is said about the content of these prayers, but ready citation of the Psalms in this chapter suggests that it would have included petitions and praise like that found in the Psalms and in the Pauline texts described above. The Lord's response to these petitions is described as a vision of tongues of fire, which is associated with an outpouring of the prophetic Spirit (Acts 2:2-4, 17, 33).[34] This charismatic experience resulted in a visionary exegesis of Psalm 16:8 (LXX, "I saw the Lord always before me") very much like that which is found in Rabbinic discussions of prayer practice ("directing the heart") described above in chapter 2 (Acts 2:25; cf. *b. Sanh.* 22a).[35] There is a clear nexus here between prayer, vision, and the use of biblical models.

Acts 13:2 describes a similar assembly in Antioch, where a group of prophets and teachers fast and "worship the Lord" together (the Greek verb is *leitourgeō*, a cultic term associated with prayer).[36] This preparatory ritual results in an audition that is once again attributed to the Holy Spirit and is couched in the language of commissioning that is characteristic of Kyriocentric visions (Acts 13:2b, 4; cf. Exod. 3:10; Isa. 6:9; Jer. 1:7-10; Ezek. 2:3).[37]

A very similar scene is described in one of Paul's speeches in Acts 22. Here Paul is described as praying in the Jerusalem temple, when he fell into a trance and saw the Lord (Jesus) speaking to him and delivering a new commission (Acts 22:17-21). The scene is reminiscent of the commissionings of Isaiah and Enoch (Isa. 6; *1 En.* 13–14).[38] The reminiscence is not surprising provided we understand early disciples of Jesus to have been like other visionary Jews in reciting the Psalms and rehearsing the theophanies of the prophets. They would visit (or direct their hearts toward) the temple and invoke the Lord's presence using the language of the Psalms just as their ancestors and spiritual mentors had done for centuries.

These three texts from Acts suggest a nexus of prayer and vision like that found in the Psalms and Second Temple literature and suggested (tentatively) by the letters of Paul.

Late first- and second-century Christian apocalypses indicate a similar setting for Kyriocentric visions. In the book of Revelation, John the Apocalypticist states that he was an exile on the island of Patmos (in the Aegean Sea, Rev. 1:9). In other words, the time in which he wrote was one of local persecution (probably that under Domitian in the 90s CE). John describes himself as being "in the spirit" on the Lord's day, when he first heard a loud voice. We understand this audition to be the voice of the Lord because it answers to the devotional setting of Lord's day worship and because it immediately commissions him to a new task (Rev. 1:10-11). Immediately after this, John saw that the source of the divine voice was a human form ("one like a son of man"), clearly recalling the anthropic form of YHWH in the

Old Testament (Rev. 1:12-18). Some form of cultic praxis is assumed here, and, as we shall see in chapter 5, John's vision is based on standard models of Kyriocentric visions, particularly those of the prophet Ezekiel.[39] Recent scholars have interpreted John's visions as oral re-enactments by a Christian prophet who assumes the persona of "John" and shares his experience with his community.[40]

Another early pseudepigraphal apocalypse is known as the *Martyrdom and Ascension of Isaiah*. Although this lengthy story of ascents and visions of the Lord is attributed to Isaiah, we may reasonably associate it with the practice of a circle of early Christian prophets who re-enacted the legendary vision of Isaiah 6 (*Ascen. Isa.* 3:8-9; 6:3-7, 16; 11:16).[41] In the present narrative, "King Hezekiah" and an assembly of prophets listen to Isaiah speak "words of righteousness and faith." In the context of this performance, they hear the voice of the Holy Spirit, and they respond in worship by praising and ascribing glory to the "God of righteousness" (*Ascen. Isa.* 6:3-9; cf. Acts 13:2).[42]

Like the book of Acts, these two early Christian apocalypses maintain the nexus of performance, prayer, and vision and thereby indicate continuity with the practices of other Jewish apocalyptic circles that we have studied.[43]

An excellent example of visionary praxis along with the recitation of psalms is found in the *Odes of Solomon*, the work of an inspired Christian psalmist in the vicinity of Antioch in the late New Testament era (around 100 CE).[44] As in the Acts of the Apostles, the odist's visions and psalms are attributed to the work of the Holy Spirit (*Odes* 6:1; 11:2, 6; 14:8; 16:5; passim). *Ode* 7, for example, speaks of the nearness of the Lord and describes seers going out to meet him with joy, while chanting "psalms of the coming of the Lord" (7:16-17).[45] As in Psalm 67, the tone here is one of exultation rather than sorrow.

About the same time as these *Odes*, Clement's Letter to the Church in Corinth (c. 95 CE), exhorted its readers to visualize the Lord (*idou ho kyrios, 1 Clem.* 34:3 rehearsing Isa. 40:10; 62:11) and cited Daniel's vision of the Ancient of Days as precedent (Dan. 7:10; *1 Clem.* 34:6). Presumably in keeping with the practice of the Roman church, the writer instructed the Corinthians to gather for worship to pray for the realization of the Lord's promises. They were to pray the Sanctus "with one voice" in order that they might see what the Lord has prepared for those who wait for him (*1 Clem.* 34:7-8, rehearsing Isa. 6:3; 64:4; cf. *1 En.* 47:2).

By the end of the fourth century, the need to defend orthodox Christology against the Arians (who viewed the pre-incarnate Logos as an archangel) led some theologians to condemn the practice of visualizing the divine form in prayer (so Evagrius Ponticus and John Cassian, discussed in ch. 9).[46] The condemnation clearly points to the fact that Kyriocentric visions were still practiced, at least, in ascetic circles. As a rule, we would not cite such late fourth-century texts to illuminate first-century practices, but the evidently conservative nature of the visionary praxis being condemned clearly points to a longstanding tradition (the rule applies more to ideas and practices that are being advocated than ones being rejected).

The visionary praxis is independently illustrated in the *Life of Pachomius*, the reputed founder of cenobite monasticism, versions of which originated in fourth-century monastic communities of upper Egypt. Our earliest version, the "First Greek Life" (c. 390 CE) describes a conversation between Pachomius and one of his associates, where Pachomius warns that sinful men ought not to ask God for visions. In spite of this warning, the abbot claims such visions for the saints, who enjoy "uninter mittent clairvoyance" in which they see the Lord in a bodily form.[47] Here Pachomius cites Psalm 16:8 (LXX, "I saw the Lord always before me") as Scripture proof, and chastises those monks who do not emulate this pattern by "setting God before them" as the Psalmist did.[48] The fact that Pachomius's understanding of the psalm text was exactly the same as that of the *Bavli* (*b. Sanh.* 22a) suggests that Christian and Rabbinic interpretations were independent developments of a common tradition going back to earlier centuries (Acts 2:25).

As we shall see in chapter 9, there was an ongoing struggle at the time between monastic visionaries and some of their ecclesiastical superiors. The Pachomians (a.k.a. "Anthropomorphites") rehearsed texts like Psalm 16 in order to direct their prayers and invoke the immediate, concrete presence of the Lord.[49] Pachomius's warning about "sinful men" seeking visions also suggests that there may have been some abuse of the visionary prerogative, perhaps related to the sin of pride (cf. Paul in 2 Cor. 12:1-7).

We have just reviewed a wide range of texts from the New Testament (Paul, Acts, and Revelation) and early Christian literature (*Ascension of Isaiah*, *Odes of Solomon*, *1 Clement*, and the *Life of Pachomius*), and we have found substantive evidence for the practice of prayer in preparation for Kyriocentric visions. We have also found several points of contact with the visionary prayer practices witnessed in Second Temple literature (fasting, prayers for the Lord to come and to save, prayers of thanksgiving and blessing, recitation of the Psalms, the appearance of the Lord in anthropic form, commissioning to a new task) and the later Rabbinic models ("directing the heart," *kavanah*). We may safely conclude that, if the impetus to deity Christology came from Kyriocentric visions, as we have conjectured, and if those visions were cradled in the practice of prayer and psalm recital, we may expect some of these very features to recur in New Testament texts about the Lord Jesus (chs. 5, 6).

Conclusion on Conditions Associated with Kyriocentric Visions

Our long-range objective in this study is to locate the origin of early deity Christology within the parameters of early Judaism by means of the Kyriocentric vision conjecture. Visionary practices are not much in vogue in modern academia, even in biblical and theological institutions (of which I am a member). Nonetheless, I believe that the material summarized in these last two chapters has shown a continuous (and fairly widespread) tradition of such visions and their attending prayers in the Second Temple era and in early Judaism and Christianity. In texts of the first century CE, it was a common topos.

The texts we have reviewed in these two chapters extend from the third century BCE to the fourth century CE, and they originate from regions of Judeo-Christian presence extending from upper Egypt and Mesopotamia to Rome. Most often, the accompanying prayers reflect situations of severe distress or persecution. In most cases, they involved calling upon YHWH for salvation. In some cases, particularly in psalms and odes, the prayers were the result of the some kind of deliverance and were the occasion of praise and rejoicing.

It should be clear by now that the earliest disciples of Jesus could conceivably have experienced Kyriocentric visions as they called on the Lord for salvation, particularly in the period of distress that they experienced after the execution of their beloved teacher.[50] Thus far, we are very much within the bounds of early Judaism, and, as we shall see in chapters 5 and 6, many of the features of deity Christology can readily be accounted for. The question that needs to be addressed first is whether the anthropic form of YHWH could plausibly be identified with a deceased teacher of living memory.

Notes

1. Moshe Idel, *Enchanted Chains: Techniques and Rituals in Jewish Mysticism* (Los Angeles: Cherub, 2005), 24–25, 32, 38–39, 65. I cannot agree with Idel's statement that the experiential side of visionary experience is more important than the theological status of its content (ibid., 66, obviously intended to be provocative), but I do appreciate the way he has redressed earlier scholarly emphasis on theological formulations (see p. 75, for a more balanced both-and statement). The reason for Idel's suspicion is his personal experience that theological and metaphysical perspectives tend to iron out the apparent inconsistencies in Jewish mysticism; Idel, "Theologization of Kabbalah in Modern Scholarship," in *Religious Apologetics—Philosophical Argumentation*, Religion in Philosophy and Theology 10, ed. Yossef Schwartz and Volkhard Krech

(Tübingen: Mohr Siebeck, 2004), 123–73; Idel, "Torah: Between Presence and Representation of the Divine in Jewish Mysticism," in *Representation in Religion: Studies in Honor of Moshe Barasch*, Studies in the History of Religions 89, ed. Jan Assmann and Albert I. Baumgarten (Leiden: Brill, 2001), 197–236 (60).

2. Bilhah Nitzan points out that the dramatic concerns of the Psalms and some Second Temple texts (impending death, threat of enemies, natural disasters) did not carry over to the same extent to Qumran and Rabbinic modes of prayer; Nitzan, *Qumran Prayer and Religious Poetry*, STDJ 12, trans. Jonathan Chipman (Leiden: Brill, 1994), 82–87. Indeed, the visionary practice involved in gazing at the four blue cords of *tzitzit* (*Sifrei Bamidbar* 115) was more like meditation than the urgent petition of the psalmist. However, Nitzan relies too much on the actual content of prayers and overlooks Rabbinic statements about *kavanah* in prayer (as discussed in ch. 2). As a result, he overly typologizes the difference between the occasional prayers of the Psalms (existential) and the statutory prayers of the Rabbis (fixed, eternal, non-individual, national, ideological, etc.).

3. *1 Enoch* 13–14 is a good example of what Crispin Fletcher-Louis says about early Jewish mysticism in general: "In the Jewish sources, a routine, liturgical, encounter with heavenly and divine (or mystical) realities and the individual's experience of 'ecstasy' are closely connected. . . ."; Fletcher-Louis, "Jewish Mysticism, the New Testament and Rabbinic-Period Mysticism," in *The New Testament and Rabbinic Literature*, JSJ Supplement 136, ed. Reimund Bieringer et al. (Leiden: Brill, 2010), 429–70 (430). Fletcher-Louis also stresses the connection of such "liturgical" practices to the Jerusalem temple (geographically or symbolically); ibid., 432–35, 455.

4. Michael Fishbane, *Biblical Myth and Rabbinic Mythmaking* (New York: Oxford University Press, 2003), 234–35, 236, 237; cf. Idel, *Enchanted Chains*, 38–39, 74.

5. Louis F. Hartman and Alexander A. Di Lella, *The Book of Daniel*, AB 23 (Garden City, NY: Doubleday, 1978), 245–49.

6. Michael Fishbane comments on Dan. 9: "Behind this stylized account we have a clear case of a ritual praxis in which study leads to supplicatory frenzy, and this to an ecstatic vision and audition"; Fishbane, "Response to Ithamar Gruenwald [cited below]," in *Gershom Scholem's Major Trends in Jewish Mysticism, 50 Years After*, ed. Peter Schäfer and Joseph Dan (Tübingen: Mohr, 1993), 49–57 (52). On the psychology of mourning as a prelude to apocalyptic visions, see Daniel Merkur, "The Visionary Practices of Jewish Apocalypticists," *The Psychoanalytic Study of Society* 14 (1989): 119–48 (125); reprinted in *Psychology and the Bible: A New Way to Read the Scriptures*, ed. J. Harold Ellens and Wayne G. Rollins, 4 vols. (Westport, CT: Praeger, 2004), 2:317–47 (323–27). Merkur cites the communal lament in Josh. 7:6-9 as an interesting biblical precedent (ibid., 323). He also suggests a meditative rehearsal aspect for some visions (ibid., 339–41, citing Dan. 7:8, 11; 9:4-19), but the models he cites do not include a theophany as part of the performance.

7. Angela Kim Harkins has called attention to the role of blessings (*berakhot*) in Enoch's transition from mundane experience to heavenly visions: "the blessing formulae [in *1 Enoch*] can be understood as marking spatial shifts into the heavenly realm, and they can be said to signal the phenomenal experience of a theophanic encounter with heavenly beings . . ."; Harkins, *Reading with an "I" to the Heavens: Looking at the Qumran Hodayot through the Lens of Visionary Traditions* Ekstasis 3 (Berlin: de Gruyter, 2012), 251; cf. ibid., 263–65 on the use of blessings as spatial transition markers in the Qumran Hodayot.

8. According to George Nickelsburg and James VanderKam, the imagery of divine wings and hiding "denotes how in a time of trouble the pious find protection shelter, or refuge with their God"; George W. E. Nickelsburg and James C. VanderKam, *1 Enoch: A Commentary on the Book of 1 Enoch*, Hermeneia, ed. Klaus Baltzer, 2 vols. (Minneapolis: Fortress Press, 2001, 2012), 2:123b. On the probable context for this persecution, see ibid., 63–64, 161.

9. As Daniel Olson points out, the title *righteous one* comes from Isa. 53:11; Olson, *Enoch: A New Translation* (North Richland Hills, TX: BIBAL Press, 2004), 90 (on 47:1). It is not likely, however, that this representative figure is the same as the Son of Man/Messiah, who appears in the

next chapter as mighty champion (48:2-10). In fact, the following verse speaks of "the blood of the righteous ones" in the plural (47:2).

10. The vision in *1 Enoch* 47:3 is sandwiched between verses in which (a) the holy ones in heaven urge that prayer of the righteous not be in vain (47:2), and (b) the righteous rejoice that their prayer has been heard (47:4).

11. A fourth example might be *4 Ezra* 5–7, where Ezra fasts seven days and addresses his supplications to YHWH (5:20-30; 6:35-59). As in the case of Dan. 9, the prayers are answered by the sending of a messenger or angel (5:31; 7:1). Nonetheless, Ezra addresses the messenger as YHWH, and the messenger speaks to him as YHWH (5:38, 40; 7:17, 28-9; cf. 5:23). Note that the prayer in this case is strictly for information (5:28, 38; 6:59). For the relation between liturgy and visions in later Heikalot texts like *Shi'ur Qomah*, see Phillip S. Alexander, "Prayer in the Heikhalot Literature," in *Prière, mystique et judaïsme*, Travaux du Centre d'histoire des religions de Strasbourg 2, ed. Roland Goetschel (Paris: Presses Universitaires de France, 1987), 44–64 (57–59); Michael D. Swartz, "Jewish Visionary Tradition in Rabbinic Literature," in *The Cambridge Companion to the Talmud and Rabbinic Literature*, ed. Charlotte Elisheva Fonrobert and Martin S. Jaffee (Cambridge: Cambridge University Press, 2007), 198–221 (210, 212–13).

12. Translated by E. Isaac; "1 Enoch," in *Old Testament Pseudepigrapha*, ed. James Charlesworth, 2 vols. (Garden City, NY: Doubleday, 1983), 1:65. Hereafter cited as *OTP*.

13. Rivka Nir has made a case for the Christian provenance of *2 Baruch*, but her arguments have been effectively rebutted by James Davila, *The Provenance of the Pseudepigrapha: Jewish, Christian, or Other?* SJSJ 105 (Leiden: Brill, 2005), 130–31.

14. L. H. Brockington inserts "a vision" in brackets after "I saw," in his revision of R. H. Charles's translation of *2 Baruch* in H. F. D. Sparks, ed., *The Apocryphal Old Testament* (Oxford: Clarendon, 1984), 853.

15. Other examples of the divine double vocative include Gen. 22:11-12 ("Abraham, Abraham"); 46:2 ("Jacob, Jacob"); Exod. 3:4 ("Moses, Moses"); 1 Sam. 3:10 (discussed in ch. 4); *4 Ezra* 14:1 ("Ezra, Ezra"); *Apoc. Ab.* 8:1; 20:1 ("Abraham, Abraham"; contrast the address by the angel Yao'el in 10:5); *T. Job* 3:1 ("Jobab, Jobab," from the hypostatic light/angel); *Jos. Asen.* 14:3, 7 ("Aseneth, Aseneth," from the "Chief of the house of the Lord"). The topic is taken up again in ch. 5.

16. See, for instance, Martin Hengel, *Studies in Early Christology* (Edinburgh: T&T Clark, 1995), 270–71; Larry Hurtado, *How on Earth Did Jesus Become a God?* (Grand Rapids: Eerdmans, 2005), 84.

17. Peter Brown, "The Saint as Exemplar in Late Antiquity," in *Saints and Virtues*, ed. John Stratton Hawley (Berkeley: University of California Press, 1987), 3–14 (12).

18. Mark S. Smith, "'Seeing God' in the Psalms: The Background to the Beatific Vision in the Hebrew Bible," *CBQ* 50 (1988): 171–83. It should be noted that, unlike the Kyriocentric visions described above, none of the visions in the Psalms are accompanied by direct address to the psalmist or commissioning by the Deity.

19. Ithamar Gruenwald, "Reflections on the Nature and Origins of Jewish Mysticism," in *Gershom Scholem's Major Trends in Jewish Mysticism*, 25–48 (39–41 on Pss. 18, 42, and 68). In a performative reading of the Psalms, the crises described need not be "historical." They are described in general enough terms to be applicable to common experiences. As Bilhah Nitzan put it, while citing the book of Psalms as a classic example, it is "possible for the experiences and feelings of the individual to be expressed in his songs in a standard manner, so that other individuals in his generation, or even in other generations, may identify with them"; Nitzan, *Qumran Prayer and Religious Poetry*, 325.

20. Arthur Weiser comments, " . . .the whole cult community together with the worshipper experience, in the traditionally fixed form of the theophany, the God of Sinai as the God who is present and now appears before them so that they can see and hear him"; Weiser, *The Psalms: A Commentary*, Old Testament Library, trans. Herbert Hartwell (Philadelphia: Westminster, 1962), 189. Weiser points out the connection of the Sinai theophany with the Temple sanctuary (and the

Covenant Festival) and suggests that the cherubim replace the clouds as the divine chariot, ibid., 29, 38–39, 484.

21. Gruenwald, "Reflections on the Nature and Origins of Jewish Mysticism," 39. Michael Fishbane corrects Gruenwald's use of the term incantation and prefers "invocation," but is sympathetic with the overall idea; Fishbane, "Response," 51–52. Terence Fretheim had stated the point already in 1984: "God has provided for structures of worship and prayer in the context of which God has promised to come to God's people"; Fretheim, *The Suffering God: An Old Testament Perspective* (Minneapolis: Fortress Press, 1984), 82–83.

22. Psalms 42–83 constitute what is known as the "Elohistic Psalter," in which the preferred divine name is Elohim, "God," rather than YHWH, "Lord." For details, see Laura Joffe, "The Elohistic Psalter: What, How and Why?" *SJOT* 15 (2001): 142–69.

23. Gruenwald, "Reflections on the Nature and Origins of Jewish Mysticism," 41.

24. Again see the comments of Gruenwald, "Reflections on the Nature and Origins of Jewish Mysticism," 41.

25. Weiser insists that the congregation's praise in 68:4 is directed to the God who has already appeared; Weiser, *The Psalms*, 484. I rather doubt that temporal sequence is quite so precise in cultic acts.

26. The recycling of themes associated with Psalm 64 is evident in *Heikalot Rabbati* 26:3, which refers to the one "who rides above the all" (along with motifs from Exod. 34:6; Ezek. 1;26; Isa. 6:2); ET in David R. Blumenthal, *Understanding Jewish Mysticism: A Source Reader*, Library of Jewish Learning 2, 4, 2 vols. (New York: Ktav, 1978, 1982), 1:83.

27. As David Rhoads has argued, "Taking oral performance into account may enable us to be more precise in our historical re-constructions . . ."; Rhoads, "Performance Criticism: An Emerging Methodology in Second Testament Studies—Part II," *BTB* 36 (2006): 126a.

28. I assume here the consensus reading of *marana tha* as a petition, "Our Lord, come!" The alternative reading *maran atha*, "Our Lord has come," is also possible, but it would still refer back to a liturgical prayer believed to have been answered in a Kyriocentric vision.

29. The motif of the coming of the Lord is also familiar from texts like Pss. 96:13; 98:9; Isa. 35:4; 40:10; 66:15; Mal. 3:1b; *1 En.* 1:9. The Aramaic form *marana* may also appear in the Aramaic scroll, 4QEnochb 3:14 (though it is not in Ethiopic *1 En.* 9:4), where it refers to the "Lord of the worlds"; Joseph Fitzmyer, *To Advance the Gospel* (New York: Crossroad, 1981), 227.

30. The idea of "turning to the Lord" in 2 Cor. 3:16 implies conversion and devotion and may reflect the similar usage in Ps. 22:27, where it parallels worshiping the Lord, but Paul does not make this clear.

31. *Acts of Paul and Thecla* 23; ET in J. K. Elliott, ed., *The Apocryphal New Testament* (Oxford: Clarendon, 1993), 364–74 (368).

32. Bert Jan Lietaert Peerbolte, "Paul's Rapture: 2 Corinthians 12:2-4 and the Language of Mystics," in *Experientia, Volume I: Inquiry into Religious Experience in Early Judaism and Christianity*, SBLSS 40, ed. Frances Flannery, Colleen Shantz, and Rodney A. Werline (Atlanta: SBL, 2008), 159–76 (170). In support of Peerbolte's view, note that the legendary Baruch also fasted in a "cave of the earth" and there prayed for the Lord to show his glory (*2 Bar.* 21:1, 25). In performative terms, Baruch provided the kind of model Paul would have followed.

33. Examples of such "upper room" assemblies in early Jewish literature are *m. Shab.* 1:4; *t. Shab.* 1:16; 2:5; *t. Sotah* 13:3; *y. Ber.* 9d; cf. Catherine Hezser, *The Social Structure of the Rabbinic Movement in Roman Palestine*, TSAJ 66 (Tübingen: Mohr Siebeck, 1997), 209–10. The important point is that devotional (performative) exercises could be carried out in private domiciles.

34. The role of the Holy Spirit in prophetic visions (not just inspired prophecy) was not a significant feature of the Kyriocentric vision performances discussed in chs. 2, 3. For the most part, it reflects realization of the promise in Joel 2:28, which is foundational in the development of New Testament Christology (Rom. 10:12-13 ; 1 Cor. 1:2; 2 Tim. 2:19; Acts 2:21, 38-40; 3:16; 4:12, 30; 7:59; 8:12, 35-36; 9:14, 21, 27; 10:43; 15:11; 16:31; 22:16). In Tannatic midrash (*Mekilta of Rabbi Ishmael* [hereafter *MRI*] Beshallah 3 on Exod. 14:9; Shirata 10 on Exod. 15:20; ET in Jacob Z.

Lauterbach, trans., *Mekilta of Rabbi Ishmael*, 3 vols. [Philadelphia: Jewish Publication Society of America, 1933], 1:210-11, 2:81), "The Lord stands by you" (Amos 9:1; 1 Sam. 3:10) actually means "The Holy Spirit rests upon you" (cf. Acts 2:3). Targum Pseudo-Jonathan translates Num. 7:89 ("Moses would hear the voice [of the Lord] speaking" in the wilderness tent) as "Moses would hear the voice of the Spirit"; cf. Martin McNamara, *Targum and Testament Revisited: Aramaic Paraphrases of the Hebrew Bible: A Light on the New Testament* (Grand Rapids: Eerdmans, 2010), 172. For other Rabbinic parallels, see Arthur Marmorstein, "The Holy Spirit in Rabbinic Legend," in Marmorstein, *Studies in Jewish Theology: The Arthur Marmorstein Memorial Volume*, ed. J. Rabbinowitz and M. S. Lew (Oxford: Oxford University Press, 1950), 179–224 (133–34).

35. On the Christian use of Ps. 16:8 with respect to the Lord Jesus, see David P. Moessner, "*Two* Lords 'at the Right Hand'? The Psalms and an Intertextual Reading of Peter's Pentecost Speech (Acts 2:14-36)," in *Literary Studies in Luke-Acts: Essays in Honor of Joseph B. Tyson*, ed. Richard P. Thompson and Thomas E. Phillips (Macon, GA: Mercer University Press, 1998), 215–32 (216, 226, 228–30). According to Moessner, Luke understood the addressee in Ps. 110:4-5 to be David, which would correlate the "Lord at your right hand" in 110:5 with the "Lord at my right hand" in Ps. 16:8 = Acts 2:25 (ibid., 230). Unfortunately, Moessner assumes (without argument) that "Lord Jesus" is different from Lord YHWH (ibid., 220), so he sees this use of Psalm 16 in Acts 2 as being disjunctive, contrary to the thesis of this study.

36. Ernst Haenchen, *The Acts of the Apostles: A Commentary*, trans. Bernard Noble, Gerald Shinn, and R. McL. Wilson (Philadelphia: Westminster, 1971), 395.

37. Praying to the Lord and hearing back from the prophetic Spirit is apparently a Lukan pattern for the Church in the book of Acts. The underlying idea is stated in Acts 2, which cites Joel's promise of the Spirit (and salvation) to those who call on the name of the Lord (Acts 2:17-21). In contrast, Paul's earlier citation of Joel in Rom. 10 focused on the person of the Lord Jesus (Rom. 10:5-13). It is possible that Luke has substituted the Holy Spirit for the more traditional vision of YHWH (cf. Acts 2:25) in order to limit postresurrection appearances (already attributed to the agency of the Holy Spirit in 1:2) to the forty-day sojourn of the risen Christ and thereby maintain the quasi-physical nature of the resurrection body (Paul's trance in Acts 22:17-18 being exceptional).

38. Christopher Morray-Jones examines the relation between Acts 22:17-21 and Isa. 6:1-8 and concludes that Paul saw "Christ as the enthroned *kavod*." Morray-Jones also identifies this vision with the "vision of the Lord" that Paul described in 2 Cor. 12 (and possibly in 1 Cor. 9:1 as well); Christopher Rowland and Christopher Morray-Jones, *The Mystery of God: Early Jewish Mysticism and the New Testament*, CRINT 3, Jewish Traditions in Early Christian Literature 12 (Leiden: Brill, 2009), 411–12 (citing the earlier work of Otto Betz). In the context of this paper, I prefer to say that Paul saw the Kavod, according to Luke, and recognized it as the man whose followers he was persecuting.

39. David Aune pointed out the cultic context for Rev. 1 (along with Acts 9; 26 and the Christophanies in the Gospel of John); Aune, *The Cultic Setting of Realized Eschatology in Early Christianity*, NovTSup 28 (Leiden: Brill, 1972), 95.

40. David L. Barr, "The Apocalypse of John as Oral Enactment," *Interpretation* 40 (1986): 243–56 (249, 251–52, 256).

41. See, for instance, Darrell Hannah, "Isaiah's Vision in the Ascension of Isaiah and the Early Church," *JTS* 50 (1999): 80–101 (esp. 85–87).

42. In contrast to Rev. 1, the content of the first-person visions of Isaiah (to which *Ascen. Isa.* 1–5 serves as a preface) are constructed in terms of a hierarchical cosmology that makes it difficult to identify the biblical models being rehearsed; cf. Jonathan Knight, "The Origin and Significance of the Angelomorphic Christology in the *Ascension of Isaiah*," *JTS* 63 (2012): 66–105 (77–78, 91–93, 95). The closest model I can find is Ezek. 8:1-4, where Ezekiel prophesies in the presence of the elders of Judah and envisions the anthropic form of *HaShem* (but with no accompanying ascent).

43. A very similar setting is portrayed for the ascent (lit. "descent") of R. Nehuniah in *Heikalot Rabbati*, the codification of which was too late to be of immediate relevance for our study. See esp. *Heikalot Rabbati* 18:3; 20:4 (*Synopse* §§216, 228), which describes a select group (the *havurah*) that accompanies and supports the performance leader as he descends to the merkavah, apparently in the process of leading the statutory (Yom Kippur) prayers; ET in Blumenthal, *Understanding Jewish Mysticism*, 1:64, 70–71, n. 75; Philip S. Alexander, ed., *Textual Sources for the Study of Judaism*, Textual Sources for the Study of Religion (Chicago: University of Chicago Press, 1984), 123 (for the latter passage). The textual models in this case are Ezek. 1 and Gen. 28:12 (Jacob's ladder).

44. James Charlesworth, "Odes of Solomon," *OTP* 2:725–71 (727).

45. Ibid., 740; cf. the translation by S. P. Brock in *The Apocryphal Old Testament*, 683–729 (696). "Psalms of the coming of the Lord" might have included verses like Pss. 96:13; 98:9, "sing for joy before the Lord, for he is coming to judge the earth."

46. See John Cassian, *Conferences* 10.2 on the festal letter of Theophilus of Alexandria (399 CE).

47. The ability to behold the Lord in unapproachable glory is also attributed to those who are worthy by Pseudo-Macarius (probably referring to Messalians), a contemporary of Pachomius who lived in northeastern Syria; Pseudo-Macarius, *Homily* 2.4.11; ET in George A. Maloney, trans., *Pseudo-Macarius: The Fifty Spiritual Homilies and the Great Letter*, Classics of Western Spirituality (New York: Paulist, 1992), 55–6; cf. 7–8 on date and provenance.

48. *Greek Life of Pachomius* 48, ET in Armand Veilleux, trans., *Pachomian Koinonia*, 3 vols., Cistercian Studies 45–47 (Kalamazoo, MI: Cistercian Publications, 1980–82), 1:330–31.

49. The *Bohairic Life of Pachomius* 184 (dating from c. 400) also attributes a Kyriocentric vision to Pachomius disciple Theodore using the language of the Sinai theophanies (Exod. 19:17-18; 20:18-19; 24:10); Veilleux, trans., *Pachomian Koinonia*, 1:219–20.

50. The context of devastation following the execution of Jesus is important not only for explaining the passionate rehearsal of OT models that provided the conditions for Kyriocentric visions, but for explaining why such visions may not have occurred during the relatively peaceful days of Jesus' ministry. The Gospels suggest that their prayer life (particularly that of Peter, James, and John) lacked the single-minded devotion characteristic of hasidim (Mark 14:38; Luke 9:32).

PART II

Kyriocentric Visions as the Impetus for Early Deity Christology

4

Conditions under which a Kyriocentric Vision Might Be Identified with a Deceased Human Being

According to our Kyriocentric vision conjecture, some of the followers of Jesus experienced a theophany, one in which YHWH appeared to them with the form, voice, and name of their deceased teacher. Our task at this point is to try to match what we know about theophanic traditions and the life and death of this teacher.

JESUS AMONG THE HASIDIM: THE PROBLEM OF HISTORICAL UNIQUENESS

At this point, we confront the phenomenon of historical uniqueness, particularly the uniqueness of deity Christology within the bounds of Judaism. Christian claims concerning the uniqueness of Jesus are usually couched in terms of theological assertions. Thus, there were many Jewish holy men (hasidim, zaddikim, hakamim), all servants of God, but only one of them was raised from the dead, or only one was an incarnate Son of God, and so forth. These theological assertions are an important part of the historical picture, and we shall return to them in chapter 7 to show how they could have been generated by the primary Lord-Jesus identification.[1]

The uniqueness we have to deal with in this chapter, however, is not primarily about Jesus: as far as we know historically, he was a fairly typical Jewish hasid.[2] Here we are concerned rather about the historical conditions under which the Lord-Jesus identification occurred. We have many accounts of Jewish hasidim: some of them were historical (particularly in post-Talmudic times), and some of them met with violent deaths for their beliefs and practices. However, none of these accounts describes Kyriocentric visions among their disciples as the sequel.[3] According to our conjecture, therefore, the case of Jesus was unique because the confluence of conditions was unique. For all we know, the latter uniqueness might be an artifact of the limited nature and number of the texts that are available to us. The class of instances in which the execution of a beloved teacher was followed by Kyriocentric visions has only one member that we know of, but there might have been other such instances about which we know nothing.

I shall refer to this singularity in the case of Jesus as the "fortuitous uniqueness" of the Lord-Jesus identification. It is fortuitous in the sense that only the coincidence of conditions seems to be unique; the conditions themselves (revered teacher, execution, Kyriocentric visions) were fairly common in contemporary Judaism.[4]

Our task in this chapter is similar in some ways to that in the previous one. We are still trying to assess the plausibility of Kyriocentric visions by discerning the conditions under which they might occur based on biblical and Second Temple texts and Rabbinic literature. In the previous chapter we tried to reconstruct the ritual context for Kyriocentric visions (assuming much of this to be performative). Here the context in question is broadened to include circumstances surrounding the life and death of Jesus.

Accordingly, we shall begin our inquiry by revisiting biblical and postbiblical traditions about self-revelations of YHWH in order better to ascertain their potential for identification with specific human roles. First, we survey some points about representations (and self-representations) of YHWH in the Hebrew Bible, early Jewish texts, and early Christian literature. These representations include descriptions of the visual appearance and voice of YHWH and the names by which YHWH identifies himself. Finally, we shall return to the awkward problem of fortuitous, coincidental uniqueness in the case of Jesus.

Diverse Appearances of the Lord in Anthropic Form

There is no question but that YHWH was known to appear in anthropic (humanlike) form, but the details were often rather vague—it might only be "something that seemed like a human form" (Ezek. 1:26). The form was so brilliant that prophets normally deflected their gaze, often falling to the ground in doing so. To behold the divine form could be overpowering or even fatal (e.g., Exod. 3:6b; 33:20-23; Isa. 6:5; contrariwise Exod. 24:10, discussed below).[5]

Even though the details of the divine form were never clearly defined, general features could be specific enough to give rise to contrasting impressions.

The prophet Ezekiel differentiated the appearance of what he saw above the loins of the figure ("like gleaming amber") from what was below ("like fire," Ezek. 1:27). The overall appearance of this composite figure, here termed *the glory of the Lord*, was something like a rainbow (Ezek. 1:28)—a marvelous image that underscores the idea of diversity in appearance. Daniel described YHWH as one who sat on a throne just like the vision of Ezekiel, yet was "Ancient of Days" (Dan. 7:9), giving a rather different impression of the anthropic form.

The diversity of appearances apparently became a matter of controversy in early Rabbinic times. Tannaitic (third–fourth century CE) midrashim addressed the problem, ostensibly in order to contradict contemporary polytheists (the "nations").[6] In one daring exegesis (*Mekilta of Rabbi Ishmael*, hereafter *MRI*), they cited several theophanic texts and concluded that *HaShem* could alter his form to suit the occasion: he was a young warrior at the Red Sea ("YHWH is a warrior," Exod. 15:3, according to the Hebrew text[7]), but a wise old man "full of mercy" on Mount Sinai (Exod. 24:10; cf. Dan. 7:9).[8] This midrash suggests that the differences reflect the variety of circumstances and the fact that *HaShem* assumed various roles and appearances of human beings, as suited to the occasion. The hermeneutical strategy is the same as in the parallel identification of YHWH with Jesus, except that the latter is understood to be a specific person, rather than just a role. In the midrash, *HaShem* is said to be one who was in the past and also one who will be in the future, or "the first and the last" (citing Isa. 41:4; cf. Rev. 1:8; 1:17; 2:8; 21:5-6; 22:13).[9] Nonetheless, there was only one true God, no matter what the gentile nations might say.

Slightly later texts like *Leviticus Rabbah* (fifth century) address the same issue but take a slightly different tack: the prophets saw a multiplicity of images because they were seeing *HaShem* in a variety of mirrors that were imperfect and so gave different impressions (*Lev. R.* 1:14; cf. 1 Cor. 13:12)—this midrash suggests that the differences reflect the disposition of the beholder (or the execution of the performance) rather than differences in the divine form itself.[10]

The diversity of forms might also include individual human beings. Kabbalistic writers of the Middle Ages sometimes spoke of the glory (*kavod*) of the Lord being revealed in the form of Moses, not just at Mount Sinai when Moses was absorbed into the divine cloud (Exod. 24:15-18; cf. 34:29), but from the very day of his birth. Even if we allow for the possibility of Christian influence at this late date (thirteenth century), we are left with the fact that nothing has been said about this embodiment being incompatible with Judaism, whether by medieval rabbis or by present-day Jewish scholars like Moshe Idel.[11]

If, as hypothesized here, some followers of Jesus did perceive the divine in the form of Jesus, they were still well within their Jewish heritage to affirm the complete unity of YHWH. Although Trinitarian discourse would quickly develop (at least as early as the letters of Paul), we must set aside Trinitarian associations if we are to understand the foundational experiences (performances) that gave rise to them. The followers of Jesus may have prayed for the Lord to come as a young "man of war" (Exod. 15:3, Heb.) or to appear as a wise old man "full of mercy" (Exod. 24:10), but what they saw (so we have conjectured) was the Lord coming to them as their crucified teacher, *Kyrios Iēsous*. The difference undoubtedly reflected the new circumstances (*MRI*), but it might also have had something to do with the change in "mirrors" (*Lev. R.* 1:14).

Based on the texts just cited, I claim that, even though the Lord–Jesus identification was unique (fortuitously), it was well within the bounds of common Judaism. There was no "duality" of powers in the early visions among Jesus' disciples—they were strictly Kyriocentric (YHWH surrounded by angels and other powers).[12]

It is worth noting that a variety of early Christian texts parallel these Rabbinic midrashim in portraying the Lord (Jesus) as both young and old.[13] Here are some examples. The *Shepherd of Hermas* (mid-second century CE) saw the divine Son of God as both an ancient rock and a new gate: an ancient rock because he was older than creation; a new gate because he was manifested in recent times (*Herm.* 79:1-2; 89:1-3).[14] The *Epistle to Diognetus* (mid-second or early third century) stated that the divine Logos (Word) was proved to be old and yet appeared young when he was born anew in the hearts of the saints (*Diog.* 11:4).[15] The *Acts of Peter* (170s CE?) described visions of the Lord (Jesus) in a variety of forms, some old and some young, each in accordance with the capacity of the seer[16]—as in *Leviticus Rabbah*, the diversity was due to the dispositions of the beholders. The Coptic *Apocryphon of John* (Nag Hammadi Codex II,1) describes a similar vision and, like the *Mekilta*, stresses the fact that there was no real plurality, only a variety of forms.[17]

While some of these Christian visions may well be literary constructs,[18] they testify to the kind of features—variable, yet specific—that described appearances of the Lord in the Old Testament and also in contemporary Judaism. In this respect, there was no conflict with the affirmation of the unity of God (Deut. 6:4) in either case.

Diverse Voices in which the Lord Revealed Himself

In Jewish imagination, as we have seen, *HaShem* could appear in a variety of forms, both young and old. Similarly, he could speak with a variety of voices, both loud and soft. The thunderous voice of YHWH is well known from Scripture (Job 37:4-5; 40:9; Ps. 29:3-5; John 12:28-9), and so is the "still small voice" (1 Kings 19:12, King James Version). But could this voice be a recognizably human one?

According to a late midrash (redacted in the tenth century) about Moses at the burning bush (Exod. 3:2-6), *HaShem* deliberated concerning how best to reveal himself to Moses. Since Moses had no previous experience in prophetic matters, he would be terrified if *HaShem* were to speak in a loud voice. On the other hand, he might not take it seriously if *HaShem* were to speak in a soft voice. So *HaShem* decided to address him in the voice of his father—familiar, yet authoritative (*Exod. R.* 3:1).[19] The idea may sound like an unwarranted complication of a simple narrative, but it was almost necessitated by a close reading of YHWH's opening words to Moses in Exodus 3:6—not "I am the God of your fathers, Abraham, Isaac, and Jacob," but "I am the God of your father [singular], the God of Abraham, the God of Isaac, and the God of Jacob." Clearly four ancestors were in view here, and the first of them was Moses' father. Even though our midrash is late, it could hardly have taken perceptive exegetes like the Rabbis eight centuries to notice the problem and experiment with such solutions.

As a matter of fact, the idea of YHWH speaking with a familiar voice was long familiar to readers of the Hebrew Bible: when YHWH first revealed himself to Samuel, his voice sounded just like that of his master Eli (1 Sam. 3:4-6).[20] Something of the same sort may have occurred during the performative prayers of the first disciples. Not knowing what the voice of YHWH sounded like, they may have prayed for the Lord to comfort them with a whisper or to thunder from heaven, but what they ended up hearing (so we have conjectured) was the more familiar voice of their crucified teacher saying something like "Do not be afraid; I am the first and the last" (Rev. 1:17; cf. Mark 5:36; 6:50; Luke 5:10; 12:7, 32). The Lord-Jesus identification was still within the bounds of common Judaism.

DIVERSE NAMES BY WHICH THE LORD IDENTIFIED HIMSELF

In Jewish imagination, as we have seen, *HaShem* could appear in a variety of forms and be heard in a variety of voices. He could also reveal himself with a variety of new names, both cosmic and historic.

The idea of the Lord adopting (or revealing) a new name was familiar to readers of the Hebrew Bible.[21] The Tetragrammaton (YHWH) is said to have been revealed for the first time to Moses, who otherwise would not have known what name to use in exercising his mission (Exod. 3:13-15; cf. Gen. 32:29; Judg.

13:17). Prior to that self-revelation, according to one tradition, the Deity had been known by other names like "God Almighty" (*El shaddai,* Exod. 6:2-3). Those earlier names continued to be used; the new name was simply added to embody the new revelation.

Such innovations could also be read back into earlier narratives. The Masoretic (Hebrew) version of Abraham's pledge in Genesis 14:22 added the Tetragrammaton to the traditional, cosmic name "God Most High" (*El elyon*).[22] In terms of our conjecture concerning the emergence of deity Christology, these innovations suggest that any Kyriocentric vision that followed the life and death of Jesus might be expected to reveal a new name.[23]

Among the names that YHWH used were some that identified him with historical objects. In the patriarchal narrative (a northern Israelite tradition), for example, the Lord named himself "God-Bethel" ("I am *El-beit-el*") after an historic cult center where he had previously manifested himself (Gen. 31:13;[24] cf. Jer. 48:13). Old Testament scholar Benjamin Sommer suggests that the Lord's assumption of this name was a way of identifying himself with the cult stele that was also known by that name (*Beit-el,* "House of God").[25] Onomatological associations with cultic locations like Dan and Beersheba also appear to be evidenced in the Hebrew text (Amos 8:14) as well as in Roman-period inscriptions.[26]

What is particularly interesting in these cases is the way self-revelations of the Lord are portrayed as incorporating loci of divine action—places and objects that were believed to bear the divine presence and make it accessible to others.[27] With regard to our conjecture about the origin of deity Christology, they suggest that a Kyriocentric vision that immediately followed the life and death of a hasid like Jesus might similarly be expected to bear the name of the person who was believed to have born the divine presence.

If we may look briefly beyond the New Testament era, Heikalot traditions systematized the idea of diverse manifestations by compiling a set of seventy divine names. Each of these names is said to have proceeded from the throne of glory and circuited the heavens, being escorted and hymned by hosts of angels using the words of the *Kedushah* (the Sanctus, *3 En.* 48B).[28] In contemporary Greek magical papyri, the so-called "Hebrew formula" had similar strings of divine names—some of these strings actually contained the word "Jesus" (*Iēsous*) as the name of the God of the Hebrews.[29]

In short, the name of the God of the Jews was as diverse as the appearances and voices. In addition to being diverse, the divine name was cumulative, acquiring new attributes and titles that supplemented, even though they did not displace, the older ones. New names could be those of holy objects like the stele at Bethel. In principle, they might also include the names of holy people (hasidim) like Jesus, although, as it is, we only know of one case in which this actually happened (fortuitous uniqueness). In spite of the varied appearances and the variety of voices, the name of the God of Israel was believed to be one (Deut. 6:4; Zech. 14:9). Like the rainbow of Ezekiel's vision, the unique Deity could be diffracted into a variety of modes or "measures" (middot).[30] Some of these names were used across a wide variety of Jewish circles (God of Abraham, God Most High, YHWH). Others were primarily current among subgroups: for example, "God Bethel" in circles associated with the cult site at Bethel and "Lord Jesus" among the followers of Jesus.[31]

So far we have focused on continuities between the practices of Judaism and those found in the New Testament and found that they are far more prevalent than usually supposed. However, this revisionist emphasis needs to be counterbalanced by revisiting the uniqueness of the case of Jesus—what I have termed "fortuitous uniqueness."

Jesus Among the Hasidim: Fortuitous Uniqueness Revisited

The variety of forms, voices, and names just illustrated points again to the value of comparing the sequel of Jesus' tragic death with that of other Jewish holy men (hasidim). If it were merely a matter of a familiar identity being followed by a new one, any identification of the two might be deemed purely functional, as was the case with Moses and Samuel. In the case of Samuel, Eli finally realized that it was the Lord who was calling, and he set the boy straight. So the next time YHWH called out, he stood right next to the sleeping boy and addressed him with the characteristically divine double vocative, "Samuel, Samuel" (1 Sam. 3:8-10).

In the later midrash about Moses, HaShem waited until he had Moses' attention, and then immediately differentiated himself from Moses' father. The entire narrative is designed to explain the YHWH's singular self-identification: "I am the God of your father" (Exod. 3:6a). As the midrash paraphrases the verse: "I am not actually your father, but the God of your father; I have come to you gently so that you would not be afraid."[32] So HaShem's use of the voices of Eli and Moses' father was functional and temporary in this case. Once its intended effect had been accomplished, the initial impression could be (and had to be) corrected. Otherwise Moses would go around telling people that his father was HaShem or, rather, that HaShem was his father!

These parallels are instructive for their obvious differences from the situation with Jesus and his followers as much as they are for their similarities.

We have not the slightest hint in New Testament narratives that YHWH at first identifies himself as Jesus (his form, face, voice, name) and then immediately reverses himself (yielding something like, "I am not actually Jesus; I am the God of Jesus!"). There is not even the slightest suggestion of such temporary, functional identification in noncanonical Christian literature, in spite of its diversity in other respects. Nor is there any evidence of a counter-strategy to refute such a suggestion ("Our enemies spread a rumor").

I conclude that the absence of any identification-reversal in the early Christian traditions is a good indication of the strength and permanence of the Lord's identification with Jesus. The strength and permanence of the identification is evidenced in the confession, "The Lord is Jesus" (which can also be read as "Jesus is Lord")—both in its form and in the fact that it was regarded as necessary for salvation (Rom. 10:9; Acts 16:31).[33] This confession clearly originated in the performance of Kyriocentric visions,[34] but it codified the Lord-Jesus identification in a pithy formula that could be abstracted and reiterated in any context, features that, as far as we know, were unprecedented in the history of Judaism. Moses was uniquely intimate with the Lord (Num. 12:7-8; Deut. 34:10), but we never hear anything like "the Lord is Moses" (or "Moses is Lord"). Jacob (Israel) was sometimes viewed as an archangel, perhaps even the glorious human figure on the throne in Ezekiel 1:10,[35] but we are never told to "believe in the Lord Jacob, and you will be saved." Enoch was eventually identified as the angelic Son of Man (1 En. 71:14), but his name is not included in a revised version of the Shema like "there is one God, the Father, and one Lord, Enoch, the Son of Man."[36] There is no good historical reason to deny the uniqueness of the christological confession in this particular sense.

On the other hand, there is no good reason to overstate the uniqueness of the christological confession. As conjectured here, the confession was rooted in the sequel—a Kyriocentric vision—to a particular context—the execution of a beloved teacher, and both aspects had antecedents and parallels in the history of Judaism. In fact, the christological confession may be unique simply because we do not know of any other such a coincidences to compare it with. From an historical viewpoint, it is important to keep an open mind concerning the possibility of other such coincidences.

The fortuitous, coincidental uniqueness of the Lord-Jesus identification can be further explicated by revisiting the traditions concerning Moses and Samuel.

According to tradition, Moses was a teacher who had no Jewish teacher or master of his own: in Jewish tradition, he was only instructed in the broader wisdom of the Greeks and Egyptians.[37] There was no Jewish hasid to address him with God's word or to embody God's power for him—a hasid who could therefore have served as a model for YHWH's later self-identification.

Adding the case of Samuel allows us to triangulate the fortuitous uniqueness issue. Unlike Moses, Samuel clearly had a teacher, the priest Eli. As we have already noted, YHWH used the voice of Eli to break the ice with Samuel. However, Eli was still very much alive at the time, so he could not have served as a viable model for YHWH's self-identification (nor, according to the story text, was Eli worthy of such an honor). What can we conclude from these cases?

Just to say that the historic Jesus was a hasid (a Jewish holy man), someone who mediated the divine for his followers, and a potential messiah, would not by itself make him unique in the history of Judaism (much less would it make him truly divine).[38] However, being a hasid would make his face and voice an appropriate model for subsequent Kyriocentric visions.

To state the point more systemically, there was always a partial homology (a structural parallel) between the Jewish hasid and anthropic form of the Lord: the one is a human being who embodies the divine and is to be emulated; the other is the divine being who assumes a human form and is to be worshipped.[39] In other words, hasid and anthropic form share the same dyadic structure. The homology is not perfect,[40] but it could well have been sufficient to make the face and voice of a hasid like Jesus an appropriate model for appearances of the Lord in anthropic form.

From a strictly historical standpoint, therefore, there is no reason why followers of a Jewish holy man should not envision the Deity in his particular form (as remembered and somewhat idealized), particularly following his death. We know that this happened in the case of Jesus, but there is no reason to suppose that followers of other (deceased) hasidim would not have had visions of *HaShem* clothed in their forms and bearing their names.[41] It is simply the case that we have no trace in the extant literature.[42]

This supposition assumes some degree of flexibility in auditions and visualizations of the divine form. According to students of mystical experience, visions are usually not as focused and specific as later descriptions make them appear. As a result, new variations are always possible and often do occur. In anthropological terms, this flexibility undoubtedly reflects the malleability of unconscious levels of the human psyche as well as the variability of oral performances (in the case of visions associated with ritual practices).[43] In performative terms, the quest for divine response was implicit in the very nature of petitionary prayer, and the expectation of a new revelation was often made explicit in the performance itself (e.g., Isa. 21:6-10; Ezek. 3:17; Dan. 9:3; Joel 2:17; Hab. 2:1; 4 Ezra 5:28, 38; 6:59).

We have already documented such variability in the rehearsal of biblical visions and the way these features were interpreted in apocalyptic and Rabbinic literature (e.g., the commissioning of the prophets in Exod. 3:10; Isa. 6:8-9; Jer. 1:7-10; Ezek. 2:2-3; *1 En.* 15:1-2; 71:14-15). In spite of all the obscurity and variation of these visions, or perhaps because of it, the pious Jew was credited with the ability to recognize the unique persona, the identity of *HaShem*, particularly in definitive redemptive manifestations like that at the Red Sea.[44] This is exactly what happened according to the Tannaitic midrash on Exodus, *Mekilta of Rabbi Ishmael*:

> When the Holy One, blessed be he, revealed himself at the Sea, no one had to ask, "Which one is the King?" But, as soon as they saw him, they recognized him, and they all opened their mouths and said: "This one is my God, and I will glorify him [Exod. 15:2]." (*MRI*, Shirata 3:36-39)[45]

This uncanny ability to differentiate the true anthropic form from other heavenly (and equally visible) powers was apparently more than a literary conceit for the Rabbis. According to *Sifrei Devarim* 343, it was precisely the degree of discernment that differentiated the average Jew from the gentile nations.[46] Even if this degree of demarcation from other peoples is judged to have been self-serving, it is relevant to our study insofar as it was also characteristic of the early disciples of Jesus (1 Thess. 1:9; Gal. 2:15; Acts 14:15, 26:17-18)—the Lord-Jesus identification was based on the prior (and probably repeated[47]) identification of the anthropic form as YHWH, just like that attributed to the Israelites at the Red Sea. Once the Jewish followers of Jesus were absorbed into the Great Church (in the fourth–fifth century), of course, deity Christology became associated with the gentile nations, and it was quite natural for Jewish critics to detect another form of gentile idolatry.

CONCLUSION REGARDING IDENTIFICATION OF A KYRIOCENTRIC VISION WITH A DECEASED HUMAN BEING

To sum up our results thus far, our conjecture has yielded the following historical scenario:

- In the eyes of his disciples, Jesus was a hasid, a holy man who mediated the divine presence and power.[48]

- Like many other Jewish conventicles of the first century, the disciples were trained to perform Kyriocentric visions like those of Isaiah, Ezekiel, Enoch, and the theophanic Psalms (ch. 2).[49] In rehearsing these models, they utilized traditional prayer forms and hoped to re-experience the visions as their ancestors had and to reap the same benefits (chs. 3, 6).
- Following the violent death of Jesus, the disciples prayed and rehearsed these visionary models with great urgency in an effort to invoke their Lord's presence and experience his saving power. In accordance with their usual practice, they prayed for salvation and envisioned YHWH coming in a glorious anthropic form (ch. 4).
- In the context of these prayers and performances, the disciples were rewarded with a compelling vision of their Lord (ch. 5). This one was their God, and they glorified him with psalms and hymns of thanksgiving (Exod. 15:2 paraphrased).
- Though a theophany like this would normally be terrifying (Isa. 6:5; 1 En. 14:24), the disciples recognized (at some point) the face and voice to be those of their own teacher, now in a glorified body. This Lord-Jesus identification was the "primary revelation" on which subsequent early Christology was based.
- Informed by the vision, the disciples were compelled to confess, "The Lord is Jesus" (Kyrios Iēsous).

In short, the identification of YHWH with a particular human being resulted from a remarkable coincidence: a Kyriocentric vision occurred immediately following the violent death of a beloved hasid. This scenario is plausible within the context of early Judaism—plausible even though the result (as far as we know) was unique.

By way of disclaimer: conjecturing that disciples of Jesus experienced Kyriocentric visions with the form and voice of Jesus does not mean that the Lord-Jesus identification was necessary or automatic. For some of the disciples, the identification was clearly strong and durable, but there may have been others who did not share this conviction. In the absence of evidence, we can only speculate, but it is worthwhile keeping these possibilities in mind. Some of those who did not experience the new vision firsthand may have accepted it on the word of others and subsequently rehearsed it as their own.

Other disciples may have demurred, however, either doubting the credibility of those who experienced the vision (Luke 24:11), or simply thinking that it was too great a step (John 20:24-25). Some of the latter group may well have continued to celebrate Jesus traditions and to rehearse Kyriocentric visions in a more traditional vein (not identified as Jesus), but they would probably not have had the dramatic sense of commissioning and the urgent new message, a "gospel," to promulgate. As a result, their oral traditions, if such existed, were never recorded and lie beyond our ken.[50]

So far, I have only shown that the Kyriocentric vision conjecture is plausible in the context of early Judaism and provides a sufficient ground for the deity Christology of the New Testament. I have also suggested that there are traces of the performance of such visions in the New Testament (ch. 3, "Visions Associated with Prayer in Early Christian Literature"). If readers will grant me that much, it becomes relatively straightforward to extend our scenario as follows:

- As the disciples confessed the Lord-Jesus identification and continued to rehearse Kyriocentric visions, performances rapidly assumed features of the historic Jesus, based on memories of his life and death. Conversely, in an equal and opposite reaction, proclamations and narratives concerning Jesus began to take on characteristics of the Kyriocentric visions.
- When Christian communities began to compose letters and Gospels, they frequently made references that assumed knowledge of these confessions and performances, thereby leaving us with the written texts upon which we base our questions and from which we develop our conjecture.

Here we move on to questions that provide a few more tests for the plausibility of the Kyriocentric conjecture. First, does the New Testament retain any traces of performances of Kyriocentric visions—performances in which YHWH was invoked in traditional appellations and subsequently identified himself as Jesus? We take up this pivotal question in the following two chapters (chs. 5, 6). Following that we further test our conjecture for predictions concerning the effect that memories of the life and death of Jesus would have had for the Lord-Jesus identification (ch. 7).

The primary confession of the New Testament, *Kyrios Iēsous*, came to mean many different things for later believers. In its original setting, however, it meant just what it says: the Lord God who had appeared to Abraham as *El shaddai*, to Jacob as *El Bethel*, and to Moses as YHWH (*Adonai*) had also appeared to the disciples as YHWH (*Adonai*) *Yeshua*, "Lord Jesus." We cannot claim to have proved that things happened in this way, but the scenario is not as implausible as later theological revisions (to be discussed in the final chapter) might make it seem.[51]

Notes

1. The idea of the uniqueness of the Lord-Jesus identification needs some qualification. The ark of the covenant, identified as the throne and footstool of the Lord (1 Chron. 28:2; Ps. 99:1), was the only object housed in the holy of holies (prior to its being hidden prior to the Babylonian Exile), so its uniqueness matched that of YHWH. YHWH was identified with the ark in Num. 10:35-36; 1 Sam. 3:3-4, 6:19-20; 2 Sam. 7:2, 6; Ps. 132:8; cf. G. Henton Davies, "The Ark in the Psalms," in *Promise and Fulfillment: Essays Presented to Professor S. H. Hooke*, ed. F .F. Bruce (Edinburgh: T&T Clark, 1963), 51–61. Similar things could be said about the bronze altar: according to *m. Sukkah* 4:5 (possibly a post-mishnaic gloss), *Sukkot* pilgrims associated YHWH (here *YFY*) so closely with the altar around which they processed while chanting pleas for salvation (*hoshanot*) that R. Eliezer had to correct their song by differentiating the two; cf. *t. Sukkah* 3:1, and see the more harmonized reading of this text by Ephraim E. Urbach, *The Sages: Their Concepts and Beliefs* (Cambridge, MA: Harvard University Press, 1987), 128. *HaShem* was similarly associated with the sequel to the ark of the covenant, the synagogue ark containing the Torah scroll (e.g., *m. Ta'anit* 2-5). The Torah scroll was an inanimate object, yet, in the case of a scroll being burnt or torn, the traditional "rending of the garment" (*keriah*) had to be performed, just as in the case of a deceased relative; William Scott Green, "Romancing the Tome: Rabbinic Hermeneutics and the Theory of Literature," *Semeia* 40 (1987): 148–68 (156–60).

2. *Hasid* ("godly/pious one") is a useful Hebrew term here in that that allows for the gifts of both prophets and sages (thereby avoiding the idea of distinct offices so popular among Christian scholars). The term *zaddiq* ("righteous one") is used in much the same sense by David Flusser, *Jesus*, trans. Ronald Walls (New York: Herder & Herder, 1969), 32, 93. The rough equivalence of the terms *hasid* and *zaddiq* is shown by the parallel usage in the thirteenth benediction of the *Amidah* (*al hatzaddikim ve al-hahasidim*); *My People's Prayer Book* (hereafter MPPB), ed. Lawrence A. Hoffman, 10 vols. (Woodstock, VT: Jewish Lights, 1997–2013), 2:98. I shall use the tem *hasid*, largely out of dereference to the use of this term by Geza Vermes (based on the prototype of Elijah), "Jesus the Jew," in *Jesus' Jewishness: Exploring the Place of Jesus within Early Judaism*, ed. James H. Charlesworth (Philadelphia: American Interfaith Institute, 1991), 108–22 (113–18), repr. in Vermes, *Jesus and the World of Judaism* (London: SCM, 1983), 1–14 (5–11); Vermes, *The Changing Faces of Jesus* (Harmondsworth: Penguin, 2001), 257–60, 267, 269.

3. The relation of martyrdom and postmortem visions in Jewish literature deserves further study. Legendary martyrs include the "Isaiah" of the *Ascension of Isaiah* and Rabbis Ishmael and Aqiva in the "Legend of the Ten Martyrs" (*Midrash Eleh Ezkerah*, fifth–seventh cent. Palestine). Some parallels between Rabbi Ishmael in the "Legend" and Jesus in the Gospels may be due to the influence of Christian ideas of miraculous conception and atonement; Ra'anan S. Boustan, *From Martyr to Mystic: Rabbinic Martyrology and the Making of Merkavah Mysticism* TSAJ 112 (Tübingen: Mohr Siebeck, 2005), 147, 197–98, 291, passim; cf. Daniel Boyarin, *Dying for God: Martyrdom and the Making of Christianity and Judaism* (Stanford, CA: Stanford University Press, 1999), 113–14. Even though they were largely fictitious, they served as models for communal performances as explained in ch. 1.

4. A partial analogue to the execution theophany sequence might be the auditions of the *Shekinah* after the violent death of Shelomo Molkho (1532); Rachel Elior, "R. Joseph Karo and Israel Ba'al Shem Tov—Mystical Metamorphosis, Kabalistic Inspiration, Spiritual Internalization," *Studies in Spirituality* 17 (2007): 267–319 (269–71). Speaking through the mouth of Joseph Karo, the *Shekinah* described herself as being elevated after having been cast to the ground (cf. Rev. 1:18); ET in Louis Jacobs, *Jewish Mystical Testimonies* (New York: Schocken Books, 1996), 123–30; cf. R. J. Zwi Werblowsky, *Joseph Karo: Lawyer and Mystic*, 2nd ed. (Philadelphia: Jewish Publication Society of America, 1977), 19–22, 108–9, 266–68. In other respects, however, the two cases were quite different. Karo was not a personal disciple of Molkho (although his associate Shelomo Alkabetz was), and the audition from the *Shekinah* or *Maggid* was not accompanied by a

Kyriocentric vision (visible appearances rather took the form of Elijah/Metatron; Werblowsky, *Joseph Karo*, 270)—so there was not the continuity needed for the *Shekinah* to assume the form or the face (or even the voice) of Molkho himself. In fact, Karo's *Maggid* had more in common with the Mishnah, which he had committed to memory than it had to any hasid or teacher, living or deceased; Jacobs, *Jewish Mystical Testimonies*, 124–25, 134–35, 138, 141; Werblowsky, *Joseph Karo*, 18–19, 99 (and note), 107, 109, 159, 257–61, 267–68, 274.

5. For a balanced treatment of this difficult, paradoxical subject, see Ira Chernus, "Visions of God in Merkabah Mysticism," *JSJ* 13 (1982): 123–46.

6. Benjamin D. Sommer traces the fluidity and multiplicity of divine representation back to the J and E strata of the Pentateuch; Sommer, *The Bodies of God and the World of Ancient Israel* (Cambridge: Cambridge University Press, 2009), 38–57. Jill Middleton views the visions of Ezekiel in similar terms, but treats the text in strictly literary and rhetorical terms and concludes that such fluidity is necessarily anti-anthropomorphic; Middleton, "Transformation of the Image," in *Transforming Visions: Transformations of Text, Tradition, and Theology in Ezekiel*, ed. William A. Tooman and Michael A. Lyons (Eugene, OR: Pickwick Publications, 2010), 113–37 (134, 136).

7. Note that this meaning of Exod. 15:3a is lost in the Greek Septuagint, which changes the wording to "the Lord shattering wars."

8. *MRI* Shirata 4:19–22; Bahodesh 5:20–23; ET in Jacob Z. Lauterbach, trans., *Mekilta of Rabbi Ishmael*, 3 vols. (Philadelphia: Jewish Publication Society of America, 1933), 2:31, 231. The two major theophanies described are associated with the Tetragrammaton (YHWH) and *Elohim* ("God"), respectively. Evidently the pavement under the feet of the "God of Israel" in Exod. 24:10 was taken to imply sympathetic identification with the children of Israel in Egypt (Exod. 1:14).

9. Philip Alexander, "Jewish Believers in Early Rabbinic Literature (2d to 5th Centuries)," in *Jewish Believers in Jesus: The Early Centuries*, ed. Oskar Skarsaune and Reidar Hvalvik (Peabody, MA: Hendrickson, 2007), 659–709 (684); Peter Schäfer, *The Jewish Jesus: How Judaism and Christianity Shaped Each Other* (Princeton, NJ: Princeton University Press, 2012), 56–58. Interestingly, Schäfer refers to these different appearances of *HaShem* as "different incarnations" (ibid., 61), an idea consonant with our Kyriocentric vision conjecture (provided we do not press the literal meaning of incarnation).

10. ET in Jacob Neusner, *Judaism and Scripture: The Evidence of Leviticus Rabbah*, Chicago Studies in the History of Judaism (Chicago: University of Chicago Press, 1986), 159–60. The major proof text here is Num. 12:8 where Moses is differentiated from other prophets by his being able to see the true form of *HaShem*; cf. M. David Litwa, "Transformation Through a Mirror: Moses in 2 Cor. 3.1," *JSNT* 34 (2012): 286–97 (291).

11. According to R. Shemayah ben Isaac ha-Levi (writing in the 1280s), Moses embodied the divine Glory from birth. Moshe Idel emphasizes the ontological implications of this description as a theophany (not just as an apotheosis); Idel, *Enchanted Chains: Techniques and Rituals in Jewish Mysticism* (Los Angeles: Cherub, 2005), 87–89. Elsewhere, Idel makes a distinction between embodiment in any sort of material and incarnation in the flesh of a living person; *Ben: Sonship and Jewish Mysticism*, Kogod Library of Judaic Studies 5 (London: Continuum, 2007), 4, 62, 451. In these terms, the statement by R. Shemayah concerning Moses seems to imply "incarnation" from the time of Moses' birth.

12. As early as the Gospel of Mark, we have narratives of visions portrayed in terms of two powers. In ch. 7, I shall argue that these binitarian constructs were an adjustment required by the interweaving of these Kyriocentric visions with Jesus traditions.

13. A helpful study on this subject is Andrew Hofer, "The Old Man as Christ in Justin's *Dialogue with Trypho*," *VC* 57 (2003): 1–21 (12–13).

14. The title *Son of God* was often used to refer to angels, and is here used to describe the visible form of God reconceived in binitarian terms; see ch. 7. The fact that the divine Son was "manifested in recent times" refers to the incarnation, which raises problems that will be discussed in ch. 9.

15. In the New Testament and early Christian apologies (beginning with Justin Martyr), the divine Logos was another label for the visible form of God.

16. *Acts of Peter* 20, 21; ET in J. K. Elliott, ed., *The Apocryphal New Testament* (Oxford: Clarendon, 1993), 413–15.

17. *Apocryphon of John* 2:1-9; ET in James M. Robinson, ed. *The Nag Hammadi Library in English*, 3rd ed. (San Francisco: Harper & Row, 1988), 105.

18. See the discussion by Paul Foster, "Polymorphic Christology: Its Origins and Development in Early Christianity," *JTS* 38 (2007): 66–99 (74–75).

19. *Exodus Rabbah* 3:1, ET in H. Freedman and Maurice Simon, eds., *Midrash Rabbah*, 10 vols. (London: Soncino, 1939), 3:58.

20. On the Greek gods' habit of appearing in the form of friends and relations, see Robin Lane Fox, *Pagans and Christians* (New York: Knopf, 1987), 108. The phenomenon is known in Jewish and early Christian literature as well. In *Joseph and Aseneth* 14:9 (10), Michael appeared to Aseneth in the form of a glorified Joseph. In the *Acts of Paul and Thecla* 3:21, the Lord (Jesus) took on the form of Paul (after which he returns to heaven). According to Irenaeus (*Haer.* 1.24.4), Basilides taught that Jesus was an "incorporeal Power" who avoided the cross by assuming the form of Simon of Cyrene. In the *Acts of Peter and the Twelve Apostles* (NHC VI,1) 2–9, Jesus appeared as a pearl salesman who at first identified himself as Lithargoel (Robinson, ed. *The Nag Hammadi Library*, 290–93). According to Paulinus of Nola, *Ep.* 49.3-4, the Lord (Jesus) appeared as St. Felix, oscillating back and forth in character. For a summary of Jesus' "metamorphoses" in apocryphal New Testament literature, see Paul J. Achtemeier, "Jesus and the Disciples as Miracle Workers in the Apocryphal New Testament," in *Aspects of Religious Propaganda in Judaism and Early Christianity*, Studies in Judaism and Christianity in Antiquity 2, ed. Elisabeth Schüssler Fiorenza (Notre Dame, IN: University of Notre Dame Press, 1976), 148–86 (167–8).

21. Terence Fretheim, *The Suffering God: An Old Testament Perspective* (Minneapolis: Fortress Press, 1984), 83–84.

22. This striking observation is based on the absence of the Tetragrammaton in the texts of the Septuagint (Greek), Peshitta (Syriac), and 1QapGen ar 22:21 (Aramaic). Mark S. Smith tentatively dates this textual addition to the second century BCE (the Seleucid era); Smith, *God in Translation: Deities in Cross-Cultural Discourse in the Biblical World*, Forschungen zum Alten Testament 57 (Tübingen: Mohr Siebeck, 2008), 212–13. Smith points out that the addition of the Tetragrammaton asserts the status of the God of Israel as *El Elyon*, the supreme God; ibid., 229, 241. In other words, the phrase "YHWH *El Elyon*" is a confessional statement comparable (in function) to *Kyrios Iēsous*.

23. Judging by Matt. 1:21, the Hebrew name *Yeshua* was also associated with the appellation *yeshuah* ("salvation"), as in the acclamation, "The Lord has become my/our salvation [*li-yshu'a*]" (Exod. 15:2; Ps. 68:19; 118:21; Isa. 12:2). Note that Matt. 21:9, 15 has the crowds address the Hosanna ("Save us, O Lord") of Ps. 118:25 to Jesus (as the son of David); cf. Herbert W. Basser, "Planting Christian Trees in Jewish Soil," *Review of Rabbinic Judaism* 8 (2005): 91–112 (96–98).

24. The Greek Septuagint changes the meaning by translating Gen. 31:13a as "I am the God who appeared to you at Bethel"; cf. E. A. Speiser, *Genesis*, AB 1 (Garden City, NY: Doubleday, 1964), 244.

25. Benjamin D. Sommer, *The Bodies of God*, 50. Sommer here uses the terms *incarnate*, *small-scale manifestation*, and *avatar* to describe YHWH's presence in the sacred stele; ibid., 40. For a nuanced treatment of various terms for the anthropomorphic representation of *HaShem*, including terms like embodiment and incarnation, see Moshe Idel, *Ben*, 60.

26. A Greek inscription to the "God-who-is-in-Dan" and an Aramaic inscription to the "God of Dan"; see Avraham Biran, "Tell Dan, 1976," *Israel Exploration Journal* 26 (1976): 201–6 (204–5). For the identification of YHWH with Samaria and Teman at iron-age Kuntillet 'Ajrud, see Graham I. Davies, *Ancient Hebrew Inscriptions: Corpus and Concordance* (Cambridge: Cambridge University Press, 1991), 81, §8.15-17, 21, nicely summarized in B. A. Mastin, "Yahweh's Asherah,

Inclusive Monotheism and the Question of Dating," in *In Search of Pre-Exilic Israel: Proceedings of the Oxford Old Testament Seminar*, JSOTSup 406, ed. John Day (London: T&T Clark, 2004), 326–51 (326–27).

27. The Lord incorporating prior actions in new self-revelations is a common theme in the books of Genesis and Exodus. Note, for example, the sequence: "I am the God of your father Abraham"; "I am . . . the God of your father Abraham and the God of Isaac"; "I am the God of your father, the God of Abraham, the God of Isaac, and the God of Jacob" (Gen. 26:24; 28:13; Exod. 3:6).

28. *Old Testament Pseudepigrapha*, ed. James Charlesworth, 2 vols. (Garden City, NY: Doubleday, 1983), 1:310–311. Hereafter cited as *OTP*. Karl Erich Grözinger describes this later systematization as an "onomatological system"; Grözinger, "The Names of God and the Celestial Powers: Their Function and Meaning in the Hekhalot Literature," in *Jerusalem Studies in Jewish Thought* 6 (1987): 53–85 (esp. 54, 57–58) (English section).

29. See, for example, PGM 4, 3019–20: "I adjure you by the God of the Hebrews, Jesus!" ET in Hans Dieter Betz, *The Greek Magical Papyri in Translation, Including the Demotic Spells*, 2nd ed. (Chicago: University of Chicago Press, 1992), 96. Pieter Willem van der Horst argues that, even if *Iēsous* were an interpolation (which he doubts), it would still be the case that the interpolator (sometime between the first and fourth centuries) found it suitable to give this name to the God of the Hebrews; van der Horst, "The Great Magical Papyrus of Paris (PGM IV) and the Bible," in *A Kind of Magic: Understanding Magic in the New Testament and Its Religious Environment*, Library of New Testament Studies 306, ed. Michael Labahn and Bert Jan Lietaert Peerbolte (London: T&T Clark, 2007), 173–83 (178). Regardless of whether the redactor was a Hebraizing pagan or an eclectic Jew, the motifs cited were clearly Hebraic and may even have been based on a first-century Jewish text (ibid., 182–83, citing Morton Smith). *Iēsous* (Hebrew, *Yeshua*) could, of course, be a transliteration of *yeshuah* ("salvation"), one of the designations of *HaShem* in the Old Testament (Exod. 15:2; Ps. 118:21; passim). However, Tosefta gives some concurrent evidence (not noted by van der Horst) of use of the name of Jesus among the rabbis, in this case, for the healing of a snakebite (*t. Hullin* 2:22). Still the magical papyrus cited above is unique in its placing the name of Jesus in an attributive position alongside other Hebrew names of God (not possessive as in the "God of Abraham").

30. On the use of the term, "measure" (*middah*) in regard to *HaShem*, see our discussion of *Sifrei Devarim* 355 in ch. 2. The idea of the Creator having finite attributes or measures implies some kind of self-projection and diffraction of the Deity in the realm of space and time. I developed this idea in relation to the problem of deism in C. B. Kaiser, *Toward a Theology of Scientific Endeavour: The Descent of Science*, Ashgate Science and Religion Series (London: Ashgate, 2007), 38–46.

31. This aspect of New Testament Christology is what theologians like Apollinarius termed *a flesh-bearing God*; Apollinarius, Fragment 109; ET in Richard A. Norris, trans. *The Christological Controversy*, Sources of Early Christian Thought (Philadelphia: Fortress Press, 1980), 110; cf. Gregory of Nazianzus, Ep. 102 to Cledonius (LCC 3:227). Cf. Deut. 33:1, where Moses is referred to as a "man of god"(*ish ha-elohim*); Isa. 9:2, 6, where the king is referred to as "god" and bears divine light and authority (Lxx *archē*); *1 En.* 49:3, where the Elect One bears the spirit of wisdom; 4QShir^b frags. 48–59 2:1-5, where the Sage bears God's intelligence and speaks with God's voice to exorcise demons; *Sifra Vayikra* 8:1, where Aaron is clothed with the Divine Presence; *Odes Sol.* 1:1, "The Lord is on my head like a crown" (*OTP* 2:735). Also note Peter Brown's description of Christian holy men as "bearers or agents of the supernatural on earth"; Brown, "Eastern and Western Christendom in Late Antiquity: A Parting of the Ways," in Brown, *Society and the Holy in Late Antiquity* (Berkeley: University of California Press, 1982), 166–95 (179).

32. *Exod. R.* 3:1, ET in Freedman and Simon, eds., *Midrash Rabbah*, 3:58 (modified).

33. The strength and permanence of the Lord-Jesus identification is further evidenced by the apparent eclipse of the minimalist option of dating that identification from the time of the

resurrection, as we shall see in ch. 7 ("When and How Did the Lord Become Identified with the Man Jesus?").

34. The performative nature of the confession is clearest in Paul's attributing it to the work of the Spirit in 1 Cor. 12:3, where it appears at the head of a long list of charismatic gifts. Most likely, the performance was part of a baptismal rite, based on Deut. 30:10-14 (turning to the Lord) and Joel 2:32 (calling on the name of the Lord), as in Rom. 10:6-13; Acts 2:38-39; 22:16. The performative nature of early confessions like "Jesus is the Messiah" and "Jesus is the Son of God" (to be discussed in ch. 7) is reflected in Gospel narratives that evoke these very responses (or participation in them) from the performative community (e.g., Mark 1:11; 4:41; 8:29; 9:7; 14:61; 15:39).

35. The pseudepigraphal *Prayer of Joseph* (Fragment A) identifies Jacob as the embodiment of the archangel Israel. Manuscript Montefiore (H.116) of *Tg. Tos. Ezek.* reflects an alternate reading of the anthropic figure in Ezek. 1:26 as "the form of Jacob our father"; Nils Armstrong Dahl, "The Johannine Church and History," in *Current Issues in New Testament Interpretation,* ed. W. Klassen and G. F. Snyder (New York: Harper, 1962), 124–42, 284–88 (136); David J. Halperin, *The Faces of the Chariot: Early Jewish Responses to Ezekiel's Vision,* TSAJ 16 (Tübingen: Mohr, 1988), 121; cf. Jarl Fossum, *The Image of the Invisible God: Essays on the Influence of Jewish Mysticism on Early Christology,* NTOA 30 (Göttingen: Vandenhoeck & Ruprecht, 1995), 143–44; Elliot Wolfson, *Along the Path: Studies in Kabbalistic, Myth, Symbolism, and Hermeneutics* (Albany: State University of New York Press, 1995), 8, 13. Jacob may also have been identified as the Demiurge (by way of Jer. 10:16) in *Midr. Tanh.,* Toledot 11; Wolfson, *Along the Path,* 117 n. 35. Possible parallels between Jesus and Jacob are suggested in John 1:51 ("descending on the Son of man"; cf. *Gen. R.* 68:12; 69:3) and possibly in 1 Tim. 3:16 ("seen by angels"; cf. *Tg. Neof. Gen.* 28:12). Another possible link is found in Ps. 24:6, "Such is the company of those who seek him [YHWH], who seek your face, O Jacob."

36. The same could be said of archangels like Gabriel in spite of the fact that they bore the divine name (*El,* YHWH) and could even be called by that name (Exod. 23:21; *2 En.* 21:4). Neither Gabriel, Michael, Melchizedek, nor Metatron is ever cited in a salvific confession of faith like "confess with your lips that Michael is Lord . . . you will be saved" (cf. Rom. 10:9).

37. Philo, *Life of Moses* 1.21; Josephus, *Jewish Antiquities* 2.286; Acts 7:22.

38. Geza Vermes points out the parallel between Hanina ben Dosa's being one of the "men of deeds" (*anshei ma'aseh, m. Sot.* 9:15), and Jesus' mighty deeds in Matt. 11:20 (note also Matt. 11:2, 19; 13:54) ; Luke 24:19; Acts 2:22; Josephus, *Ant.* 18.63; Vermes, *Changing Faces of Jesus,* 258, 277; cf. Shmuel Safrai, "Teaching of Pietists in Mishnaic Literature," *JJS* 16 (1965): 15–33 (16–18). One significant difference is that, as a rule, Jesus was remembered to have healed by direct command, whereas hasidim like Hanina healed through the fluency of their prayers to God (*b. Ber.* 34b); cf. Dan Jaffé, "L'Identification de Jésus au modèle du hasid charismatique Galiléen: Les thèses de Geza Vermes et de Shmuel Safrai revisitées," *NTS* 55 (2009): 218–46 (223). The main exception to this "rule" comes in the Johannine story of the raising of Lazarus (John 11:22, 41-43), where Jesus is said to ask the Father prior to issuing the command. The fact that John was spinning down his Christology (contrary to common wisdom) is discussed in ch. 7.

39. Moshe Idel aptly describes two forms of exemplarism: imitation of a teacher and worship of a divine hypostasis. The fact that Christianity combines the two in a single figure has no parallel that we know of in the history of Judaism; Idel, *Ben,* 38.

40. The homology between the hasidic dyad and the anthropic dyad is not perfect. The former is a dyad of conjunction as in classic Antiochene Christology. The latter is a dyad of divine self-projection as in Alexandrian Christology. But both dyads share a revelational structure, and the immanent poles of both dyads reside in the intermediate world. In Hebrew Scripture, there is no sharp line between an angel of the Lord who bears the divine name and the Great Angel who is the anthropic (or angelomorphic) form of YHWH (giving rise to the problem of proto-Arianism, as discussed in ch. 8); cf. Idel, *Ben,* 18, 29–30.

41. In the Nicene Creed, Christians confess the Lord Jesus to be the "only" (*monogenēs*) Son of God, but this uniqueness refers to the "one Lord" (*hen kyrios*) as he was "before all worlds."

42. In ch. 7, we will examine some of the ways in which the "high" Christology of the primary confession was spun down in order to accommodate traditions about the historic Jesus. If other context-sequel coincidences ever did occur, they may have been spun down to the point of not leaving traces in extant literature. The question of uniqueness against commonality (continuity) would then have to be replaced by one of robustness against fragility of the identification.

43. Gershom Scholem once held that mystic experience was fundamentally amorphous and could be interpreted in a variety of ways, Scholem, *On the Kabbalah and its Symbolism*, trans. Ralph Manheim (New York: Schocken Books, 1965), 8. As Bernard McGinn has pointed out, Scholem overemphasized the amorphous side of mystic phenomena; McGinn, *The Foundations of Mysticism* (New York: Crossroad, 1991), 336. A more moderate view of the flexibility of mystical experience has been developed by Elliot Wolfson, *Through a Speculum that Shines: Vision and Imagination in Medieval Jewish Mysticism* (Princeton, NJ: Princeton University Press, 1994), 57–58. Angela Kim Harkins adapts critical spatial theory and proposes a "Thirdspace" level that goes beyond the "Secondspace" reenactment of a text and produces significantly new religious experiences; Harkins, *Reading with an "I" to the Heavens: Looking at the Qumran Hodayot through the Lens of Visionary Traditions*, Ekstasis 3 (Berlin: de Gruyter, 2012), chap. 4 (esp. 122–23), 261–62.

44. As Terence Fretheim aptly states, Old Testament theophanies "do not necessarily suggest that God was seen in all of God's fullness. . . . sufficient sight was allowed so that the manifestation could be recognized and reported"; Fretheim, *The Suffering God*, 92. A parallel in our present-day societies might be the ability of nationals to recognize cartoon caricatures of their president or prime minister even though the specific features vary widely from one cartoonist to another.

45. ET in Lauterbach, trans., *MRI*, 2:25; cf. *Sifrei Devarim* 343, and Daniel Boyarin's marvelous riff on the *MRI* text (the sequel concerning R. Akiva): "Deixis [pointing to Hashem in Exod. 15:2] is the very figure of presence: this which I am pointing at; this which you can see. The absent moment of [past] theophany is thus transformed into an evocation of a present moment of vision of God both in the form and in the content . . . of the midrash"; Boyarin, "The Eye in the Torah: Oracular Desire in Midrashic Hermeneutic," *Critical Inquiry* 16 (1990): 532–50 (546). In *b. Hag.* 15b-16a, R. Akiva was similarly credited with the ability to differentiate *HaShem* from his myriad angels. Compare exegetical speculations about the confusion (among the angels) between *HaShem* and the man created in his image as described in *Gen. R.* 8:10.

46. *Sifrei Devarim* 343 to Deut. 33:2; ET in Hammer, trans., *Sifre*, 354–55, and, for a slightly different translation, see Steven D. Fraade, *From Tradition to Commentary: Torah and its Interpretation in the Midrash Sifre to Deuteronomy*, SUNY Series in Judaica (Albany: State University of New York Press, 1991), 42, 203 n. 72. According the *Apoc. Zeph.* 6:4-10 (original Greek dated to 100 BCE to 175 CE), when Zephaniah first saw the accusing angel in Hades, he thought it was the Lord Almighty and cried to him for salvation. However, he quickly realized his mistake and prayed to the Lord Almighty to save him from the angel.

47. From experience, we know that it is possible to see a face or hear a voice several times before being able to recognize its full identity. Given the indirectness of most Old Testament theophanies (and their rehearsals), it is likely that the disciples only recognized the face and voice of Jesus after a number of visionary performances.

48. That Jesus was believed to mediate divine wisdom and power like one of the prophets is perhaps the most certain thing we know concerning the historic person. Divine wisdom was manifest in his teachings, and divine power was evidenced in his healings and miraculous deeds (e.g., Mark 6:2; Luke 11:19-20 [Q]). This aspect of New Testament Christology is what later theologians like Eustathius of Antioch would term the *God-bearing man*; J. N. D. Kelly, *Early Christian Doctrines*, 4th ed. (London: A&C Black, 1968), 284; cf. Gregory of Nazianzus, Ep. 102 (LCC 3:227).

49. Possibly, the disciples were trained to perform Kyriocentric visions by Jesus himself, but the influence of earlier teachers like John the Baptist should also be considered (John 1:35-37). All we know for sure is that they remembered being taught to pray to God as their Father (Luke 11:2, 13 [both from Q]). If these prayers had resulted in Kyriocentric visions, they would have been associated with the name of God as Abba/Father rather than the Lord Jesus (cf. Mark 14:36; Rom. 8:15; Gal. 4:6).

50. It is tempting to try to find traces of such traditions—lacking the Lord-Jesus identification—in first and second-century texts that suggest an adoptionist Christology (e.g., GT 15, 31; GH frag. 6; *Hermas* 59:5-6; Cerinthus and the "Ophites" as described by Irenaeus, *Haer.* 1.26.1; 30.4; "Ascents of James" apud Ps.-Clementine *Recognitions* 37.2; Ebionites as described by Tertullian, *On the Flesh of Christ.* 14). As we shall see in ch. 8, however, a proto-adoptionist stance would have been part of the Jesus traditions shared by all early Christians. Such a stance could be readily combined with Kyriocentric motifs and later incorporated into writings by groups who were not as observant as we are about theological consistency. It would be extremely risky, therefore, to try to reason backwards to putative dissidents concerning the Lord-Jesus identification itself—diverse emphases are present in the New Testament itself (e.g., Q 3:22; 7:35; Phil. 2:8-9; 1 Pet. 1:17-21).

51. It is worth noting that medieval sources like *Sefer ha-Zohar* ("Book of Splendor") were more explicit concerning the oral rehearsal of psalm texts like Ps. 118. Here the adept (a donkey driver who represents the teaching office of the principal author of the *Zohar*, R. Moshe ben Shem Tov de Leon) recites Ps. 118:6-8 in order to realize the presence of YHWH and overcome his fear of divulging his secret knowledge of Torah (*Zohar* 1:95a); cf. Daniel Matt, "New-Ancient Words: The Aura of Secrecy in the Zohar," in *Gershom Scholem's Major Trends in Jewish Mysticism, 50 Years After*, ed. Peter Schäfer and Joseph Dan (Tübingen: Mohr, 1993), 181–207 (192 and n. 54).

5

Traces of Kyriocentric Visions in the New Testament

We have reviewed a wide range of material in the Hebrew Bible, Second Temple apocalypses, early Rabbinic texts, and early Christian literature, and we have found good evidence for the performance of Kyriocentric visions, particularly in contexts of crisis and petitionary prayer, both corporate and private. The pivotal question for this investigation is this: are there any traces of the performance of Kyriocentric visions in the New Testament itself? And, if there is such evidence, how could it have escaped notice in prior treatments of the origin of deity Christology?

A partial answer to the latter question is that such texts are susceptible to different interpretations, particularly when they are written for purposes that had nothing to do with investigations like our own. In fact, many New Testament texts appear to be addressing problems that arose from the charismatic practices of the early church—charismatics at Corinth, a theology of glory in the Gospel of Luke, and so forth—the very kind of practices that we are now trying to retrieve from the texts. Nonetheless, we may assume enough transparency and conservatism in the early traditions to allow us to expect some traces of Kyriocentric visions—now identified with the name of Jesus—even if they are modulated by the need to address other concerns. To put it the other way around, the complete absence of such traces would make our conjecture far less plausible.

The answer to the former question, whether there are any traces of the performance of Kyriocentric visions in the New Testament, will accordingly depend on the pre-understanding one brings to the texts. If one reads them from the perspective of any one of the three familiar explanations of how Jesus was included within the divine identity (as reviewed in the Introduction), the answer would probably be a resounding "no." The externalist, evolutionary scenario of Maurice Casey postpones all notions about the deity of Jesus to later stages of development, when gentile influence came into play—it was not historically possible for such notions to arise in a Palestinian Jewish context, so "Lord Jesus" was more like a Hellenistic savior than the God of Israel. The resurrection scenario of N. T. Wright views the post-execution sightings of Jesus as empirical rather than visionary and finds strong support in the empirical emphases of the later Gospels. Finally, the binitarian, neo-Canaanite scenario of Margaret Barker views these sightings as special cases of a form of Canaanite and Jewish binitarianism in which YHWH was a second god—New Testament Christology may have been visionary, but it was binitarian from the outset.

We are confronted here with the problem of circularity between pre-understanding and interpretation. In such cases, it is best to be explicit about one's pre-understanding so that it can be judged on its own merits. In our case, it is not gradual evolution (Casey) or empiricism (Wright) or proto-binitarianism (Barker)—valuable as these perspectives are in many cases—but a performative understanding of the communities who produced the New Testament texts.

A PERFORMATIVE APPROACH TO NEW TESTAMENT VISION TEXTS

Because we are working with a scenario based on a conjecture (picking up the discussion in ch. 1), we cannot advance the argument simply by citing isolated texts as "evidence" without incurring the charge of circular reasoning. It is precisely the selection and meaning of such texts that is in question. The most we can do here is to build on the plausible notion that New Testament communities performed their visionary traditions (defended in chs. 1–3) and then to point out features of various New Testament texts that likely reflect such performances. The value of the conjecture is found in its fruitfulness for adding depth and coherence to otherwise disparate features of the texts.

If there are such texts in the New Testament, we can assume that the performances and discussions they reflect occurred decades later than the "historical" events they describe. In technical terms, the horizon of each text is synchronic: it is based on narratives and performances as they were known in the community that produced them. Nonetheless, they were not created out of nothing. In most cases, they reshaped earlier narratives and performances, largely (but not exclusively) stored in the memories and imaginations of the community, and put to work to serve the current needs of its members. In short, we cannot expect our texts to address all of our historical questions but, like changing technologies today (examples of which were cited in ch. 1), they may still retain relics of earlier usages that can be identified by the discerning reader—hence the role of pre-understanding. In each case we examine, therefore, we should be able to identify the rehearsal of a received (mental) script and also to identify some of the alterations that adapted it to new contexts and demands.

What are some likely candidates for texts that might reflect Kyriocentric visions? They obviously include descriptions of "Christophanies" (standard theophanies reworked using Jesus/Christ language), particularly the ones in Acts and Revelation that appear to come out of nowhere as far as the narrative is concerned (e.g., Acts 9:3-6 and parallels; 22:17-21; Rev. 1:10-20). At first sight, the Gospels might not seem to be a likely source because they are narratives about Jesus. Everything has been fitted into a life-death-resurrection schema, and any "revelations" that were not originally part of that master plot have long since been reworked—as a result of the Lord-Jesus identification. As described in chapter 4, however, there is an equal and opposite reaction whereby the gospel narratives often take on characteristics of the Kyriocentric visions. Even in the Gospels, therefore, one should consider texts that use typical visionary words like "glory" (*doxa*), "vision" (*optasia*), and "seeing" or "beholding" (*oraō/ ōphthēn/ eidon* and *theaomai*), particularly in those cases where these are used in combination with each other and associated with the title *kyrios* (Mark 6:49-50, Luke 9:32; Acts 9:17, 27; John 1:14; 12:41; 17:24; 20:18, 20; cf. 1 Cor. 9:1; 2 Cor. 3:18; 12:1).

Our objective of this chapter is not exhaustively to review all of this evidence, as we should be if we were taking a purely inductive approach. The point I wish to make is that New Testament visionary texts can be read more strongly if viewed through a different lens—one that begins with apostolic visions centered in the God of Israel, rather than encounters with a glorified human being (although these too may have occurred[1]). In accordance with this Kyriocentric vision scenario, our working assumption is that the repeated performance of Kyriocentric visions morphed into visions of the Lord with a voice and a form that were recognized as those of Jesus (*Kyrios Iēsous*). These Kyriocentric (now understood as being Jesu-centric) visions continued to be rehearsed in various ways, and they had to be adapted to what was recalled about the life, the teachings, and the violent death of the teacher.

These adaptations will be studied in more detail in chapter 7, but it will help to preview them here because they will intrude into the discussion already in this and the following chapter. On the basis of the Kyriocentric vision conjecture, we can predict that several tensions would arise. Audiences who were familiar with the story of Jesus (and not having the benefit of the church's later teachings) would have had lots of questions:

- How could a dead man be the anthropic form of the living God?
- How could this Lord God be Jesus, when Jesus himself was "remembered" to have prayed to God in heaven (Luke 10:21; 11:2, passim [Q])?
- When and how did the eternal Lord become Jesus (or vice versa)?
- How do we deal with the jarring inference that the eternal Lord died on a cross?

These questions would have arisen immediately in the wake of the Lord-Jesus identification. They no doubt occasioned a variety of creative responses (to be detailed in ch. 7), and the scripts and performances for Kyriocentric visions must have changed accordingly. The question is whether the New Testament texts that date from decades later look anything like what we might expect as the result of such a conflicted process. In a handful of cases, they do, as we shall see.

INTRODUCING SIX REPRESENTATIVE VISIONARY TEXTS

I shall focus on six candidate texts, restrict myself to one in any given corpus, and refer to a few more supporting texts of the same corpus in passing. One candidate text comes from Paul's epistles, one each from the (Synoptic) Gospels of Mark and Luke, one from the Acts of the Apostles, one from the Revelation of John, and one from the Gospel of John.[2] Extensive studies have already been done on each of these texts. It is sufficient for our purposes here to point out features that plausibly refer to, or even originate in, performances of a Kyriocentric vision. Before discussing the texts individually, I shall summarize the results in a table and handle some technical matters in footnotes.

Table 3 lists these six texts (in approximate chronological order), briefly summarizes their contents, and lists the quotations and allusions[3] to Kyriocentric visions (citing the text of the Greek Septuagint) that are rehearsed in these texts.[4] Old Testament texts with asterisks are ones that are noted in the footnotes of the United Bible Society edition of the Greek text. From a scholar's (etic) perspective, these parallels may look like "intertextual" citations, but, as explained in chapter 1, in their original context (emically), they simply reflected the joint reception of a variety of known visionary motifs in communal performances. As David Rhoads has described New Testament performances, the transmission of texts did not go from one manuscript to another, the way we view them, but rather from one audience and reception to another.[5] These Old Testament citations are *inter-performative* rather than intertextual.

Table 3: Kyriocentric visions in New Testament texts and their scriptural models

New Testament Text with Relevant Phrases	Kyriocentric Vision Models (Septuagint version) Asterisks indicate UBS citations
1 Cor. 9:1-2 (Paul justifies his apostleship on the basis of his having seen the Lord Jesus): *ton kyrion eoraka* *apostolos . . . moutēs apostolēs*	 Isa. 6:1, 5 (*eidon ton kyrion*);[6] Amos 9:1 (*eidon ton kyrion*); cf. Job 42:5 (*eōrake se*) Isa. 6:8-9 (*aposteilō, apostelon me*); Jer. 1:7 (*exaposteilō se*); Ezek. 2:3 (*exapostellō se*)[7]
Mark 6:48b-50 (the disciples see a ghostly human form walking on the stormy sea; as it passes by, they cry out and then hear the "I am" and "Fear not," whereupon the storm ceases): *peripatōn epi tēs thalassēs* *parelthein autous* *idontes auton . . . auton eidan* *anekraxan . . . etarachthēsan*	 Job 9:8 (*peripatōn epi thalassēs*)[8] Job 9:11 (*parelthē mē*); cf. Exod. 33:19 (*parelouromia*); 34:6 (*parelthē Kyrios*); 1 Kgs. 19:11 (*pareluesetai Kyrios*) Isa. 6:1, 5 (*eidon ton kyrion*); Amos 9:1 (*eidon ton kyrion*) Ps. 107:27-28 (*etarachthēsan . . . ekekraxan pros Kyrion*)

egō eimi	Exod. 3:13-15 (*egō eimi ho ōn*);[9] Isa. 41:4, 43:10b, 11, passim (*egō eimi*)
mē phobeisthe	Isa. 41:10; 43:1-2a, 5 (*mē phobou*)[10]
ekopasen ho anemos	Ps. 107:29 (*esigēsan ta kumata*)
Luke 9:28-36 (together with Moses and Elijah, Peter, James, and John see the Glory and enter the cloud):	
sunelaloun autō . . . en doxē	Exod. 34:29b (*dedoxasatai . . . lalein autō*)
eidon tēn doxan autou	Num. 12:8 LXX (*tēn doxan kyriou eide*); Deut. 5:24 (*eidexen hēmin . . . tēn doxan autou*); Isa. 6:1, 3, 5 (*eidon ton kyrion . . . tēs doxēs autou*)
eiselthein autous eis tēn nephelēn	Exod. 24:18a LXX (*eisēlthe Mōusēs eis to mesen tēs nephelēs*)
Acts 9:3-6; 22:6-10; 26:12-16 (within a blinding light Saul sees the Lord, who identifies himself as Jesus and commissions him):	
"brighter than the sun"	1 Enoch 14:2 "shining more brightly than the sun"[12]
"fallen to the ground"	Ezek. 1:28c "I fell on my face"
	1 Enoch 14:15, 24 "I fell on my face"
ēkoúosa phōnēn légousan	Deut. 5:24 (*tēn phōnēn ēkoúosamen*)
	Ezek. 1:28c (*ēkoúosa phōnēn laloúntos*)
"Saul, Saul"	Gen. 22:11-12 "Abraham, Abraham" (the Angel of YHWH[13])
	Exod. 3:4 "Moses, Moses"

	1 Sam. 3:10 "Samuel, Samuel"
"I am Jesus . . ."[11]	Exod. 3:6 "I am the God of your father . . ."
stēthi epi tous podas sou "to appoint you" (*procheirisasthai se*)	Ezek. 2:1* (*stēthi epi tous podas sou*) Jer. 1:5 "I appointed you" (*tetheika se*)
"from your people and the Gentiles to whom . . ." (*ek tou laou kai ek ethnōn eis hous*) "I am sending you . . . ." (*apostellō se*)	Jer. 1:5 (*eis ethnē*) Ezek. 2:3 (*pros ton oikon Israēl*) Jer. 1:7* (*exaposteilō se*) Ezek. 2:3 (*exapostellō se*)
Rev. 1:10, 12–18 (while "in the spirit," John hears the voice and sees an anthropic form):[14] 1:10b–11 "I heard behind me a loud voice like a trumpet saying [*ēkousa . . . phōnēn . . . legousēs*]."	Ezek. 1:25 "And there came a voice [*phōnē*] from above the dome."[16] Ezek. 1:28c ᴷ "I heard the voice of someone speaking [*ēkousa phōnēn lalountos*]."[17]
1:13a "in the midst of the [seven] lampstands I saw one . . ."	Zech. 4:2 "I see a lampstand . . . seven lamps . . . the eyes of the Lord."[18]
1:13b ". . . one like a son of man [*homoion huion anthrōpou*] . . ."[15]	Ezek. 1:26ᴷ "something like a human form [*homoiōma hōs eidos anthrōpou*]"
1:14a "his head and his hair were white like white wool, white like snow" [*hē kephalē autou kai hai triches leukai hōs herion, leukon hōs chiōn*].	Dan. 7:9* (the Ancient One's clothing was white as snow [*leukon chōrei chiōn*], and the hair of his head like pure wool

1:15b ("his voice like the sound [*hē phōnē . . . ōs phōnē*] of many waters").	[*hē trix tēs kephalēs autou hōsei herion katharon*]).[19] Ezek. 1:24* (the living creatures sound like the sound [*tēn phōnēn . . . hōs phōnēn*] of mighty waters, like the thunder of Shaddai [not in the lxx]). Ezek. 43:2* (the coming of the Glory of God sounds like [*hē phōnē . . . hōs phōnē*] mighty waters).
1:17a "When I saw him, I fell [*hote eidon auton epesa*] at his feet. . ."	Ezek. 1:28c [K] "When I saw it, I fell [*idon kai píptō*] on my face."
John 12:41 Isaiah saw Christ's glory (*eiden tēn doxan autou*)	Isa. 6:1, 3 Isaiah saw YHWH (*eidon ton Kyrion*), whose robe filled the Temple and whose glory filled the earth.

The three Gospel narratives cited here are told in the third person (the authors being separated from the events they describe by decades). The other three texts are all narrated in the first person singular. As in the apocalyptic vision texts discussed in chapter 2, this dramatic feature could well have aided the communities' efforts to relive the visionary experiences described.

Let us look at the texts individually in order to identify some specific visionary motifs and practices.

Paul's Initiatory Vision as Described in 1 Corinthians 9

Paul's epistles have quite a few references to his visions of the Lord Jesus, all of which have been well covered in scholarly literature (the difficulties of interpreting 2 Cor. 12:1 were already discussed in ch. 1). Here I shall treat just one of these, 1 Corinthians 9:1-2, which, chronologically speaking, is the earliest reference to a Kyriocentric vision that we have in the New Testament.

Because of the laconic nature of Paul's writing here, it is helpful to look at the exact wording:

> Am I not an apostle? Have I not seen Jesus our Lord [*Iēsoun ton kyrion hēmōn eoraka*]? Are you not my work in the Lord? If I am not an apostle to others, at least I am to you; for you are the seal of my apostleship in the Lord. (1 Cor. 9:1-2)

Typically, Paul assumes that the leaders of the churches he is addressing know what he is talking about (based on earlier interchanges) and can interpret his words to others in their churches. Evidently, his revelatory visions had been the topic of many of his own sermons and other performances at Corinth (1 Cor. 2:6-13; 12:3; 2 Cor. 3:15-18 2; 12:1).

Paul's language here is clearly visionary—he had never seen Jesus in the flesh (Gal. 1:11-12, 15).[20] The Kyriocentric nature of the vision he describes is indicated by the combination of the verb *to see* (*orao*) with the title *Lord* (*ho kyrios*). It is inconceivable that a biblically literate Jew like Paul would use this combination without consciously intending to recall the Kyriocentric visions of prophets like Isaiah and Amos, the Septuagint version of which were couched in exactly the same terms (as shown in Table 3).[21]

Based on our treatment of performative visions in chapters 1 and 2, we may infer that the early Paul (then known as Saul) had been trained in the rehearsal of these prophetic visions, probably as a member of an apocalyptic conventicle of Pharisees. In writing 1 Corinthians 9, therefore, he was recalling a time when one of those rehearsals had refocused itself as the very man whose followers he had been persecuting. Our reading is supported by the fact that 1 Corinthians 9:1-2 includes the ideas of apostleship and mission just like the classic Kyriocentric visions (Exod. 3:10; Isa. 6:8-9; Jer. 1:7-10; Ezek. 2:3; *1 En.* 15:2). It is far more likely that Paul inherited this cluster of motifs from Jewish traditions concerning the praxis of prayer and vision (discussed in ch. 3), than that he patched it together while his mind was focused on challenges to his ministry in Corinth.[22]

From an historical viewpoint, this Kyriocentric scenario is fairly plausible: Paul certainly did belong to a pietist sect of Pharisees (Gal. 1:14; Phil. 3:5). He was familiar with visionary imagery from the Old Testament and the *Book of Enoch* ("visions of the Lord" in 2 Cor. 12:1; "the Lord of glory" in 1 Cor. 2:8[23]). In short, the rehearsal of Kyriocentric visions could very well have been part of Paul's devotional life, as it was for the "ancient pious ones" (*hasidim rishonim*) described by the Rabbis in the Mishnah (*m. Ber.* 5:1, discussed in ch. 2).

A note of caution is also in order, however. Historically speaking, the least likely step in this reconstruction is the one in which one of his rehearsals refocused itself as the voice and form of the man Jesus. In the case of Jesus' immediate disciples, already discussed in chapter 4, such identification could plausibly have happened as Kyriocentric visions were rehearsed soon after his execution—the disciples certainly remembered what Jesus looked like and could recognize his voice, and they very likely were engaged in urgent petitionary prayer for the coming of the Lord. Paul had never seen Jesus in the flesh, however, and he certainly did not mourn his violent death as the disciples did. The scenario we have constructed does not run so smoothly here.

There are various ways to deal with this problem. If Saul's moment of recognition was not the result of personal acquaintance with the voice and face of Jesus, perhaps his vision was initially incomprehensible to him and only took on focus when he interrogated one of the disciples who had experienced (or performed) similar visions (cf. Acts 9:17 on Ananias and a storyline similar to Philip's informing the Ethiopian eunuch in 8:30). This possibility would be consistent with Paul's repeated admission that his own visions were only partial and dim or enigmatic (1 Cor. 13:12; 2 Cor. 3:18; cf. Num. 12:8). This possibility would have to be squared with Paul's vehement avowal that he did not receive his gospel message from any human source (Gal. 1:12), but one might conclude, in the latter case, that he protested a little too much.

Alternatively, Saul's moment of recognition might have been based on an imaginal figure that Saul had formed in his mind as he investigated the gatherings of Jesus' followers (cf. Acts 9:1-2). If he knew of their intense prayer life, it is also possible that he ratcheted up his own in order to prepare for the planned confrontation—a confrontation that was then preempted by the Kyriocentric vision. In the absence of any clear textual support for these speculations, however, we may have to follow the lead of Larry Hurtado and classify Paul's initiatory vision as an inexplicable "mutation."[24]

Paul himself, no doubt, would rather have spoken of this mutation in terms of the unmerited grace of God (Gal. 1:15-16). It was as if a veil had been covering his face, and he could only see the divine glory as Moses, Isaiah, Ezekiel, and Enoch had seen it. Then, suddenly, the veil was removed, and he could see the divine light "in the face," or "in the person," of Jesus (2 Cor. 3:12-18; 4:6).[25] In the last analysis, we can only agree with the Apostle, that he saw what he saw as though reflected in a "mirror of enigmas" (1 Cor. 13:12; 2 Cor. 3:18; cf. Lev. R. 1:14).

THE SEA THEOPHANY IN MARK 6

There are clear echoes of Kyriocentric vision performances in the Synoptic Gospels. It is true that Luke (and Matthew) stressed the tangible, physical nature of the resurrection body of Jesus, but Mark, probably the earliest of the four Gospels, is the least emphatic of the Synoptics in this regard. If the initial steps in deity Christology were rooted in visionary experiences, as argued here, it stands to reason that the imaginal or spiritual nature of these experiences would be advocated in some circles and that pro-resurrection traditions like those in Matthew and Luke would need to counter these views with accounts of the bodily nature of the risen Lord (discussed further in ch. 7).

The first six chapters of Mark are laced with "Yahweh texts,"[26] many of which are thought to go back to a pre-Markan source.[27] According to the scenario we have sketched out, the presence of these deity motifs was not due to intertextual citations, motivated by some theological agenda. It was simply the result of the Lord-Jesus identification and the consequent superposition of two portraits of Jesus: coming Lord and beloved hasid (further discussed in ch. 7). As a result, proclamations and narratives concerning Jesus had taken on characteristics of Kyriocentric visions long before the Gospels were composed.

A particularly dense cluster of these "Yahweh texts" is found in the account of the Lord walking on the waves of the sea in Mark 6, which reads exactly like the performance of an Old Testament style theophany (Mark 6:48b–51). As noted in Table 3, the Gospel draws upon motifs found in Psalm 107 and Job 9—both of which reflect situations of deep despair (Ps. 107:13, "they cried to the Lord in their trouble"; Job 9:15, "I must appeal for mercy")—as well as the more familiar divine utterances of Exodus and Deutero-Isaiah (*egō eimi*). In the language of oral performance theory, these motifs serve as "special formulas" that direct the attention of the audience to imagine a theophanic context.[28] As we found in our discussion of apocalyptic visions in chapter 3, it seems more likely that these motifs gradually accumulated in successive performance (inter-performatively) than that the author of the Gospel (Markan or pre-Markan) somehow managed to call them all to mind and weave them together so seamlessly.

As audiences listened to Mark's narrative unfold, they knew that the numinous figure walking toward the disciples was Jesus. In fact, the writer had told us that Jesus was praying on a nearby mountain when he saw his disciples out on the sea and decided to walk out toward them (Mark 6:46–48a). Once the surreal sea-walking part begins, however, the name of Jesus is not even mentioned. In terms of the narrative, there was no need for it. In terms of oral performance, however, the combination of "Yahweh texts" and the absence of any name nicely fit the Kyriocentric vision conjecture.

Significantly, the appearance of the numinous figure occurs late at night (6:48)—the prototypical time for divine visions (e.g., Gen. 15:17-21; the "Song of the Four Nights" discussed below). As noted in the table, it is introduced by the typically theophanic term *parelthein* ("to pass by," 6:48)[29] and framed by repeated use of the verb *oraō* ("to see," 6:49-50), which was the standard Greek equivalent of the Hebrew theophanic verb, *ra'ah*.[30] The appearance is referred to as an "apparition" or a "phantasm" (*phantasma*), a potentially "docetic" feature of the narrative that Matthew, Luke, and John would later spin down, each in their own way.[31] If, as I suppose, this narrative reflects performances of Old Testament theophanies in the Markan community, the leader of the performance must have assumed the persona of the Psalmist[32] (or possibly Moses?[33]) and identified the divine object of their Kyriocentric visions as the Lord Jesus.

THE TRANSFIGURATION OF JESUS ACCORDING TO LUKE 9

The Gospel of Luke is particularly insistent concerning the physical nature of Jesus' resurrection body (Luke 23:55; 24:3, 12, 39-43; cf. Acts 1:9-11). So it is not surprising that postmortem encounters with the Lord Jesus are not described in visionary terms in the Gospel itself (cf. Luke 24:23 on a "vision of angels"). It appears, however, that this Gospel (and the performance tradition it reflects) was acquainted with the standard features of Kyriocentric visions. I infer this connection from the fact that Luke modified Mark's account of the transfiguration of Jesus (Mark 9:2-8) with "special Lukan" material that connects the narrative to the practice of prayer and incorporates standard theophanic features (Luke 9:28-36).[34]

A few of these theophanic features are as follows. Luke specifies that the disciples' experience was centered in the glory of the Lord Jesus (*tēn doxan autou*, 9:32)—a standard theophany motif best known from the visions of Moses and Isaiah (Num. 12:8 LXX; Deut. 5:24; Isa. 6:1-3[35]). As in these well-known theophanies, Luke's unique version uses the aorist *eidon*, the verb commonly used in the Greek Septuagint for beholding the glory of YHWH in anthropic (humanlike) form (9:32; cf. Acts 9:27).[36] In view of the fact that Moses was seen (together with Elijah), talking with the Lord Jesus (*synelaloun autō*), the parallel to the Septuagint of Numbers 12:8 is particularly striking. There too the Lord spoke with Moses and appeared to him in glory (*lalēsō autō en eidei kai . . . tēn doxan kyriou eide*, Num. 12:8 LXX). In Luke's narrative, therefore,

Moses was a Christian prophet, one who had known the Lord Jesus all along, and the disciples were now standing on the very same mountain, entering the same numinous cloud, and seeing the same glorious form that Moses had (9:30b, 34b; cf. Exod. 24:15-18; 33:18, 21-23; *Jub.* 1:2-3; cf. 1 Kgs. 19:11). A rehearsal of the Sinai theophanies by a pre-Christian community whose leader assumed the persona of Moses was the deep structure underlying these special Lukan features.[37] For followers of Jesus, of course, the Lord at the center of the vision was Jesus, here transfigured, and the persona of Moses was supplemented (or replaced) by that of Peter as the leading protagonist, the one whose proposal evokes a heavenly voice (9:32, 33, 35).[38] This Christianized performance would have been one of a number of traditions that Mark and Luke (and Matthew) inherited from Petrine sources.[39]

It is particularly significant that Luke's narrative places the transfiguration at night (9:32; cf. 22:45).[40] As noted in the case of Mark 6, theophanies were known to have occurred at night in the Old Testament (e.g., Gen. 15:12-21). An exegetical tradition cited in the Palestinian Targumim locates the pivotal manifestations of the Lord at nighttime.[41] In fact, there are said to be four such occasions, beginning with the moment of creation (Gen. 1:2-3), "when the Lord was revealed" (*Tg. Neof.* Exod. 12:42), and concluding with the eschaton, when a new exodus will be led by Moses and the Messiah with the Word (or Glory) of the Lord leading between the two of them.[42] If our reading is correct, then Luke's version of the transfiguration would comfortably fit within these roughly contemporary traditions.[43] By splicing the theophany motifs into Mark's account of the transfiguration (where the role of Moses was already set) and adding a reference to the exodus that Jesus was about to accomplish in Jerusalem (9:28a, 31, 37), the Gospel writer skillfully blended the visionary material of his tradition into the narrative of Jesus' life. Other readings of Luke 9 are certainly possible (new Moses, promised Messiah, etc.), and there is no need to exclude them (as we shall see in ch. 7), but this Kyriocentric reading has the advantage of explaining many of the special Lukan features of the narrative.[44]

If this interpretation is valid, it points to a visionary performance in the Lukan community, rehearsed in the name of Peter, in which the Lord appeared in the form of Jesus, accompanied by two angelified prophets (cf. Isa. 6:1-3). While the vision was still Kyriocentric, a role was set aside for God the Father in accordance with the Synoptic model (Luke 9:35; cf. Mark 9:7), which was based, in turn, on the tradition of Jesus praying to his Father in heaven (Mark 14:36; passim). Implicitly, therefore, the vision was binitarian (cf. 3:21-22).[45] We will discuss the reasons for this significant alteration of the Old Testament theophany in chapter 7.

Paul's Initiatory Vision according to Acts

With this background in the Gospel, Luke's three distinct versions of Paul's Damascus Road vision in the Acts of the Apostles are also worthy of discussion (Acts 9:3-6; 22:6-10; 26:12-16).[46] While the "historicity" of Acts can be questioned on many points, we can assume that the descriptions of Paul's visions were consistent with traditions about Paul as they were rehearsed in the Lukan community.[47] Variation among the three accounts simply reflects the fluidity in the storyline that we expect from oral performances.[48] It is not likely that they were merely literary devices of the writer (the issue we discussed in ch. 2 concerning apocalyptic visions).[49] As in the Gospel of Luke, however, there are some obvious literary features that adapt the visionary material to suit the purposes of the overall narrative, for example, in the way visionary accounts are spliced together with the story of Ananias in Acts 9 and 22. For simplicity, therefore, I shall primarily work with the account in Acts 26, which is closer to Paul's own account (Gal. 1:11-17) both in being narrated in the first person and in lacking the Ananias sequel. Still, the same basic points could be made from any one of the three accounts in Acts.[50]

The account of Saul's vision in Acts 26 is told in the first person as was standard with the Kyriocentric visions in apocalyptic literature (see Table 1 in ch. 2). As it stands, the account is a typical example of the "vision-dialogue form" (*Erscheinungsgespräch Gattung*). This type of narrative, familiar from both Hebrew Bible and apocalyptic theophanies, was a script that consisted of four basic features:[51]

(1) The heavenly Lord appears on the scene and opens with a double vocative (here "Saul, Saul," 26:14)—other examples of which we have encountered in previous chapters.[52]

(2) The human recipient takes fright and wonders what is happening (here Saul falls to the ground and asks, "Who are you, Lord?").

(3) The heavenly Lord identifies himself with a "presentation formula" (here "I am Jesus")—this formula is often couched in terms of previous history (e.g., Gen. 31:13, "I am the God Bethel"; Gen. 26:24, "I am the God of your father Abraham").

(4) The speaker commissions the recipient to a task ("I appoint you to serve and testify," 26:16).[53]

These phrases are probably not Paul's own very words regarding his Damascus Road experience (Acts was written several decades after his martyrdom), but they likely represent the terms in which Paul's vision was rehearsed in the communities that were familiar with Paul's story (see above on 1 Cor. 9:1)—at least, in the communities with which Luke was familiar. In terms of oral-performance theory, we may read the basic features of the vision-dialogue as "mnemonic cues" for those who led liturgical re-enactments of the vision while assuming the persona of Paul.[54] Instead of reading a text (the way the Scriptures are read in synagogues and churches), the lead performer would rely on mental cues like these in order to recall the details of the dialogue and rehearse them in a recognizable order.[55] Unfortunately, our text says nothing about "Paul" calling on the Lord in an attitude of prayer (as in our standard scenario), but other Pauline visions in the book of Acts suggest that such a liturgical setting could be assumed (Acts 22:17-18).

THE INAUGURAL VISION IN REVELATION 1

A remarkably similar vision account occurs in the first chapter of the Revelation of John, which, like the transfiguration in Luke 9, is set in the context of eschatological expectation and the offering of prayer ("Look! He is coming . . . I was in the spirit on the Lord's day," Rev. 1:7, 10a; cf. 3:20; 22:20).[56] Intertextual aspects of the Apocalypticist's inaugural vision have been analyzed by scholars with results oscillating among the options of deity Christology, archangel Christology, and a Danielic "Son of Man" Christology.[57]

As many commentators have noted, the overlapping of a diversity of traditions incorporated does not imply inconsistency of intent.[58] As we saw in chapter 2, motifs from a variety of visionary traditions could coalesce into a single performance (inter-performatively). In the case at hand, the addition of Son of Man and Great Angel motifs (particularly from the visions in Dan. 7 and 10) can be understood as a way of meshing the inaugural vision with later visions that describe the Lamb alongside the enthroned Deity.[59] These latter, binitarian visions had themselves been formulated (according to our scenario) as a way of ensuring consistency with traditions about Jesus praying to God his Father, as in the case of Luke 9 (discussed above).[60] Evidently, efforts to achieve theological consistency in performance and proclamation began already in the first century, long before the theologians and councils of later times.[61]

Since our present goal is simply to evaluate a conjecture by testing its implications over as wide a range of textual material as possible, it will be sufficient to show the plausibility of the Kyriocentric origin of the inaugural vision without being obliged to negate other layers of meaning.[62] The intertextual (or rather inter-performative) references to the Kyriocentric vision in Ezekiel 1 alone (shown in Table 3) are enough to make that case. Historically speaking, it is easier to explain how such direct identifications could have been toned down by subsequent "angelomorphic" references than it is to explain the rise of deity Christology from such binitarian traditions by themselves.[63]

A further argument for the Kyriocentric vision reading can be made if scholars like Jan Fekkes and Steve Moyise are correct in thinking that the Apocalypticist identified himself with the prophet Ezekiel.[64] This identification can be seen not just in the intertextual material but also in the style of presentation, particularly in the repeated use of the qualifiers, "as" (hōs) and "like" (hōmios), which protect the hiddenness of the Deity just as they do in performances of Ezekiel 1 (Rev. 1:10, 13-15; cf. Ezek. 1:26-27). Whereas these scholars are thinking in terms of a single prophet or visionary, however, I find it more realistic to think in terms of a community performance under the leadership of the Apocalypticist (or a succession of apocalypticists), in which the prophet Ezekiel was the principal model to be emulated.[65]

In any case, Ezekiel was now a Christian prophet just like Moses in Luke's transfiguration account. Isaiah was another prophet who, according to the early disciples, knew the Lord Jesus. For that piece we turn to our last representative text, this one from the Gospel of John.

Isaiah's Vision according to John 12

The Gospel of John is often said to exhibit the most developed or "highest" Christology of all the New Testament documents.[66] This familiar picture should be modified from the perspective of the Kyriocentric vision conjecture we have developed here. The christological affirmations of John resonate with echoes of the practice of Kyriocentric visions, but they are not consistently "higher" than what we have already seen in the Synoptic Gospels.[67] For example, the vision of the Lord walking on the waves (earlier attested in Mark 6; Matt. 14) is also found in John in what appears to be an independent performance (John 6:16-21).[68]

John also includes several visionary motifs that are not found in the other Gospels. Clear examples occur in the prologue (1:14, "we have seen his glory"),[69] in Jesus' "high-priestly prayer" (17:24, "to see my glory"), and in the intermediate chapters (e.g., 6:40, "all who see the Son and believe in him"; cf. 8:56; 9:35-38; 14:18-23). Such visionary motifs even occur in Johannine narratives of resurrection appearances (esp. John 20:18, "I have seen the Lord"; 20:20, "they saw the Lord"), in spite of the fact that John stressed the physical nature of Jesus' resurrection body just as much as Matthew and Luke did.[70]

What is most revealing from the perspective of an oral performance scenario is John's claim in 12:40-41 that the glory Isaiah saw in the Temple

(Isa. 6:1-5) was the Lord Jesus.[71] This identification is clearly indicated in context by a voice from heaven (the Father's) that promises to glorify Jesus (here titled the "Son of Man") as he had been glorified in the past (12:23, 28; cf. 17:5). Immediately following this announcement, John cites the commission that YHWH gave to Isaiah to harden the hearts of the people (John 12:40; cf. Isa. 6:10)—the citation here looks like a loose paraphrase as we would expect in an oral performance (parallel to the citation in Mark 4:12). Finally, John adds the comment that Isaiah "saw his glory and spoke of him" (Isa. 6:1-6; cf. *Tg. Isa.* ad loc.[72]).

If we may take the contemporary *Ascension of Isaiah* as a fair parallel, we may infer that the Johannine version assumes the existence of a conventicle in which the vision of Isaiah served as the principal model for visionary practices (*Ascen. Isa.* 6:3-16, discussed in ch. 2).[73] The performance assumed was clearly Kyriocentric—it probably included the angelic *Kedushah* or *Sanctus* ("Holy, holy, holy," Isa. 6:3) and directed it to the Lord Jesus[74]—but, as in Luke 9 and Revelation 1 (discussed above), the Lord-Jesus identification was adapted to conform to Jesus' teachings about the Father.[75] If John's Christology was not higher than what we find in other parts of the New Testament, it was far more creative in its binitarian constructions (Logos, Son of Man, *Shekinah*/Glory, name of the Father). If anything, John was more insistent on the primacy of the Father than earlier Gospels had been (John 1:14, 18; 5:19-24; passim). Over the course of the first century, Christology appears to have been getting somewhat lower (rather than higher, as is often assumed).

SUMMARY OF THE ARGUMENT FOR KYRIOCENTRIC VISIONS IN THE NEW TESTAMENT CHURCHES

Is there convincing evidence of the performance of Kyriocentric visions in the New Testament? Probably not, if we confine ourselves to eking out the context from the texts themselves. All of the writings examined here are amenable to other interpretations, as they should be, given the fact that they are embedded in larger epistolary, narrative, and apocalyptic schemas that were designed to address more immediate concerns. A study that focuses on any one of these writings in its immediate context, oblivious to the dilemma of early deity Christology (identity of the God of Israel with Jesus), might reach very different conclusions.

My argument to the contrary is based on a certainty. We can be sure that the writing and reading of the New Testament documents, as important as it is for present-day purposes, was only a small part of the life of the early church, most of which had to do with the regular practice of worship and service.[76] The New Testament texts provide the starting point without which we would have nothing to go on, but they have to be viewed as chips from a much larger block of praxis, and not reified as though they tell us everything we need to know about emergent Christianity.

One of the main features of this larger block was deity Christology—it is found in all strata of the New Testament, sometimes qualified by binitarian constructs, but often not (e.g., 1 Thess. 3:13; Mark 6:28-50; Luke 13:34 [Q]; Matt. 14:40). Strictly inductive approaches have considerable difficulty in accounting for the occurrence of deity Christology in such early strata, which are generally supposed to be dominated by Jewish beliefs and practices. The result is a dilemma. Which are we to give up: clear evidence for the divine identity of Jesus in the New Testament, or the Jewish origins of early Christology?

The best way to resolve this dilemma is to shift the focus from the theology and exegesis of the texts to the worship and service in which they were written and read. We must suppose that the unqualified ascriptions of deity (identity of the God of Israel with Jesus) were rooted in the monotheistic (or henotheistic) practices of Judaism and later adapted to accord with traditions about Jesus in relation to his heavenly Father. In this study I have tried to show that assuming the occurrence of Kyriocentric visions in the context of liturgical performances among the early followers of Yeshua can account not only for the immediate rise of deity Christology but also for visionary traditions that we find in New Testament texts ranging from Paul and Mark to the Apocalypse (Revelation) and the Gospel of John.

As far as we know, this concrete identification of the God of Israel with a revered teacher is unique in the history of Judaism. Even though this uniqueness is foundational for Christian theology, however, it may be fortuitous from a strictly historical point of view. Where else in the vast literature of Judaism do we find Kyriocentric visions occurring immediately following the violent death of a teacher who was believed by his followers to mediate the divine presence?

Even though the New Testament contains unqualified statements of the identity of the God of Israel with Jesus (the focus of our attention so far), it also contains a variety of qualifications of this identification (Son of God, Son of Man, Word, etc.). We need to determine whether the Kyriocentric vision conjecture can account for these qualifications, and we shall do so in chapter 7. Before doing so, however, we should say more about the prayers and devotional forms in the context of which Kyriocentric visions were most often rehearsed. As we saw in chapter 3, these prayers ranged from petitions for salvation to blessing and benediction for divine intervention. If the identification of the Lord with Jesus occurred in this performative context, we should expect these prayers and their terminology to carry over to the worship of the Lord Jesus in the New Testament church (a further test of our conjecture). We must also consider the possibility that some prayers and devotional forms were dedicated to God the Father. In the following chapter, we review the evidence for both continuity in the case of the Lord Jesus and also some apparent limits to such worship.

Notes

1. N. T. Wright and others would argue that there were independent traditions about encounters with the glorified Jesus. That may be true, but it is not necessary to appeal to such traditions for our purposes, and we can leave them out for simplicity. Rehearsals of Kyriocentric visions could have morphed into stories about the risen Jesus once the identification of YHWH/Adonai and Jesus was established and the narrative of Jesus' life and death was extended to incorporate postmortem events. The issue of independent traditions is indeterminate for the purposes of this study.

2. The three most obvious lacunae here are Hebrews, James, and the Petrine epistles, the first and third of which will be discussed in ch. 9 (Movement 1). Hebrews models its visions of the Lord on the high priest's entry into the holy of holies on Yom Kippur, but also transfers the sanctuary from Jerusalem to heaven (Heb. 9:24; 10:19-22; 12:22-24).

3. In terms of oral-performance theory, quotations and allusions are two distinct ways in which traditions could be handled—what Martin Jaffee calls "dual-track oral tradition." "Fixed texts" (quotations) were memorized and quoted word for word (with slightly varying degrees of constancy). "Free texts" (allusions) were likewise stored in memory, but in a more malleable form, based on mnemonic cues, and were more creatively performed; Martin Jaffee, "Oral Tradition in the Writings of Rabbinic Oral Torah: On Theorizing Rabbinic Orality," *Oral Tradition* 14 (1999): 3–32 (24, 26). In relation to Talmud and midrash, Jaffee describes a mixed model: free text material was associated with a fixed text like a Scripture verse or a Mishnah text (ibid., 250). The way Jesus' disciples performed their visions (and other material) would be something like this mixed model, except that the two kinds of text would interpenetrate more thoroughly than in the exegetical setting of a Rabbinic house of study; see ch. 7.

4. Although the earliest oral performances were undoubtedly rehearsed in some combination of Hebrew and Aramaic, the New Testament texts are (largely) in Greek, and the Septuagint provides the best verbal comparison. In fact, the original Hebrew may in some cases have been closer in substance to the LXX than to the Masoretic text on which traditional English translations of the Hebrew Bible are based. Each case must be examined on its own merits.

5. David Rhoads, "Performance Criticism: An Emerging Methodology in Second Testament Studies—Part II," *BTB* 36 (2006): 124a.

6. On the use of Isa. 6:1, 8 in 1 Cor. 9:1, see Seyoon Kim, *The Origin of Paul's Gospel*, WUNT 4 (Tübingen: Mohr Siebeck, 1981; Grand Rapids, Eerdmans, 1982), 94; Kim, *Paul and the New Perspective: Second Thoughts on the Origin of Paul's Gospel* (Grand Rapids: Eerdmans, 2002), 241. Christian performances of the vision described in Isa. 6 are also found in the *Ascension of Isaiah* (late first or early second cent.).

7. On Paul's understanding of his vision and call in terms of Ezekiel's classic vision, see, for example, Gordon Fee, *Pauline Christology: An Exegetical-Theological Study* (Peabody, MA: Hendrickson, 2007), 194.

8. The recollection of Job 9:8, 11 in Mark 6:48-49 has been discussed by scholars including William L. Lane, *Gospel According to Mark*, NICNT (Grand Rapids: Eerdmans, 1974), 236–37; H. Ritt, "Der 'Seewandel Jesu' (Mk 6, 45-52 par), Literarische und theologische Aspekte," *BZ* 23 (1979): 71–84 (79); John Paul Heil, *Jesus Walking on the Sea* (Rome: Biblical Institute Press, 1981), 59, 69–72, passim; Adela Yarbro Collins, "Rulers, Divine Men, and Walking on the Water (Mark 6:45-52)," in *Religious Propaganda and Missionary Competition in the New Testament World*, NovTSup 74, ed. Lukas Bormann et al. (Leiden: Brill, 1994), 212–13, 226–27; W. Richard Stegner, "Jesus' Walking on the Water: Mark 6:45-52," in *The Gospels and the Scriptures of Israel*, Studies in Scripture in Early Judaism and Christianity, ed. Craig A. Evans and W. Richard Stegner (Sheffield: Sheffield Academic Press, 1994), 212–34; Catrin H. Williams, *I Am He: The Interpretation of 'Anî Hû' in Jewish and Early Christian Literature*, WUNT 2, 113 (Tübingen: Mohr Siebeck, 2000), 219–21, 226–28; Andrew R. Angel, "*Crucifixus Vincens*: The 'Son of God' as Divine Warrior in Matthew," *CBQ* 73 (2011): 299–317 (306–7 on the Matthean parallel). Richard B. Hays concludes that "the story of Jesus' epiphanic walking on the sea read against the background of Job 9, can be perceived as the signature image of Markan Christology"; Hays, "Can the Gospels Teach Us How to Read the Old Testament?" *Pro Ecclesia* 11 (2002): 402–18 (410).

9. Hays, "Can the Gospels Teach Us How to Read the Old Testament?" 411.

10. Heil, *Jesus Walking on the Sea*, 59. Henderson points out that the context of passing through the waters in Isa. 43:2 matches that in Mark 6 exactly; Henderson, *Christology and Discipleship in the Gospel of Mark*, 231.

11. "I am Jesus" is the usual translation of *egō eimi Iēsous* in Acts 9:5, but a case can be made for *egō eimi* as the divine name as the response to Saul's question, "Who are you, Lord?" If so, *egō eimi Iēsous* is Luke's equivalent to the confession *kyrios Iesous*; cf. Acts 2:36; 11:17, 20; 16:31. Note the contrast to Luke 22:67-68, where Luke leaves out the *egō eimi* of Mark 14:62 (where it occurs in response to a very different question).

12. Confirmation of the occurrence of early church performances of the vision described in *1 Enoch* 14 is found in the *Testament of Levi* (mostly Christian); cf. George W. E. Nickelsburg, "Enoch, Levi, and Peter: Recipients of Revelation in Upper Galilee," *JBL* 100 (1981): 575–600 (588–9). Nickelsburg views Matt. 16:13-19 as a revelation of the risen Christ modeled on *1 Enoch* 14. What is interesting about these parallels that describe Paul's initiatory vision in Acts is the fact that there is no hint of ascent into heaven like Enoch's (or Levi's).

13. The double vocative, "Abraham, Abraham," is also read into Gen. 12:1 and 15:1 in the postbiblical *Apocalypse of Abraham* (8:1; 9:10), where Abraham is addressed by the "voice of the mighty One" (*Apoc. Ab.* 8:4; 9:3). On the motif of the hypostatic voice (Acts 26:14) in Hebrew Bible theophanies, see, for instance, Deut. 4:33, 36, passim; Job 37:4-5; Pss. 18:13; 29:3-5; 68:33; Isa. 6:8; Ezek. 1:28; cf. James H. Charlesworth, "The Jewish Roots of Christology: The Discovery of the Hypostatic Voice," *SJT* 39 (1986): 19–41 (29–31, 36–37) on the Targumim and Pseudepigrapha. Contrary to the fascinating article by Charlesworth (ibid., 35), the divine voice in Rev. 1 is clearly a substitute for YHWH.

14. I omit Rev. 1:11, 19-20. Rev. 1:20 is clearly an interpretation added to the vision itself. Rev. 1:11, 19 have no connection to the content of the vision; their role is to position the vision as an introduction to the messages for the seven churches.

15. The NRSV of Rev. 1:13 reads "one like the Son of Man," but there is no definite article in the Greek text; cf. Ian Boxall, *The Revelation of Saint John*, Black's New Testament Commentaries 18 (London: Continuum, 2006), 41–42. Moreover, the occurrence of *the Son of Man* as a title prior to the New Testament era is doubtful, the first clear indication aside from the Synoptic Gospels being the (first-century) Similitudes of Enoch (discussed in ch. 2). In fact, John 9:36; 12:34 assume that such a figure was still unknown to ordinary Jewish people (cf. John 4:25 on the known Messiah); cf. Richard Bauckham, "Jewish Messianism According to the Gospel of John," in Bauckham, *The Testimony of the Beloved Disciple: Narrative, History, and Theology in the Gospel of John* (Grand Rapids: Baker Academic, 2007), 207–38 (235, 237). The phrase "one like a son of

man" (*homoion huion anthrōpou*) in Rev. 1:13 is more likely a description of the anthropic Glory and should be paraphrased, "one who looked like a human being," or "one who appeared in a human form." As a pious Jew, the Apocalypticist refrained from describing the divine form in detail; cf. Ezek. 1:26.

16. For simplicity, I only cite Kyriocentric vision models with parallels in the books of Ezekiel and Daniel. Other models to consider include Exod. 19:16; 20:1; Isa. 6:3b; 41:4, 44:6; 10; 48:12; 60:1-3; Zech. 4:2, 10b; *1 En.* 14:19-20; 46:1; 71:10; Sir. 18:1; *4 Ezra* 14:38, 45; cf. Jan Fekkes, *Isaiah and Prophetic Traditions in the Book of Revelation: Visionary Antecedents and Their Development*, JSNTSup 93 (Sheffield: Sheffield Academic Press, 1994), 70–78, 122, passim. Parallels to Dan. 10:5-6 (probably Gabriel) have also been noted by Christopher Rowland, *The Open Heaven: A Study of Apocalyptic in Judaism and Early Christianity* (New York: Crossroad, 1982), 100–101; Adela Yarbro Collins, "The 'Son of Man' Tradition and the Book of Revelation," in *The Messiah: Developments in Earliest Judaism and Christianity* ed. James H. Charlesworth (Minneapolis: Fortress Press, 1992), 536–68 (558); Loren T. Stuckenbruck, *Angel Veneration and Christology: A Study in Early Judaism and in the Christology of the Apocalypse of John*, WUNT 2, 70 (Tübingen: Mohr, 1995), 209–21; Steve Moyise, *The Old Testament in the Book of Revelation*, JSNTSup 115 (Sheffield: Sheffield Academic Press, 1995), 37–44 (noting Kyriocentric parallels as well); and Charles A. Gieschen, *Angelomorphic Christology: Antecedents and Early Evidence*, AGAJU 42 (Leiden: Brill, 1998), 246–48; For further bibliography, see Adela Yarbro Collins and John J. Collins, *King and Messiah as Son of God: Divine, Human and Angelic Messianic Figures in Biblical and Related Literature* (Grand Rapids: Eerdmans, 2008), 191 n. 75.

17. The superscript K indicates an Old Testament text that is included in Beate Kowalski's "Comprehensive List of Allusions to Ezekiel in the Apocalypse of John"; Kowalski, "Transformation of Ezekiel in John's Revelation," in *Transforming Visions: Transformations of Text, Tradition, and Theology in Ezekiel*, ed. William A. Tooman and Michael A. Lyons (Eugene, OR: Pickwick Publications, 2010), 279–311 (302–7).

18. On iconography that identifies the lampstand with the deity, see Tryggve N. D. Mettinger, *The Dethronement of Sabaoth: Studies in the Shem and Kavod Theologies*, Coniectanea Biblica, Old Testament Series 18 (Lund: CWK Gleerup, 1982), 110–11. As J. Massyngberde Ford states in her commentary: "The menorah, the seven-branched candlestick, was a symbol of the unity of God. The position, therefore of the figure whom he [John] sees is significant; it indicates association with the deity"; Ford, *Revelation*, AB 38 (Garden City, NJ: Doubleday, 1975), 384–85.

19. Jan Fekkes includes this citation of Dan. 7:9b among those where "it is certain or virtually certain that a specific OT text or tradition lies behind John's usage"; Fekkes, *Isaiah and Prophetic Traditions in the Book of Revelation*, 70; cf. 74, 76.

20. Paul's enigmatic statement about "once knowing Christ according to the flesh" (2 Cor. 5:16) most likely refers to his earlier assessment of Jesus as a condemned criminal. I take it that his claim to have received the words of institution "from the Lord" (1 Cor. 11:23) reflected Paul's participation in eucharistic rites in which the presiding minister represented the Lord Jesus (cf. 1 Cor. 15:3), an important case in which early oral performances of the Last Supper overlapped with later liturgical forms.

21. Isa. 6:1, 5 (*eidon ton kyrion*); Amos 9:1 (*eidon ton kyrion*); cf. 1 Kgs. (LXX 3 Kgdms.) 22:19 (*eidon theon Israēl*); Ezek. 1:28 (*hē orasis homoiōmatos doxēs kyriou*).

22. For example, Gordon Fee recognizes the deity reference in Paul's expression, but assumes that Paul simply adds it in order to solidify his defense of his apostleship; Fee, *The First Letter to the Corinthians*, NICNT (Grand Rapids; Eerdmans, 1987), 396–97.

23. The phrase *Lord of glory* comes from the same tradition as *1 Enoch* 22:14; 25:3, a blessing and an eschatological theophany, respectively; Carey Newman, *Paul's Glory-Christology: Tradition and Rhetoric*, NovTSup 69 (Leiden: Brill, 1992), 237, 244; Daniel Olson, *Enoch: A New Translation* (North Richland Hills, TX: BIBAL Press, 2004), 58, note to 22:14. The phrase *Lord of glory* probably refers back to Enoch's ascent-vision in *1 Enoch* 14, where he sees the Great Glory (14:20).

The vision is in turn modeled on the experience of Isaiah in Isa. 6 as indicated in the *OTP* margin; *Old Testament Pseudepigrapha*, ed. James Charlesworth, 2 vols. (Garden City, NY: Doubleday, 1983), 1:21. Hereafter cited as *OTP*.

24. Larry Hurtado refers to Christian binitarianism as a "mutation" within Jewish monotheism; e.g., Hurtado, *How On Earth Did Jesus Become a God? Historical Questions about Earliest Devotion to Jesus* (Grand Rapids: Eerdmans, 2005), 53, 95. Certainly there was a modification. In biological terms, however, mutations are entirely random (determinism only comes in with selection among various mutations), so the term does not do justice to the preconditions and demand-side motivations that we have described. Accordingly, I am restricting use of the term to describe Paul's identification of the God of Israel as the man Jesus (glorified), and, even then, as a statement of the limitations of our knowledge rather than a statement of fact.

25. The Greek term *prosōpon* can mean either "face" or "person." Paul contrasts the removal of the veil for himself and for others "in Christ" with the permanent veil that covers the faces of fellow Jews who did not turn to the Lord Jesus (2 Cor. 3:13-16). Here he may have put his finger on the fundamental difference between Christian Jews and Rabbinic Judaism—the degree (quality of the "mirror") to which the Lord's "face" or "person" can be seen and described. As Moshe Halbertal has explained, early Rabbinic tradition stressed the propriety of pious Jews covering their faces or averting their glances from looking directly at the anthropic form of the *Shekinah* Glory. The anthropic form was certainly present and could be seen, but only with a peek or a glance, and only for an elect few like Moses (and perhaps R. Akiva), so as to protect the honor and glory of the *Shekinah* Glory; Halbertal, *Concealment and Revelation: Esotericism in Jewish Thought and Its Philosophical Implications*, trans. Jackie Feldman (Princeton, NJ: Princeton University Press, 2007), 13–17, 171, notes 4, 6. If so, the primary difference between Paul and the Rabbis is not the name of Jesus, so much as the issues of diverting one's glance in visionary performances (1 Cor. 2:7-13; 2 Cor. 3:18, both related to the outpouring of the Spirit).

26. These features of the text were one of the starting points for my own investigation of deity Christology in the late 1970s; C. B. Kaiser, *The Doctrine of God: A Historical Survey*, Foundations for Faith (London: Marshall Morgan & Scott, 1982), 34–35, revised ed. (Eugene, OR: Wipf & Stock, 2001), 39–40.

27. According to Helmut Koester, Mark 4:35—8:26 consists of two separate catenae of miracle stories derived from earlier written sources, while Mark 5:1-20; 6:53-56; 7:31-37 were added by the author; Koester, "Suffering Servant and Royal Messiah: From Second Isaiah to Paul, Mark, and Matthew," *Theology Digest* 51 (2004): 103–24 (112–13). Werner Kelber had suggested that the organization of such pre-Markan material (including Mark 6:45-52) was a typical sign of oral clustering; Kelber, *The Oral and The Written Gospel: The Hermeneutics of Speaking and Writing in the Synoptic Tradition, Mark, Paul, and Q* (Philadelphia: Fortress Press, 1983), 106.

28. John Miles Foley introduced the idea of "special formulas" from his studies of a Serbian *guslar*, Homer, and old English poets; Foley, *How to Read an Oral Poem* (Urbana: University of Illinois Press, 2002), 90. In contrast to the performance of Kyriocentric visions, as described here, Foley's exemplars were epic poems in which the hero is projected into the distant past, rather than ones in which the hero is represented by the poet.

29. Joel Marcus points out that the verb *parelthein* had become a technical term for a divine epiphany in the LXX; Marcus, *Mark 1–8*, AB 27 (New York: Doubleday, 2000), 426, 432.

30. For example, Num. 12:8 (*tēn doxan kyriou eide*); Deut. 5:24 (*eidexen hēmin . . . tēn doxan autou*); Isa. 6:1, 3, 5 (*eidon ton kyrion . . . tēs doxēs autou*). The theophanic use of *oraō* is admittedly more clear in Acts and John (Acts 9:27; John 12:41; 20:18, 20), both of which explicitly assume a postresurrection viewpoint.

31. Luke omits the entire narrative (at the cost of leaving out his favorite theme of Jesus at prayer; cf. Mark 6:46). John reflects an independent rehearsal of Ps. 107 (John 6:21b = Ps. 107:30b), but omits any reference to a phantasm or the spooky "passing by" motif from Job 9. Matthew's tradition omits the "passing by" motif and refutes any possibility of a phantasm by having Peter sink in the water (crying "Lord, save me") and Jesus reach out his own hand to save him (Matt.

14:30-31), thereby adding new divine motifs from the Psalms (Pss. 12:1; 94:18; 109:26, passim) and avoiding all docetic interpretations at the same time. The leader of Matthean performances evidently assumed the persona of Peter.

32. Psalm composers typically assumed the persona of a model psalmist like David; see Ps. 151 (Syriac I) = 11QPsa 28:3–11; cf. 11QPsa 27:4–11 on David's composing psalms and songs for the temple service.

33. On the role of the Exod. 33–34 theophany to Moses in Mark 6:48c, see Heil, *Jesus Walking on the Sea*, 69–72; Hays, "Can the Gospels Teach Us How to Read the Old Testament?" 410–11; Suzanne Watts Henderson, *Christology and Discipleship in the Gospel of Mark* (Cambridge: Cambridge University Press, 2006), 227–28. As we see in the transfiguration account (treated in the following section), Moses was viewed as a Christian prophet in the synoptic tradition.

34. Luke suggests a post-execution setting for the transfiguration through his reference to the eighth day (Luke 9:28; cf. 24:1, 13); E. Earle Ellis, *The Gospel of Luke*, New Century Bible (London: Oliphants, 1974), 142, 276. The Gospel of Matthew also contains Kyriocentric visions that may have been displaced from a post-execution setting; see esp. the account of Lord Jesus treading on the sea with the additional feature of Peter's crying out, "Lord, save me," in Matt. 14:30. Note also Matt. 18:20 ("where two or three are gathered in my name, I am there among them"); cf. Margaret Barker, *Temple Themes in Christian Worship* (London: T&T Clark, 2007), 136. Christopher Rowland has argued that Matthew's distinctive account of the transfiguration also incorporates theophanic motifs (shining face, reaction of falling down, positive spin on Peter's tabernacle suggestion); Rowland, "Apocalyptic, the Poor, and the Gospel of Matthew," *JTS* (1994): 504–18 (508–9); Rowland and Christopher R. A. Morray-Jones, *The Mystery of God: Early Jewish Mysticism and the New Testament*, CRINT 3, Jewish Traditions in Early Christian Literature 12 (Leiden: Brill, 2009), 106–7.

35. The Isaiah Targum reads "I saw the glory of the Lord" in verse 1 and "my eyes have seen the glory of the *Shekinah* of the King of ages, the Lord of hosts" in verse 5; John F. Stenning, trans. *The Targum of Isaiah* (Oxford: Clarendon, 1953), 20–3.

36. For example, Num. 12:8 (*tēn doxan kyriou eide*); Deut. 5:24 (*eidexen hēmin . . . tēn doxan autou*); Isa. 6:1, 3, 5 (*eidon ton kyrion . . . tēs doxēs autou*). Luke's transfiguration narrative concludes with a similar visionary phrase in 9:36 (*ouden ōn eōrakan*; cf. Ezek. 1:28; John 17:24).

37. Compare Angela Harkins's interpretation of the Qumran "Teacher of Righteousness" as a *maskil* (or possibly a succession of *maskilim*) who led the performances of visionary texts; Harkins, *Reading with an "I" to the Heavens: Looking at the Qumran Hodayot through the Lens of Visionary Traditions*, Ekstasis 3 (Berlin: de Gruyter, 2012), 7–8, 109.

38. Peter similarly takes on the role of a new Moses in Acts 2:37-39 (cf. Exod. 19:7-8; Deut. 11:13-21). Luke 9 and Acts 2 both reflect revised performances of Moses: Moses on Sinai, and Moses establishing a new covenant with the people, respectively.

39. In effect, I find three distinct levels of performance underlying Luke's narrative: (1) Moses' vision of the Lord on Sinai; (2) the Christianized version of that vision in which the Lord is Jesus (transfigured) and Peter is the protagonist (Moses is just a witness); and (3) the binitarian form of the Christian vision in which a supervisory role is given to the Father.

40. Two other Lukan touches that set the scene at night are found in 9:28, which states that they "went up on the mountain to pray," and 9:37, which states that they came down from the mountain the next day. Comparison with other passages like 6:12; 22:39-41 shows that Luke's Jesus habitually prayed during the nighttime on mountains.

41. *Palestinian Fragment Targums* to Exod. 12:42 (MS Vatican Ebr 44) and to Exod. 15:18 (MS Paris Hebr. 110), Michael L. Klein, trans., *The Fragment-Targums of the Pentateuch* (Rome: Biblical Institute Press, 1980), 47–48, 126; *Targum Neofiti* to Exod. 12:42; Martin McNamara, trans. *Targum Neofiti 1: Exodus*, Aramaic Bible 2 (Collegeville, MN: Liturgical Press, 1994), 51–53.

42. The Aramaic terms for *word* (*memra*) and *glory* (*yikra*) are equivalent in the Targumim; see, e.g., *Tg. Neof.* Gen. 1:16-17. As stated in ch. 1, the Messiah is part of the picture, but not the

main focus. The primary expectation of Second Temple Jews was the coming and appearance of YHWH, beside whom the Messiah (or Son of Man) was a secondary figure.

43. If we may assume that the Targumim were based on actual synagogue and school deliveries, it is likely that some of the traditions they contain are much older than their present redactions (fourth–eighth century). Tannaitic midrashim like *Sifrei Devarim* 343 similarly look back to the appearances of *HaShem* at the exodus (the "third night") and on Mt. Sinai and forward to the appearance of the Lord in the days of Gog and Magog and the "days of the Messiah"; Reuven Hammer, trans., *Sifre: A Tannaitic Commentary on the Book of Deuteronomy*, Yale Judaica 309 (New Haven, CT: Yale University Press, 1986), 354. Even if the Lukan community was largely gentile, it still represented a "Christian Judaism" that continued to adhere to traditional Jewish fasts like Yom Kippur (Acts 27:9); cf. Daniel Stökl Ben Ezra, *The Impact of Yom Kippur on Early Christianity: The Day of Atonement from Second Temple Judaism to the Fifth Century*, WUNT 163 (Tübingen: Mohr Siebeck, 2003), 227.

44. Luke's unique use of *diachōrizesthai* ("being separated") in 9:33a (elsewhere only in Gen. 13:9, 11) suggests that Peter's assumed motive in requesting the building of three tabernacles was to keep three celestial powers together on the mountain. For the writer and his tradition, his mistake was in offering such devotion to anyone other than the one Lord, Jesus (*Iēsous monos*, 9:35-36; cf. 1 Cor. 8:6; Jude 4, 25).

45. Similar binitarian motifs are found in many branches of Judaism, ranging from Philo of Alexandria and Rabbinic traditions concerning R. Shim'on ben Zoma (really a dipolar unity; Gen. R. 2:4; 4:6; 5:4) to midrashim concerning the *galut ha-Shekinah* (exile of the *Shekinah*, Pesiq. Rab. 98) and R. Abraham ibn Ezra's speculations about the divine Kavod. On the criteria for bona fide binitarianism in Judaism (as distinct from targumic circumlocutions), see Menahem Kister, "Some Early Jewish and Christian Exegetical Problems and the Dynamics of Monotheism," *JSJ* 37 (2006): 548–93 (esp. 574 n. 74).

46. I leave Stephen's vision of the Son of Man at the right hand of God (Acts 7:55-56) out of consideration for the moment, even though Larry Hurtado sees it as being primary; Hurtado, "The Binitarian Shape of Early Christian Worship," in *The Jewish Roots of Christological Monotheism*, SJSJ 63, ed. Carey C. Newman, James R. Davila, and Gladys L. Lewis (Leiden: Brill, 1999), 187–213; Hurtado, *How On Earth Did Jesus Become a God?* 199–200. This account of Stephen's vision is probably secondary to the Synoptic description of Jesus' words before the High Priest (Mark 14:62 = Luke 22:69)—or perhaps both are based on the same visionary model. From the perspective of the current investigation, both are binitarian in their present form and can be accounted for as a secondary development from the standpoint of the Kyriocentric vision conjecture.

47. Acts was most likely written for churches who were already familiar with the basic features of Paul's story; Douglas Buckwalter, *The Character and Purpose of Luke's Christology* (Cambridge: Cambridge University Press, 1996), 73–74.

48. As John Miles Foley states with regard to the role of memory in oral performances: "The goal of memory is not retrieving data but rather re-creating and re-living an experience"; Foley, "Memory in Oral Tradition," in *Performing the Gospel: Orality, Memory, and Mark*, ed. Richard A. Horsley, Jonathan A. Draper, and John Miles Foley (Minneapolis: Fortress Press, 2006), 83–96 (92).

49. Martin Hengel and Anna Maria Schwemer point to the "threefold report" in Acts as an indication that the narrative was not mere fiction but rested on traditions, possibly going back to Paul himself; Hengel and Schwemer, *Paul Between Damascus and Antioch: The Unknown Years*, trans. John Bowden (Louisville: Westminster John Knox, 1997), 38; cf. Finny Philip, *The Origins of Pauline Pneumatology: The Eschatological Bestowal of the Spirit upon Gentiles in Judaism and in the Early Development of Paul's Theology*, WUNT 2, 194 (Tübingen: Mohr Siebeck, 2005), 191 n. 111. Nonetheless, Carey Newman's finely crafted caution is to be heeded: "The shape of the Christophany in Paul should not be blurred by looking through the lens ground by Luke"; Newman, "Christophany as a Sign of 'the End,'" in *Israel's God and Rebecca's Children: Christology and Community in Early Judaism and Christianity: Essays in Honor of Larry W. Hurtado and Alan F.*

Segal, ed. David B. Capes et al. (Waco, TX: Baylor University Press, 2007), 155–67 (157). Larry Hurtado also strikes a nice balance in advocating that one ought to refrain from basing arguments on Acts alone, but, instead of discounting its historicity out of hand, one ought to test the accounts against Paul's own statements about his past; Hurtado, "Convert, Apostate or Apostle to the Nations: The 'Conversion' of Paul in Recent Scholarship," *JBL* 22 (1993): 273–84 (279 n. 24). Note further Joseph A. Fitzmyer's conclusion that the Acts accounts of Paul's "conversion" were derived from a Pauline source and then "dramatized" by Luke; Fitzmyer, *First Corinthians: A New Translation with Introduction and Commentary*, AYB 32 (New Haven, CT: Yale University Press, 2008), 420–21.

50. Benjamin J. Hubbard, "Commissioning Stories in Luke-Acts: A Study of Their Antecedents, Form and Content," *Semeia* 8 (1977): 103–23 (120).

51. Robert F. O'Toole, *Acts 26: The Christological Climax of Paul's Defense (Ac.22:1—26:32)* (Rome: Biblical Institute Press, 1978), 6–7, 64; O'Toole, *Luke's Presentation of Jesus: A Christology* (Rome: Pontifical Biblical Institute, 2004), 217–18, 223. Another parallel to consider is the appearance of Michael in *Joseph and Aseneth* 14, where Aseneth sees a "great light" from heaven and falls on her face (2-3); a man comes to her and calls her, "Aseneth, Aseneth" (*Jos. Asen.* 14:3-4); she responds, "Here I am, Lord. Who are you?" (14:7); the man identifies himself as the commander of the host of the Most High (Michael) and commands her to rise up and converse (14:8); she sees a man exactly like Joseph except for the unexpected radiance of his face and body (14:9). There are remarkable similarities to the Acts 9 theophany in spite of the fact that that both the voice and reference to "seeing the Lord" are missing (Acts 9:4, 27). But Ross Shepherd Kraemer seriously questions the Jewish provenance of *Joseph and Aseneth*; Kraemer, *When Aseneth Met Joseph: A Late Antique Tale of the Biblical Patriarch and His Egyptian Wife Reconsidered* (Atlanta: Scholars, 1996), cited and amplified by James Davila, *The Provenance of the Pseudepigrapha: Jewish, Christian, or Other?*, SJSJ 105 (Leiden: Brill, 2005), 190–95. As Davila states, he "would not use texts in this category at all for New Testament background or the reconstruction of ancient Judaism"; Davila, "The Old Testament Pseudepigrapha as Background to the New Testament," *ExpTim* 117 (2005): 53–57 (57a and n. 6).

52. For the double address by YHWH, see Gen. 22:11-12 (angel of the Lord speaking for YHWH); 46:2; Exod. 3:4; 1 Sam. 3:10 (discussed in ch. 4); *4 Ezra* 14:1; *2 Bar.* 22:2 (discussed in ch. 3); *Apoc. Ab.* 8:1; 20:1 (contrast the address by the angel Yao'el in 10:5); *T. Job* 3:1 (hypostatic light/angel); *Jos. Asen.* 14:3, 7 (chief of the house of the Lord). The visionary aspect of Saul's revelation is made explicit in Acts 26:16, 19; cf. 9:4, 17, 27.

53. In Acts 9 and 22, the Lord Jesus simply tells Saul to enter the city of Damascus where he will be told what to do (9:6). Ananias uses theophany language to describe the Lord Jesus who had appeared to Saul (*ho kyrios ho ophtheis soi*, Acts 9:17; cf. 7:2 on the appearance of the "God of glory" to Abraham) and takes over the role of delivering the commission (9:15-17; 22:14-15, note the binitarian form). The account in Acts 22 adds that Saul "called on his name" while being baptized (Acts 22:16; cf. Joel 2:32 [Hebrew 3:5]), which is consistent with what Acts 2 and Romans 10 tell us about in the practice of "calling on the name" of YHWH in (Acts 2:21, 38; Rom. 10:10-13). As Charles Gieschen has argued, the name on which early Christians called was not *Jesus*, but the divine Name, YHWH/Kyrios, which was Jesus' true identity; Gieschen, "The Divine Name in Ante-Nicene Christology," *VC* 57 (2003): 115–58 (137).

54. For an impressive demonstration of the role of mnemonic cues in Rabbinic literature, see Martin Jaffee, "What Difference Does the 'Orality' of Rabbinic Writing Make for the Interpretation of Rabbinic Writings?" in *How Should Rabbinic Literature Be Read in the Modern World?* ed. Matthew Kraus (Piscataway, NJ: Gorgias, 2006), 11–33 (21, 25, 29–30, 32). Such cues can be purely formal, or they can be substantive; ibid., 25. In the case of the *Erscheinungsgespräch Gattung*, they are both. As Walter Ong already pointed out, such mnemonic patterns continued to appear in early manuscripts in order to aid the reader's memory; Ong, *Orality and Literacy: The Technologizing of the Word* (London: Methuen, 1982), 119. Even though scripts might be written

down somewhere (leaving us with something to work with), most people of that time continued to experience them as oral performances. On the performative nature of the written text of Revelation, see Rhoads, "Performance Criticism, Part I," 127a.

55. As Robert Culley pointed out in an important review article, repeated patterns and other mnemonic cues are rarely sufficient to prove oral performance on their own and must be viewed in the light of analogies to known oral cultures and models of orality that students of orality have constructed; Culley, "Oral Tradition and Biblical Studies," *Oral Tradition* 1 (1986): 30–65 (57–59).

56. Massey H. Shepherd Jr., argued that "day of the Lord" in Rev. 1:10 simultaneously referred to the first day of the week (or else the Pascha) and to the *parousia*; Shepherd, *The Paschal Liturgy in the Apocalypse* (London: Lutterworth, 1960), 78, 81. As G. B. Caird commented (on Rev. 1:7), the Apocalypticist was as interested in the immediate coming of the Lord in personal prayer (cf. Rev. 3:20) as he was in the eschatological parousia; Caird, *A Commentary on the Revelation of St. John the Divine*, Harper's New Testament Commentaries (New York: Harper & Row, 1966), 19.

57. Suggested similarities between the "one like a son of man" of Rev. 1 and the angels include having a golden sash across the chest (1:13b; cf. 15:6) and a face shining like the sun (1:16c; cf. 10:1, which may be the Lord Jesus himself). For parallels to descriptions of angels in Jewish literature, see Christopher Rowland, "The Vision of the Risen Christ in Rev. i.13ff.: The Debt of an Early Christology to an Aspect of Jewish Angelology," *JTS* 31 (1980): 1–11. As Loren T. Stuckenbruck has pointed out, the main difference between the divine figure in Rev. 1 and angels elsewhere in Revelation is the fact that that veneration was not forbidden; Stuckenbruck, "An Angelic Refusal of Worship: The Tradition and Its Function in the Apocalypse of John," *SBLSP* 25 (1994): 679–96 (694).

58. See M. Eugene Boring, *Revelation*, Interpretation Commentary (Louisville: John Knox, 1989), 83. What Boring refers to here as John's "theocentrism" holds true for the document as a whole (esp. Rev. 4–5).

59. In the visions of Rev. 4 and following chapters, God (the Father) is the one at the center, surrounded by elders, living creatures (cherubim) and thousands of angels (4:2-11; 5:11), providing us with the best example of a New Testament vision in which the *Kyrios* is God the Father. Even though the Lamb is secondary to the one on the throne, however, it is still said to share the center as in the inaugural vision (Rev. 5:6; 7:17; Charles A. Gieschen, "The Lamb (Not the Man) on the Divine Throne," in *Israel's God and Rebecca's Children*, 227–43 (236).

60. The Apocalypticist uses various strategies to reconcile his Kyriocentric visions with the teachings and practices of Jesus: invoking Son of Man imagery, positing a shared throne and temple, and exploiting apparent dualities in OT descriptions of YHWH (e.g., Isa. 2:19 in Rev. 6:16; Isa. 60:19b in Rev. 21:23); cf. Fekkes, *Isaiah and Prophetic Traditions in the Book of Revelation*, 162–63, 267–68.

61. James M. Robinson famously argued that Rev. 1:13-16 was the only first-person account of a "resurrection appearance" other than the brief references in Paul's epistles (e.g. Phil. 3:21); Robinson, "Jesus from Easter to Valentinus (or the Apostles' Creed)," *JBL* 101 (1982): 5–37 (10, 13).

62. The fact that the vision in Rev. 1 originally stood on its own is readily seen from incongruities with the surrounding material, such as the double use of the "first and last" motif (Rev. 1:8 for the Lord God and 1:17 for the Lord Jesus) and the contrasting images of a royal warrior (Rev. 1:13-16) and a slaughtered lamb who is yet to be invested with royalty (Rev. 4:12). Steve Moyise has shown that the visionary images in Rev. 1 provided the material for the seven letters in Rev. 2–3, rather than the other way around; Moyise, *The Old Testament in the Book of Revelation*, 21 and ch. 2.

63. I borrow the term *angelomorphic* from Charles A. Gieschen, *Angelomorphic Christology*, 248–49. It simply means that the author is using the same language that is used to describe angels and does not necessarily imply the ontological status of an angel.

64. Fekkes, *Isaiah and Prophetic Traditions in the Book of Revelation*, 73; Moyise, *The Old Testament in the Book of Revelation*, 78–79, 136 (noting some deviations from Ezekiel on pp. 80–83).

65. On the joint nature of prophetic performances, see the description of the school of prophets under the leadership of Pseudo-Isaiah as described in the *Ascen. Isa.* 6, which is roughly contemporaneous with the Revelation of John and possibly of the same provenance; see David Frankfurter, "The Legacy of Jewish Apocalypses in Early Christianity: Regional Trajectories," in *Jewish Apocalyptic Heritage in Early Christianity*, ed. James C. VanderKam and William Adler, CRINT 3, 4 (Assen, Netherlands: Van Gorcum, 1996), 129–200 (132–42).

66. See, for instance, the popular book by Elaine Pagels, *Beyond Belief: The Secret Gospel of Thomas* (New York: Random House, 2003), 37–38, which states that Mark and the other evangelists only saw Jesus in a human role. The notion that John was the first evangelist to make the deity of Christ clear actually goes back as far as Theodore of Mopsuestia; Frederick G. McLeod, "The Christology in Theodore of Mopsuestia's *Commentary on the Gospel of John*," *TS* 73 (2012): 115–38 (121–22). Theodore's comment that John was making up for a deficiency in the Synoptics was mainly a way of explaining the prologue, in which he made the idea of incarnation explicit (1:14).

67. John's Jesus says several times that God (the Father) cannot be seen (John 1:18a; 5:37; 6:46; cf. 1 John 4:12), and this feature leads some scholars to think John was opposed to visionary experiences; see Michael Goulder, "Vision and Knowledge," *JSNT* 56 (1994): 53–71 (69–70). Even if John wanted to dissuade believers from seeking new visions (John 20:29), the performance of traditional Kyriocentric visions is clearly in evidence (as shown here). The fact that they are now focused on Jesus makes it possible for God the Father to be known through him (John 1:18b; 5:38; 14:7-9).

68. John 6:21 includes the final part of the Psalm narrative, "he brought them to their desired haven" (Ps. 107:30b), which is missing in the Synoptic versions.

69. According to Rudolf Schnackenburg's reconstructed pre-Christian *Logos-Hymnus*, the visionary parts of John's prologue, 1:14b and 1:18, were John's own additions; Schnackenburg, "Logos-Hymnus und johanneischer Prolog," *BZ* 1 (1957): 69–109 (84–85), the *Logos-Hymnus* being translated in Reginald H. Fuller, "Christmas, Epiphany, and the Johannine Prologue," in *Spirit and Light: Essays in Historical Theology*, ed. Madeleine L' Engle and William B. Green (New York: Seabury, 1976), 63–73 (65–66).

70. The first two appearance narratives in John 20 appear to be based on mental scripts for rehearsing visions of YHWH/*Kyrios*, now identified as the risen Jesus (John 20:13-17, 19-23). For likely Kyriocentric models, see the wording of 1 Kgs. (LXX 3 Kgdms.) 22:19 (*eidon theon Israēl*); Isa. 6:1, 5, 9 (*eidon ton kyrion ... kai eipe*); Ezek. 1:28—2:3 (*hē orasis homoiōmatos doxēs kyriou ... kai eipe pros mē*); Amos 9:1 (*eiden ton kyrion kai ... eipe*); cf. the Gospel of Mary (BG 7) 10.10-14 ("I saw the Lord ... he said"). Rehearsal of the first of these appearance narratives, the appearance to Mary Magdalene (or the model underlying it), can be seen as late as the story of Brother Sarapion in Cassian's *Conferences* 10.3.5 ("They have taken my God from me, and now I have no one to hold on to" to be discussed in ch. 9; cf. John 20:13, 17a). The third appearance narrative in John 20, that including Thomas (John 20:26-29), is probably a corrective maneuver intended to stress the physical nature of the risen Lord.

71. Larry Hurtado is uncertain whether John's Isaiah saw the glory in his own time, or merely foresaw Jesus in his postresurrection glory; Hurtado, *God in New Testament Theology*, Library of Biblical Theology (Nashville: Abingdon, 2010), 67–68, 121 n. 28, 125 n. 36. In support of the contemporary glory reading, he points to John 17:5 as an indication that that the Son's glory existed long before the incarnation (ibid., 125 n. 36). The resurrection-glory possibility could be supported equally well by appealing to John 12:16, 23, 28, which identify the glorification of Jesus with the cross and resurrection; cf. 8:56 on Abraham's seeing the day of Jesus' resurrection (as in Heb. 11:19). However, it would be a mistake to assume that biblical writers were working with a timeline with events separated by long spans. From the perspective of performance criticism, the

vision of Isaiah was contemporary with the community in which it was reenacted. John used narratives to structure his Gospel, but, as far as his community and its practices were concerned, the Lord Jesus appeared to them in the glory that they imagined and experienced during the performance of Isaiah's vision.

72. See note 35 on the Isaiah Targum.

73. Peter Schäfer perceives a close parallel between the conventicle of *Ascen. Isa.* 6 and the *havurah* of Heikalot literature; Schäfer, *The Origins of Jewish Mysticism* (Tübingen: Mohr Siebeck, 2009), 95; see also our discussion in ch. 3, "Visions Associated with Prayer in Early Christian Literature."

74. The *Kedushah* was directed to the enthroned Deity (God the Father) in Rev. 4:8-9, but was devoted to Lord Jesus in 1 Pet. 3:15a ("sanctify Christ as Lord in your hearts"); *1 Clem.* 34:3-7 ("Behold the Lord [comes] . . . his angels cried Holy, Holy, Holy . . . we too must cry . . ."); the Coptic Gnostic Treatise published by Charlotte Baynes (Arthur Green, *Keter: The Crown of God in Early Jewish Mysticism* [Princeton, NJ: Princeton University Press, 1997], 30–31); the Anaphora of Addai and Mari (ante-Nicene Syria) §3 (ET in Frank C. Senn, *Christian Liturgy, Catholic and Evangelical* [Minneapolis: Fortress Press, 1997], 81); and the Syrian (Antiochene) Rite Eucharistic Liturgy (Nikolaus Liesel, *The Eucharistic Liturgies of the Eastern Churches*, trans. David Heimann [Collegeville, MN: Liturgical Press, 1962], 72–74). In Rabbinic midrash, the *Kedushah* could not be addressed to the primordial Adam (lest he be confused with *HaShem*, Gen. R. 8:10), but it (the attribute, "holy") would in the age to come be recited before all the righteous (*b. B. Bat.* 75b, citing Isa. 4:3). Needless to say, such attribution is quite different from the worship offered to *HaShem* in the statutory *Kedushah*. In the communities of John, 1 Peter, and *1 Clement*, therefore, the *Kedushah* was clearly offered to Jesus as *HaShem*, not as a righteous person.

75. Other visionary performances are reflected in the John's narratives. See particularly John 20:19-23, where, while the fearful disciples were meeting together on the first day of the week (in prayer?), Jesus came, stood alongside the disciples in classical theophanic fashion (Gen. 28:13; Exod. 33:9; 1 Sam. 3:10; Amos 7:7), and addressed them in divine terms ("Peace be with you"; cf. Isa. 57:19; *1 En.* 71:15; cf. Mark 6:48b-50). The disciples rejoiced when "seeing the Lord" [*idontes ton kyrion*]. Finally, Jesus commissioned them: "As the Father sent me; so I send you." Only at this terminal point was the script adapted to conform to Jesus traditions about the Father.

76. According to Justin Martyr (mid-second century), the public reading of the Apostles and Prophets lasted only as long as time permitted, after which the service moved on to exhortation, prayers, the eucharist, and contributions for the poor; *1 Apol.* 67.3-6.

6

Kyriocentric Prayers and Devotions in the New Testament

A most important aspect of Kyriocentric visions was that they were rehearsed in the context of prayer and worship (ch. 3). In the previous chapter, we found some evidence for the performance of these visions in the New Testament, but a brief review will indicate that the prayer dimension was only suggested in the visionary-performance texts we examined.

Paul said nothing about prayer or worship in his brief autobiographical comments;[1] nor is there anything about it in any of the three accounts in the book of Acts. Luke's account does not even fit Rabbinic halakot concerning prayer on a journey.[2]

According to the theophany narrative in Mark 6, the disciples were fully occupied with managing their boat (Mark 6:48), and they responded to the Kyriocentric vision with terror rather than praise (6:49). Performatively speaking, the Markan account appears to be based on Psalm 107, which begins with "O give thanks to the Lord" and states four times that the seafarers "cried out to the Lord in their trouble" (Ps. 107:1, 6, 13, 19, 28), but the narrative simply describes the disciples as crying out (to God?) and the element of thanksgiving is completely lost. Even after the sea-walking figure had identified himself with the divine "It is I" and made the winds cease, the disciples were simply astounded and lacking in understanding (Mark 6:50-52, a characteristically Markan spin).

In Luke's account of the transfiguration, Peter, James, and John accompanied their teacher up the mountain in order to pray (Luke 9:28), but Jesus did most of the praying, and the disciples responded to the subsequent vision with confusion, fear, and silence (9:29a, 33, 34, 36). Admittedly, the elements of confusion (on Peter's part) and fear were adapted from an earlier version of the transfiguration (cf. Mark 9:6, 9, both omitted by Matthew), and

Luke may have intended the initial focus on prayer as an exhortation to his readers (cf. Luke 22:40, 46), but we are left at this point with speculations.

With better reason, we may infer a context of prayer when the Apocalypticist spoke of "being in the spirit on the Lord's day" (Rev. 1:10), and when John the Evangelist recounted the vision of Isaiah in the Temple (John 12:41), where the seraphim ceaselessly chanted the *Kedushah* (*Sanctus*, Isa. 6:3). However, we should be able to find more ample evidence that visions of the Lord Jesus were couched in prayer if our conjecture about Kyriocentric visions and our findings about their relation to prayer are deemed to be valid. Fortunately, much of this inductive work has been done by others.

WAS PRAYER AND WORSHIP DIRECTED TO THE LORD JESUS?

Recent discussions of early high Christology have demonstrated the use of prayers and devotional language in relation to Jesus in the New Testament. Larry Hurtado builds his case for early high Christology on evidence for "cultic devotion" to Jesus.[3] Richard Bauckham has similarly called attention to the New Testament practice of petitionary prayer and devotion to Jesus.[4] On the other hand, James Dunn has called attention to the fact that important devotional language appears to have been "reserved" for God the Father. Dunn finds little or no evidence for motifs like worship, blessing, prayer, and thanksgiving being addressed to Jesus.[5]

We need to sort through various cases here (working inductively for the moment), but not just because this is a moot subject in current discussion. More importantly, our conjecture that the occurrence of Kyriocentric visions occurred in the context of prayer implies that continued performance of those visions should result in continued prayer to the Lord (Jesus) using much the same devotional language that was used in the Old Testament and in Second Temple Judaism.[6] Since non–Christian Jews continued to pray to *HaShem*, we should also expect to find these themes in Rabbinic texts and the Jewish prayer book (the *Siddur*). Although not formalized until the late first millennium (and beyond), these prayers are particularly helpful in showing how scriptural prayer motifs continued to be used in postbiblical Judaism.[7]

One reason for the lack of resolution on the question of prayers dedicated to the Lord Jesus is the large amount of textual material that needs to be included. There are dozens of prayer formulas in the Old Testament and the texts of early Judaism. Similar motifs turn up all through the New Testament and early Christian literature,[8] not just in formal prayers and hymns, but also in letters and gospel narratives. In fact, the primary vectors for biblical material in early Christian documents are not quotations of specific texts as much as the citation of prayer formulas.

There was a symbiotic relationship between Scripture, prayer, and discourse in early Judaism. We have already mentioned the "scripturalization of prayer" that Judith Newman has called to our attention for the Second Temple era (ch. 2).[9] This vector for biblical material was accompanied by an ongoing liturgicalization of everyday discourse, whereby stock prayer formulas were spontaneously introduced into everyday speech. Even today we can hear scriptural motifs like "God willing" or "Bless you," used by people who would not know where to look for such phrases in the Bible. Such oral fragments can frequently be seen in the narratives and letters of the New Testament, thereby completing a cycle (one or more cycles) from Scripture to oral performance and from oral performance to Scripture. The documents we have are permeated with prayer motifs, and these can serve as good "genetic markers" for biblical motifs, particularly those centered in YHWH, in early Christian discourse.

In order to get a better view of this vast array of prayer motifs in the New Testament, it will be helpful to arrange the material in a series of tables. These tables will document various prayer motifs in the Old Testament and postbiblical Judaism and indicate how they were distributed in the New Testament era—whether they were addressed to Lord Jesus or to God the Father (or to both). Viewing the material in this way will help us to pinpoint areas that require special attention without trying to plow through every single text.

For simplicity, as well as reasonable accuracy, I assign texts with the title "Lord" to the Lord Jesus, and those with the title "God" to God the Father. This distribution is widely recognized, particularly in the letters of Paul,[10] and we shall offer a rationale for it, based on the Kyriocentric conjecture, in the following chapter ("Didn't Jesus pray to God as his Father?"). Some details of particular assignments of these titles are treated here in footnotes.

As it turns out, the material can be divided fairly nicely into three sets of prayer motifs: those addressed to both Jesus and his Father (Table 4), those that are predominately addressed to the Lord Jesus (Table 5), and those that are addressed predominately to the Father (Table 6). The first set is important in that it indicates awareness of a degree of parity between Jesus and his Father in New Testament era literature. The second set suggests that there were some constraints on the piety shown toward the Father, and the third suggests a reciprocal constraint on the piety shown to Lord Jesus.

In other words, both sides of the debate (Hurtado and Bauckham versus Dunn) are right with regard to the observations they make about New Testament prayers. The importance of the approach taken here is not just in adjudicating the differing emphases but in showing how to account for the distribution of prayer motifs on the basis of known traditions about the historic Jesus together with our Kyriocentric vision conjecture.

PRAYER MOTIFS ADDRESSED TO BOTH LORD JESUS AND GOD THE FATHER

First, let us look at ten prayer motifs that are shared by Jesus and his Father. For completeness, I add an eleventh motif that appears to belong to this set even though the evidence (as gathered here) is inconclusive (hence the question mark in the last row of the table). New Testament texts with asterisks are ones for which one or more of the Old Testament texts listed in the first column is cited in the footnotes of the United Bible Society edition of the Greek text.

Table 4: Prayer Motifs addressed to both Lord Jesus and God the Father
(Asterisks indicate UBS citations)

Prayer Motifs in the Old Testament and Postbiblical Judaism	New Testament Era Texts that Address these Motifs to the Lord Jesus	New Testament Era Texts that Address these Motifs to God the Father
Bend the knee and confess/ praise[11] the Lord (1 Kgs. 8:33, 35; Ps. 18:49; Isa. 45:23 LXX; Pss. Sol. 15:2; *Aleinu* prayer 6;[12] *Nishmat Kol-Hai* prayer[13])	Rom. 10:9 (confessional formula); 14:11a* (citing Isa. 45:23);[14] Phil. 2:10-11* (citing Isa. 45:23)	Rom. 14:11b* (citing Isa. 45:23); 15:9*; Luke 11:21 (Q); Heb. 13:15
"Lord of lords," "King of kings" (Ps. 136:3 [the Great *Hallel*]; *1 En.* 9:4; 84:2; Sir. 51:12 [xiv];[15] 3 Macc. 5:35; 1QM 14:16; 4Q381 frags 76–77 1:7, 14; t.	Rev. 17:14*; 19:16*[3]	1 Tim. 6:15* (part of a blessing)

Ta'an. 2:17; *Shema Barchu* 5;[16] *Aleinu* prayer 2[17])		
Worthy to receive power, glory, blessing (1 Chron. 29:10-13; *Pss. Sol.* 3:1; *m. Pesah.* 10:5;[18] *Nishmat Kol-Hai* prayer;[19] *Kaddish* 5[20]).	Rev. 5:12	Rev. 4:11; 5:13; Jude 25
Sanctify the (name of) the Lord, often with "Holy, holy, holy" (Deut. 32:51; Isa. 6:3; 8:13; *1 En.* 39:12; 11QPs[a] 26:9; *t. Ber.* 1:9 [the *Kedushah* from Isa. 6:3];[21] *Kedushah de-Yotzer* 11-13;[22] *Kedushah de-Amidah* 1-5;[23] *Kaddish* 1; Passover Haggadah[24])	1 Pet. 3:14-15; *1 Clem.* 34:6;[25] John 12:38-41 (implied)[26]	Luke 11:2b (Q, the Lord's prayer); Rev. 4:8
"Turn to the Lord/God" (Exod. 32:31; 34:33-4; Deut. 30:10; Ps. 22:27; Isa. 45:22; Lam. 5:21; Dan. 9:3 [by prayer and supplication]; Hos. 3:5; 6:1 ; Tob. 13:6; 14:6 [in worship; *m. Sukkah* 5:4;[27] *t. Ber.* 3:14 [in prayer]; *Amidah* Benediction 5:12 [citing Lam. 5:21];[28] *Aleinu* prayer 5	2 Cor. 3:16; Acts 9:35; 11:21[30]	1 Thess. 1:9; Acts 14:15; 15:19; 26:18, 20; *1 Clem.* 8:3

[calling on the Name][29])		
May the Lord direct my/our way (Ps. 37:23; Jth. 12:8; Sir. 37:15)	1 Thess. 3:11	1 Thess. 3:11
Glorified in/among his holy ones (Ps. 89:7 LXX; Ps. 154:1 (Syriac[31]); Isa. 49:3; Ezek. 28:22; 11QPs[a] 18:1)	2 Thess. 1:10a[32]	1 Cor. 6:20; Gal. 1:24; cf. Luke 2:14
To him be glory/praise (Pss. 29:1, 2; 96:7, 8; 115:1; 4Q334 frag. 2 ["words of praise"])[33]	2 Tim. 4:18; 2 Pet. 3:18[34]	Rom. 15:9; Phil. 2:11b; Luke 2:14; 17:18
"Magnify (the name of) the Lord/God"; "The Lord be magnified" (Ps. 69:30; Sir. 43:31b)	Acts 19:17	Luke 1:46; Acts 10:46
Serving/worshipping the Lord/God[35] (Exod. 20:5; Deut. 4:19; 32:43 LXX; Josh 23:19; passim)	Matt. 28:9, 17; Luke 24:52; Heb. 1:6 (citing Deut. 32:43); John 9:38;[36] Rev. 5:14?[37]	1 Cor. 14:25; Luke 4:8 (Q); John 4:21-24; Rev. 4:10; 7:11; passim[38]
? Sing psalms/hymns to the Lord/God (Exod. 15:1-2, 21; Judg. 5:3; 1 Chron. 16:7, 9; 2 Chron. 29:27, 30; Neh. 12:46; Pss. 12:6; 13:6 LXX; 21:13; 27:6; 33:2, 3;	Eph. 5:19*; *Odes Sol.* 7:17; Pliny the Younger[42]	Col. 3:16*?[43]

passim; Pss. Sol. 3:1; *m. Pesah.* 10:5;[39] *t. Rosh. Hash.* 2:2 [citing Pss. 47:6-7; 98:6]; *Ge'ullah* blessing 19 (paraphrasing Exod. 15);[40] Passover Haggadah[41])		

Scholars looking over this list will undoubtedly notice a text that has been overlooked here or there. I will proceed on the assumption that such minor revisions will not alter the overall picture, which is our primary interest. This assumption is partly validated by looking at the last row in Table 4 and the last three rows in Table 5—the ones labeled with question marks. Including these motifs in our conclusions would not significantly change the picture.

The most obvious feature of the motifs listed in Table 4 is that most of them involve liturgical acclamation and praise. As we might expect, doxology and sanctification were often directed to God the Father in New Testament literature. These motifs evidently carried over from traditional prayers to YHWH and continued to be used in the New Testament church—even Jesus was remembered to praise and sanctify the Father (Luke 11:2 [Q]). But the very same motifs are directed to Lord Jesus as predicted (prescribed) by our Kyriocentric conjecture (for example, in performances of the vision of Isaiah).[44] In other words, there is parity between God the Father and the Lord Jesus as far as these doxological motifs are concerned. This parity is especially seen in the Pauline texts cited in Table 4. In what are possibly Paul's earliest writings we find:

- "And they glorified God [the Father] because of me [*endoxadzon en emoi*]" (Gal 1:24).
- "when he [the Lord Jesus] comes to be glorified by his saints [*endoxasthēsai en tois hagios*]" (2 Thess 1:10a).

In slightly later texts we read

- "every tongue shall give praise to God [*exomologēsetai tō theō*]" (Rom. 14:11b).
- "confess . . . that Jesus is Lord [*homologēsēs . . . Kyrion Iēsoun*]" (Rom. 10:9).

- "every tongue should confess that Jesus Christ is Lord [*exomologēsētai hoti Kyrios Iēsous Christos*] to the glory of God the Father"[45] (Phil. 2:11).

An even tighter combination of usages is found in the prayer 1 Thessalonians 3:11—in this case, a prayer of intercession rather than one of praise: "Now may our God and Father himself and our Lord Jesus direct our way to you."

As shown in Table 4, the language Paul uses in 1 Thessalonians 3:11 is standard in prayers of the Hebrew Bible and the Greek Septuagint (including the Apocrypha).[46] The remarkable feature of this petition is that this divine motif is addressed to God the Father and the Lord Jesus in the very same breath. In effect, we have a binity in which the two principal divine names, God and Lord, are dedicated to the Father and to Jesus, respectively. This theological formulation is not uncommon in the New Testament, but it is all the more remarkable in view of the fact that 1 Thessalonians is probably the earliest of all the New Testament documents.

In writing to the churches in this way, Paul assumed that these forms of prayer were shared by his fellow Christians. At least, he made no attempt to explain or defend his usage. In other words, Paul was not presenting these doxologies and petitions as an innovation, based on some personal revelation or on gentile influence. As in the case of God the Father, these prayer motifs continued to be offered to YHWH, who was now identified as the Lord Jesus, and who continued to be acclaimed and praised along with the Father. Sanctification and praise of the one did not exclude devotion to the other.

Thus far the Kyriocentric conjecture holds up quite well. As noted in our discussion of vision performances in chapter 5, devotion to the Lord appears to have taken on a binitarian form at some stage (to be discussed in ch. 7), but the unity of the one being praised was not an issue.

PRAYER MOTIFS PREDOMINATELY ADDRESSED TO LORD JESUS

Next, we look at five prayer motifs that are predominately (exclusively in three cases), dedicated to the Lord Jesus. For completeness, I add four others that appear to belong to this set even though the evidence (as gathered here) is inconclusive—hence the question marks in the last four rows. As before, I leave these inconclusive cases aside in drawing conclusions.

Table 5: Prayer Motifs Predominately Addressed to Lord Jesus
(Asterisks indicate UBS citations)

Prayer Motifs in the Old Testament and Postbiblical Judaism	New Testament Era Texts that Address these Motifs to the Lord Jesus	New Testament Era Texts that Address these Motifs to God the Father
Call on (the name of) the Lord/God[47] (Gen. 4:26 LXX; 33:20; 2 Sam. 22:7 = Ps. 18:6; 1 Chron. 16:8, 35; Pss. 4:1; 17:6; 18:6; passim; Joel 2:32; Amos 4:12 LXX; Jonah 2:2; 3:8; Jth. 6:21; Add Esth 4:8; Ws. 7:7; 2 Macc. 12:15; 13:10; 15:21, 22; 3 Macc. 6:1; *Pss. Sol.* 5:5; 15:1; 4Q511 frag. 10 1:9; 11QPs[a] 24:3, 16; Josephus, *J.W.* 2.394; *Sifrei Devarim* 26 [citing 2 Sam. 22:7]; *Aleinu* prayer 5[48])	1 Cor. 1:2; 2 Cor. 12:8; Rom. 10:9–13; Luke 6:46 (Q);[49] Acts 2:21; 4:12; 7:59; 9:14, 21; 22:16[50]	Matt. 26:53;[51] 1 Pet. 1:17[52]
"Lord come" (Pss. 96:13; 98:9, passim)	1 Cor. 16:22 (*Marana tha*[53]); Rev. 22:20; *Did.* 10:6; cf. 1 John 5:20 (the Son of God has come)	None? (cf. Mark 14:62; John 14:23)[54]
"Lord save/help!" (Pss. 6:4;[55] 12:1; 20:9;[56] 106:47; 118:25;[57] 152:1 (Syriac[58]); Add Esth 4:8; 14:19; 2 Macc. 8:14; *Pss. Sol.* 12:1; *m. Ber.* 4:4;[59] 4Q511 (4QShir[b]) frag. 10 1:9; *m. Sukkah* 4:5; [60] *Lamnazeah* (Ps. 20) 8–10;[61] *Amidah* benediction 8:1–2)[62]	Matt. 8:25; 14:30; 15:25[63]	None

"Lord/God of all" (Num. 16:22; 1 Chron. 29:11–12; Ps. 97:5; Let. Aris. 16; many Qumran texts;[64] *T. Mos.* 4:2; Josephus, *Ant.* 12.22; 20.90;[65] *Amidah* benediction 1:1 [*Koneh hakkol*];[66]*Aleinu* prayer 1 [*Adon hakkol*]; [67]*Nishmat Kol-Hai* prayer[68])	Rom. 10:12; Acts 10:36 (both confessional formulas)	*1 Clem.* 64:1 ("Lord of all flesh[69]"); Eph. 4:6 ("one God and Father over all")?[70]
"Rejoice in the Lord!" (Pss. 32:11; 89:16; 104:34; Isa. 41:16b;[71] Add Esth 14:18; 4Q510 frags. 1 1:8; 10 1:7; 4Q511(4QShir[b]) frag. 1 1:5; *Shema Barchu* 5[72])	Phil. 3:1; 4:4, 10[73]	None
? "Faithful and true" (3 Macc. 2:11 [prayer of Simon the high priest]); cf. *Ge'ullah* blessing 1	Rev. 19:11	None
? "Merciful and gracious"[74] (Exod. 34:6; Neh. 9:17; Pss. 85:10; 86:15;[75] 103:8; 111:4; 145:8; Joel 2:13; Jonah 4:2; Pr. of Man. 7a; Philo, *Flaccus* 121;[76] *Ashrei* prayer [Ps. 145];[77]*Selihot* prayers [citing Exod. 34:6–7][78])	Jas 5:11c*(?)[79]	Jas 5:11c*(?)
? The Lord make you increase Deut. 1:11; Pss. 71:21; 115:14; Jer. 30:19 [LXX 37:19]; *Sifra* to Lev. 9:1 [citing Deut. 1:11]; *Sifrei Devarim* 11 [citing Deut. 1:11])	1 Thess. 3:12	None

? For whose sake we are being killed (Ps. 44:22; t. Ber. 6:7; Sifrei Devarim 32, 343; MRI Shirata 3:52-53)	Rom. 8:36*? (citing Ps. 44:22);[80] cf. Mark 13:9b, 13; Acts 5:41;[81] 15:26	Rom. 8:36*? (citing Ps. 44:22)

As the following discussion will show, the dedication of these five motifs to the Lord Jesus makes good sense in light of the Kyriocentric vision conjecture. As before, the pattern might shift a bit if other texts are added or moved from one table to another. The conclusions we shall draw should not be much affected, however. They would not be affected, at any rate, by including the motifs in the last four rows of the table.

As far as we can tell from the New Testament texts listed here, none of the early Christian writers looked for the coming of the Father or called on the Father to save them (cf. 1 Pet. 1:17).[82] These most accessible, dynamic aspects of the Old Testament Deity were clearly dedicated to the Lord Jesus, as we would expect based on the Kyriocentric vision conjecture. If the disciples had, in fact, seen the Lord in glory while calling on his name and pleading for him to come and to save them, and if he had identified himself with the face and voice of Jesus thereby giving us the *Kyrios Iēsous* confession, then these prayer motifs would readily have continued to be employed in devotion to this same Lord Jesus as Table 5 shows.[83] The dedication of the "Lord of all" (*kyrios pantōn*) acclamation to the Lord Jesus also makes sense here—it appears as a variation of the primary confessional formula in both Romans 10:12 and Acts 10:36. "Rejoicing in the Lord" would similarly follow, provided we assume that the assurance of salvation for which the disciples had prayed was granted and that, following the model of the Psalmist, they responded with rejoicing (Pss. 32:6/11; 89:9/16; 104:30/34; cf. Isa. 41:14/16). Other motifs of praise like thanksgiving and blessing will be treated in the following section.

The material in Tables 4 and 5 should be enough to demonstrate the plausibility of the Kyriocentric vision conjecture—that the impetus needed for deity Christology consisted in a vision of the Lord in response to prayers for salvation—but we still need to consider prayer motifs that were predominately (almost exclusively) devoted to God the Father.

PRAYER MOTIFS PREDOMINATELY ADDRESSED TO GOD THE FATHER

Next, let us look at four prayer motifs that are exclusively, or at least predominately, addressed to God the Father.

Table 6: Prayer Motifs Predominately Addressed to God the Father

Prayer Motifs in the Old Testament and Postbiblical Judaism	New Testament Era Texts that Address these Motifs to the Lord Jesus	New Testament Era Texts that Address these Motifs to God the Father
Give thanks to (the name) of the Lord (1 Chron. 16:8; 29:13; Neh. 12:46; Pss. 30:4, 12; passim; Jth. 8:25; Ws. 16:28; Sir. 51:1, passim; *Song of Three* 67–68; 2 Macc. 1:11; 3 Macc. 7:16; *Pss. Sol.* 16:5; 1QH 13:20 (deleted); 4Q409 1:10, 11; 4Q504 [4QDibHam[a]] frag. 1–2 7:4; 4Q510 (4QShir[a]) frag. 1 1:1-2; 4Q511 (4QShir[b]) frags. 8 1:10; 63–64 2:5; Passover Haggadah;[84] cf. Josephus, *Ant.* 7.208 [*tō theō charin hōmologei*])	None? (cf. Luke 17:16;[85] 1 Tim. 1:12 [*charin echō . . . Christō Iēsou tō kyriō hēmōn*])	1 Thess. 1:2; 2:13; 3:9; 2 Thess. 1:3; 2:13; 1 Cor. 1:4, 14; 10:30; 14:18; Rom. 1:8; 7:25; 14:6; Phil. 1:3; Col. 1:3, 12; 3;17; 1 Tim. 4:3, 4; Philem. 1:4; Mark 8:6 (Eucharist-like); 14:23 (words of institution); Luke 18:11; 22:19 (words of institution); Acts 27:35; 28:15; Rev. 4:9; 7:12; 11:17; John 6:11, 23 (Eucharist-like); 11:41; *Did.* 9:2, 3; 10:2-4; cf. Luke 10:21 (*exhomologeō*, Q); Paul's *charis tō theō* formula (1 Cor. 15:57; 2 Cor. 2:14; 8:16; 9:15; Rom. 6:17; 7:25);[86] 2 Tim. 1:3 [*charin echō tō theō*][87]
Blessing[88] (Gen. 14:20; 24:27, 48; Exod. 18:10; Deut. 8:10; Ruth 4:14; 1 Sam. 25:32, 39; 2 Sam. 18:28; 1 Kgs. 1:48;	None? (cf. Rom. 9:5;[95] Rev. 5:12[96])	Mark 6:41 (Eucharist-like); 14:22 (words of institution); Luke 1:68; Rom. 1:25; 9:5; 1 Cor. 10:16 (Eucharist-like); 2 Cor. 1:3; 11:31; Eph.

8:15, 56; 10:9; 1 Chron. 29:10; 2 Chron. 2:12; Ezra 7:27; 1 Chron. 16:36; 29:10; Neh. 9:5; Job 1:21; Pss. 18:46; 28:6; 31:21; 41:13; passim; Dan. 2:19-20; 3:28; Zech. 11:5; Tobit 3:11; 8:5, 15-17; passim; Sir. 51:12; 1 Macc. 4:30; 2 Macc. 1:17; 15:34; *Song of Three* 3, 28-66; *Jub.* 8:18; 23:1; 49:6; 50:9; *1 En.* 9:4; 22:14; 25:7; 27:3, 5; 36:4; 39:14; 61:11-12; 81:3; 90:40; *L.A.B.* 26:6; 27:13; 31:9; many Qumran texts;[89] *m. Ber.* 9:1; *m. Ta'an.* 2:4; *t. Ber.* 1:9 [the *Barukh* from Ezek. 3:12]; 6:1 [citing Deut. 8:10], passim; *t. Ta'an.* 1:11-12[90]); *Sifrei Devarim* 303; *Barchu* 2;[91] *Ge'ullah* blessing 23;[92] *Amidah* benedictions, passim; *Kaddish* 4, 5;[93] Passover Haggadah)[94]		1:3; 1 Pet. 1:3, and probably Rom. 9:5[97]
Pray to the Lord[98] (Exod. 15:1-2, 21; Judg. 5:3; 1 Kgs. 8:44; Neh. 12:46; Pss. 5:2; 6:9; 12:6; 13:6 [LXX]; 21:13; 27:6; 33:2, 3, 8; passim; Isa. 37:4;	None?[101]	1 Thess. 3:10; Rom. 1:10; Eph. 1:17; Luke 1:13; 2:37; 5:33; 10:2; 18:11; Acts 4:31; 10:2[102]

42:10; 56:7; 60:6; Dan. 9:4; Tobit 12:17–18, 22; Jth. 16:1, 13; 2 Macc. 10:7; 3 Macc. 7:16; Ws. 10:20; *1 En.* 10:21; 4Q403 [4QShirShabb[d]] 1:39–42; Philo, *Agriculture* 79, 82 [based on Exod. 15]; Philo, *Moses* 1.180; *Contempl Life* 85 [based on Exod. 15]; Josephus, *Ant.* 2.346; *1 En.* 48:5 [Lord of spirits]; *t. Ber.* 3:14 [citing 1 Kgs. 8:44][99]); *MRI* Beshallah 7[100] [citing Exod. 15:1])		
Worshipping the Lord[103] (Exod. 3:12; Deut. 6:13; Josh. 22:27; 1 Chron. 28:13; *1 En.* 10:21).	None?[104]	Rom. 1:9; 12:1; Phil. 3:3; 2 Tim. 1:3; Luke 2:37; 4:8 (Q, citing Deut. 6:13); Acts 7:7 (citing Exod. 3:12); Heb. 9:14; 12:28

The degree to which these particular prayer motifs were dedicated to God the Father is truly striking.[105] Given the facts that early prayers reflected a high degree of parity between the Lord Jesus and God the Father (Table 4) and that several prayer motifs were clearly dedicated to Lord Jesus (Table 5), it makes perfect sense to suppose (in a general way) that some would also be dedicated to the Father. But why these particular motifs?

As we already noted in chapter 5, features of Kyriocentric vision performances appear to have been adapted in order to conform to Jesus' teachings about the Father. One possibility for us to consider is that this same kind of adjustment has taken place in the cases cited here. The first two of these cases are, in fact, rather easy to explain in these terms.

Of all the church's traditions about Jesus, the one that was most frequently remembered in a performative way was the celebration of the Lord's Supper (1 Cor. 11:23-26; Mark 14:22-24; Acts 2:42; *Did.* 14:1). Although there are several different versions of what Jesus said and did at the Last Supper, they all include the idea of "giving thanks" to God.[106] The Greek verb used, *eucharisteō*, is the one from which we get the term *Eucharist*, commonly used in churches for the Lord's Supper. Jesus was also remembered as giving thanks to God on Eucharist-like occasions such as the feeding of the four thousand (Mark 8:6; cf. John 6:11, 23).

No doubt, these eucharistic words would have been preserved by Jesus' disciples even if he only had been remembered as a great hasid. They would have become even more authoritative, however, once it was understood that this hasid was actually a new manifestation of YHWH (details of this identification to be discussed in ch. 7, "When and How Did the Lord Become Identified with the Man Jesus?"). So the fact that "giving thanks" took on special meaning and was dedicated to God the Father makes good historical sense for communities that treasured these Jesus traditions as the "word of the Lord" (1 Cor. 11:23).

A secondary function of this dedication of thanksgiving words could have been to articulate a distinction between the Lord Jesus and his Father. For Paul, this distinction can be seen from texts like Romans 14:6 that honor the two figures using distinctly different verbs: "Also those who eat, eat in honor of the Lord [Jesus[107]], since they give thanks to God [for the food]; while those who abstain, abstain [lit. "don't eat"] in honor of the Lord and give thanks to God [*eucharistei tō theō*]." The Lord Jesus is to be honored by eating and rejoicing in his presence,[108] and God the Father is to be thanked for the blessing of food. Reserving thanksgiving for the Father did not imply any particular subordination of the Lord Jesus here. The fact that the authority behind this dedicated usage was the Lord Jesus may also account for one of the more puzzling Pauline formulas: "we always thank God the Father of our Lord Jesus Christ" (Col. 1:3)—it meant something like, "we always thank God the Father whom we know through the teaching and thanksgiving of our Lord Jesus Christ" (compare the alternative formula "thanks to God *through* the Lord Jesus Christ," Rom. 1:8; 7:25; Col. 3:17). This formula bravely juxtaposed the two primary portraits of Jesus: the one who thanked God as his Father (cf. Luke 10:21 [Q]), and the one who appeared to his disciples as the coming Lord (further discussed in ch. 7).[109]

Similar considerations apply for the verb "to bless" (*eulogeō*), which appears in three of the four eucharistic texts that "give thanks" does (1 Cor. 10:16; Mark

14:22; Matt. 26:26)—in general usage, the two terms were interchangeable. There is nothing to suggest that the Lord Jesus was not worthy of blessing—he was confessed to be "Lord of all" (Table 2), one of the titles traditionally used in blessings.[110] However, the first disciples vividly remembered him as blessing the Father (not the bread or the cup, as sometimes thought[111]). If, as we have conjectured, the disciples were devoted to the Lord (YHWH) in the person of Jesus, these eucharistic words and acts would also have been normative "words of the Lord" for the communities they founded. As in the case of "giving thanks" to God, Jesus' distinction between himself and his Father was evidently honored by dedicating formulas of blessing, not only in the Eucharist, but also in the standard epistolary benediction: "Blessed be the God and Father of our Lord Jesus" (2 Cor. 1:3; 11:31; Eph. 1:3; 1 Pet. 1:3), another example of a formula that superimposes the portraits of Jesus as the hasid who blessed God and as Lord.[112]

Our third case, the dedication of words for prayer and praying (*deomai* and *proseuchomai*) is also striking, particularly in view of the fact that, in practice, prayers and hymns were frequently directed to the Lord Jesus in the New Testament and other early Christian literature.[113] Apparently the use of these particular words for prayer was more dedicated than was the practice—the reason again being respect for traditions that portrayed Jesus praying to his Father (Mark 1:35; 6:46; passim, using *proseuchomai*) and instructing his disciples to do the same (Luke 11:1-2 [Q, *proseuchomai*]; 10:2 [Q, *deomai*]; cf. Mark 14:32-39 [*proseuchomai*]). Here again, the dedicated usage was attributed to the Lord Jesus, if not by Paul himself, then at least in a Pauline formula: "I pray [to] the Father of our Lord Jesus Christ" (Eph. 1:17), which could mean something like "I pray to the Father to whom our Lord Jesus Christ taught us to pray." Jesus was portrayed both as the one who prayed to God as his Father and as the one who appeared to his disciples as the Lord in anthropic form.

The case for "worship" (the primary Greek verb is *latreuō*) is similar, but somewhat more complex. As in the previous three cases, there are synonyms and parallels that dedicate equal honor to the Lord Jesus in practice. The book of Revelation, for example, used the same verb to describe worship before the heavenly throne that was shared by God and the Lamb (Rev. 22:3; cf. 7:15-17). Revelation also described the martyrs as "priests of God and of Christ" (Rev. 20:6; cf. 14:4), an office that clearly included worship and service.[114] Paul spoke of those who "worship [*latreuontes*] in the Spirit of God and boast in Christ Jesus" (Phil. 3:3). The book of Acts uses *leitourgeō*, a parallel term for worship and service,[115] to describe the worship of the Lord (Acts 13:2; cf. Acts 27:23-4).[116] The Gospels of Matthew and Luke used a similar word, *proskyneō*, to describe the worship of the risen Lord Jesus (Matt. 28:9, 17; Luke 24:52, already displayed in Table 4), and the Letter to the Hebrews cited an early rendition of Deuteronomy 32:43, "Let all God's angels worship him [*proskynēsatōsan autō*]"[117] in reference to the firstborn Son of God (Heb. 1:6).[118]

As in the previous case, that of Greek words for prayer, this particular word for worship (*latreuō*) seems to have been dedicated to God the Father, even though the practice that the word describes was common to both God and the Lord Jesus. If we may assume that one of the better known Jesus traditions was operative here, as in the previous three cases (so we have argued), it could well have been the narrative of the temptation (Luke 4:8 [Q]), in which Jesus was remembered as citing Deuteronomy 6:13 (cf. Deut. 10:20), "You shall fear the Lord your God; him alone you shall serve [or 'worship']." The Greek verb for "serve" that is used in the Septuagint is *latreuō*, precisely the one dedicated to the Father in the New Testament texts listed in Table 6.[119]

Based on the evident relation of these four prayer motifs to Jesus traditions, we may conclude that the early disciples respected those traditions as constraints on their devotional language even though they dedicated other prayer motifs to the Lord Jesus himself. Some readers may view these constraints as evidence of a relatively low Christology. The scenario presented here indicates that they can more readily be viewed as evidence of deity Christology—the teachings of Jesus were remembered as words of the Lord.

CONCLUSION REGARDING KYRIOCENTRIC PRAYERS AND DEVOTIONS IN THE NEW TESTAMENT

In this chapter, we have resorted to inductive methods and compiled biblical terminology for prayer and worship and sorting it all into three categories: motifs used for both Lord Jesus and God the Father—sometimes in binitarian formats; those dedicated to the Lord Jesus; and those dedicated to God the Father.

The Kyriocentric vision conjecture cannot be inferred from the texts, but it does an excellent job explaining them. All that is required is the context of calling on the Lord to come and to save (Table 5) and early traditions about what Jesus said and did in relation to the Father (Table 6). The main point for our purposes is that forms of worship typically used by first-century Jews did carry over to Jesus in early Christian practice—not because Jesus was an exceptional hasid (historically speaking), but because the disciples prayed to their God (YHWH), and the Lord appeared to them in anthropic form and identified himself as the man Jesus. The pattern of usage thus supports the Kyriocentric conjecture. Prayer motifs were not transferred to Jesus (as is sometimes supposed[120]). They carried over directly from standard forms of devotion to YHWH, except in those cases where such usage conflicted with the teachings and practices of the Lord Jesus himself. According to our conjecture, Christology did not start at a "low" level and gradually get higher; it started "high"—as high as YHWH himself—and was subsequently modified in various ways.[121]

To this point we have been referring to Jesus traditions in an ad hoc manner in order to explain the usage of terms in descriptions of Kyriocentric visions and of worship in the New Testament. In the following chapter, we discuss the role of Jesus traditions more systematically. Accordingly, we shall return to our hypothetico-deductive procedure and try to predict (or prescribe) the issues that Jesus traditions would have raised in the wake of the Kyriocentric vision. That procedure will allow us to generate several of the christological (and Trinitarian) affirmations in the New Testament, including those upon which standard explanations for the origin of deity Christology usually rely (resurrection and binitarian affirmations).

Notes

1. A possible exception is 2 Cor. 12:8, where Paul prays three times to the Lord (Jesus) to have a thorn removed. It is not clear how these prayers are related to the "visions and revelations of the Lord" that Paul had previously described (12:1-4). "Turning to the Lord" in 2 Cor. 3:16 is another possibility to consider, particularly if it reflects a performance based on Ps. 22:27. However, there is no mention of prayer or worship in Paul's most extensive autobiographical narrative in Galatians 1–2, which includes two passing mentions of his vision of Jesus as God's Son (Gal. 1:12, 15-16).

2. *Mishnah Berakhot* 4:5 specified that someone who journeys on a donkey must dismount and face toward Jerusalem before reciting the *Amidah* benedictions. Even expounding the merkavah of Ezek. 1 required dismounting and assuming a prayer-like posture (*t. Hag.* 2:1). An exception was allowed for a lone traveler who had no one to hold his steed (*t. Ber.* 3:18), but this situation would not have applied in the case of Saul as he was described in the first two accounts (Acts 9:7-8; 22:9, 11).

3. Larry Hurtado, *Lord Jesus Christ: Devotion to Jesus in Earliest Christianity* (Grand Rapids: Eerdmans, 2003), 137–51, 179–82, 197–203; Hurtado, *How On Earth Did Jesus Become a God? Historical Questions about Earliest Devotion to Jesus* (Grand Rapids: Eerdmans, 2005), 122, 136, 149, 198–99, passim.

4. Richard H. Bauckham, "The Worship of Jesus," in *Anchor Bible Dictionary*, ed. D. N. Freedman. 6 vols. (New York: 1992), 3:812–19, repr. in Bauckham, *Jesus and the God of Israel: God Crucified and Other Studies on the New Testament's Christology of Divine Identity* (Grand Rapids: Eerdmans, 2008), 127–51.

5. James D. G. Dunn, *The Theology of Paul the Apostle* (Grand Rapids: Eerdmans, 1998), 258–59; Dunn, *Did the First Christians Worship Jesus? The New Testament Evidence* (Louisville: Westminster John Knox, 2010), 7–28.

6. Even though prayer motifs in Second Temple texts were often subordinated to narrative or didactic concerns, in most cases they appear to have reflected prayer forms that were current at the time of composition; see M. David Flusser, "Psalms, Hymns and Prayers," in *Jewish Writings of the Second Temple Period: Apocrypha, Pseudepigrapha, Qumran, Sectarian Writings, Philo, Josephus,* CRINT 2, 2, ed. Michael E. Stone (Assen: Van Gorcum, 1984), 551–77 (556, 570, 572). The least useful texts for our purposes are ones in which the didactic purposes overwhelmed the devotional as in the prayers in the Book of Biblical Antiquities (*L.A.B.*), ibid., 574–75.

7. Ruth Langer applies Judith Newman's idea of "scripturalized prayer language" to Rabbinic (statutory) prayers and works out the detailed allusions for the *Amidah Avot* benediction; Langer, "Biblical Texts in Jewish Prayers: Their History and Function," in *Jewish and Christian Liturgy and Worship: New Insights into its History and Interaction,* Jewish and Christian Perspectives 15, ed. Albert Gerhards and Clemens Leonhard (Leiden: Brill, 2007), 63–90 (65, 81–83). Langer points out that the practice of scripturalized prayer dated back to Second Temple Hebrew prayer; ibid., 67. As Richard Sarason has explained it, the Rabbis gave statutory prayers their present form, but they worked with prayer themes that they inherited from the Second Temple era; Sarason, "The 'Intersections' of Qumran and Rabbinic Judaism: The Case of Prayer Texts and Liturgies," *DSD* 8 (2001): 169–81 (177–78).

8. I include New Testament era texts like the *Didache, 1 Clement, Odes of Solomon,* and Pliny the Younger to provide a broadened sample and not to limit the search to what was later deemed canonical by the Catholic Church.

9. Judith Newman, *Praying by the Book: The Scripturalization of Prayer in Second Temple Judaism,* Early Judaism and its Literature 14 (Atlanta: Scholars, 1999); Newman, "The Scripturalization of Prayer in Exilic and Second Temple Judaism," in *Prayers that Cite Scripture,* ed. James L. Kugel (Cambridge, MA: Harvard University Press, 2006), 7–24.

10. This distribution of names has been widely recognized since the work of Lucien Cerfaux, *Christ in the Theology of St. Paul* (London: Herder & Herder, 1951), 473, 516; Arthur W. Wainwright, *The Trinity in the New Testament* (London: SCM, 1962), 92, and others. Even if this distribution of titles is questioned in individual cases, our results should not be greatly affected.

11. The Greek verb (*ex*)*homologeo*, like the Hebrew *yadah*, can mean either "confess," "praise," or "thank." In other words, confession of faith was more devotional than present-day usage would lead us to expect and acts of praise were more propositional.

12. *My People's Prayer Book* (hereafter MPPB), ed. Lawrence A. Hoffman, 10 vols. (Woodstock, VT: Jewish Lights, 1997–2013), 6:133. Daniel Landes dates the *Aleinu* to the fourth century (MPPB 6:143). Joseph Heinemann attributes this part of the *Alein,* which addresses Adonai in the second person, to ancient synagogue usage; Heinemann, *Prayer in the Talmud: Forms and Patterns,* SJ 9 (Berlin: de Gruyter, 1977), 244–45, 270, 278.

13. *Nishmat Kol-Hai* is now part of the Sabbath morning service; ET in Joseph Heinemann, *Literature of the Synagogue,* ed. Jakob J. Petuchowski (New York: Behrman House, 1975), 11–12. It is also part of the Passover Haggadah (Cecil Roth, ed., *The Haggadah* [London: Soncino, 1959], 63). Heinemann argues that this prayer originated in the early centuries CE; Heinemann, *Prayer in the Talmud,* 241–43.

14. Rom. 14:11b is an example of a diffracted "Yahweh text," a text describing YHWH, one part of which is referred to the Lord Jesus (cf. 14:9) and the other to God the Father; cf. Bauckham, *Jesus and the God of Israel,* 209. James McGrath justly questions that possibility that Paul could have expected Jewish listeners to have picked up a novel alteration of the *Shema* in an oral/aural context, but overlooks the possibility that Paul was citing a binitarian confessional formula that was already familiar (in its basic outline) to his friends in Corinth; McGrath, "On Hearing (Rather Then Reading) Intertextual Echoes: Christology and Monotheistic Scriptures in an Oral Context," *BTB* 43 (2013): 74–80. In spite of his citation of some orality studies, McGrath ignores the liturgical and performative contexts within which Paul and his churches conversed.

15. Sirach 51:12 i–xvi is a sixteen-verse psalm inserted between verses 12 and 13 of the Hebrew text of Sirach 51 (MS B).

16. The congregational doxology in response to the *Barkhu*; MPPB 1:27.

17. MPPB 6:133. Joseph Heinemann views this part of the *Aleinu*, including the epithet "King of kings" as having its origin in midrashic exposition associated with the *Ma'amad* service in the Temple rather than in the synagogue prayer service; Heinemann, *Prayer in the Talmud*, 270–74.

18. *Mishnah Pesahim* 10:5 here refers to the Passover Haggadah (cf. Roth, ed., *Haggadah*, 36, according to the Ashkenazi rite), the earliest known version of which is found in the *Siddur* of Rav Amram, Ga'on of Sura (857–71 CE). Although most Jewish scholars date the Passover Haggadah to the third century or later, Joel Marcus has argued for the existence of an early version prior to 70 CE; Marcus, "Passover and Last Supper Revisited," *NTS* 59 (2013): 303–34.

19. Heinemann, *Literature of the Synagogue*, 11–12; Roth, ed., *Haggadah*, 66–67.

20. For the *Kaddish Shalem* ("May his great name be blessed forever . . . . Blessed, praised . . . and adored be the name of the Holy One—blessed be he"), see MPPB 6:129. For the *Kaddish Yatom* (Mourner's *Kaddish*), see MPPB 6:149. The basic form of the *Kaddish* is cited as part of the synagogue prayer service in *Sifrei Devarim* 106, ET in Reuven Hammer, trans., *Sifre: A Tannaitic Commentary on the Book of Deuteronomy*, Yale Judaica 309 (New Haven, CT: Yale University Press, 1986), 349. Marc Brettler and Lawrence Hoffmann suggest that the basic form was composed as early as the first century and point to the parallel in 1 Chron. 29:11; MPPB 6:152–53 (cf. 160), based on Heinemann, *Prayer in the Talmud*, 24–25, 256. Like *m. Pesah.* 10:5 (which refers to the Passover Aggadah) and Rev. 5:12, the *Kaddish* has seven or eight terms of praise (though verbal rather than nominal).

21. Ruth Langer interprets *t. Ber.* 1:9 as crediting R. Yehudah with participation in the angelic liturgy; Langer, *To Worship God Properly: Tensions Between Liturgical Custom and Halakhah in Judaism* (Cincinnati: Hebrew Union College Press, 1998), 193–94, 199. Langer's research supports our view that what look to us like esoteric, "mystic" practices were often included in Jewish liturgical settings.

22. For the *Kedushah de-Yotzer* (based on Isa. 6:3 and Ezek. 3:12), see MPPB 1:42–43. Heinemann concludes that both versions of the *Kedushah* originated (independently) by the time of the Tannaim (first cent.); Heinemann, *Prayer in the Talmud*, 24; cf. Ismar Elbogen, *Jewish Liturgy: A Comprehensive History*, trans. Raymond P. Scheindlin, ed. Joseph Heinemann et al. (Philadelphia: Jewish Publication Society, 1993), 59–61. Ruth Langer dates the formalized practice of the *Kedushah* to the third century CE, but suggests that it was based on earlier customs and oral traditions; Langer, *To Worship God Properly*, 192 n. 10, 200, 245.

23. For the *Kedushah de-Amidah* (based on Isa. 6 and Ezek. 3), see MPPB (following the Babylonian version) 2:59 ("Let us sanctify your name on earth"); cf. Heinemann, *Literature of the Synagogue*, 78 ("We will reverence and sanctity you in words of the holy Seraphim who hallow your name in the sanctuary"). Some scholars date the angelic *Kedushah de-Amidah* to the time of R. Aqiva (mid-second century); M. Liber, "Structure and History of the *Tefilah*," *JQR* 40 (1950): 331–57 (339 n. 20). The *Kedushah* itself must have antedated its inclusion on the *Amidah* benedictions.

24. Roth, ed., *Haggadah*, 67.

25. On the attribution of the Trisagion to Lord Jesus in *1 Clem.* 34, see our discussion in ch. 3, "Visions Associated with Prayer in Early Christian Literature."

26. On the implied attribution of the Trisagion to Lord Jesus in John 12, see our discussion in ch. 5, "Isaiah's Vision according to John 12."

27. *Mishnah Sukkah* 5:4 describes a procession around the Temple. Elliot Wolfson translates it: "we are [turned] to the Lord and our eyes are [turned] to the Lord"; Wolfson, "Iconic Visualization and the Imaginal Body of God: The Role of Intention in the Rabbinic Conception of Prayer," *Modern Theology* 12 (1996): 137–61 (143).

28. MPPB 2:39.

29. MPPB 6:133.

30. Robert F. O'Toole, *Luke's Presentation of Jesus: A Christology* (Rome: Pontifical Biblical Institute, 2004), 198–99 ("one can turn to the Lord Jesus as one turns toward God"). This motif had the force of *kavanah* (directed concentration) in the Jewish sources (discussed in ch. 2). The fact that it was used to describe the conversion of the gentile nations in Ps. 22:27 and Isa. 45:22 made it a particularly appropriate motif for describing the response of gentiles to the gospel in Acts and 1 Thessalonians. If the context there was baptismal, the element of *kavanah* was probably still operative in spite of the broader audience (cf. Acts 2:38-42).

31. J. A. Sanders, ed., *The Dead Sea Psalms Scroll* (Ithaca, NY: Cornell University Press, 1967), 104–5.

32. In earlier writing, James Dunn argued that Paul used *doxadzō* only for God the Father: "For Paul, properly speaking, only God is to be glorified"; Dunn, *The Theology of Paul the Apostle*, 258–59.

33. Note the distinct absence of any Rabbinic texts and synagogue prayers to illustrate these doxologies. It has been suggested the Rabbis were reluctant to encourage such doxological formulas due to their popularity in Christian circles; Bilhah Nitzan, *Qumran Prayer and Religious Poetry*, STDJ 12, trans. Jonathan Chipman (Leiden: Brill, 1994), 80 n. 97.

34. Dunn mentions the doxologies addressed to Jesus in 2 Tim. 4:18; 2 Pet. 3:18; Rev. 5:12, 13 (the latter two are listed in Table 5 here); Dunn, *Did the First Christians Worship Jesus?* 24. Larry Hurtado describes these doxologies devoted to Jesus as "proto-orthodox"; Hurtado, *Lord Jesus Christ*, 152–53.

35. The lxx and New Testament use the verb *proskyneō* here; Hurtado, *How On Earth Did Jesus Become a God?* 141–48; Dunn, *Did the First Christians Worship Jesus?* 10–12. As J. Lionel North and James Dunn have pointed out, *proskyneō* is also used for respect shown to fellow humans; North, "Jesus and Worship, God and Sacrifice," in *Early Judaism and Christian Monotheism*, ed. Loren T. Stuckenbruck and Wendy E. S. North (London: T&T Clark, 2004), 186–202 (195); Dunn, *Did the First Christians Worship Jesus?* 8–10.

36. John 9:38 exhibits a typical act of devotion to the Lord, involving both confession of belief and acclamation as Lord, as well as *proskyneō* worship; Hurtado, *How On Earth Did Jesus Become a God?* 143.

37. I omit Synoptic Gospel texts where *proskyneō* is used for reverence to Jesus as a teacher and healer. Hurtado makes a strong case for including Matthew's use of the term; Hurtado, *How on Earth Did Jesus Become God?* 145–8. Adding some of these Matthean texts would not change the overall pattern here.

38. Note that the texts ascribing *proskyneō* worship to the Father are somewhat earlier than those for the Lord Jesus. If we were only considering early New Testament texts like the Letters of Paul, this term for worship would belong in Table 6. See below on the parallel verb, *latreuō*, which is dedicated exclusively to the Father. Both verbs are used in parallel in Luke 4:8 (Q).

39. *Mishnah Pesah.* 10:5 speaks here of chanting the Egyptian *Hallel* (Pss. 113–18). Talmud's attribution of its first recital to Moses and the Israelites (along with Exod. 15, *b. Pesah.* 117a) tells us more about the Rabbinic performance than about a historical Moses.

40. MPPB 1:119.

41. Roth, ed., *Haggadah*, 67.

42. Pliny, governor of Bithynia, wrote in 111 ce that Christians "sang a hymn in alternate verses to Christ as to a god" (*Ep.* 10.96).

43. Reading *theō* ("to God") with P[46], Codex Aleph, A, B, C*, D*. This is the preferred reading (grade B) in the United Bible Society edition. If the reading *kyriō* ("to the Lord") were preferred, all New Testament era uses of this motif would be dedicated to the Lord Jesus and this phrase would belong in Table 5.

44. This is a good example of inductive and hypothetico-deductive methods working together—something like digging a tunnel from both sides of a river. The objective is to meet somewhere in the middle (depending on obstacles in the way).

45. In the New Testament as a whole, the secondary motif of giving glory is shared by Jesus and his Father, as noted in the third, seventh, and eighth rows of Table 4.

46. See Ps. 37:23 (*para Kyriou . . . kateuthunetai . . . tēn hodon autou*); Jth. 12:8 (*tou Kyriou . . . kateuthunai . . . tēn hodon autēs*); Sir. 37:15 (*euthunē . . . tēn hodon sou*).

47. The Greek verbs here are *kaleō* and derivatives like *epikaleō* and *parakaleō*.

48. MPPB 6:133.

49. *Kyrie Kyrie* is the standard LXX translation of the Hebrew vocative, *Adonai* YHWH; Albert Pietersma, "Kyrios or Tetragram: A Renewed Quest for the Original Septuagint," in *De Septuaginta: Studies in Honour of John W. Wevers*, ed. Albert Pietersma and Claude Cox (Mississauga, ON: Benben, 1984), 85–101 (96–97). John Strazicich bases the usage on a liturgical formula for calling on the name of the Lord; Strazicich, *Joel's Use of Scripture and Scripture's Use of Joel: Appropriation and Resignification in Second Temple Judaism and Early Christianity*, Biblical Interpretation 82 (Leiden: Brill, 2007), 293–94. In the earliest stratum of the Gospel tradition (Q), it was understood as a formula for calling on the Lord Jesus (Luke 6:46a) and was paired with obedience to the Lord's commandments. Parallels with the earliest Tannaitic accounts of the *Shema* and its Blessings (*m. Ber.* 2:2) suggest that Q deliberately paired affirmation of the Lordship of Jesus ("Lord, Lord"; the "yoke of the kingdom") with acceptance of his commandments ("do what I tell you"; the "yoke of the commandments"); cf. Reuven Kimelman, "Polemics and Rabbinic Liturgy," in *Discussing Cultural Influences: Text, Context and Non-Text in Rabbinic Judaism*, Studies in Judaism, ed. Rivka Ulmer (Lanham, MD: University Press of America, 2007), 59–97 (67). In an optimistic attempt to reconstruct chronological stages of development, Kimelman dates this Rabbinic innovation to the second century CE (ibid., 71). If our suggested parallel to Q holds up, however, the innovation must have been at least a century earlier than R. Akiva and his students.

50. We should also note the motif of casting out demons and healing in the name of the Lord Jesus (Mark 9:38-39; Acts 3:6; 9:34); cf. Sigurd Grindheim, *Christology in the Synoptic Gospels: God or God's Servant?* (London: T&T Clark, 2012), 49, 121. On the use of the divine name *Kyrios* as the "name of Jesus"; cf. Charles A. Gieschen, "The Divine Name in Ante-Nicene Christology," *VC* 57 (2003): 115–58.

51. "Do you think that I cannot appeal to [*parakalesai*] my Father . . ." (Matt. 26:53). Note that the two texts dedicating this motif to the Father are much later than the Pauline texts in column two.

52. "If you invoke as Father [*patera epikaleisthe*] the one who judges all people impartially . . ." (1 Pet. 1:17).

53. For simplicity, I assume the consensus reading of *marana tha* as a petition, "Our Lord, come!" The alternative reading *maran atha*, "Our Lord has come," would still refer back to a liturgical prayer believed to have been answered in a Kyriocentric vision. On the use of *Maran* or *Marna* as a divine name in the Levant of Jesus' time, see M. David Flusser, "Paganism in Palestine," in *The Jewish People in the First Century: Historical Geography, Political History, Social, Cultural and Religious Life and Institutions*, CRINT 1, 1, ed. S. Safrai and M. Stern (Assen: Van Gorcum, 1974), 1065–1100 (1078–79). Flusser's antithesis of the "primitive community" and Hellenistic (or Canaanite) syncretism reflected ideas that were standard fare prior to the work of Frank Moore Cross, *Canaanite Myth and Hebrew Epic: Essays in the History of the Religion of Israel* (Cambridge, MA: Harvard University Press, 1973); and Martin Hengel, *Judaism and Hellenism: Studies in Their Encounter in Palestine during the Early Hellenistic Period*, trans. John Bowden, 2 vols. (London: SCM, 1974).

54. Mark 14:62 is ambiguous. Does the fact that the Son of Man is "seated at the right hand of the Power" and "coming with the clouds" imply that "the Power" (God) is also coming? In any case, the focus is on the coming of the Son of Man as the expected Lord. John 14 is complicated,

but the main focus is on the sending and coming of the Holy Spirit as the representative of Father and Son (John 14:16, 26).

55. Psalm 6 ("David's Tahanun") is recited in the Ashkenazi Tahanun liturgy (MPPB 6:71).

56. Ps. 20:9 was also incorporated into the Ashkenazi Tahanun liturgy; MPPB 6:101.

57. Ps. 118 is one of the six *Hallel* Psalms (the Egyptian *Hallel*, Pss. 113–18) that are mandated for Passover in *m. Pesah.* 5:7; 9:3; 10:5 and are included in the *Siddur* under the Egyptian *Hallel* for Sabbath mornings on Pesah, Shavuʿot, Sukkot, Hanukkah, and New Moons. Although the Egyptian *Hallel* originally included only Pss. 113 and 114 (*t. Pesah.* 10:9), Ps. 118 was also said to have been recited as *Hallel* in Temple times (*m. Sukk.* 3:9-10; 4:1, 8, where it was mandated for the Feast of Tabernacles).

58. Sanders, ed., *Dead Sea Psalms Scroll*, 142.

59. *Mishnah Berakhot* 4:4 contains an apotropaic prayer for travelers in danger.

60. *Mishnah Sukkah* 4:5 contains a prayer for priests circumambulating the temple altar.

61. For the *Lamnazeah* (Psalm 20) see MPPB 6:101. The plea, "Adonai, save us," also occurs in *Vehu rahum*, lines 3, 9. 47, part of the Ashkenazi Tahanun liturgy for Mondays and Thursdays (MPPB 6:34–39), on the antiquity of which, see Elbogen, *Jewish Liturgy*, 71.

62. *Amidah* benediction for Healing (*Refuʾah*): "Heal us, Adonai, that we shall be healed; save us that we shall be saved"; MPPB 2:96. The exact wording was variable, as shown by the three parallel versions, one of which leaves out the words *save us*; cf. Avigdor Shinan, "Synagogues in the Land of Israel: The Literature of the Ancient Synagogue and Synagogue Archaeology," in *Sacred Realm: The Emergence of the Synagogue in the Ancient World*, ed. Steven Fine (New York: Oxford University Press, 1996), 130–42 (144).

63. Matthew's uses of the exclamation, "Save, Lord" (*kyrie sōson; kyrie boēthei*) probably reflect his own community's prayers to the Lord Jesus.

64. Qumran texts with the phrase *Lord/Master of all* include 1Q20 (Genesis Apocryphon) 20:12-13, 15; 4Q202 (4QEnoch[b]) 3:14; 4Q403 (4QShirShabb[d]) 1:28 = 4Q404 (4QShirShabb[e]) frag. 2 1:10; 4Q409 (4QLiturgy) 1:6, 8; 4Q503 (4QPrQuot) frags. 48–50 1:8 (nonsectarian?); 4Q510 (4QSihir[a]) frag. 1 1:2 (nonsectarian?).

65. Josephus in *Ant.* 20.90 describes a proselyte king praying to the "Lord of all" (*tōn pantōn kyrios*).

66. *Amidah* benediction for the Fathers (*Avot*), MPPB 2:57. The text of the *Avot* blessing is likely to be close to the original wording. Ruth Langer argues this point on the basis of the facts that an appeal to the merit of the ancestors was prerequisite to the rest of the prayer, and that there is no mention of divine kingship, as later mandated in the *Yerushalmi* (*y. Ber.* 1:8, 3b); cf. Langer, "The Amidah as Formative Rabbinic Prayer," in *Identität durch Gebet: Zur gemeinschaftsbildenden Funktion institutionalisierten Betens in Judentum und Christentum*, Studien zu Judentum und Christentum, ed. Stephan Wahle (Paderborn: Schöningh, 2003), 127–56 (144–5).

67. MPPB 6:133; cf. Philip Segal, "Early Christian and Rabbinic Liturgical Affinities," *NTS* 30 (1984): 63–90 (89). Note the doxological pairing of universal lordship and universal worship in the *Aleinu* as in Rom. 10:12-13; Phil. 2:9-11. Joseph Heinemann views this part of the *Aleinu*, including the epithet "Lord of all," as having its origin in midrashic exposition associated with the *Maʿamad* service in the Temple rather than in the synagogue prayer service; Heinemann, *Prayer in the Talmud*, 270–77.

68. ET in Heinemann, *Literature of the Synagogue*, 11.

69. *First Clement* 64:1 uses the phrase, "Lord of all flesh" (*kyrios pasēs sarkos*), in a prayer to the God who chose the Lord Jesus Christ.

70. Eph. 4:6 uses the phrase, "one God and Father over all" (*heis theos kai patēr ho epi pantōn*) in a Trinitarian confessional formula. I judge this phrase to be rather different from that used in the model phrase "Lord of all."

71. The LXX of Isa. 41:16 reads, "rejoice in the holy ones/things of Israel," but the Hebrew reading of the Masoretic text ("rejoice in the Lord") is supported by 1QIsa[a]; Martin Abegg Jr.,

Peter Flinch, and Eugene Ulrich, trans. *The Dead Sea Scrolls Bible* (San Francisco: HarperSanFrancisco, 1999), 336. Isa. 41:16 is cited in *Gen. R.* 83:5 and *Cant. R.* 7:3 as a promise of the eschatological rejoicing of Israel; cf. Marc G. Hirshman, *A Rivalry of Genius: Jewish and Christian Biblical Interpretation in Late Antiquity*, SUNY Series in Judaica (Albany: State University of New York Press, 1996), 15–16.

72. The congregational response to the *Barkhu*; MPPB 1:27.

73. Paul's "rejoice in the Lord" (*chairete en kyriō*) is clearly dedicated to the Lord Jesus, as shown by the prior confessional formula in Phil. 2:11 (*Kyrios Iēsous Christos*) and the parallel phrase in Phil. 3:2 (*kauchōmenoi en Christō*).

74. As shown here, variations on the phrase "merciful and gracious" were so common that it must be regarded as a stock phrase in the tradition pool rather than a reference to a particular biblical text.

75. The context of Psalm 86:15 reads like the script for a rehearsal of Moses' theophany in Exod. 34:5-10.

76. Philo describes a prayer of thanksgiving by the Jews of Alexandria that uses the phrase, "you have taken pity and compassion on us" (*oikton kai eleon hēmōn*); *Against Flaccus* 121, Loeb ed., 9:368-9.

77. The *Ashrei* prayer (Ps. 145) is the first of the Concluding prayers in the Shaharit and Minhah services and is found in several other places as well. In fact, its liturgical use can be dated back to the *Yahad* at Qumran; Lawrence H. Schiffman, "The Dead Sea Scrolls and the Early History of Jewish Liturgy," in *The Synagogue in Late Antiquity*, ed. Lee I. Levine (Philadelphia: American Schools of Oriental Research, 1987), 33–48 (36). According to *b. Ber.* 4b, whoever recites Psalm 145 three times per day is assured of the world to come. The phrase "gracious and merciful king" also occurs in the *Vehu rahum* prayer line 29 and in other parts of the Tahanun liturgy (MPPB 6:36, 63); cf. Heinemann, *Prayer in the Talmud*, 125 (citing Elbogen), on the possible origin of the Tahanunim in the people's prayers that followed the offering of incense in the Temple.

78. *Selihot* prayers are non-statutory prayers that enumerate the thirteen divine attributes in Exod. 34:6-7 and that later became a part of the *Amidah* framework, esp. in poems called *piyut*.

79. Among commentators who understand James 5:11 to refer to God the Father, see Peter H. Davids, *The Epistle of James: A Commentary on the Greek Text*, NIGTC (Grand Rapids: Eerdmans, 1982), 188; Martin Dibelius, *James: A Commentary on the Epistle of James*, Hermeneia, rev. Heinrich Greeven, trans. Michael A. Williams, ed. Helmut Koester (Philadelphia: Fortress Press, 1976), 247b. As Bo Reicke has pointed out, however, James 5:7, 8, and 10 all use *Kyrios* for the Lord Jesus; Reicke, *The Epistles of James, Peter, and Jude*, AB 37 (Garden City, NY: Doubleday, 1964), 54–55.

80. It is not clear from the immediate context to whom Paul addressed the Psalm verse in Rom. 8:36. The previous verses speak of the death, intercession, and love of Christ, while the following verses speak of the love of God in Christ. If Paul's first-person affirmations in Gal. 2:20; Phil. 3:7-8 are any guide here, the Psalm verse was likely addressed to the Lord Jesus.

81. "For the sake of the name" in Acts 5:41 clearly refers to the Lord Jesus; cf. Acts 4:10, 18, 30; 5:28. On the use of the divine name *Kyrios* as the "name of Jesus"; cf. Gieschen, "The Divine Name in Ante-Nicene Christology," 115–58.

82. Even though "Save, Lord" was the most common prayer for salvation in the Old Testament, calling on God (or the name of God) for salvation was also common, and, in *Selihot* prayers like *Abinu malkenu* in the later *Siddur*, we also find the combination, "our Father . . . save us"; Philip Birnbaum, *Daily Prayer Book, Ha-Siddur ha-Shalem* (New York: Hebrew Publishing Company, 1949), 101, 102. On the likely temple origin of the *Selihot*, see also Heinemann, *Prayer in the Talmud*, 151.

83. Our conjecture also makes sense of the fact that disciples cast out demons and healed in the name of the Lord Jesus, rather than in the name of God (Mark 9:38-39; Acts 3:6; 9:34).

84. Roth, ed., *Haggadah*, 47, 57 (citing Ps. 118:1), passim.

85. In Luke 17:16, the Samaritan leper returned to thank Jesus for healing him. Dennis Hamm notes that the Samaritan's actions of falling at Jesus' feet and thanking him (*eucharistōn autō*) together implied the perception of deity in Jesus. As a counterexample, Hamm cites Acts 10:25-26, where Peter forbade Cornelius to fall at his feet and worship him; Hamm, "What the Samaritan Leper Sees: The Narrative Christology of Luke 17:11-19," *CBQ* 56 (1994): 273–87 (284). On the other hand, Dunn states that the Samaritan leper's thanks is probably only thanks for a service rendered; Dunn, *Did the First Christians Worship Jesus?* 20. C. Kavin Rowe does not treat this text in his book *Early Narrative Christology: The Lord in the Gospel of Luke*, BZNW 139 (Berlin: de Gruyter, 2006).

86. The functional equivalence between Paul's uses of *charis* and *eucharisteō* is seen in 1 Cor. 10:30.

87. Dunn, *Did the First Christians Worship Jesus?* 20.

88. For a helpful review of the biblical, pseudepigraphal, Qumran, and Tannaitic blessings, see Nitzan, *Qumran Prayer and Religious Poetry*, 72–78. I ignore the scholarly distinction between direct and indirect blessings here; it is only meaningful for the texts that quote the actual words of prayers like 1 Chron. 29:10 (therefore, we have no way of knowing which one Jesus used). I also ignore the distinction between blessings that are presented in biblical narratives as prayers and those that are kerygmatic utterances in soliloquies or conversations; W. Sibley Towner, "'Blessed be YHWH' and Blessed Art Thou, YHWH': The Modulation of a Biblical Formula," *CBQ* 30 (1968): 386–99 (389). Narratives and conversations were never hermetically sealed from devotional practices (the "liturgicalization of everyday discourse") and offer some of our best evidence for prayer motifs.

89. Among the six dozen or so Qumran blessings of the Lord are 1QS 1:19; 10:13-16; 11:15; 1QM 13:2, 7; 14:3-4, 8; 18:6-7; 1QH 4:20; 13:20 (as emended); 18:14; 19:27, 29, 32; 1QapGen ar 20:12; 4Q286 (4QBer) frag. 7 1:7, 8; 4Q379 (Psalms of Joshua) frag. 22 2:5; 4Q403 (4QShirShabb^d) 1:28-29 = 4Q404 (4QShirShabb^e) frag. 2 line 10 (the Lord, King of all); 4Q405 (4QShirShabb^f) frags 20–22 1:8 (image of the throne chariot); 4Q409 (4QLiturgy) 1:1-11 (the Lord of all); 4Q491 (4QMa) frags. 8–10 1:6; 4Q502 frag. 24 1:2; 4Q503 (4QPrQuot) passim (nonsectarian?); 4Q504 (4QDibHam^a) frag. 3 2:2, passim; 4Q507 frags. 2 1:3; 3 1:1; 4Q510 (4QShir^a) 1:1-2 (Lord of all the holy ones); 4Q511 (4QShir^b) frag. 63–64 2:2; 4:2 (nonsectarian?); 4Q512 passim; 11QPs^a 19:7; 26:14; 11Q14 (11QBer) 1:3-4. Eileen Schuller has counted at least seventy-five of them; Schuller, "Some Observations on Blessings of God in Texts from Qumran," in *Of Scribes and Scrolls: Studies on the Hebrew Bible, Intertestamental Judaism, and Christian Origins*, College Theology Society Resources in Religion 5, ed. Harold W. Attridge, John J. Collins, and Thomas H. Tobin (Lanham, MD: University Press of America, 1990), 133–43 (134).

90. *Tosefta Ta'anit* 1:11, 12 cites Pss. 106:48 and 72:19 as ancient temple prayers.

91. For the *Barkhu* ("Blessed be Adonai who is to be blessed forever") at the beginning of the *Shema* prayer service, see MPPB 1:27, and Lawrence Hoffman's comment on p. 33. For the identical *Barkhu* prior to the first *Birkhat ha-Torah*, see MPPB 4:103. The *Barkhu* is cited as part of the synagogue prayer service in *Sifrei Devarim* 106.

92. MPPB 1:119.

93. For the *Kaddish Shalem* ("May his great name be blessed forever. . . . Blessed, praised . . . and adored be the name of the Holy One—blessed be he"), see MPPB 6:129. For the *Kaddish Yatom*, see MPPB 6:149. This formula is also cited as part of the synagogue prayer service in *Sifrei Devarim* 106. Brettler and Hoffmann suggest that it was composed as early as the late first century; MPPB 6:152, 160.

94. Roth, ed., *Haggadah*, 6–8, 14, 18, 36, passim.

95. Romans 9:5 is sometimes said to refer to the Messiah as "God over all." Raymond E. Brown prefers this translation, although he claims "no more than plausibility"; Brown, *An Introduction to New Testament Christology* (New York: Paulist, 1994), 182–83.

96. Revelation 5:12 states that the Lamb is "worthy to receive honor, glory, and blessing" and was included in Table 5.

97. Dunn, *Did the First Christians Worship Jesus?* 26.

98. The Greek LXX and New Testament use two pairs of terms here, *deēsis, deomai,* and *proseuchē, proseuchomai,* but they are synonymous as in Pss. 5:2; 6:9, passim.

99. Like New Testament prayers to the Father, *t. Ber.* 3:14 interprets praying to the Lord as "turning toward their Father in heaven." In other words, prayer is directed to a person with no particular sense of spatial direction (unlike *kavanah* in *m. Ber.* 2:1; 5:1, *t. Ber.* 3:4, 20 as treated in ch. 2).

100. Jacob Z. Lauterbach, trans., *Mekilta of Rabbi Ishmael,* 3 vols. (Philadelphia: Jewish Publication Society of America, 1933), 2:252–53; 254–55.

101. In Luke 21:36, Jesus commands his disciples to pray (the verb is *deomai*) in order to survive the coming tribulation and stand before the Son of Man. Presumably, this prayer was intended for God in heaven, rather than to the Son of Man.

102. Dunn, *Did the First Christians Worship Jesus?* 33, where the author rightly concludes that "*deēsis* is used in the Epistles always for prayer; that is, prayer to God [the Father]."

103. The Greek LXX and New Testament use the verb *latreuō* here; Dunn, *Theology of Paul the Apostle,* 259; Dunn, *Did the First Christians Worship Jesus?* 14–15, 27.

104. In Acts 27:23, Paul states that an angel who stood by him was the angel of the God to whom he belonged and whom he served (the verb is *latreuō*). The "God" in question is evidently God the Father.

105. I speak of these motifs being "dedicated" rather than "reserved" for the Father (as James Dunn does) partly to avoid the problems raised with the latter usage by Larry Hurtado, "The Binitarian Shape of Early Christian Worship," in *The Jewish Roots of Christological Monotheism,* SJSJ 63, ed. Carey C. Newman, James R. Davila, and Gladys L. Lewis (Leiden: Brill, 1999), 187–213 (207–8). Unfortunately, this part of Hurtado's paper seems to have been omitted in the revised version in Hurtado, *Lord Jesus Christ,* 134–53. "Dedication" also has a more positive, generous resonance than "reservation" does.

106. Claus Westermann argued the Hebrew verb *yadah* could better be translated "praise" than "thank," because it does not so much express a personal attitude of thankfulness as exalt the one being thanked (or praised); Westermann, *Praise and Lament in the Psalms,* trans. Keith R. Crim and Richard N. Soulen (Atlanta: John Knox, 1981), 25–30.

107. For the identity of the "Lord" in Rom. 14:6 as Lord Jesus, cf. Rom. 13:14 ("put on the Lord Jesus Christ"); 14:9 ("Christ died and lived again that he might be Lord of both the dead and the living").

108. I take it that Paul's phrase *esthiō kyriō* (lit. "eat to the Lord") in Rom. 14:6 is a compact form of the liturgical phrase, *esthiō enantion tou Kyriou* ("eat in the presence of the Lord"). As is clear from its context in Deut. 12:7; 14:26, such "eating" was a form of rejoicing and thanksgiving for produce of the land. In fact, Deut. 12:7 exhibits the same two-part structure that Paul assumes in Rom. 14:6, "eat in the presence of the Lord your God . . . rejoicing in all the undertakings in which the Lord your God has blessed you." The tradition Paul cites in Rom. 14 has distributed these two parts to the Lord Jesus and God the Father, respectively, thereby articulating the distinction.

109. Credit goes to James Dunn for calling our attention to the importance of the "God of our Lord Jesus Christ" texts in Paul and 1 Peter; Dunn, *Did the First Christians Worship Jesus?* 3, 110. In attributing such formulas to a superposition of two distinct portraits of Jesus (discussed in ch. 7), I hope to have presented a plausible explanation for this seemingly paradoxical usage.

110. In several Qumran texts, the One who was blessed was designated by this title; see 4Q403 (4QShirShabb^d) 1:28 = 4Q404 (4QShirShabb^e) frag. 2 1:10 ("blessed be the Lord, King of all"); 4Q409 (4QLiturgy) 1:6, 8 ("bless the Lord of all"); 4Q510 (4QShir^a) frag. 1 1:1-2 ("blessings to the King of glory; thanksgiving to the Lord of all the holy ones"). At least one of these texts was

nonsectarian (4QShirShabb and possibly 4QShir^a), indicating usage prior to and more widespread than the *Yahad* itself. For partial confirmation, see the *Amidah Avot* benediction (*Barukh attah . . . Koneh hakkol*), the wording of which is thought to be close to the original as noted above.

111. The NRSV of Mark 14:22; Matt. 26:26 states that Jesus "took a loaf of bread, and after blessing it . . ." However, the Greek texts simply say that he "blessed," implying that he blessed God; cf. *Sifrei Devarim* 303 ("I did not forget to bless you and mention your name over it"). In 1 Cor. 10:16, Paul speaks of "the cup of blessing that we bless," but again the blessing is understood in context to be directed to God, who was "Creator of the fruit of the vine" (cf. Ps. 104:14); 1QS 6:3, 8; *t. Ber.* 4:3; Passover Haggadah (Roth, ed., *Haggadah*, 8, 40, 52, 67, 68). Theologically, Christians understand the bread and cup as signifying the divine presence—in this case, the presence of the Lord Jesus.

112. Semantically, the opposite of blessing was cursing (or damning), and formulas for the two were often paired together and followed by "Amen" (Deut. 27:12-26; 28:3-6, 16-19; 1QS 2:1-18; 1QM 13:1-5; 4Q286 frag. 7 1-2; 4Q379 frag. 22 2:5-10; Jas. 3:9). It is striking that Paul paired cursing Jesus (*anathema Iēsous*) with affirming his Lordship (*Kyrios Iēsous*), instead of blessing him as we might otherwise expect (1 Cor. 12:3).

113. In addition to 1 Thess. 3:11, discussed above, see 1 Thess. 3:11-12; 2 Thess. 2:16; 3:5(?), 16; 1 Cor. 1:2; 12:8-9; 16:22; 2 Cor. 12:8; Rom. 10:12-14; Eph. 5:19; 1 Tim. 1:12; 2 Tim. 2:22; 4:18(?); Acts 1:24(?); 7:59-60; 9:14, 21; 13:2(?); 22:16; Heb. 13:21; 1 Pet. 3:15; 4:11; 2 Pet. 3:18; Rev. 1:5-6; 5:8-14; 22:20; John 14:14; cf. *Did.* 10:6; *Odes Sol.* 6:7; 14:1, 8; 16:2, 4; 17:17; 18:4; 20:10; 21:7; 26:1; 38:19; 40:2; Ignatius, *Eph.* 4:1; Ignatius, *Rom.* 4:2; *Mart. Pol.* 14:2; 19:2; 21; 22:1, 3; 23:5.

114. James Dunn sets the Revelation texts aside as a special (late?) development in the New Testament; Dunn, *Did the First Christians Worship Jesus?* 130–31.

115. The two verbs for serve/worship are used in parallel in Exod. 28:35 (Aaron in the Tabernacle); Jth. 4:14 (high priest in the Temple); Sir. 4:14 (serving Lady Wisdom alongside the Most High); 45:15 (Aaron in the Tabernacle).

116. Here I follow Richard Bauckham, who sees the title "Lord" as referring to Jesus; Bauckham "The Worship of Jesus," 813a; reprinted in Bauckham, *Jesus and the God of Israel*, 129. The identification is doubted by Dunn, *Did the First Christians Worship Jesus?* 14, but the parallel expression, "teaching about the Lord" (Acts 13:12) supports Bauckham's reading.

117. The Masoretic Hebrew text lacks this part of Deut. 32:43, but it is found in the Qumran Hebrew, 4QDeut^q (Abegg et al., trans. *Dead Sea Scrolls Bible*, 193), which is centuries older than the Masoretic, as well as in the Septuagint.

118. The reason that the Letter to the Hebrews contravenes the earlier dedication of the verb *proskyneō* was evidently that the author deliberately collected texts (or relied on an earlier catena) that would demonstrate the superiority of the divine Son to the angels. In other words, the need to exalt the Son in exegetical terms trumped the tradition of dedicating this phrase to God the Father in actual practice.

119. Interestingly, the first verb found in the LXX of Deut. 6:13; 10:20 is "to fear" (*phobeō*), a motif that is used for the Lord Jesus in the earliest Gospel (Mark 4:41) as well as for God the Father (in later texts). In Jesus' quotation of Deut. 6:13 in Luke 4:8 (Q), however, this verb is replaced by the verb *proskyneō*, which means "to worship" (a similar shift is reflected in the Old Latin version of Deut. 6:13).

120. James McGrath, for example, discussed the possibility that acts of worship were transferred to the Lamb (the Lord Jesus) in the book of Revelation, and concludes (rightly) that this was unlikely; McGrath, *The Only True God: Early Christian Monotheism in its Jewish Context* (Urbana: University of Illinois Press, 2009), 76.

121. The logic of plausibility that I am developing here is similar to standard *lectio difficilior* reasoning in textual criticism. Other things being equal, the "more difficult reading" is likely to be the original one because more conventional readings can then be more readily explained as derivative than the other way around.

PART III

Modifications of the Lord–Jesus Identification in the New Testament and the Early Church

7

Superposing Jesus Traditions and Deity Christology

The focus of our discussion thus far has been visions of the Lord in their immediate contexts in performance and prayer as the necessary ground for an early emergence of deity Christology and the worship of the Lord Jesus. Our conjecture that it all began with Kyriocentric visions has been tested against visionary texts of Second Temple literature (primarily apocalypses and Psalms), early Rabbinic (Tannaitic) literature, and the New Testament itself. We may conclude that our conjecture is plausible (not implausible) on its own terms.

Thus far I have generally avoided using conventional christological phrases like Messiah (Christ), Son of Man, Son of God, Word of God, incarnation (the Word becoming flesh), crucifixion, resurrection, and atonement (to say nothing of "substance" and "person")—none of which had a place in the Kyriocentric vision itself. However, some of these terms have appeared in cited texts (e.g., Son of Man in John 12:32-41; Son of God in Heb. 1:1-6; 1 John 5:20), and, when they did, I suggested that these texts incorporated modifications of the Kyriocentric vision that were needed to make it conform to Jesus' teachings about the Father.[1] I resorted to the same suggestion in order to account for the four devotional formulas dedicated to God the Father. This particular part of the argument clearly needs more work. In this chapter, therefore, I shall try to treat the impact of Jesus traditions more comprehensively and show that our conjecture also allows us to explain the origin of these aspects of New Testament Christology as consequences of the Kyriocentric vision. Even though these explanations cannot be proven on their own terms, they will further demonstrate the fruitfulness of the Kyriocentric vision conjecture and thereby enhance its plausibility.

According to our scenario, the early disciples had to work out their memories of Jesus using two distinct portraits. One portrait was that of the man Jesus, remembered as a hasid (a pious Jew or servant of God), who was

179

seen as the bearer of God's words and healing power.[2] The second portrait was that of the Lord (YHWH) coming to earth in a glorious anthropic form, now perceived with the face and voice of Jesus. Previously these two images had always been distinguished very clearly,[3] but they were brought together in an unprecedented way by the Lord-Jesus identification and the corresponding confession *Kyrios Iēsous*. This confession can be viewed from either side: starting from the first portrait, we have "Jesus is Lord," which is the more familiar form even though it reverses the Greek terms. Starting from the second portrait, we get "The Lord is Jesus."[4] Either way, the two portraits were superimposed, one upon the other, and the result was predictably thought provoking, if not chaotic.[5]

The metaphor of portraits is useful for our purposes, and I shall continue to use it, but it does have its limitations. Portraits are rather inert—they get framed and are hung on walls at different locations. It will help to think alternatively in terms of two film-exposures that can be superposed to produce a double-exposure. Even better, we could think in terms of two narratives—one of the Lord's comings to earth (theophanies), as remembered and rehearsed by the community, and one of the succession of chosen servants of the Lord. The task of the disciples would be to superimpose the two exposures, or interweave the two narratives, without unduly sacrificing coherence.[6] The New Testament letters and Gospels indicate that they did this in a variety of ways. In this chapter, we try to reconstruct the history (really a prehistory) of these efforts, building on the Kyriocentric conjecture and utilizing a simple hermeneutic of supply and demand.

As noted in the Introduction, an adequate historical explanation of an innovation must work within the constraints of a "tradition pool" of beliefs and practices that were available to a community—what we have termed *the supply* side. In order to be truly explanatory, however, it must also identify the problems that historical events created for the community: problems that motivated them to revisit their tradition pool and select those beliefs and practices that would help resolve the problem—what we have termed the *demand side* (a.k.a. "demand system"). Our procedure here will be first to reconstruct the problems that arose from the Lord-Jesus identification, and then to show that distinctive christological formulations can be understood to have resulted from attempts to resolve these problems.

We are dealing here with mental (or spiritual) processes that defy any clear definition, particularly as viewed two thousand years after the fact. It would be unrealistic to expect to come up with a sequence of steps, or even to identify specific individuals involved with any certainly (although apostolic leaders like

Peter were often cited by name and were probably impersonated in ecclesial performances). As Martin Jaffee has argued, innovations normally occurred in early Judaism in the mutual discourse of discipleship circles, not in the minds of singular individuals.[7] The results were emergent (an "emergent logos") and, as far as we can tell from such a distance, they were synchronous.[8]

In spite of the chaotic nature of the cognitive processes we are describing, some general areas of discussion would have emerged.[9] It should be possible, for instance, to retrieve some of the more obvious questions that arose among the early disciples and to identify christological motifs in the New Testament documents that were selected from the tradition pool and formulated as answers.

In plotting out the initial questions that were generated by the Lord-Jesus identification, we are safe in assuming that the disciples remembered the basic features of Jesus' prayer life and his violent death. These memories would undoubtedly have raised a number of difficulties for the communication of the new vision of the Lord with the name and face of Jesus:

- How could Jesus be the anthropic form in which the Lord appeared when he was dead and buried?
- When and how did the Lord become identified with Jesus?
- If the Lord was identified with Jesus already during his lifetime, how could he have prayed to God as his Father in heaven?
- If the Lord was identified with Jesus already during his lifetime, what justification was there for saying that he experienced death on a cross?

For reference, I shall refer to these four questions as "first-order questions": they were first-order in the sense that they arose directly from the primary identification of the Lord as Jesus.

If answers to some of these questions (particularly the first two) might seem rather obvious for those of us who have received the teachings of the church, keep in mind that the disciples did not have the benefit of the church's theological framework. In fact, the answers to these questions that we find in the New Testament are rather more diverse—and sometimes rather more creative—than present-day sermons and Bible studies might lead us to expect.

The order in which I have placed these first-order questions is not meant to be chronological. (It has more to do with the clarity and simplicity of their resolution in the New Testament.) As stated earlier, the issues were probably addressed synchronically and interactively. And, because of the ad hoc nature and diversity of the answers we find, they inevitably led to more questions (second-order questions) that branch out in various directions, answers to which can also be found in our texts. In other words, the development is not an orderly linear one. It is best to think of the development as a fractal process like the multidirectional growth and symmetrical branching of a snowflake or the more irregular limbs of a tree, each of which gives rise to more branches and even twigs.[10] The following considerations will fill out this picture.

I have stated the first-order questions in discursive form for the purpose of organizing the material of this chapter into sections, each with a clear agenda. It should be clear, however, that these questions were not merely a matter of theological speculations. They were existential issues for the early disciples as they tried to communicate their new vision of the Lord. Each of these questions potentially led to a crisis of faith, and so had to be addressed by drawing on available traditions and putting those traditions to work in novel ways. The traditions that were thus exploited were distilled into creedal formulas. Like the primary confession, "The Lord is Jesus," these creeds were already regarded as traditional by the time the New Testament documents were written. They were so important that they were regarded as essential for a proper reception of the primary revelation and hence for salvation.

The very first of these beliefs was that Jesus had been raised from the dead.

WASN'T JESUS DEAD AND BURIED? (BELIEFS CONCERNING THE RESURRECTION AND ASCENSION)

Thus far, we have said nothing about a resurrection from the dead. The fact is that the New Testament never claims that any of the disciples had actually observed such an event.[11] Not even the angels, of whom there were several on hand, are said to have observed it (Mark 16:5-6; Matt. 28:2-6: Luke 24:4-5). Therefore, it is not unreasonable for us to view this belief as an inference from some other experience or belief. I contend that the Kyriocentric vision would most likely have supplied such a prior experience and belief.

There are certainly other options like N. T. Wright's argument that visible appearances of Jesus, risen from the dead, were the starting point for deity Christology, but they involve several difficulties (see the Introduction). There was diversity of views about the future life in early Judaism, and belief in the resurrection of the body was far from universal.[12] It is not even clear that the disciples themselves believed in it prior to the death of their teacher (cf. Mark 9:10; Luke 24:45-46; John 20:9). Moreover, there was little or no precedent for the idea of a single individual rising from the dead on his or her own (without the healing touch of a holy man). In the case of Jesus, there may have been reports of an empty tomb, but the absence of a body by itself would simply have raised questions.[13] The Emmaus disciples in the Gospel of Luke had heard reports of an empty tomb, but they had no idea what to make of it (Luke 24:21-24). Even the Gospel of John is quite honest about this: the "beloved disciple" saw that the tomb was completely empty and is said to have "believed," but the Gospel immediately adds that "as yet they did not understand the scripture that he must rise from the dead" (John 20:8-9). In the light of Old Testament ascension narratives (Enoch, Elijah, and possibly Moses[14]) and the transfiguration account (Moses and Elijah), moreover, an empty tomb would have pointed to an immediate elevation into heaven more likely than to a physical resurrection (cf. Luke 9:51; Acts 1:2, 11 with 2 Kgs. 2:1). In short, there are more than enough difficulties with the assumption that the resurrection was a primary datum to invite consideration of a viable alternative.

What we can say with some confidence is that there were various pieces on the supply side: vivid memories of Jesus' death and burial, belief in the *possibility* of God raising the dead,[15] and evidently some reports of an empty tomb. But it is difficult to explain significantly new ideas merely on the basis of possible precedents. What is required in addition is an intentional, focused interpretation (really a re-interpretation) of those pieces from the demand side. The appearance of the Lord with the face and voice of Jesus would have provided just such a demand for the early disciples.

If we now turn the problem around and start with the Kyriocentric vision (hypothetico-deductively), we recognize that there was more than ample biblical precedent for the idea of the Lord God rising up or ascending to heaven (albeit not from death), particularly in the Psalms.[16] This ascension motif was frequently associated with theophanies in the Hebrew Bible,[17] and it continued to be invoked in the prayers of the synagogue.[18]

If we take the Kyriocentric vision as the starting point, there were basically two possibilities for the disciples. One would be to infer that the Lord Jesus had not actually died or been buried: instead he must have risen up to heaven while still living and appeared to his disciples thereafter (as the bodily form of the Lord). We know that some Christians were accused of coming to this conclusion, at least, by the beginning of the second century (Ignatius's "atheists" in *Trall.* 10:1; cf. 1 John 4:2), and we shall look at this "proto-docetist" option in some detail in the following chapter. Here we need to focus on the other possibility, the majority view in the New Testament communities, that the Lord Jesus had died and risen (or been raised) from the dead and then ascended (or been transported) to the heaven from which he appeared to the disciples. The latter option comports with the features of the tradition pool that we have already noted: memories of Jesus' death and burial, the possibility of God raising the dead, and reports of an empty tomb. More importantly, it provides the needed problematic that would have motivated the early disciples to select the idea of resurrection from the vast pool of eschatological traditions and adapt it to the special case of the Lord Jesus.

The resurrection option is, of course, widely attested in the New Testament. It is found in the earliest strata of the New Testament, where it was already codified in terse confessional formulas (1 Cor. 15:4, 20; Rom. 8:34; 10:9b; Mark 16:6). If the primary confession of the disciples was "The Lord is Jesus" (*Kyrios Iēsous*, see Introduction), then it was immediately associated with the confession that "he was raised on the third day" or that "Christ has been raised from the dead" (1 Cor. 15:4b, 20). In fact, our very earliest source, the Letters of Paul, makes a point of placing the two confessions side by side:[19]

- ". . . confess with your lips that Jesus is Lord [*kyrion Iēsoun*] and believe in your heart that God raised him from the dead" (Rom. 10:9).[20]
- "Christ died and lived again that he might be Lord [*kyrieusē*] of both the dead and the living" (Rom 14:9).
- ". . . to know him ['Jesus my Lord,' 3:8] and the power of his resurrection" (Phil 3:10).

For Paul, the Lordship and resurrection of Jesus were bound together at the most foundational, salvific level of the faith,[21] as should be the case if one had been an immediate inference from the other.[22] The Lordship of Jesus was the center (together with memories of Jesus) of the growing (fractal) structure. The resurrection and ascension of Jesus[23] form a branch of this tree-like structure, from which other branches were growing at about the same time.

Another intriguing feature of Paul's confessional proclamation is the repeated statement "God raised the Lord" (*theos ton kyrion ēgeiren*, 1 Cor. 6:14; 2 Cor. 4:14; Rom. 4:24; 10:9). Comparison with the confessional formulas just cited indicates that these statements also combine the ideas of Lordship and resurrection, the difference being that this formula is inherently binitarian: God and Lord (treated in its own terms later in this chapter).

So the first disciples shared a vision of the Lord as Jesus, and those disciples who were to pass down the New Testament traditions also concluded that he had risen (or been raised) from the dead. Thus far we have the nucleus of the second article of the later "apostolic" creed: Lordship, death on the cross, and resurrection/ascension.

Although these results represent an amazing advance toward orthodox Christian faith, as it would later be defined, they are far from a coherent, systematic theology. For one thing, we still have three first-order questions to address. Even with respect to the first question and belief in the resurrection of Jesus, however, there were many loose ends. As soon as the disciples posited the novel idea of the resurrection of a single individual, several more questions immediately arose, each of which evidently exercised the early Christians:

- Exactly what sort of body did the risen Lord Jesus have? Was it still an imaginal (spiritual) body?
- Did God raise Jesus from the dead, or did he rise on his own?
- How does the resurrection and ascension of Jesus relate to our own salvation?
- How does the resurrection of Jesus relate to the general resurrection in the future?
- How do the resurrection and ascension of Jesus relate to the original expectation of the coming of YHWH as savior and final judge?
- Are the resurrection and ascension aspects of a single movement, or are they somehow distinct and sequential?
- What did the Old Testament ever have to say about the resurrection of a unique individual?
- Even if this particular hasid had been a potential Messiah and was now raised from the dead, could he actually be the expected Messiah?

We could think of these as second-order questions—perhaps not as urgent as the first-order ones we focus on here, yet of sufficient concern that different answers for each of them appear in parts of the New Testament (answers to each of which could raise further questions). If belief in the resurrection and ascension of Jesus can be thought of as a branch growing out of the central belief in the Lordship of Jesus, these questions and their possible answers are offshoots of that branch.

We will take up the last of these questions (Messiahship) later in this chapter in relation to the first-order question concerning the crucifixion.[24] The other secondary questions can be left for now as an "exercise to the reader." Enough has been said on the first primary question to demonstrate the method, to illustrate the dynamic nature of early Christian theological endeavor, and to support the plausibility of the Kyriocentric vision conjecture.

When and How Did the Lord Become Identified with the Man Jesus? (Diverse incarnational Scenarios)

The starting point of our journey through early Christian beliefs and practices is the identification of the Lord (YHWH) with Jesus, that is, the Lord's assumption of the name, face, and voice of Jesus, which we have attributed to one or more Kyriocentric visions that occurred in the course of petitionary performances soon after Jesus' execution. The disciples who performed those visions certainly remembered the things Jesus said and did over a period of years. They also had inherited and cherished some stories about his earlier life—his family, his birth, his education, and so forth. So the disciples' task, as commissioned in the Kyriocentric performances, was to proclaim the new revelation, and in order to do so they had to interweave these stories about Jesus with their visions. Accordingly, they had to decide (in one way or another) at what stage in his life to introduce the divine identity of Jesus. There was no escaping the idea (given our previous results) that some sort of "embodiment" had occurred, but there was very little precedent to work with for this idea in received traditions.

On the supply side, there was a variety of possible models for a divine figure coming to earth, though none of them quite fit the case of the Lord Jesus.[25] Old Testament theophanies normally envisaged YHWH in an anthropic, bodily form (the prerequisite for the performance of Kyriocentric visions). According to some of the better-known narratives (eating with Abraham, wrestling with Jacob), these forms could even be tangible manifestations in everyday space. However, nothing was ever said about YHWH becoming a flesh-and-blood human being—he simply appeared out of nowhere (empirically speaking) as in other Kyriocentric visions.

A higher level of continuity is found in texts describing the personified Glory (*Kavod*) and Wisdom of God (*Hochmah*). The last chapter of Exodus describes the glory-cloud descending on the tabernacle and filling it (Exod. 40:34-35; cf. 1 Kgs. 8:10-11 on Solomon's temple). The deuterocanonical Wisdom of Yeshua ben Sira (second century BCE) has Wisdom describing her being sent by the Creator to dwell in Israel and to serve in the holy tent (Sir. 24:8-10). The book of the Wisdom of Solomon (slightly earlier than the New Testament) has Solomon praying God to send forth his Wisdom to labor at his side (a feminine attribute, Ws. 9:10). The book of the scribe Baruch even claims that Wisdom "appeared on earth and lived with humankind" (Bar. 3:37). In these latter three cases, the figure of Wisdom is a metaphor for divine knowledge and, more specifically, for the Torah (Sir. 24:23; Bar. 3:29-30; 4:1). She is housed on earth, but not in a material form. In short, neither of these biblical motifs came close to being a precedent for YHWH assuming a human being.

Although the Lord-Jesus identification could not have been derived from this pool of traditions, the early disciples did eventually utilize them to help communicate their message about the Lord coming to earth in the form of Jesus. For example, Paul spoke of "the Lord Jesus" becoming poor in order that we might become rich (2 Cor. 8:9) and of Jesus as "the form of God" who set aside his status and became a servant (Phil. 2:7), apparently combining the idea of the descending Glory with the prototypical human (Ps. 8:1-9).[26] The same idea appears in the Letter to the Hebrews: "Jesus, who for a little while was made lower than the angels, now crowned with glory" (Heb. 2:9).[27] Both texts are rather vague about the timing or the procedure of the descent, but they both assume that it occurred sometime prior to the crucifixion.

Elsewhere in the New Testament, the "when and how" question was answered in a variety of ways, thus exemplifying the creativity that we should expect to have been stimulated by the Kyriocentric visions. In other words, the difficulties the disciples encountered in answering this question gave rise to another branch of the treelike fractal structure that grew out of the disciples' Kyriocentric vision performances, and this branch would have many different offshoots. I review them here, beginning with the simplest imaginable option, that the "Lord is Jesus" identification first occurred in conjunction with the resurrection (with which it was so closely associated), and working back to the conception and birth of Jesus (the church's conventional answer), and beyond.

Several New Testament texts reflect traditions that associated the Lord-Jesus identification with either the resurrection or the ascension. Here are some examples:

- ". . . the gospel of God . . . concerning his Son, who was . . . declared to be Son of God with power according to the spirit of holiness by resurrection from the dead, Jesus Christ our Lord" (Rom 1:1-4).
- " . . . if you confess with your lips that Jesus is Lord and believe in your heart that God raised him from the dead, you will be saved" (Rom. 10:9).
- "Christ died and lived again that he might be Lord of both the dead and the living" (Rom. 14:9).
- "Therefore God also highly exalted him and gave him the name that is above every name" (Phil. 2:9).
- "This Jesus God raised up . . . exalted at the right hand of God . . . God made him both Lord and Messiah" (Acts 2:32-36).[28]
- ". . . he sat down at the right hand of the Majesty on high, having become as much superior to angels as the name he has inherited is more excellent than theirs" (Heb. 1:3-4).

All six of these texts appear to associate the divine name with the resurrection of Jesus, and most of them explicitly identify the divine name as the highest of all names, the Tetragrammaton (YHWH).

What makes these six verses particularly difficult to interpret is the fact that all three authors clearly regarded Jesus to be the Lord and divine Son of God prior to his rising from the dead (1 Cor. 2:8; Gal. 4:4; Phil. 2:7; Luke 9:32, 35;[29] Heb. 1:6, 10). Moreover, the writers all assumed that the identification of the Lord with Jesus would be permanent—the coming of the Lord at the eschaton would still display the familiar name and face (1 Thess. 3:13; 1 Cor. 16:22; Acts 1:11; Rev. 21:20; passim). Part of the answer must be that most of these texts appear to be based on confessions, sermons, and hymns that antedated the writings themselves.

I must leave it to specialists to examine these texts in detail on a case-by-case basis, but, in view of this puzzling collective feature, I hazard to suggest that at least some early interpreters thought of the resurrection (or the ascension) as the time when the Lord first assumed the name, face, and voice of Jesus. There is very little evidence for such a view in the New Testament or early Christian literature,[30] but it did gain some traction, centuries later, with "Antiochene school" theologian, Theodore of Mopsuestia (by whose time Christian theology had become officially Trinitarian).[31] As far as we are concerned here, the striking lack of support for this very reasonable view testifies to the deep impression that the Kyriocentric vision must have made on the first disciples and the consequent strength of the Lord-Jesus identification.[32]

The implications of such a post-crucifixion embodiment of the Lord in Jesus would be corroborative as far as the present first-order question is concerned: the identification of the Lord with Jesus could well have generated such a belief, particularly for early believers who wished to avoid the shocking suggestion that the one on the cross was the Lord himself (discussed in the final section of this chapter). It would run into difficulties, however, in light of our treatment of the first-order question about the prayers and teachings of Jesus (covered in the following section).[33]

If Jesus was not viewed as the Lord already during his lifetime, there would have been no compelling motive for developing binitarian formulas. A unitarian theology in which the Lord (Jesus after the resurrection) was the same as God the Father would have done quite well, thank you very much.[34] Yet five of the six the texts cited above are clearly binitarian, so we have an apparent anomaly, at least, from the standpoint of the Kyriocentric conjecture and the scenario so carefully developed.

Our best hope for a consistent scenario, in this case, would be to argue that the original versions of these five formulas were "monarchian" (lacking any differentiation of God and Lord), and that they were all altered so as to conform with binitarian language without any awareness of what appears to be a blatant contradiction. A more consistent approach from our vantage point would have been to revise the timing of the identification along with the binitarian reformulation. The best we can do at this stage is to speculate that the use of binitarian language was so well established by the time that these monarchian formulas were revised that neither Paul, Luke, nor the author of Hebrews sensed the incongruity.

Leaving these speculations aside, our scenario for early Christology works rather better for the other New Testament answers to the question of "when and how," ones that locate the identification or union of the Lord with Jesus prior to the resurrection.

The most famous example, of course, comes from the prologue to the Gospel of John: "And the Word became flesh and lived [lit. 'tabernacled'] among us, and we have seen his glory, the glory as of a father's only son, full of grace and truth" (John 1:14). This familiar text deftly combines Kyriocentric and binitarian formulas by simultaneously affirming Jesus as the Word of God (cf. 1:1, 23), the Son of God, and the glorious Lord (YHWH), "full of grace and truth."[35] In the context of the prologue as a whole, it appears to date this "incarnation"—the time when the Lord first assumed the name and flesh of Jesus—sometime prior to Jesus' coming to John the Baptist and being endowed with the Spirit (John 1:29-34), but it does not pin it down further than that.[36] There is no interest in the birth or early years of Jesus' life in the Gospel of John.[37]

The Gospel of Mark is more specific in describing Jesus' baptism as the time when he was empowered by God's Spirit and first called "my Son" (Mark 1:10-11; no birth narrative here either). In view of the prophecies about the coming Lord that are cited from Malachi and Isaiah (Mark 1:2-3), it appears that the Lord-Jesus identification began in conjunction with Jesus' baptism rather than the resurrection.[38]

The Gospels of Matthew and Luke have baptismal narratives similar to Mark's, but they have already introduced the descent of the Holy Spirit and Jesus' identity as Son of God and located them at the moment of his conception in the womb of Mary (Matt. 1:18, 20; Luke 1:32, 35). It is not entirely clear how these birth narratives relate to the Lord-Jesus identification: in Matthew's story about the magi, a glorious star travelled ahead (to the south of Jerusalem) and stopped right "over the place where the child was," suggesting that some sort of union took place soon after Jesus' birth (cf. Num. 9:15-16; Ws. 10:17 on the fiery glory or starry flame). Luke evidently tried to develop a more dynamic picture: Jesus was "Lord" from conception and birth (1:28, 38, 43, 46, 76), yet he also grew toward a higher level of divine identity (1:80; 2:52). The idea of identification with the divine from the moment of birth was not new in itself; we have noted it already in Paul for whom the divine Son was "born of a woman" (Gal. 4:4).

As far as these New Testament writings are concerned, therefore, the Lord-Jesus (or "Word-flesh") identification could have taken place almost any time between the conception and the resurrection of Jesus. Consistent with these ways of answering the question are the instances in the Gospel narratives in which the disciples are said to have noticed something more than human about Jesus even though they did not realize the full story until much later (Mark 4:41; 6:51-52; passim).

What was the situation then before Jesus' conception and birth? A few New Testament texts appear to use the name *Jesus* (or *Christ*) for the preexistent Lord (YHWH), thereby suggesting that the face and voice of Jesus were the ones that the patriarchs and prophets had seen long before the birth of Jesus as a human being (1 Cor. 10:9 [if reading *ton Christon*, rather than *ton kyrion*];Phil. 2:5-6; Jude 5 [reading *Iēsous*]).

Although this usage would quickly be corrected today (and may already have been "corrected" by some New Testament scribes), it could have made perfect sense to the early disciples.[39] How else could they explain the fact that Moses and Elijah recognized the face and voice of Jesus as the transfiguration narrative indicates (Mark 9:4)?[40] In fact, this preconception identification was cited by Christian theologians like Irenaeus and Tertullian (late second to early third century CE) as a way of explaining the Lord's promise to Moses that someday he would be able to see his face directly.[41] The face of the Lord must always have been that of Jesus.[42] For our purposes, this backward projection further testifies to the strength and permanence of the Lord-Jesus identification that resulted from the Kyriocentric visions.

No doubt we would like more clarity on the issue of when and how the Lord was first identified with the man Jesus. Our conjecture never promised a theology that is consistent from start to finish. It is generative rather than systematic.

Consistent with this degree of uncertainly is the fact that beliefs about the "incarnation" of the Lord did not appear in confessions of faith with as much clarity as the resurrection, binitarian formulas, and the Messiahship of Jesus (next to be considered) did.[43] The closest we find in the New Testament is a formula in one of the later Pauline texts, 1 Timothy 3:16, according to which "he was revealed in flesh, vindicated in spirit" (the "he" in question being "our Lord Jesus Christ," 1 Tim. 6:14; cf. 1:2). Evidently, most churches were willing to live with uncertainly on this particular issue for the better part of a century. We have to wait until the time of Irenaeus (late second century) before we find rules of faith that more clearly date the incarnation to the time of the conception and birth of Jesus (combining the language of John 1:14 with that of Matthew and Luke).[44]

For our purpose, the main point is not pinning down the "when and how" of the identification, but the fact that the Lord was seen by the earliest disciples with the face and voice of Jesus. There is ample evidence here that the first-order questions raised by these (conjectured) visions were present in the minds of the early believers and that they were addressed in a variety of ways. If we compare the results of this section with the New Testament material related to the question we discussed before this one, we sense that the issue of "when and how" was important to the early disciples, but not as urgent as those raised by the death and burial of Jesus and by his prayers and teachings.

Our fractal pattern of a tree now has two major branches and a number of smaller branches and twigs. We turn now to a third branch.

DIDN'T JESUS PRAY TO GOD AS HIS FATHER? (BINITARIAN AND TRINITARIAN FORMULAS)

We have already encountered binitarian formulas in several visionary and devotional texts of the New Testament, and we have postponed developing a rationale for this until now. In this section, I return to the conjecture that the original visions of the disciples were Kyriocentric, like the majority of those performed in pre-Christian and Rabbinic arenas, and argue that binitarian modifications must have arisen as a way of accommodating traditions concerning the prayers and teachings of Jesus.[45]

Since the influential work of Joachim Jeremias, New Testament scholars have recognized the prayers of Jesus and his addressing God as *Abba* (Aramaic for "Father") as one of the most archaic features of the Jesus traditions (Mark 14:36).[46] New Testament texts suggest that Jesus also taught his disciples to pray to God as their Father (Luke 11:2, 13 [both from Q]; cf. Rom. 8:15; Gal. 4:6).[47] If so, it would not have taken the disciples very long after the first Kyriocentric visions to realize that they had a problem in articulating their experiences.[48] In this section, I shall argue that this problem provided the disciples with a motivation for developing a third branch of the confessional tree that grew out of their Kyriocentric vision performances, a branch with several different offshoots.

First, we need to consider the major alternative in current literature, the contention that the initial vision was binitarian from the outset (cf. Acts 7:55-56).[49]

WERE JESUS AND THE DISCIPLES BINITARIAN ALL ALONG?

It is generally recognized that Judaism was henotheistic (or monolatrous)—in our terms, their devotions and prayers were Kyriocentric. It is also clear, however, that that there were binitarian traditions in both the Hebrew Bible and apocalyptic literature—traditions in which a mediating figure like lady Wisdom (Prov. 8:22-30), or an archangel like Michael (Dan. 10:21; 12:1), or an exalted human being like Enoch (in the Similitudes of Enoch) could serve as a second power beside YHWH.[50] Several scholars, both Jewish and Christian, have suggested that Christian ideas about a plurality in the Godhead actually derived from such Jewish "binitarianism."[51] In the Introduction, I referred to this suggestion as a "continuing binitarianism" scenario (exemplified by Margaret Barker).

Undoubtedly, these "binitarian" traditions played an important role in the development of New Testament Christology, particularly on the supply side. However, trying to derive early deity Christology from such traditions by themselves would run into several problems. For one thing, it would not explain why Jesus and his disciples adopted these traditions (not being universal), and, for another, it would not explain why the early disciples applied them to their deceased teacher—something without precedent in Judaism (as spelled out in ch. 4).[52]

Beyond that, starting out with binitarian Judaism would not do justice to the amazing variety of binitarian formulas in the New Testament: God and Lord, God and Son of Man,[53] God and Image of God, God and God's glory, God and God's name,[54] God and God's word (or wisdom), God and God's voice,[55] Father and Son of God. If binitarianism were simply the result of a continuing sectarian usage, we would expect one or two of these formulas to have been passed down and to be used almost exclusively. If, on the other hand (as argued here), binitarian formulas were generated by the problem of communicating the Kyriocentric vision, we would expect to find such a variety of binitarian pairings experimented with.

Finally, deriving deity Christology from binitarian traditions would leave a huge gap between the ontological status of these mediators (second powers beside YHWH) and the deity Christology embedded in the earliest strata of the New Testament. Of all the pre-Christian Jews who speculated on mediator figures, none ever prayed to them "Lord, come!" or "Lord, save!" or produced a confession like "The Lord is Jesus" (*Kyrios Iēsous*), or "believe in your heart that God raised him from the dead [and] you will be saved," or he is "Lord of all" (Rom. 10:9, 12; Acts 10:36). Evidently there was a stricture on such usage like the one the Jerusalem Talmud placed in the mouth of *HaShem* three centuries later:

> If a person faces trouble, he should not cry out to the angels Michael or Gabriel. But he should cry out to me, and I will immediately answer him. In this regard, *All who call upon the name of the Lord shall be delivered* [Joel 2:32]. (*y. Ber.* 9:1, 13a)[56]

Old Testament "Yahweh texts" were sometimes applied (albeit disjunctively) to patriarchs like Moses and to angels like Michael but never, to my knowledge, was Joel 2:32 applied to any figure other than the Lord God of Israel.[57]

These difficulties do not imply that the "continuing binitarianism" scenario has no merit. Binitarian formulas were certainly an important part of the tradition pool. In view of the difficulties mentioned, however, and in order to provide a viable alternative, I suggest that many of the binitarian formulas found in the New Testament could have been selected from that pool for a very important reason: to address the apparent conflict between Kyriocentric visions and the prayers of Jesus.

As in the case of problem raised by Jesus being dead and buried, there were basically two possibilities for those disciples who adhered to the Kyriocentric vision. One solution would have been to infer that the Lord who identified himself with Jesus was the same as the God to whom Jesus prayed (the Father)—YHWH was capable of such seemingly contrary manifestations (as discussed in ch. 4).[58] Moreover, we know that some Christians came to a similar conclusion as early as the mid-third century (Origen's "simple ones," Paul of Samosata), and we shall look at this "proto-modalist" option in more detail in the following chapter.

Here we shall focus on the other possibility, which also happens to be the majority view in the New Testament: that the Lord who was embodied (incarnate) in Jesus truly prayed to a God in heaven whom he called his "Father." The latter option comports with the memories of the disciples concerning the prayers Jesus taught them and Jesus' own prayers (taken at face value). More importantly, it provides the needed motivation for the early disciples having selected from the pool of binitarian traditions and adapted them to account for their visions and memories.

The amazing variety of binitarian formulas in the New Testament testifies to the amount of prayer and deliberation that went into preparing the new message about Kyriocentric visions. One thing that all of these formulas have in common is that they dedicate the name "God" (*Theos*) to God the Father and never to Jesus. Rather than try to cover all of the options (most of which have been adequately treated by other scholars), I focus here on these two: the God-Lord distinction and the Father-Son alternative.

ONE GOD, ONE LORD (THE PROBLEM OF SUBORDINATION)

There is only a handful of New Testament texts where Jesus is referred to as "God" (*theós*), but they are all in later strata (Titus, Hebrews, John, 1 John, 2 Peter), and the exact meaning of the title is ambiguous in all these cases save one (John 20:28).[59] The phenomenon that concerns us here is the fact that title *Lord* (*Kyrios*, the Greek form of the Tetragrammaton) was addressed to Jesus, particularly in salutations and confessional formulas where he was mentioned together with God the Father.[60] Here are a just few examples that illustrate this usage:[61]

- 1 Thess. 1:1 (a salutation): "To the church of the Thessalonians in God the Father and the Lord Jesus Christ: Grace to you and peace."
- 1 Cor. 8:6 (a binitarian confession): "for us there is one God, the Father . . . and one Lord, Jesus Christ."
- 1 Cor. 12:4-6 (a Trinitarian confession): "Now there are varieties of gifts, but the same Spirit; and there are varieties of services but the same Lord; and there are varieties of activities, but it is the same God."
- 2 Cor. 13:14 (a Trinitarian benediction): "The grace of the Lord Jesus Christ, the love of God, and the communion of the Holy Spirit."
- Phil. 2:11 (a confessional hymn): "confess that Jesus Christ is Lord to the glory of God the Father."
- Eph. 4:4-6 (a Trinitarian confession): "one Spirit . . . one Lord . . . one God and Father of all."
- James 1:1 (self-description): "a servant of God and of the Lord Jesus Christ."[62]

The fact that these phrases occur in liturgical and confessional formulas indicates that they antedated their occurrence in writing and were likely quite early in the overall scheme of things. Several things should be noted here.

First, we should note that three of the texts just cited not only use the two divine names, *God* and *Lord*, but also attach the attribute of unity to each of them, giving us "one God," and "one Lord" (1 Cor. 8:6; 12:4-6; Eph. 4:4-6, together with "one Spirit"). As several scholars have pointed out, this binitarian formula effectively amends the traditional Jewish confession of the unity and uniqueness of the Lord God (Deut. 6:4), which formed the initial verse in the *Shema* prayer.[63] This confession of the oneness was viewed as the condition for saving faith, just as in traditional Jewish belief, at the same time that the "one Lord" was identified as Jesus.

It is sometimes argued to the contrary that the authors of these texts were unlikely to have had the *Shema* in mind as background knowledge because such a binitarian confession would have been without parallel in the history of Judaism.[64] Our Kyriocentric conjecture makes it possible to take them at face value within a Jewish context, however, and this option is clearly preferable in view of the widespread use of the *Shema* prayer in Judaism.[65] It would be hard to imagine a pious Jew like Paul writing as he did without any awareness of this association. Citation of Deuteronomy 6:4 was lodged in Jesus traditions (Mark 10:18; 12:29) and Paul referred to it several times in his writings, including one instance that occurs just two verses prior our earliest binitarian text (1 Cor. 8:4*; cf. Gal. 3:20; Rom. 3:30a*[66]).

We have previously argued that the earliest christological confession was "The Lord is Jesus" (stemming from the performance of Kyriocentric visions). It now appears that memories of the prayers and teachings of Jesus motivated a more generalized form of the confession that made room for the Father as "God the Father."[67] As James Dunn put it (in one of his earlier writings) so perceptively: "It is evident from Paul that the first Christians soon became aware that they stood in a dual relationship—to God as Father, and to Jesus as Lord."[68]

A second point is that the formulas cited implied some degree or kind of subordination of the Lord Jesus to God the Father. The ultimate intent of confessing Jesus as Lord was to glorify God the Father, the one who is "over all" (Phil. 2:11; Eph. 4:6). From the perspective of the scenario developed here, this construction reflects the superposition of the two New Testament portraits of Jesus.[69] It is consistent with the subordination implied in traditions about Jesus praying to God as his Father. It also comports with our conjecture that Kyriocentric visions had identified Jesus with the more accessible, dynamic aspect of the deity of the Hebrew Bible—the one who comes to save his people and appears in anthropic form in order to reassure them of his accessibility.[70]

In other words, the subordination in question was not a novel feature of the New Testament. It was already implied in the transcendent and immanent aspects of the deity in the Old Testament.[71] The new confessional formulas remained Kyriocentric, therefore, in so far as they preserved the Lord-Jesus identification, but they also made room for a second center in the figure of the God to whom Jesus had prayed and who had raised him from the dead. Confessionally speaking, the one being included in the divine identity was God the Father not the Lord Jesus.[72]

As a result of this superposition of these two portraits, the disciples portrayed Jesus in a double-exposure and thereby left us with a seemingly paradoxical combination: the identification of the Lord God with Jesus alongside his evident subordination to God the Father. This paradox (double-exposure) is concisely expressed in the binitarian formulas we have just reviewed. It also appears in several other ways in the New Testament.

One way that this paradox was expressed is in the use of Old Testament "Yahweh texts" to describe God the Father. In these cases, we often find that the divine names used in the Hebrew and Greek models have been altered to conform to the God-Lord distribution that we have just noted. Either the divine name *God* (*ho theos*) was added to the text (Acts 2:17), or the name *Lord* (*Kyrios*) was left out (Rom. 15:9), or (most often) the name *Lord* was changed to *God* (Rom. 14:11b). The fact that these alterations conformed to the binitarian pattern we have been discussing makes it likely they were intentional.

One of the most striking examples of such intentional alterations is the change of divine names in New Testament citations of Psalm 110:1. In the Old Testament (whether Hebrew or Greek), this psalm verse reads: "The Lord [*yhwh, ho kyrios*] said to my lord [*ladoni, tō kyriō mou*], 'Sit at my right hand.'" In a few instances, this Psalm verse is quoted word-for-word (Mark 12:36; Acts 2:34), where the first "Lord" is taken to be the Father, and the second "Lord" apparently is understood to be a title of the Messiah. In the majority of citations, however, the Psalm verse is cited more loosely, and the first "Lord" is changed to "God" (Rom. 8:34; Eph. 1:20; Col. 3:1; Acts 5:31; 7:55, 56; Heb. 5:5-10; 10:12; 12:2; cf. Rev. 7:10; 22:1; 22:3), or to some other divine epithet.[73] These alterations are far too common to be coincidental, and clearly were designed to avoid referring to God the Father as "Lord." Even though these texts do not refer to Jesus explicitly as "Lord" (instead, we find Jesus, Messiah, Son of Man,[74] high priest, and Lamb), they apparently defer to that dedication, or, at least, resonate with its usage.

Binitarian formulas, the double ascription of "oneness," subordination of the Lord to God, alterations of the divine names in "Yahweh texts"—all of these features of the New Testament are fairly well known. What is new in our presentation is the straightforward explanation in terms of the posited superposition of portraits of Jesus: the coming Lord and the pious Jew (*hasid*) who prayed to God. It is this explanatory power that contributes to the plausibility of the Kyriocentric conjecture on which it is based.

We have seen that the title *Lord* derived directly from the Kyriocentric vision and that it was lodged in the primary confession, "The Lord is Jesus." It also matched the more accessible, dynamic aspect of the deity (as seen from Table 5 in ch. 6) and thereby placed the Lord Jesus in a dyadic relationship with the Father as "one Lord" in relation to "one God" (1 Cor. 8:6; Eph. 4:5-6). It is rather breathtaking to realize how much theology is packed into the New Testament use of these two divine names, *Lord* and *God*, particularly in view of the fact that most Christians recite a creed that enshrines this usage without giving it a thought.

One thing the God-Lord distribution did not do was to describe the relationship of the two divine figures in terms that would be accessible to those who were coming to the disciples' performances and proclamations for the first time. For most purposes, the titles of "God" and "Lord" were interchangeable. Both were enshrined in the *Shema* verse, "The Lord is our God" (Deut. 6:4), recited on a twice-daily basis, and the two titles were also often used sequentially, as in the combination "Lord God" (e.g., Deut. 3:24). Moreover, use of these titles must have raised serious questions about the origin of the second divine figure, the "Lord." Was he a separate, eternal being (contrary to the *Shema* and its adaptations in the New Testament)? If not, how did he originate and what was his relationship to God the Father?

It is unlikely that believers waited until the fourth century (the Arian controversy) to raise such problems. The variety of alternative binitarian formulas bears witness to the fact that more relational formulations were in some demand already in the first century. The Lord Jesus was sometimes portrayed as God's image and glory (2 Cor. 4:4, 6; Col. 1:15; Matt. 18:20; John 1:14)—emanating from God in a quasi-material fashion.[75] He was also said to be God's Wisdom and Word—conceived and uttered by God in a more spiritual or intellectual way (1 Cor. 1:24; 10:4; 2 Cor. 4:4; Col. 1:15-17; John 1:14).[76]

It seems that these titles were intended to supplement the God-Lord formulas, rather than replace them. We may infer the merely supplemental character of these titles from the fact that the pairing of *God* the Father and the *Lord* Jesus continued to be used in salutations and confessional formulas through the New Testament era and beyond. It is also significant in this regard that whenever Jesus was referred to as the glory or wisdom or word, it was always the glory or wisdom or word *of God* (1 Cor. 1:24; 2 Cor. 4:4;[77] Col. 1:15; Rev. 19:13; John 1:1), never the glory or wisdom or word of *the Lord*, in spite of the fact that the latter phrases were far more common in the Hebrew Bible. The influence of the Kyriocentric vision was evidently still in force.

Of all the alternative ways of describing the relationship of the Lord Jesus to God in the New Testament, the most common one was that of a Son in relation to his Father. We must try to account for this important distribution of titles before moving on to the fourth primary question.

FATHER AND SON (PROBLEMS RAISED BY HAVING A DIVINE SON OF GOD)

The major alternate binitarian pairing in the New Testament was that of *Father* and *Son*. Its serviceability in communicating the new revelation is most clearly indicated by the high frequency of its use in the New Testament (other than in salutations and confessional formulas). It is also indicated by the way in which it met the demand occasioned by problems with earlier binitarian formulas using the titles *God* and *Lord*.

Like most of the other alternative formulas, the Father-Son dyad conveyed an actual relationship between the two figures being confessed (as demanded). Unlike the other formulas, however, it brought out the personal character of the divine figure (the Lord) who was embodied in Jesus, and it did justice to the intimacy and reciprocity that characterized Jesus' prayers.[78] Based on the work of later theologians like Origen and Athanasius, the titles of Father and Son would become the preferred terminology, and Christians would thereafter use this terminology almost exclusively. So it is worthwhile focusing on these titles and addressing some of the problems they raise for our understanding of New Testament Christology.

For Christian believers it is axiomatic that Jesus is the Son of God or "God the Son." For scholars, however, the idea of a divine Son of God is one of the most puzzling features of the New Testament—the main reason being the fact that it had no precedent in pre-Christian Judaism. For our purposes, this anomaly presents a further opportunity to test the fruitfulness of the Kyriocentric conjecture.

Like other scholars, we must begin with the Old Testament (and Second Temple) precedents. The title *son of God* was used for a variety of figures, including the people of Israel, Joseph (Ephraim), the anointed king of Israel, angels, righteous servants of the Lord (hasidim), and others.[79] In none of these cases, however, was there any suggestion of divinity in the proper sense of identity with the Lord God.[80] In fact, most of these Old Testament texts clearly distinguish the two, for example:

- "I [YHWH] will be a father to him, and he shall be a son to me" (2 Sam. 7:14)
- "He [YHWH] said to me, 'You are my son; today I have begotten you'" (Ps. 2:7).
- "if the righteous man is God's child [*huios theou*], he will help him" (Ws. 2:18).

Prior to the New Testament, there was no truly divine "Son" in the history of Judaism.[81] In fact, the New Testament itself often follows this convention, evidently in recognition of Jesus' being a hasid ("pious one"), or even a potential Messiah (Rom. 1:3; Mark 12:6; 13:32; 14:61-62; Matt. 16:16; 27:43; passim).[82] On the other hand, a large number of New Testament texts also use "Son of God" in the sense of a unique relationship with God the Father that is theological and clearly goes against the earlier convention. Of course, binitarian formulas exhibiting this kind of uniqueness are a well-known feature of the Gospel of John (e.g., John 10:15, 38; 14:10-11, 20; 17:1, 21), but it also occurs in the earlier strata of the New Testament. Some examples are

- "But when the fullness of time had come, God sent his Son" (paralleled with God's sending his Spirit in Gal. 4:4-6).
- ". . . no one knows who the Son is except the Father, or who the Father is except the Son" (Luke 10:22 [Q]).

At some early stage, in fact, the identity of Jesus as "the Son of God" became a confessional formula, either in its own right or alongside his identity as Messiah (the latter yet to be discussed). Here are some texts where this confession is cited or, at least, assumed:[83]

- ". . . concerning his Son, who . . . was declared to be Son of God" (in a spirit-flesh contrast to his descent from David in Rom 1:3-4).[84]
- "Are you the Messiah, the Son of the Blessed?" (Mark 14:61)
- "Truly this man was God's Son!" (Mark 15:39)
- "You are the Messiah, the Son of the living God" (Matt 16:16; cf. Mark 8:29, which only confessed Jesus as Messiah).

The confessional nature of these statements implies that they were not just optional beliefs. Unlike the traditional attribution of "sonship" to kings, angels, and holy men, this belief was a gospel message, and one's salvation depended on believing it. Jesus was the Lord God of Israel, but was also distinct from God the Father, to whom he prayed and to whom he taught his disciples to pray (Rom. 1:3; Matt. 16:16; 1 John 4:15; 5:5).[85] Clearly, then, the New Testament usage was quite different from all that came before.

There are two things that need to be explained here. Why did the early Christians give such unprecedented meaning (uniqueness and deity) to the title *Son of God* and why was belief in such a controversial idea regarded as being salvific? Various explanations are possible. For example, it could be argued, as William Horbury, Adela Yarbro Collins, and John Collins have done, that the older idea of the "Son of God" as the expected Messiah already implied preexistence and, at least, some degree of "divinity" (Pss. 72:5, 17 LXX; 110:3 LXX; *1 En.* 48:2-3).[86]

This "supply-side" explanation leads to several problems. For one thing, it is not clear that any of the pre-Christian texts cited actually refer to an expected Messiah.[87] Even if we leave out the Messiah identity so that the main idea—that of divine sonship—can be sustained, moreover, it would not readily explain why such a belief suddenly became salvific in the case of Jesus. In plain terms, we need more than a pool of traditions to explain the novelty of the New Testament usage. We need something on the demand side to explain the selective appropriation of this particular image from the tradition pool.

The point I wish to argue is that the New Testament elevation of the title *son*, from human to divine and from generic to unique, receives a ready answer in our scenario, based on the Kyriocentric conjecture. The point can be made as follows.

We have already seen that the first disciples tried to superimpose the two portraits of Jesus by developing various binitarian formulas. The one that remained closest to the Kyriocentric vision, preserving the divine title *Lord*, was the God-Lord formula, but it had several insufficiencies, as we have seen. A variety of other options were explored, apparently in an attempt to bring out the relationship of the two divine figures, but most of them did not fully convey the personal character of both—hence the need for a more interpersonal alternative.

In view of the facts that Jesus' intimacy with God was expressed in his use of the title *Father* (a traditional divine name) and that he was remembered as *a* "son of God" (in the traditional sense of the term), the need to find an alternative formula that was both relational and interpersonal would have been sufficient reason for adapting the older son of God usage and pairing God the Father with Jesus as his one and only Son. Confessing the Son of God was therefore equivalent to confessing the Lord Jesus, and the salvific value of the one confession carried over to the other.[88] Linkage between the two confessions is supported by the fact that nowhere in the New Testament was Jesus ever called "the Son of the Lord" (in spite of this usage in texts like Deut. 14:1; Ws. 2:13).

Appealing to the questions raised by the Kyriocentric vision is just one way—not the only way—of explaining the origin and prevalence of the Father-Son dyad in the New Testament era. However, this ability to give account for the origin of the New Testament's unprecedented use of the title *Son of God* in terms of motivation as well as tradition (demand as well as supply) goes a long way toward demonstrating the fruitfulness, and hence the plausibility, of the Kyriocentric conjecture.

CONCLUSION WITH RESPECT TO BINITARIAN FORMULAS

There were plenty of binitarian formulas in the New Testament, and also some accounts of binitarian visions (Mark 14:62; Acts 7:55-56; Rev. 5:6-7).[89] From the perspective of our scenario, it makes sense to view them as adaptations of prior ascriptions of Lordship to Jesus, both in confessional formulas (*Kyrios Iēsous*) and also in the performance of Kyriocentric visions. Various binitarian formulas were constructed to address an apparent conflict between this portrait of Jesus as the coming Lord and memories of the life and ministry of Jesus as a Jewish hasid.

Binitarian pairings like God-Lord and Father-Son addressed that problem quite successfully. However, they also raised new questions and created new problems, some of which are still with us. For starters, the early disciples appear to have wondered about the two principal subjects of their faith:

- Does God the Father have a human form like that the Lord Jesus? If so, could this form also be seen?[90]
- If the Lord Jesus (the Word or Son of God) always appeared in a human form, is he less than God (the Father), perhaps an angel of some kind?
- How does the Holy Spirit relate to the binity of God and his Word/Son? Is the Spirit that empowered Jesus the same as the Word of God, or different?[91]
- Do we still have just one God, or are there two, or even three?

Reading the New Testament with these questions in mind should highlight theological motifs that address each of them. The most important one, for our purposes, is the question concerning the status of the Son in relation to the angels, and it will come up again in the following chapter. In preparation for this exploration, it is fitting to look more carefully at the binitarian formula that would be used most widely in the churches, that of Father and Son.

Most of the binitarian formulas we have mentioned remained squarely within the linguistic field of early Judaism. The God-Lord formula was based on the principal divine names for the deity. Other titles for Jesus like *Word*, *Glory*, and *Image* were based on divine attributes (sometimes hypostatized) that also played important roles in biblical traditions. In contrast, the idea of a divine Son of God was a radical novelty in the history of Judaism.[92] Its widespread use reflects the fitness of the title in confessing and proclaiming the identity of Jesus in an intimate relationship to God the Father, but its novelty also tended to obscure features of the original portraits, the combination of which led to the demand for new formulations. Jesus was a Jewish hasid (a son of God) and also the one who had appeared to patriarchs and prophets from the beginning of history.

One example of the shift occasioned by the new Father–Son usage is found in the beginning of the Letter to the Hebrews, where God and his Son are clearly differentiated. In reviewing the history of revelation, the author states that the one who spoke to the Jewish ancestors through the prophets was God (the Father), and that he only spoke through the Son "in these last days" (Heb. 1:1–2).[93] The fact that subsequent citations from the Old Testament describe this "Son" as the "Lord" who founded the earth (Heb. 1:10, citing Ps. 102:25), makes it clear that the author was still cognizant of the Lord–Jesus identification and thereby adhered to the preexistence of the Son. However, confusion could and would arise as the Father–Son imagery became the predominant model in the Church's discourse. Where was that Son during all those years of the history of Israel? If no one ever heard or saw him, what was the basis for the vision of the first disciples? The subsequent loss of the prehistory of the Kyriocentric vision will be taken up at the conclusion of this work in chapter 9.

Another problem that would vex the church was the question of the origin of the Son (as distinct from his preexistence). The idea of being a Son brought along with it the attribute of being "begotten" by God the Father, a motif with some biblical precedent, particularly with regard to the king of Israel and the divine Word (Philo's *Logos*).[94] However, "begottenness," in the temporal sense, could easily be confused with the idea of being created (prior to the redefinition of Nicea, 325 CE), and the alternate idea of an "eternal generation" would raise difficulties of its own. (I know from experience that theology students balk at this language to this day.) I point these things out, not to fault the theology of the church, but to indicate that theological endeavor must be ongoing and should take realistic historical scenarios into account.

The second-order questions raised by the use of binitarian formulas were evidently not as urgent as the first-order ones. Yet the theological endeavor of the early disciples was thorough enough that different answers for each of them appear in the New Testament (each of which would raise still further questions).

We have said enough on the first-order question raised by the prayers of Jesus to illustrate the dynamic nature of early theological endeavor and to illustrate the fruitfulness of the Kyriocentric vision conjecture. Our fractal pattern of a tree now has three major branches, each of which has smaller branches and twigs. We turn now to a fourth branch, one that almost became a tree on its own.

How Could the Lord Have Suffered and Been Crucified? (Identification of Jesus as Suffering Servant and Messiah)

If the Lord had identified himself as Jesus, and this identification went back to the baptism of Jesus or even earlier, and we remember that Jesus was crucified, we are forced to conclude that the eternal Lord (YHWH) actually died on a cross. According to the Apostle Paul, the message of the cross was the major "stumbling block to Jews," as well as "foolishness to Gentiles" (1 Cor. 1:23). Six decades later, the "apostolic father" Ignatius encountered Judaizers (or Christian Jews) within the churches that he visited who accepted the gospel he preached but doubted the crucifixion (and resurrection) because it had no precedent in the Old Testament (*Phld.* 8:2; significantly, Ignatius could offer no precedent in reply). In neither case, was the identity of Jesus as the Lord in question (1 Cor. 1:2, 7, 8, 10, 31, passim). The problem was that the one who was crucified was supposed to be the "Lord of glory" (1 Cor. 2:8; cf. Ignatius, *Phld.* preface), not a common criminal.[95]

Texts that reflect the problem raised by the cross could fill a book by themselves. So the pervasiveness and severity of this problem calls for an explanation. It will not do simply to say that the early disciples expected Jesus to be a victorious Messiah or a prophet like Moses. To begin with, it is doubtful that either Jesus or his disciples had identified him as the expected Messiah prior to his death.[96] As explained in the Introduction, it is equally unlikely that they inferred messiahship from his being raised from the dead—there was no precedent for such an individual resurrection in Jewish traditions (Christian readings being a different matter).

In fact, executions and crucifixions were all too common in the ancient world, and they included some of the most respected Jewish leaders. In 37 BCE, Herod the Great had crucified forty-five priests and a handful of Pharisees for supporting a rival king. There were also popular traditions about the persecution and violent death of the prophets (e.g., 1 Thess. 2:15; Mark 12:3-8; Luke 6:23 [Q]; 11:50 [Q]; 13:33).[97] If, therefore, the primary claim of the early Christians had been that Jesus was the Messiah or a prophet like Moses, the problem would have been limited to those who rejected such traditions and would not have included the communities from which our texts have come.[98]

Looking in a more promising direction, it is a fact that early New Testament texts like the letters of Paul identified the one who died on the cross as "the Lord" (1 Thess. 2:15; 1 Cor. 2:8 ["the Lord of glory"]; 11:26, 27; cf. Acts 3:15).[99] Since it would be difficult to explain these rather shocking texts if the original expectation was that of Messiah or prophet, it is worth turning the problem around and beginning with what we have taken to have been the result of Kyriocentric visions, the identification of the Lord as Jesus.

Accordingly, I suggest that the problems that are raised by starting with messianic expectations can be avoided and that better justice can be done to the acuteness of the issue of the cross, if we begin (or assume that the disciples began) instead with the primal confession "The Lord is Jesus." Starting with the Lord-Jesus identification would immediately have generated the needed problematic or "stumbling block": how could anyone in his right mind claim that the Lord God of Israel had been executed?[100]

Before proceeding with this line of inquiry, however, we need to say more about the background of the problem. If there were popular traditions about suffering prophets and holy men, could there not also have been similar traditions about the Lord of the prophets?

HOW TO AVOID PROCLAIMING A DYING AND RISING GOD

In the ancient Near East, as a whole, there was no lack of stories about dying and rising gods: Ishtar, Ba'al, Anat, Andonis, Tammuz, and Horus/Osiris, to name but a few.[101] There are no such stories about the Lord God of Israel, however. The prophets intentionally portrayed their Lord as the "living God" (fifteen times in the OT),[102] and in all likelihood, this emphasis was intended to contrast their God with the Canaanite god Ba'al.[103] Belief in a "living God" was one of the distinctive features that set Jews apart in the ancient world.[104]

This point needs qualification to a degree. In spite of all the intentional dissociation from suffering and death, the God of Israel was far from being impassive. YHWH was never far removed from the cries of his children (Exod. 3:7), and he shared in their distress (Isa. 63:9[105]). In texts of Second Temple and early Rabbinic provenance, *HaShem* was often associated with the people's suffering in dramatic ways. For example, the Wisdom of Solomon (slightly earlier than the New Testament) described Wisdom descending with Joseph into the dungeon so as not to desert him (Ws. 10:13-14). Mishnah tractate *Sanhedrin* stated that the *Shekhinah* complains of an aching head or a sore arm whenever a human being suffers, particularly in the case of righteous ones (*m.*

Sanh. 6:5).[106] The *Mekilta of Rabbi Ishmael* (*MRI*) described the *Shekhinah* Glory as suffering exile along with her people.[107] *Leviticus Rabbah* (fifth century) allegorized the behavior of eagles in Job 39 to make the point that YHWH is present as a mourner at the side of slain bodies ("wherever the slain are, there *he* is," *Lev. R.* 20:4).

For all that amazing empathy, however, the God of Israel never suffered or experienced death in his own body, and this firm "line in the sand" presented a major problem for the first disciples who were commissioned to "proclaim the Lord's death until he comes" (1 Cor. 11:26). Paul was confrontational enough simply to say that "the princes of this age . . . crucified the Lord of glory" (1 Cor. 2:8) and "the Judeans . . . killed the Lord Jesus" (1 Thess. 2:14b-15, my translation).[108] It was not until the writing of the Gospel of John, however, that the cross of Jesus was actually presented as a victory over Satan,[109] and not until Ignatius and Tatian in the second century that Jesus was actually celebrated as the suffering, dying God.[110]

But the problem did not go away. The idea of a dying god was never accepted by all Christians,[111] and, more to the point, it has never been accepted by non-Christian Jews, even by those of a "non-normative" stripe. As modern writer Harold Bloom has stated in his perceptive comparison of the two religions: "Yahweh cannot be regarded as dying. . . . I find nothing in Christianity to be more difficult for me to apprehend than the conception of Jesus Christ as a dying and reviving God."[112] "Non-normative" as he may be, Bloom speaks for Jewish critics of Christianity across the millennia. Moreover, he leaves us with the question of how the problem would have been handled by a group of first-century Jews who were repeatedly confronted with such criticisms of their message.

The fact that imagining the Lord on a cross was such an acute problem for Jewish audiences suggests that the issue had to be addressed at the outset. It also leads us to expect that attempted solutions to the problem would make as much use as possible of verses and motifs from their Scriptures (the Hebrew Bible and Septuagint). Although the appeal to Old Testament proof texts may seem like an obvious strategy for apologetically minded Christians today, it represented a significant shift in the practices of the first disciples. According to our scenario, at least, their previous practices had been largely performative. At this stage, however, they had to supplement their oral performances of biblical visions with the exegesis of isolated biblical texts, an endeavor that required a rather different set of skills.[113]

Moreover, the severity of the problem, especially with critics for whom there was no previously recognized precedent for the disciples' message, leads

206 | Seeing the Lord's Glory

us to expect some radical re-readings of the Old Testament—re-readings in service of what Barnabas Lindars once called a "passion apologetic."[114] In other words, early performances of Kyriocentric visions and the resulting Lord-Jesus identification could only be supported by developing a more "exegetical" approach to Scripture (rather than purely performative[115]), based on a search for scriptural precedents, comparable to the midrashic approach that was developed by the Rabbis.[116] The result, as we shall see momentarily, would be a shift in confessional focus from the Lord (the primal confession) to an alternative superhuman figure, the Davidic Messiah. In order to understand the need for such a shift, it will help to consider the various options that were available to them.

The early disciples really only had three options here. One was simply to date the Lord-Jesus identification from the time of the resurrection—an option that we have already mentioned several times in previous sections (at least until the time of Theodore of Mopsuestia) and that seems previously to have been disallowed by the strength and permanence of the Lord-Jesus identification. The other options were the same two that were available in the question we reviewed in the first section of this chapter: Wasn't Jesus dead and buried? The first of these was to accept the full force of the Lord-Jesus identification but downplay or sidestep the terrible reality of the crucifixion (we shall discuss this "proto-docetist" option further in ch. 8). Here we must focus on the other possibility, the majority view in the New Testament, that the one who suffered and died on the cross was the Lord himself and this was just what Scripture had prophesied (somewhere) for the end times.[117]

So the problem here was very much the same as the problem of Jesus' death and burial that we discussed earlier. In the previous case, as we described it, believers were only concerned with the fact that Jesus had died, and they found ideas in the Scripture tradition pool—ideas like the resurrection of the dead—that could be fairly readily adapted to the purpose (shifting the focus from the future and general to the past and individual). In the present case, believers had to address the shocking idea that the one who died was the Lord himself, and, as we have seen, there were no adequate biblical precedents for such a contingency. But perhaps a different approach would reveal something that they had not anticipated.

As it turns out, several New Testament texts resolved the issue by turning the tables and arguing that the cross was quite clearly prophesied in the Old Testament. They were able to achieve this resolution, however, not by appealing to texts about YHWH, but through texts that were readily associated with the Davidic Messiah. Even the idea of a dying Messiah was a novelty, as attested by the fact that most Jewish listeners did not accept it at the time.[118] But at least the disciples could make their case—a pretty strong one, as we shall see—provided that the minds of listeners were opened to new readings of Scripture by the Lord or by his Spirit (Luke 24:32, 45; John 14:26).

From the perspective of our Kyriocentric vision conjecture, the point here is that such a radical rereading of Old Testament texts was motivated by the need to proclaim the Lord in his newly revealed identity as Jesus. The mandate to proclaim the Lord-Jesus identification provided the motivation for the early disciples' searching for suffering figures in the Old Testament, selecting any that would comport with glorification and an exalted status comparable to the glory of YHWH, and adapting them to the case of the Lord Jesus.[119] In other words, the message of the texts for the disciples depended to a large degree on what they were searching for. The logic may sound rather baroque, but such a retrospective reading of the scriptures was widely practiced in Second Temple and Rabbinic circles.[120] It can also be substantiated by looking at some of the New Testament texts that appealed to the idea of a Davidic Messiah for this very purpose. I shall briefly review these well-known texts in two overlapping groups.

First, let's look at texts which baldly assert that the Messiah was predestined to suffer and die and that the prophets knew this all along (even if no one had been bright enough to understand them):

- ". . . that Christ died for our sins in accordance with scriptures, and that he was buried, and that he was raised on the third day in accordance with scriptures" (1 Cor. 15:3-4).
- "Was it not necessary that the Messiah should suffer these things [crucifixion, death, and burial] and then enter into his glory?" (Luke 24:26) [121]
- "Thus it is written, that the Messiah is to suffer and to rise from the dead on the third day" (Luke 24:46).
- "Paul argued with them [the Jews of Thessalonica] from the Scriptures . . . that it was necessary for the Messiah to suffer and to rise from the dead" (Acts 17:2-3).
- "So I stand here . . . saying nothing but what the prophets and Moses said would take place, that the Messiah must suffer . . . being the first to rise from the dead" (Acts 26:22-23).
- ". . . the Spirit of Messiah within them [the prophets] testified in advance to the sufferings destined for Messiah and the subsequent glory" (1 Pet. 1:10-11).
- ". . . the Lamb that was slaughtered from the foundation of the world" (Rev. 13:8, NRSV footnote; cf. Rev. 17:8).

All seven of these texts emphasize the idea that the Messiah was destined to suffer, and it is evident, particularly in Luke and Acts, that the motive was to counter the problem of the cross. In spite of the fact that this explicitly apologetic tone is limited to these relatively late texts, the underlying idea very likely reflects (and defends) earlier teachings.[122] In fact, we find several places in Paul's letters where the cross is directly attached to the name *Christos* (Greek for Messiah) in what appear to be brief confessional fragments:

- "*Christos* died for our sins in accordance with scriptures" (1 Cor. 15:3; as cited above).
- "For the love of *Christos* urges us on, because we are convinced that one has died for all" (2 Cor. 5:14).
- "*Christos* died and lived again" (Rom. 8:9).

As scholars have noted, the fact Paul used *Christos* as an honorific cognomen for Jesus assumes a prior identification as the Messiah.[123] Accordingly, one can readily see a deep structure underlying these texts that deliberately associated the name with the death of Jesus on the cross as something that was necessary for our salvation. Therefore, the novel association of Messiah and cross must already have been there in pre-Pauline tradition, and with it, the novel way of reading the Old Testament so ably described by Luke, 1 Peter, and (possibly) the Revelation of John.

We have argued at length that this Jesus-Messiah identification was not well rooted in the events of Jesus life (the first portrait), and was rather motivated by the need to defend the Lord-Jesus identification (second portrait). It will be helpful here to restate the four main reasons for this conclusion and add one that is yet to be explored:

- The primary hope of first-century Jews was for the coming of the Lord (YHWH). The coming of a Messiah (or Son of Man) was far less common (even though highly prized by modern scholars) and was secondary to the central expectation even when it did occur (ch. 2).[124]
- The historic Jesus was known primarily as a hasid (or prophet), perhaps as a *potential* Messiah, but probably nothing more than that (ch. 4).
- Even if some of the disciples hoped that their teacher would be the Davidic Messiah, the events surrounding his authoritative condemnation and execution clearly refuted that possibility (note the realism in Matt. 16:22; Luke 24:21).

- Proclaiming the death of an embodiment (or incarnation) of Lord (YHWH) had no biblical precedent ("a stumbling block to Jews," 1 Cor. 1:23) and therefore called for biblical justification relating to some figure other than the Lord.
- Since the early disciples were themselves pious Jews, they had to believe that there was support for this idea in their scriptures. They could surely find texts describing a suffering, dying figure that could be identified as the Messiah.

All would be well with the proclamation of the Kyriocentric vision if adequate textual support could be mustered. But where was such support to be found?

Looking at New Testament texts once again, we can see that the early believers focused on two main figures, the servant of Deutero-Isaiah and the son of David in the Psalms. Choice of the first of these figures, the servant, is fairly straightforward and can be treated rather briefly to exemplify the methodology before we tackle the more difficult problem of the Messiah son of David.

Jesus as the Suffering Servant

The texts that were most suited for this purpose were those describing the "suffering servant" in Deutero-Isaiah (Isa. 40–55). The best known and most widely used was Isaiah 52:13—53:12, which describes a righteous servant who will be exalted on high (Isa. 52:13), but was (previously?) cut off from the land of the living, buried in a grave, and promised some sort of satisfaction (Isa. 53:6-11).

There are plenty of references (some of them oblique) to this text in the New Testament. Part of the reason for this may have been memories of Jesus having cited these texts in relation to his own ministry and identity (Mark 9:31; 10:45 [both about the Son of Man[125]]; 14:24; Luke 11:22 [Q]; cf. 4Q491 frag. 11 1:15-16). But allusions to Isaiah 53 also appear in the Letters of Paul, where the wording is quite different from that in the Gospels (Rom. 4:25; 1 Cor. 11:23; 15:3; Phil. 2:7-9). Regardless of what Jesus was remembered to have said (on the supply side), the fact that the early disciples selected and emphasized these verses (or Jesus' citations of them) can best be explained by attributing a keen apologetic interest (on the demand side). The acuteness of the problem of the Lord suffering on a cross would clearly have provided such a motive.[126]

In short, the early disciples' special interest in the figure of the suffering servant can be explained in terms of the problem of the cross that was raised by the Lord-Jesus identification. On its own, however, this figure could not have matched the acuteness of the problem the disciples started with. The servant of the Lord (or hasid) was a common role in Judaism. It could be pressed into service in an extended apologetic like Justin Martyr's in the mid-second century (*1 Apol.* 50-51), but it lacked the specificity needed to match Jesus' death on a cross, on the one hand, and the eschatological grandeur needed to match the Lord's overcoming death in order to reveal himself. The search for these features in the scriptures would lead the early believers away from the book of Isaiah to the Psalms of David.

JESUS AS THE MESSIAH, SON OF DAVID

For the disciples, the problem was how to explain the suffering and death of the Lord Jesus. For us as modern scholars, the problem is how to account for their claim that Jesus was the Messiah, the "Christ." From the perspective of the Kyriocentric vision conjecture, I suggest that these two problems have one and the same answer: the early disciples found texts, mostly in the Psalms of David, that described the suffering and death of a Davidic figure and that could be interpreted (mostly for the first time) as prophecies concerning the eschatological Messiah. In other words, the claimed Messiahship of Jesus was based on the problem of the cross, not on an experience of the resurrection (contrary to the resurrection scenario discussed in the Introduction). It was not an inference from an event, but an answer to an acute problem.

The disciples had to be selective in their use of the Psalms or their efforts might easily have backfired. Some psalm verses were far too triumphalistic to fit Jesus as he was remembered. Jesus did not gird a sword on his thigh and fill his enemies' hearts with arrows or make them lick the dust (Ps. 45:3-5; 72:8)—Gospel traditions had established a very different picture (Luke 6:27 [Q]; 9:54-55; 22:49-51). Other psalm verses were far too derogatory (e.g., Ps. 89:39-45). And none of them was messianic in the proper, eschatological sense of the term.[127] Yet the Psalms of David were widely regarded as being prophetic,[128] and, as it turned out, there was one particular group that suited the purpose almost perfectly, a set of nine Psalms each of which was labeled (in the Greek Septuagint), "For the end . . . a psalm of David" (*eis to telos . . . psalmos tō David*).[129] Here are some of the most relevant verses from these Psalms with citations of the New Testament texts in which they are used to describe Jesus noted in the following parentheses:

- Ps. 8:5b—"You [Lord] have made [the son of man] a little lower than God, and crowned him with glory and honor." (A template for Phil. 2:7-10 [Messiah Jesus] and quoted in Heb. 2:6-9)[130]
- Ps. 18:4, 16—"The cords of death encompassed me. . . . The Lord reached down from on high and took me."

- Ps. 22:1a, 15, 16c, 18a—"My God, my God, why have you forsaken me? . . . You lay me in the dust of death. . . . They have pierced [Qumran Mss, LXX] my hands and my feet. . . . they divide my clothes among themselves, and for my clothing they cast lots." (Mark 15:24, 34; Matt. 27:35, 46; cf. John 19:24)[131]
- Ps. 31:5, 17—"Into your hand I commit my spirit, O Lord." (Luke 23:46 with "Father" instead of "Lord")
- Ps. 40:2—"The Lord drew me up from the desolate pit."
- Ps. 41:9—"Even my bosom friend who ate of my bread has lifted the heel against me." (Mark 14:18)
- Ps. 42:5, 7, 9—"Why are you cast down/troubled, O my soul . . . All your waves and billows have gone over me." (John 12:27)
- Ps. 69:9, 21b—"Zeal for your house has consumed me; the insults of those who insult you have fallen on me. . . . they gave me vinegar to drink." (Rom. 15:3 [the Messiah]; Mark 15:23 [King of the Jews]; 15:36; John 2:17) [132]
- Ps. 88:1, 3, 5—"O Lord, God of my salvation . . . incline your ear to my cry. For my life draws near to Sheol . . . like the slain that lie in the grave."

As the parentheses indicate, six of these nine Psalms were utilized to describe the suffering and death of Jesus in the New Testament, five of those citations being in the Gospels (though none in Q).[133] I take the prominence of these otherwise fairly obscure psalm verses as an indication that the early disciples had found what they needed: scripture texts that described a unique, arguably eschatological figure, who shared at least some of the attributes of the Lord ("crowned with glory and honor" in Ps. 8:5b), and who would suffer a violent death (Ps. 22:15, 16c; 88:3, 5). The match with Jesus was not perfect, but it was good enough to meet the need. Or, to put it the other way around, the acuteness of the need made these psalm texts look too good to ignore.

One essential piece of the puzzle that was not so clear in these Davidic Psalms was the mode of the Messiah's death, death by crucifixion. Surprisingly, New Testament writers did not cite Psalm 22:15, which in some Hebrew manuscripts, as well as the Greek Septuagint, reads: "They have pierced my hands and my feet."[134] Some of them turned instead to an intriguing, but difficult text found in the prophet Zechariah:

And I [YHWH] will pour out a spirit of compassion and supplication on the house of David and the inhabitants of Jerusalem, so that, when they look at me [NRSV note], whom they have pierced, they shall mourn for him . . . as one mourns for an only child. (Zech. 12:10)[135]

What makes the second half of this verse so difficult to translate (or understand) is the shift from first-person to third-person in the Hebrew pronouns. Taken by itself, it could be understood as referring to human shepherds of the house of David (so the Septuagint), or to the servant of the Lord (cf. 13:7, "'Awake, O sword, against my shepherd"), or even to the Messiah (son of Joseph) as the one who was pierced.[136] From the context, however, it appears that YHWH is the one speaking and referring to himself as having been pierced.

It is easy to see how this ambiguity must have drawn the attention of early disciples who were searching their Scriptures, as it did for other groups of Jewish scholars. For the disciples, it formed a needed bridge between the two portraits of Jesus—the servant of the Lord and the Lord himself—and it tied both to the idea of being pierced and mourned over.

Zechariah 12:10 is cited at least three times in the New Testament. The Gospel of John applies it directly to the crucifixion and death of Jesus as the fulfillment of prophecy (John 19:33-37*, "they shall look on the one whom they have pierced"), thereby picking up on the humanity of the one being pierced. The two other texts, Matthew 24:30* and Revelation 1:7*, seem to pick up on the divine identity in Zechariah 12:10. Both of these texts use it to describe visions of the Son of Man, portrayed in typically divine language as coming with the clouds, and anticipate his being mourned by all of humanity (for impending judgment as much as for his prior suffering).[137] The fact that this verse from Zechariah was seen to straddle the two portraits of Jesus may help to account for its having displaced Psalm 22:15 ("they have pierced my hands and my feet") in the disciples' search for prophecies about the cross.

The New Testament does not report everything that the disciples found in their Scriptures, but based on what we do find, it appears that they did a remarkably good job cobbling together scriptural material that would support their primal confession "The Lord is Jesus." Although prior hopes that Jesus might be the Messiah had seemed futile, particularly following the crucifixion, they took on added strength as Davidic Psalms and this verse from Zechariah came to the attention of those who were trying to proclaim the gospel to Jewish audiences. The newly discovered (or confirmed) identity of Jesus as Messiah was so important in this regard that it was formalized in a confessional formula, "The Messiah is Jesus" or "Jesus is the Messiah."[138] This confession is found (or alluded to) exclusively in the Gospel narratives (and related texts), which were designed to lead the reader to the cross from the very beginning.[139] Moreover, Jesus' identity as Messiah was formally conjoined with images of the cross in stock formulas like "the cross of Christ,"[140] "the blood of Christ,"[141] and "Christ died for our sins."[142] Given the success of this strategy, numerous other royal (potentially messianic) Psalms were also read in terms of Jesus' life, death, and resurrection, Psalm 110 being one of the most widely cited.[143]

The importance and force of this new confession cannot be overstated. For one thing, it straddled the two New Testament portraits of Jesus, the Davidic Messiah being an intermediate figure, "made lower than the angels, now crowned with glory" (Heb. 2:9). Moreover, it transformed the horror of Jesus' execution into a messianic act that was part of God's plan for salvation. The disciples, who had called on the Lord to deliver them in their distress (Ps. 107:13; Joel. 2:32), found that deliverance in the cross of Jesus as the son of David (Matt. 21:9; Luke 2:11;[144] Acts 2:25-36). As Alan Segal has pointed out, such a superposition of portraits, both Lord and Messiah, was unprecedented in the history of Judaism.[145] It had to be unprecedented simply because the necessary impetus for this novel superposition was itself unprecedented—a vision of the Lord with the face and name of a beloved teacher of recent memory.

In order to avoid any suggestion that the disciples had their theology all worked out, it is helpful to recall the image of fractal growth. Discovering the ancient promise of a suffering Messiah resolved the primary question about the crucified Lord, but it also inevitably raised a host of other questions in its train.

- What had the first disciples missed in what Jesus said and did that intimated his Messiahship?
- Did this Messiah have the expected Davidic ancestry?
- In what sense is this Messiah a conquering hero for Israel?
- Exactly how did the crucifixion of the servant/Messiah accomplish our salvation?
- Has the self-offering of this Messiah somehow replaced the Mosaic cult and covenant?
- Where was this Messiah and what was he doing during all those years that Israel was waiting for him?[146]

The fact that the New Testament makes assertions that addressed these questions gives us some assurance that we are reasonably close to the thinking of the early disciples.

Of course, appealing to questions raised by the Kyriocentric visions is just one way of explaining the origin of belief in Jesus as a Jewish Messiah. We cannot claim that it is the best way—only that it gives a realistic account for the origin of such an improbable idea in terms of motivation as well as tradition (i.e., demand as well as supply). This account further supports the plausibility of our Kyriocentric conjecture.

CONCLUSION REGARDING JESUS TRADITIONS AND DEITY CHRISTOLOGY

It is often assumed that the first Christians' beliefs about Jesus began at a relatively low level and were gradually elevated in the direction of deification (usually associated with the Gospel of John). Having pointed out that such a development would have been out of the question for pious Jews like the first disciples, and building on the work of scholars who have demonstrated an extremely early origin for deity Christology, we have turned the problem around and started from the other direction.

We have shown that, if we conjecture the performance of Kyriocentric visions in which the anthropic form was identified (or identified itself) as Jesus, "now crowned with glory" (Heb. 2:9), we can readily account for the primal confession, "The Lord is Jesus" (*Kyrios Iēsous*), together with the dedication of prayer motifs and "Yahweh texts" to the Lord Jesus (chs. 4–6). Once we combine this Lord-Jesus identification with the traditions about the teachings and prayers of Jesus, moreover, we can account for several other affirmations of the New Testament, including the raising of Jesus from the dead, some notion of an embodiment or incarnation, various binitarian formulas, and a clear affirmation of Jesus as the Davidic Messiah. Those affirmations no doubt led to further questions and so could also account for many other features of theological endeavor in the New Testament era. The fruitfulness of our Kyriocentric vision conjecture is in its explanatory value.

All of the ingredients of this scenario are well within the bounds of first-century Judaism—allowing that those bounds were somewhat elastic and could be stretched in various directions as they were by Rabbinic as well as by early Christian movements. What made the Christian gospel unique was an unprecedented combination, the superposition of two portraits or the interweaving of two narratives—that of a hasid (a potential Messiah) and that of the Lord—that had thereto been kept quite separate.[147]

Our intention thus far has been to make sense of the early christological developments that are evidenced in the canonical New Testament. It is time to turn our attention to the variety of other viewpoints and traditions of the early centuries, many of which were not represented in the New Testament, or, at least, not represented in a favorable light. Can our scenario account for these other tradition histories? Did they find a place in the early church? If not, when and why were they rejected? These questions will be taken up in the following chapter.

Notes

1. Once a Gospel or letter was "published" as an "edition" (*ekdosis*), it was much harder for tradents to make such modifications in language (although scribes sometimes did just that). On the significance of "publishing," whether in writing or in fixed-text performance, see Saul Lieberman, *Hellenism in Jewish Palestine; Studies in the Literary Transmission, Beliefs and Manners of Palestine in the I Century B.C.E.-IV Century C.E.* (New York: Jewish Theological Seminary of America, 1950), 85–90. Lieberman cites Horace's treatise on *Poetic Art*: "You can delete what you did not publish. The word that is sent abroad you can never revoke" (ibid., 89). In this chapter, we are concerned only with pre-publication modifications.

2. Christopher R. A. Morray-Jones similarly refers to Paul's two distinct ("contrasted") selves as being conformed to the "earthly Jesus" and being conformed to "Christ-as-*kabod*"; Morray-Jones, "Paradise Revisited (2 Cor. 12:1-12): The Jewish Mystical Background of Paul's Apostolate," *HTR* 86 (1993): 177–217, 265–92 (273). Another Pauline letter that shows the two portraits side by side is Phil. 3: "conformed to his death" (3:10), and "conformed to his body of glory" (3:21). Along similar lines, C. K. Barrett spoke of a "double tradition" in the Gospel of John, which he described as "historical tradition, conveying deeds and words attributed to Jesus, and christological tradition, confessing faith in the heavenly *kýrios*"; Barrett, *Essays on John* (Philadelphia: Westminster, 1982), 9; cf. p. 32. Barrett preferred that John had not combined the two traditions and had kept them quite separate instead: "It is simply intolerable that Jesus should be made to say [in John 8:28], 'I am the supreme God of the Old Testament [*ego eimi*], and being God I do what I am told [by the Father]"; ibid., 12. What Barrett found offensive theologically, however, can be helpful for historical reconstruction.

3. In spite of the fact that the ideal hasid (or servant/son of God) mediated the presence and power of YHWH, texts explicitly differentiated the two, e.g., Pss. 2:2; 110:1 (an anointed king/priest); Isa. 11:2-3 (a Davidic figure); Micah 5:4 (future ruler); Ws. 2:12-18 (righteous servant); *1 En.* (Similitudes) 48:6-7 (Son of Man).

4. The two portraits I have described are rather different from the "two-natures" of Chalcedonian Christology. Instead of deity and humanity, they are the Lord in anthropic form and a human who bore the divine. In terms of later christological discourse, they more like the Alexandrian ideal of a "man-bearing God" and the Antiochene ideal of a "God-bearing human." Both natures are evident in each portrait.

5. Descriptions of visions in apocalyptic literature typically involved perplexity on behalf of the seer leading to some explanation or interpretation, often by an angel; cf. Dan. 8:15-17; 9:21-23; Rev. 1:1-2; 17:6-7. As before, I take the heroes of apocalyptic texts to be representatives of their communities.

6. As Terence Fretheim has suggested in a pioneering study of New Testament Christology: ". . . two stories . . . are woven into a single tapestry, namely the story of Israel [her prophets and sages] and the story of God"; Fretheim, "Christology and the Old Testament," in *Who Do You Say that I Am?: Essays on Christology*, ed. Mark Allan Powell and David R. Bauer (Louisville: Westminster John Knox, 1999), 201–15 (215). The image of weaving is particularly propitious in view of the use of the term *massekhet* ("woven fabric") for a tractate of the Mishnah or Talmud.

7. Martin S. Jaffee, "Oral Tradition in the Writings of Rabbinic Oral Torah: On Theorizing Rabbinic Orality," *Oral Tradition* 14 (1999): 3–32 (13–14). Jaffee cites several earlier scholars, particularly Jacob Neusner and Alberdina Houtman. See Jacob Neusner's treatment of the various "stages of logic" in the formulation of the Mishnah, most of which appear to have been simultaneous; Neusner, *Oral Tradition in Judaism: The Case of the Mishnah*, Garland Reference Library of the Humanities 764 (New York: Garland, 1987), 142–43. But most parts of the New Testament would fall between Neusner's two categories of "systematic" (synchronic) and "sedimentary" (diachronic) documents; Neusner, loc. cit., 145.

8. This motivation is what Jacob Neusner terms a "critical" or "generative problematic," which includes a "program of questions and inquiries framed essentially among themselves"; Neusner, *Oral Tradition in Judaism*, 136, 139, 140.

9. In terms of modern chaos theory, these defined areas of discussion would play the role of Lorenz attractors. Chaotic systems are those for which small perturbations make it impossible to predict future states with any desired degree of accuracy. An "attractor" is a terminal state to which the system's states converge even though the approach to the final state is chaotic; see most recently Adilson E. Motter and David K. Campbell, "Chaos at Fifty," *Physics Today* 66 (2013): 27–33.

10. In this chapter, I switch from the metaphors of portraits and narratives to that of trees in order to bring out the quality of fractal growth. The analogy to fractals brings out the multi-directionality, synchronicity, and the progressive nature of theological endeavor. A particular advantage of the tree image is that one can readily imagine other plants growing out of the same ground and even intertwining limbs at some level. What these fractal analogies do not illustrate so well is the interaction among branches in the various directions. For example, belief that Jesus had risen from the dead could have catalyzed (though not caused by itself) the (second-order) belief that he was the expected Messiah (discussed in the fourth section of this chapter). Conversely, belief that Jesus was the Messiah could have occasioned a more "empirical" (third-order) view of the resurrection. Further modes of such interaction will be discussed in the following chapter, where I resume use of the metaphor of narrative threads.

11. The *Gospel of Peter*, in which several Roman soldiers are said to have seen Jesus leave the tomb on the shoulders of two giant angels (*Gos. Pet.* 10.38-40), dates from the late second century.

12. Among Second Temple writings that affirm continued, independent existence of the soul after death, often in an astral or angelic body, see *1 En.* (Epistle) 104:1-2; *Jub.* 23:31; Dan. 12;2-4; 1QS 4:6-8; *T. Job* 52:10-11; *Apoc. Zeph.* 1:1-2:1; *Ws.* 1:12-15; 2:23-4; 3:2-4; 4:7-14; 5:5, 15; 15:3; 4 Macc. 7:19; 13:13-17; 16:25; 17:18; 18:23; Philo, *QG* 3.11; Josephus, *Ant.* 1.230-31; *J.W.* 7.343-6 (describing the Essenes); *L.A.B.* 32:13; *1 En.* (Similitudes) 39:4-8; 70:1-4. *1 Enoch* (Epistle) 92:3-4 prophesies the rising of "the righteous one" (an individual?) from sleep, but this rising presumably refers to the "raising up" of a leader for Israel, not a resurrection from the dead.

13. Of course, there could also have been "sightings" of Jesus in the flesh as claimed by Luke and John (and argued by N. T. Wright). However, the results of this study suggest that they could also have been modifications of the original Kyriocentric visions, either in oral tradition or oral performance. The "pistis formula" in 1 Cor. 15:3-4 cites unspecified scripture as having predicted the death and resurrection of the Messiah ("Christ"), but, as generally recognized, this novel interpretation of Scripture was developed by the disciples in the wake of their experience of the risen Lord (cf. Luke 24:25-27, 44-47), sometime prior to the time that Paul received it (mid 30s CE?).

14. For Moses' elevation to heaven from Mount Nebo, see Philo, *QG* 1.86; *4 Ezra* 14:9; *2 Bar.* 59:3; *Sifrei Devarim* 357; John Macdonald, trans., *Memar Marqah: The Teaching of Marqah* BZAW 84 (Berlin: Töpelmann, 1963), 208.

15. There were just enough traditions at hand to establish belief in the *possibility* of God's raising the dead, e.g., Isa. 26:19; 2 Macc. 7:9, 14, 23, 29; cf. the Targum to the Prophets, where the third day in Hos. 6:2 is paraphrased as "the day of the resurrection of the dead"; Martin McNamara, "Targum and the New Testament: A Revisit," in *The New Testament and Rabbinic Literature*, SJSJ 136, ed. Reimund Bieringer et al. (Leiden: Brill, 2010), 387–427 (414–16). For all of the confusion of the disciples (just mentioned), the one person who was quite clear on this, according to John, was Martha, the sister of Lazarus (John 11:24).

16. The Lord is said to rise up or ascend in Pss. 3:7; 7:6; 9:19; 10:12, passim, where the LXX uses various forms of the same verb (*anistēmi*) often used to describe the resurrection of the Lord Jesus in the New Testament. The problem of the Lord's death is the last of the four primary questions we shall address in this chapter.

17. YHWH is said to "rise up" in theophanies like 1 Sam. 2:10 LXX (*anabainō*); Pss. 47:5 (*anabainō*); 68:1 (LXX *anistēmi*); Isa. 2:19-21; 28:21 (*anistēmi*); Isa. 60:1-2 (*hē doxa kyriou epi se anatetalken*); Mal. 4:2 (*anatelei . . . hēlios dikaiosunēs*).

18. Num. 10:35 ("Rise up, O Lord") is cited in the Torah service (*Keri'at ha-Torah*) at the opening the ark. Note also the conclusion of the *Ge'ullah* blessing after the morning *Shema* ("arise to help Israel").

19. "Lord" (*kyrios*) is the divine name (YHWH) in these texts, as can be seen from neighboring verses that use "Yahweh texts" and motifs with reference to Jesus. See, for example, "intertextual" reference in Rom. 10:9-13 to 1 Kgs. 8:33, 35 (=2 Chron. 6:24); Isa. 28:16c LXX (*ep' autō*); Ps. 103:6-8; Joel 2:32 (MT 3:5). For a more complete listing of New Testament "Yahweh texts" and their Old Testament citations, see the appendix to C. B. Kaiser, "The Biblical and Patristic Doctrine of the Trinity," in *Theological Dialogue between Orthodox and Reformed Churches*, ed. Thomas F. Torrance, vol. 2 (Edinburgh: Scottish Academic Press, 1993), 161–92 (189–92).

20. Werner Kramer argued that the original confessional formula used the name "Christ" (as in 1 Cor. 15:3-5), and that Paul substituted "Lord" for "Christ"; Kramer, *Christ, Lord, Son of God*, Studies in Biblical Theology 50, trans. Brian Hardy (London: SCM, 1966), 23–26, 44. Kramer's reasoning (loc. cit., 24–25) shows that he wants to explain away the outliers for his hypothetically constructed "pistis formula." As Magnus Zetterholm has pointed out Kramer was "anxious to find reasonable explanations"; Zetterholm, "Paul and the Missing Messiah," in *The Messiah in Early Judaism and Christianity*, ed. Magnus Zetterholm (Minneapolis: Fortress Press, 2007), 33–56 (38). The confessional formula makes more sense in terms of Paul's references to his own personal revelation, the majority of which use the title of "Lord" (1 Cor. 9:1; 2 Cor. 3:15, 18; 12:1; cf. Eph. 5:8; Acts 9:5a). Hence, the original (hypothetical) pistis formula was more likely "the Lord Jesus is risen," which then gave rise to alternate formulas like "God raised the Lord Jesus" (reflecting memories of the prayers of Jesus) and "Christ is risen" or "God raised Christ" (in response to the problem of the cross)—just the reverse of Kramer's reconstruction.

21. The association of Lordship and resurrection was not limited to Paul. See, for example, the Kyriocentric vision text in Rev. 1 that we examined in ch. 5, where the Lord Jesus says, ". . . I am the First and the Last, and the Living One [titles of YHWH]. I was dead, and see, I am alive forever" (Rev. 1:17b-18a, repeated in 2:8). The fact that the resurrection was included in confessional formulas may also indicate understandings of the atonement that was accomplished by the Lord's death and resurrection, as in "the firstfruits of those who have died" (1 Cor. 15:20), "raised for our justification" (Rom. 4:25), "raised from the dead . . . so that we too might walk in newness of life" (Rom. 6:4), "the power of his resurrection" (Phil. 3:10), and "I have the keys of Death and of Hades" (Rev. 1:18b).

22. Paul (Saul) was no doubt familiar with the claim that Jesus had risen from the dead prior to his "conversion," but his own conviction must have been the combined result of his personal Damascus Road vision and subsequent instruction from disciples like Ananias.

23. These confessional formulas emphasize the resurrection of Jesus, but for Paul there was no separation between the resurrection and the ascension (Rom. 8:34; Col. 3:1). Nor was there any separation in Hebrews (Heb. 1:3; 10:12; 12:2) or even in some of the traditions cited in the book of Acts (2:31-35; 5:30-31, in contrast to Acts 1:2-3).

24. Approaching belief in the messiahship of Jesus from the problem of the cross avoids some of the difficulties in the traditional approach discussed in the Introduction. Nonetheless, it is a good example of the interaction among developments in the various directions that indicates some sort of "entanglement" and thereby goes beyond the fractal analogy.

25. There were also precedents for archangels assuming human form and living on earth, such as the archangel Israel in the form of Jacob (*Prayer of Joseph* 1-3, 7-8), and Raphael in the form of Azariah, son of Hananiah (Tob. 5:13); cf. Philip Munoa, "Raphael, Azariah and Jesus of Nazareth: Tobit's Significance for Early Christology," *JSP* 22 (2012): 3–39. Significant as these models may have been for the development of New Testament Christology, they do not pertain to the origin of deity Christology as reviewed here. In this regard, it may be significant that the

nearest parallel to the angelic Jacob Israel occurs in the Gospel of John (John 1:51 on the Son of Man), which also spins deity Christology down in other ways.

26. Paul explicitly cites Ps. 8:6 in 1 Cor. 15:27; cf. Markus Bockmuehl, *The Epistle to the Philippians*, Black's New Testament Commentaries 18 (London: A&C Black, 1997), 136, 142, who points out that the LXX superscription reads "for the end."

27. The writer of Hebrews explicitly cites Ps. 8:4-6 in Heb. 2:6-8.

28. I take "Lord" here to represent the Tetragrammaton rather than being a synonym for Messiah, based partly on the "both . . . and" (*kai . . . kai*) construction and partly on previous uses of the title of "Lord" in Acts 2:21, 25 (both referring to the risen Lord Jesus). The idea of Jesus being designated Messiah (Son of David and Son of God) at his resurrection also recurs in Acts 13:32-33, but this passage lacks the paradoxical nature of the account in Acts 2, as explained in the final note of this chapter.

29. For an extensive treatment of the Lordship of Jesus in the Gospel of Luke, see C. Kavin Rowe, *Early Narrative Christology: The Lord in the Gospel of Luke*, BZNW 139 (Berlin: de Gruyter, 2006), 22, 27, 29, 39, 77, 105, 157, 165, 193, 202. Sigurd Grindheim aptly states that the Gospel of Luke must be read at two levels: a historical level, at which Jesus is the servant or agent of God, the savior; and a narrative level at which the reader is expected to have prior knowledge of Jesus as divine Lord, the object of saving faith; Grindheim, *Christology in the Synoptic Gospels: God or God's Servant?* (London: T&T Clark, 2012), 122, 142.

30. In chapter 8 (section on proto-adoptionism), we shall look at evidence for this option among the Christians who were opposed in the letters of John and Ignatius.

31. Theodore of Mopsuestia worked out a comprehensive, developmental Christology in which the divine Word and the man Jesus coexisted as distinct entities in "dynamic unity" (*synapheia*), comparable to that of YHWH and the temple, right up until the resurrection and ascension, when the two became fully united; Theodore, *Homily on the Nicene Creed*, 6.6, ET in Alphonse Mingana, trans., *Commentary of Theodore of Mopsuestia on the Nicene Creed* Woodbrook Studies 5 (Cambridge: Heffer, 1932), 66 n. 68; Theodore, *Catechetical Homily* 6, ET in Mingana, *Commentary of Theodore of Mopsuestia on the Lord's Prayer and on Sacraments of Baptism and the Eucharist*, Woodbrook Studies 6 (Cambridge: Heffer, 1933), 99; Theodore, *Against Apollinarius* 3; cf. Frederick G. McLeod, *Theodore of Mopsuestia*, Early Church Fathers (London: Routledge, 2009), 51, 149. Theodore was an orthodox Trinitarian for his time but, under pressure from Alexandria, his christological views were condemned at the Fifth Ecumenical Council (Second Council of Constantinople) in 553.

32. The fact that this "proto-adoptionist" option was not pursued more forcefully than it was among the early disciples indicates how strongly the primary Kyriocentric visions must have evoked the face and voice of the teacher with whom the disciples had lived. For them, the Lord-Jesus identification was evidently not just a last-minute change in the divine plan (1 Cor. 2:7-9; Rom. 16:25; Col. 1:26-27; passim).

33. Associating the identification of the Lord with Jesus at the resurrection would also create problems for the last first-order question to be discussed: the problem of the cross. If Jesus was a holy man and nothing more, the cross should not have posed such a problem for early believers.

34. Beginning the Lord-Jesus identification with the resurrection would be "unitarian" in the sense of denying multi-personality to the Deity. Unlike historical unitarianism, it would not deny the deity (Yahwehness) of the risen (Lord) Jesus.

35. The Lord-Jesus identification is encoded in texts. On the Lord's dwelling in the tabernacle, see Exod. 25:8-9; Lev. 26:11; Ps. 78:60; Joel 3:17, 21; Zech. 2:10. On seeing the glorious Lord, see Exod. 33:19, 22 LXX; Num. 12:8 LXX; 14:22; Deut. 5:24 LXX; Ps. 17:15; Isa. 6:1, 3, 5. The motifs of tabernacling and seeing his glory might be taken to identify Jesus merely as the glory or wisdom of God (cf. Sir. 24:8-10), but the attribute of being "full of grace and truth" is specific to YHWH (Exod. 33:18, 22; 34:6; Num. 14:18; Neh. 9:17; Pss 85:8-10; 86:5, 15; 103:8; Joel 2:13; Jonah 4:2).

36. Contra Reginald H. Fuller, who argued that John 1:1-16 was a commentary on Jesus' baptism as the beginning of his ministry and that John 1:32-33 equated the Logos with the Spirit who also descends on Jesus; Fuller, "Christmas, Epiphany, and the Johannine Prologue," in *Spirit and Light: Essays in Historical Theology*, ed. Madeleine L'Engle and William B. Green (New York: Seabury, 1976), 63–73 (69). Fuller attempted to avoid the label of "adoptionism" by holding that God took the initiative in raising up Jesus and preparing him for his role in life (loc. cit., 70). Francis Watson comes closer to the text in suggesting that John's idea of the "adoption" is a "high adoption" (i.e., permanent adoption), one in which "divinity and humanity became one"; Watson, "Is John's Christology Adoptionistic?" in *The Glory of Christ in the New Testament: Studies in Christology in Memory of George Bradford Caird*, ed. L. D. Hurst and N. T. Wright (Oxford: Clarendon, 1987), 113–24 (121–24).

37. Jesus' "high-priestly prayer" in John 17 twice states that he possessed the divine glory before the world was made (John 17:5, 24), presumably speaking here as the Son or Word of God. In John 18:37, Jesus says, "For this I was born [*gegennēmai*], and for this I came into the world . . .", but neither the grammar nor the immediate context make it clear what he meant or in what capacity he was speaking. The exact same expression (*erchomai eis ton kosmon*) is used for the coming of the light of the world and the Christos/Son of God in John 3:19; 11:27; 12:26; 16:28.

38. This particular way of answering the question has been championed by Michael Goulder in his *St. Paul versus St. Peter: A Tale of Two Missions* (Louisville: Westminster John Knox, 1995), 111, 136.

39. Evangelical theologian Stanley Grenz offered Phil. 2:5-6 as evidence that Paul believed that human nature (in Chalcedonian terms) was always part of the divine identity of the Logos, with the result that it was never anhypostatic; Grenz, *Theology for the Community of God* (Grand Rapids: Eerdmans, 1994), 311–13. Grenz's idea has not been widely accepted in spite of his exegetical and theological acumen.

40. Luke's account of the transfiguration makes it particularly clear that Jesus was the Lord whom Moses (and Isaiah) saw (see Table 3 in ch. 5).

41. Irenaeus, *Against Heresies* 4.20.9; Tertullian, *Against Marcion* 4:22; Tertullian, *Against Praxeas* 14. The cited promise is based on a conflation of Num. 12:6-8 with Exod. 33:18-22, where the "rock" is read as the type of the Mount of Transfiguration. Irenaeus's understanding of prophetic visions will be discussed in ch. 9 (Movement 2).

42. This notion of a preexistent celestial humanity would not survive late fourth-century controversies in which Apollinaris was charged with upholding Valentinus's idea of a preexistent body that entered into Mary; cf. Apollinaris, *Anacephalaiosis* 12-13, as understood by Gregory of Nazianzus, *Ep.* 101, 102, 202; Gregory of Nyssa, *Oration against Apollinaris* 13-21; Rowan A. Greer, "The Man from Heaven: Paul's Last Adam and Apollinaris' Christ," in *Paul and the Legacies of Paul*, ed. William S. Babcock (Dallas: Southern Methodist University Press, 1990), 165–82, 358–60. On Valentinus's idea of the heavenly body, see Irenaeus, *Haer.* 3.11.3; 5.1.2 and *Gos. Philip* (NHC II,3) 71.4-11.

43. I take it that the confessional formulas about Jesus having "descended from David" (Rom. 1:3; 9:5; cf. Matt. 22:42; John 7:42; Acts 2:30; Rev. 22:16) are more about his messianic identity than about an incarnation.

44. Irenaeus, *Proof of the Apostolic Preaching* 53 (c. 200 CE): "Christ . . . being the Word of the Father, was to take flesh and become man and come into being through birth and be born of a virgin"; Joseph P. Smith, trans., *St. Irenaeus: Proof of the Apostolic Preaching*, ACW 16 (New York: Newman, 1952), 82; cf. Irenaeus, *Haer.* 1.10.1

45. Binitarian constructs like Mark 14:62 and Acts 7:55-56 may also have been performed as visions in early Christian communities. However, they may simply have been the result of New Testament "apologetics"—a way of making sense out of seemingly incompatible ideas; cf. Barnabas Lindars, *New Testament Apologetic: The Doctrinal Significance of the Old Testament Quotations* (London: SCM, 1961), 75–137. I see no way to differentiate these possibilities in the texts themselves.

46. Joachim Jeremias, *The Prayers of Jesus*, Studies in Biblical Theology 2, 6 (Philadelphia: Fortress Press, 1978). The two Aramaic prayer bytes, *Abba* ("Father") and *Marana tha* ("Our Lord, come!" 1 Cor. 16:22) nicely anchor the two portraits (or narratives) of Jesus in the New Testament: the Jewish holy (hasid) man praying to God as his *Abba*, and the Lord coming to earth in response to his people's prayers.

47. There probably was a connection between the disciples learning how to pray from Jesus and their performance of Kyriocentric visions. If so, the anthropic form in which Jesus envisaged God in his prayers was that of his Father. Once the anthropic form was identified with Jesus (risen from the dead), visions of the Father in anthropic form receded into the background (Col. 1:15; John 1:18), but they were still evidenced in Mark 14:62; Matt. 23:21; Rev. 1:4, 8; 4:3, 9-11, passim.

48. I am indebted here to Arthur Wainwright's idea of the "problem of the Trinity" in the New Testament; Wainwright, *The Trinity in the New Testament* (London: SPCK, 1962), 3–14, 265–67.

49. Larry Hurtado claims that three visionary traditions (Stephen's binitarian vision in Acts 7, the transfiguration vision in the Synoptic Gospels, and John's in Rev. 4–5) were an "indirect reflection" of those visions experienced by early Christians; Hurtado, *How On Earth Did Jesus Become a God? Historical Questions about Earliest Devotion to Jesus* (Grand Rapids: Eerdmans, 2005), 199–201. Note that two of these three visionary traditions involved an opening of the heavens that revealed the celestial throne (Acts 7:56; Rev. 4:1)—apparently a different phenomenon from the theophanies that occurred just after Jesus' execution. At least, there was no mention of a throne in the six New Testament texts that we studied in ch. 5 (contrast Isa. 6:1; Ezek. 1:22, 26; *1 En.* 14:18-19; 47:3; 60:2; Dan. 7:9-10).

50. Larry Hurtado developed a three-category organization of these divine agents in *One God, One Lord: Early Christian Devotion and Ancient Jewish Monotheism* (Philadelphia: Fortress Press, 1988). The categories are not watertight. Figures from one category can function like a member of another. For example, Wisdom/Word can appear as an angel; the angel of the Lord may be the hypostatization of a divine attribute or name; a patriarch may be viewed as the embodiment of an angel or even of the *Shekhinah* itself; cf. Nathaniel Deutsch, *Guardians of the Gate, Angelic Vice Regency in Late Antiquity*, Brill Series in Jewish Studies 22 (Leiden: Brill, 1999), 28, 34–35, 42–43, 47.

51. Prominent Jewish scholars who have popularized the idea of Jewish binitarianism include, Alan F. Segal, *Two Powers in Heaven: Early Rabbinic Reports about Christianity and Gnosticism*, SJLA 25 (Leiden: Brill, 1977), 150, passim; Daniel Boyarin, *Border Lines: The Partition of Judaeo-Christianity* (Philadelphia: University of Pennsylvania Press, 2004), 131, passim.

52. Margaret Barker's scenario avoids this problem by positing YHWH himself as the second power, leading to problems that we discussed in the Introduction. Following up on the work of Pierluigi Piovanelli, Daniel Boyarin argues that the role of the Son of Man as a second power was actually part of mainstream Judaism in the first century; Boyarin, "The Parables of Enoch and the Foundation of the Rabbinic Sect: A Hypothesis," in *"The Words of a Wise Man's Mouth Are Gracious" (Qoh 10,12)*, SJ 32, ed. Mauro Perani (Berlin: de Gruyter, 2005), 53–72 (70); Boyarin, "How Enoch Can Teach Us About Jesus," *Early Christianity* 2 (2011): 51–76 (55); Boyarin, *The Jewish Gospels: The Story of the Jewish Christ* (New York: New Press, 2012), 72–73, passim. The point remains moot, however, because the supporting texts that Boyarin cites from *1 Enoch* and *4 Ezra* are contemporary with the New Testament. Note also the assumed novelty of the idea of a Son of Man in the Gospel of John (John 9:36; 12:34) in contrast to a known figure like the Messiah (John 4:25).

53. Since the seminal work of Rudolf Bultmann, it has been customary to divide the "Son of Man" sayings of Jesus into three categories: Jesus' predictions of the glorious coming of the Son of Man, his predictions of the death and resurrection of the Son of Man, and his reference to himself and his ministry in the present; Bultmann, *Theology of the New Testament*, trans. K. Groebel, 2 vols. (New York: Scribner, 1951), 1:30. The binitarian use we are concerned with here corresponds to Bultmann's first category. Helmut Koester and others trace this coming of the Son of Man motif to

the time of the Jewish revolt (Mark and a hypothetical second stratum of Q); Koester, *From Jesus to the Gospels: Interpreting the New Testament in its Context* (Minneapolis: Fortress Press, 2007), 230–31; cf. Andrew R. Angel, *Chaos and the Son of Man: The Hebrew Chaoskampf Tradition in the Period 515 BCE to 200 CE*, Library of Second Temple Studies 60 (London: T&T Clark, 2006), 128. Due to the uncertainties involved in its origin, I shall only discuss this usage in footnotes below.

54. On the role of the hypostatic name in early Christianity, see Jarl Fossum, *The Name of God and the Angel of the Lord: Samaritan and Jewish Concepts of Intermediation and the Origin of Gnosticism*, WUNT 36 (Tübingen: Mohr, 1985), 239–56; Charles A. Gieschen, "The Divine Name in Ante-Nicene Christology," *VC* 57 (2003): 115–58.

55. On the possible use of the "hypostatic voice" as a model for early Christology, see James H. Charlesworth, "The Jewish Roots of Christology: The Discovery of the Hypostatic Voice," *SJT* 39 (1986): 19–41. This interesting subject could be enriched by including the voice-figure connection in Ezek. 1:25-26 (the nearest parallel to Rev. 1:10-18 as discussed in ch. 5) and *MRI* Bahodesh 9 on Exod. 20:18 ("The saw the fiery word," citing Ps. 29:7); Jacob Z. Lauterbach, trans., *Mekilta of Rabbi Ishmael*, 3 vols. (Philadelphia: Jewish Publication Society of America, 1933), 2:266 (hereafter cited as *MRI*).

56. Jacob Neusner et al., trans., *The Talmud of the Land of Israel*, Chicago Studies in the History of Judaism, 35 vols. (Chicago: University of Chicago Press, 1982–87), 1:314. The warning is more likely to have been directed against possible magical uses of the names of angels rather than cultic devotion. As Peter Schäfer has stated, magical texts that invoke the help of angels "don't necessarily imply that angels were actually worshiped in Second Temple Judaism"; Schäfer, *The Jewish Jesus: How Judaism and Christianity Shaped Each Other* (Princeton, NJ: Princeton University Press, 2012), 193 (citing the *Yerushalmi* text on 194–95).

57. By a "disjunctive use" of an Old Testament Yahweh text, I mean an interpretation that takes the text to refer to someone (like Moses) other than Yahweh. Charles Talbert uses *y. Ber.* 9:1 to interpret the Lordship of Jesus in the New Testament; Talbert, *The Development of Christology during the First Hundred Years and Other Essays on Early Christian Christology*, NovT Sup 140 (Leiden: Brill, 2011), 16–17. In doing so, he ignores the telltale absence of either Joel 2 or use of the title *Lord* (as in the New Testament) in the parallel texts he cites (e.g., Dan. 10:12 and *T. Dan.* 6:1-2).

58. Identification of the Father with the Lord Jesus could also have resulted from limiting the Lord-Jesus identification to the time of the resurrection and thereby limiting Jesus' prayers and teachings to Jesus as a hasid and nothing more.

59. The ambiguity arises from two factors. The title *god* could be used to describe angels or even the king of Israel in the Hebrew Bible (e.g., Pss. 45:6; 82:1, 6; Isa. 9:6; Zech. 12:8). Unlike use of the title *Lord*, use of the title "God" for Jesus is not accompanied by "Yahweh texts" and motifs, the confessional formula in John 20:28 being the one exception (cf. Ps. 35:23; Rev. 4:11).

60. Both Jesus and the Father are called "God" in John 1:18 (Papyrus 66, Aleph*, A); Heb. 1:8-9 (citing Ps. 45:6-7). Both are called "Lord" in Mark 12:36; Acts 2:34 (both citing Ps. 110:1).

61. Some early discussions of this well-known usage are in Lucien Cerfaux, *Christ in the Theology of St. Paul*, trans. Geoffrey Webb and Adrian Walker (London: Herder & Herder, 1951), 473, 516; Wainwright, *Trinity in the New Testament*, 92. The only "Lord-Lord" texts in the New Testament are in direct quotations of Ps. 110:1 (Mark 12:36; Acts 2:34). More recently, see Gordon Fee, *Pauline Christology: An Exegetical-Theological Study* (Peabody, MA: Hendrickson, 2007), 42, 134, 274.

62. Elsewhere (other than in liturgical material), James seems to have used God and Lord interchangeably for the Lord God of Israel. Compare James 1:5 with 1:7; 1:27 with 3:9, and 4:7-8 with 4:10; cf. J. Ramsey Michaels, "Catholic Christologies in the Catholic Epistles," in *Contours of Christology in the New Testament*, McMaster New Testament Studies, ed. Richard N. Longenecker (Grand Rapids: Eerdmans, 2005), 268–91 (271–72, 273, 274).

63. The fact that the *Shema* is the basis for the confessional formula in 1 Cor. 8:6 was pointed out already by Theodore of Mopsuestia, *Catechetical Homily* 3.2; ET in Gerard H. Ettlinger, *Jesus, Christ and Savior*, Message of the Fathers of the Church 2 (Wilmington, DE: Glazier, 1987), 166. Among recent scholars on the use of the *Shema* verse in 1 Cor. 8:6, see James D. G. Dunn, *Christology in the Making: A New Testament Inquiry into the Origins of the Doctrine of the Incarnation* (Philadelphia: Westminster, 1980), 180; Dunn, *The Partings of the Ways between Christianity and Judaism and their Significance for the Character of Christianity* (London: SCM, 1991), 180, 182; Dunn, *The Theology of Paul the Apostle* (Grand Rapids: Eerdmans, 1998), 253; D. R. de Lacey, "'One Lord' in Pauline Christology," in *Christ the Lord: Studies in Christology Presented to Donald Guthrie*, ed. Harold H. Rowdon (Downers Grove, IL: InterVarsity, 1982), 191–203 (200–201); N. T. Wright, "Constraints and the Jesus of History," *SJT* 39 (1986): 189–210 (208); Wright, "One God, One Lord, One People," *Ex Auditu* 7 (1991): 45–58 (48); Wright, *The Climax of the Covenant: Christ and the Law in Pauline Theology* (Minneapolis: Fortress Press, 1992), 121, 125–32; Richard Bauckham, *Jesus and the God of Israel: God Crucified and Other Studies on the New Testament's Christology of Divine Identity* (Grand Rapids: Eerdmans, 2008), 27–28, 97–104, 210–18; Ben Witherington III and Laura M. Ice, *The Shadow of the Almighty: Father, Son, and Spirit in Biblical Perspective* (Grand Rapids: Eerdmans, 2002), 73–74; Hurtado, *Lord Jesus Christ: Devotion to Jesus in Earliest Christianity* (Grand Rapids: Eerdmans, 2003), 114; Fee, *Pauline Christology*, 17, 89–92. In a 2011 overview, Andrew Chester concluded that "Christ is given the supreme, distinctive divine name *YHWH* (denoted as *kýrios*). Paul's usage here cannot conceivably be casual or accidental; the fact that he uses the *Shema* shows that beyond any doubt. Thus he makes Christ fully one with God, in the strongest possible Jewish terms, sharing in the divine name as well as the divine act of creation"; Chester, "High Christology—Whence, When and Why?" *Early Christianity* 2 (2011): 22–50 (36–37).

64. Following the critique of previous scholars by James F. McGrath, Dunn has reversed his earlier view and now reads 1 Cor. 8:6 as a confession of the "one God" plus a separate confession of "one Lord" that is unrelated to the *Shema*; Dunn, *Did the First Christians Worship Jesus?* 109. McGrath had based his case on the observation that such a "splitting of the *Shema*" was "without any parallel"; McGrath, *The Only True God: Early Christian Monotheism in its Jewish Context* (Urbana: University of Illinois Press, 2009), 40. Actually, there are some parallels, at least, in medieval Jewish literature about *kavanah* ("spiritual concentration") in prayer, and, as will be seen, these parallels cannot be attributed to Christian influence. Joseph Dan gives an example from an early thirteenth-century text by R. Asher ben Saul of Lunel in which the two occurrences of *Adonai* (the Tetragrammaton) in the *Shema* are referred to the *sefirot* of *Keter Elyon* and *Tiferet Yisra'el*, respectively; Dan, "The Emergence of Mystical Prayer," in *Studies in Jewish Mysticism*, ed. Joseph Dan (Cambridge, MA: Association for Jewish Studies, 1982), 85–120 (111). Dan also calls attention to instances where different portions of the *Amidah* benedictions are directed (by *kavanah*) toward different (transcendent and active) *sefirot*; ibid., 108–9. Perhaps McGrath should simply have said that such a splitting was without any precedent, rather than "without any parallel." Nonetheless, the medieval parallels indicate that such a splitting could occur under appropriate circumstances.

65. The functional equivalence between the *Kyrios Iēsous* confession and the traditional *Shema* might be confirmed by Luke's baptismal phrase, "proclaiming the good news [*evaggelizomenō*] about the kingdom of God and the name of Jesus Christ [as Lord]" (Acts 8:12; cf. 8:16; Matt. 7:21-22). This pairing of divine sovereignty (*malkhut*) with confessing the divine Name (*Shem*) matches the congregational response to the enunciation of the divine name that the Mishnah attributed to the Temple era (*m. Yoma* 3:8; 4:1, 2; 6:2; *t. Pesah.* 3:19; cf. *MRI* Pisha 16:138; *Sifrei Devarim* 31), "Blessed be the name of the glory of his kingdom forever." On the composition of this congregational response (in the second cent.), based on Pss. 72:19; 145:11, see Reuven Kimelman, "Polemics and Rabbinic Liturgy," in *Discussing Cultural Influences: Text, Context and*

Non-Text in Rabbinic Judaism, SJ, ed. Rivka Ulmer (Lanham, MD: University Press of America, 2007), 59–97 (68).

66. The asterisks indicate that Deut. 6:4 is cited in the footnotes to these verses in the United Bible Society edition of the New Testament.

67. In the Old Testament, the Tetragrammaton was associated with the title *father* (e.g., Deut. 32:6; 2 Sam. 7:11-14; Isa. 63:16; 64:8; Sir. 23:1, 4). In the New Testament, however, the *Kyrios* is associated with the title *Father* only once each in Q and James (Luke 10:21 [Q]; James 3:9).

68. James Dunn, *Jesus and the Spirit* (London: SCM, 1975), 526. Dunn immediately added, "This relationship, and awareness of it, was attributed by them to the Spirit (Rom. 8.15-16; I Cor. 12.3)."

69. The superposition of portraits or interweaving of narratives is also found in Rabbinic traditions. In ch. 4, we discussed the way in which *MRI* Shirata 4:19-22; Bahodesh 5:20-23 describes the appearance of *HaShem* in two distinct roles: that of a young warrior and that of a wise old man. According to this interpretation, these appearances involved the interweaving of the narrative history of *HaShem* with the narrative of humans: warriors in one case, sages in the other.

70. Texts that describe appearances of the Lord Jesus in relation to the throne of God (cited below) imply an anthropic form also for God the Father (possibly based on Jesus' own vision-performances). However, anthropic features of the Father are not usually made explicit in the New Testament (Rev. 4:3 being a partial exception).

71. Christopher Kaiser, *The Doctrine of God: A Historical Survey*, rev. ed. (Eugene, OR: Wipf & Stock, 2001), 19–26.

72. Note the difference between our scenario and Richard Bauckham's idea of Jesus' being "included in the divine identity," by which he means that New Testament writers regarded Jesus as an integral part of the eternal divine identity from the beginning; see, for example, Bauckham, *The Theology of the Book of Revelation* (Cambridge: Cambridge University Press, 1993), 58. From a scholar's ("etic") standpoint, Bauckham's formulation of deity Christology is perfectly correct, but it should not be confused with the actual ("emic") process of confessional formulation, which probably began with the confession *Kyrios Iēsous* and then expanded to include the God to whom the Lord Jesus had prayed.

73. Various formulations are found in Mark 14:62 (Power); Luke 22:69 (Power of God); Heb. 1:3; 8:1 (Majesty); 12:2 (throne of God); cf. Rev. 5:13; 6:16; 7:10 (the one seated on the throne).

74. The title *Son of Man* may be a substitute for YHWH, intended to bring the Kyriocentric vision into conformity with the new binitarian pattern. The anthropic form of the Son of Man and the motif of his "coming/flying with the clouds" (Dan. 7:13; cf. *4 Ezra* 13:3) were the common elements (on the supply side) that made the transfer possible (in spite of the absence of his sending out angels or gathering his elect); the need to differentiate the Lord Jesus from God (Power) was what made it work (on the demand side). In fact, Andrew R. Angel argues that the identification of the Divine Warrior (YHWH) as the Son of Man (and the resulting binity) was a distinct innovation of the Gospel of Mark; Angel, *Chaos and the Son of Man*, 128, 134. If so, early Christology was significantly spun down by these revisions of Kyriocentric visions that identified Jesus with the Son of Man rather than with the Ancient One (YHWH). In the visions of Daniel 7 and the Similitudes of Enoch (both discussed in ch. 2), the "one like a son of man" or "Son of Man" was merely a secondary figure, quite distinct from and subordinate to the Ancient One (YHWH). Daniel Boyarin (following J. A. Emerton) claims to the contrary that "one like a son of man" in Dan. 7:13 was the same as the divine anthropic form of Ezek. 1:26 from the outset; Boyarin, "Daniel 7, Intertextuality, and the History of Israel's Cult," *HTR* 105 (2012): 139–62 (149, 158). The almost seamless manner in which the title *Son of Man* was substituted for YHWH in Synoptic texts (Mark 8:37; 13:26a; 14:62; cf. Mark 13:35; Matt. 16:28b*; 19:28a*; 25:31b) lends some support to Boyarin's claim. It might be safer, however, to regard Dan. 7:13-14 as inherently ambiguous in view of (a) the alternate LXX reading of Dan. 7:13b, "he came as [or 'like'] the Ancient of Days"

(Cologne Pap. 967, MS 88 [Chisianus], Syro-Hexapla), and (b) the Rabbinic idea that the thrones in Dan. 7 were for two attributes of God (justice and mercy) rather than two separate figures (*b. Hag.* 14a). Boyarin refers to this Rabbinic idea as a "Modalist interpretation"; Boyarin, "Beyond Judaisms: Metatron and the Divine Polymorphy of Ancient Judaism," *JSJ* 41 (2010): 323–65 (340–42).

75. Texts describing Jesus as the divine Glory have been thoroughly treated by Charles A. Gieschen, "The Real Presence of the Son Before Christ: Revisiting an Old Approach to Old Testament Christology," *Concordia Theological Quarterly* 68 (2004): 105–26 (120–21).

76. Rev. 19:11-13 portrays Christ as the Word of God in more material, angelomorphic terms.

77. I omit 2 Cor. 3:18, which speaks of the "glory of the Lord" because "Lord" here must refer to Jesus Christ rather than the Father; cf. 2 Cor. 3:16; 4:5.

78. Here again, I am inspired by Wainwright's *Trinity in the New Testament*, 38, 263–64; cf. Kaiser, *Doctrine of God*, 46, 48.

79. Many of the citations for these usages are found in Pierre Benoit, *Jesus and the Gospel*, trans. Benet Weatherhead, 2 vols. (New York: Herder & Herder, 1973–74), 1:56–57.

80. The title *god* could be used to describe angels or even the king of Israel (e.g., Pss. 45:6; 82:1, 6; Isa. 9:6; Zech. 12:8). In these cases, "god" simply meant "a mighty one" like God.

81. Partial exceptions are Philo's descriptions of personified Wisdom (*Sophia*) as a "daughter of God" and of the Word (*Logos*) as the "firstborn Son" of God; Philo, *Agriculture* 51; *Flight* 108-9 (with Wisdom as the mother); *Dreams* 215; *QG* 4.97 (cf. Prov. 8:30). However, the divine status of Philo's Logos is not very clear, and the first-century date and Alexandrian provenance make it extremely unlikely that his ideas influenced the earliest disciples.

82. Outside the New Testament, the earliest explicit identification of the eschatological Messiah as the unique "son of God" occurs in the late first century in *4 Ezra* 7:28-29; cf. Joseph A. Fitzmyer, *The One Who Is To Come* (Grand Rapids: Eerdmans, 2007), 107, 119; cf. ibid., 104–5, on the absence of messianic identity in 4Q246 (4QSon of God).

83. The "Son of God" confession is not found in Q (barring Luke 3:22), making it difficult to tell just how early the confession was.

84. Paul was clearly downplaying the idea of messianic descent from David "according to the flesh" in Rom. 1:3; 9:5; cf. 1 Cor. 15:50; 2 Cor. 5:16. Paul frequently referred to Jesus as "Son of God" in the unique sense, but Rom. 1:3-4 is the only instance in which he cited it as a mandated belief in spite of the fact that Luke attributes the confession to him several times in the book of Acts (9:20, 22; 17:3; 18:5). Possibly, Paul felt that the title was still too closely linked to the idea of Jesus as the Jewish Messiah—a title that also is absent from confessional formulas in Paul's letters. The distinction between the two titles was implicit in the new idea of a divine Son, but that distinction was rarely made explicit in the New Testament (see Luke 22:67, 70).

85. According to Philo, verbal confession was required of Jewish penitents and proselytes; *Rewards and Punishments* 163; cf. *b. Ber.* 13a on the necessity of verbal recitation of the *Shema* verse (Deut. 6:4).

86. William Horbury, *Jewish Messianism and the Cult of Christ* (London: SCM, 1998), 86–108; Horbury, *Messianism among Jews and Christians: Twelve Biblical and Historical Studies* (London: T&T Clark, 2003), 12–19, passim; Adela Yarbro Collins and John J. Collins, *King and Messiah as Son of God: Divine, Human and Angelic Messianic Figures in Biblical and Related Literature* (Grand Rapids: Eerdmans, 2008), 57–58, 61, 62, 90, 94, 100, passim.

87. Joseph A. Fitzmyer disputes all of the texts cited except those in the Similitudes of Enoch, which probably date from the New Testament era; Fitzmyer, *The One Who Is To Come*, 77–79, 85.

88. The attribution of divine sonship also elicited comparison with Abraham's willingness to offer his son Isaac, which was widely believed to have been salvific in early Judaism (e.g., Rom. 8:32). This offering was later referred to by the Hebrew term *akedah* ("binding"), which first occurs in *m. Tamid* 4:1 in relation to the binding of the lamb for the daily *tamid* (burnt offering).

89. These binitarian visions may have been performed as adaptations of the original Kyriocentric visions like the ones discussed in ch. 5, but the greater displacement from the biblical, apocalyptic models discussed in ch. 2 makes it more difficult to use the same methodology in assessing their performative nature. The nearest precedents (on the supply side) would have been visions of the Ancient of Days and (one like) the son of man in Daniel 7 and the Similitudes of Enoch, in which case the figure who revealed himself as Jesus would have shifted from a primary figure (YHWH) to a secondary one (the Son of Man).

90. I have suggested, as an extension of the Kyriocentric conjecture, that Jesus envisaged the *Abba* to whom he prayed in an anthropic form (ch. 4, "Conclusion"). How else would his disciples have become trained in this practice so soon after his execution? The question was still open, however, and ascription of visible form to the Father had been muted, sometimes even denied, by the time of the New Testament texts (e.g., Mark 14:62a; John 1:18a).

91. The name of the Spirit was included in confessional formulas as early as Paul (1 Cor. 12:4-6; 2 Cor. 13:14; Eph. 4:4-6), but the ontological status of the Spirit was not as clear as that of the Lord Jesus, and the issue would occupy Christian communities for centuries thereafter (particularly in the late fourth century).

92. Stories about the sons and daughters of the gods were commonplace in pagan mythologies. As Martin Hengel argued, these gentile models do not provide good parallels or likely input for the New Testament belief in Jesus as the Son of God; Hengel, *Son of God: The Origin of Christology and the History of Jewish-Hellenistic Religion* (Philadelphia: Fortress Press, 1976). In a very important book, Moshe Idel has documented traditions concerning a divine "son of God" in later Judaism; Idel, *Ben: Sonship and Jewish Mysticism*, Kogod Library of Judaic Studies 5 (London: Continuum, 2007). Idel argues that reference to a hypostatic, cosmic mediator as "son" was largely suppressed in response to Christian usage of the term; ibid., 49–50, 148–49.

93. The idea of a hidden "son" also occurred in Jesus' parable of the vineyard (Mark 12:2-6), but the "beloved son" in that case was a conclusion to the line of prophets, rather than a divine being (as discussed in ch. 8). Interestingly, Clement of Alexandria's *Stromateis* ("Miscellanies") substituted names of Jesus ("Lord" or "Christ") for "God" in his uses of the phrase, "in many and various ways" (Heb. 1:1), thereby referring the prophetic revelations of the Old Testament to the Lord Jesus; *Strom.* 5.6.35; 7.16.95 (ANF 2:452b, 551a). Clement had apparently associated the principle of variety with Christ as the manifold wisdom of the one God; *Strom.* 1.3; 6.7 (ANF 2:305a, 493b).

94. The verb *gennaō* ("beget") was used of the king of Israel in the LXX of Ps. 2:7 (cited with reference to Jesus in Luke 3:22 D, it[a, b, c, d]; Heb. 1:5) and Ps. 110:3 ("from the womb I have begotten you before the morning"). The term was also used of the origin of the Logos by Philo (*Confusion of Tongues* 63), and it later became part of the creedal tradition (e.g., Eusebius's baptismal creed). In addition to the two Psalms just cited, church fathers added Isa. 53:8 (LXX, "Who shall declare his generation"), regarding the servant of the Lord, in order to support the idea; see Justin, *1 Apology* 51.1; Justin, *Dial.* 43.3; 63.2; Tertullian, *Against Praxeas* 11 (against modalism); Eusebius, *Demonstration* 4.15.47-49; Athanasius, *Deposition of Arius* 3; *Orations against the Arians* 2.57. The disproportion between the popularity of the idea in comparison with the meager biblical support is an indication of the demand for some way of relating the Lord Jesus to God the Father.

95. For simplicity, I ignore here the hypothetical minority view that the Lord assumed the name and face of Jesus after he had died on the cross (already discussed in the previous section). In that case, there would have been no problem of the cross, whereas the texts we hope to explain appear to address that very problem.

96. Donald Juel argued that early Christians believed that their teacher was the Messiah already during his lifetime (based largely on the early date of the tradition behind 1 Cor. 15:3-7); Juel, *Messianic Exegesis: Christological Interpretation of the Old Testament in Early Christianity* (Philadelphia: Fortress Press, 1988), 24–25, 29. Major studies that call this supposition into question are Nils Alstrup Dahl, "The Crucified Messiah," in Dahl, *The Crucified Messiah and Other Essays*

(Minneapolis: Augsburg Publishing House, 1974), 10–36, repr. in Dahl, *Jesus the Christ: The Historical Origins of Christological Doctrine*, ed. Donald H. Juel (Minneapolis: Fortress Press, 1991), 27–47, and Paula Fredriksen, *Jesus of Nazareth, King of the Jews: A Jewish Life and the Emergence of Christianity* (New York: Knopf, 1999), 241–59.

97. See also the (first-century) "Lives of the Prophets"; *Barn.* 5:11; *Ascen. Isa.* 5:1-14; cf. John Downing, "Jesus and Martyrdom," *JTS* 14 (1963): 279–93 (285–86, 292); T. E. Pollard, "Martyrdom and Resurrection in the New Testament," *BJRL* 55 (1972): 240–51 (248–49).

98. Nor would it have included the community of *4 Ezra* 7:29, according to which the Messiah would die along with all other humans. On expectation of a military messiah, see *Pss. Sol.* 17–18; 4Q285 (4QSerek ha-Milhama) frag. 5; *4 Ezra* 13; *2 Bar.* 40. Kenneth E. Pomykala stresses the Messiah's use of wisdom and words, rather than horses and bows, in the Psalms of Solomon (17:23-24; cf. 17:33); Pomykala, *The Davidic Dynasty Tradition in Early Judaism*, Early Judaism and its Literature 7 (Atlanta: Scholars, 1995), 162–65.

99. As Larry Hurtado points out, these texts run counter to Paul's normal use of the name *Christ* in association with the cross; Hurtado, "Lord," in *Dictionary of Paul and his Letters*, ed. Gerald F. Hawthorne and Ralph P. Martin (Downers Grove, IL: InterVarsity Press, 1993), 560–69 (568b). The association of Christ (Messiah) and cross will be explained below.

100. Some later Christian theologians addressed the problem by restricting the crucifixion to the human nature of Jesus, rather than his identity as Lord (e.g., Athanasius, *On the Incarnation* 16), but I see little or no evidence of this incipient two-nature strategy in the New Testament era itself (barring 1 Tim. 3:16).

101. Tryggve N. D. Mettinger, *In Search of God: The Meaning and Message of the Everlasting Names*, trans. Frederick H. Cryer (Philadelphia: Fortress Press, 1988), 82–85, 90; Mark S. Smith, *The Early History of God: Yahweh and the Other Deities in Ancient Israel* (San Francisco: Harper & Row, 1990), 164–65.

102. Deut 5:26; Josh 3:10; 1 Sam 17:26, 36; 2 Kgs. 19:4, 16; Pss. 42:2; 84:2; Isa. 37:4, 17; Jer. 10:10; 23:36; Dan. 6:20, 26; Hos. 1:10 (MT 2:1). In addition there are ninety-two verses that state that "the Lord/God lives"; cf. Mettinger, *In Search of God*, 91.

103. Mettinger argues that, in Hosea at least, YHWH was defined as "living" and "immortal" in contrast to the Canaanite god Ba'al; Mettinger, *In Search of God*, 85–86, 90 (second bullet). Mark S. Smith suggests that this dissociation from the realm of death (as well as from sexuality) was not an original attribute of YHWH; it derived from the program of Levitical priesthood whose central concern was ritual purity; M. S. Smith, "Yahweh and Other Deities in Ancient Israel? Observations on Old Problems and Recent Trends," in *Ein Gott Alein? JHWH-Verehrung und biblischer Monotheismus im Kontext der israelitischen und altorientalischen Religionsgeschichte*, Orbis biblicus et orientalis 139, ed. Walter Dietrich and Martin A. Klopfenstein (Freiburg: Universitatsverlag, 1994), 197–234 (222–23); cf. M. S. Smith, *The Early History of God*, 164–65. Similarly, J. Massyngberde Ford states rather pithily that "Life is the essential property of Yahweh"; Ford, *Revelation*, Anchor Bible 38 (Garden City, NJ: Doubleday Anchor, 1975), 383. In short, Old Testament writers saw no place for a dying and rising God (Hab. 1:12 NRSV, JPS *Tanakh*).

104. Note the emphasis on the attribute of "living" (*zōn*) in Matt. 16:16; John 6:57 (for God the Father) and John 6:51; Rev. 1:18a (for the Lord Jesus), all of which are contiguous with statements about Jesus suffering and death (Matt. 16:21; John 6:51; Rev. 1:18b).

105. Here I follow the JPS *Tanakh* translation of Isa. 63:9 (based on early traditions), which is relegated to a footnote in the NRSV.

106. See also *t. Sanh.* 9:6, where the parable about a man whose crucifixion makes people think of the King who is his twin brother is interpreted in terms of the image of God in suffering humanity; cf. Abraham Heschel, *Heavenly Torah as Refracted through the Generations*, trans. Gordon Tucker and Leonard Levin (New York: Continuum, 2005), 264. See also *MRS* 1:1, where the clairvoyance and mindfulness of *HaShem* in Exod. 3:7 is taken to mean that *HaShem* experiences

the same blows (drowning and being incarcerated in a wall) as the sons of Israel; W. David Nelson translates the name as the "glory of God" (grammatically equivalent); Nelson, trans., *Mekhilta of Rabbi Shimon Bar Yohai* (Philadelphia: Jewish Publication Society of America, 2002), 2–4 (hereafter cited as *MRS*); Nelson, "Orality and Mnemonics in Aggadic Midrash," in *Midrash and Context: Proceedings of the 2004 and 2005 SBL Consultation on Midrash*, ed. Lieve M. Teugels and Rivka Ulmer (Piscataway, NJ: Gorgias, 2007), 123–37 (136).

107. *MRI* Pisha 14:86-89, which cites Isa. 63:9, ET in Jacob Z. Lauterbach, trans., *Mekilta of Rabbi Ishmael*, 3 vols. (Philadelphia: Jewish Publication Society of America, 1933), 1:113; cf. *MRI* Shirata 3; *1 En.* (Similitudes) 42 on Sophia (Wisdom) being forced to return to heaven.

108. The NRSV of 1 Thess. 2:14b-15 reads, "the Jews, who killed both the Lord Jesus and the prophets," but the Greek word *Ioudaioi* should be translated "Judeans," in view of the clearly sociopolitical term *hē Ioudaía* (NRSV, "Judea"), in 2:14a.

109. According to John Ronning, John portrayed Jesus' path to the cross as the divine warrior going forth to battle the forces of evil (rising up, being lifted up); Ronning, *The Jewish Targums and John's Logos Theology* (Peabody, MA: Hendrickson, 2010), 126, 130–34, 142. If so (Ronning's textual connections may be questioned), John has preserved the original form of the gospel message (concerning the suffering of the Lord, according to our reading) and portrayed it as divine warfare.

110. Ignatius (*Eph.* 1:1; *Rom.* 6:3) used the expressions "God's blood" and "God's passion." Tatian described himself as "the minister of the suffering God" (*Address to the Greeks* 13). Tertullian included God's having died in his version of the baptismal creed (*Against Marcion* 2.16).

111. The idea of a suffering, dying God has been opposed by theologians from Ambrose, Gregory of Nyssa, and Theodore of Mopsuestia to Wolfhart Pannenberg in our own time.

112. Harold Bloom, *Jesus and Yahweh: The Names Divine* (New York: Penguin, 2005), 6. Bloom describes himself as Jewish in culture, but "not part of normative Judaism" on p. 2.

113. Note how Matthew's Jesus refers to his followers as scribes who are "trained for the kingdom of heaven" (Matt. 13:52). Contrast Paul's list of gifts in 1 Cor. 12:3-11, which reflects the practices (confessions of faith, utterances, deeds, prophecies, tongues) of a more charismatic community than Matthew's must have been. Paul subsequently reminded his people of the need for apologetic exegesis (1 Cor. 15:3-4), as did Luke's Jesus, risen from the dead (Luke 24:25-27, 44-47; cf. Acts 8:30-35; 17:2-3, 11; 18:28), and John's Jesus even before death (2:19-22; 5:39; 10:34-36; passim).

114. Lindars, *New Testament Apologetic*, 75–137. In contrast to Lindars, I understand the problem to have been generated by the primal confession of Jesus as Lord.

115. Exegesis could itself be performative, particularly in regard to meditative ascent, as we shall see in ch. 9. Philo, the major exponent of this type of mystical exegesis in the New Testament era, regarded the exercise as an individual one; Philo, *On the Creation* 70-71; passim; cf. John Levison, "Inspiration and the Divine Spirit in the Writings of Philo Judaeus," *JSJ* 26 (1995): 271–323.

116. As Daniel Boyarin argues, however, the Rabbinic midrash often conceals at least the desire to relive the moment of the divine revelation (as in Exod. 15); Boyarin, "The Eye in the Torah: Oracular Desire in Midrashic Hermeneutic," *Critical Inquiry* 16 (1990): 532–50 (546), reprinted in Boyarin, *Sparks of the Logos: Essays in Rabbinic Hermeneutics* (Leiden: Brill, 2003), 3–23.

117. A fourth option, of course, would have been simply to downplay the sufficiency of the Old Testament for prophetic purposes. This tack would not have been an option for pious Jews like the early disciples, but Ignatius of Antioch said something along these lines when confronted by Christian Jews (or Judaizers) who refused to accept the gospel message about the cross because it was not plainly stated in their ancient scriptures (*Phld.* 8:2). Ignatius's response, that the crucifixion, death, and resurrection were themselves the only scriptures that were uncorrupted (*athikta atcheia*), indicates how difficult it still was to address this problem in the early second

century. The Council of Constantinople (381 CE) would later make the inspired nature of the prophets a confessional matter ("who spoke through the prophets"; cf. 1 Pet. 1:10–11).

118. Jewish rejection of a crucified Messiah is well portrayed in Justin's figure of Trypho the Jew (*Dialog.* 32.1; 79.1; 90.1). In some Jewish traditions, the Messiah would die of natural causes (as in *4 Ezra* 7:29), but, as N. T. Wright puts it: "There are no traditions about a Messiah being [martyred and] raised to life"; Wright, *The Resurrection of the Son of God*, Christian Origins and the Question of God 3 (Minneapolis: Fortress Press, 2003), 205; cf. Fitzmyer, *The One Who Is To Come*, 141–42. Strikingly, all the apparent allusions to the Isaianic Servant in the Similitudes of Enoch completely avoid the idea of the Servant's suffering; James C. VanderKam, "Righteous One, Messiah, Chosen One, and Son of Man in 1 Enoch 37–71," in *The Messiah*, ed. James H. Charlesworth, 177–85 (190); Fitzmyer, *The One Who Is To Come*, 87, 141.

119. The early disciples and writers did such a good job of refitting the Davidic Messiah to the prior ideas of Jesus' identity as Lord and his death on a cross that many New Testament scholars have assumed that their original realization of the Lordship of Jesus followed the same course of reasoning: from death and resurrection, through messianic status, to Lordship (see the discussion of N. T. Wright in the Introduction).

120. I refer to the *pesher* style of exegesis to find precedent for contemporary events in some Qumran texts (e.g., 4QFlor, 4QTest). In debate (as remembered with the Sadducees), for example, the Rabbis found "assurances which hint at the resurrection of the dead" in texts like Num. 23:10; Deut. 32:39; 33:6; Hos. 6:2 (*Sifrei Devarim* 329; cf. Reuven Hammer's comment on this phenomenon in his note to this text in his translation of *The Classic Midrash: Tannaitic Commentaries on the Bible*, Classics of Western Spirituality [New York: Paulist, 1995], 375).

121. Joseph Fitzmyer concludes that the idea of a suffering Messiah was Luke's "own theologoumenon"; Fitzmyer, *The One Who Is To Come*, 141–42. However, the existence of a broader tradition that Luke must have drawn from is suggested by independent traditions: (a) Mark 8:31, which attributes suffering to the "Son of Man," a title paralleling Messiah in Mark 14:61-2 (as pointed out by Fitzmyer, loc. cit., 138, 142); (b) Synoptic Gospel texts like Mark 15:34; Matt. 27:35, which cite texts like Ps. 22:1, 18 (Davidic Psalms interpreted messianically); and 1 Pet. 1:10–11, cited below.

122. An earlier stage of apologetic exegesis may be reflected in the "pistis formula" of 1 Cor. 15:3 (cited below) and in Mark's statements about the suffering Son of Man (Mark 8:31; 9:12, 31). C. H. Dodd famously argued that the idea of a suffering Son of Man was based on an original Christian synthesis of Dan. 7 with Isa. 53; Dodd, *According to the Scriptures: The Sub-Structure of New Testament Theology* (London: Nisbet, 1952), 116–19. If so, these texts in Mark are closely related to the idea of a suffering servant, which is discussed below.

123. As Douglas A. Hare argues, *Christos* in 1 Cor. 15:3 is used as a proper name with titular, messianic significance; Hare, "When Did Messiah Become a Proper Name?" *ExpTim* 121 (2009): 70–73.

124. Even the clearest pre-Christian statement of a Davidic Messiah, *Pss. Sol.* 17, is couched in a prayer to the Lord who is "our King forevermore" and "God our savior."

125. Jesus' use of the title *Son of Man* is sometimes explained by cross-reference to the enigmatic figure in Dan. 7:13, for example, by Daniel Boyarin, who appeals also to Dan. 7:25; Boyarin, *The Jewish Gospels: The Story of the Jewish Christ* (New York: New Press, 2012), 135–48. However, the Danielic "one like a son of man" is not said to suffer or die, even in the Similitudes of Enoch; cf. Joseph Fitzmyer, *The One Who Is To Come*, 85–87. The New Testament idea of a suffering son of Man can best be explained by reverting to the original Hebrew use of "son of man" as a way of describing a visionary prophet (esp. Ezek. 2:1 with its death and resurrection imagery) and tapping the tradition of suffering prophets and hasidim (e.g., Luke 7:33-35). This usage corresponds to the second of the three categories proposed in Bultmann, *Theology of the New Testament*, 1:30.

126. Much the same can be said for the Gospels' use of the marvelous image of the righteous servant (Greek: *paidos kyriou, dikaios*) from the Wisdom of Solomon 2–5 (esp. Ws. 2:13-20; 3:1-6,

alluded to in Matt. 27:39-43; Luke 9:31). Like Isaiah's servant, this wisdom figure would be exalted by God (Ws. 3:7-8).

127. Fitzmyer, *The One Who Is To Come*, 19–25, 43–46, 77–78.

128. David was regarded as a prophet (without specific reference to the Psalms) in 2 Sam. 23:1-2 ("The oracle of David") and by Josephus, *Ant.* 8.109; see James L. Kugel, "David the Prophet," in *Poetry and Prophecy: The Beginnings of a Literary Tradition*, Myth and Poetics, ed. James L. Kugel (Ithaca, NY: Cornell University Press, 1990), 45–55, 198–200. As Menahem Kister points out, the Qumran commentaries and *pesharim* treated the Psalms of David as prophetic literature; Kister, "A Common Heritage: Biblical Interpretation at Qumran and Its Implications," in *Biblical Perspectives: Early Use and Interpretation of the Bible in Light of the Dead Sea Scrolls*, STDJ 28, ed. Michael E. Stone and Esther G. Chazon (Leiden: Brill, 1998), 101–111 (108–9). In other words, the Psalms were interpreted eschatologically, often messianically, in Jesus' time, whether or not earlier generations of Jews had seen them in that light.

129. The Hebrew incipit was "To the leader" (*la-mnaseh*); Richard B. Hays, "Christ Prays the Psalms: Paul's Use of an Early Christian Exegetical Convention," in *The Future of Christology: Essays in Honor of Leander E. Keck*, ed. A. J. Malherbe and W. A. Meeks (Minneapolis: Fortress Press, 1993), 122–36 (127). We may assume that early discipleship circles included Greek-speaking participants (cf. Acts 6:1-6).

130. The Hebrew for "than God" is *me-elohim*, which the lxx took to refer to angels (*par' aggelous*). At least since the time of John Calvin, exegetes have realized that New Testament authors "do not actually explain the [original] meaning of the text [Ps. 8], and instead accommodate it to a different sense"; G. Sujin Pak, *The Judaizing Calvin: Sixteenth-Century Debates over the Messianic Psalms* (Oxford: Oxford University Press, 2010), 98.

131. The Hebrew of Ps. 22:16c is either *karu*, "they have pierced" or *ka'ri*, "like a lion." The lxx follows the former reading with *ōruxan*, "they pierced." Mitchell Dahood has argued that that reading was also in the original Hebrew; Dahood, *Psalms*, 3 vols., AB 16–17A (Garden City, NY: Doubleday, 1966–70), 1:140–41. Rufinus of Aquileia cited Ps. 22:15 to support the early Christian confession that Jesus descended to the nether regions (*in inferna*) in his burial; *Commentary on the Apostles' Creed* 18.

132. As Richard Hays sums up the case, the early Christians read Psalm 69 as "a poetic depiction of the suffering and vindication of Jesus, the Messiah, whose voice 'David' had anticipated"; Hays, "Can the Gospels Teach Us How to Read the Old Testament?" *Pro Ecclesia* 11 (2002): 402–18 (412–14).

133. It could be significant that all three of the Psalms that are not cited in the New Testament refer to the "Lord" as someone separate from the Davidic protagonist (Pss. 18:16; 40:2; 88:1).

134. See the note above on the Hebrew of Ps. 22:16c. In spite of the availability of this reading, Ps. 22:16c was never quoted by New Testament writers. However, the noted citations by Mark, Matthew, and John indicate that the language of Psalm 22 was well known, and verse 16 was later cited by Justin, *1 Apol.* 35.7; *Dial.* 97; Irenaeus, *Haer.* 4.34.4 (obscure); Tertullian, *Against Marcion* 3.18. So the lack of textual evidence for earlier citation does not mean that this motif was not used orally at an earlier stage.

135. The lxx of Zech. 12:10 reads, "they shall look to me because they have danced triumphantly," which appears designed to avoid the problem. The Qumran scroll, 4QMinor Prophets[e], confirms the reading, "look at me whom they have pierced, and they shall mourn," but lacks the sequel; Martin Abegg, Jr., Peter Flinch, and Eugene Ulrich, trans. *The Dead Sea Scrolls Bible* (San Francisco: HarperSanFrancisco, 1999), 475.

136. The lxx seems to identify the pierced party as the shepherds against whom the sword is drawn in 13:7. The language is reminiscent of the servant in Isa. 52–53, as pointed out by David C. Mitchell, "Messiah ben Joseph: A Sacrifice of Atonement for Israel," *RRJ* 10 (2007): 77–94 (91 and sources cited in n. 41). Centuries later the Talmud would refer this verse to the Messiah of the

house of Joseph (*b. Sukkah* 52a). Roy Rosenberg has argued that Zech. 12:10 already contained the idea of a slain messiah (based on intertextuality among Zech. 3:8 and Jer. 23:5, along with Isa. 53:2; 53:11; Rosenberg, "The Slain Messiah in the Old Testament," *ZAW* 99 (1987): 259–61. As Fitzmyer has argued in detail, however, there was nothing properly messianic (in the eschatological sense) about any of the Old Testament texts cited; Fitzmyer, *The One Who Is to Come*, 52, 63 n. 22.

137. Texts describing YHWH coming with the clouds include Exod. 13:21; 19:9; 34:5; Lev. 16:2; Pss. 18:9-11; 97:2-5; 104:3b-4a LXX; Isa. 19:1; Ezek. 1:4, 27-28, a motif, according to Tryggve Mettinger, that derives from the Zion cult tradition; Mettinger, *Dethronement of Sabaoth: Studies in the Shem and Kavod Theologies*, Coniectanea Biblica, Old Testament Series 18 (Lund: CWK Gleerup, 1982), 33–35, 104–5, 122. Similar language is used for the "one like a son of man" in Dan. 7:13 (cf. *4 Ezra* 13:3), which could well be the source of title *Son of Man* as used by Matthew (the motive being another matter).

138. The words of the confession appear in either order: *ho Christos Iēsous* (Acts 5:42; 18:5, 28), or *Iēsous (estin) ho Christos* (John 20:31; 1 John 2:22; 5:1). Dale C. Allison suggests that the compound name "Christ Jesus" (or "Jesus Christ") is really a remnant of this early confession (Aramaic, *Yeshua meshiha*); Allison, *Constructing Jesus: Memory, Imagination, and History* (Grand Rapids: Baker Academic, 2010), 179–80. The confession of Jesus as "Son of God" is closely associated with it and undoubtedly had the same force (Mark 14:61-2; Matt. 16:16; Luke 22:70; 23:35 D; Acts 9:20; John 1:49; 11:27; 20:31; 1 John 2:23; 5:5). In other words, the messianic sense of "Son of God" continued alongside the binitarian (Father-Son) sense discussed above.

139. Martin Kähler "somewhat provocatively" described the Gospels as "passion narratives with extended introductions"; Kähler, *The So-Called Historical Jesus and the Historic, Biblical Christ*, trans. Carl E. Braaten (Philadelphia: Fortress Press, 1964), 80 n. 11. The confession of Jesus as Messiah is alluded to (drawing on readers' prior knowledge) in Mark 8:29; 15:32; Luke 22:67; John 4:25-26; 7:41; 9:22; 10:24-26; 20:31. Contrariwise, the sayings source Q lacks an account of the cross and makes no reference to this confession, even though it does contain the primal confession of Jesus as Lord (Luke 6:46, cf. Mark 2:28; 12:37). Outside the Gospels, the confession of Jesus as Messiah is found only in the New Testament writings with which they are most closely associated, Acts and the Johannine Epistles (Acts 2:36; 5:42; 9:22; 17:3; 18:5, 28; 1 John 2:22; 5:1).

140. 1 Cor. 1:17; Gal. 6:12, 14; Phil. 3:18. See Kramer, *Christ, Lord, Son of God*, 26–28; Hurtado, *Lord Jesus Christ*, 100–1.

141. 1 Cor. 10:16; Eph. 2:13; Heb. 9:11-14; 1 Pet. 1:2, 19; 1 John 1:7; cf. Rom. 3:24-25; 5:8-9; Rev. 1:5.

142. The confessional formula, "Messiah died for us/our sins," first appears in 1 Cor. 15:3; Rom. 5:6, 8. Although it uses the title *Messiah*, it also reflects the idea of the servant in the LXX of Isa. 53:5-6 (*tais/dia tas hamartias hēmōn*).

143. Among the royal Psalm texts cited in the New Testament are Pss. 2:2, 7; 45:6-7; 110:1 (now binitarian); and 132:11. As Joseph Fitzmyer points out, Christian applications of these texts gave an explicitly messianic interpretation to what previously had been just a Davidic psalm; Fitzmyer, *The One Who Is To Come*, 144–45 (on the use of Ps. 2:2 in Acts 4:26-7; Rev. 11:15). I respectfully differ from David M. Hay in relegating Psalm 110 to a secondary (really a tertiary) role in early Christology; cf. Hay, *Glory at the Right Hand: Psalm 110 in Early Christianity*, SBLMS 18 (Nashville: Abingdon, 1973).

144. The angels announced to the shepherds, "To you is born this day in the city of David a savior who is Messiah, the Lord [*christos kyrios*]" (Luke 2:11). C. Kavin Rowe perceptively asks, "how can Jesus be both *the Lord* (kyrios) and the Christ *of the Lord* (kyríou)? . . . it appears that Luke here uses both words together in a mutually determinative manner"; Rowe, *Early Narrative Christology*, 53–54. If Rowe is correct in his reading, Luke superimposed the two portraits from the very start of his Gospel and implied that salvation was accomplished by that very overlap.

145. "No other movement [in Judaism] so far has shown any interest in conflating 'Lord' with 'the messiah'"; Alan Segal, "The Afterlife as Mirror of the Self," in *Experientia, Volume I:*

Inquiry into Religious Experience in Early Judaism and Christianity, SBLSS 40, ed. Frances Flannery, Colleen Shantz, and Rodney A. Werline (Atlanta: SBL, 2008), 19–40 (34–35). Segal's "so far" indicates that the uniqueness in question is fortuitous, not absolute, as we also concluded in ch. 4.

146. The hiddenness of Messiah Jesus will be an issue to discuss in ch. 9 (Movement 1).

147. The writer of Acts 2 expressed this superposition of two portraits succinctly in saying that God had made Jesus "*both* Lord *and* Messiah" (a *kai . . . kai* construction, Acts 2:36). I interpret this to mean that no such combination was known prior to Jesus (why else make such a point of it?), and that only God could bring it about.

8

Four Alternative Tradition Histories or Textures in Early Christology

We have tested the Kyriocentric vision conjecture in a variety of ways using three bodies of material: Second Temple apocalypses, early Rabbinic (Tannaitic) literature, and the canonical New Testament. We have seen that the conjecture accounts quite well for the basic features of New Testament Christology: the confession of the Lord as Jesus (*Kyrios Iēsous*), the dedication of divine prayers and devotions to Jesus (as well as to God the Father), the raising of Jesus from the grave, various notions of the embodiment of the Lord in Jesus, binitarian formulas, and the proclamation of Jesus as the Messiah, son of David.[1]

In spite of these confirmations, our conjecture would be weakened, however, if it could not do justice to the variety of alternatives in the New Testament and other early Christian literature (at least through the second century). In this chapter, we shall develop a method for approaching that subject and support it with a few examples from that literature. First, we need to differentiate our method from a leading predecessor.

FROM TRAJECTORIES TO TEXTURES (A MODEL OF DEVELOPMENT)

As a result of the work of James M. Robinson and Helmut Koester, scholars have often thought in terms of texts that lie on different "trajectories" in early Christianity. The main idea was that only one of those trajectories would lead to proto-orthodox theologians like Irenaeus and the early baptismal creed (the "Roman Symbol").[2] The idea of trajectories was clearly helpful for illustrating the diversity of early Christian beliefs and practices and freeing historical theology from the "triumphalistic" accounts of orthodox heresiologists.

However, thinking in terms of trajectories can be misleading if its use suggests that written texts were intentionally composed in order to articulate a comprehensive, unified point of view, or that they represented the sum total of the beliefs and practices of their communities.[3] It is more realistic to shift the focus from written texts to the communities that produced them. It will also be helpful to think in terms of overlapping tradition histories or textures in order to avoid the assumption that divergent developments were separate trajectories (like those of projectiles or comets). The idea of trajectories is based solely on the differences among various traditions, whereas that of a woven texture allows for commonalities as well as the differences.

In the following discussion, we shall find that several documentary sources can be used to illustrate more than one tradition history.[4] If the texts had been written with a view toward giving us a full account of the beliefs and practices of their communities, the overlap of traditions (or interweave of narrative threads) would undoubtedly have been even greater. In general, one cannot assume that the absence of a certain idea in a particular text reflected a lacuna in the community that produced it. We can assume that the challenges and demands of their times induced them to select some traditions and work with them, more than with others, to be sure, but we must also allow that only a few of these challenges were met by putting these traditions into writing.[5]

Our own method has been to think in terms of communities that rehearsed received traditions (on the supply side) and augmented or revised those traditions in order to address challenges that arose both within their fellowship and in their efforts to present their case to other parties (the demand side). According to our conjecture, most of these challenges arose from the need to superpose two distinct portraits, or interweave two distinct narratives, for Jesus. In the line of sages and prophets (*hasidim*), Jesus was remembered as a flesh-and-blood teacher, with whom the disciples had walked for years, who had prayed to and taught about God as his Father, and whose ministry was cut short when he was condemned to death and crucified. In the history of Kyriocentric visions, however, Jesus was the name (or his was the voice and face) with which the Lord identified himself when the disciples cried out to him in their distress in the wake of Jesus' death and burial. For those who tried to account for this paradoxical superposition, there was a pool of traditions to draw from: traditions about theophanies, the resurrection, embodiments, intermediary figures, and suffering servants (ch. 7).

In short, the tradition pool had lots of different pieces. From the viewpoint of the Catholic Church, as it emerged in the third and fourth centuries, it would simply be a matter of fitting it all together in a creed. For earlier generations, however, there was no "all" to start with: there was only a diversity of traditions, some new and some old, and some of which were celebrated and preserved in certain communities more than in others. Some of this diversity is represented by documents that were later excluded from the canon of the Old and New Testaments—the *Gospel of Thomas* being the most prominent example. However, we do not have to limit ourselves to "lost scriptures" in order to discover theological diversity. There was plenty of it even within the canonical documents, some of which had little or nothing to say about Jesus' teachings and prayers, and others little to say about his death on a cross or his resurrection from the dead (the Letter of James, for example; cf. Jas. 5:6). Some New Testament traditions spun the story of Jesus up in order to match the Kyriocentric vision; others spun the visionary traditions down in order to account for the memories of Jesus (as we have documented in chs. 6, 7), and some did both (e.g., Phil. 2:6-11).

Our task at this point is to sort out the options in the early days of the church (first and second centuries). Based on the scenario that we developed in the previous chapter, the tradition pool the churches had to work with had two portraits or narratives concerning Jesus, and these narratives could only be woven together if various other beliefs were adopted from the tradition pool. The result was three major narrative threads: the self-revelation of the Lord as Jesus (the primary vision); recollections of Jesus as a hasid or servant of the Lord who had been crucified and buried (leading to beliefs concerning Jesus' resurrection and Messiah identity); and recollection of his teachings and prayers to his heavenly Father (giving rise to dyadic formulas).[6] Most of the time, New Testament writers tried to weave all three of these threads into a single fabric, but the threads could more readily be combined by toning down (not necessarily denying) one or more of them.[7] As a result, there were at least four major options.[8] I list them here to provide an outline of the four sections that follow in this chapter:

- Work with the teachings of Jesus, and (in most cases[9]) acknowledge his mortality, but tone down the Kyriocentric vision and the Lord-Jesus identification (proto-adoptionist).[10]
- Work with Kyriocentric visions and the teachings of Jesus, resulting in binitarian formulas, but tone down Jesus' mortality and death on a cross (proto-docetist,)[11] thereby lessening the need for either Jesus' resurrection or his identity as Davidic Messiah.
- Work with Kyriocentric visions and the mortality of Jesus, but tone down (or reinterpret) Jesus' teachings about the Father (proto-modalist,)[12] thereby lessening the need for binitarian reformulations of the vision.
- Work with Kyriocentric visions and Jesus' teachings about the Father, resulting in binitarian formulas, but tone down both Jesus'

deity and his mortality just enough to portray him as a secondary
figure like an angel (subordinationist, proto-Arian.)[13]

Here I have attached some labels from later theological disputes to these options
in order to aid reader-recognition, but the options being considered at this
point were initially quite innocent of the systematic forms of polemic that were
later labeled heretical. In order to have the advantage of hindsight without
prejudicing the issues, I have used the prefix *proto* in order to differentiate these
options from later, more entrenched views.

There is more than enough textual material to document all of these
tendencies in the late first and second centuries. The purpose of the following
sections will be to cite just enough of it to illustrate the options involved and
further thereby assess the fruitfulness of the Kyriocentric vision conjecture in
this regard. In other words, our purpose will be to appreciate these options for
the traditions that they preserve, rather than to discredit them for what they
leave out (from the standpoint of the later canon and creed).

The Proto-adoptionist Option

Given the fact that the interweaving of these threads was an ongoing process
(which has never been completely settled), we expect to find texts that celebrate
the portrait of Jesus as a hasid who, like all Jewish holy men, was inspired and
energized by divine power, without reference to the Kyriocentric vision and
the resulting Lord-Jesus identification.

This particular texture might go back to the early disciples themselves.
April DeConick has reconstructed an early kernel of the *Gospel of Thomas* that
she attributes to an Aramaic-speaking group of Christian Jews who gathered
under the leadership of James, the brother of Jesus (30–50 CE). In this earlier
stratum, according to DeConick, Jesus was remembered primarily as the
greatest in the line of prophets. Deity Christology only emerged (or gained
more attention) in later strata of Thomas (80–120 CE).[14]

If, for the sake of discussion, we take DeConick's reconstruction at face
value,[15] it fits rather nicely into the scenario for early Christology that we
have sketched here. The *Gospel of Thomas* consists of a long series of logia
that recall the sayings of Jesus, which were originally oral. Like some of the
parables and sayings of Jesus in the canonical New Testament, many of these
sayings are difficult to understand and call for thinking and discussion among
the audience. Many of them also deal with issues of lifestyle (with an ascetic,
encratite leaning). Evidently the demand for such material in the Thomas

community led to a strong emphasis on Jesus' role as teacher and a relative neglect of other threads of christological tradition.

As a matter of fact, the Thomas community was quite aware of the Kyriocentric vision and its repercussions. There is plenty of evidence for a deity Christology. Within the limits of DeConick's kernel, for example, we find logia that evidently portray Jesus as the *Shekhinah*/Glory (GT 30; cf. Matt. 18:20) and the Logos (GT 82).[16] Clearly, there was no attempt to deny the portrait of Jesus as the divine Lord; it simply was not relevant to the interests of this particular Gospel. The Thomas community provides an excellent example of the risks one takes in basing judgments about unfamiliar communities on their writings alone. Accordingly, it is best to think of this early kernel as being naively adoptionist or proto-adoptionist, rather than self-consciously or systematically so.

Several strata of the canonical New Testament provide a very similar emphasis to that in Thomas: Jesus was a Spirit-empowered teacher like Moses and the prophets. You find this emphasis in Q (another hypothetical sayings source[17]), which belongs to the same early timeframe as DeConick's proposed kernel of *Thomas* (see Luke 3:22; 7:33-35; 10:8-9; 11:20). Jesus is also located in the line of the prophets in the synoptic "parable of the vineyard" (Mark 12:2-6, paralleled in Matthew, Luke, and *Thomas*)[18] and in the first chapter of Hebrews (Heb. 1:1-2). In the first chapter of 1 Peter, the Father is the one who is invoked for salvation and in whom believers trust, and Christ is described as someone destined to be revealed, rather than as a preexistent figure in the Old Testament (1 Pet. 1:17-21).

Clearly, neither Q, Mark, Hebrews, nor 1 Peter can be described as "adoptionist" (monarchian) in the exclusive, systematic sense of the term, because they all contain traditions that clearly identify Jesus as the Lord God of Israel (e.g., Luke 3:4; 7:27; 13:35; Mark 1:2-3; Heb. 1:10-12; 1 Pet. 2:8; 3:12, 14-15). In none of these cases, however, was the Christology thought through systematically. As in the case of *Thomas*, therefore, it is best to think of these particular passages as being naively adoptionist or proto-adoptionist.

Plenty of further examples of such a proto-adoptionist emphasis can be found in second-century texts like the *Gospel of the Hebrews*, the *Shepherd of Hermas*, the *Testament of Levi*, and probably the mysterious group called "Ebionites" (as reported by Tertullian and others).[19] All of these texts place emphasis on the portrait of Jesus as an inspired teacher or a prophet like Moses. On the other hand, none of them deny the Lord-Jesus identification (though heresiologists like Tertullian belabored the little-known "Ebionites" for such negations). If we cannot see a well-defined trajectory here, we can at least see a distinct pattern of interwoven traditions.

The picture of the second century is further complicated by the fact that several other texts combine this portrait of Jesus as a teacher or prophet with binitarian formulas. In these cases, the man Jesus was empowered by a divine figure like the eternal *Christos* (so the "Ascents of James," the "Preaching of Peter," and Cerinthus as reported by Irenaeus)[20] or the imperishable Son of Man (The Testimony of Truth).[21] It is difficult to say whether these statements were carefully considered opinions or simply reflections of earlier traditions like those we reviewed in chapter seven where Jesus' identity as Lord was rephrased in the same binitarian terms (Son of God, Son of Man, Word, etc.). In any case, they were continuing one of the options that had been open to early Christians since the time of *Thomas* (according to DeConick's kernel), Q, and Mark, and they continued to coexist with other textures and traditions.[22]

That situation began to change when Paul of Samosata championed similar views in the mid-third century. Like the proto-adoptionists we have discussed, Paul placed Jesus in the succession of Moses, David, and the later prophets—all inspired by the divine Logos.[23] What was different about the case of the Samosatene was the fact that he was not an anonymous writer (like pseudo-Peter) or the construct of a heresiologist (like Cerinthus). He was the bishop of Antioch, one of the four major centers of Christianity, and he is said to have issued a ban on the singing of hymns to Christ.[24] Apparently, Paul had begun with a proto-adoptionist texture and then developed its logical implications, thereby becoming a dogmatic adoptionist.

A series of local synods subsequently condemned Paul and his teachings (264–68 CE), and his brand of adoptionism (called "dynamic monarchianism" by modern historians[25]) was pronounced a "heresy"—a label that simply meant a sectarian view that selects one thread of tradition to the exclusion of others.[26]

Even from the few texts we have cited, it should be clear that what we have termed the "proto-adoptionist" option was experimented with and promulgated by a variety of groups in the early church, which is what we should expect based on our scenario. Even though these groups did not fit on a single "trajectory," they had much in common with each other and with other threads of christological tradition. In fact, the great value of these early sources consists in their reminding the church that Jesus was in fact a Spirit-empowered *hasid*, thereby preserving continuity with the traditional idea of a succession of prophets and sages. Some of these traditions celebrated the divine Spirit or *Christos* that Jesus was said to have borne. Many of them also celebrated the portrait of Jesus as the coming Lord (Mark, Q, 1 Peter, *Thomas*, and *Hermas*).

So, even if the proto-adoptionist option did not always do justice to that second portrait, it still fit comfortably in the life of the church of the second century.

THE PROTO-DOCETIST OPTION

Perhaps the greatest sticking point in superposing the two portraits or narratives of Jesus was the suggestion that YHWH had permanently assumed flesh and blood (at some stage of Jesus' life).[27] The issue was not just that such a concrete manifestation was unprecedented.[28] The real problem was the suffering and death of the Lord that such incarnation implied, even if that incarnation only began with the baptism of Jesus.[29]

Our Kyriocentric scenario suggests that we should find a variety of texts that downplay the human flesh of Jesus and/or his crucifixion, while celebrating the other two threads of christological tradition: the hasid who prayed to God the Father, and the coming, saving Lord. This objective could readily be accomplished in one of two ways: either by absorbing the flesh of Jesus into his divine identity and making it impervious to suffering, or by modeling Jesus' departure on figures who were transported into heaven like Enoch, Elijah, and Moses.[30]

There were many possibilities here. Based on our previous work, however, we should expect a constraint on Messiah language. In chapter 7, we argued that the identification of Jesus as the Messiah (as distinct from a hasid) was motivated by the need to address the problem of the cross. If we are on the right track, we should expect to find a noticeable absence of explicit Jesus-Messiah identifications in the proto-docetist options we are about to review (other than the occurrence of *Christos* as a name for a second divine power as in the proto-adoptionist option).

Most scholars would agree that there are no clear proto-docetist views among the New Testament writers themselves,[31] but we do find possible evidence of proto-docetist views in Paul's altercations with his opponents at Corinth and similarly in the Letters of John. Even though these texts are very brief (addressed to people who already knew the situation) and are therefore subject to various interpretations, it is worthwhile looking at them if only to get a sense of the problem that was confronting first-century disciples and that would become more prominent in later generations.[32]

According to Paul, "the message about the cross is foolishness to those who are perishing, but to those of us who are being saved it is the power of God" (1 Cor. 1:18). It is fair to take this powerful statement as a critique of a particular party at Corinth (cf. 1:10). Given Paul's emphasis on the cross of Jesus, however, it would be over-reading the text to attribute an actual denial of Jesus' death to that party—more likely, they only played it down in an attempt to appear "wise" and appeal to their audiences (1 Cor. 1:17, 20, 25).[33] As in the case of the proto-adoptionists, we are dealing here with a matter of emphasis—in this case, naive rather than systematic docetism.

The situation reflected in the Johannine Epistles (near the turn of the century) appears to have been more serious. Here it was not just a matter of toning down the cross; John's opponents were accused of actually denying the flesh of Jesus Christ (or of "Jesus as the *Christos* come in the flesh," 1 John 4:2-3; 2 John 7)[34] and denying the shedding of his blood ("not with water only," 1 John 5:5).[35]

Clearly, the epistle writer did not approve of his opponents' understanding of Jesus' flesh and sacrifice. What is not so clear from these brief references, however, is the *manner* in which John's opponents failed to live up to these traditions. It might have been a simple matter of their being reluctant to follow Jesus' example in a literal way and to offer their own lives as martyrs, or at least to offer their material goods in charitable giving ("we know love by this," 1 John 3:16-17; cf. 2 John 6). However, the Johannine writer viewed the issue as a theological one, not just one of discipleship.

In theological terms, John's opponents may have dated the identification of the *Christos* and Jesus from the time of the resurrection ("not confess Jesus as the *Christos* come in the flesh," 1 John 4:2-3; 2 John 7; cf. ch. 7, "When and How Did the Lord Become Identified with the Man Jesus?"). From the perspective of our scenario, this possibility is particularly interesting because "John" also accused his opponents of "deny[ing] that Jesus is the *Christos* [Messiah]" (1 John 2:22). He also repeatedly included the title *Christos* in counterstatements like "Jesus *Christos* has come in the flesh" (1 John 4:2; 2 John 7; cf. 1 John 5:6), implying that the opponents' view of the Jesus-*Christos* identity was not sufficiently strong. It is quite possible that "John" and his opponents were working with different definitions of the term *Christos*. For the Johannine writer, the *Christos* was Jesus as the Davidic Messiah ("after the flesh" to use a Pauline expression), while for the opponents it was a divine being, like the Lord or the Word, who was at some stage embodied in Jesus. In other words, John's opponents were more devoted to the Lord as the supernatural *Christos* than they were to the Lord as the flesh-and-blood man Jesus.

According to our argument in chapter 7, separating the divine identity (Lord, *Christos*) from the one on the cross in this way would also have removed the most compelling rationale for invoking the Davidic psalms in which Jesus' identity as Davidic Messiah was discerned. The texts certainly do not provide proof of our conjecture, but they do suggest some interesting possibilities. In any case, as with Paul's opponents, we are probably dealing here with naive docetists—those who either played down the cross or avoided some of its implications.[36]

Similar observations can be made about the charges that Ignatius of Antioch and Polycarp of Smyrna made against their opponents in western Asia Minor (Turkey). Polycarp repeated the thought of the Johannine Epistles and quoted the famous statement in 2 John 7 almost word for word (most likely from memory, Polycarp, *To the Philippians* 7:1). Ignatius was more specific and described very realistic conversations with his Judaizing opponents (*Phld.* 8:2).[37] He accused these opponents of being led astray by "old fables" and denying the flesh of Jesus and his suffering and death (*Magn.* 8:1; *Trall.* 10:1; *Smyr.* 5:1-7:1; cf. 1 Tim. 1:4).

From what Ignatius stated more positively about these opponents, we can infer that they regarded the Old Testament as authoritative (hence they were not gnostics; *Phld.* 8:2), that they adhered to Sabbath observance and other Jewish practices, and that they embraced the life-giving power of the risen Christ (*Magn.* 8:1; 9:1).[38] On the other hand, they were not persuaded by Ignatius's advocacy of self-offering and care for the poor as the only true form of discipleship (*Trall.* 5:2; 10:1; 11:2; passim)—in Ignatius's words, "they care nothing about love" (*Smyr.* 6:2). This is not much to go on, but similarities to the issues described in the Johannine Epistles (1 John 3:15-16) suggest that Ignatius was dealing with similar proto-docetist opponents—Christians who shared the foundational Lord-Jesus identification (at some stage), but did not view the cross of Jesus as an essential part of the gospel for one reason or another. It is difficult to know for sure when we only have records of the charges made against these supposed docetists without anything in their own words.

In none of the four texts we have reviewed so far do we have the actual words of a proto-docetic party, but we do find such ideas in two early second-century Christian sources: the *Odes of Solomon* and the *Ascension of Isaiah*, both of which derive from Syria or possibly Asia Minor in the late first or early second century.[39] In other words, they are comparable in provenance to the Johannine and Ignatian literature we have just reviewed.

The *Odes of Solomon* consists of forty-two psalm-like compositions with a variety of devotional patterns. Some of the Odes celebrated the cross as the way to heaven: the celebrant spread out hands in prayer in imitation of the sign of the Lord Jesus on the cross (*Odes* 27:1-3; 35:7; 42:1-2). Here the cross was a symbol of the Lord's deity and victory over death (cf. John 3:13-15; 12:31-33).

In other Odes, the psalmist channeled the Lord (Jesus) himself and stated that he was neither rejected nor did he perish, meaning that death and Hades could not hold him (*Odes* 28:9-10; 42:10-13).

The latter statements would seem unduly hazardous from the standpoint of later orthodoxy, but they were clearly intended to stress the deity and victory of the Lord Jesus just as the more orthodox-sounding ones did.[40] These sentiments may well have been similar to the ones that the Letters of John and Ignatius found offensive. As in the latter cases, there is nothing in the Odes about the value of self-sacrifice:[41] the cross is a symbol of prayer and ascent into heaven rather than of "discipleship" in the Ignatian sense. It therefore answers quite well to Ignatius's charges against his proto-docetic opponents.[42]

The *Ascension of Isaiah* gives us an unprecedented account of the Lord descending into the world in order to judge and destroy the evil powers (*Ascen. Isa.* 10:12). It clearly affirmed the Lord's birth, his nursing at Mary's breast, his crucifixion, and his bodily resurrection (*Ascen. Isa.* 3:13-18; 9:26; 11:3-8, 17, 19-21).[43] This pseudepigraphal work was not "docetic" in the dogmatic sense of the term, therefore, any more that the *Odes of Solomon* were.

The *Ascension* did portray the Lord as taking on a variety of angelic forms before assuming a human form and fooling the powers into believing that he was simply mortal flesh (*Ascen. Isa.* 9:13-14; cf. Phil. 2:7), but there was nothing particularly novel about this strategy of deceit. Similar ideas were expressed by Ignatius, though in less detail.[44] Like Ignatius, and unlike the *Odes*, the *Ascension* glorified the way of martyrdom of Isaiah. His cruel death, like that of the prophet Micaiah, was occasioned by his visions and prophecies concerning the coming Lord (1:9-13; 2:12-16; 5:1-16; 8:12). In making these points, *Ascension of Isaiah* also pilloried the officers of the church (3:21-31). Ignatius would no doubt have opposed these latter ideas if he had known of them (as Athanasius apparently did in his famous *Festal Letter* of 367[45]), but he would not likely have faulted the Christology of the *Ascension*.

All the proto-docetic sources cited so far were of Syrian or Anatolian provenance and date from the early second century at the latest. We have found varying emphases (or de-emphases) among early Christians who, for all we can tell, were equally devoted to the Lord Jesus and committed to proclaiming his gospel (albeit with different understandings of its implications).

The first clear evidence of what later became known as "docetism" in the dogmatic sense comes from the metropolis of Alexandria. Our primary source here is the heresiologist, Irenaeus of Lyons, whose treatise *Against Heresies* (*Haer.*) was written late in the second century (178–89 CE). The most prominent figure that Irenaeus charged with dogmatic docetism was the Christian philosopher Basilides who had begun his teaching career in Alexandria in the 130s, just a few decades after 1 John and Ignatius.[46] According to Irenaeus (*Haer.* 1.24.4), Basilides viewed Jesus as the embodiment of the divine Mind (*Nous*), who is also called *Christos*. This divinely embodied *Christos* worked miracles, but he never suffered or died on the cross—instead he ascended straight back to the Father. Accordingly, anyone who believes in him who was crucified is still a deluded slave of the lower powers (including the God of Israel).[47]

We know that Irenaeus's description was fairly accurate because it is consistent with the main features of the Alexandrian style of Gnosticism. The best parallel is a Nag Hammadi treatise called *The Second Treatise of the Great Seth* (NHC VII,2), which was probably written by a follower of Basilides. According to "The Great Seth," the *Christos* described himself as invading the body of a man (Jesus) and frightening the powers into trying to kill him. However, the powers only managed to nail "their man" to the cross, while *Christos* ascended to the height and laughed them to scorn (51.20-34, 55.3—56.14).[48]

The significance of Irenaeus's exposé of Basilides for our purposes is twofold. The title *Christos* occurs here, as well as in "The Great Seth," only as a name for the divine Mind, just as in the proto-adoptionist texts cited earlier. The *Christos* was quite separate from Jesus and had nothing to do with the crucifixion (other than provoking it). As in the case of the opponents of the Johannine Letters, there was no motive for invoking the Psalms in order to identify Jesus himself as the Messiah in the Davidic sense of the term. The main difference from the Johannine opponents was that Basilides clearly dated the embodiment of the *Christos* from the beginning of Jesus' ministry (hence the miracles) and made the crucifixion into a charade.

More importantly, however, there was a qualitative difference in the way that Irenaeus drew a line in the sand between the Catholic faith and heresy, compared to the in-house fighting we found in the letters of Paul, John, and Ignatius.[49] Irenaeus's treatise was evidently commissioned by other bishops in the church (*Haer.* 1 Pref. 2; 3 Pref. 1), and the following decades would see several bishops clamp down on this more dogmatic form of docetism. The most famous example of such proscription was that by Bishop Serapion of Antioch, who condemned a group of those who based their Christology on the apocryphal *Gospel of Peter*—Serapion was probably the first to use the term "docetists" to describe such views.[50] About the same time (late second century), the *Second Treatise of the Great Seth* expressed frustration with officers of the

Alexandrian church, indicating that the Basilidean groups involved were also experiencing some degree of persecution (59.19—61.24).[51] The battle had been joined, and days of naive proto-docetism were over.

In the late second and early third centuries, the church began to legislate what language could and what could not be used in articulating faith in the Lord Jesus, his flesh-and-blood humanity, and his cross. We have seen enough evidence of earlier forms of proto-docetism (as well as proto-adoptionism), however, to illustrate the way these options had been explored in the late first and second centuries.

There are two conclusions here for our project. The main conclusion is that there is ample evidence for early groups that experimented with ways of weaving the narrative threads together: in this case the threads of the Kyriocentric vision and memories of Jesus. Only in retrospect (ahistorically) can these experimental fabrics be tagged with the labels of various heresies.

A second, somewhat less certain conclusion is that several of these groups who belittled the cross were less likely to identify Jesus as the Davidic Messiah (as distinct from the celestial *Christos*). Thus far, the texts are quite consistent with our conjecture and the scenario developed from it.

THE PROTO-MODALIST OPTION

If one option in the Kyriocentric scenario was to tone down the Lord-Jesus identification, and a second was to tone down the significance of the cross (at least as a model for discipleship), then a third option was to tone down the distinction of the Lord Jesus and the Father that was implied by Jesus' prayers and teachings. One way of doing this was to limit the Lord-Jesus identification to the resurrection and its aftermath, thereby separating it from the prayer life of Jesus (with the exception of John 14:16). Another was to identify the Lord Jesus as the Father in his earthly (perhaps temporary) manifestation. When taken to its logical conclusion, this latter option implied that the one who died on the cross was really God the Father, a systematic form of modalism, later labeled "patripassianism" (the Father was the one who suffered), for which there was clearly no room in the New Testament itself. Given the difficulties involved in superposing the two portraits of Jesus—righteous teacher (hasid) and coming Lord—however, we should expect to find some less developed, more naive versions of the idea in the early church, just as we did in the cases of proto-adoptionist and proto-docetist teachings.

It is a remarkable fact, then, that we do not find evidence for even such naive, proto-modalistic views in the New Testament[52] (as we did in the case of proto-adoptionism). As we saw in chapter 7, the New Testament writers from Paul to John were quite clear that the Lord Jesus had prayed to God as his Father and inferred some sort of differentiation of the two.[53] Nor is there any evidence for opposition to proto-modalistic views (as there is in the case of proto-docetism).[54]

The earliest possible record of such proto-modalist views does not come until the mid-second century.[55] A good example is found in Justin's *Dialogue with Trypho* (c. 160 CE), where Justin states:

> He [the Holy Spirit in Ps. 96:1-13] bids the inhabitants of all the earth, who have known . . . the suffering of Christ, by which he saved them, sing and give praises to God, the Father of all things, and recognize that he is to be praised and feared and that he is the Maker of heaven and earth, who effected this salvation on behalf of humanity, who also was crucified and was dead and who was deemed worthy by him to reign over all the earth. (*Dialogue* 74:3)[56]

There is no question here of Justin denying a distinction between God the Father and the Lord Jesus, who is his begotten Son, Word, and Wisdom (e.g., *Dial.* 61.2). In the sentence quoted, however, it is virtually impossible to disentangle the roles of God the Father and Jesus.[57]

Part of the reason for Justin's confusion of the two figures here was that he understood both the Lord Jesus and his father to be the Lord God described in the Psalms.[58] His general rule was that portions describing the Deity in a visible, anthropic form had to be referred to the Lord Jesus, an association that dated back to the primal Kyriocentric visions.[59] In Psalm 96, however, Justin saw a transcendent God, particularly in verse 2, "Sing to the Lord, and bless his name," as well as the concrete, anthropic form of the Lord in verse 10, "the Lord is king."[60] In this instance, Justin's interpretation appears to have been constrained by the dedication of blessing to God the Father, just as it was in the New Testament (discussed in ch. 7). The takeaway point for our present investigation is that Justin was comfortable seeing both divine figures in an Old Testament text and could be rather imprecise about differentiating them. He could lapse into such a jumble of roles because he tended to think more about the unity of God and his Word (they are likened to one fire kindling another in *Dial.* 61.2) than he was about Jesus praying to the Father.[61] The sentence as it stands is a good example of unsystematic proto-modalism.

A decade or so after Justin, Melito, bishop of Sardis (in Asia Minor), made a similar kind of statement in verse form:

For he was born a son . . .
and slaughtered as a sheep,
and buried as a man,
and rose from the dead as God,
being God by his nature and a man.
He is all things.
He is law in that he judges . . . .
He is grace in that he saves.
He is father in that he begets.
He is son in that he is begotten . . . .
This is Jesus the Christ,
to whom be the glory forever and ever.
Amen." (*Poem on the Pascha* 8-10)[62]

Three features of this marvelous poem stand out. First, Jesus Christ is said to be a "father" who begets as well as a "son" who is begotten. It is clear from the other verses just cited that Melito was extolling Jesus in a series of contrary attributes: son-sheep, man-God, and law-grace. The final pairing of begetting father and begotten son should therefore be understood as part of this doxological strategy rather than as a literal identification of Jesus with his heavenly Father. In fact, we find the two divine figures clearly distinguished elsewhere in the poem (*Pascha* 76, 82, 103-5). Melito's view has been termed "naive modalism."[63]

An even more interesting feature of the poem is the single doxology at the end. As discussed in chapter 6, doxologies were addressed to God the Father in the New Testament, and occasionally also to the Lord Jesus. Here and elsewhere in Melito's poem, they are consistently addressed to the Lord Jesus alone (*Pascha* 10, 45, 65, 104-5), which is in striking contrast to the binitarian form of New Testament prayers that we reviewed in chapter 6.[64] For our purposes, Melito's emphasis is important in being consonant with the Kyriocentric nature of the visionary practices of the early disciples, particularly when described in isolation from memories of Jesus' prayers to the Father. Stuart George Hall and Alistair Stewart-Sykes have appropriately described this emphasis as "christocentric monotheism."[65]

This observation leads us to another important feature of Melito that supports the Kyriocentric scenario, the absence of any reference to Jesus' prayers or teachings about praying to the Father (as with Justin). At least three times in his poem, Melito proclaimed the main features of Jesus' ministry: he judged; he taught; he healed; he cleansed; he illumined; he raised the dead (*Pascha* 9, 72, 89, 104). Melito's evident silence concerning Jesus' own prayers does not imply that he was unaware of that part of the tradition, only that it was not foremost in his mind as he wrote. We can easily imagine that a different set of challenges might have drawn Melito's attention to Jesus' prayer life and consequently altered the language that he used in passages like the one cited above. The least we can say is that what we read here is consistent with our rationale for the generation of binitarian Christology.[66]

These few texts will suffice to show that the proto-modalist option was represented among the teachings of second-century church leaders, just as proto-adoptionism was (proto-docetism was anonymous except for Basilides). This freedom of expression began to be curtailed in the early third century, however, when several theologians developed a more dogmatic strain of modalism.

The most prominent of these theologians were like Noetus (from Smyrna, c. 200 CE) and Sabellius (perhaps from Libya). According to heresiologists, Hippolytus and Epiphanius, these two theologians identified God the Father as the one who had appeared to Israel, who was then born of Mary, and who died on the cross: in other words, God the Father of Israel morphed into the Son who is described in the Gospels.[67] This Father-Son identification meant that the prayers of Jesus were not simply overlooked, they were rendered nonsensical—a development that offended Christians who believed that the way they prayed was the way the Lord Jesus himself had taught his disciples. Here Melito's earlier "christocentric monotheism" became what modern scholars call "modalistic monarchianism."[68] Noetus was officially condemned by a synod in Smyrna around 200 CE. Sabellius was excommunicated by Pope Callistus around 220 CE.[69] These moves occurred at approximately the same time as the less formal pronouncements against systematic docetism (the condemnation of Paul of Samosata was decades later).

There is much more to the story of modalistic options, but we have covered enough to demonstrate that even if there is no evidence for proto-modalism in the New Testament itself,[70] second-century church leaders were free to experiment with this option as long as no one took it too far. In Alexandria, a naive form of modalism (or "christocentric monotheism") continued to be professed as late as the mid-third century by "simple-minded" Christians who prayed to the Son as the supreme God. By that time, however, antipathy to the idea was so entrenched that it began to foster a reaction in a subordinationist direction. As Origen contended in response to these simple ones: "we believe him who said: 'The Father who sent me is greater than I' [John 14:28]."[71] We shall take up this fourth, subordinationist option in the following section.

THE SUBORDINATIONIST (PROTO-ARIAN) OPTION

The three options we have explored so far involved toning down a single aspect or thread of the christological tradition pool of the early church. When carried too far, all three ran into stiff resistance from leaders of the church, particularly in the late second and early third centuries, resulting in the formalization of beliefs that Christians were expected to affirm upon baptism.

Our fourth option is rather different: instead of toning down a single thread of the tradition, subordinationism exploited the re-visioning of the Kyriocentric vision in binitarian terms, based on the teachings of Jesus, and toned down the Kyriocentric vision (the Lord-Jesus identification) to the level of a secondary figure like an angel. In order to see just how this option could be so appealing, we need to review some of what we covered in previous chapters.

First, we recall that Kyriocentric visions typically envisioned YHWH in anthropic (humanlike) form and placed him in the midst of a hierarchy of angels (examples given in ch. 2). For the purposes of devotion, YHWH was the center figure in the vision. With respect to his imaginal form and location, however, he was roughly on a par with the highest of his angelic associates (or archangels). In fact, Old Testament narratives sometimes portrayed YHWH's appearances and utterances as those of an "angel of the Lord" who bore the divine name (e.g., Exod. 3:2-6; 14:19; 23:20-22; the Hebrew term *mal'ak* simply means a "messenger"). Even if these traditions were relatively unproblematic in a temple-based world that was filled with heavenly visions and theophanies,[72] what could they possibly mean in the space-time world of an average person? Was the anthropic form God himself, or a subordinate entity? If the latter, was this entity an emanation from God like an image or the divine glory (two of the binitarian models mentioned in ch. 7), or was it created like an ordinary angel? There was room for a good, long conversation here.

As we have seen, the straightforward implications of the Kyriocentric vision and Lord-Jesus identification had to be spun down in order to take seriously the Lord's own teachings and his death on the cross (ch. 2). In relation to the cross, the Lord Jesus was commonly described as the Servant or the Messiah. In relation to God the Father, the Lord Jesus was commonly described in the terms of various binitarian formulas.

The earliest of these binitarian terms was the divine title *Lord*, as differentiated from *God*—this usage evidently originated in the Kyriocentric vision itself. There was no hint of subordination here: *Lord* and *God* were the two primary names for the Deity in both Hebrew and Greek. In fact, they were almost interchangeable,[73] and both were used together in the *Shema* (Deut. 8:6, even in its Christianized form in 1 Cor. 8:6; Eph. 4:2-6). This God–Lord usage occurs frequently in the New Testament, particularly in the Epistles, where liturgical formulas are most in evidence, and it has been preserved to this day in liturgical salutations, benedictions, and confessional formulas.

We have also described how other binitarian terms were selected from the tradition pool: Son of Man, image of God, anthropic Glory, Word of God, and Son of God. In addition to the fact that these terms had biblical precedent, there was an unmet demand, evidently occasioned by the fact that the terms *God* and *Lord* did not help believers to understand how the two divine figures were related. However, all of these terms (as well as the titles *Servant* and *Messiah*) suggested some degree of subordination of Jesus to God the Father. So what exactly did it mean for the Lord Jesus to be projected as an image, or spoken as a word, or begotten as a son? Here again, there was plenty of room for differing viewpoints, at least up to a point. In this section, we shall review some of the more subordinationist statements found in early Christian texts and briefly trace this usage up until a more extreme form of subordinationism that was anathematized at the Council of Nicea (325 CE).

As in the cases of proto-adoptionism and proto-docetism, we find a number of subordination-leaning passages in the New Testament itself, particular in eschatological contexts. One of the most famous examples occurs in 1 Corinthians 15, where Paul envisioned the final realization of the kingdom of God in clearly subordinationist terms:

> When all things are subjected to him [Christ], then the Son himself will also be subjected to the one who put all things in submission under him, so that God may be all in all. (1 Cor. 15:28)

The distinction here between the Son and God makes it clear that the latter is God the Father (cf. 15:25). Even though Paul used the title *Son*, rather than *Lord*, it is clear that he was thinking of the glorified anthropic form in which he was called on as Lord (1 Cor. 15:6-8, 25-27, 58). As we argued in the previous chapter, it was this very recognition of Jesus' identity as Lord that compelled Paul to adhere to Jesus' teachings about the primacy of God the Father (note also 1 Cor. 11:3, "the head of Christ is God").[74]

A similar eschatological subordination is seen in the Gospel of Mark, where Jesus says to his disciples, "about that day or hour no one knows, neither the angels in heaven nor the Son, but only the Father" (Mark 13:32). As far as the Gospel writer was concerned, Jesus clearly classified himself with the angels (cf. Mark 8:38; 13:26-27 regarding the Son of Man), and in this capacity he did not know the time of the end—a startling, counterintuitive statement that was followed almost word-for-word by the Gospel of Matthew[75] (but not by Luke).[76]

So was Mark consistently subordinationist in its Christology (cf. Mark 10:18)? We have already discussed Mark's celebration of the Kyriocentric vision and deity Christology (ch. 5). We have also found a proto-adoptionist passage in Mark 12. If we insist on viewing this Gospel from the standpoint of later dogmatic formulations, it was proto-Nicene (deity Christology), proto-adoptionist, and at least naively subordinationist, all at the same time. Evidently, early attempts to interweave the holy-man and Lord-Jesus threads of tradition could produce a variety of results, all of which would seem contradictory from the viewpoint of later theological systems.

The Gospel of John is commonly supposed to have the highest Christology in the New Testament, largely due to its use of the word God in reference to Jesus (John 1:1, 18; 10:33; 20:28). However, we find much the same ambiguity regarding the status of the Jesus in relation to the Father that we have in Paul and Mark. For John, such subordination was implied in the fact that the Son was sent by God the Father, a motif that occurs seventeen times in the Gospel, using the same verb as for the sending of John the Baptist.[77] This subordination was regularly placed in the mouth of Jesus himself. Here are four of his more striking utterances:

- ". . . the Son can do nothing on his own, but only what he sees the Father doing" (John 5:19).
- ". . . the Father is greater than I" (John 14:28).
- "I am ascending to my Father and to your Father, to my God and to your God" (John 20:17b).
- "Father . . . glorify your Son so that the Son may glorify you" (John 17:1).

It would be difficult to attribute all of these sayings to a "state of humiliation" (*status inanitionis*) in the Gospel of John. The third one actually looks forward to his resurrection and ascension.

One cannot dispute the importance of deity Christology for John: in chapter 5, we have found good evidence that the initiatory Kyriocentric vision (modeled on Isaiah's) was still performed in the Johannine community, as it was in the case of Mark. Yet efforts to superpose the two portraits (or interweave the three major threads) were still yielding varied results in the late first century church.

There is even some evidence that Jesus was regarded as the angel ("messenger") of the Lord in late New Testament texts. The Letter to the Hebrews stressed the deity of the Son of God by way of polemicizing against the idea of associating him with the angels (Heb. 1:3—2:18), thereby implying that some Christians were doing just that.[78] Some scholars have seen the idea that the Lord Jesus was an angel in Jude 5, though this interpretation is rather uncertain.[79] Others have found an "angelomorphic" Christology in the book of Revelation.[80] On the other hand, both Jude and Revelation clearly identified Jesus as YHWH, the Lord.[81] In short, the New Testament stance toward subordinationism appears to be somewhere between its stance toward proto-adoptionism (quite open) and that for proto-docetism (strictly negative). This ambiguity in language would continue until the Council of Nicea, as we shall see next.

This degree of fluidity in early Christological language would continue through the second and third centuries and well into the fourth. Because we have two centuries' worth of material to consider here, it is best to review it topically. Most Christian texts of this era mixed the language of deity with the language of subordination in just the way that we should expect based on the need to interweave the christological narratives in the same way that New Testament writers did themselves. Some texts, like the *Ascension of Isaiah* and the *Apostolic Constitutions*, described Jesus as the very Lord that Isaiah had seen the seraphim worshiping in glory (Isa. 6:2-3), thereby reflecting ongoing performances of the Kyriocentric vision, while at the same time describing the Lord Jesus as a worshiper of the "Great Glory."[82] Others, like the Apostolic Father Hermas,[83] portrayed him as an angel whose superiority to all other angels as the Lord or Son or Word of God was demonstrated by his greater stature.[84] These seemingly contradictory images clearly evidence the ambiguity that surrounded the anthropic form of the Lord and the use of the terms *Son of God* and *Word of God* up until the ecumenical councils of the fourth century.

A marvelous example of this complex language and the issues it would raise can be found in a treatise entitled, *On the Hundredth, the Sixtieth, the Thirtieth* (*De centesima, sexagesima, tricesima*)—long attributed to Cyprian of Carthage, but probably written a few generations later (late third to the fourth century). This text viewed the Son as being supernatural and preexistent, but described his origin as primordial creation:

> When the Lord created the seven archangels from fire, he determined to make one of them his Son. He it is whom Isaiah declares to be Lord Sabaoth [Isa. 6:3]. (*De centesima*, lines 216-20)[85]

In the last part of this quote, our author was clearly referring to the vision of Isaiah in the Temple, where the "Lord Sabaoth" ("Lord of hosts") was the Holy One of Israel. In biblical terms, this was a deity Christology. In an attempt to differentiate this "Lord Sabaoth" from the transcendent God (the Father), however, the author introduced the category archangel—of which there were seven—and made his unique status as God's Son an act of primordial adoption ("to make one of them his Son") that resulted in a divine binity.[86]

For the most part, this Pseudo-Cyprianic text was unexceptional for its time: the Lord Jesus was associated with angels in the Kyriocentric vision and the New Testament, and Apostolic Fathers like Hermas could include him among the most glorious angels (*Hermas* 89:7-8).[87] Prior to the Council of Nicea (325 CE), the word *creation* or *creature* (*ktisma*) was also used to describe the origin of the Son or Word of God.[88] This usage actually found biblical precedent in Septuagint texts like Proverbs 8:22, where one reads that Wisdom was created at the beginning of God's work (*ektise me archēn hodōn autou eis erga autou*).

As we have noted, Wisdom (*Sophia*) was one of the titles for the Lord Jesus in the New Testament, and it was commonly used in early Christian writings. In the mid-second century, Justin Martyr could unselfconsciously refer to the Son as an angel (the angel of the Lord) and cited Proverbs 8:22 in order to demonstrate his preexistence (*Dial.* 61.1, 3).[89] Athenagoras also cited the Proverbs proof text, apparently following Justin in this, but then he avoided referring to the son as an angel and tried to differentiate this kind of "creation" from the ordinary creation of finite beings. The awkwardness of Athenagoras's explanation indicates how difficult it was at this stage to make this distinction.[90]

In contrast to Athenagoras (and probably unaware of his writing), though in line with his predecessor, our Pseudo-Cyprianic writer believed that he was exalting the Son of God by saying that he was created in the same way that the angels were, namely out of fire (Ps. 104:4b). By the third century, however, this use of angel language and the idea of originating by creation would be pushing things too far in the direction of differentiating the Son from God the Father.

The first explicit disapproval of this kind of angel Christology had occurred already in the early third century, in the writing of Tertullian, who also happened to be the first theologian to use the Latin term *trinitas* and to develop the terminology of the later doctrine of the Trinity (*Against Praxeas* 2, 3, passim). In a treatise defending the physicality of the flesh of Christ, Tertullian took on an unnamed party who said that Jesus bore an angel (*angelum gestauit*). He admitted that Isaiah had prophesied Jesus would be the "angel of great counsel" (Greek for "wonderful counselor") in the Septuagint of Isaiah 9:6, but, he argued, this title was only an indication of his function, not his nature. In short, Christ was not to be regarded as an angel at all, not even a top-ranked angel like Gabriel or Michael (*On the Flesh of Christ* 14.35). It is not clear exactly whom Tertullian was arguing with here, but similarities to the Christology of the Pseudo-Cyprianic treatise described earlier provide a general idea of the emerging debate.[91]

One of the principal ways in which Tertullian tried to affirm the solidarity of God the Father and the Lord Jesus (and the Holy Spirit) was to declare a "unity of substance" (*unitas substantiae, Apology* 21.11). In the Eastern Mediterranean, Origen appears to have said something similar, using the Greek term *homoousios*, "of the same substance."[92] The reason these terms sound familiar to us today is that they would be canonized as "orthodox" Christology at the Councils of Nicea and Constantinople. Many critics view them as philosophical (Greek) jargon, but they can also be treated as contextual paraphrases of Paul's affirmation that Jesus Christ is the "one Lord," alongside "one God the Father," who had appeared to the patriarchs, the prophets, and the first disciples.

Seven decades before Nicea, however, Bishop Dionysius of Alexandria denied that the Son was of the same substance as the Father—evidently, he found Origen's language contradictory and was concerned to avoid the kind of "modalism" for which Sabellius had been charged a few decades before that. When some parties reacted against this denial and complained to the Bishop of Rome, who was also named Dionysius, he in turn condemned as polytheists all who said that the members of the Trinity were three separate "hypostases" (entities). Upon receipt of this charge, the Alexandrian Dionysius happily corrected himself.[93] In the mid-third century, then, the language of the later doctrine of the Trinity was being worked out on a case-by-case basis, but it would take more than a century more before it was formalized (the Council of Constantinople in 381).

As in previous options we have discussed, what would bring things to a head was someone with a penchant for logical reasoning, rhetorical negations, and personal skill in broadcasting new ideas. The primary irritant, in this case, was Arius, an ecclesial teacher in Alexandria, who first came to public attention in 318 CE. Arius taught that the Son was created as an archangel and the beginning (*archē*) of the overall process of creation (referring to Prov. 8:22; cf. Col. 1:15, 18)—this much was similar to what Justin and Pseudo-Cyprian had said. Contrary to the Christology of Athenagoras, however, Arius drew the logical conclusion from these ideas and denied that the Son had existed in God before he was thus created. As a result, he said, the Son was neither coeternal nor of the same substance as the Father. In the latter negation, Arius was clearly bothered by the impious suggestion that the divine substance could be subdivided so as to produce the Son as separate "hypostasis."[94]

Arius gave some good reasons for his contentions, and he found support among some prominent bishops (notably Eusebius of Nicomedia, who later baptized Emperor Constantine). However, he was vehemently opposed by his ecclesial superior, Alexander of Alexandria, and he was subsequently condemned by synods in both Alexandria and Antioch and finally, in 325 CE, by the Council of Nicea—later to be recognized as the first "ecumenical council." According to the "Creed of the Three Hundred and Eighteen Fathers," written up by members of that council,[95] being begotten by the Father was not the same thing as being created. The Son was begotten from the substance of God the Father as "God from God," not created out of nothing, and he was therefore of the same substance as the Father (*homoousion tō patri*). These phrases eventually became the official language of deity Christology.

Although Arius was formally anathematized, he had considerable political support, including that of the Emperor Constantine, and his subordinationist language continued to be used in various forms of "Arianism," particularly by theologians who had been offended by the modalism of Sabellius (as Dionysius of Alexandria had been a century earlier). We shall pick up the story at that point in our next chapter.

The main point of this part of our study is that several subordinationist ideas were developed in the early church, just as we should expect from a scenario starting from the performance of Kyriocentric visions combined with the teachings and prayers of Jesus. In fact, naive forms of this subordinationist option remained open for centuries after the New Testament, and it was championed by second-century theologians who were regarded then, and who continue to be regarded, as legitimate (e.g., Hermas and Justin). It required the promulgation of a more systematic, dialectical form of this idea to provoke reactions from ecclesiastical officials, first by Dionysius of Rome in the mid-third century, and then at Nicea in the early fourth.

A further legacy of Nicea, or rather of its acclamation five decades later at the Council of Constantinople (381 CE), is that the conversion of the Roman Empire to Christianity became closely associated with the church's official affirmation of deity Christology. This legacy is still very much with us today. Once the exposés of the eighteenth-century Enlightenment predisposed scholars to detect "corruptions" in the developing traditions of the church, deity Christology began to look like the imposition of a dogma by a political hierarchy just as indulgences had done to the sixteenth-century reformers.

The larger issue of maintaining fidelity in the process of doctrinal development goes beyond the scope of this book. There is one aspect of it that we shall have to examine, however, because it pertains to the issue of the anthropic form of the Lord God of Israel with which our investigation began (ch. 1). The important point is that much present-day historical research that tries to free itself of church dogma is based on assumptions that are artifacts of this peculiar history of history and counter-history. A realistic, contextual study of deity Christology that places it within the bounds of early Judaism must set those assumptions aside and allow for a "high" starting place (or a combination of high and low), as we have tried to do here.

CONCLUSION REGARDING THE DIVERSITY OF TEXTURES IN EARLY CHRISTOLOGY

Eight decades ago, historian Walter Bauer showed that the traditional ecclesial story of the teachings of Jesus' apostles being corrupted by self-willed heretics does not do justice to the historical data.[96] We must recognize the existence of a diversity of christological traditions from the outset.

This diversity does not necessarily imply merely random opinions, however. An adequate historical framework should be able to explain why these diverse christological traditions emerged, why they were tolerated, and why they eventually led to conflict and condemnation. From the perspective of the Kyriocentric vision conjecture proposed here, the four principal alternative christological traditions that we have discussed were really textures that resulted from different ways of interweaving three main narrative threads: those of the Kyriocentric vision, Jesus as a servant of the Lord who had been crucified, and Jesus' teachings and prayers to his heavenly Father. In short, diversity was the result of complexity.

As a rule, one texture did not rule out the others. In fact, as we have seen, several textures could coexist in the writings of one and the same party (the Gospel of Mark, *Ascension of Isaiah*, *Shepherd of Hermas*, and Justin Martyr). Even though they occasioned conflict in later years, particularly as a few adherents began to insist that their texture ruled out others, they are not to be attributed to evil motives on the part of their tradents.

Leaders of the Catholic churches of the third and fourth centuries insisted on preserving all three of the christological threads we have described (although some other aspects of Jesus' teachings received rather less attention), and they began to restrict the language that could be used in prayers and creeds accordingly. Nonetheless, christological controversies would continue for centuries, most of them within the bounds of the church's creeds, and such controversy still goes on today. Some readers may conclude that the endeavor is hopeless and ought to be abandoned. Others may feel that the energy, creativity, and spirit that were released by the interaction of the primal Kyriocentric visions with memories of Jesus can still provide impetus for creative thinking and even open up some new options for discussion.[97]

Before concluding this chapter, we should note a significant shift in christological discourse over the last few chapters. We began with the performance of traditional visions in the context of prayer and singing—visions that were themselves centered on the Lord God of Israel. In chapters 6 and 7, we noted an early shift toward binitarian formulas and a more exegetical, rather than performative, approach to Scripture (particularly in seeking biblical precedent for the cross). In this chapter, we have seen a further shift toward logical conclusions and systematic reasoning (on all sides). I have no intention of belittling the use of systematic thinking and logic in theology but, in our day and age, convincing explanations must be historical, not just exegetical or systematic. So it may well be that future theological endeavor will require reconsideration of the impetus that gave rise to all of these performances, exegeses, debates, and creedal formulations.

That impetus, we have argued, came from the performance of visions in which the Lord was seen in anthropic form, surrounded by hosts of angels, and coming to save his people. The early disciples recognized (or reconstrued) the anthropic form as the familiar figure of Jesus, now risen from the dead, and this recognition, codified in the *Kyrios Iēsous* confession, set the wheels of early Christology in motion. There was lots of room for diversity and controversy leading to the need for the church to define itself liturgically and confessionally.

As we shall see in the following chapter, some of the church's early efforts at self-definition led to reforms that discouraged attributing an anthropic form to the Lord (prior to his incarnation). The effects of these reforms are still with us (as discussed in ch. 1), and they may make the historical reconstructions we advocate that much harder to achieve. On the other hand, just the awareness of the problem may help us to recover some of the primal energy, creativity, and spirit that motivated the early disciples.

Notes

1. Note also the two main anomalies that our scenario has run into: Saul's recognition of the face and voice of a man whom he had never met (ch. 5), and the small group of texts that associate the Lord-Jesus identification with the resurrection and yet formulated this association in binitarian language (ch. 7, "When and How Did the Lord Become Identified with the Man Jesus?").

2. James M. Robinson and Helmut Koester, *Trajectories through Early Christianity* (Philadelphia: Fortress Press, 1971). The Roman Symbol was a collection of early versions of what later became known as the Apostles' Creed.

3. Thus J. M. Robinson described his efforts "to plot the course of specific trajectories, moving from one document to another, from one generation to another, seeking to trace the connections where one fixed point leaves off and another begins"; Robinson and Koester, *Trajectories through Early Christianity*, 16.

4. In practice, J. M. Robinson also recognized that texts like *Exegesis on the Soul* (Nag Hammadi Codex II, 6) combines terminology from two separate trajectories; Robinson, "Jesus from Easter to Valentinus (or the Apostles' Creed)," *JBL* 101 (1982): 5–37 (19–20).

5. The truth of this idea hit me in 2007 when I innocently asked my cell phone-toting son how he could keep track of the time when he didn't wear a watch (what a look I got!). The current plethora of technological options is a good example of the roles of supply and demand: some of us choose to follow one particular option or set of options, and some choose others, all within the same system.

6. This shift reflects a significant change in the two (originally separate) narratives. Suffering and death was common in the narratives of hasidim just as much as teaching and prayer were. The identification of the Lord with one such hasid effectively drove a wedge between these two aspects of this narrative, however, and made it possible, even advantageous, to focus on one aspect more than the other.

7. Such "toning down" might have been conscious or it might have been an unreflective weaving together of those threads that were at hand (omitting others).

8. Mathematically speaking, there were only three ways of pairing the three major narrative threads (the first three options listed here), but there was also an option with a single major thread. For a single thread to stand on its own, it had to include the teachings and prayers of Jesus because these were so fundamental to the liturgies and teaching ministry of the churches). A fifth option would have been simply to demonize the God of the Hebrews (and limit use of the Old Testament to polemics). The first concrete evidence we have of this option are some Nag Hammadi treatises like the *Sophia of Jesus Christ* (NHC III,4, late first century?), the *Letter of Peter to Philip* (NHC VIII,2, second–third century), and the *Apocryphon of John* (NHC II,1, also second–third century).

9. The reason I say "in most cases" is that sources like the *Gospel of Thomas* and Q lacked passion narratives simply because they were collections of Jesus' sayings and conversations.

10. "Adoptionism" is the view that Jesus was primarily a holy man (hasid), who bore the divine presence (Spirit, power, Logos, Christos) and transmitted it to others in healing power. Note that the combinations of narrative threads here and in the following options are much the same as those in ch. 7. The difference is that here we are examining fabrics produced by different blends of narrative thread, whereas in ch. 7 we were following the questions raised by those blends.

11. "Docetism" is the view that the divine figure that Jesus channeled did not suffer on the cross, either because it was impervious to suffering or because someone else was crucified in its place.

12. "Modalism" is the view the divine figure that Jesus channeled was none other than God the Father.

13. "Subordinationism" is the view that Jesus was more than human, but not truly divine (less divine that God the Father). Arianism is a special case in which the divine aspect is said to be an archangel.

14. April D. DeConick, *Recovering the Original Gospel of Thomas: A History of the Gospel and Its Growth*, Library of New Testament Studies 286 (London: T&T Clark, 2005), 123; DeConick, *The Original Gospel of Thomas in Translation: With a Commentary and New English Translation of the Complete Gospel*, Library of New Testament Studies 287 (London: T&T Clark, 2006), 25–31, 34–36. The sayings in Thomas never deny, or even play down, the death and resurrection of Jesus;

they simply ignore it. Logion 13 has Peter compare Jesus to a "righteous angel," which most likely is a way of saying a hasid ("pious one") or zaddik ("righteous one").

15. One of Nicholas Perrin's criticisms of DeConick's method of reconstruction is that it uses oral-performance theory to account for gospel traditions in the mid-first century; Perrin, *Thomas: The Other Gospel* (London: SPCK, 2007), 59, 62. In this study, we have used aspects of the theory for the Gospels as late as Luke and John.

16. For the identification of Jesus as *Shekhinah* and Word in Thomas, compare the language of Matt. 18:20; *Odes Sol.* 5:15; *m. Avot* 3:6; Tatian, *Oration* 5 (the Logos as fire).

17. "Q" stands for *Quelle*, the German word for the hypothetical "source" of non-Markan material that is common to the Gospels of Matthew and Luke.

18. On the pre-Markan origin of the parable and the Honi-like use of the label *son*, see James H. Charlesworth, "Jesus as 'Son' and the Righteous Teacher as 'Gardner,'" in Charlesworth, ed., *Jesus and the Dead Sea Scrolls*, ABRL (New York: Doubleday, 1992), 140–75 (152–56).

19. *Gospel of the Hebrews* frags. 2, 6; *Hermas* 58:2; 59:1, 5-6; *T. Levi* 16:2-3; Tertullian, *On the Flesh of Christ* 14.

20. The idea of the *Christos* as a preexistent divine light occurs already in the Gospel of John, where the Messiah (1:20; 11:27) is the same as the light of the world (1:4-8; 3:19; 12:46), and it may have roots in pre-Christian traditions; William Horbury, *Jewish Messianism and the Cult of Christ* (London: SCM, 1998), 99, 125.

21. *Kerygmata Petrou* in the Pseudo-Clementine *Recognitions* 1.36.1-4; 37.2 (Syriac); 39.1-2; 43.1; 44.2; 60.4, 7; Irenaeus, *Haer.* 1.26.1; the *Testimony of Truth* (NHC IX,3) 30.19-28.

22. The reason that Irenaeus condemned Cerinthus and the Ebionites probably had to do with their supposed connections to Gnosticism.

23. On Paul of Samosata's banning hymns, see the excerpt from the Riedmatten collection cited by Robert M. Grant, *Gods and the One God*, Library of Early Christianity 1 (Philadelphia: Westminster, 1986), 134.

24. See ch. 6 (third section) on New Testament hymns and prayers dedicated to the Lord Jesus. Similar prayers were common in second-century literature, e.g., *Odes Sol.* 7:17; 17:17; *Ascen. Isa.* 7:17; 8:18; 9:28-32; 10:15; 11:23-32; *Acts of Paul and Thecla* 42; Ignatius, *Eph.* 4:1; *Rom.* 4:2; *Mart. Pol.* 14:3; 19:2; 21; 22:1, 3; 23:5; Justin, *1 Apol.* 6.1; Melito, *On Pascha* 45, 65, 105.

25. Adolf Harnack, *History of Dogma*, trans. Neil Buchanan, 7 vols. (Boston: Little, Brown, & Co. 1905-7), 3:14–50

26. For a brief history of the dispute, see J. N. D. Kelly, *Early Christian Doctrines*, 4th ed. (London: A&C Black, 1968), 115–19. For a useful collection of excerpts, see Arland J. Hultgren and Steven A. Haggmark, eds., *The Earliest Christian Heretics: Readings from their Opponents* (Minneapolis: Fortress Press, 1996), 137–41.

27. YHWH assumed a quasi-physical body in some patriarchal narratives (Gen. 15:17; 32:24-30; Exod. 33:22-23; 34:6), and his Spirit and Wisdom were temporarily embodied in his prophets (2 Chron. 24:20; Ws. 7:27; 10:16).

28. Tertullian (*Against Praxeas* 16) saw just enough concreteness in the theophanies of the Old Testament that he could describe them as the Lord's preparations for the incarnation and thereby downplay the apparent discontinuity.

29. This problem of the cross would have been avoided in New Testament traditions that dated this embodiment from the resurrection, as discussed in ch. 7 ("When and How Did the Lord Become Identified with the Man Jesus?"). There is no indication, however, that this particular option was available to the proto-docetist parties whose traditions are explored here.

30. On Moses' elevation to heaven from Mount Nebo, see Philo, *Questions on Genesis* 1.86; *4 Ezra* 14:9; *2 Bar.* 59:3; *Sifrei Devarim* 357; *Memar Marqah: The Teaching of Marqah*, BZAW 84, trans. John Macdonald (Berlin: Töpelmann, 1963), 208.

31. Ernst Käsemann noted the triumphalistic Christology of John and described it as a naive form of docetism; Käsemann, *The Testament of Jesus: A Study of the Gospel of John in the Light of*

Chapter 17, trans. Gerhard Krodel (Philadelphia: Fortress Press, 1968). While it is true that John (in striking contrast to Paul) described Jesus as raising himself from the dead (10:17-18), the Gospel's portrayal of the crucifixion itself was quite realistic, even to the point of having a spear thrust into his side and blood gushing out (19:17-30, 37). For John, moreover, the marks of Jesus' mutilation were not effaced by the resurrection (20:27).

32. Another source to consider is Q, for which there is no evidence of a passion narrative. But Q was a sayings source, so the omission of a passion narrative may have been a simple matter of genre. Moreover, Q does strongly associate discipleship with the way of the cross (evidently relying on prior knowledge of its audience, Luke 14:26-27).

33. Compare Phil. 3:10, 18 where Paul describes Christians who do not share in Jesus' sufferings as "enemies of the cross."

34. As translated by Maarten J. J. Menken, "The Opponents in the Johannine Letters," in *Empsychoi Logoi—Religious Innovations in Antiquity: Studies in Honour of Pieter Willem van der Horst*, Ancient Judaism and Early Christianity 73, ed. Alberdina Houtman, Albert de Jong, and Magda Misset-van de Weg (Leiden: Brill, 2008), 191-209 (193, 202-3, 204). The advantage of Menken's translation is that it brings out the repetition of "confess Jesus" (with "as the *Christos* come in the flesh" taken for granted in the second instance).

35. Francis Watson points out that John 6:51 associates the flesh of Jesus with his self-offering for the life of the world; Watson, "Is John's Christology Adoptionistic?" in *The Glory of Christ in the New Testament: Studies in Christology in Memory of George Bradford Caird*, ed. L. D. Hurst and N. T. Wright (Oxford: Clarendon, 1987), 113-24 (116 n. 20).

36. Among scholars who see John's opponents as docetists who viewed the *Christos* as a supernatural being like an angel are Christopher Rowland, "Christ in the New Testament" in *King and Messiah in Israel and the Ancient Near East: Proceedings of the Oxford Old Testament Seminar*, JSOTSup 70, ed. John Day (Sheffield: Sheffield Academic Press, 1998), 474-96 (482-83); Larry Hurtado, *Lord Jesus Christ: Devotion to Jesus in Earliest Christianity* (Grand Rapids: Eerdmans, 2003), 421; Menken, "The Opponents in the Johannine Letters," 191-209 (196, 205-6).

37. Although Ignatius mentioned these particular conversations with Judaizers only in his letter to the church of Philadelphia (*Phld.* 8:2), we do not know for sure when and where he encountered them. William Schoedel reasonably assumes that the debate took place during Ignatius's visit to the church in Philadelphia; Schoedel, *Ignatius of Antioch*, Hermeneia (Philadelphia: Fortress Press, 1985), 207. However, Clayton N. Jefford points out that Ignatius may also have tried (unsuccessfully) to suppress Jewish traditions like Sabbath observance in his home church in Antioch; Jefford, *The Apostolic Fathers and the New Testament* (Peabody, MA: Hendrickson, 2007), 167-68.

38. In *Magn.* 9:1, Ignatius described how Jews who turned to the Lord Jesus "came to a new hope, no longer keeping the Sabbath but living according to the Lord's Day, on which also our life arose through him and his death—which some deny"; Bart D. Ehrman, trans., *The Apostolic Fathers*, LCL 24-25, 2 vols. (Cambridge, MA: Harvard University Press, 2003), 1:248-52. I take it that Ignatius credited his opponents with receiving life from the risen Lord, even though they did not view the death of Jesus as the means for this grace.

39. On the *Odes*, see J. H. Charlesworth in *Old Testament Pseudepigrapha*, ed. James Charlesworth, 2 vols. (Garden City, NY: Doubleday, 1983), 2:727. Hereafter cited as *OTP*. On the *Ascension of Isaiah*, see Torleif Elgvin, "Jewish-Christian Editing of the Old Testament Pseudepigrapha," in *Jewish Believers in Jesus: The Early Centuries*, ed. Oskar Skarsaune and Reidar Hvalvik (Peabody, MA: Hendrickson, 2007), 278-304 (292-95).

40. The same could be said for the painless birth from the Virgin Mary in *Odes Sol.* 19:7-10.

41. The Odist claimed to have been persecuted and rejected like Jesus, but hoped to escape and did not hold up martyrdom as an ideal form of discipleship (*Odes Sol.* 5:4-7; 23:20; 25:5-6; 42:7).

42. The Odist claimed to have the Lord's branches blossoming within and yielding fruit full of salvation (*Odes Sol.* 1:1-5). Ignatius similarly described the "atheists" he opposed as "wicked

offshoots" rather than "branches of the cross" in that they made the Lord's suffering a sham [*to dokein*]" (*Trall.* 10:1-11:2). However, I see nothing in the *Odes* that would suggest patterning the ascension of the Lord on that of Moses (nor are there any relevant citations of ascent texts in Charlesworth's marginal notes in *OTP* 2:735-71).

43. For a complete coverage of this issue, see Darrell D. Hannah, "The Ascension of Isaiah and Docetic Christology," *VC* 53 (1999): 165-96 (170-72).

44. Ignatius, *Eph.* 19:1. Hannah argues that *Ascen. Isa.* 6-11 is a midrash on Paul's statement about the deception of the "rulers of this age" in 1 Cor. 2:6-8 ("None of the rulers of this age understood this; for if they had, they would not have crucified the Lord of glory"); Hannah, "The Ascension of Isaiah and Docetic Christology," 191-92.

45. The major reason that Athanasius rejected this Isaiah pseudepigraphon was apparently that the Melitian schismatics cited it in support of their critique of the Alexandrian bishop; see *Festal Letter* 39.21, 24, 32; ET in David Brakke, "A New Fragment of Athanasius's Thirty-Ninth *Festal Letter*: Heresy, Apocrypha, and the Canon," *HTR* 103 (2010): 47-66 (61, 63 [line 33], 65). Athanasius's pairing of the Arians with the Melitians ("their parasites") in his list of enemies suggests that they may have appealed to the same work in support of their dogmatic subordinationism, as explained in a note in the final section of this chapter.

46. Irenaeus traced these teachings back to Simon Magus, who had supposedly lived during the time of Jesus' first disciples (*Haer.* I.23.3). Even though Irenaeus may have based this account on a lost work by Justin, the historical value of his portrait is doubtful. Unfortunately, the surviving fragments of Basilides do not fill out his teachings about the incarnation and the cross; for a convenient collection, see Bentley Layton, *The Gnostic Scriptures*, ABRL (New York: Doubleday, 1995), 427-44.

47. I leave out the part about Jesus assuming the form of Simon of Cyrene and vice versa. According to Birger Pearson, this body-switching stunt was added by Irenaeus based on a misunderstanding of his source; Pearson, "Basilides," in *A Companion to Second-Century Christian 'Heretics'*, VCSup 76, ed. Antti Marjanen and Petri Luomanen (Leiden: Brill, 2005), 1-31 (22); Pearson, *Ancient Gnosticism: Traditions and Literature* (Minneapolis: Fortress Press, 2007), 140, 240. It is not clear whether the one who was crucified is Simon or Jesus—perhaps the ambiguity was deliberate.

48. Similar ideas are found in another Nag Hammadi treatise, the Coptic *Apocalypse of Peter* (NHC VII,3), also dating from late second or early third-century Egypt; see Pearson, *Ancient Gnosticism*, 242-44.

49. Pearson therefore dates "The Great Seth" to the episcopacy of Demetrius of Alexandria (189-232 CE); Pearson, *Ancient Gnosticism*, 241-42.

50. Eusebius, *Ecclesiastical History* 6.12.2-6. The apocryphal text discovered in 1884 that has been termed the "Gospel of Peter" is similar in many ways to the *Ascension of Isaiah*. For comparison to the text that Serapion condemned, see Fred Lapham, *An Introduction to the New Testament Apocrypha*, Understanding the Bible and its World (London: T&T Clark, 2003), 89-94. Lapham suggests some relationship between the known *Gospel of Peter* and Christian Jews like the Nazarenes.

51. Pearson, *Ancient Gnosticism*, 241-42.

52. In the third century, followers of Noetus and Sabellius would appeal to John 10:30; 14:9-10 to support their view that the Son was the Father incarnate (*Against Noetus* 7.1, 4, attributed to Hippolytus; cf. Epiphanius, *Panarion* 62.2.3). The same group interpreted the Logos of John figuratively (*Against Noetus* 15.1).

53. Such clarity on this distinction of divine figures must have reflected the combined force of memories of Jesus at prayer and the primal Kyriocentric visions. The same cannot be said of the distinction between the Lord Jesus and the Holy Spirit in the New Testament. Texts in which the spirit is closely identified with the risen Lord include 2 Cor. 3:2-18; Rev. 1:10; 2:1, 7; 4:1-2; 14:13-14. Hans Dieter Betz also sees the Spirit whom God sends forth in Gal. 4:6 as the "present

reality of Christ"; Betz, *Galatians: A Commentary on Paul's Letters to the Churches in Galatia* (Philadelphia: Fortress Press, 1979), 210b.

54. One can always imagine such opposing views in the background when New Testament writers state their views with emphasis. So, for instance, Jesus' saying that he will ascend to his Father and his God in the Gospel of John (John 20:17) could be taken to imply that the author was attacking the idea that Jesus had completely merged with the God the Father. This text can be explained more simply, however, in terms of John's subordinationist Christology (discussed in the next section of this chapter) and his Jesus preparing the way for the coming of the Spirit (cf. John 14–16).

55. I ignore texts that simply refer to the Lord Jesus as "father" without more specific qualifications; such as *Odes Sol.* 6:6-10; *2 Clem.* 1:3-4; *Akhmimic Apoc. Elijah* 1:5-7. In the second-century *Apocryphon of John* (NHC II,1) a multiform anthropos (man) identifies himself as father, mother, and son (2.13-14), but these epithets represent different forms of Christ rather than an alternative trinity (cf. *Apocryphon* 5.7 on the trinity of Mother-Father, first man, and Holy Spirit).

56. ET adapted from ANF, 1:235b. Thomas Falls's translation omits the name "God" and paraphrases the Greek text; Fall, *St. Justin Martyr: Dialogue with Trypho*, Selections from the Fathers of the Church 3 (Washington: Catholic University of America Press, 2003), 115.

57. Larry Hurtado has worked out a neat binitarian reading of this text; Hurtado, "'Jesus' as God's Name, and Jesus as God's Embodied Name in Justin Martyr," in *Justin Martyr and His Worlds*, ed. Sara Parvis and Paul Foster (Minneapolis: Fortress Press, 2007), 128–36 (134).

58. New Testament writers already were interpreting Old Testament "Yahweh texts" in such a way that one part referred to the Lord Jesus and another to God the Father. In addition to the Christianized *Shema* verse in 1 Cor. 8:6; Eph. 4:5, which we discussed in ch. 7 ("Didn't Jesus Pray to God as His Father? One God, One Lord"), see Rom. 14:11; Eph. 4:8; Mark 1:2; Luke 7:27 (Q); Luke 9:32, 35; Acts 2:17-21, 38-39; Heb. 1:6; Rev. 6:16; 21:23; John 12:40; 19:37. A thorough study of texts like these would shed further light on early Christian understanding of the God-Lord binity.

59. On Justin's differentiation of an invisible Father and a visible Son, see *1 Apol.* 63 (citing Matt. 11:27); *Dial.* 56.1-3; 114.3; 127.1-4, and the discussion in ch. 9. The fact that Justin had such a difficult time convincing Jewish listeners that Jesus was the Lord who revealed himself to the patriarchs and to Moses may help (as much as his Platonism) to account for his stressing alternate categories like Word and Glory of God to establish the prehistory of Jesus.

60. In *Dial.* 73:1, this part of Ps. 96 is referred to the Lord Jesus; cf. *1 Apol.* 41, which also describes the Lord Jesus as "the Father of the ages" and has him reigning "from a tree" (a type of the cross). In the very next sections of the *Dialogue* (74:2-3), Ps. 96:1-3 is referred to the Father, even though Justin had referred the exact same portion to the Lord Jesus in *1 Apol.* 41.

61. Although Justin described congregational prayers, he never once mentioned Jesus praying to the Father or the Lord's Prayer.

62. Alistair Stewart-Sykes, trans., *On Pascha with the Fragments of Melito and Other Materials Related to the Quartodecimanians*, by Melito of Sardis, Popular Patristics Series (Crestwood, NY: St. Vladimir's Seminary Press, 2001), 39–40. Compare the Greek text and translation in Stuart George Hall, trans., *On Pascha and Fragments*, by Melito of Sardis (Oxford: Clarendon, 1979), 4–7.

63. The term *naive modalism* is used by Campbell Bonner, ed. *The Homily on the Passion by Melito, Bishop of Sardis with Some Fragments of the Apocryphal Ezekiel*, Studies and Documents 12 (London: Christophers, 1940), 28; Stuart George Hall, "The Christology of Melito: A Misrepresentation Exposed," *Studia Patristica* 13 (1975): 154–68 (164); and Stewart-Sykes, *On Pascha*, 29, 39 n. 3.

64. Single doxologies are also dedicated to the Lord Jesus in 2 Tim. 4:18; Heb. 13:21; 2 Pet. 3:18; and the *Acts of Peter* 20, 21, 39.

65. Stewart-Sykes, *On Pascha*, 29, which refers back to Hall's *Studia Patristica* article cited in a previous note.

66. Justin did not say anything about the prayers of Jesus either, but he cannot be cited in this regard because his apologies focus on charges raised by pagans and Jews and only refer to Jesus' teachings for their ethical content (Hall, trans., *On Pascha*, 15–17).

67. Hippolytus, *Refutation of Heresies* 9.5; 10.27 [labeled 10.23 in ANF, 5:148]; Epiphanius, *Panarion* 57, 62. What convinces me of the authenticity of Noetus, as described by Hippolytus, is the fact that he adheres to the New Testament teaching about the continuity of the visible form of the Lord God and the incarnate Lord Jesus (*Refutation* 10.27). In other words, his modalism is a straightforward inference from the Kyriocentric vision at the expense of traditions about Jesus' teachings and prayers.

68. Harnack, *History of Dogma*, 3:51–118.

69. For a brief history of this dispute, see Kelly, *Early Christian Doctrines*, 120–22. For a useful collection of relevant texts, see Hultgren and Haggmark, *The Earliest Christian Heretics*, 144–51.

70. For the reasons stated above, I ignore the Johannine texts (John 10:30; 14:9-10), to which followers of Noetus and Sabellius would appeal in the third century.

71. Origen, *Against Celsus* 8.14; cf. Origen, *On Prayer* 16.1. Gunnar af Hällström describes the practice that Origen opposed as a "popular modalist view," as distinct from "doctrinally motivated modalism"; Hällström, *Fides simpliciorum according to Origen of Alexandria*, Commentationes Humanarum Litterarum 76 (Helsinki: Societas Scientarium Fennica, 1984), 69–70. The naive modalism we have described above would include the teachings of elites like Justin and Melito as well as this "popular modalism."

72. The anthropic form of YHWH was seen residing in the highest heaven by both Enoch and Paul (*1 En.* 14:8-23; 39:3-8; 2 Cor. 12:1-4, assuming an objective genitive in 12:1).

73. I say "almost interchangeable" in recognition of the fact that the Tetragrammaton (YHWH, Lord) was more common in texts describing people calling on the name of the Deity and in those describing the Deity coming to earth and/or appearing in a concrete, visible form.

74. Joseph Kreitzer attributes the eschatological subordination in 1 Cor. 15 to Paul's continued respect for Jewish monotheism; Kreitzer, *Jesus and God in Paul's Eschatology*, JSOTSup 19 (Sheffield: Sheffield Academic Press, 1987), 158–59. James Dunn attributes it to Paul's understanding of Jesus as the Logos or Word of God; Dunn, *Did the First Christians Worship Jesus? The New Testament Evidence* (Louisville: Westminster John Knox, 2010), 111–12. Both of these suggestions are helpful, but other scholars have raised questions concerning the meaning of Jewish "monotheism" and Paul's commitment to a Logos or Wisdom Christology. All in all, our appeal to more definitively known traditions concerning the prayers and teachings of Jesus provides an alternate and perhaps simpler answer.

75. So Matt. 24:36. Even though Matthew follows Mark's narrative fairly closely here, he also adds touches that stress Jesus' knowledge of the times (11:25-27 [Q]; 26:2, 18).

76. The time of the end is also known to God alone in the clearest pre-Christian statement of hope for an eschatological Davidic Messiah, the *Psalms of Solomon* (*Pss. Sol.* 17:21). The motif of angels not knowing the time of "the day of vengeance" was traditionally derived midrashically from Isa. 63:4; see *b. Sanh.* 99a. Mark's own reason for downplaying Jesus' knowledge may have been to temper speculations of the time of the end that were raised by Jesus' previous pronouncements (Mark 13:7, 14, 26, 30).

77. For John, Jesus' being sent by and coming *from* the Father appears to have displaced the more traditional motif of his praying *to* the Father (here only in John 14:6 and then negated in 16:26).

78. Michael Goulder, for example, has argued that the antagonists in Hebrews were proto-Ebionites (or Cerinthians) who viewed Jesus as possessed by an angelic Christ/Spirit; Goulder, "Hebrews and the Ebionites," *NTS* 49 (2003): 393–406 (399–400).

79. Darrell Hannah finds this angelomorphic Christology by reading Jude 5 as "Jesus who saved a people out of the land of Egypt, afterward destroyed those who did not believe" and comparing it with Exod. 23:20-21; Num. 20:16; Isa. 63:9; Hannah, *Michael and Christ: Michael*

Traditions and Angel Christology in Early Christianity, WUNT 109 (Tübingen: Mohr Siebeck, 1999), 139–42. Compare Acts 23:9, where the "scribes of the Pharisees' group" interpret Paul's visions of the Lord Jesus as the appearance of "a spirit or an angel."

80. Rev. 1:13-18 (discussed in ch. 5); 10:1; 14:14-15. See Adela Yarbro Collins and John J. Collins, *King and Messiah as Son of God: Divine, Human and Angelic Messianic Figures in Biblical and Related Literature* (Grand Rapids: Eerdmans, 2008), 189–203.

81. See Jude 14-15, which cites *1 En.* 1:9 regarding the coming Lord Jesus; Rev. 1:6-8*, 10-18* (discussed in ch. 5); 2:17*, 23*; 3:19*; passim.

82. For example, *Ascen. Isa.* 9:27-40 (the Lord is here paired with the Holy Spirit); *Apostolic Constitutions* 8.12.6-27 (a eucharistic liturgy). The term *Great Glory* in *Ascen. Isa.* 9:37 may reflect performances of the vision of Enoch (*1 En.* 14:20; 25:3, noted in the margin of *OTP* 2:172). If so, the performers have dedicated the vision of Isaiah to the Lord Jesus, dedicated the vision of Enoch to God the Father, and woven the two together in an extended binitarian (really Trinitarian) narrative. Evidently, Egyptian Arians cited these verses from *1 Enoch* and the *Ascension of Isaiah* to support their theology. Athanasius named the Arians and singled these two texts out as being noncanonical in *Festal Letter* 39.21, 24; ET in Brakke, "A New Fragment of Athanasius's Thirty-Ninth *Festal Letter*," 61, 63, line 32.

83. *Hermas* 89:7-8 portrayed a vision of the Son of God leading a group of six angels. The writings known as the "Apostolic Fathers" is a group of eight texts from the two generations following the death of the last apostles (approx. 95–150 ce). The list was first compiled by J-B. Cotelier in 1672, and the *Didache* (arguably the earliest of the group) was added in the nineteenth century.

84. In addition to *Hermas*, cf. Justin, *1 Apol.* 63 (Angel of God, Son of God); Justin, *Dial.* 128.2 (Power, Angel, Word); the "Book of Elchasai" (two giant angels called the Son of God and the Holy Spirit); the *Testament of Dan* 6:1-7 (Angel of peace, the Lord who will not depart from Israel); the *Teachings of Silvanus* (NHC VII,4) 106.21-28 (Wisdom, Word, Light, Angel); 113.6-7 ("Light of the Eternal Light").

85. Hannah, *Michael and Christ*, 172; cf. Jean Daniélou, *The Theology of Jewish Christianity: A History of Early Christian Doctrine before the Council of Nicea*, trans. John A. Baker (London: Darton, Longman & Todd, 1964), 123. Origen attributed a similar midrash on Isaiah 6 to his Hebrew instructor (*On First Principles* 1.3.4). According to this latter interpretation, Isaiah saw the Son and Holy Spirit as two seraphim on either side of God the Father.

86. Not all uses of the idea of adoption are adoptionist or even proto-adoptionist. In this case, the one who was made Son of God is not the hasid Jesus, but a preexistent archangel.

87. As Jean Daniélou comments with regard to Hermas: "there could be no question of the Word's being considered as an angel"; Daniélou, *The Theology of Jewish Christianity*, 122.

88. For instance, in Origen, *First Principles* 4.4.1, frag. 32.

89. For Justin's descriptions of the Son as an angel, see *1 Apol.* 63.5, 14; *Dial.* 34.2, 61.1, 126.6, 127.4, 128.1. To put this usage in perspective, note that the messianic king was called an "angel" (*aggelos*) in the lxx of Isa. 9:6, and YHWH himself was called *mal'ak*, meaning "angel" or "messenger," in Gen. 48:16; Hos. 12:4-6.

90. Athenagoras insisted that the Son was always within God as his Word and so "did not come into existence" (*oux hōs genomenon*), but only came forth (*proelthōn*) in order to give form and actuality to material things (*Plea on Behalf of Christians* 10.3). Athenagoras's explanation has come to be known as a "two-stage Christology"; Harry A. Wolfson, *Philosophy of the Church Fathers* (Cambridge, MA: Harvard University Press, 1956), 204–17.

91. Epiphanius attributed a similar teaching to a little-known group called "Ebionites" (*Panarion* 30.3.4-5; 30.16:4). Michael Goulder lumps the Ebionites together with Tertullian's target group; Goulder, "A Poor Man's Christology," *NTS* 45 (1999): 332–48 (335 n. 11). Hannah argues that the latter were Valentinians instead; *Michael and Christ*, 180–82. One should also consider the

parallel discussion in the *Yerushalmi*, whether one is forbidden to call on Gabriel or Michael for salvation (*y. Ber.* 9:1,13a).

92. Origen, Fragment on Hebrews 24.359; Fragment on Psalms 54.3-4; cf. Ilaria L. E. Ramelli, "Origen's Anti-Subordinationism and its Heritage in the Nicene and Cappadocian Line," *VC* 65 (2011): 21–49 (33).

93. Our principal source here is Athanasius, *Defense of the Nicene Definition* 25–26; Athanasius, *On the Opinion of Dionysius* 4, 18. The Greek term *hypostasis* means something like "individual entity" or "recognizable individual." Later in the fourth century, the term would be used to describe the distinct personages (*prosōpa*) of the Trinity.

94. Arius's short writings are conveniently available in volumes like Edward Rochie Hardy and Cyril C. Richardson, eds., *Christology of the Later Fathers*, LCC 3 (Philadelphia: Westminster, 1954), 329–34; William G. Rusch, ed., *The Trinitarian Controversy*, Sources of Early Christian Thought (Philadelphia: Fortress Press, 1980), 29–32.

95. The "Creed of the Three Hundred and Eighteen Fathers" is not as elaborate as what we know today as the "Nicene Creed," which contains additions from the Council of Constantinople (381) and is really "neo-Nicene," as explained in ch. 9.

96. Walter Bauer, *Rechtgläubigkeit und Ketzerei im ältesten Christentum*, BHT 10 (Tübingen: Mohr, 1934). A second edition was translated into English as *Orthodoxy and Heresy in Earliest Christianity*, ed. Robert A. Kraft and Gerhard Krodel (Philadelphia: Fortress Press, 1971). See here pp. xxi–xxiii. Bauer's revisionist history portrayed pockets of heresy and orthodoxy existing side by side in the early church; ibid., 69, 77, passim. Our scenario suggests more of a mixture of contrasting tendencies within the very same groups (and even the same individual writers), from which more militant, systematic views emerged in the late second and third centuries.

97. Semi-popular literature commonly contrasts ecclesial definitions of faith to Rabbinic allowance of a plurality of meanings and interpretations, particularly as described in the Talmud (edited c. 600 CE); cf. *b. Hag.* 3a-b ("All of them were given from one shepherd") and *b. Eruv.* 13b ("The words of both houses are the words of the living God"). David Stern has pointed out that such Talmudic tolerance was more of an ideal envisioned by the anonymous editors, than a literal, historical reality; Stern, "Midrash and Indeterminacy," *Critical Inquiry* 15 (1988): 132–61 (155, 159–60). In fact, the Tannaim believed they could pronounce certain parties (esp. the Sadducees) to be excluded from the world to come (*m. Sanh.* 10:1) and were said to stone the coffins of fellow Rabbis who would not adhere to the majority decision (*m. Ed.* 5:8, 5:6 in Danby, trans., *The Mishnah*). On the other hand, Lawrence Schiffman argues, they did not thereby exclude them from the covenant people of Israel; Schiffman, *Who Was a Jew? Rabbinic and Halakhic Perspectives on the Jewish Christian Schism* (Hoboken, NJ: Ktav, 1985), 41–42, 52, 61. Apostates (*meshummadim*), on the other hand, were believed to have reneged on the covenant and were temporarily excluded from the community; Schiffman, *Who Was a Jew?* 48–49. The material reviewed in this chapter suggests that the divergent, exploratory nature of early Christian discourse was similar to the ideal of the Talmudic editors, at least until the time that various synods and rules of faith began to regularize christological language in the third and fourth centuries. In any case, simple, bifurcated comparisons of the two traditions need be qualified.

9

Three Movements that Marginalized Visions of the Anthropic Form of the Lord

The scenario we have reconstructed depends on one major conjecture: that Jesus and his disciples were among those groups of first-century Jews who celebrated visions of the Lord of glory. We have tested this conjecture in a variety of ways, but there is still one outstanding problem that needs to be addressed.

The problem is best formulated in terms of a paradox. On the one hand, the Old Testament speaks of YHWH appearing and being seen in anthropic (humanlike) form, and the New Testament identifies this very Lord as Jesus. On the other hand, Christians tend to think of the God of Israel as having been invisible prior to the incarnation and view the Lord Jesus as hidden throughout the history of Old Testament Israel.[1] Old Testament descriptions of the anthropic form are usually classed as "anthropomorphisms" and are taken to be figures of speech rather than literal encounters.[2] How could this be?

This paradox raises the following question. If we have outgrown anthropomorphic language, is it not likely that the founders of our faith also eschewed such primitive, archaic ideas? Or, to turn the question around, if our conjecture is valid, the early disciples did in fact believe that the Lord appeared to them in anthropic form, and such appearances were the main impetus for early Christology, how is it possible that the performance of such visions became such an embarrassment to the church?

Our task in this chapter will be to review some of the opinions that early Christians held about the relation of the incarnation to the Old Testament theophanies.[3] I will try to show that early Christian leaders altered their views of these theophanies in various ways in order to commend their beliefs to gentile audiences and to protect them against the challenges of hostile parties like the Gnostics and the Arians (though earlier traditions were also preserved). For convenience, I shall describe this re-envisioning process in three overlapping movements:

> 1. Stressing the uniqueness and novelty of the incarnation (largely against Judaism and Judaizers in a gentile context)
> 2. Playing down concrete aspects of Old Testament theophanies (against Gnostics and Manicheans)
> 3. Re-visioning the Logos as invisible and immutable (against Eunomian Arians and Anthropomorphites)

Much of this material has been covered by other scholars, so there is no need for extensive detail here.[4] Our main task will be to document the historical transition from the performance of biblical and apocalyptic visions within the bounds of early Judaism to a distinct religion with very little in common with Judaism.

This analysis is intended to be descriptive rather than evaluative. Some readers may well mourn the loss of early performative Christology and its fractal growth. Others, however, may have little patience for such informal, experiential ways of doing theology. If it is true that the Lord of the disciples was capable of taking on different appearances and speaking with various voices, it must at least be allowed that faith in that Lord could continue to take on new forms as new challenges arose.

Movement 1: The Incarnation was Unprecedented (Contra Judaism and Gentile Judaizers)

In chapter 4, I argued that the unprecedented nature of the Lord-Jesus identification was a case of "fortuitous uniqueness." The two principal portraits of Jesus—as Jewish holy man and as coming Lord—were common enough in the history of Judaism, particularly in pietist circles. The circumstances that led to the superposition of these portraits were also common: the violent death of the holy man, and the manifestation of the Lord in a new form or with a new name. What made the Christian gospel unique was the coincidence of these circumstances and the superposition of the two portraits, which led to novel understandings of Old Testament ideas like *Son of God* and *Messiah* (discussed in ch. 7). If such a coincidence ever occurred at any other time in the history of Judaism, the message of the performers involved must have been lost or perhaps suppressed.

In spite of the fact that this uniqueness was coincidental (historically speaking), a number of early church leaders and teachers stressed the uniqueness of Jesus in sharp contrast to the alleged barrenness of non-Christian Judaism. Here we shall look at some examples in the New Testament, some second-century theologians, and two fourth-century writers.

HEBREWS AND 1 PETER

Some late New Testament epistles already stressed the uniqueness and novelty of their Lord, either to wean their readers away from continuing Judaism or to accommodate their message to a gentile audience.

Ironically, such an anti-Judaic stance was first evidenced in the writings of Christian Jewish writers who wished to differentiate their faith and distance their congregations from their Jewish coreligionists. For example, the writer of the Letter to the Hebrews emphasized the utter novelty of God speaking though his Son ("in these last days")—prior to the advent of Jesus, God had only spoken to the Jewish ancestors through prophets (Heb. 1:1). Although the Son was the same as the Lord who created heaven and earth (1:10) and eventually took his place in the succession of prophets (1:1-2; cf. Mark 12:2-6), he had never been known by either the patriarchs or the people of Israel.

Hebrews claimed that the coming of the Lord was prophesied in the Torah, the Prophets, and the Psalms (1:5-13), but cited no precedent whatever for that coming in Old Testament theophanies, the performance of which was so instrumental for the origin of deity Christology.[5] In fact, the Lord seems never to have dwelt in the Jerusalem temple (Heb. 8:5; 9:12, 24), even though it was well known that prophets like Isaiah and Ezekiel had personally witnessed that presence. In place of the priestly service of Aaron that was so central to the Temple cult, Hebrews offered an alternative priesthood, one after the order of Melchizedek by which believers could enter a heavenly sanctuary (5:5-6; 6:19-20; 7:25; 10:19).[6]

This distancing from temple-based Judaism is particularly interesting in that the author spoke of himself directing the community in their visionary ascent to the heavenly sanctuary and hence into the presence of the Lord Jesus and God (Heb. 2:9; 10:19-22; 12:22-24). This way of ascent is said to have been pioneered by Jesus (6:20; 12:2), but it was clearly modeled on the entry of Aaron, as high priest, into the holy of holies on Yom Kippur (6:19; 8:1-2; 9:11-12, 24; 10:19-22)—this in spite of the author's polemic against the Levitical priesthood in Hebrews 7.

From a performative perspective, it appears that the writer was accustomed to assume the high-priestly role in such performances, evidently following the example of Jesus' own ascent.[7] Michael Swartz has documented a similar development in the *Avodah piyutim* (Yom Kippur poems of the third century and later), which were also based on the Yom Kippur account in Lev. 16. The synagogue poets (*payetanim*) identified themselves with the high priest and led their congregations in a similar imaginal entry into the holy of holies to "bask in the divine presence."[8] This parallel suggests that the author of Hebrews was in the habit of performing Kyriocentric visions (now binitarian) just as much as Paul, the Gospel writers, and John the Apocalypticist (ch. 5). The difference was that the Kyriocentric performances in Hebrews had become so Christianized that the author could afford to devalue the Hebrew Bible models they were based on (contrast John 12:41 on the vision of Isaiah).

Two reasons can be offered for this significant development in early Christology. First, as explained in the previous chapter, the writer of Hebrews tried to combine a strong deity Christology ("Son" in the binitarian sense) with the idea of Jesus as a prophet-like hasid ("son" in the proto-adoptionist sense). The original portrait of Jesus as the Lord in line with Old Testament theophanies, however, was displaced by Jesus as a "son" in the line of the prophets ("he has spoken to us by a son"). Manifestation of his divine Lordship, prior to the resurrection, was thereby limited to the time of creation (Heb. 1:10–12).

The second reason for Hebrews ignoring Old Testament theophanies was that the writer wanted to stress the superiority of the atonement accomplished by Jesus to the sacrifices that had been offered in the Jerusalem Temple. The former cleansed sin once and for all and admitted believers into the true sanctuary in heaven. This polemic was clearly an attempt to wean recipients away from their continuing allegiance to older Judaic practices (10:1–23; 12:18–25).

The subtlety of Hebrews' Christology can be appreciated by exegetes who have the patience to sort through the complex imagery. For the ordinary believer, however, the impact of this New Testament letter has had more to do with what was distilled and liturgicalized for common usage, and the focus here was God's Son being revealed without reference to earlier theophanies. For example, the Alexandrian "Anaphora of Saint Basil" dedicated the Sanctus (Trisagion) to God the Father and then continued: "You did not disown us forever, but always watched over us through your holy prophets, and in these last days, you manifested yourself to us who sit in darkness and the shadow of death through your only-begotten Son [Heb. 1:1-2 supported by Isa. 9:2; Matt. 4:16; Ps. 23:4]."[9] Liturgically, we (gentiles) acknowledge the prophets as the forerunners of Jesus, but entirely forget their actually encounters with the living Lord.

The writer of 1 Peter trumpeted the novelty of what was revealed in Jesus in similar terms. As a Messiah who redeems by shedding his blood, Jesus "was predestined before the foundation of the world, but was revealed at the end of the ages" (1 Pet. 1:19-20). Although the letter has several references to Jesus as YHWH, the Lord (e.g., 2:8; 3:12; 3:14-15), the author was thinking of him more as the Son of Man or Messiah, who was hidden from the time of the foundation of the world (cf. *1 En.* 48:6-7; 62:7; *4 Ezra* 12:32; 13:25-26). This emphasis comports with the fact that the intended audience for this letter was likely gentile converts, for whom details of Old Testament history may not have been so meaningful. Everything prior to the reception of the gospel, according to the author, was spiritual darkness, alienation from God, and ignorance of the law (1 Pet. 2:9-10; 4:3). From the perspective of our Kyriocentric conjecture, the implication of this emphasis is that performances of Kyriocentric visions had been so adapted to the gospel narrative that their origin in Old Testament visions had nearly been eclipsed.

IGNATIUS, IRENAEUS, AND THE ACTS OF PETER

The notion that the Lord Jesus was completely unknown to Israel before his incarnation recurs in Ignatius, bishop of Antioch, in the early second century. We have seen that Ignatius was particularly upset by a group of Judaizing Christians who kept Sabbath and based their faith and life on the Jewish Scriptures alone. Several striking passages from his letters illustrate his anti-Judaic reaction:

- "... entrusted with the ministry of Jesus Christ, who was with the Father before the ages [cf. John 1:1] and has been manifest at the end [cf. 1 Pet. 1:20]" (*Magn.* 6:1).[10]
- "... there is one God who manifested himself through Jesus Christ his Son, who is his Word that came forth from silence" (*Magn.* 8:2).[11]
- "Await the one who ... is invisible, who became visible for us, the one who cannot be handled, the one who is beyond suffering, who suffered for us" (*Pol.* 3:2).[12]

If one were to hear (or read) these lines by themselves, one would have to conclude that the Lord Jesus had never been seen or heard of until the life of the historic Jesus.

By way of explanation for this emphasis, Ignatius, like 1 Peter, was thinking in terms of Jesus as the Messiah, the Christ, who was hidden from the time of the creation of the world.[13] He was also writing to largely gentile churches (e.g., *Phld.* 6:1). In its immediate context, Ignatius's formulation was appropriate (he could have had no idea how influential his personal letters would be). In the broader context of the history of Israel and the origin of deity Christology, however, it overwrote the traditions of divine appearances that prepared the way for the incarnation. The residue of christological faith was ably defended, but the historical trail leading back to the origin of that faith had been covered up. (Admittedly the latter has only become a concern in the wake of Renaissance humanism.)

The effect of tailoring the gospel to gentile audiences became even clearer toward the end of the second century, especially in the writings of Irenaeus of Lyons. Irenaeus emphasized the role of God the Father in the Old Testament narratives as a way of countering Gnostic claims that the Father was completely unknown before the teachings of Jesus—we take up this motivation in the following section (Movement 2). The point to note here is that Irenaeus consciously accommodated his message to the mindset of his gentile audience (in southern France). We particularly see this in his *Demonstration [Epídeixis] of the Apostolic Preaching* (c. 200 CE), where Irenaeus made a clear distinction between what is theologically true of the Son of God and what is most meaningful for gentiles whom he was catechizing:

> But we must necessarily believe . . . that there was born a Son of God, that is, [born] not only before his appearance in the world, but also before the world was made . . . for the Son was as a beginning for God before the world was made [cf. Prov. 8:22], but, for us [gentiles] at the time of his appearance [in the flesh], but, before that, he did not exist for us in that we knew him not. (*Epídeixis* 43, emphasis added; cf. §45 for the gentile context)[14]

In theology, there was an important role for the Son in the Old Testament narratives, particularly his cosmic role as Wisdom in Proverbs 8. In popular preaching, however, what mattered was his being made known to the nations in the wake of his incarnation, crucifixion, and resurrection as one who recapitulated and corrected the mistakes of Adam. Irenaeus's contextual, pastoral approach to theology has often been noted for its strengths, particularly in its accommodation to the language and culture of lay audiences quite different from those for whom Jesus and the disciples proclaimed their message.[15] Here we see one of the weaknesses of this contextual approach, its loss of the performative context in which the message originated.

The Old Testament roots of deity Christology were still clear enough for educated elites like Irenaeus, but some more popular expositions only presented one side of the picture, particularly when they spoke rhetorically in terms of antitheses. A good example of such a popular account is the apocryphal *Acts of Peter* (also late second century), in which Peter proclaims the faith in these catchy lines:

He will also comfort you, so that you may love him . . .
this Young Man and Old Man,
appearing in time, yet invisible in eternity . . .
whom flesh has not seen, and now sees;
    who has not been heard [before], but is known now as the
Word which is heard;
never chastised, but now chastised;
who was before the world, and is now perceived in time. (*Acts of Peter* 20)[16]

The idea here is much the same as Irenaeus's presentation of the faith, except that there is no room left for a prehistory of the incarnation, even in principle. Irenaeus had contrasted a beginning before creation with a beginning for us at the incarnation, but this popularized gospel had only an eternity of invisibility and a recent appearance in time (cf. Ignatius, *Pol.* 3:2).

ATHANASIUS AND EPHREM SYRUS

The extent to which the prehistory of the Lord Jesus could be truncated for gentile audiences is also illustrated by Athanasius's treatise, *On the Incarnation of the Word*, which was written as a manual for preachers and catechetical instructors in Egypt (sometime between 313 and 337 CE, based on earlier lecture material). In his later writings, Athanasius showed considerable awareness of the history of appearances of the Logos (Word, Reason) in the Old Testament.[17] In this early, semi-popular work, however, the history of the Logos was greatly simplified: in the beginning, God gave all humans a share in his image, the Logos (as divine Reason) so that they might have some idea of God the Father. When this knowledge was lost and humans (i.e., gentiles) fell into idolatry, the Logos assumed a human body in order to heal our mortality and direct us back to the Father (*Incarnation* 11). Athanasius made a passing mention of the law and the prophets as auxiliary helps (§12), but said nothing about the theophanies of the Old Testament. Appearances in anthropic form would not have been very helpful to gentiles who were worshiping visible gods in the form of idols. In fact, talk about such concrete appearances would have given the wrong impression to audiences who were brought up on stories of Zeus, Kronos, and Apollo (§47) and some of the more enlightened of whom preferred to think in terms of an invisible, impassible Logos (§§1, 33, 41, passim).

An example of popular theology from the mid-fourth century is the hymns of the great Syriac poet Ephrem. As in the cases of Irenaeus and Athanasius, we find here a mixture of emphases, depending on context. In his *Hymns on Virginity*, Ephrem struck a balance, making use of a parable. In the Old Testament, the Logos appeared to the prophets in an ordered sequence of images (colors, symbols, types), just like a king who leaves different images of himself around the countryside, each one representing a different stage of his earlier (pre-coronation) life. On one hand, these historic images were just shadows of the king's mature presence, and, in the same way, the words of prophets and were "swallowed up" by the real incarnation. On the other hand, the old images still existed and were to be cherished (worshipped) as mementos of real events in the life of the King. If the error of the Jews was to reject the new, real presence, that of the Marcionites was to disdain the older images (*On Virginity* 28).[18]

Ephrem took a less balanced approach, however, in his *Hymns on the Nativity*. The purpose of these hymns was simply to exalt the birth of the Christ child. The challenge of the Marcionites was not in view, and Ephrem targeted the Jews (as well as Arians) instead. In the following two excerpts, he stressed the utter novelty of the incarnation and the prior distance of all the Old Testament saints from the Lord:

I.59 By the Spirit, Abraham perceived that the birth of the Son was distant;
for his own sake, he eagerly desired even in his day to see him [cf. John 8:56a].[19]
III.3-4 Glory to that One [the Father] who came to us by his Firstborn. . . .
Glory to that Hidden One, who even to the mind
is utterly imperceptible to those who investigate him.
But by his grace through [the Son's] humanity
a [divine] nature never before fathomed is [now] perceived.[20]

Ephrem magnified the birth of Jesus here, as called for by the liturgical occasion, but he did so at the expense of recognizing divine appearances prior to that event. Even though he cited John's Gospel, his emphasis here was strikingly different from John's statements that "he [Abraham] saw it and was glad," and "Isaiah . . . saw his glory" (John 8:56b; 12:41) and even from his own emphasis in the *Hymns on Virginity*, cited earlier. Ephrem could project very different images of the patriarchs and prophets depending on the liturgical occasion for which he was writing and the opponents against whom he was arguing.

Other texts could readily be cited to illustrate the ways in which early theologians played down the Old Testament appearances of the Lord. These few examples from the first to the fourth century will suffice to make the point and to show the way such adaptations were called for by new audiences, challenges, and liturgical occasions. Before leaving this part of our survey, however, some counterexamples should be mentioned in order to keep things in perspective and avoid an oversimplified picture of the early church.

SOME IMPORTANT COUNTEREXAMPLES

As long as they were not trying to downgrade Judaism, many early theologians and synods continued to teach that the Lord (or the Logos) had appeared in human form to the patriarchs and prophets (even if they did not yet know him as God's Son). In the early third century, Tertullian described the Old Testament theophanies as preparations for the incarnation:

> For he it was [the Son] who came down to converse with humans, from Adam even to the patriarchs and prophets, always from the beginning preparing beforehand, in dream and in a mirror and in an enigma [Num. 12:6, 8; 1 Cor. 13:12; 2 Cor. 3:18], that course which he was going to follow out to the end. Thus he was always also learning how, as God, to [keep] company with humans, being none other than the Word who was to be flesh [John 1:14]. (*Against Praxeas* 16)[21]

Similar treatments of Old Testament theophanies can be found in Novatian, Origen, Eusebius of Caesarea, Cyril of Jerusalem, Hilary of Poitiers, Athanasius (writing against the Arians), Didymus, and Paulinus of Nola.[22]

As late as the mid-fourth century, the Second Council of Sirmium (351 CE) explicitly condemned those who said that the one who appeared to Abraham and wrestled with Jacob (Gen. 18:1; 32:24) was not the Son, but the Father ("the unbegotten God").[23] This historic synod was directed by the Homoiousian theologian, Basil of Ancyra, who characteristically emphasized the subordination of the Son (and hence the distinction of the divine hypostases) in order to counteract Sabellianism.[24] The creed was specifically designed to counter the monarchian (unitarian) views of Bishop Photius, who viewed the Father as the only true God and had denied the preexistence of the Son. Once theologians realized that such a subordination of the Son played into the hands of the Arians (Eunomians), a very different way of interpreting the theophanies would emerge, as we shall see a bit later (Movement 3).

MOVEMENT 2: THEOPHANIES WERE PREVIEWS OF THE INCARNATION (CONTRA GNOSTICS AND MANICHEANS)

Along with this stress on the uniqueness of Jesus, there was a concurrent tendency to downplay the experiential reality of Old Testament theophanies in comparison with the incarnation.[25] This strategy was more complex than that of asserting uniqueness or novelty: it fully recognized the history of Old Testament theophanies, but differentiated them from the incarnation as figures or shadows of what was yet to come. The major challenge that occasioned this shift came from hardcore gnostics,[26] and later from the Manicheans, both of which claimed that the God of the Old Testament was a visible being, having quasi-material hands and feet, and therefore could not be the supreme God. Many gnostics also held that the human body of Jesus Christ was only apparently material (the latter view being an extreme form of docetism).

Next we shall look at two major theologians who responded to these challenges.

IRENAEUS OF LYONS

Even though he was not the first to take up the gnostic challenge, Irenaeus was the first whose writing on this subject has survived. The full title of his work was *A Refutation and Overthrow of Knowledge Falsely So-Called*, but it is generally cited by its short title *Against Heresies* (*Haer.*, written in Lyons, c. 178–89 CE).

First, regarding Old Testament theophanies: Irenaeus countered the claim of his Gnostic opponents as follows in Book Four of *Against Heresies*:

> These things did the prophets set forth in a prophetical [predictive] manner, but they did not, as some [Gnostics] allege, say that he who was seen by the prophets was a different god, the Father of all [to the contrary] being invisible [cf. John 1:18; Col. 1:15] .... The prophets, then, indicated beforehand that God would be seen [in the future] by humans. (*Haer.* 4.20.5)[27]

According to this passage, the theophanies were not appearances of an inferior, visible god—a demiurge—as his opponents had claimed. Instead, they were prophetic previews of the future incarnation. Clearly, Irenaeus was embroiled in an argument here, no doubt based on his personal experience. Accordingly, he stated the two positions in either-or terms—either the prophets said they had seen an inferior God, or they said that humans would see God at some future date (the incarnation). These alternatives leave out the possibility that the prophets really did see something in their own time, and what they saw was the one true God.[28]

The gnostic opponents were prepared to back up their claim, however. In this case, they apparently cited Isaiah's claim that he had seen the Lord with his own eyes and claimed it as proof that the God of the Hebrews was a visible being. Thus cornered, Irenaeus countered that this vision was really a spiritual matter and should not be taken to refer to literal seeing with the eyes:

> For the prophets used to prophesy, not in word alone, but in visions also . . . according to the suggestions of the Spirit. After this invisible manner, therefore did they see God, as also Isaiah says, *I have seen with my eyes the King, the Lord of hosts* [Isa. 6:5], pointing out that humans should [in the future] behold God with their eyes and hear his voice [cf. John 5:37]. In this [spiritual] manner, therefore, did they also see the Son of God as a man conversant with men [e.g., Gen. 3:9-19; 18:3, 22-33], while they prophesied what was to happen, saying that he who had not yet come was present. (*Haer.* 4.20.8)[29]

Here Irenaeus grants that Isaiah said that he saw the Lord of hosts with his own eyes, but counters that such visions were the work of the Spirit, presumably operating on the imagination of the prophet (cf. 1 Cor. 2:10-12). Accordingly, we should read his words as prophesy, in this case a preview of the eschaton when all believers will see God together (Matt. 5:8 was cited in 4.20.5). The same spiritual interpretation should be applied to biblical narratives in which the Lord appeared as a man in the Old Testament narratives and conversed with patriarchs like Abraham. We must treat these accounts as prophecies of the coming incarnation.

If Irenaeus wanted the Old Testament appearances to be less material that his gnostic opponents claimed they were, he wanted the body of Jesus to be more far material than they allowed. In fact, it was more material than the visions of the patriarchs and prophets. In Book Five of *Against Heresies*, Irenaeus referred back to the passages cited above, and continued his case:

> But I have already remarked that Abraham and the other prophets beheld him [the Lord Jesus] in a prophetic manner, foretelling in

vision what would come to pass. If, then, such a being has now appeared [only] in outward appearance . . . there has been a certain prophetic vision made to humans [in Jesus], and another advent of his must be looked for. (*Haer.* 5.1.2)[30]

We have here a second motive for Irenaeus's rethinking the Old Testament theophanies. Allowing too much continuity between those visionary appearances and the incarnation would not only play into the hands of the gnostics who declared the Old Testament deity to be corporeal, but, given the truth about the spiritual nature of those theophanies, it would suggest that the body of Jesus was a purely spiritual, divine body like the one Isaiah saw—the "heresy" of docetism.

From Irenaeus's writings, we conclude that visionary practices that had been so instrumental in the spirituality of the Second Temple and New Testament eras (and continued to be in the Rabbinic period) had become problematic and even something of an embarrassment as a result of second-century Gnosticism.

AUGUSTINE OF HIPPO AND GREGORY OF NYSSA

In the fourth century, the perceived threat of Manichaeism replaced that of Gnosticism in the minds of church leaders. Manicheans were even more sharply dualistic than gnostics (judging the world of material elements to be evil rather than simply a mistake), but they taught the same ideas that Irenaeus most feared in the gnostics: the denigration of the Lord God of Israel and the spiritualization of the body of Jesus. These twin features of Manichaeism stand out in Augustine's *Confessions* (397–401). Augustine's main purpose here was to trace the ups and downs of his spiritual development and examine them in prayer before God. As the bishop of Hippo recalled before God, his ten years as a Manichean constituted the nadir of his development. Accordingly, his *Confessions* give us one of our most realistic pictures of Manicheans and their teachings, at least, as an orthodox Christian bishop viewed them in retrospect.[31] Although the general story of Augustine's life is well known, it will help to mention a few details that might otherwise have escaped notice.

While Augustine was a student in Carthage (beginning 371 CE), he met several Manichean disciples who ridiculed the anthropomorphisms of the Old Testament: "Is God confined with a corporeal form? Does God have hair and nails?" (*Conf.* 3.12).[32] This young man had been brought up in the provincial, fundamentalist Christianity of Numidia, and nothing had prepared him for this kind of challenge (he was only nineteen or so at the time). Consequently, as

Augustine later confessed: "I thought it shameful to believe you to have the shape of the human figure and to be limited by the bodily lines of our limbs" (*Conf.* 5.19).[33] At this stage in his life, Augustine was not too clear about his way forward, but, whatever it might be, it could not lead back to the simple, literal reading of the Old Testament narratives that he was brought up with.

About a decade later (384 CE), Augustine moved to Milan, Italy, and he soon came under the influence of Bishop Ambrose and Christian Neoplatonism. Ambrose preached on the Scriptures using the anagogical (spiritualizing) method of Origen. According to this way of reading Scripture, Old Testament passages could be treated as figurative expressions of spiritual truths, particularly in cases where the plain, literal sense of a text would lead to an absurdity like the idea that the Lord God was confined to a body.[34] Other aspects of Augustine's life were already moving him toward making his peace with the church, but hearing Ambrose resolve the problem of biblical anthropomorphisms removed one of the major remaining obstacles (*Conf.* 5.24). At least, this was the way Augustine described the situation as he looked back a decade or so later (after he had become a bishop):

> "And I was glad, my God, that your one church . . . did not hold infantile follies, nor in her sound doctrine maintain that you, the Creator of all things . . . are bounded on all sides and confined within the shape of the human body." (*Conf.* 6.5)[35]

Even if Augustine's intellectual problems did not clear up quite that easily,[36] the long-term result was a clear break with any reading of the Old Testament that gave credence to the anthropic form of the God of Israel. Given the exegetical methods of the time, there was no Christian alternative to this anti-anthropomorphist tactic.

The general direction of Augustine's exegetical procedure is clear enough, but what difference would that make for particular biblical texts? Let us look at one text that played an important role in the Old Testament and in subsequent theology—the manifestation of the Lord's glory in Exodus 33–34, in which he turned his back on Moses as he passed by. This text is of particular importance in our present investigation because the theme of the Lord's "passing by" was an essential part of the performances reflected in the Gospel narrative of Jesus walking on the sea (Mark 6:48-50) as we saw in chapter 5. But first a little background on previous handlings of this text.

The Cappadocian theologian Gregory of Nyssa had carefully treated this Exodus passage in his mystical treatise *On the Life of Moses* (c. 390 CE).[37]

Gregory was primarily concerned here with the problem of the Lord having a "back" that he could turn on Moses as he "passed before him" (Exod. 33:22-23; 34:6). One could not take such a passage literally because it would confuse people about the nature of God and play right into the hands of the Manicheans, whose criticisms were well known to this Eastern church father (Does God have a backside?).[38] Fortunately, a simple solution was at hand, and even the simplest believer could understand it.

As everyone knows, servants have to watch the back of their superiors when they follow them. So the Lord was really commanding Moses to follow him, just as the disciples were commanded by the Lord Jesus when he had come in the flesh (*Life of Moses* 2.249-51). Therefore, the Lord's "passing by" Moses was not to be taken literally—what value would there have been in such a silly story? It was rather a figurative way of saying that Moses should follow the Lord, and, in that figurative sense, Moses really did behold his glory. In Gregory's own words:

> So Moses, who eagerly seeks to behold God [Exod. 33:18], is now taught how he can behold him: to follow God wherever he might lead is to behold God. His "passing by" [Exod. 33:22; 34:6] signifies his guiding the one who follows. (*Life of Moses* 2.252)[39]

Gregory gave no indication here that he was aware of Jewish and early Christian performances of Moses' encounter with the Lord.[40] In ecclesial settings, these prophetic and apocalyptic traditions had long since been superseded by the performance of gospel narratives (as discussed in ch. 5) and the liturgical ascent to the Lord in the celebration of the Eucharist.[41] Gregory's silence in this instance does not mean that such archaic traditions were not still being rehearsed—we shall see evidence to the contrary in the next section (Movement 3)—only that they were no longer encouraged by most intellectual leaders of the church, concerned as they were with the risks of heresy.

Augustine followed the lead of the Cappadocian theologians in many ways. In the case of Exodus 33–34, he certainly agreed that the literal reading, the reading that had been exploited by the Manicheans, was out of the question.[42] Instead, of allegorizing the idea of seeing the Lord's "back" as his obeying the command to follow, however, Augustine could appeal to a typological interpretation that he inherited from Irenaeus and Tertullian (either from his own reading or through Ambrose).[43] Like Rabbinic midrash, this interpretation was predicated on an obvious difficulty in the text: how could Moses see anything if he was inside a rock and covered by the Lord's hand

(Exod. 33:22)? Evidently, Moses saw nothing at that time: the Lord only passed (Exod. 34:6) and promised to reveal his glory to Moses at some future time. From the Gospel narrative we know that promise was fulfilled on the Mount of Transfiguration, when Moses and Elijah talked with the glorious Lord Jesus face to face (Mark 9:4). In other words, the "back" of the Lord in Exodus 33 was not a present, immediately accessible body, but rather a type of his future manifestation in the flesh.[44] Augustine stated it this way:

> Not unfittingly, it [Exod. 33:23] is commonly understood to prefigure the person of our Lord Jesus Christ: that his "back parts" are to be taken to be his flesh, in which he was born of the Virgin and died and rose again . . . but that his "face" was that "form of God" in which he "thought it not robbery to be equal with God" [Phil. 2:6], which no one certainly can see and live [Exod. 33:20]. (*On the Trinity* 2.17.28)[45]

Note that Augustine referred the phrase *form of God* (Phil. 2:6) to the divine nature of the Lord Jesus here. In interpreting the Lord's "back," an Old Testament anthropomorphism, as the incarnate presence here, Augustine was clearly following the tradition of earlier exegetes like Irenaeus and Tertullian.[46] However, these earlier exegetes (Tertullian, Novatian, and Origen) had understood the "form of God" in Philippians to be the pre-incarnate anthropic form.[47] Given Augustine's background and experience with the Manicheans, that part of the tradition was still too risky, and the connection of Latin Christology with the Kyriocentric visions from which it originated was further weakened.

The task of these three church theologians, Irenaeus, Gregory of Nyssa, and Augustine, was to defend the faith they had received from the first disciples of Jesus. The fact that they were free to interpret texts about the anthropic form of the Lord in such figurative ways was due to the availability of anagogical methods in their time (on the supply side). The fact that they felt *impelled* to reinterpret texts in such a sweeping way is an indication of their sense of the threat to the honor of their God coming from the criticisms of Gnostics and Manicheans: "Is God confined with a corporeal form? Does God have hair and nails?" (*Conf.* 3.12). As far as our theologians and their audiences were concerned, it was more compelling, rhetorically speaking, to challenge the heretics' exegesis than it was to try to argue with their logic.

Movement 3: The Lord is Invisible and Immutable (Contra Eunomian Arians and Anthropomorphites)

In the previous chapter, we reviewed the development of various subordination interpretations of the Lord-Jesus identification, including portrayals of Christ as a great angel who was created (rather than just begotten). At the end of that section (the subordinationist option), we noted how this usage led to Arius's denial of the Son's coeternity and consubstantiality with the Father. An ecumenical council was convened at Nicea in 325, and the overwhelming majority of attending bishops voted to condemn Arius and his teachings. Contrary to much popular writing, the Council of Nicea did not settle the issue (even less so Constantine)—no one knew at the time that Nicea would later be regarded as the first of a series of definitive ecumenical councils.

In fact, Arius was eventually reinstated by Emperor Constantine, and Arian supporters of various stripes continued to hold important bishoprics for more than half a century. The issue was largely addressed at a political level for several decades (mostly through the acquisition of bishoprics and exiling opponents). The theological aspects only came to the fore in the mid-350s, when seemingly irrefutable, dialectical arguments were developed by Arian bishops like Aëtius and Eunomius (temporarily bishop of Cyzicus). In a syllogistic nutshell, these theologians argued that all beings must belong to one of two categories: the unbegotten or unoriginate, on the one hand, and the begotten or created, on the other. As monotheists, however, Christians believe there to be only one who is unbegotten, and that is God the Father, who is also invisible and impassible. Therefore, the Son of God (and the Holy Spirit as well), must be in the originate, created category (as Arius had taught)—all the more so in that he was both visible and passible, not only in his incarnate form, but even in his "divine form" before the incarnation.[48] As a consequence (at least, for the Homoian Arians), the Son could not possibly be of the same nature as God the Father (as the fathers of Nicea had taught).[49]

This Eunomian argument clearly contravened the Nicene distinction between being begotten and being created, as if the "Creed of the Three Hundred and Eighteen Fathers" ("begotten, not made") had never been mandated. What made the Eunomian argument so compelling, however, was that it built on the ideas that had been important part of the church's discourse since the time of Justin Martyr (mid-second century). It will be helpful at this point to take another look at the subordinationism of Justin and Origen (only mentioned in ch. 8), which set up the Eunomian dilemma, and then also to note the contribution of Origen that would eventually provide the orthodox response.

JUSTIN AND ORIGEN

In his *Dialogue with Trypho the Jew*, Justin argued for the presence of the Lord Jesus in the Jewish Scriptures (the Old Testament) by pointing to the well-known theophanies and insisting that they could not have been God the Father as Jewish teachers supposed.[50] The important thing here is the reason that they could not have been sightings of the Father: because the Father is ineffable and so never descends or ascends and is never confined to a particular place as the theophanies were (*Dial.* 127.2, citing Gen. 3:8; 11:5; 18:22 as examples).

Justin's intent here was to exalt the Lord Jesus as the visible God of the Old Testament—perfectly in line with the views of the first-century disciples. As we have seen in the previous chapter, such a sharp differentiation between the Father and the Son or Word of God was common in the second and third centuries, and it was virtually canonized by Homoiousian theologians at the Second Council of Sirmium (351 CE). Whatever the intent of its exponents, this strategy would eventually play into the hands of the Eunomians, according to whose dialectic such a subordinate, visible god must be created.

The most influential theologian in the eastern Mediterranean churches was Origen, working primarily in Alexandria and maritime Caesarea, whose anagogical method of interpretation has already been noted (as background for Ambrose and Augustine in the previous section). Although he is sometimes regarded as the father of systematic theology, Origen's writings are mostly exploratory (beyond the clear teachings of the baptismal creed) and impossible to systematize. Consequently, his influence with respect to Trinitarian theology would lead in contrary directions.

On the one hand, Origen could refer to the Son as a "second God" (*deuteros theos*, a familiar phrase in Middle Platonism), or simply as a "creature" (*ktisma*) inasmuch as he was begotten by God the Father.[51] In this respect, Origen set the stage for the Arians and the Eunomians (both of whom also started out in Alexandria).

On the other hand, Origen adhered to a Platonic dichotomy between the intellectual world and the visible-material world and consequently insisted that the visible forms that the patriarchs and prophets had observed were not a true indication of the transcendent (intellectual) divine nature—only simple-minded Jews and Christians took them literally.[52] In the context of the third-century, the primary motivation for this move was to counter the objections of gnostics who claimed that the God of the Hebrews could not be the true God if he could be seen (citing John 1:18).[53] Here is how Origen put it in his influential textbook, *On First Principles* (written in Alexandria in the 220s):

It is one thing to see, another to know. To see and to be seen is a property of [spatial] bodies; to know and to be known is an attribute of intellectual existence. Whatever, therefore, is proper to [visible, spatial] bodies must not be believed either of the Father or of the Son, the relations between whom are such as pertain to the nature of deity. (*First Principles* 1.1.8)[54]

Origen understood all visible bodies to be spatial entities with shape, size, and color (cf. *First Principles* 2.4.3). The Rabbinic idea of an "imaginal body" that we invoked in chapter 1 would have been highly suspect to him. Although mystically inclined, Origen never advised his readers to direct their hearts to the imaginal body of an anthropic Deity (as in the texts cited in ch. 2, "Visionary Motifs and Practices in Rabbinic Literature"). Instead, at least for those who were capable, he advocated contemplating the Deity with a disembodied mind.[55]

Origen was dealing with the challenges of Gnosticism at the time he wrote, but his anti-anthropomorphic reading of the Old Testament would provide a needed response to the Eunomian challenge over a century later.[56]

The Eunomians and Gregory of Nazianzus

The Eunomian Arians could certainly agree with Justin and the Homoiousians that the invisible Father could not possibly have been present in Old Testament theophanies. They also agreed with the subordinationist ideas of Origen: the Son was a creature in the sense that he was not unoriginate, but rather "begotten" by the Father. According to Eunomian dialectic, however, the conclusion must be that the Father was only true, unoriginate God, as Arius had contended all along.

Aside from being impeccably logical, the Eunomian case took on added plausibility in a historical context where Christianity was striving to differentiate itself from pagan "myths," among which there was an abundance of stories about gods who had come down to earth (in more ways than one) in visible, tangible forms.[57] Just as Christianity was finally beginning to win the battle against paganism, Eunomians could claim to be more Christian than their Nicene opponents.[58]

Under these circumstances, belief in the Lord-Jesus identification on which the Nicene faith was based would not stand up to criticism. The only way to salvage the fruit of that identification, in which salvation was located by most Christians, was to abandon the connection to visible theophanies. Here is where Origen's idea of an intellectual perception of the Son (as well as the

Father) provided the anti-anthropomorphite interpretation needed to counter this part of the Eunomian challenge (the inescapable "begottenness" of the Son was another matter).

Historians refer to advocates of this new interpretation of the faith of Nicea as "neo-Nicene" to recognize these changed circumstances and the way they shifted theological language (if not substance) away from the original "Creed of the Three Hundred and Eighteen Fathers." A few examples from the Greek fathers and from Augustine in the Latin West will illustrate this new trend.

The most influential exponent of neo-Nicene theology was the Cappadocian Gregory of Nazianzus who had been commissioned by Emperor Theodosius to assist in the attempt to eliminate all forms of Arianism from the church by providing a new, more compelling theological framework (379–380).[59] A major part of this effort was the delivery of five "Theological Orations" (Or. 27-31), in which Gregory definitively articulated the neo-Nicene view of the Trinity and fiercely defended it against Eunomian dialectics (as well as Homoian positivism).[60]

The pivotal biblical text on which Gregory based his foray was the account of Moses (partial) vision of God on Mount Sinai in Exodus 33–34. We have already seen how Gregory of Nyssa interpreted Moses' seeing the "back" of the anthropic form in terms of the Lord's guiding and Moses' following (Movement 2, against the Manicheans). In his Second Theological Oration (Or. 28), Gregory of Nazianzus took a different tack and identified the "back" of the Lord as the immanent energy of the triune God—the glory that fills heaven and earth. As this shift in focus from the individual hypostases to their common energy would become a new tenet of Trinitarian theology for coming generations, it is worthwhile noting exactly how Gregory made his move.[61]

As was common for theologians of his time, Gregory began his Second Theological Oration with a prayer for illumination. Normally that prayer would have been addressed to God the Father (or to God and the Lord Jesus), requesting the guidance of the Spirit.[62] Gregory began in much the same vein, asking "that the Father may be well pleased, and the Son may help us, and the Holy Spirit may inspire us," but then shifted the focus with the following correction: "or rather that one illumination may come upon us from the one God, one in diversity, diverse in unity" (28.1).[63] In view of the general principle that the "order of prayer" establishes the "order of theology" (ordo orandi, ordo credendi), Gregory was already alerting his congregation to a major shift in Trinitarian theology—one that would avoid the problems raised by the visibility of the Son prior to his incarnation.

Along these lines, Gregory proceeded to rehearse Moses' ascent of Sinai for his congregation. Although this ascent had been described as climbing a mountain in the typical Exodus narrative (conflating Exod. 19, 24, and 33) and also in its New Testament rehearsals (esp., Luke 9:28, 34), it was often taken as a type of a mystic ascent into heaven by early Jewish and Christian exegetes.[64] Accordingly, Gregory made a point of starting out with daring boldness:

> I was running to lay hold on God, and thus I went up into the mountain and drew aside the curtain of the cloud [Exod. 24:18a; Lev. 16:2, 12][65] and entered away from matter and material things, and as far as I could I withdrew within myself. (Or. 28.3)[66]

Before continuing with this oral rehearsal, several things should be noted here. In one sense, Gregory was continuing the performative approach to scriptural traditions with which we began our study in chapter 1. Without reading from the book of Exodus, or even quoting it directly, he reenacted the experience of Moses, conflating several texts about Moses and Aaron as he did so (cf. Heb. 12:18-24),[67] and led his congregation in the performance of their joint vision just as earlier prophetic and apostolic leaders had done. However, Gregory was also changing the terms of the performance in several ways.

One way was that Gregory picked up on Origen's anagogical (anti-anthropomorphite) method of exegesis. The cloud curtain that we are to imagine ourselves passing through here is no longer a cosmic veil between heaven and earth (as in Heb. 9:24; 10:22). Instead, it is the chasm between the phenomenal and intelligible worlds and can be crossed only by the cognitive exercise of a disembodied mind ("away from matter . . . within myself") that Origen had introduced into Christian exegesis (Origen's "intellectual existence").

Another important change here has to do with the object of the performance: Gregory did not aspire to see the Lord's face, as Moses was believed to have done, or to see one of the three hypostases of the Trinity. His stated objective here was to "lay hold on" or "comprehend" the triune Godhead (hōs theon katalēpsomenos).[68] But Gregory knew, and most of his listeners knew, that his own approach to the Godhead was far more tentative. After an initial reaction of surprise, they would catch on.

At one level, Gregory was clearly parodying the Eunomians (here typified as "savage beasts"), who claimed to define the divine nature in human language (as "unoriginate")—hence the use of the provocatively aggressive verbs, run and lay hold (on God!). In another, more immediate sense, however, Gregory was warning members of his own congregation against taking traditional vision-performances at face value: hence the anagogical application of the biblical terms "mountain," "curtain," and "cloud," which we have already noted.

We can only guess at Gregory's target audience here, but the meditative performance he is critiquing could well match some of the (self-styled) "Aarons" or "initiates" (*mystoi*), whom he called out from the pulpit (*Or.* 28.2, 3).[69] Let us leave this avenue of inquiry aside for the moment—the topic will come up again when we turn to the monks of Egypt. The main point for now, is that Gregory was initiating a reform of oral performance whereby what had once been imaginal and anthropomorphite now became imageless and purely cognitive.

Returning to Gregory's imaginary ascent, we find him pretending to look up (within himself) toward God, and then being humbled (good performative stuff):

> And, when I looked up, I scarce saw the "back parts" of God, although I was sheltered by the "rock" [Exod. 33:19-23], the Word that was made flesh for us. And, when I looked a little closer, I saw, not the first and unmingled nature, known [only] to itself—to the Trinity, I mean; not that which abides within the first veil and is hidden by the cherubim, but only that nature which at last even reaches to us. And this is, as far as I can learn, the majesty, or, as holy David calls it, "the glory" which is manifested among the creatures [Pss. 8:1; 19:1; cf. Isa. 6:3], which it has produced and governs. (*Or.* 28.3 cont.)[70]

Again, we see Gregory's anagogical treatment of the terms in Exodus 33, "back" and "rock," and also of the cherubim whose wings hid the diving figure who was seated in the tabernacle (Exod. 25:20; 37:9; cf. Isa. 6:2 JPST). Still, the main point that his congregation would have taken away with them was that the nature (*physis*) of the Trinity was beyond the keenest vision of even the most spiritual humans, even beyond that of the angels[71]—their "unmingled nature" (unmingled with the phenomenal world) was only known to themselves. Even with the benefit of the incarnation ("the Word that was made flesh for us"), all we can hope to get is a glimpse of the "back parts" of the Trinity, that is, majesty of God or "the glory which is manifested among the creatures."

What Moses saw, according to Gregory (and the same applied to the Apostle Paul[72]), was neither the Father (as Irenaeus sometimes claimed) nor the Son (Justin et al.), but the divine energy that is reflected in all of creation.

The very ground on which Eunomian and Homoian arguments were based was thereby eliminated: the Son is as immaterial and invisible as the Father (so also is the Spirit). Therefore, he is in no way inferior to the Father, even if he is "begotten" within the divine substance (considered more carefully in Or. 29). The Lord-Jesus identification was secure (now couched in terms of the Nicene *homoousion*). The price of this security was jettisoning the very kind of Kyriocentric vision performance from which that identification had originated and that it was intended to codify.[73]

Gregory and his Cappadocian associates set the agenda for the ultimate victory of Nicene orthodoxy over its chief rivals, the Eunomian Arians. Similar tactics were used by major Eastern theologians like John Chrysostom and Evagrius Ponticus, and in the West by Ambrose and Augustine. Chrysostom wrote a treatise against them (*Against the Anomians*, 886–87 CE), and Augustine devoted a major part of his treatise *On the Trinity* (399–419 CE) to their arguments.[74] The variety of writings on the subject and their exegetical and practical contexts (never to be conflated) could fill a book by themselves. I take the liberty of pointing out some features that we have not seen already, before concluding with a look at the other side of the argument, as represented by certain monastic groups in Egypt.

JOHN CHRYSOSTOM AND EVAGRIUS PONTICUS

John Chrysostom was less enamored than his Cappadocian contemporaries with anagogical readings of Scripture, but he was also a great orator. Like many orators of his time, he relied on the force of sharp distinctions, particularly the distinction, inherited from Origen, between the phenomenal and the divine. Over and over, he stated that material bodies are entirely different from the divine substance: the material is confined in space and consists of divisible parts, whereas the truly divine is without finite form and absolutely simple. With regard to Old Testament theophanies, Chrysostom concluded that the perplexing variety of forms and figures that the prophets described were only ways in which God likened (*hōmoiōthēn*) himself (citing Hos. 12:10 LXX)—in other words, they were figures of (divine) speech.[75]

Chrysostom's repeated use of the verb *homoioō* ("make like," "compare") can best be understood against the background in which Homoian Arians had declared that the Son was only "like" (*homoios*) the Father, thereby driving in a theological wedge between the two divine figures. Chrysostom was effectively pulling out that linguistic wedge and redeploying it between the undivided

Trinity and the Old Testament theophanies (and thereby between the Old Testament theophanies and the incarnation).

Evagrius Ponticus was more of a contemplative theologian than an orator and was less given to sharp rhetorical contrasts. Still, he began his career working with Gregory of Nazianzus and served in Constantinople during the very years that the latter was delivering his Theological Orations (379–81 CE). Evagrius always regarded Gregory as his primary living teacher. Given his spiritual bent, he may well have been one of the "Aarons" or "initiates" that Gregory had challenged in his Second Theological Oration (*Or.* 28.2, 3).

Evagrius was later vested as a monk, and he spent the rest of his life praying and writing in the monastic settlements of the Scetis Valley (southeast of Alexandria) and the Nitrian Desert (slightly further to the east). He gave us the first written *apothegmata* ("sayings" or "maxims"), which focused on the practice of prayer, a form best known today from the later *Apophthegmata Patrum* ("Sayings of the [Desert] Fathers").

Evagrius also left us his correspondence with other monks and nuns, in which he regularly diagnosed demonic influences that interfered with the pure contemplation of God—pure, that is, from all visual images.[76] Among these spiritual diagnoses, we find repeated references to people being deluded by visions that they mistakenly ascribed to the visible form of God. As you pray, Evagrius warned his confidants, you are to:

> Beware . . . that some unusual and strange form appears so as to lead you into the presumptuous thought that God is actually situated there as in a place. This is calculated [by the demons] to persuade you . . . that God is something quantitative. But God is without quantity and without all outward form. (*Chapters on Prayer* 67)[77]

The anti-anthropomorphic theology that underlies this sage advice is familiar to us from the work of Origen, Gregory of Nazianzus, and John Chrysostom: God is not bound by a form of any kind, and even the most spiritual prophets or monks that ever lived could not see him as he truly is.

Two things are distinctive about Evagrius's warning. First is the accusation that such "unusual and strange forms" were suggested by demons (made explicit in *Chapters on Prayer* §§72, 73, 115[78]). Origen and Gregory of Nazianzus had wondered whether the visions of the prophets were imprinted on their minds, but the context then was primarily exegetical and the imprinting was done by God himself. What Evagrius did here was to declare the era of true prophetic visions over and done with[79] and to attribute any further semblances of such visions to demons, who substituted smoke for true light (*Chapters on Prayer* §68[80]). The very heavy-handedness of this tactic indicates that Evagrius probably knew of monks and nuns who aspired to the visionary states of the prophets, much as Gregory's "Aarons" and "initiates" and perhaps the earlier Evagrius, had done. From Evagrius's point of view, such a practice was inconsistent with the anti-anthropomorphic theology of his teacher Gregory and could lead these wayward monastics into Arianism. As we shall see in a moment, the Egyptian desert was full of such backward visionaries.

Another relevant feature of Evagrius's warning is his reference to people locating God, as if God were "in a place." In the context of monastic prayer, such directed concentration must have been something like the *kavanah* of the Rabbis (studied in chapter 2). In this connection, it should be noted that Origen and his fourth-century followers associated the idea that God had an anthropic form with "Jewish fables" (from Titus 1:14).[81] In view of the evidence we have reviewed for imaginal prayer in pietistic circles of early Judaism, this ridicule may well have reflected Origen's awareness of such practices among his Jewish associates as well as similar practices among pietistic (simple-minded) churchgoers. Evagrius followed Origen's lead and updated it to address the practices of Egyptian monastics.

We have seen the demonic "smoke," but where was the fire? Is it possible that the sort of Kyriocentric vision that we found in apocalyptic and early Christian literature was still being performed in some monastic circles (as it was among the Rabbis)?

JOHN CASSIAN AND THE EGYPTIAN MONKS

The clearest evidence of Kyriocentric visions is found in another of their anti-anthropomorphite critics, John Cassian. Cassian made a tour of the monasteries of Lower Egypt (the Scetis Valley) in the late 380–90s, during which time he was clearly influenced by Evagrius. Later he worked under John Chrysostom, the bishop of Constantinople at the time, and eventually he returned to southern France, founded the first cenobitic (communal) monasteries in that area (c. 415 CE), and wrote treatises based on his learning.

Cassian's treatise *On the Cenobite Institutions* (early 420s) dealt largely with theology and exegesis. Here Cassian repeated the familiar objections to views of God having a human form, with limbs "ordered like a man's," and, taking a leaf out of Chrysostom's works, insisted that the Deity is absolutely "simple and uncompounded." Accordingly, biblical references to such limbs must never be taken literally, but rather interpreted anagogically as ways of describing various powers and attributes of the Godhead (*Inst.* 8.3–4).[82]

In addition to this theological frame of interpretation, Cassian wrote up his notes from his Egyptian travels with narratives concerning his "Conferences" (*Conlationes*) with leading ascetics and spiritual directors (the first ten books were written c. 426). Of greatest relevance to the history we are tracing are his accounts of disputes that had taken place in the late fourth-century monastic world—particularly what has since become known as the "Anthropomorphite controversy." Here we read that the Bishop of Alexandria, Theophilus, had sent around an annual Festal Letter (399 CE) in which he attacked the "heresy of the Anthropomorphites," particularly with regard to the interpretation of Genesis 1:26 ("Let us make humankind in our image"). At this stage of his career, Theophilus was following the Alexandrian, Origenist tradition, according to which the "image of God" related to the intellectual nature, rather than the visible form, of humans.[83] For those of us who are used to the idea of an intellectual image of God in our minds, the response to Theophilus's letter may be a surprise.

Cassian informs us that the monks to whom this festal letter was read aloud reacted with great bitterness, thinking that the bishop contradicted the clear teaching of Scripture on the creation of Adam in the image and likeness of God. In other words, the monks at this meeting were avid Anthropomorphites. In fact, they took a vote and issued a formal decree, saying "that the aforesaid Bishop ought to be abhorred . . . as tainted with heresy of the worst kind" (*Conferences* 10.2).[84]

These last words alert us to the fact that there was more at stake here than quibbles about a particular biblical text or idea. Like Evagrius, these monks were concerned with prayer and contemplation more than with exegesis or rhetoric—in the performative sense they were very much in the spirit of the early disciples. We already have an inkling of their prayer practices from Gregory of Nazianzus's description of the "Aarons" and "initiates" in Constantinople—they aspired to "look up" into heaven and see the anthropic form of the Lord on his throne. Before continuing with Cassian's epic of the Anthropomorphite controversy, therefore, we need to look further afield in the Egyptian desert to provide some context for these practices.

Fortunately, there are several references in contemporary monastic literature to the kind of imaged prayer that Theophilus and Cassian were attacking. Some of the clearest descriptions come from the cenobite monasteries that were founded by Pachomius in Upper Egypt (Tabennisi). Pachomius lived in the first half of the fourth century (d. 346), but the writings themselves date from the late fourth or early fifth century (a two generation gap similar to that between the death of Jesus and the Gospels). Although the historical veracity of these texts can be questioned as to specific individuals and events, there are several common themes running through them that must antedate the texts in which they are found.

We read, for example, that Pachomius was praying alone once, when he fell into a trance and saw the Lord Jesus seated on a throne—not an invisible, spiritual throne in heaven, it seems, but a material one that stood in the monastery's prayer hall (the *synaxis*) like the cherubim throne in the temple (Exod. 25:22; Lev. 16:2; passim).[85] This description of visionary, imaged prayer centered in an anthropic form sounds very much like the practice that Gregory was attacking. But was it accidental or was it intentional, based on the rehearsal of Old Testament models as in the Second Temple and New Testament examples we have studied (chs. 2, 5)?

In the same Pachomian source, we read that the abbot who succeeded Pachomius, named Theodore, had similar visions of the Lord Jesus in the monastery church. In this case, the church was apparently viewed as a doorway to the heavens, much as the inner sanctum of the Jerusalem temple had been. Here we are told that:

> [Theodore's] thoughts were always in heaven beholding the glory of God [cf. 2 Cor. 3:18]. As the psalmist David said: "I began by seeing the Lord before me at all times, positioned at my right hand that I might not be shaken" [Ps. 16:8]. When he came to the doorway of the church, he looked in and saw an apparition [of the Lord whom he was seeking]. "Where his feet were," there appeared to him "something like a sparking sapphire" [Exod. 24:10b], and he was unable to look at his face [Exod. 33:20] because of the great light which unceasingly flashed forth from him [2 Cor. 4:6; Acts 22:6]."
> (*Bohairic Life of Pachomius* 184) [86]

This visionary account is similar to the one about Pachomius, except that it sets the scene in the church, apparently in a congregation of monks, rather than in a private setting.[87] The citations of Psalm 16 and two major Exodus theophanies, along with possible allusions to the visions of Paul, indicate the performative nature of the practice underlying this fascinating text. The sequel also makes it clear that Theodore took on the role of Moses in relation to his fellow monks.[88]

It is not necessary to assume that these inter-performative citations were handed down by continuous oral performance from the times of the apocalypticists and the first disciples of Jesus. We understand that biblical texts were available to the monasteries in codex form, and much of the monk's prayer life was devoted to meditation based on a hearing of those texts (*Conferences* 2.5 *ad finem*).[89] Nonetheless, there are significant similarities of this description of monastic praxis to the performance of prophetic visions among apocalypticists, rabbis, and early disciples as illustrated in chapters 2 and 5. Particularly striking is the use of Psalm 16:8, "I keep the Lord always before me; because he is at my right hand, I shall not be moved," as a meditative template. This is exactly the same Psalm verse cited by Peter in Acts 2:25 (in preparation for baptism) and by the Jewish pietists as described by the Rabbis (*b. Sanh.* 22a).

From these brief passages, we learn that in spite of the fact that such visions of the Lord had long since been narrativized in ecclesial contexts, they were still rehearsed in monastic circles, especially in Egypt, particularly in connection with prophetic visions and Psalm verses. In the eyes of Bishop Theophilus and John Cassian, as we shall see, such archaic, pre–Christian practices were to be discouraged as a "state of Jewish weakness" (*Conferences* 10.6, yet to be discussed).[90]

If we turn back now to John Cassian's account of the Anthropomorphite controversy among the monks in Lower Egypt, we learn how the church officials from Alexandria and Cappadocia tried to suppress such practices. Recall that the majority of monks had officially rejected the Festal Letter of Bishop Theophilus. Cassian singled out one particular monk named Sarapion, who evidently made a deep impression on him. Sarapion was an old man, respected for his "longstanding strictness of life"—just the kind of person that Cassian had come to learn from. To the contrary, however, we are told that his ignorance with regard doctrine was a major obstacle to ecclesial reform ("a stumbling block to all who held the true faith").[91] Sarapion was so ignorant, in fact, that he thought the Bishop's anti-anthropomorphite teaching was a complete novelty, one that was "not ever known to or handed down by his predecessors" (*Conferences* 10.3).[92] From the standpoint of Theophilus and Cassian, what was clearly needed was a crash course in neo-Nicene theology.

And a crash course is what they got. Cassian went on to relate that the Nitrian monks were visited by a deacon named Photinus, who had come from Cappadocia. We can tell that Photinus was trained in the anti-anthropomorphite neo-Nicene theology described earlier because he was specially welcomed by the local Abbot (Paphnutius) as one who could "confirm the faith" as stated in the Festal Letter of Theophilus, particularly with regard to the true, spiritual meaning of the "image and likeness" of God in Genesis 1:26 (*Conferences* 10.3).

Deacon Photinus promptly informed the literal-minded monks that all the respected leaders of the churches understood God to be "incorporeal and uncompounded and simple." Therefore, God was not "comprised in a human form and likeness" that could have served as a template for the creation of the first human being. The wording of this message undoubtedly reflected the official teaching of the neo-Nicene theologians with whom Bishop Theophilus and Cassian were trying to align themselves at the time.

The most revealing part of the story is the monks' response to this message. Previously, they had reacted hostilely to the Festal Letter of Theophilus, evidently encouraged in their resistance by the elderly monk Sarapion. This time, however, Cassian tells us that, after lengthy discussion, Brother Sarapion was "shaken by the numerous and very weighty assertions of this most learned man and was drawn to the faith of the Catholic tradition" (*Conferences* 10.3).[93] The last remnants of the Anthropomorphite heresy in Lower Egypt were being won over—won over intellectually speaking, at least. The neo-Nicene leadership had, at least, succeeded in changing the "order of theology" (*ordo credendi*).

In the immediate sequel, we are informed that the time arrived for the monks to pray, which, of course, they were prepared to do. This time, however, Brother Sarapion was completely disoriented due to the fact that "the anthropomorphic image of the Godhead which he used to set before himself in prayer was banished from his heart" (*Conferences* 10.3).[94] At length, the poor man burst out into tears, threw himself down on the ground, and groaned: "Alas! Wretched man that I am! They have taken away my God from me, and I have now none to lay hold of, and I do not know whom to worship and address" (*Conferences* 10.3).[95] It turned out that it was easier to change the "order of theology" than it was to change the "order of prayer" (*ordo orandi*).

Clearly, Cassian's narrative is tendentious: Sarapion's alleged desire to "lay hold" of God (*quem teneam*) in prayer[96] is just like that of the "initiates" (*mystoi*) that Gregory of Nazianzus had parodied in his Second Theological Oration. Yet, given the material we have covered on oral performance and spiritual concentration (*kavanah*), it would be difficult to argue that Cassian simply made up the story in order to prove a point. For one thing, the description of Sarapion's outburst strikes us as the kind of experience that would have made a deep impression on Cassian's mind—he stated quite openly that he was "terribly disturbed" (*valde permoti*) as a result and that he had fallen into "no small despair" (*prava desperatio*).[97] More importantly, the language of this obscure monk is very much the same as attributed to Abbot Theodore, who similarly "set the Lord before him" (Ps. 16:8) and envisioned the divine glory as an Anthropos (Exod. 24:10) when he prayed.[98] This accumulation of evidence makes it more than likely that the Brother Sarapion's performative approach to prayer was related to that of earlier figures that we have studied and not unlike that in the context of which the first disciples first saw the Lord as Jesus (*Kyrios Iēsous*).

Cassian concludes this part of his narrative by describing how his conversations with Abbot Isaac reassured him of the correctness of the neo-Nicene theology. The problem, the Abbot explained, was that Sarapion had lived in relative isolation and had not been instructed in "catholic doctrine" about the ineffable substance of the Godhead. As a result of his simplicity, Sarapion made the same mistake as the pagans by constructing an idol, albeit only an idol in his mind.[99] This error landed him in the heresy of the Anthropomorphites, who maintained that the infinite and simple substance of the Godhead is fashioned like the human being described in Genesis 1:26 (*Conferences* 10.5).

Like other neo-Nicene theologians, Abbot Isaac was jealous for the transcendent dignity of the divine nature common to all three members of the Trinity. Like Gregory of Nazianzus and Evagrius, he also wanted to reform the prayer life of his monks.[100] Rather than visualizing an anthropic form, they should aspire to complete purity—purity, that is, from all bounded, visual images, "which is a sin even to speak of." They should not even hang on to things they remember hearing about God's actions in history (*Conferences* 10.5 *ad finem*).[101] Such pure minds would be delivered from the state of "Jewish weakness" (*Judaica infirmitas*) and thereby enabled to see Jesus properly. As Abbot Isaac went on to explain, some minds will only see him as he was in his state of humiliation (our first portrait), but others will see him as he will appear in divine glory (second portrait). In the latter case, they must see the glory of his face with the eyes of their minds and "no longer after the flesh" (cf. 2 Cor. 5:16). In other words, what the pure mind sees is not a figure of any kind, but rather the formless godhead of Christ, like that seen by Moses and Elijah and by the apostles in the "lofty mountain of solitude" (the Mount of Transfiguration).[102] Those Christians who live in towns, and so are unable to achieve this monastic degree of solitude, can still see him in their prayers, but not with the same degree of clarity (*Conferences* 10.6).

In this foundational work of Western monasticism, Cassian constructed a world in which the eternal Godhead relates to humans primarily as disembodied minds (the sacraments were not in view in this monastic context). There is no "middle world" like the storied heavens of apocalyptic cosmology or the "imaginal world" of the Rabbis. The visions that had originated in corporate, performative settings, and then described in scriptural texts, were now interpreted as acts of individual, conceptual contemplation.

CONCLUSION REGARDING MARGINALIZATION OF THE ANTHROPIC FORM OF THE LORD

Even though the practice of envisioning the divine form would be continued through the Middle Ages and into modern times (particularly in visual art), this early history rounds out our limited investigation in two ways. We have seen how theological challenges led leaders and teachers of the church to marginalize the traditional practice of envisioning the divine form in the performance of prophetic visions. This knowledge helps us to understand why this devotional practice is so little known to us today (in spite of icons and religious art). It can also help us to factor out our prejudice against such imaging when we try to recover the beliefs and practices of the first disciples and their Jewish coreligionists.

Secondly, the material reviewed here has revealed that church leaders were well aware of such practices as late as at the turn of the fourth (to the fifth) century. In trying to discredit such practices as "Jewish fables," church leaders unwittingly gave us evidence of the performative affinities of their prophetic and apostolic predecessors. Further study would show that fifth and sixth-century leaders like Cyril of Alexandria, Theodoret of Cyrrhus, and Gregory the Great would continue to polemicize against them as well. So there is ample evidence of pietistic circles of this sort within the Great Church (particularly in monastic movements), just as there is in Rabbinic Judaism (ch. 2). Three centuries of polemics against Judaizers, gnostics, Manicheans, Arians, Eunomians, and Anthropomorphites had not entirely erased the performative foundations of deity Christology.

Notes

1. A good example of this anti-anthropomorphism is the great hymn, "Immortal, Invisible, God Only Wise," by Walter Chalmers Smith (*Hymns of Christ and the Christian Life* [London: Macmillan, 1867]). On a more academic note, Old Testament theologian Edmond Jacob described passages about YHWH appearing in visible, human form as "naive" and even "crude" and saw the fruit of "theological reflection" in the alternative belief that God is invisible and "essentially spiritual"; Jacob, *Theology of the Old Testament*, trans. Arthur W. Heathcote and Philip J. Allcock (London: Hodder & Stoughton, 1958), 74.

2. Among the first scholars to question this disregard for biblical anthropomorphisms and to differentiate literary figures of speech from the concrete human form of the Lord in Scripture were James Barr, "Theophany and Anthropomorphism in the Old Testament," VTSup 7 (1959): 31–38; and Ulrich Mauser, "Image of God and Incarnation," *Interpretation* 24 (1970), 336–56.

3. I am using the term *incarnation* here for convenience without prejudice as to its timing (as discussed in ch. 7).

4. For good overviews, see Angela Russell Christman, "What Did Ezekiel See? Patristic Exegesis of Ezekiel 1 and Debates about God's Incomprehensibility," *Pro Ecclesia*, 8 (1999):

338–63; Christman, *"What Did Ezekiel See?" Christian Exegesis of Ezekiel's Vision of the Chariot from Irenaeus to Gregory the Great,* The Bible in Ancient Christianity 4 (Leiden: Brill, 2005); Robin M. Jensen, *Face to Face: Portraits of the Divine in Early Christianity* (Minneapolis: Fortress Press, 2001); Jensen, "Theophany and the Invisible God in Early Christian Theology and Art," in *God in Early Christian Thought: Essays in Memory of Lloyd G. Patterson,* VCSup 94, ed. Andrew B. McGowan, Brian E. Daley, and Timothy J. Gaden (Leiden: Brill, 2009), 271–96.

5. In Heb. 11:27, the author states that Moses acted by faith "as seeing the Unseen One" (*aoraton hōs orōn*), a clear example of faith replacing sight (cf. 11:1, 6, 13).

6. According to Heb. 9:24, the abode of the Deity was never in the Temple, but rather in heaven (cf. 1:3; 8:1; 9:12; 10:12; 12:2, 23).

7. The writer of Hebrews saw himself following the example of Jesus as the pioneer (Heb. 6:19-20; 12:2). It is not likely that he assumed the persona of Jesus, however, because his goal was to "see Jesus" (as Messiah and high priest) in heaven (Heb. 2:9; 12:22-24).

8. Michael D. Swartz, "Judaism and the Idea of Ancient Ritual Theory," in *Jewish Studies at the Crossroads of Anthropology and History: Authority, Diaspora, Tradition,* Jewish Culture and Contexts, ed. Ra'anan S. Boustan, Oren Kosansky, and Marina Rustow (Philadelphia: University of Pennsylvania Press, 2011), 294–317, 404–10 (313–16).

9. Leonel L. Mitchell, "The Alexandrian Anaphora of St. Basil of Caesarea: Ancient Source of 'A Common Eucharistic Prayer,'" *ATR* 58 (1976): 194–206 (199).

10. Bart D. Ehrman, trans., *The Apostolic Fathers,* 2 vols., LCL 24-25 (Cambridge, MA: Harvard University Press, 2003), 1:247.

11. Ibid., 1:249.

12. Ibid., 1:315.

13. Although Ignatius certainly recognized Jesus' identity as divine Lord, his confessional formulas often stressed his second identity as the Messiah who first appeared on earth when born of Mary and who was eventually crucified, e.g., *Eph.* 18:2; 20:2; *Trall.* 9:1 (*Smyrn.* 1:1 is more nuanced in celebrating the "cross of the Lord Jesus Christ" and then describing "our Lord" as descended from David according to the flesh, born of a virgin, crucified under Pontius Pilate). Ignatius's emphasis on Jesus as Messiah comports well with his celebration and defense of the crucifixion (discussed in ch. 7, "How to Avoid Proclaiming a Dying and Rising God").

14. ET in Joseph P. Smith, trans., *St. Irenaeus: Proof of the Apostolic Preaching,* ACW 16 (New York: Newman, 1952), 75.

15. For example, Justo L. González, *The Story of Christianity,* 2 vols. (San Francisco: Harper, 1984), 1:68; González, *Christian Thought Revisited: Three Types of Theology* (Nashville: Abingdon, 1989), 30.

16. J. K. Elliott, ed., *The Apocryphal New Testament: A Collection of Apocryphal Christian Literature in an English Translation* (Oxford: Clarendon, 1993), 414.

17. For instance, Athanasius's *Orations against the Arians* (356–62 CE) 3:12, 14 on the appearances to Jacob, Moses, and Isaiah.

18. Kathleen E. McVey, trans., *Ephrem the Syrian: Hymns,* Classics of Western Spirituality, (New York: Paulist, 1989), 386–89. Marcionites rejected the Old Testament as making statements that were unworthy of the true God.

19. Ibid., 71. Elsewhere in this hymn, Ephrem stated that Moses and Elijah had not seen the Lord (on earth) prior to his incarnation. Contrast Ephrem, *On Genesis* 16.1, 3, where Gen. 18:1-5 was directly in view (rather than John 8:56a) and Abraham really did see the Lord.

20. McVey, trans., *Ephrem the Syrian,* 83–84. The phrase "those who investigate him" evidently referred to the Eunomian Arians, a challenge that will be considered later in this chapter (Movement 3). Much the same stress on the novelty of God's appearing (*theophaneia*) to human beings was made by Gregory of Nazianzus in his own Epiphany sermon (*Or.* 38.2, 3), delivered in 380–81 CE.

21. Ernest Evans, trans. *Tertullian's Treatise against Praxeas* (London: SPCK, 1948), 153 (adapted). Tertullian specifically cited the appearances of the Lord to Adam, Noah, Abraham,

Jacob, Moses, Isaiah, and Ezekiel (§§14–16). He made a similar point in *Against Marcion* 2.27; 3.9; cf. Jensen, "Theophany and the Invisible God," 281.

22. Novatian, *On the Trinity* 18, 19; Origen, *Comm. on John* 6.9, 25; *Hom. on Joshua* 6.2-3; Eusebius, *History of the Church* 1.2.4-10;*Demonstration* 5.9-11, 17-19; 7.1, 16; Cyril of Jerusalem, *Catechetical Lectures* 10.6-8, 27; Hilary, *On the Trinity* 4.27, 31-33; 12.46-47; Athanasius, *Orations Against the Arians* 3.12, 14; Didymus of Alexandria (attr.), *Comm. (Enerratio) on Jude 4–5*; Paulinus of Nola, *Ep.* 49.12. Origen is a special case (to be discussed later): he regarded the visible aspect of the theophanies to be analogous to the visible aspect of the Christian sacraments; *Hom. on John* 1.37.

23. Sirmian anathemas 14 and 15, *apud* Hilary, *On the Councils* 49 (*NPNF2*, 9:18a); cf. Epiphanius, *Panarion* 71. This creedal statement (traditionally numbered the "First" of Sirmium) is not to be confused with the creed of the Third Council of Sirmium of 357 (the "Sirmian blasphemy") or the Fourth ("Dated") Creed of 359, both of which were explicitly anti-Nicene; see J. N. D. Kelly, *Early Christian Creeds*, 3rd ed. (London: Longman, 1972), 281–82, 285–92; Mark Weedman, "Hilary and the Homoiousians: Using New Categories to Map the Trinitarian Controversy," *CH* 76 (2007): 491–510 (498–99). The positive idea in the Sirmian anathemas was identical to that of earlier theologians like Justin and Irenaeus, which were directed against Judaism (e.g., Justin; *1 Apol.* 63; Irenaeus, *Haer.* 4.7.4; Irenaeus, *Demonstration* 45).

24. Homoiousians (also spelled "Homoeousians") were moderates who held that the Son was "of like substance" (*homoiousios*) with the Father, or "like the Father in all things" including the divine substance, for example, Cyril of Jerusalem, *Catechetical Lecture* 4.7.

25. Irenaeus's hermeneutic had good precedent. On the Christian side, Justin stated the hermeneutical principle that all of the prophets' statements were in the form of parables and types that disguised the truth (*Dial.* 90.2). Rabbinic midrash also sometimes referred prophetic visions to foreseen future realities. For example, Jacob's vision of the "gate of heaven" in Gen. 28:17 was referred to the Jerusalem temple in *Gen. R.* 69:7.

26. Using the term *gnostics* here is simply a way of identifying the opponents against whom heresiologists like Irenaeus argued. There never existed a coherent gnostic theology or an organized gnostic church (in contrast to the Marcionites and Manicheans).

27. *ANF* 1:488-9 (modified). Irenaeus cited John 1:18 in the following section (4.20.6).

28. A "close reading" of this quote would leave the careful reader free to infer that the invisible God had rendered himself visible in some way, but Irenaeus's style was clearly polarizing and polemical.

29. *ANF* 1:490a (modified). A similar point was made by Irenaeus in *Demonstration of the Apostolic Preaching* 12, 44, where Gen. 3:9-19; 18:3, 22–33 were actually cited.

30. *ANF* 1:527a (modified).

31. Manichean denigration of the Old Testament God as having a human form and being obsessed with material affairs is described in *Conf.* 3.12; 5.19, 21; 6.4; 9.11). Their docetic Christology and its effect on Augustine's spiritual struggles is described in *Conf.* 5.16, 20; 9.6, 9.

32. Henry Chadwick, trans. *Saint Augustine: Confessions* (Oxford: Oxford University Press, 1991), 43.

33. Ibid., 85.

34. Origen never discounted the literal, "historical" interpretation of Scripture, but he often relegated it to a lower level of understanding, suitable only for simple-minded believers, particularly when it led to theological difficulties; see, for example, in *Hom. on Joshua* 6.2-3 (probably Caesarea, late 230s CE); *Comm. on John* 6.19; 32 (Caesarea, late 240s). In these (relatively late) writings, Origen attributed the theophanies directly to the Lord Jesus.

35. Chadwick, trans., *Confessions*, 88.

36. When Ambrose recommended that he read the prophet Isaiah, Augustine could not get past the first verse, "The vision of Isaiah . . . which he saw" (Isa. 1:1), so he "put it on one side to be

resumed when I had more practice in the Lord's style of language"; *Conf.* 9.13; Chadwick, trans., *Confessions*, 163.

37. For a comprehensive treatment of Gregory's exegesis of Exod. 33 in comparison to Philo's, see Albert C. Geljon, *Philonic Exegesis in Gregory of Nyssa's* De Vita Moysis, Brown Judaic Studies 333 (Providence, RI: Brown Judaic Studies, 2002), 142–45.

38. For example, Gregory's *Catechetical Lecture* ("Address on Religious Instruction"), in which he forewarned catechumens about the Manichean deceptions; Edward Rochie Hardy and Cyril C. Richardson, eds., *Christology of the Later Fathers*, LCC 3 (Philadelphia: Westminster, 1954), 277, 305.

39. Abraham J. Malherbe and Everett Ferguson, trans., *Gregory of Nyssa: The Life of Moses*, Classics of Western Spirituality (New York: Paulist, 1978), 119.

40. Another Cappadocian theologian, Gregory of Nazianzus, interpreted the "back" of God that Moses saw as the glory of the triune God that was manifest in all creatures; *Or.* 28.3 (Second Theological Oration). This interpretation, which will be discussed in the next section (Movement 3), at least credited Moses with seeing something real in his own lifetime.

41. Gregory of Nyssa himself described the Eucharist in very realistic terms in his *Catechetical Lecture* ("Address on Religious Instruction"); Hardy and Richardson, eds., *Christology of the Later Fathers*, 318–21. Performative aspects of the Eucharistic prayers were clearly described in other sources like the Syrian *Liber Graduum* 12.2; 28.8; John Chrysostom, *On the Priesthood* 3.4; Chrysostom, *Hom. 3 on Ephesians* (NPNF1, 13:62a, 63a, 64–65); the *Liturgy of St. James* 26 (ANF 7:543a). For other examples, see C. B. Kaiser, "Climbing Jacob's Ladder: John Calvin and the Early Church on Our Eucharistic Ascent to Heaven," *SJT* 56 (2003): 247–67. These ascensional traditions reflected the performance of binitarian visions of Rev. 4–5 (and Heb. 10:19-22; 12:22-24) more closely that they did the Kyriocentric ones in Rev. 1 and the other five New Testament texts examined in ch. 5.

42. Augustine, *Exposition on Psalms* 138:8, "Far be it from us to have any such thoughts of that Majesty!" (*NPNF1*, 8:637, where the passage is labeled 139.6); cf. Augustine, *On the Trinity* 2.17.31. A similar disdain had been expressed by Origen in response to gnostic critics of the Old Testament Deity; *First Principles* 2.4.3.

43. Irenaeus, *Against Heresies* 4.20.9 (immediately following the section quoted above); Tertullian, *Against Marcion* 4:22; cf. Ambrose, *On the Holy Spirit* 3.5.33; Ambrose, *On the Faith* 5.19.236 (mocking Arius).

44. In some later writings, Augustine saw the church as the visible "back" that would be seen by the Jewish people; *Ep.* 147.32 (to Paulina, "On Seeing God"); Augustine, *On the Literal Meaning of Genesis* 12.27.55.

45. *NPNF1*, 3:50–51 (modified).

46. Like Irenaeus (*Haer.* 4.20.9), but being more playful in his Latin, Augustine suggested that the reason the Lord referred to his coming incarnation as "his back" (Latin, *posteriora ejus*), could have been either that it symbolized human mortality (*propter posterioritiate*) or because it referred to the late stage (*posterius*) of the world (Heb. 1:2; 1 Pet. 1:20).

47. Tertullian, *On the Resurrection* 6; Tertullian, *Against Praxeas* 7; Novatian, *On the Trinity* 22; cf. §18 (on Col. 1:15); Origen, *Comm. on John* 6.19.

48. Aëtius's short tract is found in Epiphanius, *Panarion* 76.11. All but one of its thirty-seven paragraphs is written in the form: if A, then B; or, if A, then not B.

49. According to Basil Studer and Michel Barnes, the "Arians" who pressed theophanies of the Logos as evidence of his having a different substance from the Father were Homoians; Basil Studer, *Zur Theophanie-Exegese Augustins: Untersuchung zu einem Abrosius-Zitat in der Schrift 'De Videndo Deo'* (Rome: Herder, 1971), 8, 69; Michel René Barnes, "Exegesis and Polemic in Augustine's De Trinitate I," *Augustinian Studies* 30 (1999): 43–60; Barnes, "The Visible Christ and the Invisible Trinity: Mt 5:8 in Augustine's Trinitarian Theology of 400," *Modern Theology* 19 (2003): 329–56 (341). Homoians (also spelled "Homoeans") held that the Son was "like [*homoios*]

the Father" but ruled out any talk of substance as unbiblical (Creed of Ariminum, 359). In other words, they substituted a strategy of biblical positivism for the Eunomian strategy of dialectical logic. The term *homoios* could be used of any angel or even a person who became godlike through *homoiōsis* (assimilation) or *theopoiēsis* (deification). Western Homoians like Palladius of Ratiaria defined the godhead in terms of invisibility (citing Exod. 33:20; John 1:18; 1 Tim. 6:17), much as the Eunomians had defined it in terms of ingenerateness; cf. Hilary, *On the Trinity* 4.8.

50. Justin said that these Jewish teachers insulted the Son of God, and he referred to them as "Pharisaic" (*Dial.* 137.2), but his understanding of this term may simply reflect New Testament usage. More reliably, he understood these teachers to read Old Testament texts anthropomorphically (114.3; cf. 9.1), as did many of the Rabbis that we discussed in ch. 2 ("Visionary Motifs and Practices in Rabbinic Literature"). The reason that Justin found these teachers to be such a challenge, beside the fact that they were attracting proselytes (23.3; 32.5; 122.4), was that he and most Christians of his time also understood these texts anthropomorphically, though in a binitarian, christological sense.

51. E.g., Origen, *First Principles* 4.4.1, frag. 32; G. W. Butterworth, trans. *Origen: On First Principles* (New York: Harper & Row, 1966), 314. Among other texts, Origen cited Col. 1:15 (*prōtotokos pasēs ktiseōs*) and Prov. 8:22 LXX (*ektise me*) in support of this usage.

52. Origen, *Commentary on John* (Alexandria, c. 231 CE) 1.43, 124, 190, 275; Origen, *Homily on Genesis* (Caesarea, sometime after 234) 3.1.

53. Origen, *First Principles* 2.4.3, directed against the Alexandrian followers of Basilides and Valentinus.

54. Butterworth, trans. *Origen: On First Principles*, 13; cf. *First Principles* 2.4.3 (ibid., 99). In this context, Origen still attributed the theophanies to God the Father (an anti-gnostic tactic also seen in Irenaeus, *Haer.* 3.3.3; 11.7)—Christ was not entirely absent, however, being present, along with the Holy Spirit, as one of the seraphim that praise the Lord of hosts; *First Principles* 1.3.4; 2.4.1; 4.3.14. Even though the Son is the "image of the invisible God" (Col. 1:15), he is still an invisible image (*First Principles* 4.4.1, frag. 32), so invisible, according to excerpts found in the writings of Jerome, that he could not be even seen by the Spirit (Butterworth, trans. *Origen: On First Principles*, 13 n. 3, 99 n. 1).

55. In *Against Celsus* 1.48, Origen avoided locating Old Testament theophanies in the visible world by saying that they were apparitions impressed on the mind like dreams. In his *Homily on Ezekiel* 1.8, on the other hand, he stated that Ezekiel saw the divine form with the eyes of his flesh—implying a created glory like the "realist" interpretation of Rav Sa'adyah Ga'on (*Book of Beliefs and Opinions* 2.10, c. 935 CE); cf. David J. Halperin, "Origen, Ezekiel's Merkabah, and the Ascension of Moses," *CH* 50 (1981): 261–75 (265). Origen's options were limited by the fact that his ontology only had two distinct levels: one empirical and the other intellectual (as shown in the quote above). He had little or no interest in the intermediate worlds (heavens) of apocalyptic and Rabbinic (and later heikalot) literature.

56. Historical theologies that simply follow the ebb and flow of ideas (in this case the cultivation of anti-anthropomorphic readings from Origen to the Cappadocian theologians) often conflate the contexts (as the fathers did themselves, but with better reason) and consequently miss the fact that the functions of the ideas and the motives for selecting them often differ from one generation to the next.

57. On the longstanding concern to differentiate Christian beliefs from the pagan myths concerning divine appearances, see, e.g., Acts 14:11; Justin, *1 Apol.* 21.1; Origen, *Against Celsus* 7.35.

58. The fathers of Nicea only rejected the idea that the Logos was created. The two-stage Logos Christology that was traditionally associated with the anthropic form (from Justin to Eusebius of Caesarea) was still intact, at least, until it was spurned by Gregory of Nazianzus (*Or.* 20. 9).

59. Lest it seem improbable that such a great theologian would be involved in a political campaign, note how Gregory searched out Arian spies and noted with satisfaction their later

absence (*Or.* 27.2; 28.1, "so as not to sow upon thorns"). Gregory expressed second thoughts about this policy in his "Farewell Address" (*Or.* 42.3, 18, 23).

60. According to Gregory, the Eunomians argued that the Logos is the perceptible form of God (following Justin and the Second Council of Sirmium). Therefore, the Logos must be corporeal, and a literal, substantial generation of the Logos from God would involve passion and subdivision. Accordingly, piety requires that the "generation" of the Logos must be external rather than substantial; in other words, the Logos was created (*Or.* 29.4).

61. The Eastern churches developed an ontology of uncreated energies. In the Latin West, Augustine and later theologians thought in terms of the undivided external operations (*opera ad extra*); cf. Kaiser, *The Doctrine of God: A Historical Survey,* revised ed. (Eugene, OR: Wipf & Stock, 2001), 86–87, 93–95.

62. Compare the prayer of Hilary: "We look to you [Father] to give us the fellowship of that Spirit who guided the prophets and the apostles"; *On the Trinity* 1.36 (*NPNF*2, 9:50b). New Testament precedent can readily be found in John 14:16 ("he will give you another Advocate"); 14:26 ("the Holy Spirit, whom the Father will send in my name"); 15:26 ("whom I will send you from the Father").

63. ET from Hardy and Richardson, eds., *Christology of the Later Fathers,* 136.

64. Alan F. Segal, "Heavenly Ascent in Hellenistic Judaism, Early Christianity and Their Environment," *Aufstieg und Niedergang der römishen Welt* 2, 23 (1980): 1333–94.

65. Almost the same expression, "drawing aside the curtain," was used by Clement of Alexandria, *Miscellanies* 7.17 (*ANF* 2:554b). It must have been a standard expression, at least in the Eastern churches.

66. Hardy and Richardson, eds., *Christology of the Later Fathers,* 137. Although Gregory spoke in the past tense, reflecting his personal meditative practice, the context in *Or.* 28.3 makes it clear that he expected his congregation to follow him to the extent of their various abilities ("if any be an Aaron . . . if any be a Nadab or an Abihu . . . if any be of the multitude").

67. Moses' ascent to the Lord on Sinai was homologous with Aaron's entrance into the holy of holies. The inner sanctum connected directly to the heavenly throne of the Deity, as illustrated by Old Testament scholar Tryggve Mettinger in *The Dethronement of Sabaoth: Studies in the Shem and Kabod Theologies,* Coniectanea Biblica: Old Testament Series 18 (Lund: CWK Gleerup, 1982), 129–30 ("nothing to do with any analogical typology"), and explained in the Talmud: "The chamber of the Holy of holies down below is opposite the chamber of the Holy of holies up above" (*y. Ber.* 4:5, 8c).

68. The verb *katalambanō* means either "laying hold" physically (and thereby "overcoming") or "comprehending" intellectually (cf. the cognates in *Or.* 28.10, 21, 29). Clearly, Gregory was pinning this verb on his opponents here. Its only New Testament uses with respect to the Deity are found in John 1:5, "The light shines in the darkness, and the darkness did not overcome [or 'comprehend'] it," and Eph. 3:18-19, "that you may have the power to comprehend with all the saints what is the breadth and length and height and depth, and to know the love of Christ that *surpasses knowledge.*" It is unlikely that Gregory's target group used a term with such ambiguous associations to describe their own approach to God. They may, however, have use a verb like *aptō*, to "touch" or "take hold of," based on the performance of the vision reflected in John 20:17 (there attributed to Mary Magdalene).

69. Elsewhere in this *Oration,* Gregory spoke of those who have been "caught up like Paul to the third heaven" (2 Cor. 12:2) and raised to "angelic or archangelic place and dignity" (28.3), spiritual adepts who are "advanced in contemplation" (28.9), and some who "walk in the paths of the infinite" (28.12).

70. Hardy and Richardson, eds., *Christology of the Later Fathers,* 137–38.

71. On the angels' limited vision of God, see *Or.* 28. 4, 12.

72. In describing the vision that Paul described in 2 Cor. 12 (*Or.* 28.20), Gregory said the same thing and rather disarmingly expressed his anxiety lest he "appear to anyone too careful and overanxious about the examination of this matter." In the case of Old Testament theophanies,

Gregory took much the same approach as Origen (*Against Celsus* 1.48, cited above). He ascribed them either to created angels (as in the apparition to Samson's parents) or to dreams and phantasms that were somehow impressed on the mind (the visions of Isaiah and Ezekiel; *Or.* 28.19). In the final Theological Oration, on the other hand, Gregory argued that all of the Old Testament appearances were only figures of speech (*Or.* 31.22), but here he was defending the deity of the Spirit against the Macedonians (not the Son against the Eunomians) and followed the argument of his Cappadocian associate, Basil of Caesarea (*On the Holy Spirit* 15).

73. Gregory's later concern about the challenge of the Apollinarian churches reinforced his anti-anthropomorphic stance as indicated in his Epistle 202 (to Nectarius). The occasion was Apollinarius's publishing a pamphlet in which he had asserted that the pre-incarnate, heavenly Son of Man had a body, which was a kind of spiritual "flesh" (Hardy and Richardson, eds., *Christology of the Later Fathers*, 231).

74. On Augustine, see Kaiser, *Doctrine of God*, 89–95. So much attention has recently been given to differences between Augustine's ("psychological") view of the immanent Trinity and the ("social") view of the Cappadocians that their shared understanding of the external operations and theophanies is often overlooked.

75. Chrysostom, *On the Incomprehensibility of God* (386–87 CE) 4.18-19; Chrysostom, *Hom. on Isaiah 6*; Chrysostom, *Hom. on John* (c. 391) 15. The main point about God's simplicity had already been made by Origen, *Comm. John* 13.123-31 (against Stoic philosophers and literalist interpreters of Scripture), and also by Athanasius, *On the Decrees* 24 (early 350s, against Arians). The multiplicity of divine "likenesses" in Hosea 12:10 had been cited by Irenaeus, *Haer.* 4.20.6. The same text was also cited by the Rabbis (*MRI* Shirata 3:30-31; *Lev. R.* 1:14), but without the same negative spin.

76. Robin Darling Young, "Evagrius of Pontus," in Patrick W. Carey and Joseph T. Lienhard, *Biographical Dictionary of Christian Theologians* (Westport, CT: Greenwood, 2000), 187–88; Herbertus R. Drobner, *The Fathers of the Church: A Comprehensive Introduction*, trans. Siegfried S. Schatzmann (Peabody, MA: Hendrickson, 2007), 365–67.

77. John Eudes Bamberger, trans., *Evagrius Ponticus: The Praktikos; Chapters on Prayer*, Cistercian Studies 4 (Kalamazoo, MI: Cistercian Publications, 1981), 66. I am indebted here to Alexander Golitzin, "'The Demons Suggest an Illusion of God's Glory in a Form': Controversy over the Divine Body and Vision of Glory in Some Late Fourth, Early Fifth-Century Monastic Literature," *Scrinium: Revue de patrologie, d'hagiographie critique et d'histoire ecclésiastique* 3 (2007): 13–43 (32).

78. Bamberger, trans., *Evagrius Ponticus*, 67, 74; cf. Golitzin, "The Demons Suggest an Illusion of God's Glory," 32.

79. Prophetic gifts had been claimed by (or on behalf of) second-century church leaders like Ignatius, Polycarp, Amnia of Philadelphia, Quadratus, Hermas, and Melito of Sardis. Third and fourth-century leaders like Tertullian, Athanasius, Basil of Caesarea, and the Syriac author of *Liber Graduum* were more likely to claim them on behalf of the church as a whole than for themselves personally,

80. Bamberger, trans., *Evagrius Ponticus*, 66.

81. See, for instance, Origen, *Hom. on Gen.* 3.1; Arnobius, *Against the Nations* 3.12; Basil and/or Gregory of Nyssa (attr.), *Sermons on the Creation of Humanity*, in Hadwig Hörner, ed., *Auctorum incertorum, vulgo Basilii vel Gregorii Nysseni Sermones de creatione hominis; Sermo de paradiso* (Leiden: Brill, 1972), 9–10. The label of "Jewish fables" comes from Arnobius's critique of anthropomorphite Christians of the early fourth century (*Against the Nations* 3.12).

82. *NPNF2*, 11:258. It should be noted that anagogical and anthropic interpretations are not necessarily exclusive. Medieval Kabbalah successfully combined the two approaches by representing divine attributes as ten limbs (*sefirot*) of the cosmic body of HaShem (*Ein Sof*).

83. The 399 Festal Letter has not survived itself, but it was described in much the same terms in one of Theophilus's later letters and by Gennadius, *Lives of Illustrious Men* 34; see Norman

Russell, *Theophilus of Alexandria*, Early Church Fathers (London: Routledge, 2007), 22, 141–42. Bishop Theophilus later reversed himself and attacked the Origenist monks led by the Tall Brothers.

84. *NPNF2*, 11:401b.

85. *Bohairic Life of Pachomius* 86; cf. §184 on the *synaxis* as a place of prayer; Armand Veilleux, trans., *Pachomian Koinonia*, Cistercian Studies 45–47, 3 vols. (Kalamazoo, MI: Cistercian Publications, 1980–82), 1:112, 220.

86. Veilleux, trans., *Pachomian Koinonia*, 1:219–20; cf. Golitzin, "The Demons Suggest an Illusion," 22–23, who for some reason does not mention the devotional use of Ps. 16:8.

87. A corporate setting is indicated not only by the venue, but also by the following reference to Theodore's thinking of the revelation to *all of Israel* on Mount Sinai; Veilleux, trans., *Pachomian Koinonia*, 1:220.

88. According to the text, Theodore saw the Israelites designating Moses as the Lord's spokesman (thereby protecting themselves from the divine glory), as the model for his being commissioned to exhort the brethren; ibid.

89. William A. Graham describes the monastic use of Scripture as follows: "Meditation here is not abstract contemplation but determined 'exercise' in the word of God: What the mouth repeats, the heart should experience"; Graham, *Beyond the Written Word: Oral Aspects of Scripture in the History of Religion* (Cambridge: Cambridge University Press, 1987), 134, 137.

90. Note that the *First Greek Life of Pachomius* (c. 400 CE) played down the visionary aspect of these traditions. As James Goehring has shown, the redactor was sympathetic to the Alexandrian patriarchal ecclesiology (presumably before Bishop Theophilus's reversal on Origenism); Goehring, *Ascetics, Society, and the Desert: Studies in Early Egyptian Monasticism*, Studies in Antiquity and Christianity (Harrisburg: Trinity Press International, 1999), 138–39, 156, 208–11. Pachomius now tells his vision-seeking followers to look at their fellow humans who are the temple of God and above all remember the warning of Ps. 54:3 about the sin of insolence (*First Greek Life* 48). Similarly, Theodore hides his visionary gifts and advises his fellow monks that keeping the orthodox faith and God's commandments are more important than visionary gifts of the Spirit and that they ought not to think less of themselves if they do not have such visions, or too highly of themselves if they do (*First Greek Life* 135); Veilleux, trans., *Pachomian Koinonia*, 1:393–94.

91. Columba Stewart judges that Cassian's narrative is a dogmatic construction rather than an historical report; Stewart, *Cassian the Monk*, Oxford Studies in Historical Theology (New York: Oxford University Press, 1998), 10, 86–87. Fair enough, but a key part of this argument is an alleged association of the name *Sarapion* with the pagan cult of Serapis. The name *Sarapion* could also be a variant of Serapion, as in Bishop Serapion of Thmuis of *Sacramentary* fame. More recently, Mark DelCogliano has suggested that the characters had their roots in historical individuals; DelCogliano, "Situating Sarapion's Sorrow: The Anthropomorphite Controversy as the Historical and Theological Context of Cassian's Tenth Conference on Pure Prayer," *Cistercian Studies Quarterly* 38 (2003): 377–421 (415–16).

92. *NPNF2*, 11:402. For a more colloquial reading, see Colm Luibheid, *John Cassian: Conferences*, Classics of Western Spirituality (New York: Paulist, 1985), 126–27.

93. *NPNF2*, 11:402; cf. Luibheid, *John Cassian*, 126.

94. Mark DelCogliano suggests that the Latin word for "Godhead" (*deitas*) represented the Greek *theotēs* and referred to the triune God; DelCogliano, "Situating Sarapion's Sorrow," 408 n. 144.

95. *NPNF2*, 11:402b (adapted); cf. Luibheid, *John Cassian*, 127. Similar language (albeit Greek) was used in John's narrative account of the vision attributed to Mary Magdalene (John 20:13, 17a).

96. *NPNF2*, 11:402b. Luibheid's translation of *quem teneam* as "one to hold on to" (*John Cassian*, 127) is possible, but weakens the dramatic force of capturing and restraining.

97. *Conferences* 10.3, 4; ET in *NPNF2*, 11:402b. Again Luibheid weakens the force of this statement by translating *valde permoti* as "deeply moved" (loc. cit.). The past participle *permotus* has the sense of being agitated, more than just being affected or moved.

98. Further afield is the idea of "directing one's heart" as in *m. Ber.* 2:1; 5:1 (discussed in ch. 2). This devotional practice is reflected in Sarapion's having the anthropic form in his heart (and subsequently "taken away"). For Christians, the practice was based on Matt. 5:8, understood in terms of purifying the heart as a temple for the Lord; cf. Ephrem, *Hymns on the Nativity* 16.3; *Liber Graduum* 17.8. Anti-anthropomorphic readings of Matt. 5:8 emerged in Ambrose, *Exposition on the Gospel according to Luke* 1.24-27; Augustine, *On the Lord's Sermon on the Mount* 1.4.12; Augustine, *On the Literal Sense of Genesis* 12.28.56; and Pseudo-Basil, *Homily on the Construction of Humanity*: "Empty from your heart all misplaced imagination. . . . Do not imagine a form for him. Do not belittle him who is great in Jewish fashion. Do not enclose God in corporeal concepts"; cf. Gedaliahu Strousma, "Form(s) of God: Some Notes on Metatron and Christ," *HTR* 76 (1983): 269–88 (271–72), where the homily is attributed directly to Basil.

99. This sideswipe at pagan idolatry may reflect Bishop Theophilus's campaign against pagan temples, one of the main justifications for which was that they contained representations of the divine as phalluses; Socrates, *History of the Church* 5.16 (NPNF2, 2:126a); cf. Elizabeth A. Clark, *The Origenist Controversy: The Cultural Construction of an Early Christian Debate* (Princeton, NJ: Princeton University Press, 1992), 52–56 (54); DelCogliano, "Situating Serapion's Sorrow," 409 with n. 149, 412–16.

100. In addition to the material cited above, see Gregory of Nazianzus, *Or.* 18.2, 3.

101. A free translation of Cassian's "Nec ullam quidem in memorian dicti cujusdam vel facti speciem seu formam cujus libet characteris admittet"; cf. Luibheid, *John Cassian,* 128.

102. Columba Stewart offers an interesting parallel to Symeon the New Theologian's vision of the face of Christ in formless light; Stewart, *Cassian the Monk*, 197 n. 79.

Conclusion: Accomplishments and Some Unresolved Issues

The objective of this treatise has been to address a dilemma that confronts students of New Testament Christology: the writers and their predecessors were (mostly or all) pious Jews, yet they ascribed deity to their teacher, Jesus, in a way that no pious Jew could ever think of doing.

OUR CONJECTURE AND THE CASE FOR ITS PLAUSIBILITY

Our investigation has taken us from Second Temple texts like Enoch and Daniel (third to second century BCE) to the theological consensus that emerged under the leadership of the neo-Nicene Cappadocians (late fourth century CE). Our strategy has been: (1) to view these texts in relation to the communal performances they reflect; (2) to root early Christology in a particular kind of performance—the rehearsal of Kyriocentric visions in the context of communal prayer—that can be documented in Second Temple literature as well as in the New Testament; (3) to ask what sort of demands occasioned the identification of the envisioned Lord as Jesus; and (4) further to see whether the sort of demands that were created by the Lord-Jesus identification can account for other christological features of the New Testament and early Christian literature (including alternative tradition histories).

The conclusion of our investigation is that the deity Christology of the New Testament can readily be explained by conjecturing new visions of the Lord, this time having the name and face of Jesus. The primary impetus for deity Christology was therefore the belief that the Lord had appeared in anthropic form and identified himself as Jesus (*Kyrios Iēsous*). This identification was unique, but only in the sense that we have no evidence of other such occurrences in the history of Judaism. It is a case of fortuitous uniqueness. Early cultic devotion to Jesus needs no further explanation than that the first disciples were Jews who ascribed divine attributes to their Lord and addressed him in prayer.[1]

No amount of exegesis could ever prove the Kyriocentric vision conjecture to be true. Our main objective has been to establish a viable scenario alongside others and to demonstrate its plausibility and explanatory potential. This plausibility can be demonstrated in a variety of ways, in relation to its background in Second Temple literature, its foreground in early (Tannaitic) Rabbinic traditions (chs. 2, 3), and its implications for the development of Christology in the New Testament era and beyond. With regard to the latter, the Kyriocentric conjecture explains the following:

- The use of Kyriocentric vision language in an important group of New Testament narratives (ch. 5)
- The dedication of some prayer motifs to the Lord Jesus and others to God the Father (the latter indicating the constraints of Jesus traditions, ch. 6)
- The reformulation of Kyriocentric visions in terms of the resurrection of Jesus—a second-order belief that raised as many questions as it resolved (ch. 7)
- The variety of traditions concerning the initial identification of the Lord with the life of Jesus—a concurrent theological development (ch. 7)
- The reformulation of Kyriocentric visions in binitarian language—a second-order belief that raised further questions (ch. 7)
- The identification of Jesus as a suffering Messiah—a second-order belief that raised still further questions (ch. 7)
- The existence of alternative tradition histories or textures that combined the narrative threads in different ways (ch. 8)
- Reasons why leading theologians felt the need to reinterpret the anthropic form of Old Testament theophanies and even to eliminate Kyriocentric visions (ch. 9)

All of this adds up to a good case for supposing that Christology began at a high level ("The Lord is Jesus") and was subsequently adjusted in various ways out of respect for memories of Jesus' life and death. The early disciples were superimposing two portraits, or interweaving two narratives, in creative ways that made sense in terms of their performances but have never completely succumbed to systematization. The resulting structure is like the divergent fractal pattern of a growing tree more than the convergent pattern of a crossword puzzle.

SOME UNRESOLVED ISSUES

In the spirit of "truth in advertising," I should advise the reader of several important areas where our scenario has not worked so smoothly. The four areas that I am most concerned about are the following:

- If Kyriocentric visions were widely practiced in apocalyptic groups, as I have argued, why was the Qumran community so reluctant to mention the anthropic form (ch. 2)?[2]
- What is the relationship between visions that occur in the process of ascents to heaven (as in *1 Enoch*, discussed in ch. 2) and those that follow invocations on earth (as in the Psalms, ch. 3)? Was the ascent an original part of the vision performance or was it a narrativized literary feature?
- How could Saul have recognized the face and voice of Jesus in his initiatory vision when the two men had never before met (ch. 5)?
- How could several New Testament texts (arguably) have preserved traditions concerning a post-crucifixion identification of the Lord with Jesus, while rephrasing those very traditions in binitarian language—the latter being based on an identification prior to the crucifixion (ch. 7)?

I have suggested answers for these questions, but none of them is entirely satisfactory. In terms of our understanding of early deity Christology, however, we are better off with a set of speculative questions like these than with the dilemma that lies at the very heart of the New Testament. As I understand methodology, moreover, reviving old questions (the first two listed here) and raising new ones (the second pair) are strengths of a research program, not defects.

ISSUES CONCERNING OUR BELIEFS AND PRACTICES TODAY

At the end of the day, I must dare to step out of my role as a historian and outline some of the problems that must be addressed when we try to bring archaic beliefs and practices into contact with modern society, scientific cosmology, and religious faith and practice. I only intend to highlight these issues for future discussion.

From the very outset there is the problem of androcentric, hierarchical language so ably brought to our attention by Elisabeth Schüssler Fiorenza and others.[3] I have tried to put statements concerning the anthropic form of the Lord in the past tense to indicate that this was, in fact, the way early Jews and Christians thought and spoke about the Deity. (Even though the texts we possess were mostly written by men, we can assume that women of that time would have concurred). In liturgical and homiletical situations today, however, we must respect the diversity of sensitivities to language that exist among both men and women. The problem is obviously not unique to the present work, but it comes up with even greater force for its being planted (according to our conjecture) at the very root of the Christian faith. Even before the predominance of Father-Son language, the distinct assignment of the titles *God* and *Lord* was instrumental in differentiating the two divine figures, and this usage has continued in liturgical formulas to this day (ch. 7).

Another issue concerning the anthropic form of the Lord stems from our awareness of the value of all life forms and the possible existence of other forms of intelligent life elsewhere in our vast cosmos. Do we have to choose between a literal reading of the divine form as an anthropos (a human form) with hands and feet, on the one hand, and a purely anagogical interpretation like Origen's and Gregory of Nazianzus's, on the other (ch. 9)? Is there still room for understanding the divine form as a representation of the *plērōma* ("fullness") of divine attributes, both male and female, like the *plērōma* that was embodied in Jesus (Col. 1:19; 2:9) or the system of *sefirot* (numbered limbs) that was developed by medieval Kabbalists?[4]

I have personally found it helpful to use such patterns in addressing the mystery of growth and change. The anthropic form might be viewed as the visible representation of a complex invisible structure much the way "lines of force" provide a visible representation of an invisible magnetic field. Could it be possible to design a modern spiritual discipline, based on similar structures, comparable to what the writer of Ephesians called the "fullness of God" or the "measure of the full stature of Christ" (Eph. 3:18-19; 4:13)?

An even more difficult question for moderns is what to do with the "imaginal world" that was so real and seemingly "objective" for our ancient and medieval forebears.[5] A similar idea can be found in the objectivist philosophy of Karl Popper (1902-94). His "third world" is a conceptual world that includes problems and arguments as well as ideas. It is distinct from the world of individual consciousness and that of visible, empirical entities, but is still related to both by way of construction, feedback, and being encoded in artifacts like books.[6] Popper's main concern was to create some space for conjecture and refutation without appealing directly to individual creativity—an issue very similar to the place we assigned performance in relation to literary texts, on the one hand, and subjective, "mystical" experiences on the other.

As far as I know, no one has demonstrated the explanatory value of Popper's idea. Even if there is none, it does remind us that our conjectures and reasoning often take on a life of their own in ways that we neither control nor anticipate. They also produce concrete results. A good example is the way in which James Clerk Maxwell, a century and a half ago, tinkered with a few mathematical equations and discovered that he could solve them to yield the velocity of light.[7] Our visible, empirical world has been transformed several times over by the applications of this purely mental construct that we blithely refer to as "electromagnetic waves." How is this possible? Is it mere chance or is it possible that our intellects are illumined in some way from beyond? If the latter, how does this transfer of energy or information relate to the mundane energy transfers that we can measure and manipulate? Any progress we can make in understanding the creativity of our own psyches in relation to the deep structures of the material world could go a long way toward understanding the visionary practices of the ancients. Understanding ancient visionary practices might also help us understand the creative processes we rely on today.[8]

Finally, I wonder about the effects of analyzing revered traditions in terms of historical processes. An essential part of any effort to recover the history behind the biblical texts is deconstructing the narratives and explaining why and how they were constructed out of earlier traditions and subsequently altered to account for other narratives (also referred to here as "portraits"). Yet these ancient texts are the very ones that we rehearse in churches and that still inform our lives as "gospel truth."

In short, we also need to account for the verisimilitude of narratives as they exist in our Bibles, and this need leads to a series of other questions. Is our notion of objective history too naive? Can New Testament narratives that were "corrected" in hindsight from a postresurrection vantage point be as historically valid as their predecessors? On the other hand, if such revisionism is allowed, how can we compensate for the voices that were obscured or even lost in the process? Is there some way of construing New Testament narratives so that they are "thick" enough to preserve those earlier voices, including those of the disciples' Jewish forebears? Unless we can address questions like these, we end up with a "double truth" like that attributed (mistakenly) to the Latin Averroists of the thirteenth century: one narrative is true for me as an historian, while another works for me as a religious practitioner.

As indicated, I struggle with these issues and hope to get closer to that "fullness" that the Lord intends for all of us. The objective of this book is rather more modest, however. There is at least one way of doing historical justice, within the context of first-century Judaism, to the deity Christology that was assumed by the writers of the New Testament. Perhaps there are other ways yet to be discovered.

Notes

1. Larry Hurtado details cultic devotion to the Lord Jesus in terms of prayer, invocation, confession, baptism, Eucharistic language, hymns, and prophetic language; Hurtado, *Lord Jesus Christ: Devotion to Jesus in Earliest Christianity* (Grand Rapids: Eerdmans, 2003), 137–51.

2. A few Qumran texts to consider are listed in ch. 2, note 4. Perhaps other scholars will be able to make more out of these texts than I have been able to.

3. Elisabeth Schüssler Fiorenza, *Transforming Vision: Explorations in Feminist Theology* (Minneapolis: Fortress Press, 2011), 222. Even though this archaic language does not meet modern standards of inclusiveness, it still conforms to those of biblical writers, who shared a more hierarchical understanding of the world than we do (loc. cit., 17).

4. See, for example, Elliot Wolfson, "The Doctrine of Sefirot in the Prophetic Kabbalah of Abraham Abulafia, Part I," *JSQ* 2 (1995): 336–71 (357 n. 61 on *Sha'arei Zedeq*); Moshe Idel, *Ben: Sonship and Jewish Mysticism*, Kogod Library of Judaic Studies 5 (London: Continuum, 2007), 424 (on R. David ben Yehudah he-Hasid); Sandra Valabregue-Perry, "The Concept of Infinity (*Eyn-sof*) and the Rise of Theosophical Kabbalah," *JQR* 102 (2012): 405–30 (421–25 on R. Isaac the Blind).

5. On the role of imagination in medieval epistemology and meditation, particularly meditation on the crucified body of Jesus, see Michelle Karnes, *Imagination, Meditation, and Cognition in the Middle Ages* (Chicago: University of Chicago Press, 2011), esp. 4, 32–33, on the difference from modern, inventive imagination, and 135–37 on sharing in Christ's resurrection and ascension (Bonaventura).

6. Karl R. Popper, *Objective Knowledge: An Evolutionary Approach* (Oxford: Clarendon, 1972), 106–22.

7. Christopher B. Kaiser, *Creational Theology and the History of Physical Science: The Creationist Tradition from Basil to Bohr*, Studies in the History of Christian Thought 78 (Leiden: Brill, 1997), 384–88.

8. For my own efforts along this line, see Kaiser, *Toward a Theology of Scientific Endeavour: The Descent of Science*, Ashgate Science and Religion Series (London: Ashgate, 2007), 59–124.

Bibliography

Abegg, Martin, Jr., Peter Flinch, and Eugene Ulrich, trans. *The Dead Sea Scrolls Bible*. San Francisco: HarperSanFrancisco, 1999.

Achtemeier, Paul J. "Jesus and the Disciples as Miracle Workers in the Apocryphal New Testament." Pages 148–86 in *Aspects of Religious Propaganda in Judaism and Early Christianity*. Studies in Judaism and Christianity in Antiquity 2. Edited by Elisabeth Schüssler Fiorenza. Notre Dame, IN: University of Notre Dame Press, 1976.

Alexander, Elizabeth Shanks. *Transmitting Mishnah: The Shaping Influence of Oral Tradition*. Cambridge: Cambridge University Press, 2006.

Alexander, Philip S. "Jewish Believers in Early Rabbinic Literature (2d to 5th Centuries)." Pages 659–709 in *Jewish Believers in Jesus: The Early Centuries*. Edited by Oskar Skarsaune and Reidar Hvalvik. Peabody, MA: Hendrickson, 2007.

———. *Mystical Texts: Songs of the Sabbath Sacrifice and Related Manuscripts*. Companion to the Qumran Scrolls 7. London: T&T Clark, 2006.

———. "Prayer in the Heikhalot Literature." Pages 44–64 in *Prière, mystique et judaïsme: colloque de Strasbourg, 10–12 septembre 1984*. Travaux du Centre d'histoire des religions de Strasbourg 2. Edited by Roland Goetschel. Paris: Presses Universitaires de France, 1987.

———. "Qumran and the Genealogy of Western Mysticism." Pages 215–35 in *New Perspectives on Old Texts*. STJD 88. Edited by Esther G. Chazon and Betsy Halpern-Amaru. Leiden: Brill, 2010.

———, ed. *Textual Sources for the Study of Judaism*. Textual Sources for the Study of Religion. Chicago: University of Chicago Press, 1984.

Allison, Dale C., Jr. *Constructing Jesus: Memory, Imagination, and History*. Grand Rapids: Baker Academic, 2010.

Alsup, John E. *The Post-Resurrection Appearance Stories of the Gospel Tradition*. Calwer Theologische Monographien, A 5. Stuttgart: Calwer, 1975.

Anderson, Gary. "Towards a Theology of the Tabernacle and Its Furniture." Pages 161–94 in *Text, Thought, and Practice in Qumran and Early Christianity*. STDJ 84. Edited by Ruth A. Clements and Daniel R. Schwartz. Leiden: Brill, 2009.

Angel, Andrew R. *Chaos and the Son of Man: The Hebrew Chaoskampf Tradition in the Period 515 BCE to 200 CE.* Library of Second Temple Studies 60. London: T&T Clark, 2006.

———. "*Crucifixus Vincens*: The 'Son of God' as Divine Warrior in Matthew." *CBQ* 73 (2011): 299–317.

Arbel, Vita Daphna. *Beholders of Divine Secrets: Mysticism and Myth in the Hekhalot and Merkavah Literature.* Albany: State University of New York Press, 2003.

Ashton, John. "The Johannine Son of Man: A New Proposal." *NTS* 57 (2011): 508–29.

Aune, David. *The Cultic Setting of Realized Eschatology in Early Christianity.* NovTSup 28. Leiden: Brill, 1972.

Bamberger, John Eudes, trans. *Evagrius Ponticus: The Praktikos; Chapters on Prayer.* Cistercian Studies 4. Kalamazoo, MI: Cistercian Publications, 1981.

Barker, Margaret. *The Great Angel: A Study of Israel's Second God.* Louisville: Westminster John Knox Press, 1992.

———. *The Hidden Tradition of the Kingdom of God.* London: SPCK, 2007.

———. *The Risen Lord: The Jesus of History as the Christ of Faith.* London: T&T Clark, 1996.

———. *Temple Themes in Christian Worship.* London: T&T Clark, 2007.

Barnes, Michel René. "Exegesis and Polemic in Augustine's *De Trinitate* I." *Augustinian Studies* 30 (1999): 43–60.

———. "The Visible Christ and the Invisible Trinity: Mt 5:8 in Augustine's Trinitarian Theology of 400." *Modern Theology* 19 (2003): 329–56.

Barr, David L. "The Apocalypse of John as Oral Enactment." *Interpretation* 40 (1986): 243–56.

Barr, James. "Theophany and Anthropomorphism in the Old Testament." *Congress Volume: Oxford 1959* (Leiden: Brill, 1960). *VTSup* 7 (1960): 31–38.

Barrett, C. K. *Essays on John.* Philadelphia: Westminster, 1982.

Basser, Herbert W. "Planting Christian Trees in Jewish Soil." *Review of Rabbinic Judaism* 8 (2005): 91–112.

Bauckham, Richard. *The Theology of the Book of Revelation.* Cambridge: Cambridge University Press, 1993.

———. *Jesus and the God of Israel: God Crucified and Other Studies on the New Testament's Christology of Divine Identity.* Grand Rapids: Eerdmans, 2008.

———. "Jewish Messianism According to the Gospel of John." Pages 207–38 in *The Testimony of the Beloved Disciple: Narrative, History, and Theology in the Gospel of John.* Grand Rapids: Baker Academic, 2007

————. "The Worship of Jesus." *ABD* 3:812–19. Reprinted on pages 127–51 in Bauckham, *Jesus and the God of Israel: God Crucified and Other Studies on the New Testament's Christology of Divine Identity*. Grand Rapids: Eerdmans, 2008.

Bauer, Walter. *Orthodoxy and Heresy in Earliest Christianity*. Edited by Robert A. Kraft and Gerhard Krodel. Philadelphia: Fortress Press, 1971.

————. *Rechtgläubigkeit und Ketzerei im ältesten Christentum*. BHT 10. Tübingen: Mohr, 1934.

Baumgarten, Albert I. "The Akiban Opposition." *HUCA* 50 (1979): 179–97.

Ben-Amos, D., and J. R. Mintz, trans. *In Praise of the Baal Shem Tov*. Bloomington: University of Indiana Press, 1970.

Ben Ezra, Daniel Stökl. *The Impact of Yom Kippur on Early Christianity: The Day of Atonement from Second Temple Judaism to the Fifth Century*. WUNT 163. Tübingen: Mohr Siebeck, 2003.

Benoit, Pierre. *Jesus and the Gospel*. Translated by Benet Weatherhead. 2 vols. New York: Herder & Herder, 1973–74.

Berkhof, Hendrikus. *Christian Faith: An Introduction to the Study of the Faith*. Translated by Sierd Woudstra. Grand Rapids: Eerdmans, 1979.

Betz, Hans Dieter. *Galatians: A Commentary on Paul's Letters to the Churches in Galatia*. Philadelphia: Fortress Press, 1979.

————. *The Greek Magical Papyri in Translation, Including the Demotic Spells*. 2nd ed. Chicago: University of Chicago Press, 1992.

Biran, Avraham. "Tell Dan, 1976." *Israel Exploration Journal* 26 (1976): 201–6.

Birnbaum, Philip. *Daily Prayer Book, Ha-Siddur ha-Shalem*. New York: Hebrew Publishing Company, 1949.

Black, Matthew. *The Book of Enoch or 1 Enoch: A New English Edition with Commentary and Textual Notes*. SVTP 7. Leiden: Brill, 1985.

————. "The Maranatha Invocation and Jude 14, 15 (I Enoch 1:9)." Pages 189–96 in *Christ and Spirit in the New Testament*. Edited by Barnabas Lindars and Stephen S. Smalley. Cambridge: Cambridge University Press, 1973.

Blackman, Philip, ed. *Mishnayoth*. 7 vols. London: Mishna Press, 1951–56.

Blenkinsopp, Joseph. *Isaiah 56–66: A New Translation*. AB 19B. New York: Doubleday, 2003.

————. "The Qumran Sect in the Context of Second Temple Sectarianism." Pages 10–25 in *New Directions in Qumran Studies*. Library of Second Temple Studies 52. Edited by Jonathan G. Campbell et al. London: T&T Clark 2005.

Bloom, Harold. *Jesus and Yahweh: The Names Divine*. New York: Penguin, 2005.

Blumenthal, David R. *Understanding Jewish Mysticism: A Source Reader*. 2 vols. Library of Jewish Learning 2 and 4. New York: Ktav, 1978, 1982.

Bockmuehl, Markus. *The Epistle to the Philippians*. Black's New Testament Commentaries 18. London: A&C Black, 1997.

Bokser, Baruch M. *Post-Mishnaic Judaism in Transition: Samuel on Berakhot and the Beginnings of Gemara*. BJS. Chico, CA: Scholars, 1980.

———. "The Wall Separating God and Israel." *JQR* 73 (1983): 349–74.

Bonner, Campbell, ed. *The Homily on the Passion by Melito, Bishop of Sardis with Some Fragments of the Apocryphal Ezekiel*. Studies and Documents 12. London: Christophers, 1940.

Boring, M. Eugene. *Revelation*. Interpretation Commentary. Louisville: John Knox, 1989.

Bousset, Wilhelm. *Kyrios Christos*. Translated by John E. Steely. Nashville: Abingdon, 1970.

Boustan, Ra'anan S. "The Dislocation of the Temple Vessels: Mobile Sanctity and Rabbinic Rhetorics of Space." Pages 135–46 and 365–70 in *Jewish Studies at the Crossroads of Anthropology and History: Authority, Diaspora, Tradition*. Jewish Culture and Contexts. Edited by Ra'anan S. Boustan, Oren Kosansky, and Marina Rustow. Philadelphia: University of Pennsylvania Press, 2011.

———. "The Emergence of Pseudonymous Attribution in Heikalot Literature: Empirical Evidence from the Jewish 'Magical' Corpora." *JSQ* 12 (2007): 18–38.

———. *From Martyr to Mystic: Rabbinic Martyrology and the Making of Merkavah Mysticism*. TSAJ 112. Tübingen: Mohr Siebeck, 2005.

———. "Rabbinization and the Making of Early Jewish Mysticism." *JQR* 101 (2011): 482–501.

Boyarin, Daniel. "Beyond Judaisms: Metatron and the Divine Polymorphy of Ancient Judaism." *JSJ* 41 (2010): 323–65.

———. *Border Lines: The Partition of Judaeo-Christianity*. Philadelphia: University of Pennsylvania Press, 2004.

———. "Daniel 7, Intertextuality, and the History of Israel's Cult." *HTR* 105 (2012): 139–62.

———. "The Diadoche of the Rabbis; or, Judah the Patriarch at Yavneh." Pages 285–318 in *Jewish Culture and Society under the Christian Roman* Empire. Interdisciplinary Studies in Ancient Culture and Religion 3. Edited by Richard Kalmin and Seth Schwartz. Leuven: Peeters, 2003.

———. *Dying for God: Martyrdom and the Making of Christianity and Judaism.* Stanford, CA: Stanford University Press, 1999.

———. "The Eye in the Torah: Ocular Desire in Midrashic Hermeneutic." *Critical Inquiry* 16 (1990): 532–50. Reprinted on pages 3–23 in Boyarin, *Sparks of the Logos: Essays in Rabbinic Hermeneutics*. Brill Reference Library of Judaism 11. Leiden: Brill, 2003.

———. "How Enoch Can Teach Us About Jesus." *Early Christianity* 2 (2011): 51–76.

———. *The Jewish Gospels: The Story of the Jewish Christ.* New York: New Press, 2012.

———. "Justin Martyr Invents Judaism." *Church History* 70 (2001): 427–61.

———. "The Parables of Enoch and the Foundation of the Rabbinic Sect: A Hypothesis." Pages 53–72 in *"The Words of a Wise Man's Mouth Are Gracious" (Qoh 10,12): Festschrift For Günter Stemberger On The Occasion of His 65ᵗʰ Birthday.* SJ 32. Edited by Mauro Perani. Berlin: de Gruyter, 2005.

———. "Two Powers in Heaven; or, The Making of a Heresy." Pages 331–70 in *The Idea of Biblical Interpretation: Essays in Honor of James Kugel.* SJSJ 83. Edited by Hindy Najman and Judith H. Newman. Leiden: Brill, 2004.

Boxall, Ian. *The Revelation of Saint John.* Black's New Testament Commentaries 18. London: Continuum, 2006.

Braga, Corin. "'Imagination', 'Imaginaire', 'Imaginal': Three Concepts for Defining Creative Fantasy." *JSRI* 16 (2007): 59–68.

Brakke, David. "A New Fragment of Athanasius's Thirty-Ninth *Festal Letter*: Heresy, Apocrypha, and the Canon." *HTR* 103 (2010): 47–66.

Braude, William G., trans. *Pesikta Rabbati: Discourses for Feasts, Fasts and Special Sabbaths.* 2 vols. Yale Judaica Series 18. New Haven, CT: Yale University Press, 1968.

Brown, Francis, S. R. Driver, and Charles A. Briggs. *Hebrew and English Lexicon of the Old Testament.* Oxford: Clarendon, 1953.

Brown, Peter. "Eastern and Western Christendom in Late Antiquity: A Parting of the Ways." Pages 166–95 in Brown, *Society and the Holy in Late Antiquity.* Berkeley: University of California Press, 1982.

———. "The Saint as Exemplar in Late Antiquity." Pages 3–14 in *Saints and Virtues.* Edited by John Stratton Hawley. Berkeley: University of California Press, 1987.

Brown, Raymond E. *An Introduction to New Testament Christology.* New York: Paulist, 1994.

Buckwalter, Douglas. *The Character and Purpose of Luke's Christology.* Cambridge: Cambridge University Press, 1996.

Bultmann, Rudolf. *Theology of the New Testament.* Translated by K. Groebel. 2 vols. New York: Scribner, 1951.

Butterworth, G. W., trans. *Origen: On First Principles.* New York: Harper & Row, 1966.

Caird, G. B. *A Commentary on the Revelation of St. John the Divine.* Harper's New Testament Commentaries. New York: Harper & Row, 1966.

Capes, David B. *Old Testament Yahweh Texts in Paul's Christology.* WUNT 47. Tübingen: Mohr, 1992.

Carey, Patrick W., and Joseph T. Lienhard. *Biographical Dictionary of Christian Theologians.* Westport, CT: Greenwood,, 2000.

Casey, Maurice. *From Jewish Prophet to Gentile God: The Origins and Development of New Testament Christology.* Cambridge: James Clarke, 1991.

———. "Lord Jesus Christ: A Response to Professor Hurtado." *JSNT* 27 (2004): 83–96.

Cerfaux, Lucien. *Christ in the Theology of St. Paul.* Translated by Geoffrey Webb and Adrian Walker. London: Herder & Herder, 1951.

———. "*Kyrios* dans les citations pauliniennes de l'Ancien Testament." *Ephemerides Theologicae Lovanienses* 20 (1943): 5–17.

Chadwick, Henry, trans. *Saint Augustine: Confessions.* Oxford: Oxford University Press, 1991.

Charlesworth, James H. "Jesus as 'Son' and the Righteous Teacher as 'Gardner.'" Pages 140–75 in Charlesworth, ed., *Jesus and the Dead Sea Scrolls.* ABRL. New York: Doubleday, 1992.

———. "The Jewish Roots of Christology: The Discovery of the Hypostatic Voice." *SJT* 39 (1986): 19–41.

———, ed. *Old Testament Pseudepigrapha.* 2 vols. Garden City, NY: Doubleday, 1983. Abbreviated as *OTP.*

Chazon, Esther G. "Liturgical Communion with the Angels at Qumran." Pages 95–105 in *Sapiential, Liturgical, and Poetical Texts from Qumran: Proceedings of the Third Meeting of the International Organization for Qumran Studies.* STDJ 35. Edited by Daniel K. Falk, Florentino García Martínez, and Eileen M. Schuller. Leiden: Brill, 2000.

Chernus, Ira. "Visions of God in Merkabah Mysticism." *JSJ* 13 (1982): 123–46.

Chester, Andrew. "The Christ of Paul." Pages 109–21 in *Redemption and Resistance: The Messianic Hopes of Jews and Christians in Antiquity.* Edited by

William Horbury, Markus Bockmuehl, and James Carleton Paget. London: T&T Clark, 2007.

———. "High Christology—Whence, When and Why?" *Early Christianity* 2 (2011): 22–50.

Childs, Brevard S. *Memory and Tradition in Israel.* Studies in Biblical Theology 37. London, SCM, 1962.

Christman, Angela Russell. "What Did Ezekiel See? Patristic Exegesis of Ezekiel 1 and Debates about God's Incomprehensibility." *Pro Ecclesia* 8 (1999): 338–63.

———. *"What Did Ezekiel See?" Christian Exegesis of Ezekiel's Vision of the Chariot from Irenaeus to Gregory the Great.* The Bible in Ancient Christianity 4. Leiden: Brill, 2005.

Clark, Elizabeth A. *The Origenist Controversy: The Cultural Construction of an Early Christian Debate.* Princeton, NJ: Princeton University Press, 1992.

Cohen, Shaye J. D. "The Significance of Yavneh: Pharisees, Rabbis, and the End of Jewish Sectarianism." *HUCA* 55 (1984): 27–53.

Collins, Adela Yarbro. "Rulers, Divine Men, and Walking on the Water (Mark 6:45–52)." Pages 212–13 and 226–7 in *Religious Propaganda and Missionary Competition in the New Testament World.* NovTSup 74. Edited by Lukas Bormann et al. Leiden: Brill, 1994.

———. "The 'Son of Man' Tradition and the Book of Revelation." Pages 536–68 in *The Messiah: Developments in Earliest Judaism and Christianity.* Edited by James H. Charlesworth. Minneapolis: Fortress Press, 1992.

Collins, Adela Yarbro, and John J. Collins. *King and Messiah as Son of God: Divine, Human and Angelic Messianic Figures in Biblical and Related Literature.* Grand Rapids: Eerdmans, 2008.

Collins, John J. *Daniel: A Commentary.* Hermeneia. Minneapolis: Fortress Press, 1993.

———. "Gabriel and David: Some Reflections on an Enigmatic Text." Pages 99–112 in *Hazon Gabriel: New Readings.* Early Judaism and its Literature 29. Edited by Matthias Henze and John J. Collins. Atlanta: SBL, 2011.

———. "Introduction: Towards the Morphology of a Genre." Pages 1–20 in *Apocalypse: The Morphology of a Genre.* Semeia 14. Edited by John J. Collins. Missoula, MT: Scholars, 1979.

Cross, Frank Moore. *Canaanite Myth and Hebrew Epic: Essays in the History of the Religion of Israel.* Cambridge, MA: Harvard University Press, 1973.

Crossley, James. "Review of Hurtado, *Lord Jesus Christ.*" *JEH* 56 (2006): 118–20.

Culley, Robert. "Oral Tradition and Biblical Studies." *Oral Tradition* 1 (1986): 30–65.

De Lacey, D.R. "'One Lord' in Pauline Christology." Pages 191–203 in *Christ the Lord: Studies in Christology Presented to Donald Guthrie.* Edited by Harold H. Rowdon. Leicester: InterVarsity Press, 1982.

Dahl, Nils Alstrup. "The Crucified Messiah." Pages 10–36 in *The Crucified Messiah and Other Essays.* Minneapolis: Augsburg Publishing House, 1974. Reprint on pages 27–47 in Dahl, *Jesus the Christ: The Historical Origins of Christological Doctrine.* Edited by Donald H. Juel. Minneapolis: Fortress Press, 1991.

———. "The Johannine Church and History." Pages 124–42, 284–88 in *Current Issues in New Testament Interpretation: Essays in Honor of Otto A. Piper.* Edited by William Klassen and Graydon F. Snyder. New York: Harper, 1962.

Dahood, Mitchell. *Psalms.* 3 vols. AB 16–17A. Garden City, NY: Doubleday, 1966–70.

Dan, Joseph. "The Emergence of Mystical Prayer." Page 85–120 in *Studies in Jewish Mysticism.* Edited by Joseph Dan. Cambridge, MA: Association for Jewish Studies, 1982.

Danby, Herbert, trans. *The Mishnah Translated from the Hebrew with Introduction and Explanatory Notes.* Oxford: Oxford University Press, 1933.

Daniélou, Jean. *The Theology of Jewish Christianity: A History of Early Christian Doctrine before the Council of Nicea.* Translated by John A. Baker. London: Darton, Longman & Todd, 1964.

Davids, Peter H. *The Epistle of James: A Commentary on the Greek Text.* NIGTC. Grand Rapids: Eerdmans, 1982.

Davies, G. Henton. "The Ark in the Psalms." Pages 51–61 in *Promise and Fulfillment: Essays Presented to Professor S. H. Hooke.* Edited by F. F. Bruce. Edinburgh: T&T Clark, 1963.

Davies, Graham I. *Ancient Hebrew Inscriptions: Corpus and Concordance.* Cambridge: Cambridge University Press, 1991.

Davies, Philip R. "Sects from Texts: On the Problem of Doing a Sociology of the Qumran Literature." Pages 69–82 in *New Directions in Qumran Studies.* Library of Second Temple Studies 52. Edited by Jonathan G. Campbell, William John Lyons, and Lloyd K. Pietersen. London: T&T Clark, 2005.

Davila, James R. "The Old Testament Pseudepigrapha as Background to the New Testament." *ExpTim* 117 (2005): 53–57.

———. *Descenders to the Chariot: The People behind the Hekhalot Literature.* SJSJ 70. Leiden: Brill, 2001.

———. *The Provenance of the Pseudepigrapha: Jewish, Christian, or Other?* SJSJ 105. Leiden: Brill, 2005.

Dearman, J. Andrew. "Theophany, Anthropomorphism, and the *Imago Dei*: Some Observations about the Incarnation in the Light of the Old Testament." Pages 31–46 in *The Incarnation: An Interdisciplinary Symposium on the Incarnation of the Son of God.* Edited by Stephen T. Davis, Daniel Kendall, and Gerald O'Collins. Oxford: Oxford University Press, 2002.

DeConick, April. *Recovering the Original Gospel of Thomas: A History of the Gospel and Its Growth.* Library of New Testament Studies 286. London: T&T Clark, 2005.

———. *The Original Gospel of Thomas in Translation: With a Commentary and New English Translation of the Complete Gospel.* Library of New Testament Studies 287. London: T&T Clark, 2006.

———, ed. "'Early Jewish and Christian Mysticism': A Collage of Working Definitions." *SBLSP* 40 (2001): 278–304.

DelCogliano, Mark. "Situating Sarapion's Sorrow: The Anthropomorphite Controversy as the Historical and Theological Context of Cassian's Tenth Conference on Pure Prayer." *Cistercian Studies Quarterly* 38 (2003): 377–421.

Destro, Adriana, and Mauro Pesce. "The Heavenly Journey in Paul: Tradition in a Jewish apocalyptic Literary Genre of Cultural Practice in a Hellenistic-Roman Context?" Pages 167–200 in *Paul's Jewish Matrix.* Studies in Judaism and Christianity. Edited by Thomas G. Casey and Justin Taylor. Rome: Gregorian & Biblical Press, 2012.

Deutsch, Nathaniel. *Guardians of the Gate, Angelic Vice Regency in Late Antiquity.* Brill Series in Jewish Studies 22. Leiden: Brill, 1999.

Dibelius, Martin. *James: A Commentary on the Epistle of James.* Hermeneia. Revised by Heinrich Greeven. Translated by Michael A. Williams. Edited by Helmut Koester. Philadelphia: Fortress Press, 1976.

Dimant, Devorah. "Apocalyptic Texts at Qumran." Pages 177–91 in *The Community of the Renewed Covenant: The Notre Dame Symposium on the Dead Sea Scrolls.* Christianity and Judaism in Antiquity Series 10. Edited by Eugene Ulrich and James VanderKam. Notre Dame, IN: University of Notre Dame Press, 1994.

Dodd, C. H. *According to the Scriptures: The Sub-Structure of New Testament Theology.* London: Nisbet, 1952.

Downing, John. "Jesus and Martyrdom." *JTS* 14 (1963): 279–93.

Drobner, Herbertus R. *The Fathers of the Church: A Comprehensive Introduction.* Translated by Siegfried S. Schatzmann. Peabody, MA: Hendrickson, 2007.

Dunn, James D. G. *Christology in the Making: A New Testament Inquiry into the Origins of the Doctrine of the Incarnation.* Philadelphia: Westminster, 1980.

———. *Did the First Christians Worship Jesus? The New Testament Evidence.* Louisville: Westminster John Knox, 2010.

———. *Jesus and the Spirit: A Study of the Religious and Charismatic Experience of Jesus and the First Christians as Reflected in the New Testament.* London: SCM, 1975.

———. *The Partings of the Ways between Christianity and Judaism and their Significance for the Character of Christianity.* London: SCM, 1991.

———. *The Theology of Paul the Apostle.* Grand Rapids: Eerdmans, 1998.

Ehrlich, Uri. "'In the Last Benedictions He Resembles a Servant Who Has Received a Largess from His Master and Takes His Leave." Pages 41–61 in *The Experience of Jewish Liturgy: Studies Dedicated to Menahem Schmelzer.* Brill Reference Library of Judaism 31, Translated by Dena Ordan. Edited by Debra Reed Blank. Leiden: Brill, 2011.

———. *The Nonverbal Language of Prayer: A New Approach to Jewish Liturgy.* TSAJ 105. Translated by Dena Ordan. Tübingen: Mohr Siebeck, 2004.

Ehrman, Bart D., trans. *The Apostolic Fathers.* 2 vols. LCL 24–25. Cambridge, MA: Harvard University Press, 2003.

Elbogen, Ismar. *Jewish Liturgy: A Comprehensive History.* Translated by Raymond P. Scheindlin. Edited by Joseph Heinemann et al. Philadelphia: Jewish Publication Society, 1993.

Elgvin, Torleif. "Jewish-Christian Editing of the Old Testament Pseudepigrapha." Pages 278–304 in *Jewish Believers in Jesus: The Early Centuries.* Edited by Oskar Skarsaune and Reidar Hvalvik. Peabody, MA: Hendrickson, 2007.

Elior, Rachel. *Jewish Mysticism: The Infinity Expression of Freedom.* Translated by Yudith Nave and Arthur B. Millman. Oxford: Littman, 1997.

———. "R. Joseph Karo and Israel Ba'al Shem Tov—Mystical Metamorphosis, Kabalistic Inspiration, Spiritual Internalization." *Studies in Spirituality* 17 (2007): 267–319.

Elliott, J. K., ed. *The Apocryphal New Testament.* Oxford: Clarendon, 1993.

Ellis, E. Earle. *The Gospel of Luke.* New Century Bible, London: Oliphants, 1974.

Engberg-Pedersen, Troels. "The Construction of Religious Experience in Paul." Pages 147–76. *Experientia, Volume I: Inquiry into Religious Experience in Early Judaism and Christianity.* SBLSS 40. Edited by Frances Flannery, Colleen Shantz, and Rodney A. Werline. Atlanta: SBL, 2008.

Ettlinger, Gerard H. *Jesus, Christ and Savior*. Message of the Fathers of the Church 2. Wilmington, DE: Glazier, 1987.

Evans, Ernest, trans. *Tertullian's Treatise against Praxeas*. London: SPCK, 1948.

Faierstein, Morris M., trans. *Jewish Mystical Autobiographies: Book of Visions and Book of Secrets*. Classics of Western Spirituality. New York: Paulist, 1999.

Falk, Daniel K. "Qumran Prayer Texts and the Temple." Pages 106–26 in *Sapiential, Liturgical, and Poetical Texts from Qumran: Proceedings of the Third Meeting of the International Organization for Qumran Studies*. STDJ 35. Edited by Daniel K. Falk, Florentino García Martínez, and Eileen M. Schuller. Leiden: Brill, 2000.

Fall, Thomas. *St. Justin Martyr: Dialogue with Trypho*. Selections from the Fathers of the Church 3. Washington: Catholic University of America Press, 2003.

Fee, Gordon. *The First Letter to the Corinthians*. NICNT. Grand Rapids; Eerdmans, 1987.

———. *Pauline Christology: An Exegetical-Theological Study*. Peabody, MA: Hendrickson, 2007.

Fekkes, Jan. *Isaiah and Prophetic Traditions in the Book of Revelation: Visionary Antecedents and Their Development*. JSNTSup 93. Sheffield: Sheffield Academic Press, 1994.

Fine, Lawrence. *Physician of the Soul, Healer of the Cosmos: Isaac Luria and his Kabbalistic Fellowship*. Stanford, CA: Stanford University Press, 2003.

Fine, Steven. *This Holy Place: On the Sanctity of the Synagogue during the Greco-Roman Period*. Christianity and Judaism in Antiquity 11. Notre Dame, IN: University of Notre Dame Press, 1997.

Fiorenza, Elisabeth Schüssler. *Transforming Vision: Explorations in Feminist Theology*. Minneapolis: Fortress Press, 2011.

Fishbane, Michael. *Biblical Myth and Rabbinic Mythmaking*. New York: Oxford University Press, 2003.

———. *The Exegetical Imagination: On Jewish Thought and Theology*. Cambridge, MA: Harvard University Press, 1998.

———. "The 'Measures' of God's Glory in the Ancient Midrash." Pages 53–73 in *Messiah and Christos: Studies in the Jewish Origins of Christianity, Presented to David Flusser*. TSAJ 32. Edited by Ithamar Gruenwald, Shaul Shaked, and Guy G. Strousma. Tübingen: Mohr, 1992.

———. "Response to Ithamar Gruenwald." Pages 49–57 in *Gershom Scholem's Major Trends in Jewish Mysticism, 50 Years After*. Proceedings of the Sixth International Conference on the History of Jewish Mysticism. Edited by Peter Schäfer and Joseph Dan. Tübingen: Mohr, 1993.

Fitzmyer, Joseph. *To Advance the Gospel*. New York: Crossroad, 1981.

———. *First Corinthians: A New Translation with Introduction and Commentary*. AYB 32. New Haven, CT: Yale University Press, 2008.

———. *The One Who Is To Come*. Grand Rapids: Eerdmans, 2007.

Flannery-Dailey, Frances. *Dreamers, Scribes, and Priests: Dreamers, Scribes, and Priests: : Jewish Dreams in the Hellenistic and Roman Eras*. SJSJ 90. Leiden: Brill, 2004.

Fletcher-Lewis, Crispin H. T. "Jewish Mysticism, the New Testament and Rabbinic-Period Mysticism." Pages 429–70 in *The New Testament and Rabbinic Literature*. JSJ Supplement 136. Edited by Reimund Bieringer et al. Leiden: Brill, 2010.

———. "The Real Presence of the Son before Christ: Revisiting an Old Approach to Old Testament Christology." *Concordia Theological Quarterly* 68 (2004): 105–26.

Flusser, M. David. *Jesus*. Translated by Ronald Walls. New York: Herder & Herder, 1969.

———. "Paganism in Palestine." Pages 1065–1100 in *The Jewish People in the First Century: Historical Geography, Political History, Social, Cultural and Religious Life and Institutions*. CRINT 1, 1. Edited by S. Safrai and M. Stern. Assen: Van Gorcum, 1974.

———. "Psalms, Hymns and Prayers." Pages 551–77 in *Jewish Writings of the Second Temple Period: Apocrypha, Pseudepigrapha, Qumran, Sectarian Writings, Philo, Josephus*. CRINT 2, Literature of the Jewish People in the Period of the Second Temple and the Talmud 2. Edited by Michael E. Stone. Assen: Van Gorcum, 1984.

Foley, John Miles. *How to Read an Oral Poem*. Urbana: University of Illinois Press, 2002.

———. "Memory in Oral Tradition." Pages 83–96 in *Performing the Gospel: Orality, Memory, and Mark*. Edited by Richard A. Horsley, Jonathan A. Draper, and John Miles Foley (Minneapolis: Fortress Press, 2006).

Ford, J. Massyngberde. *Revelation*. AB 38. Garden City, NY: Doubleday, 1975.

Fossum, Jarl. *The Image of the Invisible God: Essays on the Influence of Jewish Mysticism on Early Christology*. NTOA 30. Göttingen: Vandenhoeck & Ruprecht, 1995.

———. *The Name of God and the Angel of the Lord: Samaritan and Jewish Concepts of Intermediation and the Origin of Gnosticism*. WUNT 36. Tübingen: Mohr, 1985.

Foster, Paul. "Polymorphic Christology: Its Origins and Development in Early Christianity." *JTS* 38 (2007): 66–99.

Fox, Robin Lane. *Pagans and Christians.* New York: Knopf, 1987.

Fraade, Steven D. *From Tradition to Commentary: Torah and Its Interpretation in the Midrash Sifre to Deuteronomy.* SUNY Series in Judaica. Albany: State University of New York Press, 1991.

———. "Literary Composition and Oral Performance in Early Midrashim." *Oral Tradition* 14 (1999): 33–51.

———. "The Temple as a Marker of Jewish Identity Before and After 70 C.E.: The Role of the Holy Vessels in Rabbinic Memory and Imagination." Pages 235–63 in *Jewish Identities in Antiquity: Studies in Memory of Menahem Stern.* Texts and Studies in Ancient Judaism 130. Edited by Lee I. Levine and Daniel R. Schwartz. Tübingen: Mohr Siebeck, 2009.

Frankfurter, David. "Beyond 'Jewish Christianity': Continuing Religious Sub-Cultures of the Second and Third Centuries and Their Documents." Pages 131–43 in *The Ways that Never Parted: Jews and Christians in Late Antiquity and the Early Middle Ages.* TSAJ 95. Edited by Adam H. Becker and Annette Yoshiko Reed. Tübingen: Mohr Siebeck, 2003.

Frankfurter, David. "The Legacy of Jewish Apocalypses in Early Christianity." Pages 129–200 in *The Jewish Apocalyptic Heritage in Early Christianity.* CRINT 3, Jewish Traditions in Early Christian Literature 4. Edited by James C. VanderKam and William Adler. Assen: Van Gorcum, 1996.

Fredriksen, Paula. *Jesus of Nazareth, King of the Jews: A Jewish Life and the Emergence of Christianity.* New York: Knopf, 1999.

Freedman, Harry, and Maurice Simon, eds. *Midrash Rabbah.* 10 vols. London: Soncino, 1939.

Fretheim, Terence. "Christology and the Old Testament." Pages 201–215 in *Who Do You Say that I Am? Essays on Christology.* Edited by Mark Allan Powell and David R. Bauer. Louisville: Westminster John Knox, 1999

———. *The Suffering God: An Old Testament Perspective.* Minneapolis: Fortress Press, 1984.

Fuller, Reginald H. "Christmas, Epiphany, and the Johannine Prologue." Pages 63–73 in *Spirit and Light: Essays in Historical Theology.* Edited by Madeleine L' Engle and William B. Green. New York: Seabury, 1976.

Furnish, Victor. *II Corinthians.* Anchor Bible 32A. Garden City, NY: Doubleday, 1984.

Geljon, Albert C. *Philonic Exegesis in Gregory of Nyssa's De Vita Moysis.* Brown Judaic Studies 333. Providence, RI: Brown Judaic Studies, 2002.

Gieschen, Charles A. *Angelomorphic Christology: Antecedents and Early Evidence.* AGAJU 42. Leiden: Brill, 1998.

———. "The Divine Name in Ante-Nicene Christology." *VC* 57 (2003): 115–58.

———. "The Lamb (Not the Man) on the Divine Throne." Pages 227–43 in *Israel's God and Rebecca's Children: Christology and Community in Early Judaism and Christianity: Essays in Honor of Larry W. Hurtado and Alan F. Segal.* Waco, TX: Baylor University Press, 2007.

———. "The Real Presence of the Son Before Christ: Revisiting an Old Approach to Old Testament Christology." *Concordia Theological Quarterly* 68 (2004): 105–126.

Goehring, James. *Ascetics, Society, and the Desert: Studies in Early Egyptian Monasticism.* Studies in Antiquity and Christianity. Harrisburg, PA: Trinity Press International, 1999.

Golitzin, Alexander. "'The Demons Suggest an Illusion of God's Glory in a Form': Controversy over the Divine Body and Vision of Glory in Some Late Fourth, Early Fifth-Century Monastic Literature." *Scrinium: Revue de patrologie, d'hagiographie critique et d'histoire ecclésiastique* 3 (2007): 13–43.

———. "The Vision of God and the Form of Glory: More Reflections on the Anthropomorphite Controversy of AD 399." Pages 273–97 in *Abba: The Tradition of Orthodoxy in the West: Festschrift for Bishop Kallistos (Ware) of Diokleia.* Edited by John Behr, Andrew Louth, and Dimitri Conomos. Crestwood, NY: St. Vladimir's Seminary Press, 2003.

González, Justo L. *Christian Thought Revisited: Three Types of Theology.* Nashville: Abingdon, 1989.

———. *The Story of Christianity.* 2 vols. San Francisco: Harper, 1984.

Goodenough, Erwin Ramsdell. *Jewish Symbols in the Greco-Roman Period.* 13 vols. Princeton, NJ: Princeton University Press, 1953–68.

Goulder, Michael. "Hebrews and the Ebionites." *NTS* 49 (2003): 393–406.

———. "A Poor Man's Christology." *NTS* 45 (1999): 332–48.

———. *St. Paul versus St. Peter: A Tale of Two Missions.* Louisville: Westminster John Knox, 1995.

———. "Vision and Knowledge." *JSNT* 56 (1994): 53–71.

Graham, William A. *Beyond the Written Word: Oral Aspects of Scripture in the History of Religion.* Cambridge: Cambridge University Press, 1987.

Grant, Robert M. *Gods and the One God.* Library of Early Christianity 1. Philadelphia: Westminster, 1986.

Green, Arthur. *Keter: The Crown of God in Early Jewish Mysticism*. Princeton, NJ: Princeton University Press, 1997.

Green, William Scott. "Romancing the Tome: Rabbinic Hermeneutics and the Theory of Literature." *Semeia* 40 (1987): 148–68.

Greer, Rowan A. "The Man from Heaven: Paul's Last Adam and Apollinaris' Christ." Pages 165–82 and 358–60 in *Paul and the Legacies of Paul*. Edited by William S. Babcock. Dallas: Southern Methodist University Press, 1990.

Grenz, Stanley. *Theology for the Community of God*. Grand Rapids; Eerdmans, 1994.

Grindheim, Sigurd. *Christology in the Synoptic Gospels: God or God's Servant?* London: T&T Clark, 2012.

Grözinger, Karl Erich. "The Names of God and the Celestial Powers: Their Function and Meaning in the Hekhalot Literature." *Jerusalem Studies in Jewish Thought* 6. English section 53–85 in *Early Jewish Mysticism*, Proceedings of the First International Conference on the History of Jewish Mysticism. Edited by Joseph Dan. Jerusalem: Hebrew University, 1987.

Gruenwald, Ithamar. *Apocalyptic and Merkavah Mysticism*. AGAJU 14. Leiden: Brill, 1980.

Gunkel, Hermann *The Legends of Genesis: The Biblical Saga and History*. Translated by W. H. Carruth. Chicago: University of Chicago Press, 1901.

Haenchen, Ernst. *The Acts of the Apostles: A Commentary*. Translated by Bernard Noble, Gerald Shinn, and R. McL. Wilson. Philadelphia: Westminster, 1971.

Halbertal, Moshe. *Concealment and Revelation: Esotericism in Jewish Thought and Its Philosophical Implications*. Translated by Jackie Feldman. Princeton, NJ: Princeton University Press, 2007.

Hall, Stuart George. "The Christology of Melito: A Misrepresentation Exposed." *Studia Patristica* 13 (1975): 154–68.

———, trans. *On Pascha and Fragments*. By Melito of Sardis. Oxford: Clarendon, 1979.

Hällström, Gunnar af. *Fides simpliciorum according to Origen of Alexandria*. Commentationes Humanarum Litterarum 76. Helsinki: Societas Scientarium Fennica, 1984.

Halperin, David J. *The Faces of the Chariot: Early Jewish Responses to Ezekiel's Vision*. TSAJ 16. Tübingen: Mohr, 1988.

———. "Origen, Ezekiel's Merkabah, and the Ascension of Moses." *CH* 50 (1981): 261–75.

Hamm, Dennis. "What the Samaritan Leper Sees: The Narrative Christology of Luke 17:11-19." *CBQ* 56 (1994): 273–87.

Hammer, Reuven, trans. *The Classic Midrash: Tannaitic Commentaries on the Bible*. Classics of Western Spirituality. New York: Paulist, 1995.

———, trans. *Sifre: A Tannaitic Commentary on the Book of Deuteronomy*. Yale Judaica 309. New Haven, CT: Yale University Press, 1986.

Hannah, Darrell D. "The Ascension of Isaiah and Docetic Christology." *VC* 53 (1999): 165–96.

———. "The Elect Son of Man of the *Parables of Enoch*." Pages 130–58 in *"Who is This Son of Man?" The Latest Scholarship on a Puzzling Expression of the Historical Jesus*. Library of New Testament Studies 390. Edited by Larry W. Hurtado and Paul Owen. London: T&T Clark, 2011.

———. "Isaiah's Vision in the Ascension of Isaiah and the Early Church." *JTS* 50 (1999): 80–101.

———. *Michael and Christ: Michael Traditions and Angel Christology in Early Christianity*. WUNT 109. Tübingen: Mohr Siebeck, 1999.

Hanson, Anthony T. *The Image of the Invisible God*. London: SCM, 1982.

———. *Jesus Christ in the Old Testament*. London: SPCK, 1965.

Hardy, Edward Rochie, and Cyril C. Richardson, eds. *Christology of the Later Fathers*. LCC 3. Philadelphia: Westminster, 1954.

Hare, Douglas A. "When Did Messiah Become a Proper Name?" *ExpTim* 121 (2009): 70–73.

Harkins, Angela Kim. *Reading with an "I" to the Heavens: Looking at the Qumran Hodayot through the Lens of Visionary Traditions*. Ekstasis, Religious Experience from Antiquity to the Middle Ages 3. Berlin: de Gruyter, 2012.

Harnack, Adolf. *History of Dogma*. Translated by Neil Buchanan. 7 vols. Boston: Little, Brown, & Co., 1905-7.

Hartman, Louis F., and Alexander A. Di Lella. *The Book of Daniel*. AB 23. Garden City, NY: Doubleday, 1978.

Hasan-Rokem, Galit. *Web of Life: Folklore and Midrash in Rabbinic Literature*. Translated by Batya Stein. Stanford, CA: Stanford University Press, 2000.

Hay, David M. *Glory at the Right Hand: Psalm 110 in Early Christianity*. SBLMS 18. Nashville: Abingdon, 1973.

Hays, Richard B. "Can the Gospels Teach Us How to Read the Old Testament?" *Pro Ecclesia* 11 (2002): 402–18.

———. "Christ Prays the Psalms: Paul's Use of an Early Christian Exegetical Convention." Pages 122–36 in *The Future of Christology: Essays in Honor of*

Leander E. Keck. Edited by A. J. Malherbe and W. A. Meeks. Minneapolis: Fortress Press, 1993.

Hayward, C. T. R. "Understanding of the Temple Service in the LXX Pentateuch." Pages 385–400 in *Temple and Worship in Biblical Israel: Proceedings of the Oxford Old Testament Seminar.* Library of Hebrew Bible/Old Testament Studies 422. Edited by John Day. London: T&T Clark, 2005.

Hecker, Joel. "Eating Gestures and the Ritualized Body in Medieval Jewish Mysticism." *HR* 40 (2000): 125–52.

———. *Mystical Bodies, Mystical Meals: Eating and Embodiment in Medieval Kabbalah.* Detroit: Wayne State University Press, 2005.

———. "Mystical Eating and Food Practices in the *Zohar.*" Pages 353–63 in *Judaism in Practice from the Middle Ages through the Early Modern Period.* Edited by Lawrence Fine. Princeton, NJ: Princeton University Press, 2001.

Heger, Paul. "*1 Enoch*—Complementary of Alternative to Mosaic Torah?" *JSJ* 41 (2010): 29–62.

Heil, John Paul. *Jesus Walking on the Sea.* Rome: Pontifical Biblical Institute, 1981.

Heinemann, Joseph. *Literature of the Synagogue.* Edited by Jakob J. Petuchowski. New York: Behrman House, 1975.

———. *Prayer in the Talmud: Forms and Patterns.* SJ 9. Berlin: de Gruyter, 1977.

Henderson, Suzanne Watts. *Christology and Discipleship in the Gospel of Mark.* Cambridge: Cambridge University Press, 2006.

Hengel, Martin. *Between Jesus and Paul: Studies in the History of Earliest Christianity.* Translated by John Bowden. Minneapolis: Fortress Press, 1983.

———. *Judaism and Hellenism: Studies in Their Encounter in Palestine during the Early Hellenistic Period.* Translated by John Bowden. 2 vols. London: SCM, 1974.

———. *Son of God: The Origin of Christology and the History of Jewish-Hellenistic Religion.* Philadelphia: Fortress Press, 1976.

———. *Studies in Early Christology.* Edinburgh: T&T Clark, 1995.

———, and Anna Maria Schwemer. *Paul Between Damascus and Antioch: The Unknown Years.* Translated by John Bowden. Louisville: Westminster John Knox, 1997.

Heschel, Abraham. *Heavenly Torah as Refracted through the Generations.* Translated by Gordon Tucker and Leonard Levin. New York: Continuum, 2005.

———. *Prophetic Inspiration after the Prophets: Maimonides and Others Medieval Authorities.* Hoboken, NJ: Ktav, 1996.

Hezser, Catherine. *The Social Structure of the Rabbinic Movement in Roman Palestine.* TSAJ 66. Tübingen: Mohr Siebeck, 1997.

Himmelfarb, Martha. *Ascent to Heaven in Jewish and Christian Apocalypses.* New York: Oxford University Press, 1993.

Hirshman, Marc G. *A Rivalry of Genius: Jewish and Christian Biblical Interpretation in Late Antiquity.* SUNY Series in Judaica. Albany: State University of New York Press, 1996.

Hofer, Andrew. "The Old Man as Christ in Justin's *Dialogue with Trypho.*" *VC* 57 (2003): 1–21.

Hoffman, Lawrence A. *Beyond the Text: A Holistic Approach to Liturgy.* Bloomington, IN: Indiana University Press, 1987.

———, ed. *My People's Prayer Book.* 10 vols. Woodstock, VT: Jewish Lights, 1997–2013. Abbreviated as MPPB.

Horbury, William. *Jewish Messianism and the Cult of Christ.* London: SCM, 1998.

———. *Messianism among Jews and Christians: Twelve Biblical and Historical Studies.* London: T&T Clark, 2003.

———. Review of Hurtado, *Lord Jesus Christ. JTS* 56 (2005): 531–9.

Hörner, Hadwig, ed. *Auctorum incertorum, vulgo Basilii vel Gregorii Nysseni Sermones de creatione hominis; Sermo de paradise.* Leiden: Brill, 1972.

Horsley, Richard. *Scribes, Visionaries, and the Politics of Second Temple Judea.* Louisville: Westminster John Knox, 2007.

Hubbard, Benjamin J. "Commissioning Stories in Luke-Acts: A Study of their Antecedents, Form and Content." *Semeia* 8 (1977): 103–23.

Hultgren, Arland J., and Steven A. Haggmark, eds. *The Earliest Christian Heretics: Readings from their Opponents.* Minneapolis: Fortress Press, 1996.

Hundley, Michael. "To Be or Not to Be: A Reexamination of Name Language in Deuteronomy and the Deuteronomistic history." *VT* 59 (2009): 533–55.

Hurtado, Larry W. "The Binitarian Shape of Early Christian Worship." Pages 187–213 in *The Jewish Roots of Christological Monotheism: Papers from the St. Andrews Conference on the Historical Origins of the Worship of Jesus.* SJSJ 63. Edited by Carey C. Newman, James R. Davila, and Gladys L. Lewis. Leiden: Brill, 1999.

———. "Convert, Apostate or Apostle to the Nations: The 'Conversion' of Paul in Recent Scholarship." *JBL* 22 (1993): 273–84.

———. *God in New Testament Theology.* Library of Biblical Theology. Nashville: Abingdon, 2010.

———. *How On Earth Did Jesus Become a God?* Grand Rapids: Eerdmans, 2005.

———. "'Jesus' as God's Name, and Jesus as God's Embodied Name in Justin Martyr." Pages 128–36 in *Justin Martyr and His Worlds*. Edited by Sara Parvis and Paul Foster. Minneapolis: Fortress Press, 2007.

———. "Lord." Pages 560–69 in *Dictionary of Paul and his Letters*. Edited by Gerald F. Hawthorne and Ralph P. Martin. Downers Grove, IL: InterVarsity Press, 1993.

———. *Lord Jesus Christ: Devotion to Jesus in Earliest Christianity*. Grand Rapids: Eerdmans, 2003.

———. *One God, One Lord: Early Christian Devotion and Ancient Jewish Monotheism*. Philadelphia: Fortress Press, 1988.

Idel, Moshe. "Adam and Enoch According to St. Ephrem the Syrian." *Kabbalah* 6 (2001): 183–205.

———. *Ascensions on High in Jewish Mysticism: Pillars, Lines, Ladders*. CEU Studies in the Humanities 2. Budapest: Central European University, 2005.

———. *Ben: Sonship and Jewish Mysticism*. Kogod Library of Judaic Studies 5. London: Continuum, 2007.

———. *Enchanted Chains: Techniques and Rituals in Jewish Mysticism*. Los Angeles: Cherub, 2005.

———. *Kabbalah: New Perspectives*. New Haven, CT: Yale University Press, 1988.

———. "Theologization of Kabbalah in Modern Scholarship." Pages 123–73 in *Religious Apologetics—Philosophical Argumentation*. Religion in Philosophy and Theology 10. Edited by Yossef Schwartz and Volkhard Krech. Tübingen: Mohr Siebeck, 2004.

———. "Torah: Between Presence and Representation of the Divine in Jewish Mysticism." Pages 197–236 in *Representation in Religion: Studies in Honor of Moshe Barasch*. Studies in the History of Religions 89. Edited by Jan Assmann and Albert I. Baumgarten. Leiden: Brill, 2001.

Jackson, Howard M. "The Origins and Development of *Shi'ur Qomah* Revelation in Jewish Mysticism." *JSJ* 31 (2000): 373–415.

Jacob, Edmond. *Theology of the Old Testament*. Translated by Arthur W. Heathcote and Philip J. Allcock. London: Hodder & Stoughton, 1958.

Jacobs, Irving. *Holy Living: Saints and Saintliness in Judaism*. Northvale, NJ: Aronson, 1990.

———. *The Midrashic Process: Tradition and Interpretation in Rabbinic Judaism*. Leiden: Brill, 1995.

Jacobs, Louis. *Jewish Mystical Testimonies*. New York: Schocken Books, 1996.

Jaffé, Dan. "L'Identification de Jésus au modèle du hasid charismatique Galiléen: Les thèses de Geza Vermes et de Shmuel Safrai revisitées." *NTS* 55 (2009): 218–46.

Jaffee, Martin S. "Oral Tradition in the Writings of Rabbinic Oral Torah: On Theorizing Rabbinic Orality." *Oral Tradition* 14 (1999): 3–32.

———. "What Difference Does the 'Orality' of Rabbinic Writing Make for the Interpretation of Rabbinic Writings?" Pages 11–33 in *How Should Rabbinic Literature Be Read in the Modern World?* Edited by Matthew Kraus. Piscataway, NJ: Gorgias, 2006.

———. "Writing and Rabbinic Oral Tradition: On Mishnaic Narrative, Lists and Mnemonics." *Journal of Jewish Thought and Philosophy* 1 (1991): 123–46.

Jefford, Clayton N. *The Apostolic Fathers and the New Testament.* Hendrickson, MA: Peabody, 2007.

Jensen, Minna Skafte. "Performance." Pages 45–54 in *A Companion to Ancient Epic.* Edited by John Miles Foley. Malden, MA: Blackwell, 2005.

Jensen, Robin M. *Face to Face: Portraits of the Divine in Early Christianity.* Minneapolis: Fortress Press, 2001.

———. "Theophany and the Invisible God in Early Christian Theology and Art." Pages 271–96 in *God in Early Christian Thought: Essays in Memory of Lloyd G. Patterson.* VCSup 94. Edited by Andrew B. McGowan, Brian E. Daley, and Timothy J. Gaden. Leiden: Brill, 2009.

Jeremias, Joachim. *The Prayers of Jesus.* Studies in Biblical Theology 2, 6. Philadelphia: Fortress Press, 1978.

Joffe, Laura. "The Elohistic Psalter: What, How and Why?" *SJOT* 15 (2001): 142–69.

Juel, Donald. *Messianic Exegesis: Christological Interpretation of the Old Testament in Early Christianity.* Philadelphia: Fortress Press, 1988.

Kadushin, Max. *The Rabbinic Mind.* 3rd ed. New York: Bloch, 1972.

Kähler, Martin. *The So-Called Historical Jesus and the Historic, Biblical Christ.* Translated by Carl E. Braaten. Philadelphia: Fortress Press, 1964.

Kaiser, Christopher B. "The Biblical and Patristic Doctrine of the Trinity." Pages 161–92 in *Theological Dialogue between Orthodox and Reformed Churches.* Edited by Thomas F. Torrance. 2 vols. Edinburgh: Scottish Academic Press, 1993.

———. *The Doctrine of God: A Historical Survey.* Foundations for Faith. London: Marshall, Morgan, & Scott, 1982. Revised ed., Eugene, OR: Wipf & Stock, 2001.

———. "Climbing Jacob's Ladder: John Calvin and the Early Church on Our Eucharistic Ascent to Heaven." *SJT* 56 (2003): 247–67.

———. *Creational Theology and the History of Physical Science: The Creationist Tradition from Basil to Bohr.* Studies in the History of Christian Thought 78. Leiden: Brill, 1997.

———. *Toward a Theology of Scientific Endeavour: The Descent of Science.* Ashgate Science and Religion Series. London: Ashgate, 2007.

Kalmin, Richard. *The Sage in Jewish Society of Late Antiquity.* New York: Routledge, 1999.

Kanarfogel, Ephraim. "Prayer, Literacy, and Literary Memory in the Jewish communities of Medieval Europe." Pages 250–70 and 397–404 in *Jewish Studies at the Crossroads of Anthropology and History: Authority, Diaspora, Tradition.* Jewish Culture and Contexts. Edited by Ra'anan S. Boustan, Oren Kosansky, and Marina Rustow. Philadelphia: University of Pennsylvania Press, 2011.

Kaplan, Lawrence. "Adam, Enoch, and Metatron Revisited: A Critical Analysis of Moshe Idel's Method of Reconstruction." *Kabbalah* 6 (2001): 73–119.

Karnes, Michelle. *Imagination, Meditation, and Cognition in the Middle Ages.* Chicago: University of Chicago Press, 2011.

Käsemann, Ernst. *The Testament of Jesus: A Study of the Gospel of John in the Light of Chapter 17.* Translated Gerhard Krodel. Philadelphia: Fortress Press, 1968.

Kelber, Werner H. "Modalities of Communication, Cognition, and Physiology of Perception: Orality, Rhetoric, Scribality." *Semeia* 65 (1994): 193–216.

———. *The Oral and The Written Gospel: The Hermeneutics of Speaking and Writing in the Synoptic Tradition, Mark, Paul, and Q.* Philadelphia: Fortress Press, 1983.

Kelly, J. N. D. *Early Christian Doctrines.* 4th ed. London: A&C Black, 1968.

Kim, Seyoon. *The Origin of Paul's Gospel.* WUNT 4. Grand Rapids: Eerdmans, 1982.

———. *Paul and the New Perspective: Second Thoughts on the Origin of Paul's Gospel.* Grand Rapids: Eerdmans, 2002.

Kimelman, Reuven. "Polemics and Rabbinic Liturgy." Pages 59–97 in *Discussing Cultural Influences: Text, Context and Non-Text in Rabbinic Judaism.* SJ. Edited by Rivka Ulmer. Lanham, MD: University Press of America, 2007.

Kister, Menahem. "A Common Heritage: Biblical Interpretation at Qumran and Its Implications." Pages 101–11 in *Biblical Perspectives: Early Use and*

Interpretation of the Bible in Light of the Dead Sea Scrolls. STDJ 28. Edited by Michael E. Stone and Esther G. Chazon. Leiden: Brill, 1998.

———. "Some Early Jewish and Christian Exegetical Problems and the Dynamics of Monotheism." *JSJ* 37 (2006): 548–93.

Klawans, Jonathan. *Purity, Sacrifice, and the Temple: Symbolism and Supersessionism in the Study of Ancient Judaism.* Oxford: Oxford University Press, 2006.

Klein, Michael L., trans. *The Fragment-Targums of the Pentateuch.* Rome: Biblical Institute Press, 1980.

Knight, Jonathan. "The Origin and Significance of the Angelomorphic Christology in the *Ascension of Isaiah.*" *JTS* 63 (2012): 66–105.

Knohl, Israel. "'By Three Days Live': Messiahs, Resurrection, and Ascent to Heaven in *Hazon Gabriel.*" *JR* 88 (2008): 147–58.

Koester, Helmut. *From Jesus to the Gospels: Interpreting the New Testament in its Context.* Minneapolis: Fortress Press, 2007.

———. "Suffering Servant and Royal Messiah: From Second Isaiah to Paul, Mark, and Matthew." *Theology Digest* 51 (2004): 103–24.

Kovelman, Arkady. *Between Alexandria and Jerusalem: The Dynamic of Jewish and Hellenistic Culture.* Brill Reference Library of Judaism 21. Leiden: Brill, 2005.

Kowalski, Beate. "Transformation of Ezekiel in John's Revelation." Pages 279–311 in *Transforming Visions: Transformations of Text, Tradition, and Theology in Ezekiel.* Edited by William A. Tooman and Michael A. Lyons. Eugene, OR: Pickwick Publications, 2010.

Kraemer, Ross Shepherd. *When Aseneth Met Joseph: A Late Antique Tale of the Biblical Patriarch and His Egyptian Wife Reconsidered.* Atlanta: Scholars, 1996.

Kramer, Werner. *Christ, Lord, Son of God.* Translated by Brian Hardy. Studies in Biblical Theology 50. London: SCM, 1966.

Kreitzer, Joseph. *Jesus and God in Paul's Eschatology.* JSOTSup 19. Sheffield: Sheffield Academic Press, 1987.

Kugel, James L. "David the Prophet." Pages 45–55 and 198–200 in *Poetry and Prophecy: The Beginnings of a Literary Tradition.* Myth and Poetics. Edited by James L. Kugel. Ithaca, NY: Cornell University Press, 1990.

———. "The Scripturalization of Prayer." Pages 1–5 in *Prayers that Cite Scripture.* Edited by James L. Kugel. Cambridge, MA: Harvard University Center for Jewish Studies, 2006.

Lane, William L. *Gospel According to Mark.* NICNT. Grand Rapids: Eerdmans, 1974.

Langer, Ruth. "The Amidah as Formative Rabbinic Prayer." Pages 127–56 in *Identität durch Gebet: Zur gemeinschaftsbildenden Funktion institutionalisierten Betens in Judentum und Christentum.* Studien zu Judentum und Christentum. Edited by Stephan Wahle. Paderborn: Schöningh, 2003.

———. "Biblical Texts in Jewish Prayers: Their History and Function." Pages 63–90 in *Jewish and Christian Liturgy and Worship: New Insights into its History and Interaction.* Jewish and Christian Perspectives 15. Edited by Albert Gerhards and Clemens Leonhard. Leiden: Brill, 2007.

———. "Revisiting Early Rabbinic Liturgy: The Recent Contributions of Ezra Fleischer." *Prooftexts* 19 (1999): 179–94.

———. *To Worship God Properly: Tensions Between Liturgical Custom and Halakhah in Judaism.* Cincinnati: Hebrew Union College Press, 1998.

Lapham, Fred. *An Introduction to the New Testament Apocrypha.* Understanding the Bible and its World. London: T&T Clark, 2003.

Lauterbach, Jacob Z., trans. *Mekilta of Rabbi Ishmael.* 3 vols. Philadelphia: Jewish Publication Society of America, 1933.

Layton, Bentley. *The Gnostic Scriptures.* ABRL. New York: Doubleday, 1995.

Lesses, Rebecca. *Ritual Practices to Gain Power: Angels, Incantations, and Revelation in Early Jewish Mysticism.* Harvard Theological Studies 44. Harrisburg, PA: Trinity Press International, 1998.

Levine, Lee I. *The Rabbinic Class of Roman Palestine in Late Antiquity.* New York: Jewish Theological Seminary of America, 1989.

Liber, M. "Structure and History of the *Tefilah*." *JQR* 40 (1950): 331–57.

Lieberman, Saul. *Hellenism in Jewish Palestine; Studies in the Literary Transmission, Beliefs and Manners of Palestine in the I Century B.C.E.-IV Century C.E.* New York: Jewish Theological Seminary of America, 1950.

Liesel, Nikolaus. *The Eucharistic Liturgies of the Eastern Churches.* Translated by David Heimann. Collegeville, MN: Liturgical Press, 1962.

Lindars, Barnabas. *New Testament Apologetic: The Doctrinal Significance of the Old Testament Quotations.* London: SCM, 1961.

Lindblom, Johannes. "Theophanies in Holy Places in Hebrew Religion." *HUCA* 21 (1961): 91–106.

Litwa, M. David. "Transformation Through a Mirror: Moses in 2 Cor. 3.1." *JSNT* 34 (2012): 286–97.

Luibheid, Colm. *John Cassian: Conferences.* Classics of Western Spirituality. New York: Paulist, 1985.

McGinn, Bernard. *The Foundations of Mysticism.* New York: Crossroad, 1991.

McGrath, James F. "On Hearing (Rather Then Reading) Intertextual Echoes: Christology and Monotheistic Scriptures in an Oral Context." *BTB* 43 (2013): 74–80.

———. *The Only True God: Early Christian Monotheism in its Jewish Context.* Urbana: University of Illinois Press, 2009.

McLeod, Frederick G. "The Christology in Theodore of Mopsuestia's *Commentary on the Gospel of John*." *TS* 73 (2012): 115–38.

McNamara, Martin. *Targum and Testament: Aramaic Paraphrases of the Hebrew Bible: A Light on the New Testament.* Grand Rapids: Eerdmans, 1972.

———. *Targum and Testament Revisited: Aramaic Paraphrases of the Hebrew Bible: A Light on the New Testament.* Grand Rapids: Eerdmans, 2010.

———. "Targum and the New Testament: A Revisit." Pages 387–427 in *The New Testament and Rabbinic Literature.* SJSJ 136. Edited by Reimund Bieringer et al. Leiden: Brill, 2010.

———, trans. *Targum Neofiti 1: Exodus.* Aramaic Bible 2. Collegeville, MN: Liturgical Press, 1994.

McVey, Kathleen E., trans. *Ephrem the Syrian: Hymns.* Classics of Western Spirituality. New York: Paulist, 1989.

Macdonald, John, trans. *Memar Marqah: The Teaching of Marqah.* BZAW 84. Berlin: Töpelmann, 1963.

Mackie, Scott C. "Heavenly Sanctuary Mysticism in the Epistle to the Hebrews." *JTS* 62 (2011): 77–117.

———. "Seeing God in Philo of Alexandria: Means, Methods and Mysticism." *JSJ* 43 (2012): 147–79.

McLeod, Frederick G. *Theodore of Mopsuestia.* Early Church Fathers. London: Routledge, 2009.

Maloney, George A., trans. *Pseudo-Macarius: The Fifty Spiritual Homilies and the Great Letter.* Classics of Western Spirituality. New York: Paulist, 1992.

Malherbe, Abraham J., and Everett Ferguson, trans. *Gregory of Nyssa: The Life of Moses.* Classics of Western Spirituality. New York: Paulist, 1978

Manning, Gary T. *Echoes of a Prophet, The Use of Ezekiel in the Gospel of John and in the Literature of the Second Temple Period.* London: T&T Clark, 2004.

Marcus, Joel. *Mark 1–8.* AB 27. New York: Doubleday, 2000.

———. "The Once and Future Messiah in Early Christianity and Chabad." *NTS* 47 (2001): 381–401.

———. "Passover and Last Supper Revisited." *NTS* 59 (2013): 303–34.

Marmorstein, Arthur. "The Holy Spirit in Rabbinic Legend." Pages 179–224 in Marmorstein, *Studies in Jewish Theology: The Arthur Marmorstein Memorial*

Volume. Edited by J. Rabbinowitz and M. S. Lew. Oxford: Oxford University Press, 1950.

——. *The Old Rabbinic Doctrine of God.* Vol. 2: Essays in Anthropomorphism. New York: Ktav, 1968.

Martínez, Florentino García, and Eibert J. C. Tigchelaar, eds. *The Dead Sea Scrolls, Study Edition.* 2 vols. Leiden: Brill, 1997.

Mastin, B. A. "Yahweh's Asherah, Inclusive Monotheism and the Question of Dating." Pages 326–51 in *In Search of Pre-Exilic Israel: Proceedings of the Oxford Old Testament Seminar.* JSOTSup 406. Edited by John Day. London: T&T Clark, 2004.

Matt, Daniel. "New-Ancient Words: The Aura of Secrecy in the Zohar." Pages 181–207 in *Gershom Scholem's Major Trends in Jewish Mysticism, 50 Years After.* Proceedings of the Sixth International Conference on the History of Jewish Mysticism. Edited by Peter Schäfer and Joseph Dan. Tübingen: Mohr, 1993.

Mauser, Ulrich. "Image of God and Incarnation." *Interpretation* 24 (1970): 336–56.

Menken, Maarten J. J. "The Opponents in the Johannine Letters." Pages 191–209 in *Empsychoi Logoi—Religious Innovations in Antiquity: Studies in Honour of Pieter Willem van der Horst.* Ancient Judaism and Early Christianity 73. Edited by Alberdina Houtman, Albert de Jong, and Magda Misset-van de Weg. Leiden: Brill, 2008.

Merkur, Daniel. "The Visionary Practices of Jewish Apocalypticists." *The Psychoanalytic Study of Society* 14 (1989): 119–48. Reprinted in volume 2 on pages 317–47 in *Psychology and the Bible: A New Way to Read the Scriptures.* Edited by J. Harold Ellens and Wayne G. Rollins. 4 vols. Westport: CT: Praeger, 2004.

Mettinger, Tryggve N. D. *The Dethronement of Sabaoth: Studies in the Shem and Kabod Theologies.* Coniectanea Biblica, Old Testament Series 18. Lund: CWK Gleerup, 1982.

——. *In Search of God: The Meaning and Message of the Everlasting Names.* Translated by Frederick H. Cryer. Philadelphia: Fortress Press, 1988.

——. "Israelite Aniconism: Developments and Origins." Pages 173–204 in *The Image and the Book: Iconic Cults, Aniconism, and the Rise of Book Religion in Israel and the Ancient Near East.* Edited by Karel van der Toorn. Leuven: Peeters, 1997.

———. *No Graven Image? Israelite Aniconism in its Ancient Near Eastern Context.* Coniectanea Biblica, Old Testament Series 42. Stockholm: Almqvist & Wiksell, 1995.

Michaels, J. Ramsey. "Catholic Christologies in the Catholic Epistles." Pages 268–91 in *Contours of Christology in the New Testament.* McMaster New Testament Studies. Edited by Richard N. Longenecker. Grand Rapids: Eerdmans, 2005.

Middleton, Jill. "Transformation of the Image." Pages 113–37 in *Transforming Visions: Transformations of Text, Tradition, and Theology in Ezekiel.* Edited by William A. Tooman and Michael A. Lyons. Eugene, OR: Pickwick Publications, 2010.

Miller, Stuart S. *Sages and Commoners in Late Antique Erez Israel: A Philological Inquiry into Local Traditions in Talmud Yerushalmi.* TSAJ 111. Tübingen: Mohr Siebeck, 2006.

Mingana, Alphonse, trans. *Commentary of Theodore of Mopsuestia on the Lord's Prayer and on Sacraments of Baptism and the Eucharist.* Woodbrook Studies 6. Cambridge: Heffer, 1933; Piscataway, NJ: Gorgias, 2009.

———, trans. *Commentary of Theodore of Mopsuestia on the Nicene Creed.* Woodbrook Studies 5. Cambridge: Heffer, 1932; Piscataway: Gorgias, 2009.

Mitchell, David C. "Messiah ben Joseph: A Sacrifice of Atonement for Israel." *RRJ* 10 (2007): 77–94.

Mitchell, Leonel L. "The Alexandrian Anaphora of St. Basil of Caesarea: Ancient Source of 'A Common Eucharistic Prayer.'" *ATR* 58 (1976): 194–206.

Moessner, David P. "*Two* Lords 'at the Right Hand'?: The Psalms and an Intertextual Reading of Peter's Pentecost Speech (Acts 2:14-36)." Pages 215–32 in *Literary Studies in Luke-Acts: Essays in Honor of Joseph B. Tyson.* Edited by Richard P. Thompson and Thomas E. Phillips. Macon, GA: Mercer University Press, 1998.

Morray-Jones, Christopher R. A. "Paradise Revisited (2 Cor. 12:1-12): The Jewish Mystical Background of Paul's Apostolate." *HTR* 86 (1993): 177–217, 265–92.

———. *The Transparent Illusion: The Dangerous Vision of Water in Hekhalot Mysticism: A Source-Critical and Tradition-Historical Inquiry.* SJSJ 59. Leiden: Brill, 2002.

——— and Christopher Rowland. *The Mystery of God: Early Jewish Mysticism and the New Testament.* CRINT 3, Jewish Traditions in Early Christian Literature 12. Leiden: Brill, 2009.

Motter, Adilson E., and David K. Campbell. "Chaos at Fifty." *Physics Today* 66 (2013): 27–33.

Mowinckel, Sigmund. *He that Cometh*. Translated by G. W. Anderson. Nashville: Abingdon, 1954.

Moyise, Steve. *The Old Testament in the Book of Revelation*. JSNTSup 115. Sheffield: Sheffield Academic Press, 1995.

Munoa, Philip. "Raphael, Azariah and Jesus of Nazareth: Tobit's Significance for Early Christology." *JSP* 22 (2012): 3–39.

Nelson, W. David. "Oral Orthography: Oral and Written Transmission of Parallel Midrashic Tradition in the *Mekilta of Rabbi Shimon bar Yohai* and the *Mekilta of Rabbi Ishmael*." *AJS Review* 29 (2005): 1–32.

——, trans. *Mekhilta of Rabbi Shimon Bar Yohai*. Philadelphia: Jewish Publication Society of America, 2002.

Neusner, Jacob. "Jewish Use of Pagan Symbols After 70 C.E." *JR* 43 (1963): 285–94.

——. *Judaism: The Evidence of the Mishnah*. Chicago: University of Chicago Press, 1981.

——. *Judaism and Scripture: The Evidence of Leviticus Rabbah*. Chicago Studies in the History of Judaism. Chicago: University of Chicago Press, 1986.

——. *Oral Tradition in Judaism: The Case of the Mishnah*. Garland Reference Library of the Humanities 764. New York: Garland, 1987.

——. *Transformations in Ancient Judaism: Textual Evidence for Creative Responses to Crisis*. Peabody, MA: Hendrickson, 2004.

——, trans. *Sifré Zutta to Numbers*. Studies in Judaism. Lanham, MD: University Press of America, 2009.

——, trans. *Sifre to Deuteronomy*. 2 vols. BJS 98, 101. Atlanta: Scholars, 1987.

——, trans. *Sifrei to Numbers*. 2 vols. BJS 118–19. Atlanta: Scholars, 1986.

——, et al., trans. *The Talmud of the Land of Israel*. 35 vols. Chicago Studies in the History of Judaism. Chicago: University of Chicago Press, 1982–87.

——, William Scott Green, and Ernest S. Frerichs. *Judaisms and Their Messiahs at the Turn of the Christian Era*. Cambridge: Cambridge University Press, 1987.

Newman, Carey. "Christophany as a Sign of 'the End.'" Pages 155–67 in *Israel's God and Rebecca's Children: Christology and Community in Early Judaism and Christianity: Essays in Honor of Larry W. Hurtado and Alan F. Segal*. Edited by David B. Capes et al. Waco, TX: Baylor University Press, 2007.

——. *Paul's Glory-Christology: Tradition and Rhetoric*. NovTSup 69. Leiden: Brill, 1992.

Newman, Judith. *Praying by the Book: The Scripturalization of Prayer in Second Temple Judaism.* Early Judaism and its Literature 14. Atlanta: Scholars, 1999.

———. "The Scripturalization of Prayer in Exilic and Second Temple Judaism." Pages 7–24 in *Prayers that Cite Scripture.* Edited by James L. Kugel. Cambridge, MA: Harvard University Press, 2006.

Nickelsburg, George W. E. *Ancient Judaism and Christian Origins: Diversity, Continuity, and Transformation.* Minneapolis: Fortress Press, 2003.

———. "Enoch, Levi, and Peter: Recipients of Revelation in Upper Galilee." *JBL* 100 (1981): 575–600.

———, and Robert Kraft. Introduction to *Early Judaism and Its Modern Interpreters.* Edited by Robert A. Kraft and George W. E. Nickelsburg. Bible and its Modern Interpreters 2. Atlanta: Scholars, 1986.

Nickelsburg, George W. E., and James C. VanderKam. *1 Enoch: A Commentary on the Book of 1 Enoch.* Hermeneia. Edited by Klaus Baltzer. 2 vols. Minneapolis: Fortress Press, 2001, 2012.

Nitzan, Bilhah. *Qumran Prayer and Religious Poetry.* Translated by Jonathan Chipman. STDJ 2. Leiden: Brill, 1994.

Norris, Richard A., trans. *The Christological Controversy.* Sources of Early Christian Thought. Philadelphia: Fortress Press, 1980.

North, J. Lionel. "Jesus and Worship, God and Sacrifice." Pages 186–202 in *Early Judaism and Christian Monotheism.* Edited by Loren T. Stuckenbruck and Wendy E. S. North. London: T&T Clark, 2004.

O'Neill, J. C. "The Use of *Kyrios* in the Book of Acts." *SJT* 8 (1955): 155–74.

O'Toole, Robert F. *Acts 26: The Christological Climax of Paul's Defense [Ac.22:1—26:32].* Rome: Biblical Institute Press, 1978.

———. *Luke's Presentation of Jesus: A Christology.* Rome: Pontifical Biblical Institute, 2004.

Olson, Daniel. *Enoch: A New Translation.* North Richland Hills, TX: BIBAL Press, 2004.

Ong, Walter. *Orality and Literacy: The Technologizing of the Word.* London: Methuen, 1982.

Pagels, Elaine. *Beyond Belief: The Secret Gospel of Thomas.* New York: Random House, 2003.

Pak, G. Sujin. *The Judaizing Calvin: Sixteenth-Century Debates over the Messianic Psalms.* Oxford: Oxford University Press, 2010.

Pearson, Birger. *Ancient Gnosticism: Traditions and Literature.* Minneapolis: Fortress Press, 2007.

————. "Basilides." Pages 1–31 in *A Companion to Second-Century Christian "Heretics."* Edited by Antti Marjanen and Petri Luomanen. VCSup 76. Leiden: Brill, 2005.

Peerbolte, Bert Jan Lietaert. "The Name above All Names (Philippians 2:9)." Pages 187–206 in *The Revelation of the Name YHWH to Moses: Perspectives from Judaism, the Pagan Graeco-Roman World, and Early Christianity*. TBN 9. Edited by George H. Kooten. Leiden: Brill, 2006.

————. "Paul's Rapture: 2 Corinthians 12:2-4 and the Language of Mystics." Pages 159–76 in *Experientia, Volume I: Inquiry into Religious Experience in Early Judaism and Christianity*. SBLSS 40. Edited by Frances Flannery, Colleen Shantz, and Rodney A. Werline. Atlanta: SBL, 2008.

Perrin, Nicholas. *Thomas: The Other Gospel.* London: SPCK, 2007.

Philip, Finny. *The Origins of Pauline Pneumatology: The Eschatological Bestowal of the Spirit upon Gentiles in Judaism and in the Early Development of Paul's Theology*. WUNT 2, 194. Tübingen: Mohr Siebeck, 2005.

Pietersma, Albert. "Kyrios or Tetragram: A Renewed Quest for the Original Septuagint." Pages 85–101 in *De Septuaginta: Studies in Honour of John W. Wevers*. Edited by Albert Poetersma and Claude Cox. Mississauga, ON: Benben, 1984.

————, and Benjamin G. Wright, eds. *A New English Translation of the Septuagint and the Other Greek Translations Traditionally Included Under That Title*. New York: Oxford University Press, 2007.

Piovanelli, Pierluigi. "'Sitting by the Waters of Dan,' or the 'Tricky Business' of Tracing the Social Profile of the Communities that Produced the Earliest Enochic Texts." Pages 257–81 in *The Early Enoch Literature*. JSJSup 121. Edited by Gabrielle Boccaccini and John J. Collins. Leiden: Brill, 2007.

Pokorny, Petr. *The Genesis of Christology*. Edinburgh: T&T Clark, 1987.

Pollard, T. E. "Martyrdom and Resurrection in the New Testament." *BJRL* 55 (1972): 240–51.

Pomykala, Kenneth E. *The Davidic Dynasty Tradition in Early Judaism.* Early Judaism and its Literature 7. Atlanta: Scholars, 1995.

Pongratz-Leisten, Beate. "When the Gods Are Speaking: Toward Defining the Interface between Polytheism and Monotheism." Pages 132–68 in *Propheten in Mari, Assyrien und Israel*. Edited by Von Matthias Köckert and Martii Nissinen. Göttingen: Vandenhoeck & Ruprecht, 2003.

Popper, Karl R. *Conjectures and Refutations: The Growth of Scientific Knowledge.* London: Routledge & Kegan Paul, 1963.

———. *Objective Knowledge: An Evolutionary Approach.* Oxford: Clarendon, 1972.

Ramelli, Ilaria L. E. "Origen's Anti-Subordinationism and its Heritage in the Nicene and Cappadocian Line." *VC* 65 (2011): 21–49.

Rand, Michael. "More on *Seder Beriyot.*" *JSQ* 16 (2009): 183–209.

Rapoport-Albert, Ada. "God and the Zaddik as the Two Focal Points of Hasidic Worship." *History of Religions* 18 (1979): 296–325.

Reed, Annette Yoshiko. "Heavenly Ascent, Angelic Descent, and the Transmission of Knowledge in 1 Enoch 6–16." Pages 47–66 in *Heavenly Realms and Earthly Realities in Late Antique Religions.* Edited by Ra'anan S. Boustan and Annette Yoshiko Reed. Cambridge: Cambridge University Press, 2004.

Reeves, John C. *Trajectories in Near Eastern Apocalyptic: A Postrabbinic Jewish Apocalyptic Reader.* Resources for Biblical Study. Atlanta: SBL, 2005.

Reicke, Bo. *The Epistles of James, Peter, and Jude.* AB 37. Garden City, NY: Doubleday, 1964.

Reif, Stefan. *Judaism and Hebrew Prayer: New Perspectives on Jewish Liturgical History.* Cambridge: Cambridge University Press, 1993.

Rhoads, David. "Performance Criticism: An Emerging Methodology in Second Testament Studies—Part II." *BTB* 36 (2006): 164–84.

Ritt, H. "Der 'Seewandel Jesu' (Mk 6, 45–52 par), Literarische und theologische Aspekte." *BZ* 23 (1979): 71–84.

Robinson, James M. "Jesus from Easter to Valentinus (or the Apostles' Creed)." *JBL* 101 (1982): 5–37.

———, ed. *The Nag Hammadi Library in English.* 3rd ed. San Francisco: Harper & Row, 1988.

———, and Helmut Koester. *Trajectories through Early Christianity.* Philadelphia: Fortress Press, 1971.

Ronning, John. *The Jewish Targums and John's Logos Theology.* Peabody, MA: Hendrickson, 2010.

Rosenberg, Roy. "The Slain Messiah in the Old Testament." *ZAW* 99 (1987): 259–61.

Roth, Cecil, ed. *The Haggadah: A New Edition.* London: Soncino, 1959.

Roukema, Riemer. "Jesus and the Divine Name in the Gospel of John." Pages 207–33 in *The Revelation of the Name YHWH to Moses: Perspectives from Judaism, the Pagan Graeco-Roman World, and Early Christianity.* TBN 9. Edited by George H. Kooten. Leiden: Brill, 2006.

Rowe, C. Kavin. *Early Narrative Christology: The Lord in the Gospel of Luke.* BZNW 139. Berlin: de Gruyter, 2006.

Rowland, Christopher. "Apocalyptic, the Poor, and the Gospel of Matthew." *JTS* (1994): 504–18.

———. "Christ in the New Testament." Pages 474–96 in *King and Messiah in Israel and the Ancient Near East: Proceedings of the Oxford Old Testament Seminar.* JSOTSup 70. Edited by John Day. Sheffield: Sheffield Academic Press, 1998.

———. *The Open Heaven: A Study of Apocalyptic in Judaism and Early Christianity.* New York: Crossroad, 1982.

———. "The Vision of the Risen Christ in Rev. i. 13ff.: The Debt of an Early Christology to an Aspect of Jewish Angelology." *JTS* 31 (1980): 1–11.

———. "Visionary Experience in Ancient Judaism and Christianity." Pages 41–56 in *Paradise Now: Essays on Early Jewish and Christian Mysticism.* SBLSS 11. Edited by April D. DeConick. Atlanta: SBL, 2006.

———. "Visions of God in Apocalyptic Literature." *JSJ* 10 (1979): 137–54.

Runia, Klaas. *The Present-Day Christological Debate.* Leicester: Inter-Varsity Press, 1984.

Rusch, William G., ed. *The Trinitarian Controversy.* Sources of Early Christian Thought. Philadelphia: Fortress Press, 1980.

Russell, Norman. *Theophilus of Alexandria.* Early Church Fathers. London: Routledge, 2007.

Safrai, Shmuel. "Teaching of Pietists in Mishnaic Literature." *JJS* 16 (1965): 15–33.

Sanders, J. A., ed. *The Dead Sea Psalms Scroll.* Ithaca, NY: Cornell University Press, 1967.

Sanders, Seth L. "Performative Exegesis." Pages 57–79 in *Paradise Now: Essays on Early Jewish and Christian Mysticism.* SBLSS 11. Edited by April D. DeConick. Atlanta: SBL, 2006.

Sarason, Richard S. "The 'Intersections' of Qumran and Rabbinic Judaism: The Case of Prayer Texts and Liturgies." *DSD* 8 (2001): 169–81.

———. "On the Use of Method in the Modern Study of Jewish Liturgy." Pages 97–172 of volume 1 in *Approaches to Ancient Judaism: Theory and Practice.* BJS 1, 9, 11, 27, 32, 192. Edited by William Scott Green. 6 vols. Missoula, MT: Scholars, 1978–85 (1978).

Schäfer, Peter. "The Aim and Purpose of Early Jewish Mysticism." Pages 277–95 in Schäfer, *Hekhalot-Studien.* TSAJ 19. Tübingen: Mohr, 1988.

———. *The Jewish Jesus: How Judaism and Christianity Shaped Each Other.* Princeton, NJ: Princeton University Press, 2012.

———. "Jewish Liturgy and Magic." Pages 541–56 of volume 1 in *Geschichte, Tradition, Reflexion: Festschrift für Martin Hengel zum 70. Geburtstag.* Edited by Hubert Cancik, Hermann Lichtenberger, and Peter Schäfer. 3 vols. Tübingen: Mohr Siebeck, 1996.

———. *The Origins of Jewish Mysticism.* Princeton, NJ: Princeton University Press, 2011.

———, Margarete Schlüter, and Hans Georg von Mutius, eds. *Synopse zur Hekhalot-Literatur.* TSAJ 2. Tübingen: Mohr Siebeck, 1981.

Schiffman, Lawrence H. "The Dead Sea Scrolls and the Early History of Jewish Liturgy." Pages 33–48 in *The Synagogue in Late Antiquity.* Edited by Lee I. Levine. Philadelphia: American Schools of Oriental Research, 1987.

———. "New Light on the Pharisees." Pages 217–24 in *Understanding the Dead Sea Scrolls: A Reader from the Biblical Archaeology Review.* Edited by Hershel Shanks. New York: Random House, 1992.

———. *Who Was a Jew? Rabbinic and Halakhic Perspectives on the Jewish Christian Schism.* Hoboken, NJ: Ktav, 1985.

Schmidt, Werner H. *The Faith of the Old Testament: A History.* Translated by John Sturdy. Oxford: Blackwell, 1983.

Schnackenburg, Rudolf. "Logos-Hymnus und johanneischer Prolog." *BZ* 1 (1957): 69–109.

Schoedel, William. *Ignatius of Antioch.* Hermeneia. Philadelphia: Fortress Press, 1985.

Scholem, Gershom G. *Jewish Gnosticism, Merkabah Mysticism, and Talmudic Tradition.* New York: Jewish Theological Seminary of America, 1960.

———. *Major Trends in Jewish Mysticism.* New York: Schocken Books, 1941.

———. *On the Kabbalah and its Symbolism.* Translated by Ralph Manheim. New York: Schocken Books, 1965.

Schremer, Adiel. *Brothers Estranged: Heresy, Christianity, and Jewish Identity in Late Antiquity.* Oxford: Oxford University Press, 2010.

Schuller, Eileen. "Prayer, Hymnic, and Liturgical Texts from Qumran." Pages 151–71 in *The Community of the Renewed Covenant: The Notre Dame Symposium on the Dead Sea Scrolls.* Christianity and Judaism in Antiquity 10. Edited by Eugene Ulrich and James VanderKam. Notre Dame, IN: University of Notre Dame Press, 1994.

———. "Some Observations on Blessings of God in Texts from Qumran." Pages 133–43 in *Of Scribes and Scrolls: Studies on the Hebrew Bible, Intertestamental*

Judaism, and Christian Origins Presented to John Strugnell on the Occasion of His Sixtieth Birthday. College Theology Society Resources in Religion 5. Edited by Harold W. Attridge, John J. Collins, and Thomas H. Tobin. Lanham, MD: University Press of America, 1990.

Schwartz, Seth. *Imperialism and Jewish Society, 200 B.C.E. to 640 C.E.* Princeton, NJ: Princeton University Press, 2001.

Schweizer, Eduard. *The Good News According to Mark.* Translated by Donald H. Madvig. Atlanta: John Knox, 1970.

Scott, Steven Richard. "The Binitarian Nature of the *Book of Similitudes.*" *JSP* 18 (2008): 55–78.

Segal, Alan F. "The Afterlife as Mirror of the Self." Pages 19–40 in *Experientia, Volume I: Inquiry into Religious Experience in Early Judaism and Christianity.* SBLSS 40. Edited by Frances Flannery, Colleen Shantz, and Rodney A. Werline. Atlanta: SBL, 2008.

———. "Heavenly Ascent in Hellenistic Judaism, Early Christianity and Their Environment." *Aufstieg und Niedergang der römishen Welt* 2, 23 (1980): 1333–94.

———. *Paul the Convert: The Apostolate and Apostasy of Saul the Pharisee.* New Haven, CT: Yale University Press, 1990.

———. "The Resurrection: Faith or History." Pages 121–38 and 210–12 in in *The Resurrection of Jesus: John Dominic Crossan and N.T. Wright in Dialogue.* Edited by Robert B. Stewart. Minneapolis: Fortress Press, 2006.

———. *Two Powers in Heaven: Early Rabbinic Reports about Christianity and Gnosticism.* SJLA 25. Leiden: Brill, 1977.

Segal, Philip. "Early Christian and Rabbinic Liturgical Affinities." *NTS* 30 (1984): 63–90.

Senn, Frank C. *Christian Liturgy, Catholic and Evangelical.* Minneapolis: Fortress Press, 1997.

Shepherd, Massey H., Jr. *The Paschal Liturgy in the Apocalypse.* London: Lutterworth, 1960.

Shinan, Avigdor. "The Aramaic Targum as a Mirror of Galilean Jewry." Pages 241–51 in *The Galilee in Late Antiquity.* Edited by Lee. I. Levine. New York: Jewish Theological Seminary of America, 1992.

———. "Synagogues in the Land of Israel: The Literature of the Ancient Synagogue and Synagogue Archaeology." Pages 130–52 in *Sacred Realm: The Emergence of the Synagogue in the Ancient World.* Edited by Steven Fine. New York: Oxford University Press, 1996.

Skarsaune, Oskar. "Jewish Believers in Jesus in Antiquity—Problems of Definition, Method, and Sources." Pages 3–21 in *Jewish Believers in Jesus: The Early Centuries.* Edited by Oskar Skarsaune and Reidar Hvalvik. Peabody, MA: Hendrickson, 2007.

Smith, Joseph P., trans. *St. Irenaeus: Proof of the Apostolic Preaching.* ACW 16. New York: Newman, 1952.

Smith, Mark S. *God in Translation: Deities in Cross-Cultural Discourse in the Biblical World.* Forschungen zum Alten Testament 57. Tübingen: Mohr Siebeck, 2008.

———. "'Seeing God' in the Psalms: The Background to the Beatific Vision in the Hebrew Bible." *CBQ* 50 (1988): 171–83.

———. "Yahweh and Other Deities in Ancient Israel? Observations on Old Problems and Recent Trends." Pages 197–234 in *Ein Gott Alein? JHWH-Verehrung und biblischer Monotheismus im Kontext der israelitischen und altorientalischen Religionsgeschichte.* Orbis biblicus et orientalis 139. Edited by Walter Dietrich and Martin A. Klopfenstein. Freiburg: Universitatsverlag, 1994.

Smith, Walter Chalmers. *Hymns of Christ and the Christian Life.* London: Macmillan, 1867.

Soloveitchik, Haym. "The Midrash, *Sefer Hasidim* and the Changing Face of God." Pages 165–77 in *Creation and Re-Creation in Jewish Thought: Festschrift in Honor of Joseph Dan on the Occasion of His Seventieth Birthday.* Edited by Rachel Elior and Peter Schäfer. Tübingen: Mohr Siebeck, 2005.

Sommer, Benjamin D. *The Bodies of God and the World of Ancient Israel.* Cambridge: Cambridge University Press, 2009.

Sparks, H. F. D., ed. *The Apocryphal Old Testament.* Oxford: Clarendon, 1984.

Speiser, E. A. *Genesis.* AB 1. Garden City, NY: Doubleday, 1964.

Stegner, W. Richard. "Jesus' Walking on the Water: Mark 6:45-52." Pages 212–34 in *The Gospels and the Scriptures of Israel.* Studies in Scripture in Early Judaism and Christianity. Edited by Craig A. Evans and W. Richard Stegner. Sheffield: Sheffield Academic Press, 1994.

Stemberger, Günter. "Dating Rabbinic Traditions." Pages 79–96 in *The New Testament and Rabbinic Literature.* SJSJ 136. Edited by Reimund Bieringer et al. Leiden: Brill, 2010.

Stenning, John F., trans. *The Targum of Isaiah.* Oxford: Clarendon, 1953.

Stern, David. "Midrash and Indeterminacy." *Critical Inquiry* 15 (1988): 132–61.

———. *Midrash and Theory: Ancient Jewish Exegesis and Contemporary Literary Studies.* Evanston, IL: Northwestern University Press, 1996.

Stewart, Columba. *Cassian the Monk.* Oxford Studies in Historical Theology. New York: Oxford University Press, 1998.

Stewart-Sykes, Alistair, trans. *On Pascha: With the Fragments of Melito and Other Materials Related to the Quartodecimanians.* By Melito of Sardis. Popular Patristics Series. Crestwood, NY: St. Vladimir's Seminary Press, 2001.

Stone, Michael E. *Ancient Judaism: New Visions and Views.* Grand Rapids: Eerdmans, 2011.

———. *Selected Studies in Pseudepigrapha and Apocrypha with Special Reference to the Armenian Tradition.* SVTP 9. Leiden: Brill, 1991.

Strack, Hermann L., and Günter Stemberger. *Introduction to the Talmud and Midrash.* Translated by Markus Bockmuehl. Edinburgh: T&T Clark, 1991.

Strazicich, John. *Joel's Use of Scripture and Scripture's Use of Joel: Appropriation and Resignification in Second Temple Judaism and Early Christianity.* Biblical Interpretation 82. Leiden: Brill, 2007.

Strousma, Gedaliahu. "Form(s) of God: Some Notes on Metatron and Christ." *HTR* 76 (1983): 269–88.

Stuckenbruck, Loren T. *Angel Veneration and Christology: A Study in Early Judaism and in the Christology of the Apocalypse of John.* WUNT 2, 70. Tübingen: Mohr, 1995.

———. "An Angelic Refusal of Worship: the Tradition and Its Function in the Apocalypse of John." *SBLSP* 25 (1994): 679–96.

Studer, Basil. *Zur Theophanie-Exegese Augustins: Untersuchung zu einem Abrosius-Zitat in der Schrift 'De Videndo Deo.'* Rome: Herder, 1971.

Sullivan, Kevin P. *Wrestling with Angels: A Study of the Relationship between Angels and Humans in Ancient Jewish Literature and the New Testament.* Arbeiten zur Geschichte des antiken Judentums und des Urchristentums 55. Leiden: Brill, 2004.

Suter, David W. "Revisiting 'Fallen Angel, Fallen Priest.'" Pages 137–42 in *The Origins of Enochic Judaism, Proceedings of the First Enoch Seminar, University of Michigan, Sesto Fioentino, Italy, June 19–23, 2001.* Henoch 24. Edited by Gabriele Boccaccini. Torino: Silvio Zamorani Editore, 2002.

Swartz, Michael D. "Jewish Visionary Tradition in Rabbinic Literature." Pages 198–221 in *The Cambridge Companion to the Talmud and Rabbinic Literature.* Edited by Charlotte Elisheva Fonrobert and Martin S. Jaffee. Cambridge: Cambridge University Press, 2007.

———. "Judaism and the Idea of Ancient Ritual Theory." Pages 294–317 and 404–10 in *Jewish Studies at the Crossroads of Anthropology and History: Authority, Diaspora, Tradition.* Jewish Culture and Contexts. Edited by Ra'anan S. Boustan, Oren Kosansky, and Marina Rustow. Philadelphia: University of Pennsylvania Press, 2011.

———. "Mystical Texts." Pages 393–420 in *The Literature of the Sages, Second Part: Midrash and Targum, Liturgy, Poetry, Mysticism, Contracts, Inscriptions, Ancient Science, and the Languages of Rabbinic Literature.* CRINT 2, The Literature of the Jewish People in the Period of the Second Temple and the Talmud 3b. Edited by Shmuel Safrai. Assen: Van Gorcum, 2006.

———. "Piyut and Heikalot: Recent Research and its Implications for the History of Ancient Jewish Liturgy and Mysticism." Pages 263–81 in *The Experience of Jewish Liturgy: Studies Dedicated to Menahem Schmelzer.* Brill Reference Library of Judaism 31. Edited by Debra Reed Blank. Leiden: Brill, 2011.

———. "Sage, Priest, and Poet: Typologies of Leadership in the Ancient Synagogue." Pages 101–17 in *Jews, Christians, and Polytheists in the Ancient Synagogue: Cultural Interaction During The Greco-Roman Period.* Baltimore Studies in the History of Judaism. Edited by Steven Fine. London: Routledge, 1999.

Tabory, Joseph. "The Prayer Book (Siddur) as an Anthology of Judaism." *Prooftexts* 17 (1997): 115–32.

Talbert, Charles. *The Development of Christology during the First Hundred Years and Other Essays on Early Christian Christology.* NovT Sup 140. Leiden: Brill, 2011.

Talmon, Shemaryahu. "The Emergence of Institutionalized Prayer in Israel in Light of Qumran Literature." Pages 200–43 in Talmon, *The World of Qumran from Within.* Jerusalem: Magnes, 1989.

Towner, W. Sibley. "'Blessed be YHWH' and Blessed Art Thou, YHWH': The Modulation of a Biblical Formula." *CBQ* 30 (1968): 386–99.

Ulmer, Rivka. "The Contours of the Messiah in *Pesiqta Rabbati.*" *HTR* 106 (2013): 115–44.

Urbach, Ephraim E. *The Sages: Their Concepts and Beliefs.* Cambridge, MA: Harvard University Press, 1987.

van der Horst, Pieter Willem. "The Great Magical Papyrus of Paris (PGM IV) and the Bible." Pages 173–83 in *A Kind of Magic: Understanding Magic in the New Testament and Its Religious Environment.* Library of New Testament Studies 306. Edited by Michael Labahn and Bert Jan Lietaert Peerbolte. London: T&T Clark, 2007.

van der Toorn, Karel. *Scribal Culture and the Making of the Hebrew Bible.* Cambridge: Harvard University Press, 2007.

von Rad, Gerhard. "Doxa." Pages 232–55 of volume 2 in *Theological Dictionary of the New Testament*. Edited by G. Kittel and G. Friedrich. Translated by G.W. Bromiley. 10 vols. Grand Rapids, 1964–1976.

Valabregue-Perry, Sandra. "The Concept of Infinity (*Eyn-sof*) and the Rise of Theosophical Kabbalah." *JQR* 102 (2012): 405–30.

VanderKam, James C. "Righteous One, Messiah, Chosen One, and Son of Man in 1 Enoch 37–71." Pages 177–85 in *The Messiah: Developments in Earliest Judaism and Christianity*. Edited by James H. Charlesworth. Minneapolis: Fortress Press, 1992.

Veilleux, Armand, trans. *Pachomian Koinonia*. 3 vols. Cistercian Studies 45–47. Kalamazoo, MI: Cistercian Publications, 1980–82.

Vermes, Geza. *The Changing Faces of Jesus*. New York: Viking Compass, 2001.

———. *The Complete Dead Sea Scrolls in English*. New York: Allen Lane, 1997.

———. "Jesus the Jew." Pages 108–22 in *Jesus' Jewishness: Exploring the Place of Jesus within Early Judaism*. Edited by James H. Charlesworth. Philadelphia: American Interfaith Institute, 1991. Reprinted on pages 1–14 in Charlesworth, *Jesus and the World of Judaism*. London: SCM, 1983.

Wainwright, Arthur W. *The Trinity in the New Testament*. London: SCM, 1962.

Watson, Francis. "Is John's Christology Adoptionistic?" Pages 113–24 in *The Glory of Christ in the New Testament: Studies in Christology in Memory of George Bradford Caird*. Edited by L. D. Hurst and N. T. Wright. Oxford: Clarendon, 1987.

Weedman, Mark. "Hilary and the Homoiousians: Using New Categories to Map the Trinitarian Controversy." *CH* 76 (2007): 491–510.

Weinfeld, Moshe. "The Day of the Lord: Aspirations for the Kingdom of God in the Bible and Jewish Literature." Pages 345–72 in *Studies in Bible*. Scripta Hierosolymitana 31. Edited by Sara Japhet. Jerusalem: Magnes, 1986.

———. *Deuteronomy and the Deuteronomic School*. Oxford: Clarendon, 1972.

Weiser, Artur. *The Psalms: A Commentary*. Old Testament Library. Translated by Herbert Hartwell. Philadelphia: Westminster, 1962.

Weiss, Zeev. "Between Rome and Byzantium: Pagan Motifs in Synagogue Art and Their Place in the Judeo-Christian Controversy." Pages 366–90 in *Jewish Identities in Antiquity: Studies in Memory of Menahem Stern*. TSAJ 130. Edited by Lee I. Levine and Daniel R. Schwartz. Tübingen: Mohr Siebeck, 2009.

Werblowsky, R. J. Zwi. *Joseph Karo: Lawyer and Mystic*. 2nd ed. Philadelphia: Jewish Publication Society of America, 1977.

Westermann, Claus. *Praise and Lament in the Psalms.* Translated by Keith R. Crim and Richard N. Soulen. Atlanta: John Knox, 1981.

Williams, Catrin H. *I Am He: The Interpretation of 'Anî Hû' in Jewish and Early Christian Literature.* WUNT 2, 113. Tübingen: Mohr Siebeck, 2000.

Witherington, Ben, III, and Laura M. Ice. *The Shadow of the Almighty: Father, Son, and Spirit in Biblical Perspective.* Grand Rapids: Eerdmans, 2002.

Wolfson, Elliot R. *Along the Path: Studies in Kabbalistic Myth, Symbolism, and Hermeneutics.* Albany: State University of New York Press, 1995.

———. *The Book of the Pomegranate: Moses De Leon's Sefer Ha-Rimmon.* BJS. Atlanta: Scholars, 1988.

———. "The Doctrine of Sefirot in the Prophetic Kabbalah of Abraham Abulafia, Part I." *JSQ* 2 (1995): 336–71.

———. "Iconic Visualization and the Imaginal Body of God: The Role of Intention in the Rabbinic Conception of Prayer." *Modern Theology* 12 (1996): 137–61.

———. "Images of God's Feet: Some Observations on the Divine Body in Judaism." Pages 143–81 in *People of the Body: Jews and Judaism from an Embodied Perspective.* The Body in Culture, History, and Religion. Edited by Howard Eilberg-Schwartz. Albany: State University of New York Press, 1992.

———. "Judaism and Incarnation: The Imaginal Body of God." Pages 239–54 in *Christianity in Jewish Terms.* Edited by Tikva Simone Frymer-Kensky. Boulder, CO: Westview, 2000.

———. "Seven Mysteries of Knowledge: Qumran E/Soterism Recovered." Pages 177–213 in *The Idea of Biblical Interpretation: Essays in Honor of James Kugel.* SJSJ 83. Edited by Hindy Najman and Judith H. Newman. Leiden: Brill, 2004.

———. *Through a Speculum that Shines: Vision and Imagination in Medieval Jewish Mysticism.* Princeton, NJ: Princeton University Press, 1994.

Wolfson, Harry A. *Philosophy of the Church Fathers.* Cambridge, MA: Harvard University Press, 1956.

Wright, Benjamin G., III. "*Sirach* and *1 Enoch*: Some Further Considerations." Pages 179–87 in *The Origins of Enochic Judaism, Proceedings of the First Enoch Seminar, University of Michigan, Sesto Fioentino, Italy, June 19–23, 2001.* Edited by Gabriele Boccaccini. Henoch 24. Torino: Silvio Zamorani Editore, 2002.

Wright, N. T. *The Climax of the Covenant: Christ and the Law in Pauline Theology.* Minneapolis: Fortress Press, 1992.

———. "Constraints and the Jesus of History." *SJT* 39 (1986): 189–210.

———. "One God, One Lord, One People." *Ex Auditu* 7 (1991): 45–58.

———. "Resurrecting Old Arguments: Responding to Four Essays." *JSHJ* 3 (2005): 209–31.

———. *The Resurrection of the Son of God*. Christian Origins and the Question of God 3. Minneapolis: Fortress Press, 2003.

Zahavy, Tzvee. *Studies in Jewish Prayer*. Studies in Judaism. Lanham, MD: University Press of America, 1990.

Zetterholm, Magnus. "Paul and the Missing Messiah." Pages 33–56 in *The Messiah in Early Judaism and Christianity*. Edited by Magnus Zetterholm. Minneapolis: Fortress Press, 2007).

Index of Contemporary Authors

Index of Biblical and Post-Biblical Texts

CPSIA information can be obtained at www.ICGtesting.com
Printed in the USA
LVOW12s1349200314

378102LV00003B/4/P

9 781451 470345